OUTSIDE, INSIDE

Diaries: Volume 5, 2003–2005

OUTSIDE, INSIDE
ALASTAIR CAMPBELL

DIARIES: VOLUME 5, 2003–2005

Edited by

Alastair Campbell

and

Bill Hagerty

Biteback Publishing

First published in Great Britain in 2016 by
Biteback Publishing Ltd
Westminster Tower
3 Albert Embankment
London SE1 7SP
Copyright © Alastair Campbell 2016

ISBN 978-1-78590-061-7

10 9 8 7 6 5 4 3 2 1

A CIP catalogue record for this book is available from the British Library.

Set in Palatino by Adrian McLaughlin

Printed and bound in Great Britain by
CPI Group (UK) Ltd, Croydon CR0 4YY

MIX
Paper from
responsible sources
FSC® C020471

*In memory of my brother Donald.
We led such different lives, and politics was
the least of his interests. But I miss him every day
and always will.*

Contents

Acknowledgements

As I say in the introduction, both Ed Victor, my literary agent, and Iain Dale, publisher of Biteback, were foremost in pressing me to publish my post-Downing Street diaries. Ed has been with me since long before the first word was published and as well as being a wonderful guide through the literary world, he has become a great friend and a charity partner in raising funds for research into leukaemia, a battle with which he has thankfully survived.

Iain Dale and his team make a remarkable commitment to political publishing and I have enjoyed the visits to his office with, appropriately, its superb view across the river to the Houses of Parliament. In particular I would like to thank Olivia Beattie, for her patience, professionalism and enthusiasm, and Victoria Gilder and Sam Jones.

Bill Hagerty was my editor on the previous volumes and has done the same superb, thorough job on this one. His attention to detail has often reminded me of what a terrific journalist he was when he was my boss at the Mirror Group many years ago.

Both Bill and I would like also to recall the role of two people who were centrally involved in the diaries but sadly were taken away from us far too young. Richard Stott, my former editor at the *Daily Mirror*, became my editor for *The Blair Years* but sadly died from pancreatic cancer aged just sixty-three, shortly after the book was published in July 2007. Bill gave a wonderful eulogy at his funeral and I know Richard would have been pleased, as I was, that Bill then took over. Taken away even younger was Mark Bennett, my researcher and assistant in Downing Street, who became my transcriber, researcher and assistant on the diaries and would have remained so in the publication of these further volumes. He died unexpectedly in 2014 aged just forty-four, and I wish once again to acknowledge his role and friendship here.

Introduction

If you are reading this, and planning on reading the whole book, and you enjoy it, there are a few names that may be familiar to you that you will have to thank. One, if I may start with a quality political diarist name drop, is Tony Benn RIP, with whom, despite our political differences, I always got on well and with whom, latterly, I would discuss the practicalities of diary writing. The second, likewise a politician of the left and a diarist of some note, is Chris Mullin. The third is Lord Bruce Grocott – Brucie to me – who before taking the ermine was Tony Blair's Parliamentary Private Secretary and a great friend and support in opposition and in government. What all three have in common – beyond long parliamentary experience and some though not all shared political opinions – is that they nagged me to make sure that, having already published my diaries up to the point when I left Downing Street in 2003, I did not stop there. They all gave me their own version of the 'owe it to history' thing. But Bruce had another point, which underlined the difference between contemporaneous accounts written up day after day, as mine, Tony Benn's and Chris Mullin's are, and the classic political memoir written towards the end of a career – most of which Bruce felt should be subtitled 'How I was right all along'. The diary, he insisted, having read mine for 1994–2003, 'tells it like it was'.

Nobody has yet to accuse me of turning the diaries into a 'how I was right all along' kind of tome. Indeed, when Tony Blair's chief of staff Jonathan Powell read those which were published in 2007, he commented that far from being self-serving, 'You come over as a complete lunatic.'

There are a fourth and a fifth man who have been part of the persistent nagging crew: my literary agent Ed Victor, and Biteback publisher Iain Dale. Iain didn't exactly beg. But any time I was on his LBC radio show he would always take me to one side and say he really, really wanted to do my post-Downing Street diaries. 'Why? I left.' 'No, you didn't. You just did it all from a different angle.'

If you are detecting a slight reluctance in me, you wouldn't be wrong. Ed Victor likes to call me his 'most complicated client' and the reasons for my reluctance are not straightforward. First off, fair to say that the publication of *The Blair Years* was what the media like to call a publishing sensation. Massive coverage, an instant number one bestseller and in a way defining for me personally because it became the point at which I was perhaps no longer Tony Blair's spokesman and strategist but also my own. The tour, the fallout, and the demands to talk about the book seemed to go on for ever. I was tired of talking.

The next part of the problem was a fault of my own making. It had been my idea to do 'extracts' for the whole period, published as the first book, admitting that I was sanitising them somewhat so as to minimise any damage to Labour, still in government, and especially to Gordon Brown. But the only way I could justify doing so was to say that one day the full volumes would be published, as indeed they have been, four of them. They were not quite the publishing sensation of *The Blair Years* but they still got a fair bit of attention and required me to do yet more media and events, facing the same questions over and over again, during four separate periods (oh, five, because I also did *The Irish Diaries*, publishing everything to do with Ireland, North and South). There were times I felt trapped as a prisoner of my own past. Proud of most of what we did. But unable ever fully to move on from it.

For another complication will become clear to the reader of this and future post-Downing Street volumes, namely the tension within me, more often closer to tortured agonising, about leaving my political life behind to focus on things like my family and my mental health, while at the same time feeling a strong sense of duty to Labour, and being pressured by many, especially but not only Tony Blair, to go back in some form. The title of this volume is *Outside, Inside*. It was almost *Never Really Left*, but the chances of that being misunderstood, in the era of Jeremy Corbyn leading the Labour Party, would have been too high. *Outside, Inside* captures the reality, however, that for much of the time Tony Blair remained as Prime Minister, and perhaps more surprisingly when Gordon Brown succeeded him, often it felt like I was as involved as ever I had been.

'Do you find your perspective changes now you are not there all the time?' Tony Benn asked me one evening when we were attending a birthday dinner for his daughter Melissa, a close friend of Fiona, my partner. The answer is yes. But not always in the same way. There are times I can read over past events and relive them with the same kind of emotional intensity as existed at the time. On other occasions, there are events and incidents which clearly seemed hugely important at the time, or else why was I recording them in such detail, yet in the real world of today, I have all but forgotten them.

One sensation I have repeatedly is that of asking myself how I found the time to write down at the end of the day all the words that I did. Now that I lead a less intense kind of life, I seem less disciplined in the keeping of the diary. But when I was centrally involved, it was almost like a coping mechanism. Writing it down was a way of making sense of it when, often, living through it, it didn't seem to make sense at all.

I left. But I didn't. I left because I was tired of it, and felt I wasn't doing it as well as I used to. Yet thereafter I kept being told, both by Tony and by Gordon, that I was needed more than ever. I left also because I wanted to show Fiona, finally, that I really did understand and appreciate her desire for a different kind of life. But the reality is it took us years to get to a place where we were happy with the role I played. This volume is bad enough for the difficulties I am having in adapting. The next one is even worse. Worse too in the next one my mental health, and the realisation that I cannot sort it out on my own, that I need – and finally get – proper help.

Some of the themes, though, will be very familiar to readers of the previous volumes, even if every word of this one is new. Perhaps the biggest narrative of all is the relationship between TB and GB. As becomes clear in the pages which follow, I became something of the go-between trying to resolve the differences between them, sufficient for them to fight the 2005 election campaign together convincingly. But much of that I had forgotten by the time I came to transcribe it all, including just how close, and how often, Tony came to throwing it in. The active efforts he was making at one point to test the waters for a possible tilt at the European Commission presidency is one of those stories I had completely blanked out of my mind, perhaps because at the time I was so scared it would leak out, and force him out before his time was actually done.

All of the past volumes have large elements of TB–GB and so will the future ones, which we will be rolling out in the coming years. It is one of those political relationships historians, political students, writers and film-makers will look at for a long time to come. The question of whether Tony should have 'dealt with' Gordon differently – namely, sack him rather than tolerate and manage him, and ultimately help him take over the leadership – is unfortunately one of the most significant of this period of history. Even having had a ringside seat, and with the benefit of hindsight, I still don't have a settled view. Some days I think he should have done. Other days I don't. But I do believe that within the fallout from their fallout we can perhaps see the seeds of Labour's current difficulties under Corbyn. We did not cement the legacy of New Labour, or organisational and cultural change in the party. And one of the side effects of the TB–GB malaise was that we did not develop talent sufficiently. Indeed, quite a lot of talent was driven away by it all. It was all about Tony handing over to Gordon. By the time Gordon went, the talent pool was shrinking, and by the time Ed Miliband went, it was shrinking even further. One thing is for sure – if I had predicted in my 2003 diaries that by the time they were published Jeremy Corbyn would be Labour leader and Ed Balls would be a former backbencher turning his hand to ballroom dancing on TV, I would have been asked to up my medication.

All that is for future volumes. This one begins on the first day of a personal freedom that took a long time in coming, and amid the ongoing debates and controversies of Iraq. I am writing this introduction a few weeks after the Chilcot Inquiry on Iraq has been published. This volume, which opens thirteen years ago, begins as we await the Hutton Inquiry on the build-up to the war in Iraq, and the convulsions that it will lead to in the BBC. TB–GB. Iraq. Whither Labour? Will the Tories get their act together? Rows with the media. What am I doing with my life and to my health and wellbeing? There are some themes and questions that run through the diaries incessantly. I hope the events and perspectives around them will be of as much interest to the reader and the historian as Tony Benn, Chris Mullin and Bruce Grocott thought they would be.

Who's Who

August 2003–May 2005

Tony Blair — Prime Minister (TB)

John Prescott — Deputy Prime Minister and First Secretary of State (JP)

Gordon Brown — Chancellor of the Exchequer (GB)

Alastair Campbell — Journalist, author, political aide, former Downing Street director of communications and strategy (AC)

Jack Straw — Foreign Secretary (JS)

Philip Gould — Political pollster and strategist (PG, Philip)

Peter Mandelson — European Commissioner for Trade, former Cabinet minister (Peter M)

David Hill — Tony Blair's chief media spokesperson (DH)

Andrew Adonis — Director of 10 Downing Street Policy Unit (AA)

John Birt — No. 10 advisor, 'blue skies thinker' (JB)

Peter Hyman — Strategist and speechwriter turned teacher (PH)

Geoff Hoon — Defence Secretary (GH)

Charles Clarke — Secretary for Education and Skills; Home Secretary from December 2004 (CC)

Robin Cook — Former Leader of the House of Commons (RC)

Lord (Bruce) Grocott — Government chief whip in the House of Lords

Cherie Blair — Wife of TB (CB)

Fiona Millar — AC's partner (Fiona, FM)

Jonathan Powell — Chief of Staff (Jonathan, JP)

Catherine Rimmer	Research and Information Unit (CR)
Lord (Charlie) Falconer	Lord Chancellor, Constitutional Affairs Secretary (CF)
Tessa Jowell	Culture, Media and Sport Secretary (TJ)
Michael Howard	Leader of the Opposition from November 2003 (MH)
Iain Duncan Smith	Leader of the Opposition until November 2003 (IDS)
William Hague	Former Leader of the Opposition
Charles Kennedy	Leader of the Liberal Democrats
Lady (Margaret) Thatcher	Former Prime Minister
David Blunkett	Former Home Secretary (DB)
Stephen Byers	Former Cabinet minister (SB)
John Reid	Health Secretary (JR)
David Miliband	Minister for Schools, Minister of State for the Cabinet Office from December 2004 (DM)
Bill Clinton	42nd President of the United States (BC)
George W. Bush	43rd President of the United States (GWB)
Jacques Chirac	President of France (JC)
Gerhard Schroeder	Chancellor of Germany
Douglas Alexander	Minister for the Cabinet Office; Minister of State for Trade from September 2004 (DA)
Neil Kinnock	Leader of the Labour Party, 1983–92 (NK)
Glenys Kinnock MEP	Wife of Neil Kinnock
Anji Hunter	Former Director of Government Relations
Ruth Kelly	Secretary for Education (RK)
Ed Balls	Chief Economic Advisor to the Treasury (EB)
Margaret Beckett	Secretary for the Environment, Food and Rural Affairs (MB)
Matt Carter	Labour Party General Secretary from January 2004 (MC)
Alan Milburn	Former Health Secretary; Minister for the Cabinet Office from September 2004 (AM, Alan)

Alan Johnson	Minister for Higher Education; Secretary for Work and Pensions from September 2004 (AJ)
Godric Smith	Prime Minister's official spokesperson; head of strategic communications from January 2004 (GS)
Alistair Darling	Secretary for Transport (AD)
Patricia Hewitt	Secretary for Trade and Industry
Sir Clive Woodward	British and Irish Lions coach (CW)
Sir Alex Ferguson	Friend of AC, manager of Manchester United (AF)
Greg Dyke	BBC director-general until January 2004
Gavyn Davies	Chairman of the BBC until January 2004
Dr David Kelly	Biological weapons expert, Ministry of Defence
Lord Hutton	Law Lord, former Lord Chief Justice of Northern Ireland
Adam Boulton	Sky News political editor
Paul Dacre	Editor of the *Daily Mail*
Sir David Frost	Broadcaster, TV host
Trevor Kavanagh	*Sun* political editor (TK)
Andrew Marr	BBC political editor
Rupert Murdoch	Chairman, News Corporation (RM)
John Sergeant	Former ITN political editor
Rebekah Wade	Editor, *The Sun* (RW)
Philip Webster	Political editor, *The Times*
Donald and Betty Campbell	Parents of AC
Rory, Calum and Grace Campbell	Children of AC and FM
Audrey Millar	Mother of Fiona
Gail Rebuck	Publisher, wife of Philip Gould

The Diaries

Saturday 30 August 2003

Though the numbers of media in the street had dwindled, I still woke to the sound of their arrival, and the subsequent chatter, and couldn't get back to sleep. I felt tired, didn't feel any of the release I had been hoping for. I guess that would take time. The papers were OK-ish. Massive in scale and, judging from media monitoring, not all negative by any means. Interesting that though they had been saying for weeks I was on the point of leaving, they reported it as a shock that I had, and a few saying bad for TB (including those who had said it would be good for him if I went). Sun headline 'Blair loses his brain'. Only the Daily Mail was truly vile, which I wouldn't have wanted any other way. Fiona [AC's partner] was in a reasonably good mood, with perhaps a little hint of triumph. It was going to take a bit of time to settle into a new rhythm, I could tell that. Calum [AC and Fiona's son] and I set off for Burnley v Crewe. Calum was definitely pleased I was out, and was great company on the way up. Every time I was mentioned on the radio, we switched channels. It was still running on the bulletins, but in a very 'It was a big story yesterday so we have to go through the motions today' kind of way, with the usual rentaquote hacks on there blathering with not much to say. The only journalist I spoke to on the way up was Kamal Ahmed [*Observer*], who was doing a big write-through. Alex [Ferguson, Manchester United manager] called, and said he thought yesterday was fine and that I got the tone right. He asked how I was feeling, and I said I wasn't sure. 'Yeah, you'll miss it,' he said. 'I'm still not sure you've done the right thing, but maybe you owe it to Fiona.'

TB called and said he had been trying to work out which other political figure would get such massive coverage for his resignation.

He had concluded that it was him, Bush and maybe GB. Six or seven pages in the broadsheets, five in the tabloids, huge coverage abroad. The Sundays doing massive write-throughs. I still felt it was a reflection of the media's self-obsession. They had built me up in part because it built themselves up. They loved it when they could make the media the story.

Mind you, it had certainly cut through, and when we stopped to get petrol and a coffee at Keele services, people were coming over to talk, more than usual. C [head of MI6, Sir Richard Dearlove] called, said he was really sad I was going, that he had always enjoyed working with me, and he felt TB would suffer because 'you always give it to him straight'. He felt I had always understood the problems and challenges faced by the Agencies and he was grateful for the support I gave them. He said he wanted to hold a lunch or dinner for me at SIS HQ. John Scarlett [chairman of Joint Intelligence Committee] told Clare Sumner [Downing Street official] he felt real personal sadness that I was leaving and his view was that though I wanted to leave, and Fiona certainly wanted us to leave, I had to some extent been hounded out by the way controversies were generated around me. I'm not sure I agreed with that but I was touched by his support.

We arrived around half past one. The photographers were out in force at the ground but Cathy Pickup [Burnley FC secretary] organised it so that they would do a few pictures at the start and then bugger off. Everyone was really warm and friendly, lots of supporters wishing me luck, and I think it brought home to Calum that there really had been a change. Stan Ternent [Burnley manager] waved at us as he got to the bench. I shouted, 'Got any jobs?' 'You can have mine,' he said. It was the best possible place to be today. I really felt at home, and for the first time a strong sense of release. I was doorstepped as we left but just got in the car and off we went.

TB was calling regularly through the day, and was talking at times as though I was still there – what we needed to do in the coming weeks, how we come out of Hutton,* go on the offensive, get back into domestic issues in a big way. He was gobsmacked that GB's only communication had been a message from his secretary to Alison [Blackshaw, AC's PA] 'thanking you for all the work you have done down the years', but also felt it typical. He then came out with a belter – he asked me

* Judicial inquiry, chaired by Lord Hutton, into the circumstances surrounding the death of David Kelly, the biological warfare expert and former UN weapons inspector in Iraq.

August '03: TB talking as though AC still there

to think about going to Iraq full time to sort things out there. I said I think not at the moment. He said he really needed someone out there who could be his person, and was able to co-ordinate people to work together. I decided not to mention it to Fiona! Later he sent through a positively compendious weekend note, fifteen pages or so. I couldn't quite face reading it. And then another one came in, even longer.

Sunday 31 August

First call of the day was from TB. He was thinking ahead to [Labour Party] conference, and wanted advice on how to prepare the ground for it. The reality was, though, that Iraq was not going well and that was likely to be the backdrop. The Tories, via IDS [Tory leader Iain Duncan Smith], were now saying that my departure should be followed by TB's, but it wasn't really flying. TB wanted me to write a paper to set out a few themes and how he might draw them together. I can't say I was enthused by the thought of spending my first Sunday out doing another note on strategy, but I settled down for an hour or so and put down a few thoughts. Then I read his note, and amended my own. Our best strengths were still that on the domestic fundamentals we were OK.

TB was holding up despite Iraq, and the Tories were pretty hopeless. He was pushing for what he called 'wholesale renewal' across government, party, policy, organisation. It sounded a little bit same old same old, only with a bit more oomph. He accepted that we had lost some of the values element to what we did, and wanted to reboot the idea of New Labour as the only really progressive force. When it came to messaging, he was a little trapped in the same old arguments about speed of change, opportunity/responsibility, relationship between citizen/state. But at least he was trying to get them wrapped into a message which combined fairness and the future. He was worried if we did not keep winning the battle on fairness then the public would not hear us on the difficult things we needed to do for the future. He was also arguing for a new set of five-year plans for the economy, public service reform, not just schools and hospitals but transport and pensions, also crime and criminal justice, and he wanted more done on the constitution. On foreign policy he wanted to focus on global warming, Africa, Iraq/Afghanistan. On Europe, he still felt we should have a clear euro entry timetable, but we needed to show we could win the reform arguments.

He told me later he felt he had lost his voice on the economy, clearly felt he had left it too much to GB, and felt business was less happy with us than they had been. Knowledge economy, science, skills, SMEs [small and medium-sized enterprises], modern manufacturing were the areas he wanted to focus on. He used the same phrase – 'lost my voice' – on welfare reform and on poverty and social exclusion, felt we were not focusing enough on the poorest children and the poorest estates. And he said he was worried they were losing direction on education. He was also going on about the need for a major internal shake-up, and for a new approach both to Cabinet and the PLP [Parliamentary Labour Party], which he now defined as dominated by 'malcontents spreading discontent'. He felt his team were not doing enough to keep the 'discarded but basically loyal' broadly onside and to give some of them a sense of a possible comeback. I was worried he was going to throw baby out with bathwater on comms, though interestingly he was thinking about moving to televised briefings.

On me, the Sundays were mixed, as expected. Loads, needless to say, on how much money I could make. TB said he expected Paul Dacre [editor of the *Daily Mail*] to make an overture because he would know I was the kind of person likely to go for him. Mrs Kelly [Janice, widow of David Kelly]* was due to give evidence to the Hutton Inquiry tomorrow, which was obviously going to be a big moment. I would love to know what she really thinks. There had been very little sense so far of what kind of relationship they had, and what her views were of what had happened. I didn't know how I felt at the moment. It was all a bit confused. I was less stressed on one level, as yesterday when driving back from Burnley and feeling that I didn't have to make half a dozen calls as soon as I got in the car; and at least there was the clarity of knowing I no longer worked there. But I was also very sad, and anxious about the future.

Coming out of the ground last night, one of the stewards had said, 'You look like a ton has been lifted off your back,' but I didn't feel like that. Also, the way TB was calling, and the tone of his calls, it was as though I was not really leaving at all. Four or five calls today, and even though one or two of them started with a kind of 'How are you?'

---

* The British scientist who had an off-the-record conversation with BBC journalist Andrew Gilligan about the government's dossier on weapons of mass destruction in Iraq and was called to appear before the parliamentary Foreign Affairs Committee after his name had appeared in the media. He was found dead three days later.

they were basically no different to the kind of calls I had had from him every Sunday for years. At one point he asked me to brief a couple of journos that I would be staying involved in a different way. I said I didn't think that was very sensible.

As for future work, I had decided I would just ignore all the phone calls and the various offers of things, and take my time. I would make a few speeches to tide us over but not sign up for anything remotely permanent. The *Sunday Mirror* said I was off to the Lords. They do just make it up, these people. One of them had a story about the kind of money I could make 'on top of a generous civil service pension'. Another made-up one, as I would be getting no pension at all, part of the bias against special advisors. Mum and Dad [Betty and Donald Campbell] said they were both a lot happier now. Dad had never said he felt the pressure, or that all the fuss had any effect on his various ailments, but I knew it did deep down. Mum was totally open about it. She just hated all the attacks and the poison and all the pressure I absorbed. She had lost so much weight there was hardly anything of her, and I knew a lot of it was the worry about me. I think she had been imagining that my resigning would mean it would be like a tap being turned off, and the media would just stop talking about me. 'They were still talking about you this morning,' she said. 'Don't listen to it.' 'But then I won't know what's going on.'

We went out for dinner with the Goulds [Philip Gould, pollster and political consultant to the Labour Party, Gail Rebuck, his publisher wife, their children Georgia and Grace] and Lindsay [Nicholson, personal friend] at the Camden Brasserie. I felt more relaxed but it also felt weird that in no time at all, I just wouldn't be involved in that never-ending chatter and running decision-making that had been my life for a decade. There were a few pieces around on Peter [Mandelson] beginning to re-exercise his influence, which was likely to give TB political problems. Peter wouldn't be able to resist trying to use it to garner a bigger role and profile again.

Later I read the second of TB's notes: a big grope right across the policy space, anxious about the economy, fine on health but keen for more reform, raging about bureaucracy in education, anxious about student finance, agitated about the lack of realism in departments' approach to transport and pensions. Sometimes these notes were just TB letting off steam and the crime and criminal justice stuff was full of it. So many things that needed to be done, he had been banging on about them for ages and yet there was a sclerosis in parts of the system.

Sentencing, and the use of non-custodial. The loss of the rehab side in prisons. Drugs, organised crime, crap IT in the courts. And then on asylum he was off again: why did he keep having to ask for the same things again and again when with the public this was no. 1 issue? He said the system was already gearing up to try to frustrate new legislation but it had to happen and in the Queen's Speech.

Monday 1 September

The papers were still groaning on and though the press I was getting wasn't that bad, Peter M was getting a bit of a kicking. Mrs Kelly gave evidence down the line and she used some pretty powerful language so we were back into another bad rash of media for the MoD [Ministry of Defence] and the government in general. It didn't add much to the overall substance and though for obvious reasons she wasn't pushed hard, I think people – including Hutton – will think there was something a bit odd that Kelly didn't discuss things with her at all until the day the statement came out about his involvement in the [Andrew] Gilligan story [the *Today* programme report which led to AC's dispute with the BBC].

TB was seeing his key people at Chequers [UK PM's official country residence] and it did feel odd to think that was going on, I wasn't there and instead was having a very nice, easy 10-mile run down by the canal. The reports back, from David Hill [AC's successor] and PG, were that he was on good form, had rediscovered a bit of his fizz and was motoring ideas wise for conference. But both DH and Philip were angry about a second meeting, which had been chaired by Peter M, with John Birt [advisor on 'blue-skies thinking'] alongside him, on political strategy. Philip said it had been a bit galling to get lessons on political strategy from JB.

I knew they were calling to try to get me involved in turning TB against the idea, but I was reluctant. I think I genuinely needed a break, and not least from the internal politics. TB would know Peter would be trying it on, for good reasons as well as bad, wanting to fill the gap I was leaving. Also, TB would be wanting him involved. But it would not be good if he started off by deliberately annoying David and Philip, or trying to undermine them. John Birt had a lot of talents but I am not convinced political strategy is his forte. I went into the office to pick up a few things, tie up a few loose ends, and deal with some of the mail that had come in. The doormen, the duty clerks and the cleaners etc.

were really nice, several of them saying words to the effect that the place wouldn't be the same, and I should change my mind.

The letters from the public, both from pre-leaving and the ones seemingly written on the day, were overwhelmingly positive. A few green-ink jobs [irate and seething readers' letters to newspapers], and a few worrying about what it said about politics that I felt I had to get out. A nice one from Anna Ford [BBC newsreader] saying she thought if the BBC had any sense they would hire me straight away. Harry Evans [former *Sunday Times* editor] called from the States. He and Tina Brown [wife of Evans, journalist and editor] had been following it all closely. He felt I was leaving with my dignity intact and that the state of BBC journalism was dreadful. 'The media will want to say this is about the state of politics, but it is actually about the state of media,' he said. He had always been a bit of a hero of mine when I was starting out in journalism, so it meant a lot to hear that from him.

I picked up in a roundabout kind of way some of the things Bob Phillis [chair of a review into government communications] was planning to say in his report. They sounded very different to what he had suggested when we met, including getting rid of the Order in Council [the special measure that allowed AC and chief of staff Jonathan Powell to instruct civil servants despite being special advisors]. I had already warned TB there would be a bit of civil service retrenching around my departure and this would send the wrong signal and undermine DH from the start. I understood why TB wanted to use my departure to signal a new relationship with the media, but long-term he must not let the changes we had made on cross-government co-ordination to slip back.

I went to see Tom Bostock [AC's GP] re my asthma, which had flared up again. He was perhaps not the best person to see, given he had been totally opposed to my leaving, and deep down felt the decision finally to leave was driven by Fiona feeling she was neglected, and not about a real assessment of why I did the job, why I needed to and why others needed me to. He said he was worried, he felt that after a while it would dawn on me what I had given up, I would feel resentful and angry and collapse into a deep depression. He also felt the kids would miss the idea of their dad being really close to the centre of events. 'You are going from virtually running a country to doing nothing. You won't be able to cope with that. You have to find a replacement and you'll find there is nothing to replace it.'

He felt it was disastrous for TB, and disastrous for me, and he really wished I hadn't done it. He said I had stomach problems, breathing problems and a record of mental problems. I had to be very careful, he said, or I would be on a downward spiral. He was so over the top I ended up laughing. 'I come to see my doctor for a prescription for Ventolin and Symbicort, and get a warning that I am probably going to go bonkers again.'

Tuesday 2 September

TB called at 7.20, asking what I thought of Mrs Kelly's evidence. He felt that it was becoming clearer and clearer that it was a personal tragedy, that the political ramifications were not as great as our opponents hoped. We both had a residual fear that Hutton himself was bound to be influenced by the media coverage, day after day projected to put us in the worst possible light, but TB said his sense was of someone who would make up his own mind based on fact, and that in so far as he had made impressions of the key witnesses, we will have come over better than [Greg] Dyke [BBC Director-General], [Gavyn] Davies [chairman], [Richard] Sambrook [head of news] and Gilligan, none of whom did well. We agreed that it was sensible for me to stay low-profile until the report was published.

Before long, we were on to the usual theme – what to do about GB? He said he was clear it couldn't go on indefinitely like this, GB pulling in a different direction while pretending not to. He felt he would have to offer him a move which he knew he wouldn't accept, and then just move him out. But as he said it, I could tell he wasn't sure. There was a hesitation and a thinness to the voice. He was aware of the scale of the problem finally, but unclear about a solution. He kept coming back to the point that though GB was impossible, in terms of sheer ability he was the only talent who got near to TB. 'The ones asking me to kick him out don't actually have to make the decision, and they are not really thinking through the consequences,' he said. 'They are just assuming that if he leaves the government, he leaves the scene and that is that. It would be very different.'

I asked him what pills he had been taking at the weekend given the compendious notes he sent over. 'What did you think?' I said I thought there was a lot of good stuff in there, but I could sense his frustration at the difficulty in making it happen. He asked me to talk to Andrew Adonis [policy advisor] and Peter Hyman [strategy advisor] about the manifesto process, which had obviously been a big part of his thinking in the notes. AA had done a good note on process, suggesting policies should be in place, and some unveiled, in the pre-election conference, alongside the themes he hoped to fight on. Both he and Pat McFadden [special advisor] felt TB had lost his ownership of the education agenda, and Pat in particular felt 'community' and especially poorer kids and families, should be TB's big progressive cause up to 2005.

AA felt a development of Sure Start* was the way to do both. He had also done a good note analysing the weaknesses of the 2001 manifesto, both in terms of content, feeling it lacked the scope and scale of '97, and also that the process had failed to involve party and policy makers properly, let alone engage the public. He also had some very good ideas for making the policy development process far more open and inclusive.

David Davies [Football Association executive] popped round. Both the FA and the Football Foundation were keen for me to work with them, and he also had a notion that he and I could go into some kind of business partnership together. I explained that for a while I was going to take it easy, not make firm commitments until I started to get clearer in my own mind what I wanted to do. I had always felt that if I was in the job, but thinking about the next one, I had effectively stopped doing the job, so although I had agonised about staying or leaving for ages, I had not really thought about what I was going to do in a post-No. 10 existence. So things felt odd now. A few days after leaving, I literally had no idea what I was going to do with myself in the future. Or today and tomorrow even.

I had a meeting with David Hill and just went over the various personnel inside No. 10 and in departments, talked him through who was who, who was good, who was less good and which departments he had to keep an eye on. In truth, compared with when we first started out, we had pretty good relations across Whitehall, and the problems we had on the co-ordination front were as much about the political side of thing as the civil service. David was definitely the right choice to take over from me. He would calm things down with the media, TB liked him, and also he wouldn't mind if TB kept a line open to me for extra advice.

I think we knew each other well enough, and liked each other well

* Government area-based initiative, announced in 1998, with the aim of giving young children the best possible start in life through improved childcare, early education, health and family support.

enough, to make sure that didn't become a problem. I told him he could always call on me if he wanted to, and likewise he could always tell me to butt out if I wasn't wanted. He said he knew TB would always rely on me to some extent and he welcomed that. I said getting the balance between foreign and domestic was always hard. Pre-empting the cross-cutting issues that needed early central co-ordination was always harder than it should be. I told him I would not be offended if he tried to develop a different style which used me as a foil. I felt DH would do a good job, though he was the first to admit he was more a hands-on media handler than a strategist.

We went out for the premiere of *Calendar Girls*, black tie and all that, and it felt a bit odd being shouted at by the paps as we went in. I had very mixed feelings about it all. There was something very superficial about it. I'd noticed in recent weeks just how much more I seemed to get recognised around the place. Sometimes I liked it, because it made me feel I had done something, and also because it indicated all sorts of options for the future. But sometimes I hated it, just wanted to feel normal again. Grace [AC's daughter] and Sissy [Matilda Bridge, friend of Grace] were loving it, of course, all the red carpet bollocks and the snappers shouting out. Fiona less so. She said having spent years walking two steps behind Cherie, now it looked like she'd have to do the same with me.

I did a gaggle of interviews on the way in, which were meant to be about promoting *Calendar Girls* and Leukaemia Research, but half of which were about me and leaving the job, which I danced around. I was also asked to do a speech to kick the whole thing off, talking about my own role with the charity, so was suddenly out on stage in front of a packed theatre, but I spoke about John and Ellie [John Merritt, AC's closest friend, who had died of leukaemia, and daughter Ellie, who was also killed by the disease] and why I got involved, made a few allusions to the recent fuss, and it seemed to go down well enough. Given the subject of the film, and the role in it of the Women's Institute, I made a joke about TB's Women's Institute slow handclap [when addressing a WI Wembley conference].

Ian Hislop [satirist, broadcaster] was there, his mother having died of leukaemia, and was asking me to do *Have I Got News for You?* I was intending to say no to most things for a while. A bloke came up to me at the dinner, and said there was something very Zeitgeist about me being there, at this film, about this illness, set in the part of the world I came from [Yorkshire] at a time I was so much in the news. He said

I should not underestimate how much people saw me as my own man, not just an extension of TB, and I should focus on that. Angela Baker, the woman played by Julie Walters in the film, knew Mum, having been a singer in the Grassington Singers [community choir]. She was also the registrar at [AC's brother] Graeme's wedding. They were such palpably good people and it was a nice evening all round.

I had a lovely chat with Lindsay [Nicholson, widow of John Merritt] and her new bloke, Mark [Johansen]. He was not what I expected, very different to John, but they seemed happy together. I had mixed feelings about that too, even if I knew I shouldn't. It was ridiculous to think someone widowed so young would never marry again, but I suppose it just hammered home even more than ever the finality of death, and the fact that memories fade with time, and life has to go on.

The film was terrific, and the girls loved it. I got a warm reception everywhere, which Fiona said was down to the fact I no longer worked for TB. I said she was going to have to get over the negativity she felt towards him. It was pointless, added to which I was still going to be involved with him in some ways, including at the next election. He called again later. He said he was aware that for the next few months it was going to be like being inside a tunnel. The media and the Tories sense his vulnerability. They think he is in a swamp and to some extent he is. 'What they underestimate is my ability to swim through it,' he said. The key is sorting domestic policy, and somehow managing GB. GB had clearly been at JP again, who last night had been echoing the line to TB that 'we just make it worse by going on about crime the whole time'.

Matthew Rycroft [Downing Street foreign affairs private secretary] called, to say that we had been informed who the other parties in the Hutton Inquiry wanted to cross-examine. The BBC wanted me, John Scarlett and Julian Miller [Cabinet Office official], so clearly they were going to focus on the dossier in the main.* The Kelly family wanted Tom Kelly [No. 10 spokesman] re the Kelly/Walter Mitty comment.† I got home to a stack more messages – offers from *The Observer*, LBC [London-based radio station], ITV, a commercial radio network, the

---

* Following an 'off-the-record' discussion between Dr David Kelly and reporter Andrew Gilligan about the government's dossier on weapons of mass destruction in Iraq, Gilligan quoted an unnamed source's allegations that the dossier had been 'sexed up'.

† In what Downing Street regarded as an off-the-record talk with journalists, Tom Kelly had referred to David Kelly as a 'Walter Mitty character', referring to a James Thurber character who constantly fantasised. Tom Kelly apologised to David Kelly's family.

[*London Evening*] *Standard* offering me a sports column, a US speaking agency, a Dutch agency. At least I had plenty to choose from when I finally decided to make some choices. For now, none of it held much appeal.

Wednesday 3 September

Angela Baker had made a real impression on me. She showed me that there are so many different ways to make a difference. She had started out trying to raise a few bob for a sofa in a hospital waiting room, after her husband [John Baker] had died, and now she was the stuff of books and films, and making loads of money for the charity. She was also such a nice and warm human being, as were the other calendar girls, but she really had something quite special. I definitely want to get more involved with the charity. I went in for a meeting re Hutton and was called into TB's meeting to discuss his next press conference.

I was arguing he needed to get back on to a values message, the same TB that was elected, pursuing policies aimed directly at improving people's lives. He kept coming back to saying that the way to deal with trust was to persuade people we were doing the right thing. We just went round in circles on it. I said I felt that people thought he had floated off. He said it didn't matter as long as we were doing the right thing and in Iraq and on public services, he remained convinced we were. But people didn't believe it because of what they were told about him, day in day out, and yet he would not attack the press.

Charlie Falconer [Lord Chancellor] called, said he felt my evidence to Hutton had gone really well and I would be fine. He felt that I would go mad if I didn't have a big project, and I shouldn't hang around. Allison Pearson's column in the *Standard* said people were obsessed with me because I was devilishly sexy, which cheered me up. The press seemed to be reacting favourably to David Hill's appointment but I still felt it was a mistake to lose the Order in Council, which had allowed me to have civil servants working to me. I wasn't convinced it would stop them going for David, and making it explicit that he could not instruct civil servants might lead to a retrenchment of sorts, which would become a real problem if they thought power was slipping back to the Tories.

Our submissions to Hutton went in, the main points that it was clear the BBC story was wrong, an explanation as to why our anger was justified and why David Kelly had to appear at the select committees.

The BBC submission had a lot of blather and rubbish in it. Insofar as there was substance, it was mainly focused on the dossier. The family's submission was a very harsh document, particularly vis-à-vis the MoD. They wanted Geoff Hoon [Defence Secretary], Bryan Wells, Martin Howard, Pam Teare and Martin Hatfield [MoD officials], and also Tom Kelly on the Walter Mitty point. They also wanted Gilligan.

Charlie got my hopes up a little when he said the feedback Garry Hart [Falconer's special advisor] got was that the judge was impressed with me and there was an outside chance I wouldn't be called back. I doubted that. The *Private Eye* front cover had me and Calum on it, pictured at the football on Saturday, with Calum saying, 'What did you do in the war, Daddy?' and me saying, 'I started it.' I thought it was quite funny but a number of people called and suggested I should do something about it. No point. It was one of four pictures on there, suggesting they hadn't been able to decide what to do as the cover. There was the one with Calum; one of me next to a desk fan in the office which had a speech bubble, 'I'm your only fan'; one with TB and David Frost asking him, 'What will you do without him?' and a blank speech bubble next to TB; then one of Peter with the bubble: 'I am the new face of no-spin Labour.' I called Hislop and asked for a proof to frame. [It now has pride of place in AC's downstairs toilet amid dozens of cartoons.]

Jonathan [Powell, No. 10 chief of staff] held a staff meeting to go over some of the changes planned following my departure, but by all accounts it didn't go terribly well, not least because he didn't have any Q&A. I got home, and ran for an hour.

Thursday 4 September
TB called when I was still in bed to resume the conversation of yesterday, namely that he didn't know what the press conference was supposed to be about. We were arguing it was about trailing the values-based message pre-conference. But he lacked confidence or purpose at the moment. I went in later to go through more files and I had barely got in the building when Alison said, as she had said so many times before, 'The Prime Minister wants you to pop round and see him.' We had two more conversations of the same ilk, round and round in circles, and at one point DH gave me a look that said, 'What have I come into?' At one point, TB just picked up the sports section of the *Telegraph* and read it for fully five minutes while the rest of us sat there

making small talk before he came back to the same point. I said to him afterwards he was giving every impression of slightly losing the plot.

The press was full of the former DIS [Defence Intelligence Staff] man Brian Jones, who said at the Hutton Inquiry yesterday that there had been real disquiet over the 45 minutes point.* John Scarlett and Julian Miller came in to see to TB to explain the background: that the DIS people on the JIC did not make John or the JIC aware of these concerns. John said that he felt that what was happening post my resignation was that things were moving away from me being the big bad beast to him being the problem because he did not heed warnings. There were also concerns that the ISC [Intelligence and Security Committee] were going to be very critical of John and David Omand [Cabinet Office Security and Intelligence Co-ordinator], even to the point of them having to resign. John was looking even more worried than usual and TB had to tell him not to be concerned. Also, [Hoon special advisor] Richard Taylor's evidence was going to add to Geoff Hoon's problems. John came round for a chat, said he was coping well, but he was clearly finding it very tough, everything being so public.

TB's press conference went OK but the tension was there between saying no change, we hold firm on the one hand, while emphasising the importance of renewal. I was just tired of having the same conversations. David H said, 'Is it always like this?' I nodded. Hutton part one came to an end. [Former United Nations Special Commission weapons inspector] Olivia Bosch's evidence was good for me and bad for Gilligan. Richard Taylor was bad for GH. Hutton was very measured and said it should not be taken as a sign of criticism if he recalled witnesses. I bought a new pair of running shoes and ran home. It was astonishing how much more often I was recognised and pointed out as I ran, and it was all a bit weird.

Friday 5 September

Some of the media were picking up on TB being a bit less confident, and some linking it to my departure. I went in later and he called me out on the terrace before his meeting with [US General John] Abizaid. He said we had lots to do. He was still talking as if I was still there, and

---

* Andrew Gilligan's claims that a government dossier on weapons of mass destruction had been 'sexed up' alleged that AC had been responsible for inserting that Saddam Hussein could deploy WMDs within 45 minutes.

going to be there in the future. I was deliberately wearing sports gear, and not a suit, to signal I wasn't really there, but I guess he was used to seeing me in running gear, so it didn't seem to have much effect. He said for the first time he felt a barrier growing between him and the country. 'It is not hostile out there, but some of the warmth from some of the people has gone.' He felt it was partly Iraq but mainly non-delivery. I said don't underestimate the drip-drip effect of all the personal stuff, lifestyle, CB [Cherie Blair]/Carole Caplin [friend and advisor to CB] etc.* The message going out the whole time is that you are no longer one of them. He didn't really want to buy into it.

He had had JP at him all morning about Peter M having been at Chequers, which sounded a total rerun of the Chewton Glen meeting in opposition, Peter there, JP not. [Chewton Glen, a Hampshire hotel, had been the venue for a Labour away-day in opposition from which JP felt excluded, to his annoyance when he found out Mandelson had been there.] Also GB was successfully winding up John against foundation hospitals and top-up fees. TB looked very down, said he couldn't see how he was ever going to get the show back on the road again. GB was hostile and now extending hostilities to try to get JP over. TB said I must do a column in the *Sunday Times*, where I'll be heard, have a voice and use it for us. I wasn't sure I could be bothered with doing something every week like that. I would rather write something when I felt like it. He was still confident on Hutton.

Neil [Kinnock, former Labour leader, Vice-President of the European Commission] came in for lunch, spent an hour or so going over his problems at the Commission, lacerating [Commission President] Romano Prodi re his management skills. I could sense he was a bit down and worried about it all. He also felt the mood was moving against Tony, and he might have only a couple of conferences left. There was definitely a whiff of departure, which I supposed I fuelled a bit with my own resignation, and TB had to act fast, decide one way or the other and then act on it. Neil felt TB had not looked after people well enough, and so created more enemies than he needed to, also that his language was less rooted in ordinary families than it used to be. And of course GB was there the whole time, breathing down his neck.

I went with Gail [Rebuck, CEO Random House] to the home of Sonny Mehta [chairman, Knopf publishing company] for a general

---

* Cherie Blair's association with Caplin became newly controversial when Caplin's relationship with Peter Foster, a convicted conman, became public knowledge.

chat about diaries and Sonny's assessment of the interest in the States. I hadn't decided what if anything to do with them, but he said he was sure there would be interest in America. Gail and I had never really discussed publishing them, but it was pretty clear if I did, I would do it with her. Then back to the office for a meeting on Hutton. Jonathan Sumption [AC's lawyer] felt John Scarlett and I were the two most likely to be recalled.

He felt it was a bit odd that Hutton had agreed almost without question to a BBC demand for further documents, but wondered if it was because he was actually basically with us and wanted to be seen to be fair. The ISC [which had carried out an inquiry into the Iraq War] was beginning to leak and it seemed that it was good for me re 45 minutes and 'sexing up', and would say I had not, but did say that with hindsight it would have been better if the 45 minutes point had not been in there because its inclusion caused the subsequent confusion. Ridiculous. It did no such thing. It only became a huge issue long after, with the BBC report.

I felt TB should speak to Ann Taylor [ISC chair] to underline how important it was that they defended the JIC's and John Scarlett's integrity in any media around the report. TB was not sure they would respond too well to any pressure. But John was worried the pressure was moving from me to him and that they would go for him on the quality of the intelligence because no WMD [weapons of mass destruction] had been found. I said it made tactical sense to get the focus back on to me. At the end of the Sumption/Hutton meeting, JS [Scarlett] took me aside and asked everyone else to leave. He said TB would miss me and so would he, because in a world where friendship was not easily built, I was a good friend to have. In a way, my going had definitely put extra pressure on him but he was just very nice, warm and supportive and I appreciated it. I felt it was inevitable we would both be recalled by the Inquiry, in my case in part for PR reasons.

Saturday 6 September
To Stoke v Burnley with Calum. Lunch with Peter Coates [Stoke chairman, Labour supporter] and his wife Deirdre. He felt we were in much weaker shape than before, but couldn't see us losing the next election. The Tories just weren't where they needed to be and showed little sign of working out how to get there. TB called from Balmoral (he and CB were there for the annual PM weekend with the Queen) halfway

September '03: Intelligence Committee report looking OK

through lunch. He said there had been a bit of booing when he arrived at the Balmoral Show, but he was not sure whether it was SNP, anti-Iraq protesters or raving Tories who thought he and CB – who was pictured yawning – shouldn't be there. He hated that kind of thing though, not least because it meant it would be the only thing anyone knew or heard about it. He said the Queen had been asking after me, but I couldn't quite tell if he was joking.

It was a great game, with Graham Branch [Burnley footballer] playing really well. I really like these guys – in whatever walk of life – who get hammered – in his case last year by the fans – but then keep going and win back respect over time. That was the thing TB had to build on. I felt it in myself too. I got a very friendly reception from the Burnley fans today, some of whom did an 'only one Ali Campbell' chant when I first arrived, and from some of the Stoke people when we were walking round to the away end, and I was thinking that if these people believed even half of the shit they had read, I wouldn't be able to walk anywhere without protection. That being said, Peter Coates had asked for a few security people to take me round. But the reaction showed people didn't believe a lot of the shit, or at least that they understood in politics, if someone had it in for you, there might be an ulterior motive. We drove over to Mum and Dad's afterwards. She was telling me how upset Calum had been when she spoke to him after I went back from France to give evidence. Calum certainly seemed a lot happier now I was out.

Sunday 7 September
Ran for an hour, then we set off home after lunch. Dad was not looking so great, a bit breathless, and his eyes tired, but he and Calum had a good chat about football, school, usual stuff. Calum was taking the mickey out of me writing a diary when I have nothing to put in it 'now that you're unemployed and basically just my driver and banker'. Out for dinner with the Goulds and the McEwans [novelist Ian and his wife Annalena McAfee, author and journalist]. Ian had been following the Hutton Inquiry very closely and had a very good take on it, had sussed out the main characters and why, on the BBC side, their arguments were so weak. He may just have been saying it to make me feel better, but he said he felt I would come out fine.

TB had sent over a note AA had done a while back on how the Tories had prepared for their third term under Thatcher, and there were some very interesting lessons for us in there. It was odd how AA was so loathed by so many in the party – not least Fiona on some of the education stuff – because what was interesting was how much he put the role and interest of the party at the centre of his thinking. He said part of what the Tories did pre-'87, from a very weak position around the time of Westland* was to develop strength through a strategic [Chancellor Nigel] Lawson budget, which got the tax cut dynamic back in play, stepping up privatisation, public service reform, especially when Ken Baker replaced Keith Joseph at Education, and above all by bringing it together under a programme totally focused on the future and a pre-election slogan 'The next moves forward', which became the title of the manifesto. AA was recommending that we have the same systemic approach, by setting up a dozen or so pre-manifesto policy groups and getting much of the reform agenda up by conference. Interestingly, his analysis barely mentioned Maggie's [Margaret Thatcher's] foreign policy profile, feeling these broader domestic changes were far more important and driven by what he called 'intellectual ascendancy'. Again, he felt we had the same intellectual ascendancy now but were not making enough of it. I sent him a message saying I thought it was a superb analysis and TB should follow his suggestions on process ASAP.

Monday 8 September

A nice warm day and I went into No. 10 to read more Hutton stuff, and did a couple of meetings. The letters were still coming in and still broadly supportive. I saw TB out on the balcony and he was very down re GB, said he couldn't see how to improve things with him. 'He is a complete nightmare at the moment.' I bumped into GB in No. 11 on my way through to my old office in No. 12, and he could not have been more charming. Real hail fellow, well met stuff. 'How're you doing, how're the kids, regards to Fiona', like he used to be. He said I looked really fit, and asked if I was happier being outside? He made a joke about my departure getting more coverage than if TB had gone, and I said something about wishful thinking and he laughed. He said

---

* The Westland affair of 1985–86 saw Margaret Thatcher and Defence Secretary Michael Heseltine publicly disagree over the future of Britain's last helicopter manufacturer, Westland Helicopters. Heseltine resigned and Westland accepted a bail-out deal from American company Sikorsky.

he was doing lots of exercise too, 45 minutes running and swimming every day if he could find the time. He was his old charming self, not a word about any of the current problems.

I spent the afternoon sorting through hundreds of files, and trying to separate what was personal and what was government. Alison and her team really had done a brilliant job for me. They had kept pretty much everything in all sorts of different files. It brought home to me just how many huge events we had been involved with in the last few years. When I was at the running track later, Catherine [Rimmer, head of research] and Clare [Sumner] called and read through the letter from the Hutton Inquiry, confirming I would be recalled to give evidence again, and going through areas for questioning and possible criticisms. These included the fact that I was involved in the dossier at all. Also, getting over-angry with the BBC. Also the fact that I suggested 'leaking' Kelly's name – which I didn't – on 3 July. Tom [Kelly] and Godric [Smith, AC's former deputy, now co-spokesman with Kelly] were also being recalled, which was ridiculous.

Everyone had said I could hardly have done better first time round, and maybe deep down I had been raising hopes I wouldn't be recalled at all. But now I felt really low, not far off being depressed, just like when I got the first letter out in France. I tossed and turned all night. It was the thought of psyching myself up again, dealing with the media circus outside again, going through what was bound to be a much tougher ordeal the second time around. Fiona was being much nicer and more supportive now that I was out. She went through the diary extracts for the first time and didn't think they were that bad, apart from the reference to 'fuck Gilligan', which of course was part of what they wanted to publish.* The first time I gave evidence, they had referred to the diaries, but now intended to publish some of the relevant parts, and 'fuck Gilligan' would be part of that, and send the media into a frenzy no doubt.

Tuesday 9 September

I was up early and off to see Les Hinton [executive chairman, News International] at his house in Hampstead. He had lots of ideas of things I could do but I wasn't keen to commit to anything. He was very down

---

* In a then unpublished diary, made available to the Inquiry, AC had written that 'it would fuck [Andrew] Gilligan' if Dr David Kelly proved to be his source.

on GB, felt he was basically old Labour and serious people noticed that he was not loyal. He even asked whether I thought TB would fight four elections, and clearly felt he should. He was probing on whether I thought anyone other than GB was up to it. He felt I was uniquely placed and agreed that I shouldn't rush. But he hoped I would consider doing something for them, and was intending to put together a big package of politics and sport across the titles. I felt more up for the sport than the politics.

In for a meeting with the government lawyers, Alan Maclean and Adam Sharples. They felt I had to co-operate with the Inquiry's request to publish some of the diary extracts and I was modestly relaxed about that. They felt that the extracts they were going for, and asking to publish, suggested it was more about GH than me. He and I were due to give evidence on the same day. TB meanwhile had received a letter warning that areas where he might be criticised – though nothing was finalised – might be having an input into the document, also whether he was vicariously responsible for an underhand naming strategy re Kelly. He was rightly worried about that, felt that if it stuck, things would be really difficult. The lawyers couldn't really understand the process, whereby we could all be cross-examined but without really knowing what the possible criticisms might be. It all felt very hostile, but both Charlie [Falconer] and Cherie thought Hutton was just going through everything he had to go through in a very thorough way. I was really fed up with it though, as was Godric. Tom was putting on a brave face. I spent three hours working on a draft supplementary statement. I was also worrying about whether I could go ahead in doing the Great North Run the day before I appeared again, and also whether I could do any private sector work at all before Hutton reported, which could be months and months away.

The ISC report arrived. It exonerated me, wasn't bad for the JIC but they were critical of GH because he had not been open re the DIS criticism. I was pleased personally, given the exoneration was pretty clear, so that meant both select committees had cleared me [AC had previously been cleared by the Foreign Affairs Committee (FAC) of wrongdoing in relation to the build-up to war] but a part of me just felt the anger once more that this had even happened. TB's general take on Hutton was that it would be OK for me, less for the government. We had a meeting on how to respond to the ISC report. John S said his wife was in a rage that he was to be cross-examined by the BBC. I knew how she felt but we just had to get on with it. Clare Sumner said she had assumed I had stopped doing my diary. I said certainly not and she laughed, then threw an orange marker pen at me.

I got a fantastic letter from Bertie Ahern [Irish Prime Minister], really personal, and a lot about the role Joe Lennon [Ahern spokesman] and I played in the Good Friday talks. He said there were times when it was only the creativity we showed in keeping the media occupied and at bay that gave him and TB and the others the space to get things done. He could not have been warmer and said TB could not have achieved what he had done as a leader and PM without the support I gave him. There was a letter from GWB [US President George W. Bush] too, saying news of my departure had reached Crawford [Bush's Texan home], he wished me well and said I had served my country and TB well. It was handwritten, and I remembered the time Karl Rove [Bush advisor] had said Bush reached the top by writing more thank-you letters than anyone else. Fiona signed up to do a fitness column for *The Guardian*. I said it was the first step to being a lifestyle guru to the chattering classes.

Wednesday 10 September

I was back to not sleeping well, waking up the whole time, fretting, Q&A going on endlessly in my head. Today's media problem was the ISC report, which was leaked to the *Standard*, who nosed on the point about GH misleading MPs, drowning out any sense that I had been cleared, but also somehow making it look like it came from No. 10. It was pretty obvious the leak came from the Tories or the Libs and it was a total set-up for IDS at PMQs. Geoff [Hoon] had been trying to persuade Ann Taylor to go a bit softer on him, but the leak made it virtually impossible. I went in to keep going through the thousands of files with Alison. I was amazed at how much stuff there was to go through. Clare Sumner felt that where I was not 100 per cent convincing in my statement was on contacts with [*Times* journalist Tom] Baldwin. That was because I couldn't remember all the many conversations with him so I worked through a note trying to figure out where I may have contributed to the various *Times* articles.

I had lunch with Jamie Rubin [former US Assistant Secretary of State] at Wiltons. He had been through something similar when he left as Madeleine Albright's spokesman, and had lots of good advice. Do lots of speeches at first, here and in the States, to make sure there are no financial worries. Use six months at least to work out what you want to do. Once the speaking bids fall a bit, do TV and punditry to raise the profile. He said he had enjoyed leaving the administration but then there came a day when he missed the phone not ringing. That's when you have to start to work it all out for yourself. On Hutton, though he had always felt we made a mistake in getting too sucked into the Bush post-9/11 agenda, he thought people could see the difference between taking the wrong decision – as he believed we did – and lying or deliberately misleading the public, which he believed we didn't. He said there were people in his social circle who didn't like me or TB, but who did not believe the conspiracy theories.

TB called and said he wasn't sure why but he was very confident that Hutton would not be bad for either of us and I really shouldn't worry. I said I do worry. He asked if there was anything in particular I worried about and I said no, but I don't like having to wait and trust the judgement of others. I was getting into the mindset of imagining the worst all the time. He said the TUC [Trades Union Congress] speech last night went OK. The press had made spin the issue by saying that TB didn't say what had been briefed in advance. He felt David would be able to get the press more onside but what he still wanted from me was strategic breadth and depth. Philip [Gould] felt that Peter M trying to fill the gap I left was not being successful because while everyone in No. 10 and around government had a basic respect for my abilities, Peter is not seen in the same way because of his independent political profile and ambition. Jamie had said over lunch that the first time he ever met Peter he had gossiped about several ministers before the starters had arrived, and he thought if that's what he's like with strangers, what's he like with people he knew?

TB did fine at PMQs, partly because Duncan Smith went OTT on Hoon, ISC, trust, me. Adam Sharples and Alan Maclean came in at 5, having done a very good job on my draft supplementary statement. I felt I had been thorough and clear but they had spotted a few gaps and also bits where it could have been clearer. I was really impressed by their work. As I left, I bumped into TB, who was at the bottom of the stairs to the flat talking to Sue Nye [GB special advisor, and wife of Gavyn Davies, BBC chairman]. For understandable reasons, I guess, she was a bit cool, though not hostile.

TB asked me up to the flat to discuss Geoff's situation. As we trudged up the stairs and he pinged in the door lock code, I was trying to think if I had had a single day since leaving without being back in for some reason. Every time I had gone in, either for Hutton meetings, or just to sort out all the files and where they should go, he found out and asked me to have a chat. He wanted to make a cup of tea but I said I wanted to get back for the football. On Geoff, he was clearly worried. I said if Ann Taylor said he should resign it would be very difficult, but anything short of that he should tough it out. On the way out, I bumped into GB again, not quite as gushing, but still clearly not wanting to discuss anything but small talk. I got home to find messages asking me to do *Desert Island Discs* and present *Have I Got News for You?* Both suggested has-beenology, and worried rather than excited me. England 2, Liechtenstein 0.

Thursday 11 September
Ninety-minute run along the canal, back through the parks. As Fiona said, it was indicative of how negatively some people saw us that anyone was prepared to believe that we would have leaked the ISC report. It was building up pressure on GH. I don't know whether it was because the run had cleared my head – at one point on the canal I realised I had gone several miles and had not really been aware of where I was – but I was already feeling a bit more distant from it. Just one brief chat with TB about my statement for phase two questioning and his letter setting out possible areas of criticism of him. Only a handful of us knew that he had received a letter. Sumption spent much of the day focusing on that and making clear that both potential criticisms – one, that nobody but the JIC should have been involved in the dossier and two, that TB was vicariously responsible for the Q&A and so a Kelly naming strategy – were unfair and wrong. My only worry was about Baldwin and which of his various stories I had contributed to because I couldn't be 100 per cent sure and I hated the possibility of it looking like I was trying to dissemble.

Catherine dug out some excellent examples to blow apart inconsistencies and inaccuracies in the BBC case: for example, Dyke briefing at the weekend of the governors' meeting and the *Sunday Telegraph* saying he and Davies rejected a deal. Also a two-way by Norman Smith [BBC political reporter] which said at the time that the reason I was at the Foreign Affairs Committee was that the story was just not going away. I was in No. 10 for several hours in the afternoon, going over it all once more. Stan Ternent called about tickets for the Burnley match on Saturday. He said if you want a man-in-the-street view, it's that the BBC should apologise. I drafted my own version to deal with the point about why I got so angry. Ann Taylor was fine today and GH did OK. Needless to say the point about me being totally exonerated was just getting buried in all the other stuff. The Tories behaving like total twats, as ever. Richard Norton-Taylor ran a horrible piece about John Scarlett in *The Guardian* saying he should go. A nice call from David Manning [diplomat, former TB chief foreign policy advisor] in the States. I felt by the end of the day that my statement was pretty strong, if a bit long. We also had to decide whether it was too personal. Both Ian Austin [GB aide] and Ed Balls [Chief Economic Advisor to the Treasury] were being very supportive when I saw them around the place, so maybe GB was trying to change things a bit.

Friday 12 September

Still not sleeping well so I went out early for a run on Hampstead Heath. The media were expecting to get the Hutton recall list today so we had crews outside again but I gave them the slip by going out through the Bridges' [AC's neighbours] house. In the event, Hutton only gave out Monday's witnesses, so the story was going to be Dyke called to give evidence. I went in for another session with the lawyers. Bruce [Grocott, MP, TB advisor] came over, helpful as ever, and said he felt I should cut out expressions of regret, which would get blown out of proportion. He felt I was on strong ground without it and if I gave an inch, the media would take a mile. He said he felt I had been part of Labour's history, the best ever at what I did and I should now make some money, have a good time for a while, but make sure I was back before the election. He was also adamant that 'you owe it to political history' to write books, firstly because I can write, but also because I had recorded it every day. I did a call with Sumption, who was starting to plan out his BBC cross-examination. Catherine's team did a really good job trying to analyse Baldwin's various sources, which clearly included the BBC.

I did a little farewell for my inner team at No. 10, and read out parts of [John Major's former press secretary] Jonathan Haslam's handover note (on the strengths and weaknesses of the press office staff) to me back in 1997. He had got some of them right and some of them very wrong. I told them they had been a superb team and I couldn't have got through the last period without them. David Hill would be starting properly next week and I wanted to get my desk totally cleared before that. Even as I was speaking, Catherine was still working away at my computer. She and Clare had been absolutely phenomenal. Sumption told me he was minded not to cross-examine Dyke, though he would make a judgement dependent on his evidence. But he felt Davies was very weak.

I had been worrying about whether to go ahead with plans to do the Great North Run so close to giving evidence again, and he said he thought it would be fine if I did it, that actually it was a good idea 'but I hope you don't die. If you do, it's better that you're murdered than that you die of natural causes. You see, I'm learning, and thinking about the presentational impact.' Everyone had said he and I wouldn't get on but I liked him and respected his ability. We agreed that he and I would meet on Monday so that he could help get my head in gear. I still felt I was being unfairly treated with regard to being the only one asked to provide my diary, and now for parts of it to be published, but when I said that, he just said, 'It has to be. You'll be fine.'

Saturday 13 September

It was nice not to have to do all the usual Saturday conference calls. JR [John Reid, Health Secretary] called, said it was really weird last week to do *Frost* without me phoning him before, during and after. We set off for Norwich v Burnley, lunch with [Norwich City owners] Delia [Smith] and [husband] Michael [Wynn-Jones] and their mothers, who were brilliant. Delia had told me her mum was my biggest fan and sure enough, she spent the whole lunch telling me so, and telling me Tony still needed me, and she hoped I saw off everyone and went back. She said she felt I would have been a better PM than Tony. It is such a nice club, and the mood in the bit where Delia has lunch very down to earth and un-corporate. They got me to do a little Q&A for fans, almost all about football, just a couple of half-political questions. Charles Clarke [Education Secretary] and family arrived and Fiona was talking to them while I was talking to Phil Webster [*Times* journalist], who said the feeling was that we would be fine, though of course nobody could know. I reckoned I would probably be challenged over relations with *The Times* and said to him it was dreadful that journalists who actually did what they believed to be right, like him and Tom, should be pilloried.

The game was OK but we lost 2–0 thanks to some dreadful defensive errors. Charles was worried TB would be a lot more vulnerable to GB attacks without me there, and that Peter would not fill the gap because he would be thinking of his own position not TB's. He felt

Gordon would be a disaster as leader, everyone knew it and yet the longer he stayed where he was the likelier it was that he would see off everyone else. We headed to Lavenham and dinner with the Goulds at the Angel. Philip had some good thoughts on my statement, mainly the need to explain what I actually did and legitimise it. There was a danger that ignorance about the need for a role like mine meant that people, even someone like Hutton, would not understand why TB had to have someone like me doing what I did. He felt it needed more context about the nature of modern politics and the modern media. He also felt I needed to make the Baldwin section less defensive, and be clearer in the explanation why I was involved in the dossier. He was going on endlessly about how much of a vacuum I had left because there was nobody there that people trusted to be strong with TB. Peter M was the only one really, but he was divisive. I wasn't missing it at all at the moment but Philip felt I should be more involved not less. He said he was not sure he could bear to be in there day in, day out if I wasn't also in there making sure TB was on the right track.

Sunday 14 September

I did a half marathon, Lavenham and Sudbury, just over 1.45, which was OK. While I was out running, an idea popped into my head, about a possible book – 'Demons' – about my nervous breakdown, and broader lessons, which I thought might be a useful and counter-intuitive first book, rather than what was expected, and I started to draft out possible structure and sections in my head as I ran. I was struck when I resigned that a few people mentioned my recovery from the breakdown as being a significant part of what I had done and achieved. Some of the mental health charities were now pressing me to get more involved.

I called C to commiserate about tomorrow, and the fact he was having to give evidence, and to wish him luck. He sounded very fed up. He felt that the media expected too much by way of openness and that one day people would realise that the strength of the secret services lay in the secrecy and their ability to work in ways that were not always understood. The oversight and the ISC had been big steps, but he felt there would be more and more pressure until they just became another service. He had been to see Hutton and James Dingemans [counsel to the Inquiry] in private, and said they were pretty apologetic, but felt they had to call him. He was happy to go, not least because he could support John re the JIC process. Hutton had made clear he didn't want a circus, and Richard [Dearlove] was going to be allowed to do it down the line from SIS HQ, rather than have to run the media gauntlet as we had done. C had been absolutely clear he wouldn't talk about methods or sources. He strongly felt that what we had done was fine and proper and like me was angry at the way John S had been treated. He was furious at [former JIC chairman] Rodric Braithwaites's piece in the *Standard* about what a JIC chairman should and shouldn't do, and said that if he saw him he would tell him he was a fucking disgrace. Both he and John got how in the modern world you have to adapt and change, maybe be more open than you want to be.

I was still working on my statement, a new Baldwin section to make it clearer, and a new section about the nature of the modern media which was why I had been involved in the dossier. Sumption decided against using the second bit. He said that while he understood what I was trying to do, in terms of public consumption of my statement, his only concern remained the judge and he felt it was unnecessary, that in the first round of questioning he did not feel Hutton shared any view that somehow my role was illegitimate.

Monday 15 September

I spent most of the day working on the statement and also agreeing the letter to go to the Inquiry about my diaries. I watched Dingemans on TV, going through the questions for phase two and who he wanted back, with the focus very much on me, Hoon and Gilligan. The news today was focused on the DIS guys, who were OK, and C, who was very good. He called me afterwards, said it was a bit weird being at the end of a microphone but he felt he got his points over, also that he had a go at Kelly when he was told that he discussed CX [classified intelligence material] with Susan Watts [BBC journalist]. Dyke was really poor and even the BBC news said it had produced some very awkward moments for him. I had a meeting with Sumption. He still felt there was no need to get Dyke recalled for cross-examination but I felt that we should. He wanted to keep the focus on Gilligan and Richard Sambrook, and felt Dyke had damaged himself anyway. He was sure that Hutton would have been unimpressed by Dyke, who he would have found cavalier. He seemed to think that the demeanour you might use on a sympathetic chat show was the one to take to a public inquiry headed by a judge.

Sumption was looking particularly shabby today, his clothes not quite fitting, very old-fashioned braces and his shoulder twitching away, but he was very welcoming and full of good humour. He said he felt I should now not over-prepare, that I was basically on top of things, and provided I adopted the same approach as first time round, things would be fine. I did feel on top of all the substance, so the most important thing was to get proper rest and make sure I was on form on the day. Bradders [David Bradshaw, No. 10 special advisor, long-time friend and colleague of AC] and Catherine were by now pretty much obsessed with the whole thing, to the point of it being almost comic. They could quote just about anything that anyone had said. Mention anyone involved in the whole story and they could reel off a stack of facts about them, quotes from their evidence, stories in the media about them.

TB called, mainly to talk about Hutton, I think looking for assurance that I was in the zone. Inter alia, he said Carole [Caplin] had told him she would never sell her story. She had got rid of Ian Monk [PR advisor] and now Martin Cruddace was in charge of her. My old lawyer at the *Mirror*! I said don't put her up anywhere. If she has to do anything, let it be an article not an interview. TB said she was a victim in all this, that the real evil people are the Paul Dacres and the Ian Monks. Martin Cruddace popped up to do a clip on her, so it was going to be difficult for a while. Some of the papers were saying she was writing a book, others saying she wasn't, and the former inventing the idea that TB would take her to court to stop it.

Tuesday 16 September

Another day working on the statement, in particular the section on the 'leak' idea post-Hoon conversation, where I wanted to say that I was not envisaging hiding the sourcing. Godric was a bit worried about it. Sumption was very against the idea of me addressing the nature of the modern media, said we had to avoid anything but fact. He said he had drafted a paragraph on the parliamentary importance of the document. I did something similar and we married them through the day and after a few cuts and a bit of tightening, got it finished. Once it was done, I took it away, hid in Gordon's little lounge in No. 11, and read it through on my own one last time before signing it off. It felt strong to me, had benefited from all the toing and froing and all the different comments. In the end, as before, I was happy to go with Sumption's judgement on anything that he felt might impact one way or the other on the judge. John Scarlett came over, said he was trying hard not to get angry. We went over what we would say on the 45-minute point and the allegations of concealment from the FAC. I felt comfortable with all the arguments.

Dyke did so badly that Sumption seemed to be enjoying himself setting out his strategy and why he didn't want to cross-examine. He really felt strongly there was no need to cross-examine Dyke, because he had been such a bad witness. He was sure that he could get what he wanted from Davies, Sambrook and Gilligan. TB likewise felt Dyke had been so bad that he could only do better next time, so leave him. Sumption and Maclean felt he was a wounded beast and we should just leave him there. Nobody felt he had done well. Catherine felt he had exposed a deep antipathy towards me, which again was unlikely to play in his or their favour. By mid-afternoon I had got my statement signed off, the letter re the diaries agreed, and I then settled down to read. The Hutton cross-examination process started. The family QC, Jeremy Gompertz, just seemed to be chasing headlines. He was pretty tough with Martin Howard. Kate Wilson [MoD chief press officer] did well, which was important. Sumption told me he really wasn't interested in the headlines, all that mattered was the judge and he intended to be very forensic. I was just trying to get in the zone now. His strong advice was to relax, not focus too much on it, but that was easier said than done. He said he was confident, based on my performance last time, and I really should not worry.

Wednesday 17 September

Gilligan and Sambrook were giving evidence. Sumption's debut. It went OK for us on substance, Gilligan and Sambrook saying sorry for getting things wrong. Needless to say the media didn't really go for them. As Tina Brown said when she called later, if that had been me or a government official, we were dead in the water based on a performance like that. I stayed at home all day, continuing to read through everything. It was a beautiful day and I felt myself getting in the zone for Monday. I was a bit up and down as to whether doing the Great North Run was the best preparation, even if Sumption seemed to think so. I missed PMQs, just forgot it was on, which was funny in a way. I did a conference call on Hutton. Philip called and said he was really worried about the way No. 10 was working. He hadn't fully realised how much I extended across the whole place, not just comms and politics. He felt the decision-making processes had become less clear, less crisp, more complicated.

Ed Victor [AC's literary agent] came round to discuss various book options. Gail had always been a fan and a friend of his, and she felt he was definitely the right guy for me if and when I decided to do the diaries. I mentioned a few other book ideas I had, e.g. sport, and also the mental health book. He said fine, but it would be odd not to do the diaries first. When I first came across Ed, I had really not imagined him to be my kind of guy, a bit too plugged in, a bit too social scene and all that, and he was a splendid name-dropper, but I liked him and I could tell he has judgement. I also liked that he wasn't rushing me, or making me feel I had to decide like right now. I went out for a half-hour run.

Thursday 18 September

All day working on cross-examination with Catherine, Clare, Adam Chapman and Stephen Parkinson [government lawyers]. The big area was my evidence to the FAC on why I didn't mention that I had made a point (in discussions on the dossier) about the 45 minutes. I was clear I didn't need to, but it could be difficult. We went over it for ages and agreed I should address it in evidence in chief. On the point about me getting too angry, which was one of the areas where I had been warned I might be criticised, I felt fine on that but they felt there were some weaknesses in the letters I wrote, so we went over how to address those if raised. I felt pretty justified in having been angry, given the nature of the allegations against me, knowing them to be unjustified, and there-fore felt confident I could explain satisfactorily why I had expressed myself as I did. Fine, they said, but do it without reliving the anger. Do not come over as angry and aggressive. John Scarlett came over for an hour or so to go over the dossier issues again. I felt we were OK on pretty much all of the questions they were putting. The areas for me to worry about were pretty clear – dossier, why was I involved? I felt fine on that. Was my evidence to the FAC misleading? Again, I didn't feel there was a question I couldn't answer, and it was only because the lens through which this was all being viewed had changed that others felt I might be vulnerable on that. Did I deliberately and wrongly raise the temperature too high, e.g. at the FAC, when I went for the BBC and said I would not leave it until they apologised, or when I did the Channel 4 interview and really went for them again? Contact with Tom Baldwin [*Times* journalist]. The leaking – so-called – of the fact of Kelly coming forward to say he was probably the source. And also the general mood I created, this idea that I was so driven on this that it created a completely different atmosphere and set of priorities within No. 10 and more broadly. I felt OK but really wanted it to be over now.

Anthony [Measures, No. 10 official] came back from court. He said the Gilligan PalmPilot stuff was inconclusive, but the general sense was that it was moving in our favour. I spoke to a couple of others who had been there who said Gilligan came over really badly, and Hutton, while not giving anything away, did not seem to take to him at all. I said that means something's bound to go wrong. GH sent me a written message from Cabinet to say could I call him on Sunday and not go through Switch [No. 10 switchboard]. Clearly he was worried his people would be listening in on him. I got home and read hours of transcripts from the first wave of evidence.

Friday 19 September

Woke up to news we had lost Brent East by-election to the Libs, then back to preparing. I was really just honing things in my own mind. I was flicking through the files, cutting them down with Clare and Catherine, not wanting to take too much up with me to Newcastle. I met Fiona, Audrey [Millar, Fiona's mother] and the kids at King's Cross and was reading through the shortened file on the train. I actually felt Sumption was probably right that a weekend out of town would do me good, and that having the family there meant I would have to switch off from preparation a bit too. But I spent most of the train journey up just flicking through various passages, then looking out of the window, imagining the worst possible questions and thinking through how I would best answer them. We were picked up at the station, taken to the hotel, then Brendan [Foster, former athlete turned businessman and TV commentator, founder of the Great North Run] came down with Sue [his wife]. He had been totally supportive, over the past few months had sent lots of little supportive messages and texts. It was a massive weekend for him, with the GNR expected to be bigger than ever, so it was great of them to give over the Friday before the race to be with us. The boys thought Brendan was a top bloke, and Rory loved grilling him about his athletics career and the guys at the top now. He said there were more people at the BBC on my side than I thought. He had been in there for a planning meeting a while back and he said people who knew he was a pal of mine had been very supportive. He said people were amazed how I had managed to stay sane. He felt I was getting in the right place mentally for Monday.

Saturday 20 September

Slept OK. I called GH to go over all the issues. I said he really had to find an opportunity to take responsibility, and be clear he was going to do that. We went over what we would be saying about the diaries. It was clear we had different recollections and just had to live with that. He felt the MoD had a better week last week, as we all did and he was very much in 'keep going' mode. There was something very plodding about his style but he was basically a decent enough bloke and it was totally unfair the way he was being done in. We went down to the quayside to watch the mile races. Grace met Basil Brush, which was a laugh. Brendan was really pushing the boat out for us. He had been so solid through all this. Steve Cram [former athlete turned BBC commentator] was there too, and Allison Curbishley [former athlete and commentator] who I'd never talked to properly before. She was nice, very lively. Cram was trying to get me to get properly involved in athletics, said it was all a bit of a shambles and could do with the kind of nous in the political world that I had.

Rory was running in the Junior GNR and did well considering he was at the low end of the age range. He was 50th after half a mile, 32nd after 2 miles, 17th at the end. I was really pleased and he looked so happy when he came back, even if he was being a bit Jack the Lad. Cathy [Gilman, Leukaemia Research director of fundraising] collected me to go and do a Leukaemia Research event. I didn't have a clue what I was supposed to be doing, but she seemed happy enough and at least it meant the BBC covered it, even if there was more of Hutton than there was of Leukaemia Research. TB called later, said he was not at all happy re the by-election. He felt we could win it back. He said David H was going to be fine on the press side but he was still going to need me to help re strategy. I know, I said.

Sunday 21 September

I was up early having not slept well. I had breakfast with Dick Caborn [sports minister] who was also doing the race, then did Radio 5 and *Breakfast with Frost*. David [Frost] asked me a few things he shouldn't, e.g.

Hutton – on which they knew I would say nothing – and the by-election, but I pushed him back to LRF [Leukaemia Research Fund] and the GNR. Cathy was thrilled with it. It was a lovely sunny day and after all the doubt about whether I should do it the day before giving evidence, I was glad that I did. The atmosphere was warm and friendly and it was a good way of taking my mind off things. We got driven out to the start, where I did some interviews with Brendan and Mark Knopfler [musician]. The organisers provided a very nice chap called Graham to run with me and it really helped having someone to pace me, fetch me water, also move in if people got a bit too close. I didn't mind, but I hated it when they started conversations. Talking slowed me down too much and interfered with my breathing. There were a few 'good luck tomorrow' people, which was nice, but I would just nod and try to keep focused on running. There were some quiet parts to the route, unlike the London Marathon, but where there were crowds, they really helped. There was a good laugh near the end, before the drop down to the sea, where there was a slight incline. I was struggling a bit and an old woman yelled out, 'Go on, Mr Hoon, you can do it.' I did 1 hr 41 which was a lot better than I expected to, though I collapsed in a heap at the end.

I did a stack of interviews then met Fiona, Audrey and the kids in the marquee, where Grace had struck up a friendship with [athlete] Sonia O'Sullivan's daughter. Lots of the BBC sports guys were there – John Motson, Ray Stubbs, Mark Lawrenson [commentators] – wishing me luck for tomorrow. I beat them all, plus plenty of former pros. I was starting to seize up and had a shower and a quick massage. Then by helicopter into Newcastle for the train home. I was back to reading all the files again, but I felt pretty much on top of it all. I just wanted it to be all over now. We got home and CR [Catherine Rimmer] came round to go over it all one more time. The files were getting thinner and thinner, thank God, as we dispensed with all the material we didn't need any more. What a total star Catherine had been. She was probably worth me hiring for the future and she was clearly interested. I was getting messages of support from the usual people, often accompanied by a warning not to lose my temper if any of the lawyers tried to rile me. Alex [Ferguson] called to wish me luck, and said just do the same as last time. Brendan called and thanked me for going up to do the run and all the media I did. But actually I had him to thank for having given me a great and in the event pretty relaxing weekend surrounded by nice people, and giving the family such a good time. TB's main worries seemed to be GH, and the diaries.

I slept a lot better, and didn't feel as stiff as I feared I would, though walking down the stairs was a bit tricky. I left home around half six. One of the photographers said her camera didn't work as I left and would I do it again? Pur-lease! I had a bit of foot repair work to do once I got in, with a couple of blisters and a bruised big toe. Catherine Rimmer and Clare Sumner came into the office with a stack of files and folders. We were just going through the honing process now. I wanted to be able to go in with a small folder and a few key points on a couple of pages, and my main points on the inside cover. Dossier process and why it was robust. Why so angry at the allegations. No naming strategy re Kelly. CR did me a single-page grid on all the post-18 September email changes. We then drove down to Brick Street Chambers for a meeting with Sumption, Alan Maclean and Adam Sharples. Sumption had a big smile on his face when I walked in, said he was looking forward to it. I said yes, I am sure this will be marvellous for your growing fame and profile.

He took me through all the areas he was going to ask me about, though I couldn't have the list – why I was involved in the dossier, why I got so angry with the BBC. Obvious stuff. He would draw out the facts he wanted to highlight, and then the other lawyers could have a go. Just answer them in the same way as you do me, he said. If any of them tried to irritate you, don't let them. Just find the actual question in what they said, and then answer it. He was clearly enjoying the whole thing. We had also developed a rapport and now had a good laugh from time to time. I told him the only lie I told first time round was that I respected BBC journalism. I got him going as well when I said I may have to give him a new name because there were now so many JSs in my diary – John Scarlett, Jack Straw [Foreign and Commonwealth Secretary], John Sawers [senior diplomat] and now him. 'Do you want to be JSu?'

I think Alan and Adam, who were clearly a bit in awe of him, as indeed were most people in the legal profession apparently, were surprised both that we got on so well, and also that I could take the mick out of him and he didn't seem to mind. He said be exactly as you were first time round, calm and factual, say it like it is, come over as the man on top of the detail. TB had said the same – don't treat these lawyers like lobby journalists. Don't get into arguments with them. Listen to the question and answer it. Sumption's last words were: 'Don't relive the row with the BBC. There is no need. He has all the facts. Just answer the questions and talk directly to the judge.' I asked how to play Andrew Caldecott [BBC lawyer]. He said he would play fair. He would not pull tricks but he may try to provoke. Just don't rise. 'He is not like Gompertz who is a Rumpolean fathead.' I said I must take a note immediately for tonight's diary. I scribbled down 'JSu calls Gompertz Rumpolean fathead.' Laughter. I asked how much I should say about the political call I made re not admitting the 45-minute observation to the FAC. He said be straightforward about it. If pressed, you'll have to, so be relaxed.

Catherine was worried I would go too far in saying I felt there had to be a plan for Dr Kelly, and it would put the MoD back in it after they had done better last week.* I said I had to say what I thought and I really thought we could have done this differently, and handled it better from Kelly's perspective. Sumption left for the court and I stayed in the meeting room at his office and carried on honing. A few good omens. A couple of days ago CR had the same cab driver I had told her about when giving evidence the first time around. He told her, 'I had that Alastair Campbell in the back of the cab. Bloody good bloke.' I walked over to the court with Adam. Several people said 'Good luck' on the walk over. A very nice security guy and a friendly usher took us to the waiting room, a bit grubby, apparently it was the old judges' robing room. Sumption came in briefly, said, 'Congratulations on your elevation to being a retired judge.' He said GH had done much better second time around. He said there was nothing new to worry about emerging from his evidence, maybe the fact that he gave a different emphasis to some of the content of the diaries, but we just have to accept that. He paced up and down while I ate a pastrami sandwich and a piece of chocolate cake. I was glad Geoff gave us nothing new to think about, and now I was just focusing on my own evidence.

The plan was that Lee Hughes [Inquiry secretary] would 'read the diaries in' and parts of them would be published. I finally went in, and got into my stride fairly quickly. First Sumption, who helped me get all the main points over. Caldecott used literally ALL his time asking about the dossier, but I felt I got the better of him. I was a bit wary early on but, as Alan Maclean said afterwards, once I got a feel of the

* AC told the Hutton Inquiry he felt once it was clear that Dr Kelly was being claimed by the BBC to be the source, No. 10, the MoD and Dr Kelly should have accepted his identity would become public and agreed how that was best done.

bowling I started to play him well. I held very firm on the 45-minute point, held firm on my role in the dossier, denied I had transformed it. Caldecott didn't seem to know where to go. At one point Hutton intervened as if to say, 'Where is this all leading?' and Caldecott waffled and suddenly looked nervous. Hutton then paraphrased something I had said and asked if he had accurately summed up my position, and I just said, 'Yes.' He seemed to me totally to get the difference between strengthening the dossier and 'sexing it up'.

After the Hutton intervention, Caldecott asked for a break. I thought he would then go to my anger with the BBC and try to show I went over the top, but he never touched it. Instead we had more on the dossier and again I didn't feel he got near me. He seemed unsettled when I just answered his questions and then stared at him, waiting for the next one. He gave me a file of papers to go through but I kept asking to see them on the screen, so that I could delay a bit and get more time to think. He was clearly a bit of a technophobe, on a par with me I suspect. At one point I accidentally knocked over a glass of water which went all over my grid of changes to the dossier, which was annoying. Nobody seemed to notice apart from the usher, who passed me some tissues to wipe it up.

I kept saying to myself, 'Be Geoff Boycott not Colin Milburn [two former England cricketers with differing styles] – dead bat, don't yield, nick a single if you can, nothing dramatic.' Then Dingemans, who as before was fairly gentle but of course the diaries were tricky. We went through them pretty much line by line. I rather underestimated how big the diary stuff would go. I hadn't done what I should have done, gone through it all line by line and worked out all difficult questions from every line. I tried to defend GH, saying the way I had recorded it in my diary risked being unfair to him. Hutton intervened, asking what I meant by 'it' at some point, and I wasn't very good on that. It was not easy being grilled line by line on words often knocked off in a rush at the end of a busy day. I was tired and flagging a bit, and whereas first time I gave evidence I felt I had got stronger as I went on, this time I felt myself fading a bit. The media were going to have a field day with the diaries, especially my reference that we would 'fuck' Gilligan, and also Dingemans's handling of them. I just had to hope Hutton didn't think it changed the substance of anything, or that he might give me points for openness. Most of Hutton's interventions were OK.

I felt I did OK but I wasn't happy with my finish, maybe tiredness after the run yesterday. I didn't feel I was as good second time around, though the lawyers seemed to think it was fine, Clare and Catherine that it was even better than the first time. I went back with Catherine and later up to see John Scarlett to go over the points for him when he gave evidence tomorrow. It was pretty clear they were heading towards saying that he allowed me to interfere. There was a mini drama over one of the documents that had been put to me purporting to show the difference in two drafts of my memo to the FAC but in fact one was indeed a draft, and the other was a memo I had written to TB to explain why I felt I should attend the FAC when I did. The lawyers decided to complain. We went over the various problem areas for John – his note to TB, our discussions, the changes to the draft. He and I had a private chat at the end. He said it had been hard to do his job properly with all this going on but now he was hoping to get back to it. He felt TB, he and I would be fine but he wasn't sure about Geoff. Geoff called later, said he felt he did better, clearly there were differences between us re the diaries but he had been grateful I had given them to him early and also that I had volunteered the point that they risked being unfair to him. I had made the point, at Sumption's suggestion, that I was happy to defend what I wrote, but that others should not have to defend what I say about them.

I watched the news, as ever slanted to the BBC line. Sumption called, said he felt I had put on another vintage performance, done really well and he was very confident. 'You honestly could not have done better,' he said, 'and I can promise you I do not say that to everyone I represent.' Would you have told me if I had been terrible? I asked him. 'I might not say you were terrible, but I would not say you were good unless you were.' I felt relieved but still on edge, and knew I wouldn't sleep properly. TB called from Chequers. I warned him the diaries would go big but it would be fine for him, just get me back in the frame for being obsessive. Everyone seemed to think Caldecott didn't lay a glove on me. I didn't really feel I got out a case about the BBC, but Sumption felt the balance was just right. I told TB about the woman 11 miles into the Great North Run shouting out, 'Go on, Mister Hoon, you can do it,' and also Stephen Hepburn [Labour MP for Jarrow] giving me his considered opinion that 'naebody up here gives a flying fuck about Hutton'.

Tuesday 23 September

The papers were absolutely wild about the diaries. As TB said, Campbell swears shock. They were totally over the top, and again left us hoping Hutton was not influenced by the media. There was next to no coverage of the dossier issue on the BBC, so presumably they had woken up to the fact they were probably on losing ground there. I felt that if I was criticised it would be for getting too obsessed and creating an atmosphere that led to Kelly being put in a difficult position. Tom and Godric did well by all accounts, as did Scarlett. He called me after giving evidence and sounded exhausted. He said, 'Just reporting in to my handler to inform you that the assignment went well.' He said he felt totally drained. I had told him after my session that Caldecott clearly didn't like being stared at and, according to Catherine and Clare, JS stared at him the whole time, didn't give an inch, stayed totally with me on the main points. ITN led on a Jonathan email which wasn't even new while of course the papers today were totally obsessed with me saying 'fuck' in the diaries. God knows what Hutton made of the whole thing. I felt I didn't deal with the diaries well and at one point Hutton made an intervention which I didn't fully understand, so I'm not sure I answered it too well. But everyone felt it was OK, so maybe I was beating myself up too much.

Wednesday 24 September

I was still having to spend most of my time on Hutton. I had been psyching myself up with the idea that once I had given evidence for the second time, I would be able to get out of things for a while, until he delivered his report, but I had to go in again, this time working on the statement of oral and written submissions which Sumption would have to present. Again, I felt it was a bit dry, that it could do more about the whole emotional impact, also that the story about the BBC was not stated clearly enough, and I wasn't terribly happy about us accepting that on Channel 4 I went over the top.* I put through a few comments, otherwise not doing very much and went home to get Grace from school. Sumption did his first draft of the closing speech. It was clever, but I put through a few ideas for changes. As

---

* Having initially turned down a request for an interview, AC had arrived at the *Channel 4 News* studio on 27 June 2003 to refute angrily the BBC's continuing claims that he had 'sexed up' the government dossier on Iraq's banned weapons.

September '03: Papers go wild on the diaries

throughout, he was playing only to the judge, not the non-existent jury or the headlines.

Thursday 25 September

A new version of Sumption's speech came through. I had a few little changes to suggest but he was now being fairly resistant. To be fair, he had built a very strong argument and I had to trust him to do that. But I wasn't keen on the way he had expressed himself about my Channel 4 interview. Godric felt the BBC had gained something by their earlier apology. Sumption's manner was getting a fair bit of attention in the press. I made a few cracks about his hair and whether he ever brushed it. He said not but that very occasionally his wife would brush it as he was running out of the door. He was absolutely clear that he needed to get the big picture over, but didn't really want to go for the BBC at this stage. People in the office were feeling that he had missed tricks all over the place, but he had said to me at the start that all he was going to focus on was the judge and I felt very confident in him, even if it meant day to day we were probably getting worse media treatment than if he played the game a bit more.

Audrey [Fiona's mother] came round and we watched all the closing submissions live. Gompertz wasn't bad, better than when questioning, and the family were pretty heavy towards Hoon and Hatfield. Sumption got through two-thirds of his speech before lunch, first on the dossier, defending our right to be involved, and also the BBC row, which I thought he put well. After lunch Kelly. I also wanted him to deal with the diaries, both the false *Mail* story claiming that I had tried to keep them out of evidence and also to protect Hoon a bit more because the family brief was clearly to go for him. Sumption was pretty tough about Kelly and the anonymity point. He was very good dealing with Hutton's interventions. Caldecott was poor on interventions but did OK with very bad material overall. Gilligan's brief, Heather Rogers, was absolutely excruciating. Dingemans was not as sympathetic towards us as we hoped, sceptical on the dossier, not remotely heavy enough on the BBC, nice to the media generally and far too many references to me, e.g. losing it on Channel 4 and also re the naming of Dr Kelly. He was also far too emotional. Hutton's summing up was OK, really just thanking everyone and then he said he hoped to report in bloody December. Jesus! It meant the next few weeks would be difficult for all sorts of reasons while the press would just go on and on about there being no WMD.

Catherine and Clare were both very down. I think they had been hoping that it would be a very clear-cut thing and over quickly. We were probably reading too much into everything but it was all a bit dispiriting, now all in the hands of a judge none of us could read. I called Ian Kennedy [personal friend, academic lawyer] who had been following it and he advised me not to read too much into Dingemans's tone. He did not believe he would be speaking to instruction, but wanting to get written up well, and also having to show he was showing no favour to any one side.

Friday 26 September

Ed Victor was due to come round but there were still photographers in the street so I went round to his flat in Regent's Park. Beautiful place, very bookish of course, but also light and airy and with some fabulous flowers on top of the table where we sat to talk. 'Well, I think anyone who didn't realise that you had diaries, and that they are colourful to say the least, will know now,' he said. He was making the fairly obvious point that the longer I waited to do memoirs or diaries, the lower the value. He couldn't believe that I didn't have a photocopy of all the diaries, or that I hadn't kept them anywhere safe. We arranged for them to be copied and put in a vault. We both assumed that at the end of the day, out of friendship, I would do something with Gail, but Murdoch and his people were already expressing a lot of interest and I wanted him to be the buffer for all that. Both he and Gail were clearly thinking I'd do something next year or the year after, but I was feeling I wouldn't do anything that might clutter things in the run-up to an election. I felt comfortable with him, enough to trust him with taking it over. Also, the volume of work required just to transcribe them was pretty overwhelming when I thought about it.

Philip G was phoning me the whole time about how bad things were, both at party HQ and at No. 10. He was basically saying I needed to get in there more. There was nobody there that TB didn't basically just tell to fuck off if they put something different to his own ideas. TB seemed to think that any idea that people inside No. 10 were putting forward was an exhortation to move to the left, whereas in fact they were simply asking for a reassertion of basic values. But he had to get the balance right between listening and leading. It was going to be very odd not going to conference. I couldn't even remember the last time I didn't, some time back in the '80s, I guess. The general feeling on Hutton was that the BBC were going to get hit; even they seemed to accept that.

Saturday 27 September

I spoke to TB before he left for conference. The press were all basically moving against him. The Sundays were working up polls trying to give a sense of a leadership crisis. GB was operating, that was pretty clear from the tone of his usual friendly hacks. TB had done an OK draft but there was a clear tension within it – on the one hand we were saying renewal/journey/transition and on the other we were saying no retreat. Philip was driving me slightly bonkers with his phone calls, which were mainly about how much harder it was for him if I wasn't there, how there was no guiding hand controlling the process of the speech writing. TB went down to Bournemouth via a visit to Southampton, where someone yelled out, 'War criminal', so ensuring that the news wasn't that great. Iraq was still the dominant problem. And of course it was all very difficult with GB motoring as he was, and clearly feeling emboldened, so that the attacks were no longer even particularly coded.

I went for a long run and then later with Calum to Milton Keynes for Wimbledon's first game there, against Burnley. We were up in the back row behind the goal but were spotted. The Burnley fans were very protective, abusing the photographers, especially the guy from the *Sunday Times* who came right into the stand. Then a kid of about seventeen came over and was asking how he could get involved in politics. He said he was worried he wasn't bright enough, but he was actually a lot more insightful than quite a lot of people in Parliament. He was very bright and it was such a shame that he thought he wasn't. The game was OK, though we threw it away from a 2–0 lead to draw 2–2.

I was still feeling a bit like a fish out of water, not wanting to do much, anxious about Hutton. Now the Public Administration Committee wanted to call me, which was a total fucking pain. How many more bloody committees? TB called just before 10 p.m. and was amazed that I was in bed. I said where do you expect me to be, I've got nothing else to do. He said he needed help on the speech. I said fine, but what do you really want to say? He said he wanted to signal change but did he really, I wonder? It was clear from his interviews that his message to the party that retreat would be a disaster was the dominant one. But he also needed to persuade people that what he believed in was what they believed in. I agreed to write a passage on trust, also why he was still up for the fight, another on the clash between courage and caution. He said it would be far better if I went down there, but though I agreed this way of working was pretty hopeless, I didn't particularly want to go. Philip was calling every hour or so, clearly trying to direct proceedings. He said it had only really just dawned on him how I had overseen everything – messaging, drafting, writing, the press, the jokes, TB's psychology, management and organisation – and they were floundering a bit.

Sunday 28 September

I spent half the morning working up a few sections for his speech. The papers weren't great, which made him even more up for a 'No surrender' kind of message. He said it must be weird for you not being here. I said it was very odd. It would be very odd watching it on TV. Philip said TB was constantly asking what I thought of this or that draft, that it was as if he felt he should not be phoning me the whole time but wanted advice and approval for what he had done. TB and I had a couple of long chats and I agreed to do a line-by-line write-through. I said don't send me every draft but when you get to the end of the evening, send me the latest version and I will get a line-by-line rewrite to you within a few hours. He said again it would be easier if I went down. I said maybe, but I am not going.

Monday 29 September

I watched GB's speech on TV, upstairs at my desk, with Philip on the phone. We lost count of how many times he said the word 'Labour'. It was endless, almost comic. It was actually quite a good speech but bound to be seen as a possible leadership effort, which in the end wasn't good for GB. He was looking much more confident than usual, though, and all his people were sitting together looking very pleased with themselves – Alistair Darling [Secretary of State for Scotland], Andrew Smith [Secretary of State for Work and Pensions], Douglas Alexander [Cabinet Office minister], Nick Brown [former Minister of State for Work], Ann Keen [Parliamentary Private Secretary to the Chancellor of the Exchequer]. NB was apparently out and about saying we had lost trust. TB was off at [Leader of the Lords] Gareth Williams's funeral (he had died aged sixty-two) but called on his way back. He said GB was really operating big time now. Delegates were being friendly but there was a part of him that was worried that there was almost something of a sympathy vote attached to it all, which was the last thing he wanted. He really wanted to hit home the message, without being arrogant, that he was staying put, and get the right balance between listening and leading. In reality, though, he really wanted to tell them they had to face some home truths and grow up about the nature of modern politics. His best message was in the area of fairness allied to the future. It was where he felt comfortable. It gave values and modernisation. I had done a line-by-line rewrite but that was the area I worked on most. He was right not to get shifted off it, but we had to watch the dynamics, particularly after GB's speech today.

After the meeting with Ed Victor, I had agreed to start transcribing as and when I could, just so that we could get everything down in a form others could read, so once GB had finished, and I had another go at TB's speech, I started to transcribe diaries from 1994. Looking at the books piled up, I couldn't even begin to work out how long it might take me. It was going to be a very slow process. Most days filled a full A4 page of my tiny shorthand and scribbles, and particularly busy days had extra scraps paperclipped in, and there was also stuff I had sometimes scribbled in notebooks when on the move, so it was all a bit of a logistical nightmare. I decided to view it as a trip to the dentist. It just had to be got through. I would not set myself a time-table, just do it as and when I could. On the content of the first few pages, it was all extraordinarily similar to what was going on now, almost ten years later. TB worrying about GB. JP worrying about not being on board. Peter M diddling with the press and undermining David Hill. I felt both better and worse about not being there. I felt frustrated that I couldn't do more from where I was but at the same time I didn't want to be all-consumed by it. I knew I was letting TB down in a way, because sometimes the best work on speeches came from being there, part of the team, part of all the conversations, open to ideas coming from all manner of different directions. TB called again and we chewed over ways of saying 'Not for turning' and came up with 'I've not got a reverse gear'. It wasn't great, to be honest, but the best we could think of right now. The general feeling down there was that GB had overshot but we would see. Rebekah Wade [*Sun* editor] called me later to say *The Sun* was going to be distancing itself, that TB was on a 'yellow card'. Really.

Tuesday 30 September

The new draft was much tighter and he felt a lot happier with it. There was no point this being anything other than his own voice. Philip must have called ten times before ten o'clock. It was a nightmare going through it page by page on the phone but there were also many literals in it, which was driving me mad. The ending still didn't work. I tried to redo the listen–lead section as an ending to go with TB's section on the letters from relatives of UK soldiers killed in Iraq. We just about got there but he would have to give a lot in the delivery. Philip said the team had risen pretty well, though TB felt a bit let down on the policy front. He called me a couple of times, really wanted me to work on the ending and was reasonably pleased with what we finished with. But the combination of the general mood, *The Sun* clearly off board and the response to the GB speech made him nervous. I felt GB had overshot. TB was late starting but got a terrific reception when he went on and seemed almost taken aback by it. He got through Iraq fine, the policy section was not as boring as usual and then he was away. The warm mention of Neil [Kinnock] really worked, so did the ending, and he got a loud 7-minute ovation. Even though the press would not be universally great, he was in far better shape than everyone predicted. As ever, the press had overshot at the weekend in terms of predicting how he would be received and GB overshot yesterday in trying to create a negative frame for TB to walk into.

I went to Watford v Burnley and so missed any of the coverage. But the message was pretty clear – that he was staying put, thank you very much, and what was absolutely clear was that even with all the problems, quite a large section of the party was more than happy with that. Not for the first time, GB had done well on an individual basis but the party had sensed that was the basis on which he was operating, looking out for himself rather than the government as a whole, and they didn't much like it.

Wednesday 1 October

I had sent Gail and Ed a few diary extracts. They were both amazed. Gail thought even the bits she had seen, which weren't even of highlights, were riveting. 'How on earth did you ever find the time to do something as detailed as this?' Philip and I had discussed it last night and agreed I had to be very careful not to be thought of as disloyal or causing problems for people I had worked with. I felt I should plough on transcribing, but keep my options open about timing, and have in mind that I won't do anything damaging to TB. I did about four hours today and covered less than two weeks. I was already well over 20,000 words. I had a long chat with Philip again. I think I was probably clinically depressed. He said the problem was I had gone from having a driving purpose to now not knowing what I wanted to do. I told him what Bostock had said, and he said maybe I should go and see him and tell him he was right. The trouble was it also meant getting lectured on Iraq and on having left in the first place. I knew that it wouldn't be enough just making money but I would need something, maybe in sport, maybe charity, maybe a political cause, maybe a mix of all of them. But at the moment I couldn't clear the fog in my head enough to do anything.

There were a stack more bids coming in for speeches, events, but I was feeling very lethargic. A speaking agency had called yesterday offering 25 grand for a speech in the south of France, and I couldn't be arsed. It didn't help that virtually everyone I spoke to from the conference, like Rebekah, David Hill, Philip, JP, went on about how TB kept saying how much the operation missed me, and how we had to find ways of getting me more involved without it becoming a big thing again. He got a good press for his speech, but it was uncanny going through the '94 diaries to see how all the same themes were running – TB–GB, JP feeling insecure, Peter M and the PLP, Carole [Caplin], the press. Jamie Rubin called to say he had been approached by Wes Clark [ex-US General, now running for Democratic presidential nomination] and was thinking about going out to help him in Arkansas and what did I think? I had been holding back a bit on Wes, probably because of [General Sir Mike] Jackson and [General Sir Charles] Guthrie, who were both pretty down on him. I said I liked him in many ways,* and he was clever, but there was something just a bit odd that stopped me from thinking he was the real deal as a politician. Jamie felt he was the most attractive of the Democrat challengers and he was clearly wanting to do it, and I said go for it and give it a few months. Jamie had made some decent money since getting out of government but was clearly keen to get back into politics, so maybe this was the best route. God knows how he and Christiane [Amanpour, wife, CNN journalist] operate.

---

* AC had established a good working relationship and friendship with General Clark, then Supreme Allied Commander Europe (SACEUR), when overseeing NATO communications in 1999 during the Kosovo War.

There was a defeat at conference on foundation hospitals but the talk was all still about TB's speech, the effect of which had been overwhelmingly good in the party. The general view was that GB, despite a formidable performance on Monday, had overall had a bad week, in part because he had been so formidable, and everyone knew he had been trying to put over the sense that he would be a better PM than TB.

Thursday 2 October
It wasn't exactly fun going through the diaries. It brought back a lot of memories, good and bad. I was also beginning to worry about issues of confidence, also the fact that so much of the material was about personality splits etc., which wasn't exactly edifying. Apart from the Hutton stuff, this was the first time I had ever gone back and read anything, and it was clear that a lot of what went down there depended not just on events, but also the kind of mood I was in. Some days it just felt like an emotional dustbin, whereas other days I got a real sense of having been involved in stuff that was big and worthwhile. But what was most surprising in a way was how much I had completely forgotten. It was odd not having the phone going the whole time, and the kids were beginning to take the mickey about me being unemployed, a dosser whose big decision was what time to get up and which daytime TV programmes to watch. We had dinner with Tessa [Jowell, Secretary of State for Culture, Media and Sport] and David [Mills, Jowell's husband]. She felt the press having whipped up the leadership issues, GB had overreached and therefore had a bad week, whereas TB did fine. But she also felt there had to be much deeper engagement with party and public.

The ISG [Iraq Survey Group] was reporting overnight and saying yes, there was evidence of programmes but no actual WMD, so that was becoming more and more difficult for GWB as well as for TB. Also Hutton was hanging over everything like a shadow, and when I read the draft submission from Sumption, I was clear that I was at the centre of every bit of difficulty and controversy. The evidence session to Hutton out of the way, and now TB's speech done, I was definitely on for a big dip. I could feel it this morning and it is even worse tonight.

Friday 3 October
Into the office to try to reply to some of the correspondence post-resignation. Very nice letter from Douglas Alexander [Chancellor of the

Duchy of Lancaster]. Warm and personal. He was sometimes seen as a GB clone, but in fact he was his own man in many ways, was able to see GB's weaknesses as well as strengths, and TB's strengths as well as weaknesses. The same could not be said for all of GB's people, either in his team or in the media. I had a good chat with Jonathan Powell about shared concerns on the Hutton submission. He agreed that there was a risk when leaving things to lawyers that they would be too blind to the political needs. But, as ever, he was managing to keep his spirits up, and seemed pretty unfazed.

We had dinner at Rachel's [Kinnock, daughter of Neil and Glenys] with Neil, Glenys and Audrey. Glenys said conference had been unreal. Everyone felt GB made a great speech, but the moment it was seen as a leadership bid, the positive impact was gone. He just overdid it, overtipped the balance. Neil felt if he had actually presented the successes of the government as a joint thing, the result of him and TB working together, he would have looked more like a leader. Neither of them were terribly keen on TB's speech and felt he only got the reception he did because the party knew he was under pressure and wanted to rally round. Neil was very down on GB, more so than I had seen or heard for a long time. He said it was a tragedy that we had a Prime Minister and a Prime Minister-in-waiting who was not mature enough, as seen by the fact that GB allowed his speech to run in the way it did. He felt GB should have done a big defence of TB and shown they were together, but he can't do it and he got rumbled. People realised he was trying to undermine him. He said it was a tragedy, that he couldn't understand it, that it's less than a decade since they were the best of friends.

He recalled taking them to a dinner with Thabo Mbeki [South African politician] around the time of [former leader of the Labour Party] John Smith's death. You were proud to take them anywhere, but now there's just this bitterness and nastiness and it can't be concealed any more. He felt that TB would probably have been ready in the not too distant future to hand over, but it would be hard to hand over to GB if this is the way he behaves. He said, 'They have to realise they are playing with the future of the Labour Party and that's why people like me get angry.' GB has got to show there's more than just burning ambition for himself, but an understanding that TB has made us the assumed party of government and we have to keep it that way. Glenys was clearly more favourably disposed towards GB but Neil felt that TB was more sinned against than sinning, which was something of a shift. Rachel and I reminded them of what we had said for a long time – GB would never get the job. Something would happen. Audrey said that TB was a terrific PM, Gordon a good Chancellor, and they should both carry on doing what they are good at.

Sunday 5 October

Out for lunch and in the evening out with the Goulds to see David Blaine [illusionist] in his glass box down by the river.* I couldn't understand the fuss but Grace Gould thought he was brilliant, a real star for our times. The tabloids were going on an alleged rape by Premiership footballers. They were virtually identified; it certainly wasn't hard to work it out. The way the media skirted around the contempt laws was pretty extraordinary. I was feeling lethargic and depressed and not remotely clear about the future. I was so not used to this kind of meandering, not-sure sort of existence and I couldn't see where or how I was going to settle it down. Added to which I was having to adapt to life without the infrastructure around me. I had barely used a computer for years. I had never used email and I was now having to learn all manner of new skills without knowing what use they would be put to. Fiona was being helpful but there was a tension there because she knew that I felt in some ways I had been forced out by her constant negativity about the impact of the job on our lives. Neither of us was yet really ready to go beyond me just feeling that, rather than bringing it out into the open, but there would come a point when we would have to. She asked why I didn't go to see Tom [Bostock, GP] and maybe get something to lift my mood, but I couldn't face it. I felt sleep was the only thing I wanted right now, but was finding it hard to sleep.

Monday 6 October

Grace was ill and off school so I sat with her the whole day just watching kids' films and doing a bit of diary transcribing. But I was hopeless on these fucking computers and for the second time I hit some random button and bang went 11,000 words. It brought back the time Fiona wiped out an entire bloody novel I'd written in 1986 or 7, when I just

* The beginning of Blaine's endurance 'experiment', suspended in the box above the River Thames without food. It was to last for forty-four days.

curled up in a ball under the bedclothes. I felt a milder version of the same thing now. Above all I felt it was a symbol of meaninglessness. What a fucking pointless thing – write 11,000 words then wipe them out and have to start all over again. I told Fiona I felt purposeless. She said why wasn't it enough of a purpose to get back to some kind of normal family life? I said that was all fine but there had to be something else. I was treading water. Bill [Wells] the messenger came round with the latest submissions to Hutton, which were vastly improved. Bill said I was really badly missed, that the place just wasn't the same. It didn't exactly help but he is such a lovely bloke. Sarah Hunter [special advisor] called – Patrick Carter was wondering if I wanted to chair a review of UK tennis. So that was football, athletics and now tennis asking if I could advise on strategy, or even take up a full-time position. Even for something like that, I couldn't muster any enthusiasm.

Tuesday 7 October

Peter Hyman [No. 10 special advisor] came round for a chat, nice as ever. He felt it would take me longer than I thought to work out what I should do, and I should take my time. He was moving towards leaving himself. The office was pretty mad at the moment. I had left a big hole and Peter M and John Birt were trying to fill it, which was not going down well. At meetings, they sat there with masses of paper, grids, plans, analyses and both went through the same material and arguments. 'Literally, Peter will go through it, and then John will go over the same thing. Some of it is fine, some of it is absolute nonsense.' It all sounded a bit odd. He reckoned he needed to move on by Christmas. Fiona was trying to be helpful but I was feeling very down and I don't think she really got it at all, the feeling of redundancy and lack of purpose or direction.

Peter M sent me a text, asking if I was free for lunch. He wanted to set up weekly meetings with him, me and Philip. I couldn't decide in my own mind if I wanted to be drawn back in like that. Philip was asking if I wanted to set up stall inside his office in the Express Newspapers building. Again, not sure. I hadn't seen any TV or listened to the radio yesterday so I had my first real instance of finding out something from the papers – Hilary Benn was the new Secretary of State for Development, Valerie Amos Leader of the Lords. Again it brought home that however much you stay in touch, willingly or less so, you are not in the loop in the same way. Godric called for a chat. He was in Rome with TB. He said TB was saying he felt I should get stuck in with a few public interventions sooner rather than later.

Wednesday 8 October

Tom Bower [journalist] did a ridiculous OTT attack in *The Times* Thunderer column on Fiona [a specialist on education and parenting issues] re her debate on comprehensive education. I had another not doing much kind of day. I did several hours on the diaries and slowly got into 1995. Ed called from the Frankfurt Book Fair. He had seen Vicky Barnsley from Harper Collins and it was obvious Murdoch's people would pay a lot, probably more than Random House. They were clearly hoping a big press deal now, as set out by Les Hinton when I saw him, would help persuade me to do the book with them too. He said he wasn't sure how I would get on with Vicky, that she had come across as a bit manipulative, trying to make a big point that it would be bad for the whole book project if I did it 'with Philip Gould's wife'. I had told Ed that I felt there were at least three volumes to be done – opposition, first term, second term, and I was not keen to do them anything other than chronologically.

Philip called, said today was exactly the kind of day I should be doing a sports column, because there was the Rio Ferdinand drugs test story, and the whole FA v players battle that was raging.* I was talking to Alison about her working for me while keeping a foot in No. 10. Arnold Schwarzenegger was elected as Governor of California, which was pretty bad news. It led to a dreadful row with Fiona later when I said how awful it was and she said I ought to be happy because 'it's your American party', at which point I switched, and eventually stormed out. I was due to do [former footballer turned broadcaster] Eamonn Dunphy's new chat show in Dublin, with Roy Keane and Bob Geldof, which they were really building up, but I was worried he would try to take me down tracks I didn't want to go. I spoke to Eamonn and he agreed he would only briefly touch on Hutton and would stay off Carole Caplin. PG said TB had been on great form today but both he and Matthew Taylor [new Downing Street policy advisor] said Peter M was really getting backs up at No. 10, effectively trying to operate as a mix of me and Jonathan.

* Manchester United player Ferdinand had been dropped from the England football squad to play Turkey after failing to take a mandatory drugs test.

The Tories were having a nightmare week and IDS really looked now like a dead man walking. He has also developed a bizarre new karate chop when he speaks, which made him look really weird. It was hard to see him surviving to the election.

Thursday 9 October

Alison came round, said she felt any civil service job would be really boring after working for me, and that obviously she expected David would do things in a different way. We worked out how she might be able to do half me, half No. 10. I did a really long run on the Heath, then went with Fiona to her education debate at the Royal Geographical Society. We went upstairs and I hung back while they briefed her and the other speakers on the pre-meeting. Chris Woodhead [former head of Ofsted], who despite his fall remained unbelievably smug, Melanie Phillips [journalist] vile and humourless, and Claire Fox, formerly of *Living Marxism* [Revolutionary Communist magazine], who was at least articulate but unpleasant in a Trot kind of way. Tony Giddens [academic] and Tim Brighouse [educationalist] were not nearly sharp enough. Fiona was the best on her side of the debate but they still lost the vote. I went to [former *Mirror* photographer] Kent Gavin's farewell, all the old *Mirror* crowd there, good fun, Gavers chuffed I went.

Later I watched a rerun of Duncan Smith's speech at his conference. It just about did the job for him internally but I found it a bit embarrassing, first because of the organised standing ovations and also because of the autocue on the floor. I read it later, and it really was a poorly put-together speech. The content was bad, the delivery dire. There is no way the Tories are going to let him fight an election campaign for them. He got very close to accusing TB of being responsible for David Kelly's death and also cracked a joke about [Lib Dem leader] Charlie Kennedy's drinking. Pathetic. He was getting bad advice from somewhere and worse, he was taking it.

Friday 10 October

TB asked me to do a note for him on the interview he was due to do with *The Times*. I was suggesting the emphasis on renewal because it hadn't really worked at conference and he was best placed at the end of the conference season to have another go. He hadn't watched IDS but said what he had heard made him pretty sure he was not long for this world [as Tory leader]. Our new accountant came round and advised setting up a company with Fiona. I had a fair few speech events now in place, and started to work on a few, but I still didn't really view it as a meaningful form of existence. We were both clear we did not want to set up a company if it was just a way to avoid tax. I flew to Dublin from City Airport. Dublin was looking great and I was staying in the Merrion hotel opposite Bertie's office. The show was being recorded at a university, and the fees they were paying, twenty grand for me and I guess similar for Roy Keane and Geldof, plus the pretty high production values, suggested they were really investing in it, and hoping to take on *The Late Late Show* [long-running, hugely popular TV show].

Dunphy was a real livewire, endless effing and blinding, terrible name-dropping, chain smoking and always telling the staff how brilliant they were. Geldof was on great form, gave me a big hug, said he wanted Fiona and me round for dinner so that he could talk me into getting more involved in Africa. He had been speaking to TB re doing a 'Blair Report' on AIDS/Africa, building it up on a par with the Brandt Report.* Bob said he had told TB he was doing this show tonight with Alastair and TB said, 'What, my Alastair?' to which Geldof said, 'Not any more.' Bob was on first so while he was on I was sitting chatting with Roy Keane and his lawyer Michael Kennedy. I took to him straight away as something of a kindred spirit. I told him TB had always called me Keano when he wanted me to calm down. He was very open and frank, said he couldn't decide who he hated more, Mick McCarthy [football manager, formerly of Republic of Ireland team] or Niall Quinn [international Irish footballer], who he said made him sick the way he posed as Holy Joe. He was clearly quite pro-Gerry Adams [Sinn Féin President], as were a lot of people I met today. The mood on Bertie Ahern wasn't great and the only hint of hostility I got from the audience was when I said how much I liked him. Dunphy was fine, very soft on me e.g. re Iraq. The audience was very warm.

Keane did a really strong interview, went over his career, possibility of future management, talking up Alex as a contrast to McCarthy. He was a lot more handsome in the flesh, and a lot more intelligent than the image. Afterwards there was a big crowd having a few drinks, including the mother of one of the three IRA guys held in Colombia. She had sixteen kids. I drove back to the hotel with Keane. He reckoned

---

* Independent Commission report on international development issues initially chaired in 1980 by former German Chancellor Willy Brandt.

Bobby Charlton was the best ever, Paul Scholes the best today. Back at the hotel, we had a bit of a teetotal bender, Keane and I swapping stories about pressure, media scummery etc. Dunphy had a pretty sharp political mind. He felt TB had blown it on EMU [European Monetary Union] because of all the capital lost on Iraq and Bush. Keane had a good sense of humour, and was OK with people who were coming over to say hi, but you always sensed a tension and anger in there. I got him to give Rory a ring and tell him to keep going with his running.

Saturday 11 October
I got to the airport and realised I had left my phone behind in Dublin. I was absolutely lost without it and got the TV people on the case. I got home and Fiona said TB had been calling. I called back and said there was a case for him watching the whole of the IDS speech because it showed up clearly both his strategy and his strategic failings. TB said he'd be wasting his time, because the guy's a goner, as early as this week. But he felt that even if they got the necessary twenty-five names to trigger a race, IDS would stay and fight and we could end up with the best of all worlds, a fight and no improvement for them.

He was no further forward on GB but felt he had really damaged himself at conference by trying to exploit the media's build-up. He said their last meeting had been dreadful, Ed Balls asking him why he didn't want to say that we believed in old Labour values. He said it was like listening to a GC [constituency general committee meeting] in the '80s. TB was not sure how to bring it to a head. He asked what I was up to and I said bits and bobs, also starting to think about books. I thought I might start with opposition, certainly do nothing about government yet. TB felt Robin Cook had really finished himself with his book. The approach wasn't serious enough. He could easily have become a European Commissioner, but not now that people would just think he was happy to shop them, and not always accurately. He was very attracted to Bob Geldof's big approach on Africa, and felt I should take up the idea of getting more involved, that I would really like working with Geldof.

There had been a very interesting example of the media still twisting things on Iraq. The coverage of [Archbishop of Canterbury] Rowan Williams's speech at the church service on Iraq was of it being very pointed criticism of TB, like a warning, but TB said in fact it was a really good speech, very measured and exactly the kind of thing he should be saying. He still felt the armed forces were onside. He had met the families of soldiers who had been killed. Most were OK, two or three very angry, some just keeping their counsel. On WMD, he felt none would be found until we got Saddam and some of the people around him. I watched Scotland beat Lithuania, then England draw with Turkey (earning a place in finals of Euro '04).

I read over some of the diary stuff. I worried there were too many confidences in there, that I would end up being seen as disloyal, somebody who did damage to Labour, including a future GB government. I needed to think this through very carefully. It didn't help that the tensions in it were so close to home. On the one hand Philip wanted Gail to land a big book but on the other he was like me in not wanting to do any damage to Labour, past, present or future.

Sunday 12 October

David [schools minister] and Louise [Miliband] came round for breakfast. David felt TB did well at conference but he was really worried about TB–GB. He couldn't see how things between them would improve from now on in. The lines and the habits were too well set, people too entrenched, and GB just not someone who would change his ways. They were still waiting for the call on adoption to say that their baby was ready to be collected. What a nightmare the whole thing must be, having life on hold waiting for a call to fly over there [the United States] and meet a child about whom you knew nothing, but knew it would change your life. Peter M was really pushing for a regular meeting with me on strategy and campaign planning, but Fiona, who had just read the diary extracts from '94, said, 'What do you think David Hill would think, remember how you felt when Peter was doing things you didn't know about or approve of?' I didn't feel that me–David would be the same as me–Peter, because David and I could be confident of each other's roles. The problem with Peter was the constant need for it to be said and thought by others that he was at the centre of everything. I decided not to do any political writing for now but instead put together a paper to send to *The Times* with the idea of a multimedia, interactive series to decide the greatest sportsman on earth. They loved it, and wanted me to get going as soon as possible. I felt that the creative juices had flowed a bit since Dublin, and when they found my phone I felt a lot better. I did a long run on the Heath, part of it reasonably fast.

Monday 13 October

Peter M and I agreed to have lunch but then he decided he needed more time to work on the speech he was doing tomorrow. He dropped into the conversation that he thought I would transmogrify in the next few months into a big media figure and then get back to working for TB in some capacity. He had also clearly been talking to either TB, Philip or both about the diaries. He said I have to work out whether and how to do them without damaging my own reputation. I was spending several hours a day now transcribing diaries on my own, all a bit of a chore even when it was interesting, and something at the back of my mind said I would probably never publish them, not for a long time anyway. I went running with the boys and heard a radio somebody was listening to at the track, a news item re TB and something he was announcing on anti-social behaviour. I was still not used to hearing the news and hearing things about TB I hadn't known about or planned.

Tuesday 14 October

I had forgotten just how dreadful the JP–GB hatreds had been back in opposition. Really dreadful. Alex F called wanting me to get involved in a dinner for a property company that had approached him. It was good money but didn't feel right, and I said I'd go with him next time, once he had sussed it out more. Then Brendan [Foster] called, said he had been dining out for ages on the walk I did into the High Court the day after the Great North Run when I was giving evidence to Hutton. He said it was a walk every athlete in the world knows, when your legs are as stiff as wood but you didn't want to show it. He wanted me to go out to Ethiopia to do the Great Ethiopian Run, which sounded brilliant. I had not been there since covering the famine for the *Mirror* in the '80s.

Keith Blackmore [sports editor] from *The Times* came round. They were dead keen on the sports series idea and willing to pay well. The basic idea I had given them was to decide a longlist of great sports stars, try to interview sporting greats and agree at the end of it who is the greatest of all, almost certainly Muhammad Ali. I liked Keith, and could tell he was really enthused about the idea. I had a long chat with Godric about his future. I felt he needed to get out and do something different, but like me he was worrying the whole time about Hutton and its possible impact on his reputation. I took Calum to Ipswich v Burnley. We lost 6–1, five down at half-time, really crap.

Wednesday 15 October

IDS/Betsygate was getting worse for them.* Fiona and I went for lunch with Joe Haines and Bernard Donoughue [former Harold Wilson advisors]. It was nice to hear some of the old stories of the Wilson era, where the divisions and enmities seemed a lot deeper, probably because there was more a policy and ideological base to them. They were both very down on GB. Bernard, who can be a terrible gossip, said he had once been driven by a cabbie who said he once had GB in the back of the cab and he was shouting at Sarah. He thought GB had all sorts of issues that made him worried about his fitness to be PM. Both of them were very down on the BBC and thought there was a case now for taking away the licence fee. They saw Gavyn Davies as a friend and former colleague but felt he had been totally out of his depth. Bernard was also vituperative about the rise of the two-way, felt it was becoming a real problem, that the news was just a collection of uninvited opinion from correspondents. Joe was on good form, and it was great that these two had stayed such good and close friends. They saw each other every week without fail.

Thursday 16 October

Another sign of newfound out-of-touchness. When I spoke to him earlier in the week, TB had suggested I go in for a chat, so I called to see what a good time would be today, to discover he was in Brussels for two days.

Friday 17 October

Breakfast with Gail and Ed Victor. I had sent them extracts from the stuff I had done so far. I told them I felt it would be difficult if not impossible to do anything while TB was there because although in all sorts of ways he came out well, so much was about the difficult personality clashes, the stuff that drove me mad, and I worried that if I did anything perceived to damage them I was not far off from being the kind of disloyal and dishonourable person that I despised in others. They looked disappointed, but seemed to accept it, and Gail had clearly half been expecting it. I said I was not even clear that I could

---

* Controversy over how much money IDS's wife, Elizabeth ('Betsy'), received as his diary secretary.

October '03: Haines and Donoughue with echoes from Wilson era do anything after TB went, if GB took over, not least because so much of the damaging stuff was about him. They seemed surprised as well as disappointed at that.

In recent weeks I had been amazed at how much I had forgotten, particularly of the bad stuff, and although we always seemed to get there in the end, the journey was often a nightmare. I just knew that having been so much part of getting us into power, I didn't want to damage this or any future Labour government. We moved to the idea of themes, maybe taking a theme that avoided the stuff I was worried about, and use it to advertise the fact of the diaries, the full version of which could be done another day, long in the future. Gail suggested the special relationship. I suggested the five major military situations we had been involved in, or maybe Ireland. So at the end of it at least we agreed there was the prospect of doing something at least within a few years, though not the full thing.

I went into No. 10 to thrash out the detail of how Alison was going to work, spending part of her time still in the civil service and part with me. Fiona wanted to write a big piece on Cherie, said she wanted to use it to draw a line. I was worried that far from drawing a line, it would open it all up again, all the stories of bad blood between me and Cherie, an area where actually the press had not really delved as they might have done. I still felt that if she damaged them in any way, even without intending to, she damaged herself. She felt that even though we had left she was still constrained in what she could say and do, and less happy than I was at just living with that. There was something in that, but the reality was a lot of the offers we were now getting were precisely because we had been there. I for one did not intend to do in TB, for all the things I could say and do to do so. I still felt the overall experience was more good than bad, and going through the diaries confirmed that, even though so much of the focus was on the bad.

David Bradshaw called, said he felt I had to get out and about a bit pre-Hutton, raise the profile, maybe soften it a bit. I was quite content at the moment doing very little, and certainly enjoying having so little contact with the media.

Saturday 18 October
I ran for over an hour but my knee was a bit dodgy. We went to West Ham v Burnley and [Labour MP] Jim Fitzpatrick's wife Sheila, who is a doctor, had a look at the knee in the car and said I had probably

been overtraining and should rest for at least a week. I had a good chat with the West Ham chairman Terry Brown, who was a runner, very interested in the whole area of pressure, and how politicians dealt with pressure. I met Alan Pardew, who had just been appointed the new West Ham manager and seemed a good bloke. He was a Labour supporter, liked TB, but said he worried he would not be so effective without me there. He told me their club pay bill was more than £17 million. Ours [Burnley's] is £3.1. There's just no way to compete on those terms. The game itself was fantastic. We should have lost about 10–0, but Brian Jensen was phenomenal in goal and we fought hard for a 2–2 draw. The fans were as good as they've been for years and we were surrounded by all the lads from Keighley, who were great fun, and started singing songs about me, none of which, thankfully, took off.

Fiona and I later went to Guildford to see Ross Kemp [actor], who was performing in *The Taming of the Shrew*. Rebekah [Wade, wife of Kemp] could not quite believe the extent to which Middle England people just stared at me as though there was something a bit odd about me being in a theatre in Guildford. I enjoyed the play, then a couple of drinks with them and off home by 12.30. She felt TB had picked up a bit since conference, but said GB and co. were still at it. The Sundays were mainly focused on the Tories and their problems. The *Sunday Telegraph* had a story about a speaking agency touting me at 25 grand a whack. This was about them getting publicity. I complained and got a grovelling letter back.

Sunday 19 October
It was very odd the way the phone rang so infrequently and how irritated I got when it did. Most Sundays in the past few years I would have spent at least a few hours on the phone. This morning, one call from TB, one from Ed Victor, that was it. It was also odd having so much time. I noticed how Ed would call after meetings or discussions, and virtually relay the whole discussion, and give a commentary, the kind of thing I just never had time for before. I liked him though and felt we were pretty much moving in the right direction, albeit a lot more slowly than he or Gail might like.

I got a message to call Rebekah Wade urgently. There was a buzz that TB had had a heart attack. In fact, he had gone from Chequers to Stoke Mandeville and then to Hammersmith because of a heart problem. He had an irregular heartbeat and it had just gone way too high for a while. I called Jackie [Blair family nanny] in the flat, who said he was fine. Media wise, the office seemed to be handling it absolutely fine. It was probably the first time there had been anything major happening in his Downing Street life that I had not been involved in and again it felt odd, added to which I was worried about whether in fact the problem was more serious than people were saying. It was obviously a big story anyway, though the kids seemed more interested in David Blaine coming out of his box.

Monday 20 October

My knee had got worse and it transpired the calf was torn and I needed to take it easy for a bit. In the diaries, I was up to the first meeting with Diana [late Princess of Wales], who was all over the news again today, courtesy of Paul Burrell [former royal butler] in the *Mirror*.* It was weird how often I seemed to be transcribing the diaries, and then a name I was writing about would pop up on the news or in my life. The TB health scare had calmed down a bit. Alex [Ferguson] called re TB as he had had something similar. Bruce [Grocott] called for a chat, said he was missing me round the place, and Alison had said some days it was like the building was in mourning. I went to [journalist] Roy Greenslade's book launch. Annie Robinson and John Penrose, Eve Pollard, Noreen Taylor [all journalists] and Natascha [McElhone, actor] looking absolutely gorgeous. Guy Black [former director, Press Complaints Commission] and Mark Bolland [public relations executive; former director, Press Complaints Commission] were there, Bolland indiscreet and gossipy as ever. It was a nice enough do, downstairs in El Vino's. I admitted to Eve I had been pretty depressed for some time, and it didn't help that everyone seemed to have ideas about what I should do but none of them really appealed. She said it would be remarkable if there had not been some kind of comedown when leaving No. 10, but I felt this probably went a bit deeper than that.

Tuesday 21 October

The main news was a sense of progress in Northern Ireland with more IRA decommissioning and Sinn Féin and David Trimble [former First

* Burrell claimed that the Princess had told him ten months before her death in a car crash of her fears that her life was in danger.

Minister of Northern Ireland] both apparently up for it. TB was due to head off for talks with Bertie [Ahern] to do the deal. Sally [Morgan, political advisor] called a.m., just for a chat. She said it was comic how much he missed me. At one meeting last week, she said he heard what he thought was my voice in the corridor and he got up, said, 'Is that Ali?', went out to see, but it was someone else and he came back looking sad. Sally was not enjoying the Peter–Birt move into the centre of things. She said they were now living in a Birtian world that she found difficult to the point of being unbearable. Alex F called again and said he would like to speak to TB because he could advise him re the heart, and how he had dealt with something similar. I said I would fix it when he was on his way back from Ireland. Alex worried maybe TB was overdoing it. He asked if I had had a big adrenalin crash, which I had, and he said it was important to stay busy. Truth is I was staying busy, but mainly via going back in, and also transcribing the diaries, which was sometimes just like living in an echo chamber of what was happening now. He was fine about the £10,000 fine and the two-week ban from yesterday [Ferguson had been found guilty by the FA of improper conduct and abusing match officials] but clearly worried about the Rio Ferdinand situation [awaiting FA punishment for missing drugs test].

Jonathan called, then TB, who said he would like me to start thinking more about strategy again. DH was a very good press handler, and in some ways gave him things I didn't because of my neuralgic relations with lots of the media. But where he really missed me was strategy. He said Peter H and Philip were on something of a work to rule because they weren't happy about Birt and some of the other changes being made. Peter M was not doing much other than organisation. So either he wanted me to get more involved again, or to find him people who could help with strategy. He seemed pretty relaxed about the heart scare though he still felt a bit weird from time to time. He had been getting these really odd, pressured feelings, like a sudden surge of intensity inside his body. He had been OK when sitting down but the moment he became active, like jumping up out of a chair and walking somewhere, he felt odd and pressured. The doctors said it was a pretty common thing. He was surprised he had not been told to rest more, but there we are.

On the political scene, he was still of a mindset that said he was in a tunnel and would remain within it for a while but eventually he would emerge from it and, provided we got the timings right, he remained confident we would do fine. His big problem remained GB. He felt we had to wait to see if the new baby* changed his approach at all, but he was doubtful. He felt it was an outrage the way GB played about on Europe with the Murdoch press, presenting himself to the party and the left-wing media as a Europhile, and to the Murdoch lot as someone only going through the motions because of TB, with the unspoken message that 'if I was PM, there could be a change'. I was trying to say to TB that things probably looked better from the outside but I felt that of all the top politicians he had easily come out best from the conference season.

He felt that if he could somehow get Iraq in a better position within a year and greater acceptance of public service improvements, things would look very different. I told him of the audience reaction in Dublin when I was supportive of Bertie. The mood there had not been great for him. He said he hoped the next few days would help him. He then set off for Belfast and although I had always enjoyed the Northern Ireland part of the job, a large part of me was glad not to be there.

Later to Peter M's 50th birthday party. I had a long chat with Charlie and Marianna [Falconer]. She felt Charlie and I were quite similar and that we could only work 100 per cent or not at all. Charles Dunstone [mobile phones businessman] was impressive, very clever without feeling he has to show it too much. It was a nice enough do, in Peter's new flat, a sort of wood-panelled thing that felt more like a cruise liner than a central London flat. Lots of the old crowd were around but it became a bit tiresome constantly being asked what I was up to these days. Peter seemed happy enough, and friendly.

Wednesday 22 October
Up before 7 for the first time in ages. The knee was still playing up but I ran into town, took 37 minutes to run to the Royal Festival Hall to meet [Lord] Clive Hollick [TV and newspaper businessman], who had suggested we meet up to discuss possible work opportunities. A mix of small talk and big talk re politics. He felt GB's speech was very ill advised, also that he had alienated so many people it would be hard for him to come back from it. He thought TB should stay there for a long time. He felt that I should steer well away from the showbiz celebrity side of life and stay as closely involved in politics as possible.

---

* GB's son John, born 17 October 2003.

He wanted me to be one of a series of speakers, also including TB and Bill Clinton, to do a big series at the Festival Hall. He was also 35 per cent owner of Five [TV channel], which wanted me to do some sort of serious chat show, or a series of films about Britain, and possibly some sort of project with Clinton. He had quite a good take on some of the issues I was mulling over, clearly felt I had lots I could do but also that wrong moves would be damaging. He reckoned I could easily get the *Mirror* editorship, and also that Murdoch might be interested. It was really odd to think that at one time in my life the idea of editing the *Mirror* would have been the seemingly insurmountable pinnacle of my ambitions, but, feeling as I did, it sort of left me cold right now.

I ran over to No. 10, in through the back and up to see TB. He looked OK. I said, 'How's the patient?', slapping my heart. He admitted he had been very worried, really quite shocked. It was whenever he tried to do anything really active that it had become a problem, and at times it had been a bit scary when the feeling came on, but he reckoned they had fixed it and he was assured about that. He was convinced IDS was a goner and we had to accept he would be facing someone else at the next election.

His main problem remained GB. GB had done a piece for the *Wall Street Journal* on the EU constitution, which was a pretty big thing and they had not even discussed it properly. He said they had had a conversation about the baby but it had been very perfunctory, without warmth, almost like two strangers. 'I'm afraid the fault line is that there are two operations and everyone knows it and I just don't know what to do about it.' He said that some in the team were telling him he had no choice, he had to sack him, or else his authority was going to be eaten away bit by bit, but he still wasn't sure: 'It is the nuclear option. The reason that I tell them that sacking him is a nuclear option is that it really is a nuclear option. It might be the end of him, but depending on how he reacts, it might be the end of all of us.' I said whether he sacks him or not, GB is determined he should be next, so it is not unreasonable to weigh up whether that is likelier from inside or outside. That would depend on how he reacted, but he would know that the party would not appreciate it if the destabilisation became even more obvious. 'So does that mean sack him or not?' I said it means I understand the complications.

He was more worried about it than I had seen him for a while. He was also really pressing me to get back into doing more political stuff more quickly. I said I would know when I was ready, and it wasn't now. I needed to come back later with more oomph and bite. He was very insistent that I couldn't actually just walk away from all this. 'You have got as much invested in this as I have, and the next election will be tougher than the last one, especially when they get a new leader.' I said I understand all that, but there is no point pretending that I can just come back and do the same stuff I had given up. I still needed a bit of time to work out a proper modus operandi.

He said Northern Ireland had been a bit of a debacle yesterday; it had all looked fine but it turned out that all the pieces weren't pinned down. [General John] de Chastelain [chairman of the Independent International Commission on Decommissioning, responsible for ensuring the decommissioning of arms by paramilitary groups in Northern Ireland], he said, gave a classic example of how not to do public presentation. He still felt that it was going in the right direction and the important thing was just to keep going on it, but it was going to be a long haul. I ran home to collect Rory and then off to get the plane to Glasgow for the Rangers–Man United game. I was impressed that we were able to manage our first e-ticket experience. Rory was getting really irritated by people looking at me at the airport. Also at Glasgow, lots of the Rangers fans wanted to talk about Northern Ireland, and some of them angry we were 'selling them down the river'. We waited for the Man United bus to arrive and saw Alex for a chat in the rather impressive main entrance and collected the tickets. They were meant to be for the away end but it turned out they were United sponsors' tickets, but in a Rangers section, which was a bit hairy, especially as we were sitting with the Ferguson sons, including Darren, who some of them recognised. I was keeping as low a profile as possible, but then a very nice copper came up and said they were keeping an eye on us.

Thursday 23 October
Donald [AC's brother] drove us to the airport and was talking in a rather maudlin way about what life would be like after Dad died. The plane was delayed and I managed to get a load of work done on speeches. Jeff Randall [BBC business editor] was on the same flight. He was a big Rangers fan because, he said, it was the most un-PC club to support. He was very right-wing, also had some very aggressive views about the BBC. He felt 95 per cent of the people who worked there were wankers. He had tried in his own way to challenge the culture but it was impossible. He intended to get out soon. He was

particularly fed up that he was to be denied the right to write a newspaper column because of Gilligan and the governors' failure to handle the issue properly. George Galloway [Member of Parliament for Glasgow Kelvin] was expelled from the party. Briefly to [Prince Charles's spokeswoman] Colleen Harris's farewell at the Palace. A few of the old brigade there and a bit of reminiscing about Diana's death and the week that followed. Colleen looked really happy.

Friday 24 October–Wednesday 29 October

To Rome for a few days. Nice time. I felt fairly relaxed most of the time, and the kids were on good form. PG was still trying to get me more involved. Fiona was very wary about it all. She had no idea of the extent to which I was still engaged and involved, and helping out. TB called a few times, and he was almost furtive when he did, like he wanted to know I wasn't with the family when we were speaking, because he knew it was all a bit explosive in that quarter. The weather was reasonably mild and I was getting in some decent runs, including a couple up to the Vatican, which was really a lot tackier than I had expected. Fantastic inside, but the outside area all a bit yucksville, touristy tat and all that.

Fiona and I had a nice lunch with Ivor Roberts [UK Ambassador], who gave us a good fill-in on the wonders of Italian politics, which sounded way madder than ours. He seemed to be enjoying it as Ambassador here, though he really missed Dublin. TB called halfway through. I'd arranged for Alex to speak to him about the heart thing and he said it had helped to hear from someone who had pretty much the same thing without long-term negative effects. He said the GB situation was as bad as ever and he wanted me thinking about a post-IDS strategy for the Tories.

We left for home after lunch on the Wednesday and got back to the news that IDS was out. There was a seemingly unstoppable process propelling Michael Howard [shadow Chancellor of the Exchequer] in. The once despised right-winger was now being presented as Mr Cuddly. I was pretty confident it wouldn't work, but boy, do the media want to give them a lift.

Friday 31 October

TB called as I was at the gym, to discuss Howard. I felt our line on him had to be that unless the party changed fundamentally, a new face at

October '03: IDS out; Howard almost certainly in

the top would change nothing. I said we, not they or the media, should be setting the bar for what change meant, and we should be setting it very high. He said why can't you do it? I said do what? He said write the strategy for dealing with him. I said I would write something, and started working on it.

Colleen Harris called. She was in a real panic, actually sounded scared and wanted to bounce something off me. She said the *Mail on Sunday* had once run a sex scandal about someone in Prince Charles's household anonymously. But they had now put the allegations to her again and she was sure they were going to run it. Should they injunct, or let them publish and be damned? Or issue a pre-emptive strike? She favoured the pre-emptive strike, and so did I. We went through the kind of thing a pre-emptive statement might say. They should try as hard as possible to make it a story as much about the press as about the royals. She was adamant the story was untrue, that the source was an alcoholic, bitter former butler. She said Charles would go with whatever she suggested. I agreed with her approach and said the public would support him if they felt it wasn't true and this was just the press peddling rubbish to get at the royals. But she needed to know it would go big and be difficult.

Tessa [Jowell] came round, wanting to know if I was interested in a big role in the team running the Olympic bid. It was about the first thing I had been asked about that was remotely tempting. I doubted, however, even if TB and Tessa wanted it, that I would be acceptable to some of the backers. The neuralgia was still pretty intense in some areas and would stay so for a while yet.

Saturday 1 November

I took Rory to a cross-country race out in west London and High-gate Harriers ended up a man short and roped me in. I ran OK for me, and came in 193rd, helped in the last lap by a really attractive woman who appeared out of nowhere and said she would lead me in. I was even overtaking at the end, and presumably these guys were all club runners, so I was moderately chuffed with myself. We went home via a pub that was showing Manchester United v Portsmouth. A bloke came up to me in the pub and asked me what I was doing these days. It was happening more and more and I never knew what to say, beyond, 'A bit of this and a bit of that.' I didn't particularly want it widely known I was working on my diaries because that led to a load more questions, to which I had not remotely decided the answers. *The Times* sent through a contract for the sports series, but it didn't specify sport so I sent it back with a few other changes too. It was 100k basic, which was a solid enough base. The speech offers were coming in. I wanted to keep options open until I finally decided what I wanted to do long-term.

Sunday 2 November

TB called to discuss Howard again. What did I think? I said I thought every one of them he had faced – Major, Hague, IDS, now MH – all said they would lead from the centre. But either because of their real beliefs, especially IDS, or in Major's case because of the state of the party, they were never able to. Howard is a genuine right-winger. That plus the party pressures will bring problems for him. He either would not or could not do it. I said you moved Labour to the centre because you believed it was the right thing to do. Howard thinks it is the right thing to say but deep down he doesn't want to do it and therefore he won't know how to do it. I felt he should be using Howard's arrival to fire up a real New Labour message again.

TB sounded a bit jumpy, as he always did when the atmosphere suddenly changed, but I felt Howard was OK for us, even if the media bummed him up for a while. His bigger problem was GB not MH. The *Mail* and *The Sun* in particular were trying to give Howard a boost, but I didn't fear what was going on, not remotely. I hope you're right, he said. He didn't like the feel of it. I reminded him of the time he was in a total panic because he was convinced Hezza [former Tory Cabinet minister Michael Heseltine] was going to take over from Major.

We went later to [Labour general secretary] David Triesman's party in SE1. Philip and I chatted re TB and the potential sense of isolation. We felt TB was right to want to do his own thing and be his own man, but what he mustn't do is allow Howard's arrival, and any move to the right, to drag himself further in that direction too. I had had no idea that David T was being pushed out as general secretary. It seemed TB had asked him to go to the Lords and be a minister. He would do a good job there. It looked like Matt Carter [member of Labour's National Policy Forum] was being brought in as his successor. David seemed down, said a lot of his problems were because he couldn't work with Ian McCartney [Labour Party chairman].

Steve Byers [Secretary of State for Transport, Local Government and Regions] seemed very down about the political situation. John Reid said he missed me, and so did TB. He felt the sharks were circling with greater intent now. He was also suspicious of Jack Straw and David Blunkett [Home Secretary], felt they were too busy watching which way the wind was blowing. He felt if Jack sensed TB was vulnerable, he would be over to GB. Hilary Armstrong [Chief Whip] was a bit down too. It didn't make me feel any better that they all kept saying TB missed me and the strategic operation was weaker. Hilary felt Howard was not getting the lift he should be. But the overall sense I had, having talked to half a dozen ministers and a stack of people from No. 10, was that the plot was being lost a bit, that the centre and the operation round TB had weakened and despite the sense of setback at conference, GB was still in a strong position and would make a move if he could.

Monday 3 November

My main focus of the day was the speech to Jewish Care [community charity], which was quite a big number and which would help me work out if I wanted to do this kind of thing. I worked on a stack of anecdotes and would decide later, once I had sussed the audience, which to use. I had a bit of a last-minute panic when the computer locked and wouldn't print but Fiona came up and sorted it. I was also working on the diaries for June and July '95, when a previous Tory leadership contest was going on. It was like living in two time zones. I would be working away then look out of the window and wonder why the weather was so bad for June when in fact it was November. I collected Audrey, who I was taking to the lunch, then off to the Marriott. Lots of photos, then to the lunch. I was sitting with Michael Levy [Labour fundraiser], David Gerrard [businessman] and Gail Ronson [wife of Gerald Ronson, businessman], who was really bright and friendly. She thought I would benefit from talking to Gerald about the difficulties of transition in big moments of personal change, though whether she felt my departure from Downing Street equated to his going into prison, or coming out, I wasn't sure.

An award was presented to Sir Nicholas Winton [humanitarian], who had done so much to get Jews out of Nazi Germany. He told me over lunch how Betty Maxwell [media owner Robert Maxwell's widow] was the one who urged him to make his story public, and he was glad he had, not because of all this praise that came his way, but because it gave him a place in the public debate and allowed him to play a part in reminding people of a story that must never be forgotten. He gave a fantastic, emotional speech, which would be a hard act to follow. I got them laughing, though, with a description of how Michael Levy, who had helped fix the event, man-snogs his way from table to table as he fundraises, and a few Maxwell stories, then my usual defence of politics in general and Labour in particular.

I was developing a narrative about the two main parts of my professional life – around a decade on each side of the fence – and how my respect for the media had fallen and my respect for politics had grown. Part of it was an analysis of the corrosive impact of a culture of media negativity. Nicholas Winton said he agreed with my overall analysis of the press, said he had never seen the story of what he did accurately presented in the media. Quite a few people came up at the end, asking if I would speak at this or that event, so it must have gone OK. Michael [Levy] was very nice and supportive, but also terribly insecure. He really wanted to be told that he was valued and respected and that it would be a disaster for the party if he walked away from it. Gilda [Levy, wife of Michael] was seemingly very keen on him giving it all up. He asked if TB really understood what he did for him. I think so, I said. Did he respect him for it? I think so, I said again. I then made the mistake of saying TB was a politician and from time to time he would calculate the value someone gave. He asked for examples. I said everyone had their downside. But e.g. Jonathan would give him 80 per cent upside, a lot. Sally not far off.

I could see him, pleading rather desperately with his eyes, wanting me to include him in the list. Eventually he asked straight out, what percentage value did I think TB gave him. I was trying to get away now, so said, 'Probably 80 to 20 – the 20 because of the baggage that seems to go with anyone involved in fundraising.' His eyes lit up. 'So I'm the same as Jonathan.' Well, you do different things but I have no doubt he values you for what you do. I said he should just carry on doing it. He said he sometimes felt TB didn't say thank you enough.

I was developing a line on Howard, about him being all tactics and no strategy because in the end he was an old-fashioned right-winger pretending to be something else. I worked on it till the early hours, in the form of an article. His record in the last government was also a problem for him.

Tuesday 4 November

I did a long run yesterday and was feeling a bit stiff and sore. I had a couple of speech planning meetings, with the Marketing Society and HBOS. I quite enjoyed meeting different people from different backgrounds who were capable of seeing things similarly but differently. I had drafted a speech for the Marketing Society and though they had one or two comments, by and large they were thrilled with it. The speaking world was going to be a lot of money for old rope. I sent the Howard article through to No. 10. DH and Bradders [David Bradshaw] were both against it. Only Philip was enthusiastic. I had sent a draft through to John Witherow [*Sunday Times* editor], who really liked it, was kind enough to say I'd lost 'none of the old touch'. Interesting meeting with Dennis Stevenson [chairman, HBOS], who was very bright. He and I both had depressive tendencies and we talked a bit about how we might work together on campaigns for better funding and awareness for mental health. He was very well connected and had a lot of drive and energy when he wasn't on a dive down. He felt TB was in need of a reboot.

Peter Hyman came round p.m. and was very down on things. He said Peter M and Birt had 'effectively carried out a coup' and were running pretty much everything they could. But there was no real political direction from TB at the moment, which gave Peter and Birt the licence they needed. Also, the policy unit was not nearly strong enough. He had an interesting take on my *Times* sportsman series, saying Ali was the greatest sports personality of all time, but is that the same as the greatest sportsman? So maybe it was an Eddy Merckx [Belgian cyclist] type.

Wednesday 5 November

Fiona was seeing a pensions expert, thinking it was time we started to get a bit more order in our finances. Witherow was very pleased with the Howard piece. 'I suspect a lot of Tories will have their legs crossed in agony when they read it,' he said. Hope so. Some of the papers, the *Mail* especially, were beyond parody in the way they were trying to give Howard a lift. I used the quote of his when he told me Labour wouldn't win till we elected TB as leader 'because he looks and sounds like a Tory'. That, allied to their belief that they were cheated out of power by me and Peter and dark arts, was one of the reasons he would almost certainly fail as Hague and IDS have done. They cannot begin the proper analysis of themselves till they accept they were properly beaten and till they see what TB was and is doing is progressive. Witherow asked me – I think jokingly – if I would ever consider working for the other side. I said No, and he said that most Tories would read the piece and wonder why they couldn't find someone who could see so clearly what they needed to do, and then help Howard do it.

GB was back from paternity leave yesterday and went to Brussels, where he did a number on the [EU] constitution and then did a piece in today's *Telegraph* of all places. He was clearly determined to keep going on setting himself in a different place to TB on Europe. TB called later, said he was up for the idea of doing something to deal with it, but had he left it too long? Philip said that when Peter Hyman saw Anthony Seldon [headteacher and author] yesterday, he had said that all PMs spend twenty years after they leave the job thinking about things they should have done and TB will spend all his time wondering why he didn't sack GB. The truth was that GB WAS at it but, as PM and leader, TB just had to hold the line that he was a great Chancellor etc., and that they were saying the same thing re the constitution as at PMQs today. It was total bollocks of course. *The Guardian* ran a story that TB blocked GB from a place on the NEC [Labour Party National Executive Committee], so straight back from paternity leave we were into a new round of TB–GB. Things cannot go on like this.

I had lunch at the Camden Brasserie with David Frost, who loved us being there, getting noticed left, right and centre. David was full of good advice. He felt I could do whatever I wanted in TV but advised against doing just politics. We discussed his pending George W. Bush interview, which I had helped to fix. I advised short straight questions, not waffling around, which he would deal with easily. I also thought it would be in both their interests if he got him to show some humour. It was useful to go over all the different strands of what I could do. We talked about some of the book ideas I could maybe do, but agreed in the end there was only one book that mattered, the full diaries.

YouGov [market research firm] called, asking me to be a non-exec. No, ta. Kamal Ahmed [political editor, *The Observer*] called. He had been asked to do a book on me, but a really serious analytical book, not like Peter Oborne's [journalist Oborne had written an unauthorised biography of AC]. Then to the reception at the Science Museum to celebrate 100 years of the *Mirror*. Briefly chatted with Sly Bailey [chief executive, Trinity Mirror]. Didn't strike me as impressive. Piers Morgan [*Daily Mirror* editor] full of pretty superficial analysis of the big political questions. Tony Miles and Mike Molloy reminders of *Mirror* editors in a more serious media age. Nice chat with Anna Ford. I thanked her for her letter at the time of my departure, and we talked about Burnley (we are her no. 1 team). I was standing with her, Michael Grade [showbusiness executive] and Robin Cook [former Foreign Secretary] as we endured Piers's overlong speech. TB arrived, and I could tell he hated it. It was one of those events he sort of felt he ought to go to, like the *Mirror* lunches at conference. But there was not much point pretending he took the *Mirror* seriously, so he went through the motions really.

We had a little chat as he left. He said he liked my Howard analysis but I should always watch out for going OTT. I said I was in a position to go a bit OTT without it damaging him necessarily. He felt that the argument was right but also that for him personally, he needed a bit more time before he started fully to articulate a strategic attack at PMQs. But he wanted me to lay the ground. Ken Livingstone* was coming back into the party.

Thursday 6 November

Alex came down from Manchester, and I arranged for us to go in and see TB. I thought it might help to get a bit of a different take on the leadership situation. He also liked Alex personally and would enjoy seeing him. Alex came round to the house and as we had a cup of tea in the kitchen, once the small talk was out of the way, I asked what his take on the GB situation was. I'd not mentioned anything specific so it was interesting to hear what he said. He said he had heard GB on TV saying that something or other was 'all a matter for the Prime Minister'. 'He didn't need to say that. He could have batted it off easily. He was saying that to create division and it's wrong.' Later Mark [Ferguson, AF's son, businessman] said when they came for dinner that in the City GB was 'unelectable'. Alex said GB was clearly 'Tony's Brian Kidd' [AF's former no. 2] and he needed to decide. 'Where there is doubt, there is no doubt.' It was one of his favourite phrases, but he said if Tony had real doubts about Gordon, then it meant he didn't

---

* Having previously stated that he would not run as an independent candidate for the London mayoralty, Livingstone did so and was expelled from the Labour Party. He was duly elected and it became known that he would be re-admitted to the party prior to the next mayoral election, in 2004.

really want him there. I said he also had doubts about getting rid of him, which is why it made it such a difficult dilemma. He knew that it was a lot harder to get rid of people in politics. You could lose them from the Cabinet team but they would still be around the whole time and could cause you problems.

Alex was great with the kids and Audrey as always, and on a roll on the football front. His big worry at the moment related to the horse [Rock of Gibraltar] and all the nastiness it was arousing.* I said these Irish guys had very deep pockets and were unlikely to stop, no matter how famous and popular he and Manchester United were. It was clearly getting him down a bit. I picked his brains on the footballers for my series on great sportsmen and women, and he reckoned Alfredo di Stefano or Pelé as best ever footballers.

We got a cab and went in to No. 10. Nice to see my old staff again, and I made a point of making sure Alex saw one or two of the United fans in the building. TB talked about his heart scare and they swapped stories on their various flutter experiences, then Alex was giving him a few thoughts on diet. He said it was one of the areas where he felt things had changed hugely since he had arrived at United, let alone when he was a player. They talked a bit about pressure and also how they dealt with people. Alex was interesting on how he dealt with players who misbehaved or how he left players out of the side, different strategies that he had for dealing with different people. He was a disciplinarian on one level, but he also gave the players a fair amount of leeway provided they bought into basic approach and understood that there could only be one boss. He also talked about the need to make sure the strong characters, like a Keane or a Cantona, were allowed to be strong, and the quieter ones were allowed to be quiet. You needed the right mix.

TB asked him how he dealt with players going through a bad patch of form, and how he dropped them without shattering their confidence. AF said sometimes there was no easy way, you just had to drop them. But it was always important to give them a sense that there was a road back. It might mean moving them out but even then you had to let them feel it was the way to a better future somewhere else. The thing about players is that most of them have a pretty good sense of their own talents. They know who the best players are. 'Not like politics

---

* Ferguson was involved in a legal dispute with a major Manchester United shareholder, Irish businessman John Magnier, over stud rights to racehorse Rock of Gibraltar, which Ferguson part-owned. The dispute was eventually settled out of court.

then,' I said and TB said, 'Alex, I've got all that too, but I have one big problem you don't.'

After our earlier conversation, Alex knew what he was talking about, and compared it with his Brian Kidd situation, where you reach the point of thinking that he is more interested in getting the job he wants – yours – than doing the job he should be doing. 'If you are worrying about it, it's a real problem. Where there is doubt, there is no doubt.' TB said GB was a great talent but he had such an ambition to be Prime Minister and he could not hide it. Everyone thought he would come back from paternity leave more mellow but in fact he had come back in an even greater rage. It was difficult though, because I really don't want to do anything that would split the party.

Alex had to take a call from a lawyer about a story the *News of the World* were planning on Rio Ferdinand. TB and I went through to the Cabinet Room. I said the problem was that there had been so many of these division stories that eventually it would get through to the public as a given, and I felt this may be the one that did it. Either they saw division; or they saw his naked ambition; or they saw TB being a bit spiteful. However they looked at it, it was bad not good for us. He said he didn't know what to do. Maybe it had all gone too far. He said he had no idea this thing with the NEC had been going on. It was a clear GB operation to present TB as villain and himself as victim. TB seemed a bit sad, a bit lonely. He said to Alex he had been really looking forward to seeing him. 'I don't get a lot of joy in the job these days.' They both agreed that the press was probably the worst part of their jobs. I sensed TB saw their little chat as a bit of a welcome break from the stack of policy meetings in his diary.

Alex and I left for Les Ambassadeurs and, in the car, he said he thought Tony was looking more careworn, less confident. I said the GB thing was playing around inside his head the whole time. We had a cup of tea and more chat about football, then left for a charity do at Chelsea. We bumped into GB, who had gone for the drinks bit, and he just walked by us with a brusque 'Hello.' He can't have seen Alex, as normally he would be all over him. I saw Gus O'Donnell [Treasury Permanent Secretary], who said that currently the situation was awful and he didn't know how to help. He liked them both but he knew instinctively that TB was a better PM, that GB was not inclusive or relaxed and big picture enough. He was incapable of hiding how hard he found it to deal with foreigners. He was in the right job, so was TB, he said, and we had to work at keeping them together.

He felt I should try to persuade TB to drop the Permanent Secretary for Communications idea, which was one of the ideas being considered in the review of government comms. Sue Nye had gone out with GB but came back in. She and Gavyn Davies were at the next table but I told her I didn't think it sensible to speak to him with the Hutton Report not yet out. He looked over and smiled a couple of times, but I still had no desire to engage. We had a nice enough time though. The charity was doing well on the fundraising front. There was a Norwegian woman at our table saying I should get involved in one of the big international bodies. The story Colleen called me about was going big, St James's Palace having put out a statement. TB and GB were having dinner, yet another kiss and make up, said JP!

Friday 7 November

TB felt the dinner with GB went OK-ish, but not much better than that. He needed to get JP in a better place to keep the pressure on GB to change. He said the old freeflowing chat, or the friendliness of exchanges when they first got together, was all gone. It was all hard work. Every word was carefully delivered because you never knew how or when he would try to use what was said, either briefed in the media, or just as part of the ongoing war of attrition. It was such a sad reflection of what had happened between them. *The Times* had a story that I'd sold my diaries to Penguin, so I was asking for a correction of that. Jack Cunningham [former Cabinet minister] was on the *Today* programme – like the old days – and making clear the party did not appreciate what GB was doing. So GB was angry again. I went up to see Mum and Dad in between sorting Rory's transport to Liverpool v Man U.

Saturday 8 November

TB and GB had finally agreed to do a 'peace and harmony' briefing operation which at least served the purpose of putting out the message that they wanted this to be resolved, even if nobody in the media was going to buy the idea that all was sweetness and light between them. Part of the problem was that even if those who spoke directly for TB did not fan the flames, others who were known to be close enough to TB did, and of course on the GB side, the journos know it goes on because they get stuff poured towards them all the time. I was talking to Mum about Dad's death and funeral plans. There was something close to acceptance by Mum that it would be happening in the not too distant future. Dad too was talking in a far more fatalistic way about things. I never once heard him complain, about pain, about anything really, and neither of them could speak highly enough of the NHS. But there was definitely something different, almost calm, about the way they approached things now. I had lost count of the times I thought it would be the last I saw him. Maybe this was it. He had been hanging in for a few years now.

Dick Caborn called. He said he had been on the phone to JP, had mentioned we were meeting at Sheffield United v Burnley, and JP had invited himself over. I went for a really nice run before we set off. Nice chat with Derek Dooley [chairman, ex-footballer, who had a leg amputated after an on-pitch collision]. JP was very funny pretending to be knowledgeable about football. Someone would mention the name of a player and he would then pretend to know something about him, and make a comment, usually getting names or clubs wrong. They gave us a table a bit out of the way and brought food over. Soup, then salmon 'without the sauce', said JP. He wanted to talk over things in general, and in particular where we were with TB–GB. He said it was all about GB wanting to take over, and wanting to know when it would happen. TB was unsurprisingly not keen to hand over at a time he felt he was being undermined by him. JP said he knew my view of GB and he shared some of the analysis. He said, 'Is this for the diary, by the way?' I said everything was, but not yet.

He said TB was leader and GB had to accept that. If he could, they could carry on and work together. But if they couldn't, it would be curtains. He felt his role was to try to steer them to the position he felt the party wanted, which was TB does the job, has a good run, and at some point we have a new leader and that is obviously Gordon. He said the party hated all the division stuff that was playing the whole time at the moment. He felt most of the bad was on GB's side, but not all of it. He said he'd told GB, 'I'm against foundation hospitals, but what I do is argue my corner and then once it's agreed I back the policy, and that's what we should all do.' He also felt Peter M had to be legitimised, either through a job in Brussels or through an open role.

He asked me what I thought TB would do afterwards. I felt UN Secretary-General was made for his skills in many ways, but the rule seems to be nobody from the United Nations Big 5 can get it, and his role in Iraq alone would make him unacceptable to a fair few of them.

I thought he might get involved in the inter-faith debate. JP said he did not want to be involved in sorting TB–GB for ever. Both of them tended to say to him, 'I know him (whichever) better than you do.' He felt TB was guilty about the past and GB played on it the whole time. He wondered whether it hadn't all gone too far. He felt both of them exaggerated differences to give themselves positioning. He asked what I thought. I thought he (TB) had two options – work with him, or sack him. But option 1 was also dependent on GB doing the same.

The match was poor and at one point I could see from our seats in the away end that JP had nodded off behind his dark glasses. I had a bit of a spat with Fiona as I drove back. She said, 'Why on earth would JP want to come over all that way to see you?' I said, 'You may think I have nothing more to offer but maybe he doesn't. You'll be pleased to know we spent almost all of the time talking about Tony and Gordon.' The *Sunday Times* did the piece on Howard dead straight. The Charles stuff was running as a big-time frenzy. I was doing *Breakfast with Frost* tomorrow on the back of the *ST* article. JP called on his way home from the match and said if I was asked about the TB–GB dinner I should say that it was normal for the three of them to meet. David Hill called, said it was out there that JP had been at the dinner.

Sunday 9 November

TB called as I was on the way to *Frost*. He said re Howard that we should be saying he talks the language of the centre but pursues policies of the right. Hit them on opportunism and having no agenda for the country. Running Britain down. On Iraq, we're there and have to stay there and mend it. On GB, they are big enough to work together. It was a bizarre role reversal, him briefing me on lines to take and on tone. I had a brief chat with John Howard [Australian PM] who was pre-recording before going to the Cenotaph ceremony. He was asking if the Aussie Labor Party had been sounding me out to help them yet; also said that he was confident the Iraqi argument would still be won.* I met some Zimbabwean journalists, which was useful given what they were engaged in [fighting restrictive legislation against the press] when it came to me launching an attack on our press. I felt the interview went fine and we got through a lot – Howard, TB–GB, Iraq, media, royals. I asked Fiona what she thought and she hadn't watched

---

* Howard had supported the coalition invasion of Iraq earlier in the year.

November: '03: TB goes for Howard 'opportunism'

it. Leaving the job had not exactly transformed things on the home front. Boris Johnson [*Spectator* editor and MP for Henley] called, offering me a front cover on any subject I wanted. Good follow-up on the Michael Howard piece. I felt the arguments were strong and would carry.

Tuesday 11 November

Fiona had done her first column for *The Guardian*, which sparked another big row because it was being spun by *The Guardian* and the BBC as her hitting back at me re the 'bog-standard comprehensive' jibe.* She hadn't shown it to me in advance and said she knew it was being spun as that which is why she hadn't. I said it was bloody obvious that's how they would run it, and she wasn't born yesterday. She went into a complete rage, saying what is the point of leaving if you haven't really left, and why should she still be constrained from saying what she thought, and generally laying into education policy, and it didn't stop until Grace's friends came to pick her up for school. After Grace had gone there was a bit more rage on both sides before we talked about it in a more civilised manner. She said that when she'd asked why did JP go all that way to see me, what she meant was, 'Why are you allowing yourself to be drawn back into it all again? He went halfway across the country to get you back in.' I said I was very proud of what I had done and when I heard her criticising the government in the way she did, I was not just going to sit there and say nothing. She said she barely criticised at all, but was expected to agree with everything I said or did, and sometimes she didn't, and now we were out she was entitled to say so.

I said I certainly didn't expect to be made to feel like shit for having done a job pretty well, and a job that was tough but needed to be done, and I didn't have to feel like I was having my ear bent by a never-ending *Guardian* editorial. I was going through the July '95 diary as part of the transcription work, and we were having some pretty explosive rows then too. But I felt this was worse, that I'd done what she wanted and got out of the job and seemed to get no recognition for it. It was sometimes as though I had never left in her eyes, but that was maybe because I had not really left in TB's eyes either, and to some extent my own. But it did not feel today like we had taken a big step forward; on

---

* AC had in 2001 controversially declared, 'The day of the bog-standard comprehensive is over.'

the contrary. As ever when we had a big row, I went through the day feeling pretty low and shitty.

Liz Lloyd [No. 10 deputy chief of staff] came round. She went through the No. 10 operation and said it had gone backwards. They had underestimated how my role cut across all sections and all departments, and the new people and structures were not really adapting. Later to Grace and Georgia's [Gould] school play. Philip said he really felt I needed to establish a role in the election campaign planning. Douglas [Alexander] was feeling a bit vulnerable because of all the different arguments flying around, but he would not mind me being in there. I did a note for TB on PMQs, felt he had to start pinning Howard for his role in the poll tax.

Wednesday 12 November

Pretty grim mood between me and Fiona, not helped when I was out last night and someone shouted across the road that he liked her piece in *The Guardian* and, to me, 'Maybe you should try criticising them now you're free.' Free did not feel like the right word. She later apologised, said she should have told me and also let me have a say, and I apologised for flipping my lid, but I was really fed up with it all. I felt I'd done what she wanted and yet here we were, still rowing the whole time. TB called pre-PMQs, and post. Pre, he wanted to say that Michael Howard was living proof that people written off under the Tories would come back to prominence under Labour. Howard was OK, but no matter how hard he tried he always came over as a rather unpleasant lawyer. TB more than held his own, though I could tell from the earlier call he had been a bit nervous. He felt there was a lot in Howard's past that would harm him in the future, and the research team really needed to get motoring.

David Blunkett came round for dinner. He was pretty chirpy at the way the identity cards policy had come out,* though he had had to fight pretty hard to get his way. He was very down on GB as ever, felt that TB could sack him if he wanted to, said he was like a big lumbering growl that was heard across government every day. He asked if I was missing it. I said I missed it a fair bit, but I didn't miss the press

* Blunkett had announced the government would introduce a 'British national identity card' as an anti-terrorism measure. The plan was scrapped when the Conservatives gained power in 2010.

or the pressure, added to which I was getting dragged in more or less every day, and that was likely to continue until I decided whether I was going to go for another full-on role somewhere or wait it out. He asked if I was going back for the election campaign, and I said probably, I would almost certainly do something, and Fiona said, 'Of course he is going back.'

Grace was very funny with him. At one point I had to take a call and was standing in the kitchen door waiting for TB to be put through. I was half listening to DB and Grace. He asked if it was nice having me home more, and she said yes. Then he asked what I did all day. She said, 'Well, when I go out to school in the morning, he's sitting on the sofa you're on. When I come back, he's lying down on it, asleep.' David laughed his head off. 'So what is so funny?' I asked him when I came back in. 'Grace was just telling me that you have finally retired.' DB was not aware of the row Fiona and I had had, though he knew what she thought of our approach to education, especially since he had left the job for the Home Office, but he was savvy enough to know transition was unlikely to be easy, and he raised it on a couple of occasions. He said to Fiona at one point, in a nice way, that she had to understand why TB would not want to let me go fully, because in these very top, very exposed jobs, you need support and good advice from people you really feel you can trust, and they do not fall off trees.

He said having someone who is as politically savvy as a politician without actually being a politician was a big help to someone in a top job and if you were able to find one, you were always reluctant to let them go. Fiona listened, didn't say much, but I think she understood. I thanked David when he was leaving and I was taking him out to the car. I said it was good to be out of the day-to-day, but I felt I was neither in nor out, and it was creating all sorts of tensions in my head, and with Fiona. He said, 'Get yourself up to Burnley and shout it all out,' and laughed. Then, as he was getting into the car, he said, 'And get yourself a seat while you're up there.'

Thursday 13 November

I wasn't sure that going through all the old diaries was doing much good on the mental or the marital front. The fact that I had just gone through the '95 holiday in Flassan, when Neil [Kinnock] tore into me – I had forgotten he almost chucked a boiling kettle at me when we were rowing about Murdoch – and I felt Fiona backed him not me, was not a good backdrop to the row going on now. I did a bit of work in the morning and then left for a lunch and a speech, which seemed to go OK. It was good money, but not terribly fulfilling. I think this was the basic problem in the situation with Fiona. Because she had felt so strongly for so long that I should be out, she couldn't see why I was finding the transition so hard. But the reality was that I was finding it hard, and she wasn't helping in the way I felt she should. I also thought she more than anyone ought to appreciate how hard it had been, and why I was keen to preserve for myself the sense that it had been worthwhile. All I seemed to hear was her belittling the government in a very offhand kind of way. She surely can't have expected me just to cut off from it, not care what went on, not want to defend what we had done and were still doing.

I had a dinner engagement, which meant I had made 30,000 quid in a day, more than most people make in a fucking year for God's sake, but I can't say it meant much. In fact I was feeling pretty down about things. It was also hard to get up for these kinds of events when inside I was feeling pretty low. Martin Gilbert [investment group Aberdeen Asset CEO] was good fun, though, and smart. Mark [Neale, university friend] came to the evening do, which was for Aberdeen Asset management, and I think was quite shocked by how big a figure I seemed to be, the way they seemed to hang on every word. We were laughing about it on the way home, recalling the time I was a busker and he was my 'bottler' [collector] in the south of France, and what if those people tonight had seen me back in those days, pissed falling off the back of his Honda with the bagpipes going as he went round with his crash helmet. He said that even though he had followed my activities from the States, he had no idea my profile was such that people would pay five-figure sums to hear me speak and have the chance to ask questions about anything and everything.

Friday 14 November
Very odd start to the day. I received a note via No. 10 that London Transport Lost Property Department wanted urgently to contact me, as they had something which they assumed to be mine. It seemed a bit unlikely as it was found on a bus route I had never been on. I needed a decent run, though, so I ran off down the canal for a bit and then back through Regent's Park to the Lost Property Department near Baker

Street. They produced a big black file which had an authentic copy of my signature at the front, lots of sketches of me inside, extracts from the Inquiry, sketches of John Scarlett, Jonathan, Hoon, others who were giving evidence to the Inquiry. It was only as I flicked through it, I realised it was almost certainly the work of the producer of a theatre production, possibly the actor playing me. I left it there, and then got the No. 10 switchboard to phone and tell them their file had been left on a bus and No. 10 was helping them to relocate it. I feel sure they can weave a new conspiracy theory out of that.

All sorts of weird and wonderful offers were still coming in, the latest to be a visiting fellow at Harvard's JFK school. I said I would give it some thought, but I knew I was going through a depressive period because virtually every time I was asked to do anything just now, the basic instinct was to feel a bit more energy flooding out of me. It was crazy in a way. As Philip said, doing a course on campaigns or on government, or Ireland, or whatever, at Harvard of all places, could be fun, could be interesting, could help get me in a new place and also get over to a new audience the benefits of progressive government; on a rational level, I knew all that, but the energy needed to take it on just wasn't there. He said he thought I ought to see someone, that the glums seemed to be lasting longer than usual.

Bush's visit was being put over as a bit of a nightmare for TB. The whole tone of the coverage was that Bush was a disaster area and any reminder of his relationship with TB was bad for TB, who I knew would be feeling embarrassed about the way Bush was being portrayed, and there was a risk he would push the boat out even further as a result. His overnight interviews went fine with the heavies. I bumped into Matthew Taylor when I went in to see Alison. He was clearly still getting used to the place. He said, laughing, 'I knew it would be right-wing and badly managed inside No. 10 but I had no idea it would be so right-wing and so badly managed.' He also said he was shocked at the badness between No. 10 and 11. 'I know I shouldn't be because I have read about it for years, but it's worse than I thought it was.' He said even getting the slightest agreement on the smallest issue seems to require Herculean effort, and there are very few policy-making processes that are simple and without rancour. Sally popped in too, and did that wonderful silent headshake and eye swivel that simply meant she was having a bad day, thanks to the usual reasons. The BBC *News at Ten* led on Murdoch hinting that he might not support us at the next election, which was getting the media terribly excited. There was something deeply offensive about the fact that that in itself, because it was basically about the media, was thought to be a lead story.

Saturday 15 November

I was up to see Mum and Dad, who was not great, just sitting there, eyes tired and puffy, breathing not so great, and I could tell it was all a bit of an effort. He had the telly on but was not really engaging with much at all. Mum was doing her best to keep spirits up but she seemed a bit down. I left with Calum for Derby v Burnley (2–0), another crap match, really poor. Back later, when the Sunday papers arrived, I just couldn't be bothered with them, couldn't even read them.

Sunday 16 November

Philip came round to watch the France v England game (Rugby Union World Cup semi-final, 7–24), but I knew he was also coming to keep an eye on me, and of course to talk re TB, the campaign planning (lack of) and suss out what more I might do. He had done some groups which showed TB doing OK, certainly the public mood not as bad as the media mood, but Howard was also picking up. We really had to guard against allowing our own views about Howard to influence what we thought was coming through to the public. Both of us had a sense that the Tories were improving their base position a lot more than our people thought. Most people saw Howard as a blank piece of paper. They didn't remember him much from government and thought he was better than IDS. I was going down with some awful bug on top of the fucking depression.

Monday 17 November

Feeling like death warmed up. Dan Bartlett [senior White House official] called to run some of the Bush speech lines by me. They knew this was a tricky visit, as much for TB as for him, and he said they did not want to add to TB's troubles, but Bush did feel he had to take the opportunity to push on with his foreign policy agenda and basic message about the war on terror. They felt his interviews had gone OK, and some of the papers had run polls which showed basic support both for the visit and for the USA in general. I said it was important they did not get too defensive. Bush had a real media problem, for sure, but the basic view of the US in Britain was still positive, and also there was probably a bigger gap between media and public opinion in the UK than in the US. He asked how I was getting on with life post the job, and I said not as well as I had hoped, not least because I didn't really feel I had been allowed to leave. 'What on earth would give you that impression?' he said, then laughed.

I was speaking at a charity do at the Langham Hotel, which went OK without being brilliant, though I felt the Q&A was a lot better than the previous ones, less defensive maybe. I was so used to dealing with the lobby that maybe I was looking for trickiness and hostility in questions when none was there. At every one of these speaking events, paid or charity, that I have done so far, I have been asked why I don't stand as an MP. I suppose in many ways it's the obvious thing to do, but it doesn't feel right at the moment, almost like starting all over again, and I'm not sure it would help much on the home front suddenly to go back into another political project. In fact I know it wouldn't. If anything, I wonder if Fiona might be more tempted than me, though right now I get the feeling she would just like us to be right out of it, right out. I did feel well placed to develop a narrative about the media and politics, having been on both sides of the fence.

Leon Symons [ex-*Daily Express*] was at the do and asked a question based on the assumption that all politicians are liars. I hit very hard at him and got a very good response. I felt that if only the political class would stand up for itself better, the public could be won round to a different position. It was also interesting to see how people seemed to respond better now that I was slightly removed from it. I was drenched in sweat when I left, because of the lighting, but the various events I had done in the last few days had helped crystallise in my own mind the idea that I should use these speeches to make a defence for politics in general, TB and Labour in particular, and emphasise that all that mattered was to make the right policy and strategic decisions and drive them through.

Wednesday 19 November

I was speaking at the Marketing Society, feeling really low, raging temperature, hadn't run for four days. But I managed to lift myself, and both speech and Q&A went well. I felt that the message was better framed as a defence of democratic politics rather than just a blunt attack on the media and defence of TB/New Labour, though I did plenty of that. The demos for the Bush visit were not as big as anticipated and his speech went pretty well. A couple of journalists called me to tell me that Guy Black was going to get the job as Howard's press secretary. It didn't surprise me terribly, but I wasn't convinced that he was the right material.

Thursday 20 November

Breakfast with Les Hinton and Vicky Barnsley, who laid out her stall as to why she thought Harper Collins would be best placed to do a book. I didn't like the way she tried to make out, not very subtly, that it wouldn't look great if I did a book with Gail, given she was a personal friend. In the end, if and when I did do a book, all that mattered was getting a publisher who knew what they were doing and took it seriously, and I had no doubt at all that Gail would do that. Harper Collins also had a perfectly good reputation but there was the Murdoch thing and they would have to come up with very good reasons, not just financial, for me to go for them above Gail. Les seemed to have a better understanding of where I was coming from, and was not just doing the pushy hard sell.

I was pretty clear there would be nothing before TB went, certainly nothing damaging, and possibly nothing before GB went either, and she couldn't really understand it. 'You have to understand, Vicky, this is a true Labour believer you're talking to,' said Les. She said it went without saying that timing was important and the longer I waited, the more the value fell. I said I understood that but though I am not pretending I don't care about the money, it is not the main thing for me. If I do books, whether diaries or an analysis based upon them, I want them to be done well and become part of the ongoing political debate about the New Labour period and politics more generally. I think Les understood more than she did. I suspect he had been hoping that having gone into the deal with *The Times* for the sporting greats series, that might make me feel more open to going with them on the books front too, but I saw them as totally separate things.

At 4 p.m., a meeting with Dave Richards [Premier League] The specific discussion was whether I wanted to work with the Football Foundation [sports charity], but it developed into whether I would be interested in trying to take over UK Sport [government sports development body] or Sport England [public sports funding body]. It was tempting, but all I had seen of the way British sports administrations worked made me think there would be a lot of head banging against walls. I met Dan Bartlett at the Park Lane Hilton. He said Bush missed having me around, and that the meetings were a lot more dull, and nobody wound up him or TB. He felt the visit had been as well set up as it could have been given the circumstances. I didn't get the impression that the Americans were under nearly as much pressure as we were on WMD. Bush knew TB was going to take a hit for having him over, especially the fact it was a full state visit, with Prince Charles having gone to meet them at the airport, and the Queen involved as much as she was.

Dan said even by their standards the security was tight. Bush was meeting British 9/11 victims, and also UK soldiers who had been in Iraq and Afghanistan. He said they had been aware of the scale of the demos, but they seemed to be directed as much at TB as at Bush. On the political front, they were thinking it was 'Howard Dean's to lose'.* Karen Hughes [counsellor to President Bush] was far less involved now but would come back for the campaign. Bush liked to have her around. Dan was not sure how long he would stay. He seemed a bit tired and said the non-stopness was a problem. He said he didn't know how I did it for so long, and he got the impression I was to all intents and purposes still doing it.

Fiona and I were out later for dinner at [media owner] Richard Desmond's. Up off Bishop's Avenue. All very '70s. A bar in his lounge, pool visible from inside, drum kit. His wife Janet was pretty sussed politically, and also about the main characters in the media. They both clearly loathed Paul Dacre. Desmond was pressing hard on getting the OFT [Office of Fair Trading] to look at how London papers were distributed, because he wanted to rival Associated Newspapers. He was far too warm about Howard for my taste, possibly the Jewish link, but also because though he liked TB, he described GB as a 'tax maniac'. Howard was clearly working him like crazy and the conversation was peppered with references to their meetings and chats. I told Janet, who seemed a solid citizen, less likely to be swayed, to keep an eye on him. He was someone whose views of politicians tended to be driven less by what they thought and did than by how much attention they gave him. I remembered him saying he didn't like Hague because he

---

* Governor of Vermont Dean was a candidate for the Democratic nomination in the upcoming US presidential election. Despite great organisational and fundraising flair, he was to lose out to Senator John Kerry.

took so long to return calls. I defended GB re the economy, but he was having none of it, said he was a maniac, 'You know it, Tony knows it, the public knows it, the only one who doesn't is Gordon.' He gave me the figures showing that if the *Mail* got the *Telegraph*, the *Express* [a Desmond-owned paper] was basically fucked.

Friday 21 November

I spent the morning working on various speeches. I called Jonathan [Powell] re Desmond. He said there was every chance the *Mail* would get the *Telegraph*. He wanted me to go in and go over some of the media issues that flowed from that. TB said he had taken consider-able offence at the Murdoch [BBC] interview and didn't like the way these people thought they could just play around.* GB had changed a little bit for the better, and realised since Howard's arrival that it was a different ball game, that IDS had been unelectable without a doubt, that Howard might be, but we couldn't be certain, and there was no doubt the right-wing media would help him all they could, and the Tories would give him the support he needed for at least as long as it took to make a judgement about whether he could do it. In any event, he had a basic competence sufficient to make sure he was there at the election. I felt that was no bad thing, because I just could not see the public electing him up against TB. He thought Howard was good at the tactical level, but that he lacked substance on strategy, and was therefore liable to make the same kind of mistakes Hague and IDS had done. The general view on Guy Black was that he wasn't impressive, and not a great choice.

Chat with TB. It was a nice enough chat but I was still feeling de-motivated. Yesterday alone, whether re books, the football job or helping Desmond go for the *Mail*, I had discussed all sorts of projects that ought normally to take my fancy, but for some reason none really did at the moment. Bad news later when Chris [Downes, family friend] died. Earlier I had got Peter M to go to the hospital and later Fiona, Audrey, Gavin and I went to see Illtyd [Harrington, Chris Downes's partner]. All incredibly sad, and I am not sure how Illtyd will cope without him. Illtyd was the political force, but Chris the life force who had kept their show on the road. TB called again. He felt the Bush visit

---

* Murdoch had signalled that his newspapers could support the Conservatives at the next general election.

November: '03: GB 'a maniac', complains media owner Desmond

had gone much better than expected, and that the Istanbul attacks had made it more relevant.

Saturday 22 November

Up early to watch England v Australia in the Rugby World Cup Final. Quite an amazing event, won (by England, 20–17) with the last kick of the game, which would make overnight stars of virtually all of them, and put Jonny Wilkinson [player whose drop-goal in the last minute won the match] into a different league. No doubt it would also get the *Mail* et al. into TB and Tessa's ribs for 'suddenly' taking an interest in rugby. It was astonishing how good sport could make a country feel, and how papers like the *Mail* saw it as their job to generate as much bad feeling as possible. No. 10 faxed through the prospectus for next week and I did a bit of work on that.

Sunday 23 November

Papers wall to wall rugby. The broadcasts ditto, and it was going to be like that for some time. It was interesting to see how in one moment, everyone involved had just moved to a different place media wise, profile wise, money wise. Wilkinson in particular was now going to be on a totally different level, while Clive Woodward [coach] was going to be able to move into the leadership space in a big way if he wanted to. Roz Preston [former advisor to CB] came round later in the day, and she and Fiona had pretty much reached the same place re CB, that she had a lot of strengths and qualities but had moved to a different place in her mind, was less easy to help and advise. Fiona was a lot more relaxed talking to Roz about how she felt about where we were on things, including saying I seemed to be as involved as ever, and without any apparent rancour.

I still didn't feel up to running, which was a pain, but I was determined to do the run in Ethiopia [Great Ethiopian 10-Kilometre Run]. I've got a week to get myself in shape. The head was in a bad place. The bug I'd had was lingering, so my breathing was shit, and I had a problem with my big toe. Tom Bostock [GP] came round and said he thought I was crazy to do it and, 'Don't blame me if you have a heart attack.' He said the GMC [General Medical Council] would 'rightly' strike him off if they thought he did anything other than warn me not to do it. He was almost comical in how over the top he went. I sensed he was keen at some point to be able to say 'I told you so' about me having left the job and then plunging into all kinds of mental and physical illness. I do like him though, and there are not that many GPs who do house visits the way he does when I am feeling like this.

I was still banging away at the American Embassy re Mark [Neale]'s visa situation. Went out with him and the Goulds. We got into another great blah when Fiona was defending Helena Kennedy [lawyer Labour peer] over some attack she had made on our record. I said she had been given the platform of a seat in the Lords by Labour, and that gave her the right to say what she wanted, but the responsibility to understand it made her part of a team, and it would simply be wrong if she felt she could become a rentaquote critic. Admittedly, with a few fucks and fuckings thrown in. Fiona said she was entitled to say what she liked and if people felt Labour's policies were going in the wrong direction they were entitled to say so. 'Your problem is you think anything Tony says or does has to be supported.' No, but there has to be some understanding of how hard his job is, and an instinct to support if you are Labour, not an instinct to oppose. Perhaps with more fs. 'Well, this is all very jolly,' chipped in Mark, which at least defused things, but the mood never recovered. These flare-ups were happening too often and then taking too long to subside.

Philip called me after we had got home and said again he thought I needed to see someone because he felt I was clearly depressed. He said Fiona was not going to change until she felt I had, and I said what more do I have to do? I have given up a job you were adamant I shouldn't ever give up. Yes, he said, but she thinks nothing has changed. Well, it has, which is why I am looking at my diary for tomorrow, which has got fuck all in it. I knew I wouldn't be able to sleep so I went upstairs to the office and worked on a note for TB on the prospectus. 'What are you doing up there?' Fiona said when she went to bed. 'Writing a note to Tony Blair, the Prime Minister of the United Kingdom of Great Britain and Northern Ireland, about how to prepare the ground for the next election.' 'What a surprise. Night night.'

I told him the draft was way too defensive. Also it didn't have a strong enough sense of the future. We have to be the party that is constantly setting out future challenges, and past achievements are useful for the purposes of a document like this only if accompanied by next steps for the future. The day when the agenda was driven by little policy nuggets was over. It had to be about basic values, future challenges, and only in that context did people buy into a policy debate.

Philip had said the Tories were slowly getting their act together and we had to get a proper operation going again soon. Even if we were perhaps overstating the sense of Tory recovery based on the media coverage about them being better than under IDS, there was no harm in putting a bit of fear into our people that the gap was closing and the next election was anything but a foregone conclusion. I finished the note, then wrote this up, and it was gone 2 a.m., but I still felt I wouldn't sleep, and so did a bit of work on the speech I was supposed to be doing on Tuesday.

Monday 24 November
Finally, for the first time in ages, I did a half-decent run. I sent Brendan [Foster] a message, the bad news that my GP had advised me against going to Addis Ababa; the good news that I intended to ignore him. I got the all-clear from the Business Appointments Commission to go ahead with the sports series work for *The Times*. The Cabinet Office told me the Lib Dems had tried to hold it up; now it was down to [Sir Andrew] Turnbull [Cabinet Secretary] but it shouldn't be a problem.

Tuesday 25 November
Fiona was off filming for her education film in Bristol, and I motored all day on the diaries. Sometimes it was interesting, and all sorts of stuff I had completely forgotten was down there. Also stuff I had totally misremembered, including some of the stories I had been telling in the speeches I was doing. A lot of the time it was just a chore, and it was going to take a long time to get them in shape. Why had it never crossed my mind to type the fucking things? I guess that would have changed the nature of them though. They are really raw, and I reckon that is partly because it is pen to paper, scribble and shorthand, not me banging them out the way I do notes or speeches. I was speaking at the Foreign Press Association Awards, black-tie job in Park Lane. Matt Peacock [Australian broadcaster, organiser] was extremely nice. He reckoned the obsessive interest of some of our media in me was in part about jealousy, that so many of these journalists would love to have been able to do what I did, and be right at the centre rather than on the outside. He reckoned there was a part of every journalist who reckoned they could do the job I had done, and a part of most journalists who imagined what it was really like on the other side of the fence.

I chatted to Prince Edward for a bit. He was very anti-press, said re Charles that the press go so low, then you think well that's it, it's impossible for them to go any lower, but somehow they do. I asked him if he had any ideas about what to do about it, and he said no, but he knew it wasn't working and he knew it wasn't good for the country. I had a silly woman from the *Standard* chasing me round the whole time. Clive Anderson [comedian and broadcaster] was the MC and was extremely funny, with some of his best jokes at my expense re WMD, lack of. I did a bit of funny stuff, but the speech was a fairly sober version of the basic argument I had been developing about the need for politics and media to respect each other more, but made it clear I thought politics deserved that respect more than the media. Mike Jackson [UK Army General] said to me afterwards I need to keep making that speech, make it a hundred times until they hear it. Betty Boothroyd [former Commons Speaker] said much the same. She said she worried that relentless drip-drip-drip against politics and politicians would eventually lead to a kind of anarchy, where respect for the rule of law eroded, and where politics was viewed so badly that nobody would think about doing it. It was a perfectly nice evening, and I tended to get on better with some of the foreign media, who were generally more serious and less in your face the whole time.

Wednesday 26 November
Fairly straight coverage in the heavies of the speech last night. I went for an hour-long run on the Heath, but felt sluggish and slow. Likewise I couldn't be bothered to do much work. I had agreed to do a piece for the Davos [World Economic Forum] magazine and just rejigged the speech to the Marketing Society. Going to the dentist to get a new crown was probably the highlight of the day. It was a big day on the political front and I watched Howard and TB do the Queen's Speech. Howard was pretty strong, really motoring on TB–GB, both of whom looked a bit uncomfortable. Howard had some half-decent lines and landed them pretty well. They clearly felt they had the fault line to work at. But I didn't feel on policy they had a clear agenda or strategy. I was also hoping that Howard having been so clear that the TB–GB fault line was to be a source of attack, GB might change his modus operandi a bit. TB was OK, better than last year, and though I know he had been a bit nervous, he did it pretty well. Out for a dinner. But didn't feel on form. Also, Chris's funeral had been set for when I was due to be in Ethiopia.

Fiona was nice about it though, said Illtyd would understand it was a charity thing, and partly about John [Merritt], who both of them liked.

Thursday 27 November

I did *GMTV* first thing re the Great Ethiopian Run, and managed to get in loads of plugs for Leukaemia Research. They also asked me about TB's health scare, the *Mirror* having splashed on a doctor going to see him about a stomach pain. Off to the airport, met Brendan and Sue in the departure lounge. We stopped in Alexandria. Ben Wilson [No. 10 press officer] had come along and was loving it, also begging me to mention him in my diary at some point. I did a couple of interviews on the plane. Stayed at the Hilton in Addis where years ago I was with [Robert] Maxwell [late media tycoon] when he decided he would single-handedly save Ethiopia.

Friday 28 November

Up early for the press conference chaired by Richard Nerurkar, who used to run marathons for the UK and now lives out here. Good event, if a bit long, but you felt that the Ethiopians were really up for this.

Haile Gebrselassie [Ethiopian distance runner] and Paul Tergat [Kenyan distance runner] were absolutely charming, even put on Watford home and away strips for Dave Hart, who worked for Brendan and wanted to get a piece in the Watford FC programme. It turned out that Richard N went to Bradford Grammar and also that Brendan taught there, which was news to me. I don't know how much it was down to my company, but Brendan seemed to hate the press as much as I did, and shared my analysis both of the *Today* programme and of *The Guardian*. He was a good person to talk to about my situation, and felt I was in the same sort of position that he was when he gave up running, having spent his whole life dedicated to that.

Ben and I left for a run and we went up to the Sheraton, which was so luxurious as to be close to obscene, given the surroundings, to hear a speech by Myles Wickstead [UK Ambassador to Ethiopia] to the Ethiopian International Institute of Peace and Development. He was an interesting bloke, very committed, and a big driving force in the whole Great Ethiopian Run project. They asked if I would speak, and the chair introduced me as a 'political superstar', which was all a bit OTT and weird, but the level of questioning revealed a phenomenal understanding of the detail of British politics. It was only when you came to places like this that you realised how big the whole TB/New Labour phenomenon was with any political audience around the world. They had a sense not just of TB's political success, but also of the commitment to Africa. One or two of the questioners had bought into the whole 'spin' thing, comms as a negative, but generally the take on the TB government was overwhelmingly positive. I did a few interviews and then ran back with Ben. We had kids running alongside us all the way, not begging, just wanting to join in, though they accepted willingly the money we gave when we arrived at the hotel.

The effect of the altitude was not as bad as I thought, though Ben was struggling a bit. I liked Myles, who managed to combine an obvious love for the country with the ability not to go totally native. Brendan said the idea for the run had effectively come from Myles, in a conversation they had a few years back. Why should countries like Britain and the US have the big mass participation events, when the greatest distance runners in the world came from this part of the world?

I was now starting to map out the first few *Times* pieces, on which Brendan had some good thoughts. I worked out of room 924, from where it was possible to see straight into the shanty town behind the hotel. It was still bad, but nothing like as bad as it had been when I stayed here before. The infrastructure had definitely improved, even if it was still light years from what we took for granted.

Saturday 29 November

Twenty-minute drive up to the mountains, scenery more and more beautiful, the air thinner and thinner. Paul Tergat was stretching, took ages to do so, and I ran with him and the Kenyan squad along a trail. It was a bit like Scotland with sunshine, not so green but really bold and stark. We came across little knots of people and donkeys in the oddest places, yet they seemed totally unfazed. The altitude was tough but I managed 40 minutes, including surviving with Tergat up a hill before he strode away. I had effectively stayed with them for their warm-up, but once they were actually running, they were gone. We headed back for lunch at the Olympic Café, part of a complex owned by Gebrselassie, who came up and joined us. I did an interview with him for *The Times*. He had absolute clarity about what it took to be a top athlete, but also a real understanding of what someone like him meant to a country like Ethiopia. He felt his background, allied to his natural talent, allied to the motivation given to him by his brother, the inspiration of Yifter the Shifter [Miruts Yifter, distance runner famed for changes of pace], and then stacks of discipline and self-control were the reasons he had made it. He had a lovely smile, and a good way with words. He was also fascinated by politics.

Later to the Ambassador's residence, which again was like stepping from one world into another. There was a golf tournament going on in the grounds. Admittedly the course was small and not exactly Muirfield, but it was still quite odd to see all these expat businessmen playing golf in Addis. Well-dressed Ethiopians serving cooling drinks from silver trays. Myles good at the schmoozing that went with the turf. Nice, small, relaxed dinner. Brendan was very down on sporting bureaucrats. Myles very positive re TB–GB approach to development, but felt sometimes the follow-through was missing. An agency photographer said he had flogged a picture to several of the Sundays of me running through a pack of donkeys.

Sunday 30 November

Fiona was getting really nervous about speaking at Chris's funeral. I sent through some ideas, then had a tepid bath to stretch. Brendan told me at breakfast he had been doing the same and said he couldn't believe that he'd been listening to my advice about pre-race preparations, all of which I'd got from an article about Paula Radcliffe [long-distance runner]. He was also complaining that John Caine [race organiser] had advised him to start two-thirds of the way back in the crowd. 'What are you telling me? That there are 12,000 people here who will beat me when I was once one of the fastest in the world?' 'Well, if you want to get run over in the rush, you go ahead to the front,' said John. We walked down from the hotel to the start. Perfect weather, fantastic atmosphere, everywhere a sea of green T-shirts with red and yellow sleeves. Gebrselassie started it off. The start was pretty chaotic and you had to be careful not to lose your feet in the holes in the road. It was hilly in parts, and I got into an OK rhythm and pulled ahead of Brendan and Myles early on. I couldn't believe I was going to beat Brendan Foster in a 10k race. And then, 300 yards from the finish, he appeared alongside me and we agreed to go through together, just under 55 minutes, about 12 minutes slower than we would have done in the UK, because of the altitude.

He had said at the start under an hour was 'not bad for a couple of middle-aged blokes'. The last 3k had been really tough but two Ethiopian guys helped me through it. As atmospheres go, it was about as good as it gets, kids singing as they ran, crowds half watching and half joining in. Back at the hotel, I had a session with Paul Tergat, who comes from a massive family, as his father had been one of the last lawful polygamists. He wasn't entirely sure of his age. He had a lovely way with him, great smile and a nice voice, and he said we ought to stay in touch, because he felt we could make change happen. He said sport had the capacity to change the world, but only if political people were involved too. We went off to the Ambassador's residence for lunch, again all a bit surreal as they served roast beef with all the trimmings and but for the heat, we might have been at home. I did a piece for *The Times* and *The Spectator*, then the race dinner at the hotel. Brendan said he had been thinking about my situation. He felt I needed 'a mission'. He felt that it might be going for the media.

Monday 1 December

OK coverage in some of the papers, but a ridiculous and largely vile piece in the *Telegraph* saying I was suffering from 'post-success syndrome', and quoting the usual anonymous friends, so-called, saying I was depressed. The depression had actually lifted a bit, the trip having been good fun and also having given me a bit of time to think. I stayed at the hotel to do a stack of interviews which had been fixed by Dave Hart or Leukaemia Research, and what with the various pieces I was doing it was closer to a working day than all the others. Then up with the Ambassador to a meeting of the Organisation of African Unity, who were holding a conference in Addis. Lots of the senior politicians there, so all a bit handshake and card-swapping, but even here, I'd say that a good third of the conversations involved them asking at some point about the TB–GB relationship. It was a defining thing, I'm afraid, though every single one of them mentioned the positive leadership role the UK was taking. Dinner at the Embassy, speeches by Myles, Brendan and me. It had been a fantastic event and a good trip. Myles a top bloke for a diplomat. Brendan as solid a citizen as you could want.

Tuesday 2 December

We had to be out at 4 for a 5.30 plane and in between watching a couple of films, I did a few more *Times* columns for the future. I had really enjoyed it, and both Brendan and Cathy [Gilman, Leukaemia Research] sent me really nice messages, but I was also glad to be home. TB called. He was on OK form, but realised things were getting difficult again. He had done his press conference largely on tuition fees and also been asked a lot about his health again. In fact, he had never really had a day off ill, but he did have low-level nagging stuff that sometimes made him feel less good than he should. He felt Howard was doing OK but that we could get them on the big questions. They were taking all the wrong lessons from us, thinking we had done it through the media rather than through sorting the big questions. He felt that he and GB were working better together but he could never be sure. I asked if GB had reacted to Howard's line of attack in the Queen's Speech. 'No, but he won't like it if the party starts to think we have gifted Howard that line of attack, which of course he has.'

Nick Brown had been out and about causing difficulty on tuition fees. Things were feeling a bit more ragged. TB said he would like me to think of a way of becoming more involved again, and what he lacked was another strategic mind constantly thinking things through. DH was doing well but more on the media handling than strategy. He was pretty resigned to Peter Hyman going, which would lose another more strategic mind. I had sensed the last time I saw Peter he was feeling the need to move on, and was keen to get into the education world in a different way. It was a good chat though, and he seemed to have a good take on his own situation.

Wednesday 3 December

Up at 5, did a long run and even after just a few days at altitude, I could feel the difference for the better. I did a Radio 5 phone-in on the argument that politics was more trustworthy than the media and was pretty combative. Jason Ferguson [agent son of Alex] was on wanting to discuss film opportunities. Fiona's TV film on schools had taken her off to Skipton for the day.

Thursday 4 December

Off to Heathrow. Picked up the *New Yorker*, which had a big piece on us and was pretty negative re the whole Kelly affair. Another speech, this time in Edinburgh to HBOS. I was putting a fair bit into these speeches, but even as I delivered them was conscious of how little they mattered compared with the speeches I used to write for TB. It was odd too how the people listening, at least some of them, seemed to think that they did matter, and maybe I should try to persuade myself that they were right. I certainly held the audience, and I think they were surprised how funny I could be, both in delivering pre-prepared lines and in the Q&A. Years with the lobby was good training for the Q&A side of things. For the moment, it just felt like taking money – this was another five-figure job, organised by Dennis Stevenson, for stating the blindingly obvious, albeit reasonably articulately.

Dennis Skinner [Labour MP] called when I was on my way back south, really worried. He said he felt the mood reminded him of 1979, that there was a wind of change and he didn't think TB got it because he always felt he could win arguments rationally. He was worried that people were drifting into a 'time for a change' place mentally, and if there was a new mood we had to find some new ways of countering it. Also, nobody really bought the line that GB was supportive of TB. He was at it, his people were at it, everyone knew it, and it was a dangerous moment. He said he didn't think GB had a clue what doing the top job was like, but he for one was in no doubt he couldn't do it as well as Tony. But TB is vulnerable right now, more than he realises maybe, and he needs to shore things up. He thought Howard was a 'nasty bastard', but he was tough and he was coming over better than he had expected him to, a different league to IDS. He also felt I should find a way of going back, because nobody was selling policy well and it was obvious the machine in No. 10 and across the government was a lot weaker. We chatted a bit about football, but he kept coming back to his basic point, that things didn't feel good, that it was a dangerous moment, TB had to watch himself.

Friday 5 December

The papers were full of the health scare for Alex [Ferguson], who called to say he was fine, and it was all being exaggerated. It was basically the same thing he had talked about with TB, a little heart scare, they had picked it up in a check-up a few months back and it had just been a case of going in for this minor op to get it fixed. He said he would be back in tomorrow ready for the match against Villa. He was aware of the chat I had had with Jason and hoped I could do some films with him. I wrote up the Gebrselassie interview, but otherwise it was quiet on the work front. I was reading with one of the special needs kids at

Grace's school, and it was a real eye opener to see just how far behind he was. I did a German, then French interview, then Alex Allan [senior civil servant] came round for a chat. Top bloke, and a shame in a way that he had only been there so briefly with us at the start. He was keen on the new Permanent Secretary for Communications job, or possibly the Department for Constitutional Affairs, and he was certainly keen to get stuck into a proper job here after all his time as High Commissioner in Australia.

TB called from Nigeria, where the CHOGM [Commonwealth Heads of Government] conference was on, so he was having to do lots of stuff involving the Queen as well as the usual never-ending round of bilaterals. CHOGM was one event I certainly wouldn't miss. He said I must go in next week, that tuition fees was a real problem though he thought in the end it would be OK. His worry was that we weren't making the argument with sufficient vigour. Cathy Gilman and I were discussing me doing the next London Marathon, when she suddenly said she didn't want me to do it, that that was last year's story, that Jeffrey Archer [author] was doing it anyway, and we needed something new to get a different sort of profile for the charity. She wanted me to do a triathlon instead, 1,500m swim, 40k bike, 10k run. It seemed bonkers, particularly as it was so long since I had swum or cycled, but as the day wore on, the idea grew on me, especially after speaking to Steve [Loraine, married to a relative, former triathlete], who agreed to coach me. Then out to the theatre in Islington with Fiona, Neil and Glenys to see Sinead Cusack in a play [The Mercy Seat] she had invited us to. I seemed to be the only one who liked it. It was about a bloke who was thought to be in the Twin Towers on September 11 but who was actually at his mistress's house, and wanted to use it for them to disappear together, but they didn't. It was pretty powerful, funny in parts, but Fiona, Neil and Glenys didn't like it. We had dinner with Sinead and [her husband, actor] Jeremy Irons at the restaurant over the road from the theatre afterwards. Neil was in a bit of a rage and Jeremy was provoking both him and Glenys. Neil went off on one about a whole series of things – UNESCO and UNICEF celebrities, someone saying the European Union was all about red tape, the media. I don't know whether Jeremy was doing it deliberately but he was certainly pressing a lot of Neil's buttons. He said Jeremy Paxman and John Humphrys [broadcasters] behaved like a mob, but it was good that politicians were held to account, which set Neil off on one, saying the subtext of their interviews was to challenge the very existence of democratic politics.

I got an approach from someone called Wendy Bailey, who managed people doing talks in theatres, asking if I was interested in doing an 'Audience With' national tour. The money wasn't great but it could be fun, and getting out and about might help me make my mind up about what I wanted to do with myself longer-term.

Saturday 6 December

I took Rory to his cross-country race, one of the big ones, which was held at Stowe public school. It was freezing cold but a beautiful setting and I just got angrier and angrier at the facilities they had compared with state schools. It took an age to drive from the entrance to the school grounds to where we had to park, past things like an all-weather hockey pitch, their own golf club, pitches galore, archery, fantastic changing rooms. Rory wasn't feeling great and didn't run well. We got back and I decided to see if I could swim a mile. I went to the gym, did a hundred times 19m in 53 minutes, which Steve [Loraine] said was not bad for a beginner. I had never particularly liked swimming and of the three disciplines it was without doubt going to be the one I least enjoyed, but at least I knew I could do a mile, and sustain the boredom of a long swim. Steve told me that the resting pulse rate first thing is a key indicator of fitness and I should start to take it every morning and send it through.

Sunday 7 December

Dinner with Jamie Rubin and Christiane Amanpour, Melanne [Verveer, Hillary Clinton staff] and her husband Phil. They were all good fun, and Fiona really got on well with Melanne, but they weren't happy with the comments I'd been making on the US and Bush. I had been out and about a bit on the media defending TB for inviting him and defending Bush over Iraq. Melanne said she had seen my clips on the US media. I said surely they of all people understood the UK had to stay close to the US, but they felt we and TB in particular had tipped too far. Jamie reminded me – again – that he had warned me after 9/11 that these neocons would use us. I did my usual defence, saying TB led the UK re Iraq out of his genuine assessment of UK interests, not because the US wanted him to. But they felt we had really pushed the boat out too far this time. Melanne said Hillary was on good form and really emerging well in her own right. There was a fair bit of talk about whether TB and CB had changed much over the years. Jamie was keen for us to do some kind of work project together.

Monday 8 December

I had a meeting with Bob Phillis re his report on government communications. There was a time I would have wanted to be across every dot on every i, and wanted to fight to make sure they did not make bad changes that they would come to regret, especially as I knew he was proposing changes I thought were a mistake. But I really couldn't be bothered engaging. He talked away for a while, with a real intensity, like this was the most important piece of work being done anywhere in the world right now, and I just wasn't engaged at all. I felt that the changes we had made had been necessary, and that some in the civil service would want to retrench, leave some of the changes as they were, but in other areas try to take things back. There was a time when I would have made sure of doing everything I needed to do to get the agenda I wanted. But I felt of all the things I was trying to leave behind, systems of media management were at the front of the queue. The rugby parade [World Cup winners] was extraordinary, absolutely massive and the players seemed overwhelmed. It showed just how big the longing was for success for the country. But so often it was only expressed through sport.

Tuesday 9 December

I ran in for a breakfast meeting with Bruce [Grocott] at 1 Parliament Street. He was adamant that I had to come back in to a central position well before the election. 'I know you have given a lot but you have to give a bit more because if you don't, our Tone is toast… Sorry to lay it on but there you are.' I told him about the call from Dennis Skinner, and he said he was right. He said TB was isolated, more than he realised. A lot of MPs were circling, not just the total GB diehard, real believers, and he felt that other than Pat McFadden and Sally Morgan there were no distinctly Labour voices in the TB inner circle arguing to move him in the right direction. He was worried Tony was veering to the right, and that the more the party or the PLP pissed him off, the more inclined he was to do so. He felt that TB should try to win the next election but go not long after – 'nine years should be enough for anyone'. He felt despite all the problems it had to be GB who took over.

And he was arguing for more 'policy red meat' to remind the party we were still Labour. He shared my assessment that Howard was better than IDS, but once the campaign pressures really mounted, the public would get him for what he was.

I had a meeting with JoP [Jonathan Powell] re the possible media policy fallout post-Hutton, assuming it went our way. He was thinking it was possible to do *Telegraph–Mail*, PCC on a statutory footing – Chris Meyer [Press Complaints Commission director] had gone totally PCC native – restrict ownership to one paper per owner, a huge hit on Murdoch. I felt that what the public would wear was moves to force accuracy, which meant some kind of regulation. But having spent so long arguing for a jihad against parts of the press, I felt it wouldn't be possible on the back of this, whatever the outcome. This had been about one report on the BBC, and though the press may have played its part in what followed, I couldn't see there would be an appetite to take them on on the back of Hutton. The general feeling seemed to be that Hutton would be OK, but we had no way of knowing, and there had not even been a hint of a leak re his thinking.

I saw TB for a chat and he seemed in OK form. He'd said to GB that they both had a nuclear option – TB's was to put him out, GB's was to try to unseat him, and he felt there had been a bit of reaction on that. He told him he would help him become leader but only if he worked with him, and that meant proper working together, proper co-operation at every level. He couldn't work out if GB had shifted or not. He felt that post-Howard's arrival he probably had but Ed Balls was still pouring nonsense into his ear. He was still pushing me to get involved in some way re Iraq, and now also Africa. I asked if he seriously thought there was any prospect of me being his man in Iraq, either from a domestic perspective or from a presentational perspective? He said that people would get over that, but people knew of my closeness to him, there would be no doubt I had his authority, I would have the clout to get in and sort some of the people who needed to make things happen.

On Africa, he was hoping to preside over a Brandt-style report for 2005 but that too had GB problems because he had his own ideas and was going down slightly different tracks. I popped round to the press office. They had all been on major ligging patrol with the Rugby World Cup squad who had come in as part of the celebrations yesterday, and lots of them were showing me their pictures taken with the Cup and some of the players.

I did a dinner for Tim Allan's company, Portland, at L'Escargot. He got an interesting bunch together for it, including James Murdoch [son of Rupert, CEO of BSkyB TV]. He was very sharp and at least didn't just echo his dad's thoughts, as so many of his executives did. But he and I had a very different take on the media. He felt the US press was biased but ours was OK!!! He claimed he was not a conservative. He was totally on board re Iraq and Afghanistan, a big admirer of TB. Did my usual spiel about the relations between politics and media, and how the balance had got way out of kilter, and the Q&A was lively enough. Alan Rusbridger [*Guardian* editor] and Robert Peston [*Sunday Telegraph* City editor] felt I should concede more, that I spoiled the argument by being so one-sided, as if I felt all of the problems in the media–politics dynamic were media-caused rather than ours, and it was more complicated, with fault and credit on both sides. But in fact I had already built in over-compensation for what I really thought – namely that a lot of the press was even worse than I was saying.

Nice chat with Tony Ball [media businessman], who is also very, very sharp, and clearly a good source of support for Tim. I chatted with Rachel Whetstone [Michael Howard staff]. I was surprised how indiscreet she was, e.g. re what she thought of the shadow Cabinet, which was in most cases not a lot. Her general complaint was that too many of them still behaved like ministers not opposition politicians.

Wednesday 10 December
I gave a long interview to Robert Crampton for the *Times* magazine. I wasn't really motoring though. *The Times* were wanting me to do loads of stuff to cement the connection re the sports stuff. He was friendly enough, asked me half-decent questions. Keen on the mental health stuff, and all the usual re TB, GB, blah. Fiona and I were having dinner with C [Sir Richard Dearlove] and Rosalind [his wife] at Vauxhall Cross [MI6 HQ], so we had to be picked up and driven in. He was his usual charming, witty self. She was more eccentric than I imagined she would be, or maybe a couple of notches up from outgoing, nice, friendly, warm, and I reckon she kept him in check a fair bit. We did a bit of small talk while admiring the view down the Thames, and he seemed genuinely solicitous about how we were adapting. I said, 'Fine.' 'No, he's not,' said Fiona. He was keen to make sure I knew the security agencies bought none of the anti-me stuff constantly flying around the media, that he for one wished I was still there.

He felt that I always gave solid advice that was genuinely intended as advice, without side or personal agenda. He reckoned there might be a few people lower down who yakked to the press about me, and told them what they wanted to hear, but he thought it more likely the press just made it up. Rosalind said she didn't know how I had put up with it for so long. She said he had only had a taste of it and for a relatively short time, but it was not pleasant, and it must be horrible for families. 'Fiona gives me a far harder battering than the press so it's fine,' I said. I said I had actually become almost immune to it, though I wasn't sure if that was a good thing.

He seemed concerned about TB's health, said he was looking more and more tired, and his persistent cough in meetings had become a given. He shared my view of Chris Meyer, another point in his favour. 'The worst kind of self-promoting egotist.' He seemed really excited about taking over as Master of Pembroke College [Cambridge] when he stepped down and asked me to visit to speak to the students. He clearly didn't want to get too drawn on who should get his job when he went but he seemed to think that maybe a current internal choice was better. We did a fair amount of small talk re Cornwall, where they had a house, and they were both very solicitous of Fiona. We talked a bit about the kind of things he would do in the future and I sensed that as I had, he would get pretty severe withdrawal symptoms. He knew that I wasn't the type to go big on the farewell dinner scene but he said as we left he really had wanted to say his own thanks for the support I gave him, and above all the role I played for TB. He felt re Iraq that there were things happening that were good for us long-term, but it was going to be a long haul and not easy. He seemed pretty unkeen re GB, said he had had a bit to do with him, e.g. over Iraq, and he felt there was something a bit odd about him, that he was certainly not TB quality. GB had done the Pre-Budget Report today which was being seen as a bit fiddly. The main news out of it seemed to be rising debt.

Thursday 11 December

Pottered around, a bit of diary transcription and working on future columns and answering letters. In between times, wondering what the fuck I was going to do with myself in the future. Harvard were chasing me re the idea of a visiting fellowship. I was quite keen but not keen enough to make it happen on the timescale they wanted, which was very soon. Les Hinton called, asking me to speak at the News Corp editors' gathering in Mexico. Kate Garvey [Downing Street special advisor] and I had developed a running joke about how I was now going in my own right to do things that before I had done as an aide to TB – different conferences, TV programmes and the like. But this was the funniest yet – for Hayman Island, read Cancun.

Friday 12 December

I needed to start getting into cycling. To the gym to hit the exercise bike. 40k, medium effort, 2 minutes per k most of the time. Read at Grace's school, which I now had as a fixed point in the diary. Meetings re future speeches. It was interesting how people wanted to have big meetings to sort stuff that could probably be done in five minutes on the phone. But they were paying well, and I suppose it helped having a face-to-face feel for what they expected. Vicky Barnsley called with a £2.5 million reverse order three-volume book deal, in other words start with Iraq and my departure, and work backwards so Volume 3 does the first election. It seemed to be more than Gail thought about offering, but I wasn't ready to sign up for this yet. I hadn't worked out how I wanted to do them, and if I went in for that kind of money now, I would lose any kind of control over the process. I didn't want to get into this until I really wanted to. I spoke to Ed [Victor], who said we needed to reflect, no rush.

I sat down p.m. and tried to do for myself what in the past I had done for others, namely write a strategic plan, try to sort out all the various offers and the things I was involved in and thinking about, and see if I could get some kind of shape to it. But the reality is that only the political part really seemed to matter. Diaries – has to be done if I'm going to do books. Sports column – fine, good fun, will meet some interesting people and go to good events, but plenty other people could do. The speeches – lucrative but felt sometimes like I was prostituting myself and didn't want to get into the habit, or of feeling that easy money was the route to a good life, because it's not. I was as ambivalent as ever about the media, and couldn't imagine myself doing a weekly column or a regular TV show. Not drawn to business, and certainly not interested in the non-exec route. So politics and charity may be the best routes. The other thing that was happening was that I was getting more and more used to seeing the kids at both ends of the day, and enjoying it.

I had lunch with Barney Jones [editor, *Breakfast with Frost*] at the Camden Brasserie. He felt I should go for sports presenting on TV, and that if the BBC had any sense they would make overtures to get me involved in some way other than current affairs. I mentioned the Africa role with Bob Geldof to Fiona. Not keen. She felt I would get sucked in to travelling the whole time. I finally told her TB also wanted me to go to Iraq for him. She thought I was joking.

Saturday 13 December

Watched the Manchester derby (Man Utd 3, Man City 1) on the telly before we headed to Tessa's for the weekend. TB was at the Brussels summit on the new EU constitution, which was clearly going to end in tears. He called, and said as much. Even his usual summit optimism, which I had seen in most EU capitals in the past, seemed to be dwindling, close to exhausted. The plan in the build-up had been to agree a draft for the new constitutional treaty, but he said they were so far off it there was no chance, so people were just going through the motions. He thought the stuff on growth and the economy, and [former Dutch PM] Wim Kok's employment stuff was fine, but it was not one of the most memorable weekends of his life. Glad I wasn't there. I really did not miss the Eurobollocks. He said this summit was very high on the bollockache-ometer.

Sunday 14 December

I was out on a 10-mile run in the Cotswolds when the phone rang. ITV news asking if I would go in and comment on Saddam's capture. It was the first I'd heard of it. Had I still been there, I'd not only have been told but with the Yanks would probably have planned how to tell the world. A big moment, and I heard it from a TV reporter. I told him I was nowhere near a studio and carried on with my run. It forced me to reflect on whether deep down I still wished I was there. I certainly liked the planning and execution of big, important moments. But did that mean I wished I was in there now, rather than running through some beautiful scenery and having time for myself and the family? I don't think so. The summit collapsed last night, as TB had predicted, and news wise was anyway going to be pretty much wiped out by Saddam's capture.

Tessa was another one telling me TB missed me badly and I ought to get back in some shape or form. David made a really nice lunch, during which he was arguing for a legal open market in drugs as the only way to destroy the criminal elements running it now. I started

December: '03: Saddam Hussein captured

out totally opposed but was partly won round by the end of it. Back home then out with the Goulds, PG just back from China and saying the Chinese only really cared about the US, not Europe, let alone UK. Not sure it was as simple as that. We got home to watch *BBC Sports Personality of the Year*, which was dreadful. Too much clever-clever telly bollocks, comedy and the like, and not enough sport.

Monday 15 December

I did a 1,500-metre swim in 40 minutes, and a 40-minute gym bike session covering 19 miles. I had a lunch speaking engagement which seemed to go OK. I was now trying to devise a different style that was basically to use my basic politics-media argument, but to speak more expansively, less from notes. I also needed to start developing different themes and arguments. Otherwise I would get bored rigid doing this, and it would show. I had a speech coming up in Scotland and started to work up a narrative about the impact of devolution. I missed TB's statement on Iraq post-Saddam's capture which was still wall to wall media wise. We had a dinner at home for John Scarlett and his wife Gwendoline, Catherine Rimmer who came with her sister, and Clare Sumner and her husband. I wanted to thank CR and CS for the astonishing job they had done for us.

Inevitably we went over what we thought Hutton would say and the general take was a bit pessimistic. Our fear was it would be a plague on both your houses. John said I was sorely missed, partly because there seemed to be less humour around but also because TB was looking more isolated. Like C, he was not sure about GB. He had not been impressed by the way he conducted himself in meetings. He said he had learned a phenomenal amount about the media in the past few months, and largely shared my analysis. It was interesting how it had become a given, now routinely used in just about any media reference to John, that I'd described him as a 'mate'. I hadn't. He said he had no regrets at all about the whole dossier business, because he was sure in his own mind we did the right thing. But he was more anxious than most in No. 10 seemed to be about which way Hutton would go.

Tuesday 16 December

Chris Shaw [Channel 5] came to see me, and though he didn't exactly say, 'Name your price' he wasn't far off it. I liked his direct approach.

He said 'I'm not going to give you loads of bullshit about how you need us because we need you more than you need us.' He said I was in a very strong position and I should exploit it. He said I could do pretty much anything I wanted – a chat show, series, interviews, personal opinion documentaries. He felt I would have far more control and flexibility than with other channels. I think he overestimated how much the other channels would rush to offer me stuff. I was pretty sure the BBC wouldn't and I'm not sure I would take it if they did. But I liked him and I thought maybe it was better to start out on a smaller channel, not worry about ratings, just see whether I liked the process of TV. I didn't have a particular desire just to be on telly, and told him so, and I didn't watch it much, other than sport.

Then a meeting with Dave Edmundson [Burnley FC CEO], who wanted to pick my brains about all sorts of things related to the future of the club. He was very lively, clearly ambitious for the club. I was happy to help him with time and ideas, but I wondered if he would get them all through. I quite enjoyed having these meetings at home, to break up the day while I was pressing on with the diaries. I'd established that three hours was about the max I could work on the diaries at any one go, usually a lot less. Cathy [Gilman] was seeing the London Triathlon people, who were keen for me to get involved. I was pretty much committed to doing it now. I did an interview with Radio New Zealand – God knows why, a bit random – then Steve Byers and Alan Milburn [former Health Secretary] arrived for dinner. Both felt we were not in good shape, that TB was more isolated than ever and did not have the strategic operation he needed. They were lobbying quite hard to say I should go back and try to do strategy without having to do media. DH was doing well on the media, they felt, but that only took you so far if strategy was weak.

Alan was of the view that JP would go a year or so into the next term and that a deputy leadership contest would lead to possible contenders v GB emerging. I was doubtful. They said pretty much everyone was down on GB because more and more of them knew the truth about how he operated, but they were not sure where TB was on it. They were clearly hoping. I said he was absolutely sick of the way he operated – which was true. But I said TB wanted to make it work with GB – which was also true. Alan said it was wishful thinking, Steve that it just wasn't going to happen. They trotted out stories galore – especially Alan from some of the spending review meetings – GB coming across as a 'rampaging lunatic' (Alan's description). He said there was no way he could change, and if TB thought so, he was just as mad as Gordon. I felt they were overdoing the weakness in TB's position, but they felt top-up fees was a real problem, though they were supportive on the policy.* They felt the argument was right but had not been made properly, and GB was putting a different line out anyway. It was interesting to see the two of them together. Alan seemed to be seen by both as the more senior of the two.

They were interested in getting an insight into what it had been like during the bad times. We had plenty of stories about how awful it had been at times but I still found myself defending TB and wanting to build the arguments to defend the difficult policy positions. They asked what I intended to do and when I ran through a few of the things I was doing, they both felt none of it would replace politics. 'You'll be back,' said Steve. 'Hope so,' said Alan. Fiona seemed a bit more relaxed about the idea.

Wednesday 17 December

I went to do a photo shoot with the French photographer sent by *The Times*, Brigitte Lacombe, in a studio not far from home. She had obviously been told I didn't like faffing around, and pretty much had it all set up to go. Painless. I had lunch with Phil Webster [*Times*], and we ended up talking most of the time about the sports column idea, and the series I was doing for his paper. It was actually a really good talking point idea – who is the greatest of all time and how do we judge? Obvious but endlessly fascinating to people who liked sport. He was sure it would end up with Ali, but wondered about [Lance] Armstrong [cyclist] in terms of the current performers. Lance was definitely Number One on my list for interviews. Phil said TB was in great form last time he saw him. Phil was another who felt the GB bandwagon had stalled a bit. He said they had miscalculated at conference and never really recovered from that. Also, Howard seemed to have improved the Tories a bit, but that had made Labour people a bit more serious about stuff.

Later I went to two very different cultural experiences – first Grace's school play, which was brilliant, and then to the Royal Opera House

---

* Despite a 2001 election manifesto pledge by Labour that it would not introduce student top-up (variable) fees, the government published proposals to allow universities to charge them. The plan received wide cross-party criticism.

with the Ronsons for *Sweeney Todd*. It was OK as these things go, but we were in one of the boxes and I'm always conscious at these top-level cultural places of being stared at. Also, Jeremy Paxman's agent was there, trying to get me to work with her.

Thursday 18 December

Office party. For once, I was not the victim of the Christmas party scam. Instead the victim was Peter Hyman, Godric and Hilary [Coffman, special advisor] setting him up by saying *The Guardian* were on to a big story about him leaving and how it was seen as a big blow to TB. I was never a great one at these boozy social events at the best of times, but I was really getting tired of the 'What are you up to?' questions, and also tired hearing all the complaints about lack of strategy or leadership. It was nice to see everyone, and the mood was OK, but I was glad to get home.

Friday 19 December

To the school to do reading, then met Robert Crampton on the Heath. He really wanted a lot of time for this interview and I felt I did better than last time, not least because a range of passers-by, some that I knew and some that I didn't, came up to talk to us while we sat outside the café, from one of the park keepers to the husband of a woman who had set herself up as a lifestyle executive consultant and wondered if I needed any help in my current transition. Everyone was very friendly, which I don't think he had expected, to the point that he was wondering if I had set the whole thing up. He was pushing a lot on the mental health history side of things, which I was happy enough to talk about. I was worried afterwards I had said too much about Hutton, having been clear since I gave evidence that I would stay shtum until he reported.

I set off for Mum and Dad's. TB called to say the Libyans were announcing that they were getting rid of all their WMD and he was going to do a statement on it later, up in Durham. This had been cooking for a while, and in a way had flowed from them being able to resolve Lockerbie.* He didn't want to be too warm re Gaddafi, but

---

* Earlier in the year Gaddafi had accepted Libya's responsibility for the 1988 bomb that destroyed a Pan Am flight over Scotland, killing 254 people. He agreed to pay compensation to the families of the victims.

he had to say it was a big step and wouldn't have happened without Gaddafi changing tack. It might also recalibrate the debate on WMD more generally. 'Would Libya have done this if we hadn't shown how serious we are re WMD in Iraq?' I said the statement should be very measured. The story will speak for itself in a way and he doesn't need to force the obvious at people. That can wait a bit. By the time everything was sorted and ready to be announced, it was late, and the BBC Ten O'Clock broke into the bulletin, a rare event, to bring a part of TB's press conference up north. He didn't look great, a bit tired and drawn, but the story was good news and in some of the two-ways and third party voices it was coming over that it only came about because of military action in Iraq.

Saturday 20 December

Bad fog, but we set off to Preston v Burnley. Later TB called on his way to a dinner he didn't want to go to. Yesterday he had had a long conversation with Gaddafi, which was 'interesting if you like your politics wacky'. He felt that because of Saddam's capture, and now this, we were in better shape on the foreign policy front, and the Iraq issue more generally. 'Surely even the thickest head can see that he did this because he saw we were serious?' Don't bank on it. What really worried him still was the lack of strategic capacity on the domestic front. He knew that Milburn and Byers had been to see me, and I think Fiona might have been right when she said she was sure TB had put them up to it. True, they had talked about GB and the ongoing nightmares, but in so far as there had been a purpose to them saying they would like to come and see me, it had clearly been to get me to think about how and when I went back, especially for the campaign. He certainly seemed well informed about what we had discussed. 'I hear Fiona might be mellowing a bit.'

He said he wanted me to do more not less, but focused on strategy, not get back into the day-to-day combat with the media. He said when Peter M had pointed out at a recent office meeting that there was no strategic capacity, people got very angry about it, and said he was just meddling, but it was true. It was not what DH did. He did a different job very well, but strategy was what he needed most. Re GB, he said they were working together reasonably well but he wondered whether they would ever really get their act together. He sounded neither up nor down. He was pleased yesterday had come together. He was fascinated by the triathlon thing, quizzing me about the distances, how much training it required, whether I thought I could really do it. I sensed he wanted to do something totally out of his ordinary day-to-day.

Unprompted, Philip sent me over a really good note about my own position in the future. He was such a good friend to have. He knew I was struggling with this, but rather than have another conversation going round in the same circles, he committed his thinking to paper, and it helped me clear a few things in my own mind. He said to think of my professional life as a story with three or maybe four big chapters. Journalism was the first career, the first chapter; TB/politics was the second; and now I was well placed to set my own terms for the writing of the third. Because Chapters 1 and 2 had gone pretty well, I was in good shape, with a strong reputation for what I was good at, a lot of recognition, and I could take my time. There was no shame in using this period of thinking to make a bit of money to provide security for the family, and also no shame in wanting and needing a bit of rest and reflection. But there would come a point where I would need to decide if I saw my future in politics, media, business or sport. He felt I would probably decide on politics or sport, or a mix of the two. He didn't really make recommendations but the setting out of it all as he saw it was really helpful.

Sunday 21 December
Ninety-minute run, now armed with Steve's triathlon schedule, a programme of running, swimming, cycling. There was a lot in it. It was going to need a fair bit of time set aside for training if I was going to do this properly.

Monday 22 December
I was now getting in the habit of taking my pulse every morning and texting through to Steve who would fine-tune the training programme accordingly. It was averaging in the low to mid-fifties, which was apparently quite good for my age. As well as the Clive Conway [motivational speakers agent] / Wendy Bailey theatre tour idea, I had another guy, Ian Osborne, who had worked up a similar plan starting in the West End. On his reckoning, we were into six-figure earnings quite easily, but it sounded a bit over-optimistic to me. I went into No. 10 to drop off some Christmas cards. DH showed me the Phillis Report [on government

December: '03: PG note on AC's future

communications], which I felt was a wasted opportunity. It was buying too much into the criticism, not enough into the needs of a modern government in the media age. One of the press officers showed me an interview with John Humphrys complaining I constantly bombarded *Today*, *The World at One*, and the *PM* programme during the war, which was totally untrue. I am not sure I called them once.

Tuesday 23 December

Last-minute Christmas shopping with Grace, then to the gym for a swimming lesson. I had basically decided to go right back to the start, pretend I had never learned to swim before, learn from scratch. As a kid, I had been taught to do breaststroke first, then backstroke, then crawl and I never really got much beyond breaststroke. Also my asthma and the mess the chlorine always made of my nose meant I was never going to love swimming. But having decided to go right back to scratch, and learn front crawl as if for the first time, I thought I could get into it. I found it very hard at first, but after a bit I got the logic.

Wednesday 24 December

Thousand-metre swim, then worked on a speech for the Yorkshire Forward [regional development agency] conference. The big story was that one of the Queen's Corgis had been killed by one of Princess Anne's terriers. Apparently it wasn't the first time Anne's dog had a go, and there were calls for it to be put down. Apparently the dog was called Dotty, but then it turned out it was actually Florence, not Dotty. But Dotty had attacked a couple of kids in a park a while back. There was something ridiculously British about the whole thing, dominating the news on the day before the country was expected to sit down after a big lunch and get a message from the Queen. John Pienaar [BBC journalist] called, pressing me to do a BBC news seminar in January. I said I wouldn't commit to anything before Hutton. Dinner at [family friend] Terry Tavener's. I had been asked to do *Desert Island Discs*, which had given me something else to think about, and the list changed every time I thought about it. Fiona had forgotten that we used to dance in [former colleague on Mirror Group training scheme] David Ireland's room, because he had a record player and I had Randy Crawford's 'One Day I'll Fly Away'. I thought I had to have bagpipes, definitely Jacques Brel, though I don't know which, Diana Ross probably, Elvis, maybe Simply Red and 'Money's Too Tight to Mention' because that was the song I played the whole time when I went mad, and 'Things Can Only Get Better', for sure.

We ended up having a very frank discussion, Fiona and I both feeling in the end that maybe she should have left when she first wanted to, pre-Iraq, and that we should have stopped thinking it had to be both or none of us. I should then have stayed, but accepted that we could have had different views and she could have expressed them publicly from the outside. [Married couple] James Carville [Clinton advisor] and Mary Matalin [advisor Dick Cheney, US Vice-President to George W. Bush] seemed to manage not just different views but different parties. I was certainly finding it harder than I thought I would to settle into a rhythm. I was doing lots of different things, but they were all very bitty, and so I spent a lot of the time feeling just a bit discombobulated. A friend of Terry's, Simon, a Lib Dem, told me that Lib Dems required more sleep than any other party.

Saturday 27 December
For the first year in ages, a fairly quiet, and relatively harmonious Christmas. Got my annual ENT problems. Saw Bostock [GP] who was pretty offside re government direction on health. He went through the big changes we were making, and explained why he felt every single one of them would have the opposite effect to that which was intended. He also asked me not to do the triathlon, thought it would end up bad for me, as did Fiona. They were both worried about the effect of the swimming on my asthma and my nose, and Fiona that it would become my next obsession. But I can think of worse things to be obsessed about.

Tuesday 30 December
To Selfridges to get a couple of suits. The Honours list was published, which made me glad I wasn't there. 'Sir' Simon Jenkins, who would take the title but not use it. Do me a favour.

Wednesday 31 December
Definitely a pre-Alzheimer's moment this morning. I drove up to the top of the road, turned left, then crashed into a bollard at 8 miles an

December: '03: Quiet, harmonious Christmas for once

hour. Fuck knows what was going on in my head. It wasn't deliberate. I just wasn't really conscious of where I was. Absolutely fucking crazy. A couple of people were standing on the pavement, really looking at me like I was a total madman. I had to reverse the car, or else was blocking the road on both sides of the bollard. It made the most extraordinary noise and I suspected I had completely fucked the engine. Fiona came up to take a look, and to be fair could have reacted a lot worse. The bollard was bent over so I made a call to the council to tell them. Later to Lindsay [Nicholson]'s, in Fiona's car, to meet Mark [Johansen], her new bloke, properly, along with some of his friends. He seemed a nice enough bloke, but so different to John. I was going to have to try hard.

Thursday 1 January 2004
Pulse 52, 70 minutes bike, 34k. Also played golf with Calum. I phoned John Reid to go over some of the issues Bostock had raised and on some of them, John could see that he had a point. We chewed the fat about football, and he became the latest to tell me GB was getting worse not better, and I would need to go back sooner rather than later. I was sorting out the car, which looked like it was a write-off. I didn't know it was possible to write off a car at 8 miles an hour. I had got into the habit over Christmas of sleeping a couple of hours during the day, but then feeling more tired and a bit depressed afterwards. I was getting anxious about Hutton again. The end-of-year reviews were full of BBC breast-beating. The only politicians I spoke to over the holiday, apart from TB, were Blunkett, who called to say Happy New Year, JR, DM [David Miliband] and Tessa.

Friday 2 January
Pulse 53, 1,500-metre swim at Barnet, best yet. Bloke came up to me in the changing room, he said he had been at my Jewish Care speech when I had talked about the press culture of negativity, and he couldn't look at the papers in the same way since, so maybe it was worth keeping going with that same argument. He was particularly struck, he said, by the point that there was no longer any real separation between news and comment, including on the telly. Most of the day revolved around various events for Fiona's birthday, and though we had got on fine in the last few days, I was still feeling a bit stressed, which I think was just a pre-Hutton thing. I was also getting annoyed with myself

at moving so slowly towards any big decisions. I was warming to the idea of doing something with Channel 5, maybe a series of interviews allied to a documentary on the triathlon, but it was annoying me that I had gone from being generally decisive to a bit dithering, constantly wanting to buy time to do not very much, or at least nothing that required real thought or commitment. I was glad we managed to get through the day without a cross word in either direction.

Saturday 3 January

Pulse 53. Rest day. Took Rory to a race. Calum went to Mansfield-Burnley on his own, which was a first. Dinner with the Goulds. Philip was looking tired and lacking a bit in energy, though he said he had had a decent break. He kept coming back to the same thing all the time – TB's operation weakened, GB's strengthened, AC needs to get more involved. He later sent me a note analysing a lot of the polling of recent months and comparing it with this period in the second term cycle, early 2000. We were behind on most of the main indicators, e.g. a double-digit lead on voting intentions now closer to neck and neck. 21 per cent lead on the economy now 6. Behind on tax. Ahead on interest rates and inflation. Massive education lead almost all gone, NHS not that much better, asylum well down. And on the right direction/ wrong direction question, which was one of the most important, we had slipped badly, with crime, NHS and asylum, rather than economy, the main drivers he said. We were still holding our own on the issues we would want up at the election, but on our negatives they were starting to make inroads.

There was also something a bit weird going on with people being broadly optimistic about their own futures, but not the country's. That was partly a media thing and we needed to challenge and grip it. It was the same on public services – good responses re their own schools and hospitals, general impressions bad. The figures on primary school improvement for example were terrific. But PG was worried we had three groups of people we were losing – anti-war middle-class and younger voters shifting to the Libs because of Iraq and tuition fees; suburban middle-class, some of them moving to the Tories over more general issues; and working-class voters switching to disengagement because of asylum and immigration in particular, and the feeling they are getting a raw deal. Asylum was definitely linking up all our negatives now, from anything bad on the economy to crime, pressure on public services, terrorism, Europe. There was an opening for populism that we had to watch out for. PG was echoing the AA [Andrew Adonis] view that the key had to be a really radical third term agenda that took people by surprise. It was not enough to say we had a good record and there would be more of the same. That being said he felt we were going to have to attack the Tories even harder than in the past, because the short memory problem meant a lot of people had totally forgotten what a Tory government had been like.

Sunday 4 January
Pulse 51. 12-mile run. Asthma at the start, but worked out OK. TB in Iraq, which brought home just how out of it I now was. He had mentioned he would be going some time soon, but for obvious reasons they hadn't talked too widely about when. He was in Basra, mainly seeing our troops, and also visiting some of the Iraqi police being trained by our guys. He had flown straight from Sharm el-Sheikh, where he and Cherie and the kids had gone for a few days. As I was running, I was thinking about how consumed I would have been by the whole thing had I still been there, but as it was I barely even saw the news all day.

Monday 5 January
Pulse 52. 1,500m swim session, 42 minutes. TB called on his return from Iraq. Felt it went well, that he could see a way forward, but he knew how much was dependent both on the Americans and on the Iraqis, and on both making the right decisions and seeing them through. It would be a long haul, and I could sense he was worried about it. I suspect some of our top brass will have been frank with him about the Americans. Any chats I had had with our people who had been there did nothing to persuade me they had gripped it properly. He sounded a little bit beaten down by it all, though he said he'd had a proper break over Christmas. He had seen Philip, and said his mind was turning to campaign structures again. He said it was worrying him that his three best people were not available, that I was out of the game, Peter M was out of the game, and GB was 'currently dysfunctional'. It was a pretty dispiriting thought as we went into New Year, he said. He said most of the time we complained that the press was a travesty against us, but recently it was a travesty in our favour, in that the reality was probably even worse than what was presented,

certainly in relation to the internal workings, and some of the relationships at the top, especially GB. 'I'm back to the same old problem – will he ever work with me properly or not?'

Philip was pushing for Milburn to be moved into a central campaigning position, even into a position inside No. 10. TB's view, and mine, was that Alan was good but maybe not good enough to run the whole campaign, that on the political side of things, he was better at analysis than solution. That seemed to apply to most of us at the moment, but if he was going to move someone into a central position, they had to be top notch. TB said that what was infuriating was that on policy, with the five-year policy plans there, he was more confident than he had been for ages. He was also confident he could win on tuition fees. But, exactly as Philip and I had been saying, we were showing no real fight or imagination re Howard. He was thinking that a combination of Byers, Milburn and I was what he needed for attack. That convinced me he had been behind the Byers–Milburn dinner. That was fine, no problem, but it was easier if he levelled with me. I still felt we need not get panicky re Howard. He had got the Tories into the position where they were an OK default option but not much beyond that. With GB, he said what they had at the moment was 'managed disagreement' which was better than unmanaged disagreement but not as good as managed agreement.

I said I had thought about the situation a lot over Christmas. It was only a few months since I had left, and he had been in agreement that I should. Since when I had not made the transition that well, things at home still had their moments, but more than anything I felt there was barely a day when I wasn't dragged back in. For sure, it was not the same as being there full time, working round the clock. But I had not really had a sense of release, and that meant I had not really managed to re-energise and re-motivate. 'So what have you decided then?' he asked, not unfriendly, but I knew he would be irritated. I said I was happy to help him, but not full time. I didn't want it to be all-consuming again. I was always happy for him to call whenever he felt like it, to look over speeches and papers, to feed in thoughts direct or through others. It was nice to talk to him but I was still reluctant to get sucked back in. Philip was back working on me the whole time. He phoned to say what great form TB had been on this morning, despite the heart problem, but how he needed help. The kids were fantastic at the moment. It seemed impossible to think that Rory would be leaving home in a couple of years. I did a two-hour sports interview for *The Times* with Alison Kervin. It seemed odd to be interviewed for my views on sport, but that's how they wanted to kick off my series, which was fine by me.

Tuesday 6 January

Pulse 54. One-hour run. *The Times* were really keen now. Chat with Keith Blackmore [sports editor] about various ideas for promoting the series. Working on the diaries, going through a period of GB–JP difficulties, which at least was a change from TB–GB. Long chats with Ian Osborne ['Audience With...' promoter] and Wendy Bailey about their respective theatre tour ventures for me. Both pissed off that I was dealing with the other. Osborne was convinced we could fill West End theatres, sell out straight away. I wasn't so sure, and the last thing I needed was a flop. Dinner with John Browne [BP CEO] at his club. He was keen for me to do something with them, but wasn't sure what. He said Philip had said to him that if they wanted somebody to develop a brief to destroy Exxon [rival group], they should hire me. He was very strong on the importance of strategy. It struck me that BP was a bit like a state, but one which crossed borders, with different levels of influence in different countries. He thought it was really important I wasn't just seen as being ex-No. 10, that I was now my own man with a lot to offer as myself. If I went into the consultancy business, he would certainly hire me. I couldn't really tease out what he thought of GB. I knew he was a big TB fan. He felt he looked tired the last time he saw him. He had nothing but praise for the way he operated, and the help he gave to big British companies. He felt Howard didn't have it. He bought my analysis on the press, said they had no interest in whether or not the country did well, just wanted to tear down anyone and anything.

I felt it was partly the media that stopped him putting his head above the parapet more, but he was clearly not somebody interested in going into government. David Simon [who had left BP as CEO to become Minister for Trade] had not enjoyed the experience, and that had made him a bit reluctant. He was odd looking, but interesting, had a very large face on top of a very small, thin body. But I liked him in the main because he was phenomenally clever and had a very good take on a lot of the big geopolitical issues. In their own way, these big business guys with companies crossing borders thought as much about the geopolitics as they did about, in his case, oil.

Wednesday 7 January

Pulse 53. 70-minute run. Met the London Triathlon people with Cathy to go over the race logistics, and put together a media plan, including a launch on 29 January. I liked the triathlon people. Very can-do. I got measured up for a wetsuit and a new bike, and also agreed the plan for a documentary focused on the preparation and the event. We then heard that Hutton was going to make a statement and assumed it would be to announce the date of publication for his report. It turned out to be rebutting the idea that we had been putting in papers to the Inquiry, but by then the press had moved on to Howard asking questions at PMQs about what TB said on the plane to Paul fucking Eastham of the *Mail* back in July, re the naming of David Kelly. The press felt they had struck a blow on this. I wrote a long note to TB, both about the issue pre-Hutton, and also more generally on his strategy for the New Year. He was due to do *Breakfast with Frost* and it was important he set the bar in the right place.

Lunch with Phil Stephens [*Financial Times*], whose son called halfway through to say he had just been mugged. I had never much enjoyed these lunches with columnists when I was doing the job, other than when I had a specific purpose, so there seemed even less point doing them now, though I liked Phil. There was far more in them for the journalists than for the lunchee. I went to see Calum play tennis, he won but lost his rag a couple of times. I had agreed to go with Wendy Bailey for the idea of the theatre tour, and that South Shields would be a good place to kick it off. Labour seat, Labour area, down to earth, not too glitzy, a bit unexpected. The money was a fraction of what I was getting for the big corporate speaking gigs, a grand, plus a share of ticket sales over a certain amount, but I felt it would be a better way of getting out there, sussing the mood and also being out of London more, which I needed to think through the question about my future more generally.

Thursday 8 January

Pulse 53. Swimming lesson, then proper session. Philip came round. He had done some focus groups last night which were pretty grim, down on us, and he said Howard was definitely making an impression. He had seen GB last night, who was adamant he wanted to improve things with TB, and PG kind of believed him. He felt it was about trying to stop TB from getting Peter M involved again. Philip also felt

I should speak to Anthony Seldon, who was moving towards the end of his book project on TB. I felt a bit between a rock and a hard place with PG and Gail. Her interest was in me pressing on, and hopefully agreeing to do some kind of book earlier rather than later. His was in getting me back at the centre. He knew how to play me as well, get me going about things not being as good as they should be operationally, tell me Howard was beginning to move and make an impression. There were good people in No. 10, and in the party, but I had no sense from outside of a political strategy being implemented, and Howard was getting away with far too much. PG felt that if I got back involved, GB would get properly involved in a way that he wouldn't if it was Peter.

Dave Edmundson called asking me to do interviews to promote a financial appeal for Burnley FC, which was fine. CR [Catherine Rimmer] called, said she was not at all confident about the operation we had in place for Hutton. The Tories had a big team working full time on it now, they felt if it went remotely against us, this was a massive moment of vulnerability for TB, whereas we were in a 'just wait and see' mode. I met Chris Shaw and said yes to the triathlon [Channel 5 TV] idea, plus six half-hour programmes on anything I wanted. I liked the idea of a series of interviews with genuinely top flight people. He was really keen for me to do stuff. Maybe I was underplaying my own appeal on the telly front. It was just that I wasn't feeling massively motivated by it. I thought of the way David Frost so clearly just loved what he did, and loved the idea of fixing an interview, big or small, and would do it pretty much with the same enthusiasm for the rest of his days, and I couldn't imagine feeling like that really.

Friday 9 January
Pulse 52. 50-minute bike, 25k, then 20-minute run. Gospel Oak School to do reading. Phil Webster called wanting to do a news story to trail the piece in the magazine tomorrow, on the line that I was still seeing TB and also re some of the big bucks offers for quick memoirs turned down. I said it was hardly a surprise, but he said he felt it was a good line for them. David Bradshaw called, said that things were all a bit flat, particularly in their part of the building, and some of the power had gone out of there, and there was insufficient politics in the policy operation. He said it was weird how much of the power dynamics in the building reflected the personalities.

Saturday 10 January

Pulse 53. The *Times* interview came out fine. Lots of nice messages from former staff. Sky, ITN and BBC were all following up and we had the cameras outside again, but I ignored them when I went out for a run. It seemed very odd that they thought me seeing TB still was a story. I suppose they would be surprised to know how much, but I think most people would think it was closer to being newsworthy if I wasn't still seeing him from time to time, but there we are. TB called, said he liked it, thought I got really good tone into the whole thing about the job, the nature of politics and the media, that I had a unique perspective which I should articulate more, and he loved the line about Dacre being the most poisonous man in British politics. GB was clearly less relaxed about it. Philip called him and apparently GB's first words were, 'What's this about Alastair wanting to run the election campaign?' Philip said I didn't, but I did want to help when the election came. It was a classic example of the way TB and GB see things differently. TB sees it, gets totally what I am saying, and sees the good side. GB sees it, totally misunderstands where I am coming from, and then sees the bad side. PG said when it came to it, GB will be at the front of the queue asking me to go back for the campaign, but an offer of help and support is taken by him as a threat.

Philip felt that TB was pretty down after yesterday's meeting at Chequers. I had a long chat with TB, which confirmed that, because he clearly felt we were not at the races in terms of overall strategy and campaign planning. On Hutton, having first decided he wanted to use the *Frost* interview to set the bar, he now felt not, that we should really just wait for Hutton, and say nothing. That was probably right. I asked myself what Sumption would advise and I am sure he would say that the least said, the better. The chances of Hutton watching were slim, and the chances of him being influenced slimmer, so far better, if he was to get any message at all, it was that we would be saying nothing until he did. TB said he wanted to talk up tuition fees, and make the case for change as being in the national interest because the universities were part of our economic future and could not be allowed to stand still. I felt that was the right area to go on with *Frost* – it was a difficult policy area, reform was needed, but it was also possible to get in a message both about fairness and the long term. By February, he wanted proper campaign structures set up again, and would I take charge of the Tory attack team? I can't say my spirits soared at the thought.

He felt Howard was a lot better in the House, and had grown more effective, but he was nasty and, second and more importantly, he was right-wing and actually wanted Thatcherism plus. Calum and I went to Palace v Burnley. Marc Apsland was doing pictures for *The Times* to go with the interview to kick off the sports series. Lots of Burnley fans coming up to discuss the club's financial crisis.

Sunday 11 January

Pulse 53. One-hour run. TB did OK on *Frost*, at his best on tuition fees, straight bat on Hutton, nice about me, he said yes, I'd be back for the campaign and whatever the media said, I was someone with integrity. He still wasn't looking great and of course the heart issue had unlodged a few worries in people's minds about whether he had the physical stamina to keep going. In fact I reckoned he would be as fit as any other major nation leader, but he did look a bit grey and when I spoke to Mum later she said he looked 'awfy peely-wally'. He called from the car afterwards and felt he was strong on tuition fees because he really believed in the argument and believed we could make it a progressive argument. On Hutton, he felt that the Tories were overdoing it and trying to politicise it, and his hunch was it would be getting on Hutton's nerves. He was now convinced we should just sit back and wait. He felt Hutton would pretty much be his own man and would not take too kindly to pressure of a political nature from any quarter, including from us. *The World at One* did a good number on the intellectual inconsistency of the Tories' position on tuition fees.

I got the train up to Leeds for Yorkshire Forward, met by a very nice driver, a former protection cop, and picked his brains with the basic argument I was going to put about Yorkshire going places, and how we should fight the culture of negativity. The *Sunday Telegraph* did a big follow-up on my interview with *The Times* and one or two others picked up what I said about depression. I had definitely been feeling down more regularly and on more days than before, mainly I think because of the lack of urgency on a day-to-day basis. I was keeping busy, but the things I was up to did not provide that sense of urgency, need to do now, now, now, and I think I was maybe literally depressing too, or decompressing might be a better word. Whatever it was, I was not feeling as good as I ought to be, and for quite a lot of the time.

Monday 12 January

Pulse 53. 15-minute run, aborted because of asthma attack. Coverage for TB's interview was low-key. I was staying at a very nice hotel on the outskirts of Harrogate. Down to the conference centre. Had a nice chat with P. Y. Gerbeau [former chief executive of the London Millennium Dome], who was speaking before me. I hated his speech though, which was just a great rant about how terrible politicians were. It was such an easy thing to do, but it was cheap-laugh territory really, and I suddenly saw him as a rather diminished figure. I said to him afterwards I thought he could do better than that; he had an interesting life and views and didn't need to do the obvious. Nice chat with David Sainsbury [Science and Innovation Minister], who I felt was a thoroughly good thing, and who had a real passion for taking his basic message about the importance of science around the country. He wore his wealth well, was not showy or flashy, spoke nicely and quietly and seemed as interested in others as he was in himself. Jim Naughtie [broadcaster] was chairing the event and he and I had a perfectly good rapport. He felt the TB operation was missing a few gears too, but he was not buying the idea of a changed Michael Howard. He said he couldn't imagine the people who had not wanted to vote for Major or Hague being won back by Howard.

I felt the speech went well and during the Q&A, there were one or two rank Tories who got me going, one who said people would never trust TB again, and another who said it would be very bad for Labour if I was back for the election. A very nice woman from Harewood House [stately home near Leeds] stood up to defend me, said the stuff about spin was rubbish and the reason people like that went at me was because I was good at my job, better than the press or the Tories. What's more, she was applauded for saying it. When I wound up at the end, I said what events like today showed was that you can have a proper engagement, people were far more interested in politics than people gave them credit for, and we did not have the media we deserved. Good reception, then a stack of interviews, first about the event, then to promote the first 'Audience With' with some of the north-east media who had come down. Of all the Q&As I had done so far, I enjoyed this one the most, really good range of questions. I bumped into Tony McNulty [junior transport minister] on the train. He felt both on tuition fees and Hutton, that we would be fine. The GB people were definitely checking in again. Ian Austin [Labour MP and GB spokesman] had called me at the weekend to ask if I fancied going out for a bike ride now that I was training for the triathlon, and today an email from Ed Balls saying we should have lunch. I wonder if they had read *The Times* and just decided to get in touch, or whether GB had put them up to it.

Tuesday 13 January

Pulse 53. Bad run. OK swim, 1,200m in just over half an hour. Asthma. *Guardian* did a number on the front page re me kicking off 'Audience With' in South Shields. I did Jeremy Vine and Radio 5, strong push on the argument that it's about time we addressed the state of the political media debate. I felt very confident in the argument. They were pretty obsessed with Hutton and wanted to debate worst-case scenarios, which was understandable though it was not hard to push back. Hutton remained like a big shadow over everything at the moment. I had slept very badly last night and I'm sure it was about that. I was also getting inundated with calls from the BBC and others about what I would do on the day of the report, media wise. Went to see Ed Victor. We agreed it was time for him to tell Gail about the Harper Collins offer. He said friendship was one thing but the gap between £2.5 million and what he imagined Gail had in mind would represent 'a very large friendship subsidy'. He had a nice way with words. He also represented Simon Jenkins and agreed his argument about his knighthood – that he would accept it but not call himself Sir – was ridiculous. I made a mental note to satirise him at some point. Ed had clearly understood that I was not going to rush into print, and he seemed to understand all the reasons. I sensed he was going to seek to enjoy my constant changing of the landscape. Re the TV deal, he advised me to get a media lawyer and put me in touch with Nigel Bennett at Michael Simpkins. I put a call in to Dan Bartlett to get a yes in principle for a Bush interview at some time in the future.

Wednesday 14 January

Pulse 57, 45-minute run, still not sleeping well. Spent the morning working on a script for the first 'Audience With'. I was conscious of John Browne's remarks about not just being seen as what I was, even if that was what people were particularly interested in. I tried to use anecdotes and episodes from the past to build an argument about the current state of politics/media, and make my central point that after a decade on either side of the fence, my respect for the media had fallen as my respect for politics had risen. Though I would always defend Labour, it was important to defend politics more broadly, so I spent a bit of time thinking about Tories and Liberals, and leaders from across the spectrum in other parts of the world, that I would put into the 'politics good' category. Philip was calling the whole time at the moment about me getting more involved.

Cathy Gilman came round with a stack of invites to sign for the launch of my triathlon appeal on the 29th. She had the old list from when I did the marathon, which included Gavyn Davies, but I decided against inviting him given the current sensitivities, even though he had been so generous in the past. Alex called and I got him to agree to put his name to supporting the Burnley fundraising appeal. He asked if he could see me tomorrow to discuss the Irish and the horse situation. A journalist friend had told me that Ian Monk [PR] was working for the Irish. I watched PMQs and felt Howard was overcooking things on Hutton and that TB handled it well. I was sure Howard's basic unpleasantness would become a problem for him. People accepted that politicians were rough with each other in the House, but with him there was a genuinely nasty streak that would become more apparent over time. We were now expecting the report on 28 January. Mum called in a real state because Dad had fallen on the steps, and she was sure he had had another mini stroke. I told her not to listen to the news because Hutton had announced the date and there was bound to be lots of speculation.

Thursday 15 January
Pulse 59, feeling crap, 30-minute run. Meeting with Nigel Bennett and I agreed he should take over the negotiations with Channel 5. Nice bloke, seemed to have his head screwed on. His advice was that I think of myself like a brand, with many different streams that could generate income. I said I had never been obsessed with money, but I didn't like being ripped off, so I would let him negotiate. Earlier *The Guardian* ran a story that I had hired a PR so I wrote demanding a correction. It then transpired the story had come from a PR firm hired by Ian Osborne, so I emailed him, said I did not wish to proceed. He sent back the most grovelling email imaginable, pleading with me to stick with him, promising he would ensure that it worked. I said I did not need a PR, I would decide what I did and asked him to come for a meeting tomorrow. As Fiona said, there were a lot of people really

trying to use me for their own ends, and I didn't want or need a PR anywhere near me at the moment. I just wanted absolute assurance that logistics were solid. Meanwhile Wendy Bailey was packing the diary with theatre dates all around the bloody country.

Tessa came on, asking me to write a peroration for her Olympic bid speech, so I worked on that for a bit, and liked what I did. We got the Hutton date officially so TB would have the tuition fees vote on the 27th, Hutton on the 28th, the day before my triathlon launch. The South Shields event had sold out and they called to say Lauren Booth [CB's half-sister] had been on trying to get review tickets. Lunch at the Caledonian Club with Alex, son Jason, his Irish and Scottish lawyers, and a PR guy from Dublin, Paul Allen. The argument was whether they hit back at some of the negative stuff in the press. I felt that if they judged it to be affecting public opinion, and informed opinion, they had to do something, they needed rebuttal, but also people around the place putting Alex's side of the story. Both Jason and the Dublin solicitor were very cautious but the PR guy with Alex's Irish brief was keen to press on. I asked if they would settle and they felt probably. If there was a lot of pressure on, some pressure had to go back the other way. Paul Allen, the PR guy, said later he was grateful because that's what he had been advising and Alex clearly took my counsel and later that's what they agreed to do. Paul said that inside his office his firm called it Operation Rossmore. Les Dalgarno, Alex's Aberdeen lawyer, who went back with him a long way, said they called it 'Operation TFH – that fucking horse'. They were talking big money though.

Jason's big worry was if they got into a situation where it looked like Alex was attacking a major shareholder of Manchester United. But all I was saying was that they needed to get to a position where it was clear there was no option but to respond to some of the attacks. Not attack anyone personally, but make sure his side of the story was heard. I had never really understood why he had got in so deep on this one. I knew he liked racing, and betting, but these were not people to be underestimated, even by him, I would say. I liked Les, who had his head screwed on, and I liked the Irish PR guy, who had seemed like he knew his way around the Irish scene. Alex looked a bit worn out with it all.

Friday 16 January
Pulse 58, too high again. Steve said take a rest day but I did 70 minutes on the bike. Nigel Bennett saw Chris Shaw to sort a deal with Channel 5.

Alex called re yesterday, felt better about it, also asked what I thought about the Rio Ferdinand situation and whether he should appeal [Ferdinand had been banned for eight months for missing drugs test]. His view, that I backed, was that if he didn't people would take it as guilt. TB and Tessa did the launch of the Olympic bid, which seemed to go well. Both spoke well and the buzz was pretty good. The papers were really cranking up now for TB's 'danger moment' with tuition fees and Hutton coming on consecutive days. Philip said it was ridiculous that a judge held the future of a Prime Minister in his hands. It was true though, that if he lost the fees vote, and then was directly criticised by Hutton, he would be close to being toast.

I started to get calls saying that Michael Foot [former MP, minister and leader of the Labour Party] had died and saying could I do tributes. So I called him at home and was told by the housekeeper that he was on his way to Plymouth for the football and was perfectly well. I spoke to Bostock again. He never failed to remind me that he thought I had been wrong to leave, and felt all my current health problems – stomach, asthma, ENT, depression – flowed from that. He felt 'the real AC story' was that I had been brilliant, unbeatable, for several years, but then was got at by a variety of factors and forces, and decided to leave, and was now in a state of relapse and morning asthma was a symptom of that. I had written to Lindsay [Nicholson] after meeting Mark to say I thought they were great together and would fully understand if she wanted me to cut down on the leukaemia fundraising and profile, given that John was usually mentioned in it all. She called to say there was no problem, that Mark understood how important John and Ellie were to her, and to me, and the past would never be erased.

Saturday 17 January

Pulse 59, rest day. The *Times* sports interview came out fine, albeit with a couple of mistakes in it. The sports route was definitely a good one for me to be going down. I took Rory to Euston as he was heading to Man Utd v Wolves. There was a big piece in *The Guardian* about Alex and the Magnier case, all focused on the smear/private investigator side of things. I called him. He was still in bed. I was surprised given they had a match on, but he said he was going through a phase of being tired. I sensed he was more worried than he let on. I had sensed at the meeting in the Caledonian that this was heading towards a denouement. Magnier and McManus were big players in the United set-up given their shareholdings, and the club surely couldn't let this drag on, him as the manager in a case against big shareholders. He had to think about where he wanted it to end, and get there, surely. 'Aye, mebbe you're right.' But he sounded a bit down and defeated by it all.

Calum and I were going to Burnley via Leeds, and on the train I worked on upcoming speeches, including the triathlon launch. TB called, said he was remarkably chipper considering. On tuition fees, he felt the problem was GB had licensed a lot of the critics to go out and criticise, and promise their local parties they would make a stand, and now it was quite difficult for some of them to come back in. He feared that some of them were treading the path that so many had taken in previous Labour governments – where thwarted ambition led to ill-discipline and self-indulgence with no regard to the broader consequences. Some of them were now into a habit they couldn't really get out of.

On Hutton, Kevin Tebbit [MoD Permanent Secretary] had cleared up all the last-minute issues with a letter to the Inquiry. TB said he was quite confident. He felt Hutton had asked all the right questions and would get to the truth, which was that the BBC story was wrong and on Kelly that he had just got in too deep and didn't tell the truth about his contacts. He really hoped not to have to get rid of Geoff [Hoon]. The important thing was that there were certain issues on which TB was explicitly cleared. He said he felt fine, and he felt it was important I got back into the game fairly soon, particularly re the Tories. It was certainly an odd position to be in though – the future of a Prime Minister effectively lying in the hands of a judge who was giving nothing away about what he was thinking or going to say.

We arrived in Leeds, met by Dave Edmundson, and in the car chatted about various fundraising ideas. He reckoned Burnley needed £700,000 to keep heads above water. They had asked me to do a press conference at the club and there was a very good turnout. I did my spiel, half a dozen questions or so, including some twat who kept trying to ask me about Hutton. Alex had given me the go ahead to say he would do an event for them, so I was able to talk up how much the club meant throughout football. I was sure we could get a lot of people in football and outside to help out. It was interesting, listening to Dave and later Barry Kilby [chairman] how many parallels there were, at least in language terms, to what we did with the Labour Party. The need to reach out to new people, consolidating a base and then building on it. The need to modernise.

Sunday 18 January

Pulse 54. 70-minute run. I watched Howard on TV and got on to David Hill to point out that he had said absolutely nothing positive about the future of the country, that he was basically just an attack dog. I actually felt pretty good about Howard. He was becoming a classic opposition politician, but that was different to being a leader. I started to sort letters from all living Labour leaders expressing support for Burnley FC's financial appeal. The main story was a huge suicide bomb in Iraq, the biggest since Saddam was captured. Around twenty dead, sixty-odd injured, right at the gates to the coalition HQ. The basic security situation was not good, and the timing was bad as Kofi [Annan, UN Secretary-General] was about to see Paul Bremer [administrator of the Iraq provisional authority] to decide whether the place was yet safe enough for the UN to go back in. Grim. They reckoned the bomb truck had about a thousand pounds of explosives and the effects were felt as much as a mile away. Most of the dead were Iraqis.

TB was starting to set out his thoughts on Hutton and how we reacted to the various possible scenarios. The Tories had set the bar at TB as PM lying to Parliament and public. That, added to the fact the whole wretched thing started with a claim we falsified intelligence – which even Tory MPs on committees, let alone an independent judge, had rejected. So he was confident if Hutton found for us on those two aspects, we could start to rebuild trust/integrity. And if the judge rules we did not lie re the naming of Dr Kelly, then our position is even stronger. We have the facts on our side, but I was still worried it would be virtually impossible for anyone, even a hard-headed judge, not to be swayed by the way the whole thing had been reported for so long.

Monday 19 January

Pulse 54. Did a full swim session and then to a spinning class, which was bloody hard, constant pace changing on an exercise bike. About twelve or fifteen in the class, and I've never sweated so much in my life. Peter M sent over an excellent note on Hutton. He too had watched Howard on *Frost* yesterday and felt he had been 'wriggling' on the issue of whether he was saying TB lied, and so it was important to get together pre-Hutton reporting all the different statements to that effect Howard had made. I was also pleased that Peter said he was not in favour of any 'cosy agreements' with Dyke etc., that their reporting on Hutton had been a complete disgrace and they needed to be reminded by third parties they were on trial here every bit as much as we were. We were obviously going to stay quiet on Hutton till he reported and he felt we should state publicly that we will not be saying anything, nor even preparing responses, until we see the report.

He seemed to share TB's view that Hutton would not, given the evidence, say we lied, but we had to be on alert for the way any slight hint of it would be blown up by the media to create an initial sense that TB had to go. He also set out a few good thoughts on tuition fees. It was pretty grim that these two potential huge problems were coming down the track together, though I guess the one positive to be drawn was they both showed TB and the government taking on the difficult issues of leadership, whereas on both Howard's response was naked opportunism. He and TB both felt the party in the country was in a better place on tuition fees than the PLP.

Tuesday 20 January

Pulse 54. 45-minute run. Clive Conway and Wendy Bailey came to plan South Shields and various other things. They had the idea of an audio book and were also talking to Channel 4 about turning the whole thing into a one-off programme, but I worried there would be bad faith issues with Channel 5. They gave me a lift into town for a meeting with DH, Clare S and Catherine R, re preparing for Hutton, later joined by Jonathan, Peter M, PG, Tim Allan, Sally M and Pat. It did not exactly fill me with confidence. The strategy was not clear. Jonathan was not his usual self, was probably doing too much and on some issues was a bit all over the place. David didn't seem to have an easily understood strategy. I know it was difficult without knowing what was coming, but it was possible to work out the broad parameters of different possible reports and different responses. PM, PG and I were in a different position to TB – tougher – on the question of how to handle the BBC.

I had seen TB earlier when I went up to the flat, learned he was in the gym and went up there. He was playing loud rock music, so loud he didn't hear me as I went in. He was doing sit-ups, resting in between groups of ten and twenty, and I stood there and watched him for a minute or so and there was something very sad and lonely about him. His face was taut, and he had a slightly haunted look around his eyes. When he finally spotted me, he clicked into a different mode, jumped up and was straight into fairly lively conversation. He said he felt fine, that on tuition fees he was confident we were going to be OK. He admitted that re Hutton he just couldn't work out where he was, he was trying not to think about it but that was not easy. Tell me about it. He couldn't work out on the procedure whether Hutton was just being very, very proper, or whether he was enjoying the attention and the feeling of power that he now had. He thought it was a very odd situation, that he might not even get the report till noon, on a day when in any event he would be dealing with tuition fees. 'If he says he thinks I lied, that's it, finished.'

He said it was odd to have put his future in the hands of a Northern Ireland judge, but there we are. He was a bit annoyed with Charlie because from the outset he had made clear he wanted an inquiry that was quick, not a circus, but the Inquiry had delivered several months' worth of circuses. To be fair to Charlie, and to Hutton, the Inquiry had to be real, and tough. He felt Howard had gone a bit far, and made a mistake in placing the bar so clearly on TB. He felt it was useful that I was out and would be able to go for them more than if I was still here. He told me he had assured Gavyn [Davies] he wouldn't directly call for his resignation, which I felt was a mistake, because that was where we might end up, depending on how it all came out. I felt Gavyn had been weak and incapable of exercising much control, and it was a mistake to give that assurance. As Bradshaw said at a later meeting, this was going to be seen as win or lose, nobody would appreciate a halfway position.

TB was looking a bit tired but generally OK. He felt the masochism strategy, tougher interviews involving critics and often angry members of the public, was going fine. He said he was enjoying my public fulminations about the press. He said of course we had to go along with all this nonsense, a la Phillis Report, that there was bad on both sides, when in truth the badness was pretty much all theirs. *The Sun* were currently running stuff on gypsies coming in under EU enlargement, which had a pretty disgusting undercurrent to it. I felt TB and his team had run a good operation on tuition fees, though Sally said it was still not clear they would win, but on Hutton I felt there was no real operation at all and I was getting worried about it. TB said he was getting on better with GB but that had been born of convenience, GB worried about Howard. He admitted the problem was he had given GB too much leeway. Equally, GB had given his own people licence to cause trouble on tuition fees, and he didn't know how to peg back on it.

I went for a run with Godric [Smith] who echoed what Bradders had said – that power had shifted away from our end of the building. John Kerry did well in Iowa [US Democratic presidential primary], as did John Edwards. TB had met Edwards, said he was bright, interesting. He felt Bush would probably win but was clearly not sure. Bizarrely, coincidentally, Ari Fleischer [former White House press secretary] was in No. 10 doing a tour, so I swapped notes with him about life on the outside. Like me, he was doing a mix of stuff, including sport. Of all the times I had been back since leaving, today was the time that I felt both in and out. In, because people were still looking to me to help formulate a response on a difficult issue, but out, because I felt less urgent about it and because all sorts of other things were going on in which I wasn't at all involved. I missed some of the people, including TB, I missed a lot of my team, and I missed the sense of involvement, but I didn't miss the pressure or the expectations, and was quite glad when I got out and waited for the 24 bus. Mum called in a real state because it emerged that Dad had broken his shoulder when he fell the other day.

Wednesday 21 January

Pulse 51, good swim session. Bad dream about Dad. I was in a hallway with Mum, who was crying. I tried to comfort her, and went through to see Dad who was lying in bed, semi-conscious, tubes and drips all over the place. I wanted to say he had been a fantastic father but I was worried he would feel it was me saying he was about to die, so I never said it. Later, Calum told me he had had a nightmare about Dad dying. He was the one who seemed to be most sensitive to other people's feelings on things like this, and the one who most wanted to know about family background. I was getting stacks of bids to do media on the day Hutton came out. I sent Jonathan an email saying I was a bit alarmed about yesterday, that there seemed to be a lack of clarity and grip. Jonathan said it was hard to know how to prepare, as we knew so little about what was coming. What was clear was that TB was in a different place re the outcome for the BBC. I felt we should go for them but clearly he didn't.

Tim Allan did a very good note, felt that we should use Howard's recent pronouncements to set the bar on the question of whether TB lied or not, and we should end up calling for an apology from the BBC and an apology from Howard. He said that having read as much as he could, he would be very surprised if Hutton said either of us lied.

I fixed an interview for *The Times* with Nick Faldo [former golfer] and was talking to his PR about the whole theme of greatness in sport, and she gave me a big number about the fact he was still going for the Ryder Cup captaincy. Dad was back in hospital, and they said he may have to go to a home for intensive therapy to try to get his legs going again. It sounded OK but also felt like we were on the last lap. I remembered something Kim Howells [Transport Minister] said when his dad died, that no matter how much you expected it, and no matter how long you had to prepare for it, it was the most brutal shock imaginable when it happened. I felt that I ought to get up there, but the Hutton thing made it difficult. I told Mum I would try to get up at the weekend.

Joan Hammell [JP special advisor] called, said that JP wanted to have a session with me and GB. She said there had been one with JP, GB and Peter, at the end of which Peter had said to her, 'You must think that we're all mad.' She said I was badly missed, and she thought JP wanted to find a way of getting me back in on my own terms. JR called after watching *Panorama*, which I hadn't bothered with. It was clearly part of the BBC's pre-Hutton spin to show themselves as being balanced. I got a transcript, and it was basically attacking the BBC in the hope that it would be seen as a show of independence, but then going on to go for me, John Scarlett, and above all TB. Philip and Bradshaw both felt it was pretty bad for us, and were furious it had gone out at all. They had obviously decided that on the merits they lost, so were hoping to manipulate opinion so that everyone got whacked. I was still of the Sumption view that Hutton wouldn't be swayed, but there was definitely a desire among the media to persuade the public we were all as bad as each other.

JP called later. He said the TB–GB situation was a bit better. He said the three of them had had dinner recently at JP's place. GB had sat down, complained the chair was too low and could he have a higher one? JP got him a new one, then said to TB, 'Do you want one?' and TB said, 'No, I've got used to him looking down on me.' He said GB had realised he needed help to become leader and that meant he had to build relationships with people who currently feared their heads would be chopped off if he became Prime Minister. JP had decided that what TB really wanted was the old magic circle around him, operating properly, and that meant GB, PM and AC, and he wanted to help put that together. He had had a good session with GB and Peter, said they had a proper discussion about strategy and although it was hard because GB still basically wanted people totally on his side, JP felt Gordon had gone away thinking there had been a proper purpose to it. He said he had mentioned the idea to GB of getting together with me and described his reaction as 'neutral to positive'. He thought he was worried about my diaries. I said the one thing that came out of my diary, from all the transcription I was doing, was that this TB–GB thing had been going on too long and had to improve. Maybe it couldn't.

JP basically felt there was a lot of guilt running through their relationship. TB had obviously made promises, or at least suggestions of a deal, and GB felt betrayed. And GB felt guilt in his calmer moments at the way he treated TB. Neither of them could really get over it. I was happy to be involved in trying to help them do that, even if I didn't hold out much hope of it happening. JP felt that TB was still a bit too soft with the rebels on tuition fees. It might have been better if they had fought it out at the start. He said he had told TB a while back that he had to threaten to sack him, and eventually he did. 'GB came to see me and said, "John, he's threatened to sack me."' He couldn't believe he had finally done it. JP said he sometimes felt like a referee at a tennis match but the reality was TB was the best we had, GB was the second best and we had to get them working together. He felt I had done the right thing in going, and he supported me at the time, but that we had to find a way of getting me involved again in a different way. He had also made it clear to TB that if he wanted to move Ian McCartney as party chairman, he would support him on that.

Thursday 22 January
Pulse 55, crap 30-minute run. I read all the Hutton transcripts. Felt there were no questions I couldn't deal with, but we now just had to wait. *Panorama* had been an effective spin job for the BBC, looking like they were prepared to criticise themselves, but there was a widespread feeling that they shouldn't be doing it at all, prejudging the Inquiry in that way. Rereading all the transcripts, it was impossible not to reflect on how much time, effort and money had now gone into this. As [Sir] Patrick Cormack [Tory MP] said when Fiona and I had dinner with him and his wife Mary at the Athenaeum, it was a private tragedy and there should not have been a public inquiry. I was both troubled and untroubled by Hutton. I was pretty sure that the public's interest in it peaked long ago, and that seemed to be borne out by news viewing figures. But I was troubled in that I feared Hutton wouldn't be able to

resist the media pressure to go for both sides equally. I doubted that he would feel able to go for Kelly at all.

I hadn't really wanted to go out at all, but Patrick had been pressing Fiona for ages. He was a nice enough bloke, totally supportive on Hutton, vile about IDS, pro-TB and against the press. He said we now had a Fourth Estate determined to do what it could to help destroy the first, second and third. I didn't like these posh clubs though. I was generally a bit depressed again, had been ever since Dad's fall. His illness, the thought of Rory leaving home, and the idea of people out there still doing books on me was combining to get me down again.

Friday 23 January

Finally went for a proper check on my chest and sinuses. Nice chat with the doctor who felt JR was basically OK but not totally on their wavelength as Health Minister. I had organised a few meetings, speeches and other events. Mark Ferguson came round later. He had paged me yesterday to say he wanted to see me urgently. They had decided they were going to settle re the horse. They were worried about the damage being done to Alex's reputation and even to his health. Mark realised they needed to keep me out of this publicly, because the press liked doing me in as much as Alex, but could I help prepare the ground, and work out the best way out of this? Both Alex and Cathy had had enough of it. I felt the only route out on this was to be in control of the process, to get some honour and strength by making clear he had made the decision to get out of this because the club was too important to have this distraction hanging around him the whole time. I had sensed from the Caledonian meeting this is where it would end. Alex didn't have the appetite for a media war on this, and it would damage him even more at the club. It was going to be a big hit to take, but would be forgotten provided he kept United winning.

Saturday 24 January

Pulse 55, did an hour on the new bike. The Hutton coverage was picking up, focusing on TB, GH, me and the BBC, pretty much in that order. The first *Times* column seemed to go down fine. I went to watch Calum play tennis at a club in Paddington, and noticed two or three people reading it. I was being chased about some rubbish out of Phil Stephens's book on TB that had been published in the States

January '04: Ferguson plans to settle re horse dispute

that I tried to get Cherie to withdraw from public life. Ridiculous. I was really fed up having to deal with this bollocks. Lots of pre-Hutton in the Sundays and tuition fees was picking up big time through a combination of what Charlie called 'the ejected, the dejected and the rejected'. But they were there in sufficient numbers to make these dangerous times for TB.

Sunday 25 January

Pulse 55. One-hour run, then off with Rory to King's Cross and then Mum picked us up at Retford station. Rory slept on the train and I worked on a couple of columns and a speech. TB called a couple of times, fairly philosophical. He was pretty fed up with it all, but said re the [tuition fees] vote, 'Oh well, if we win, we win, and if we don't, there we are. It will just show the Labour Party reverting to type, not serious about reform, not thinking about the future, believes the Tories could never come back.' He was having to go through what I felt was the humiliation of a meeting tomorrow with Nick Brown and George Mudie [Labour MPs opposed to tuition fees policy], who were helping lead the rebellion and were effectively a rival, ie GB, whips' operation. TB felt the problem was that GB had licensed these people and was unable to unlicense them. TB now accepted there was a group who would do anything to get rid of him. Peter M called me later and said he was absolutely sure GB was still at it, that he was torn because he knew he couldn't allow himself to be portrayed or seen as anti-reform. He felt TB had always underestimated GB's duplicity. He said if we lost the vote on tuition fees, it was the start of a slow death, the slow death of New Labour and reform.

I caught a phone-in in the car, where the mood was pro-TB and pro-reform, but it was pretty tough from now on in. On Wednesday, TB would be sitting there on the front bench listening to Charles [Clarke] on tuition fees as the Hutton Report arrived. We had lunch with Mum, Liz [AC's sister] and her kids and then Rory and I went to see Dad. He was in a very nice little care home, set in a nice garden in a village. He was sitting up in his chair when we arrived but still bruised from his fall, and clearly uncomfortable. His left hand was badly swollen. His eyes were very watery, his sight failing more than ever. It was a sad scene. Here was the man Donald [AC's brother] called his rock, who now couldn't see, couldn't move his legs, couldn't sit up without being lifted. Yet he was still bright up top and talked away to the three of us. I was really touched by Mum's constant stroking of his hair, fretting over him. She was clearly worried that the nurses didn't know his little ways, but he said they were fine. The doctors reckoned it would take three weeks' therapy to get his legs moving properly. I felt he would be happier at home unable to move, than here for several weeks being helped to move a little.

Rory and I sat together on the bed and I was so glad he was there. It was a very un-him thing to have asked to come, but he did and it brought back memories of when I was a bit younger than him, with Dad, when we moved his dad from Tiree to a hospital on the mainland, and nobody had wanted to make the decision he should go. I could remember Dad talking to him as he lay on a kind of trolley bed on the boat, how ill and weak my grandfather had looked. Dad looked exactly like that now.

For the first time, I heard him refer directly to the prospect of death. As we talked over the pros and cons of him being here or at home, he said 'I kind of think if I stay, maybe one of the angels will take me before the three weeks is up.' I feared he would give up if he stayed here, and the pain and disability at home were somehow preferable to managed discomfort here. I so wanted to say something comforting, but it's hard, you either mouth platitudes or you acknowledge that death is coming. So we chatted away, tried to tease out what he really wanted, to be there or to be home. Rory did a great job of keeping spirits up, though I think he was shocked at how weak Dad now looked, and said later he found it very hard to imagine that one day I would be like that. I told him the story of the journey on the boat and said the chances are that one day, he'd look like that too.

We got back to the house, Mum a bit tearful, and I wrote Dad a long letter, told him the four of us had been blessed with wonderful, loving parents, and that anything I had achieved was because of the upbringing I had had and the values I had been raised with, talked of the powerful line I felt of kinship, family and love, between his dad and him, between him and me, that I hoped I could pass that on to Rory, Calum and Grace, and that if Fiona and I could feel as loved by each other as he and Mum did so long into their marriage, that would be a life well lived. I told him I had been asked by someone what my legacy would be and how I wanted to be remembered. I had found myself answering that any legacy would rightly be seen as TB's and as for me, as long as my parents were proud of me, and Fiona and the kids loved me, I didn't really care. I recalled the time he drove me to

Cambridge and gave me the quote from Hamlet about being true to oneself, said that he had lived his life according to that code, and if I did likewise, it was because of him.

Mum read it to him later, said she was crying the whole way through and that he had been touched. She said there had always been part of him that had felt guilty about his dad leaving Tiree, and I didn't want him in that place, nice though it was. I felt it would be far better if he could be at home, die with dignity, with Mum and hopefully us with him. I spoke to him later, said that his life was so different to his own father's, as mine was to his, but there were really strong historical, cultural and above all personal links. I had sometimes felt I had not been a great son because I moved away and lived a life that was so different to theirs, in terms of the work side of things at least. He said they were both incredibly proud of me and it meant a lot to them both that I could say those things to him.

Monday 26 January

Hutton and tuition fees were now moving towards frenzy point. Mark Ferguson called, said that MUFC had put out a statement to the Stock Exchange that was supposed to have said Jason [Ferguson, Mark's brother] was not involved but that bit had been cut.* Both here and in Ireland the press was getting nasty for Alex. Mark said his mum was getting really upset about it all. Alex was even thinking about getting out of it. We agreed Alex should settle but not for his press conference tomorrow. Mark said he had never seen Alex so down. He said there weren't many people he would listen to on this kind of thing, but I was one of them and he hoped I could help. He wanted me to talk Alex out of doing his press conference tomorrow, which I did.

Then to No. 10 for a meeting with JoP, PH, Peter M, Tim Allan, Clare Sumner, CR and Bradshaw. It was good to have Tim back in there, as an insider-outsider. He was coming up with some good insights. TB had done a draft statement based on what he thought would happen. It was OK but didn't really press home the lie/lie/apology/apology strategy which Tim had suggested. Jonathan seemed to have done a good job of gripping it since last week. The briefing materials had

---

* A BBC TV investigation into the business relationship between Manchester United and Sir Alex Ferguson's football agent son, Jason, prompted an internal review of the club's transfer deals.

improved and all we really needed was a really strong message. Hutton had agreed that once Howard saw it in advance, he could brief his team on it. I felt that as a best-case scenario, TB ought to be able to use it for a strategy of rebuilding trust but it was going to be very very difficult, if only because the media would focus on the worst parts of any outcome. I had been struck going around the place though that the public were more understanding of TB's position than I sometimes felt the No. 10 people realised. The best comic moment of the morning came when Peter M was in mid-flow, suddenly stopped, looked over at me and said, 'You need a really strong moisturiser you know.'

I went in to see TB later. He was on the phone to difficult MPs. He said the asinine nature of some of them was beyond belief. He had wasted so much time on Nick Brown and George Mudie, who basically just wanted him dead. He felt the vote would go through OK, but it was very difficult. On Hutton, he felt the danger area for us was whether we were so keen to get Dr Kelly's name out that we were being disingenuous in saying we hadn't done anything. I think he felt I was the vulnerable one at the moment. He felt we were probably OK on the intelligence questions, probably OK in fact on naming but he might say there was so much of a desire for the name to be out that there was a problem. I had to sign a letter which said that I would be able to read the report in advance but could not discuss it with anyone.

Tuesday 27 January

It was a really odd feeling knowing that there was this document, already printed, and people like the judge and his team knew what was in it, and it was so important to the fate and reputations of quite a few people, including the Prime Minister, who didn't have a clue what it was going to say. I was less nervous than on the days I gave evidence. I spent most of the morning working on my *Times* column, and the speech for South Shields, but first I went out to the [Parliament Hill] lido to meet Alan Davidson [photographer], and do some pictures for the triathlon launch on Thursday. First cycling, then running, then swimming. Phil Jeal [lido manager] had got waterproof shoes and gloves to add to my wetsuit but it was still absolutely freezing, 39°F, and I could only stay in for a minute or so. Alan was happy enough. We went back to discuss the timing of putting them out. Alan felt today was best, as there was a vacuum before the report was published. Fiona agreed, but I feared it would look I was exploiting the timing and I was still worried what influence anything like this might have on the judge who might still be putting together his statement, even if the report itself was already printed.

I called Rebekah Wade for advice and she said, confirming my own view, that today and tomorrow were impossible, and I should do it on Thursday to coincide with the launch itself. Then she said something odd: 'You must be really happy.' I said, 'Why?' 'Because you've been cleared.' 'How do you know – is this a piece of Trevor [Kavanagh, *Sun* political editor] thinking?' She said, 'Mmm, a bit more than that.' Tony, me, Geoff all cleared, she said, and dreadful for the BBC. I assumed it was bullshit from her team, but then later it came out that they had been leaked it which was a total pain because it would lead to a media frenzy that would take over from the report itself if we weren't careful, and of course our bovine lot would blame us. I told Godric in passing what she had said, but neither of us took it very seriously. I got a cab in at half eleven and went to wait in Tom [Kelly] and Godric's room. There was lots of the usual black humour, working out who GB would keep, whether Tom would have to resign tomorrow or by the Sundays over his Walter Mitty remark, but the mood was good.

Catherine said David Omand wanted us all to have pink and yellow marker pens, and use pink for good and yellow for bad bits. I kept mixing them up in my mind so in the end didn't bother. I explained to Fiona that because of the thing I had signed I wouldn't even be able to tell her what was in it. But I would text her a number from one to ten, one being bad, ten being perfect.

I saw TB a couple of times who was more focused on tuition fees. He felt if we lost, it was potentially the beginning of the end. He said he found some of our MPs ridiculous and others were actually contemptible. On Hutton, like me, he had reached the point where because there was nothing we could do till we saw it, we might as well not worry. He said it all depends on whether he has gone for the facts, as the rational part of me says he will, or has been influenced by all the nonsense in the media. He seemed confident that Hutton would go for the facts. Clare said that somebody had been looking at his previous judgements, and his style was to set out a lot of evidence and then make short judgemental statements as he went along. He was going to do a fairly lengthy statement after questions tomorrow, and before the statement in the Commons. I watched the Sky pictures of the boxes being loaded into a car by Sue Gray [Cabinet Office] and Lee Hughes [Inquiry secretary] and then we just waited. We did a little press office team photo and then eventually Nicholas [Howard, No. 10 official] came through with a box and they handed out individually marked copies. Mine was no. 17.

We went through to David Hill's room. GS was first to find the conclusions, page 300 and something. We went there, and in a matter of minutes knew it was fine. 45 minutes, fine. JS, fine. BBC bad. Nothing improper re Kelly. Mild rebuke for Tom but nothing catastrophic. Relief all round. DH, CR, CS in and out, TK, GS and I with Adam Sharples, Sameena [Rizzi, No. 10 staff] bringing in teas and everyone shutting up when she did, then when she went back out, we'd have found another positive line for us, and another hit at the BBC. There would clearly have to be resignations at the top.

TB was over at the House for the tuition fees debate, which was still touch and go, Sally saying that Nick Brown turning would probably help a bit. Tessa called to say good luck and she said there was a lot of bitterness over there. Some of these people really hated TB, but GB was panicking now because he had set this whole ball rolling and it was going too fast. TB came back and we all went into the Cabinet room where Jonathan, Matthew Rycroft, David Omand, Stephen Parkinson [lawyer] had been going through it. David O said of the fifteen key questions, we won fourteen and a half to a half. I said yesterday I had been trying to work out the best-case and the worst-case scenarios. Hutton had gone beyond my best-case. TB came in and we told him it was very very good for us and dreadful for the BBC. He said, 'Are you having me on?' JoP said, 'It could hardly be better. Probably too good.' TB sat down with his glasses on and read the conclusions himself, then looked over, sighed and just nodded. We by then were into the body of the text itself. There was language even more positive for us there. Tom spotted the line that Hutton had said all this applies regardless of whether the intelligence turns out to be wrong.

I felt relief as everyone else did but going over it all again, seeing their ridiculous letters to me and the lies they told, I was still really angry. I had a nice chat with David Omand. Everyone was relieved. He said John S was fine. He could live with the point that there was a chance he had been subconsciously influenced by me. The MoD people were most relieved of all. Geoff [Hoon] came over and I could tell that he too still felt real anger. The [Sun] leak was a total pain, and GS and I asked ourselves whether it would be one step forward two steps back again. He said even they cannot present this as anything other than a win for us and humiliation for the BBC. It was nice being back in with the team, but also nice knowing that it would not be for long. It was frustrating for the rest of the office, particularly people like Bradshaw who felt so strongly and had worked so hard, that we couldn't tell them anything, but they were clearly picking up the positive vibes. And of course once the leak story took off, they assumed it was true. Bradders said he wanted heads on sticks. CS and GS worked on the Q&A while I did my own statement which to my surprise TB liked, and only toned down a little. He said he saw no point directly calling for resignations. He said this was an important moment re the media. He said all that has happened was that just for once, over one story, the media had been subject to the kind of scrutiny we get all the time, and they had been found wanting. The point I should be making is not that this was a total aberration but that these stories were all too common, that we had to deal with this kind of journalism the whole time.

Jonathan said the report was so good for us there would be a backlash in the media. They will hate the fact that TB and the government come out so well. TB had to go over to the House again, and the vote still looked touch and go. We waited for the result which was phoned through just before Jim Fitzpatrick announced it. It was a narrow win but as TB said when he came back, a win is a win. By tomorrow we would be in a very much stronger position. He was angry still at those MPs who said they finally accepted the arguments in favour of the policy, but simply said they couldn't vote with us because of the past statements they'd made. He said that some of them frankly had no idea of the implications of us losing on the second reading. It would actually have been the beginning of the end.

People were running the line that it was all a failure of policy-making, the way he worked, and it would have to change. I had heard it many times before. I thought he might be a bit more emollient re GB, who must have pulled a few round, but TB said the whole thing had been set in train by him. He had licensed these people and then found it impossible to unlicense them. If I heard him say it once… He went to the flat to work on the statement and I worked some more on mine. A number of camp beds had been laid out because we thought we would have to work through the night, but we finished about 11 and people went home. I stayed in No. 10 to avoid the scrum outside the house in the morning. I slept in the same bedroom I had for the same reason the night before I gave evidence. I also bumped into Bill [Wells] the messenger, as I did then, and he said exactly the same thing as he did then, you're a good man, Alastair and it's going to be fine. Bill had become something of a totem or mascot or whatever the word is.

I went to bed and read Anthony Seldon's draft of some of the chapters for his book on Tony, which was reasonably fair though with some inaccuracies. It brought a lot of things back. It is remarkable how much, how many events, crises, great days, bad days, we have been through, though for me personally many of the worst had been in the last few months. I was confident tomorrow would be one of the better days. I texted Fiona a nine. Phew, she said. Sleep well.

Wednesday 28 January

I woke up at five and couldn't get back to sleep, so got up and went to TB's gym. My asthma wasn't great so I did 15–20 minutes on the treadmill, then some weights, then half an hour on the steps thing. This thing had completely buggered up my training this week, and I was also missing Rory's race today which pissed me off too. I went to see TB who was sitting at the round table in the corner of the lounge overlooking the park, scribbling furiously as he tried to finish the statement. How many times had I walked in there to that scene? Dozens. Hundreds. I said he really had to nail Howard today, and should also demand an apology from Liam Fox [Tory defence spokesman], who had said on the floor of the House that the government leaked the report to *The Sun*. I had actually moved to the view the Beeb might have leaked it to create a diversion from the reality of the report. TB said he would go for the Tories, don't worry, but he would wait for Howard first. If he didn't apologise, it would show very bad judgement. I said I would love to know how Howard felt when he realised the report was a total vindication.

The duty clerk brought up Hutton's statement and TB had a quick look. It was pretty much identical to the summary conclusions. TB had written some good passages, and was in confident mood. The leak story was running huge, wiping out tuition fees even. I called Rebekah and Trevor and said they should make it clear publicly that this did not come from us. It didn't stop the Tories and journos making it out to be me. I was shocked and angry that Mike Brunson [ITN political editor] seemed to imply it was me. I called him and demanded he withdraw it. Howard and Charles Kennedy had arrived at the Cabinet Office at 6, and on the way in and out, Howard was making mischief re the leak, and saying the cops should be called in. He was a total opportunist, and deeply unpleasant. That, allied to poor judgement and the lack of an agenda, would be his problem. Andrew Turnbull [Cabinet Secretary] and others were busy having to deal with the leak issue. At one point it seemed Hutton would be announcing a leak inquiry, which would look like he was investigating us, but eventually it was agreed we would announce it, along with the categorical denials we were giving. The blather went on though, and eventually I gave a categorical denial to PA myself.

Journalists were calling the whole time and we were not returning calls. The blather machine ground on, but this was real Phil Space [*Private Eye* fictional journalist] time until the statement. TB went over for PMQs and was storming, really went for Howard over the leak, got in the theme of apology, and was strong and defiant on tuition fees. His body language was good and of course they knew he'd seen the report, so they assumed it was good, as per *The Sun*. In fact it was better. By the time Hutton came on, I was alone in Tom/Godric's office and paced up and down as he delivered it. The voice brought back the memories of sitting there for hours. It was odd, watching television and hearing a Law Lord deliver a judgement in which your name kept popping up, and bringing back memories of all these dreadful events. It was a total vindication and that came over clearly. The cutaways to the media watching him showed their irritation. These people were desperate for him to say the story was right and TB had lied. These people were idiots. If they had listened to the evidence, read the evidence, it was inevitable that this would be the judgement. The initial story was wrong, so wrong, and the BBC's handling was so woeful and dishonest. Our main concern had been whether he felt there had been any badness in the naming issue. He didn't, and that was that.

TB did well in the House, Howard was dreadful. TB said to me earlier that if he had any judgement at all, he'll just apologise. He didn't. He said he accepted the report then proceeded to pick it apart in relation to TB. He ended with loud boos from our side, and then TB skewered him, saying being nasty wasn't the same as effective, and opportunism wasn't leadership. I texted David Hill to say we should say it had taken ages to work out Major, Hague and Duncan Smith's weak points. Howard had exposed his in weeks. Opportunism. Nastiness. Bad judgement. No policy agenda for the country. We'd arranged that I would do my statement at the Foreign Press Association. I'd agreed with Nigel Bennett I would sign the Channel 5 deal in the next few days, so I got Chris Shaw round to do some filming.

I was driven over to the FPA and prepared in a basement room. The phone was going the whole time. Alex said it was absolutely fucking brilliant. He was whooping with delight. Ditto Mark. Philip really happy. Text messages were going every few seconds. But it reminded me of the election in '97. Everyone else seemed pretty euphoric, and I didn't feel it. I just wanted to move on and never have to deal with this kind of crap again. The best moment of the day was when Fiona phoned and said Rory had won the London schools cross-country. I spoke to him and felt great. I just wish I was there, not in SW1. I went out, did my statement fine, though I was still feeling really angry inside, said no questions, I would be doing *Newsnight*, and walked out. 'Did you leak the report?' Jon Smith [Press Association] shouted out. For a nanosecond, I thought about stopping and removing a few of his teeth, but then smiled to myself and walked out through the photographers and off we went. Back in the office, you could feel a different atmosphere, people had been through a bad time, and it was over.

Already the media were beginning to move the goalposts. People had said this judge was the most honest person on earth, a man of unquestionable integrity and judgement and now they're beginning to question his judgement. I really loathe these people I'm afraid. They are morally and intellectually corrupt. There was no word from the BBC for ages. Eventually they released a sort of Soviet style videotape of Greg Dyke saying they kind of accept the report, kind of saying story was right, almost apologising but not quite, no sense of where they were going, total lack of clarity. What had they been doing since they got the report? It was ridiculous. How had these people got to such senior positions when they were so clearly lacking in leadership or judgement? Then breaking news, Andrew Marr [BBC political editor], who had become something of a spokesman for the BBC's machine, saying that Gavyn Davies was going to resign. I'm afraid I couldn't feel much sympathy. He had exposed himself as weak and hadn't discharged his responsibilities. I assumed Dyke, Sambrook, Gilligan would all have to go, but maybe they would try to save their skins.

The news was pretty much wall-to-wall fine for us. TB said my statement was good but I should be making clear this is about more than the BBC. I should be defending the BBC and good journalism, attacking the bad. The office was so noisy that I went into Gordon's little office in No. 11 for a bit of peace and quiet and worked on the speech I was down to be making at a dinner tonight. I could have done without it but of course the organisers were thrilled. Bruce Grocott, Hilary

Armstrong, Razi Rahman and Darren Murphy [both special advisors] came round. Bruce and Hilary were exactly the kind of people I had in mind when I said if people knew the truth about politicians they would be pleasantly surprised and if they knew the truth about the media they would be horrified.

Bush spoke to TB, said it was great news. Matthew Rycroft said Bush had twice asked after me. TB said he was having to hold him back. Bush seemingly said 'I suppose he's doing a celebratory dance on people's heads.' Jonathan rightly spotted early that there would be a media backlash because in their eyes it was so one-sided. I left at seven to speak at Citigate's dinner, nice chat with Simon Lewis [former Buckingham Palace PR], who reckoned 75 per cent of stories in his time at the Palace were wrong. About fifty business people were there, including Jonathan Haslam. I did my usual spiel, which was fine, and a fairly lively Q&A. I was pretty heavy re the media and the PCC, said it was not a serious organisation while Dacre was on it, and was basically the puppet of the press. I had to watch the number of times I mentioned the *Mail* but I did feel strongly it was an utter poison. Haslam asked me how my views squared with the way I treated Major [when a journalist]. It wasn't a wholly unfair point.

Matthew Doyle [Labour press officer] came up with Gavyn Davies's resignation statement, which was a continuing display of defiance. I sat next to Gerald Corbett [chairman, Woolworths; ex-CEO, Railtrack] who wanted to know what Prescott thought of him. I said he thought he was a rich Tory public school tosser. He said that's good because I thought he was an incompetent oaf. He roared with laughter. It was interesting how these business people all said they could live with a Blair government but did not want GB. Matthew and I left for the BBC studios, Matthew saying I must keep calm, going over the lines and the questions. I got there, John Reid and David Cameron [Tory MP for Witney] were in the green room, and John and I did a bit of joint winding up of Cameron, talking about how bad Howard's judgement had been today.

I chatted with Jeremy Paxman before the programme and he was nervous, pacing up and down, not his usual self. I watched the start, then they came to me after Christopher Bland [former chairman of BBC board of governors] who was up as a BBC propagandist. I did fine, pretty calm, put over the points I wanted, and Jeremy was in some difficulties towards the end. I thought his hands were shaking at one point. The messages that came in were positive. I left for home. I didn't feel any sense of elation or gratification. Yes, I felt vindicated, but also knew with our media as it is, the shit wouldn't stop just because a judge had told the truth. Tessa called and said the BBC were pretty much in meltdown. I said surely Dyke will go. He has to, she said. He may try to stay on. The governors are meeting tomorrow and we will see what happens then. I got to bed after one, but didn't sleep well.

Thursday 29 January

The papers weren't as bad as I had expected them to be, one or two shouting whitewash, and there was definitely going to be a backlash. Jonathan was right, that the outcome had in some ways been too good for us. John Reid was terrific on the media, measured and clear and on top of it all. I worked a bit on the script for my South Shields event, then did a Radio 5 phone-in which was OK. I did a quick round of interviews after Richard Ryder [BBC governor, ex-Tory MP] put out a statement with the BBC apology, Dyke resigned and so the backlash grew. Dyke was coming over as a complete clown. Philip sent me a note saying it was important not to be triumphalist but emphasise that the media had to be capable of critical self-analysis. He felt that although I held it together well with Paxman last night, he could tell the anger was simmering, and I just needed to hold it together a few more days. I said to Fiona that even though mentally I had been preparing for the worst, what had been keeping me awake at night, tossing and turning and keeping her awake too, was the constant worst-case scenario Q&A preparation going on in my head. No matter how stressed I felt today at times, I just had to remind myself what some of those were to get myself in a better place. If Hutton had said TB had deliberately misled Parliament, or that I had lied, or we had deliberately set up Kelly, then heaven knows what kind of meltdown we would be in now.

I had a chat with Sumption and reminded him of that first conversation in France, when he said on the substance he felt we were fine, and it was all about the judge. He seemed really pleased with the outcome, but not wholly surprised. He said he had been somewhat shocked by how poor the BBC had been as witnesses. 'You were a model witness,' he said 'because you took the time and the care to prepare.' I wonder if I would have had the time had we not been on holiday first time around or out of the job second time around. Anyway, with his and Philip's words locked away inside my mind, I set about doing a load of interviews. I think I did OK, firm on the media and what it said about them, nothing that could be seen as triumphalist.

The only one I lost it with was Nick Robinson [ITN political editor]. He had decided he was just going to keep asking me why I had not expressed regret to the Kelly family. I imagined the interview would get used both in full somewhere but also for clips and I knew that if I allowed him to put the words down my throat, that would be the line they would take, and they would spin it up as part of their continuing 'six of one, half a dozen of the other' narrative. Also, I didn't want suddenly to drop in there that I had had the earlier exchange with Mrs Kelly via GH, because I worried it would look exploitative. So I played a straight bat as best I could but I could feel my gorge rising and he could sense it too I think. When finally the interview stopped, I knew they were still filming but I was really angry by now, and made sure he knew it. We were in a hotel where Leukaemia Research were hosting the launch of my triathlon appeal. They couldn't believe their luck that it came when it did, with loads of media there just wanting fresh pictures re Hutton/BBC.

The reception itself went fine and Trevor Beattie [advertising executive] paid ten grand for a signed [by AC] copy of the Hutton Report. I knew we would get a bit of grief for it from the usual places, but ten grand to kick off the appeal was not to be sniffed at. There was a good mix of politics and media people there, but I got quite emotional when I spoke about John [Merritt]. I hadn't really let anything out over the past few days and weeks, and seeing real friends and family there, among all the others, just made me choke up a bit. I often wondered about what he would have thought about the way my life had turned since he died. I think he would be amazed, as was Lindsay. But I think he would have been pretty horrified at the way the media had turned out too. I am pretty confident he would have been totally on my side in this one, and of course the whole Farzad [Bazoft, *Observer* journalist executed by the Iraqi regime in 1990, and buried close to Merritt in Highgate cemetery] episode meant he had always been anti-Saddam.

When I watched the news later, I thought Dyke looked ridiculous and the orchestrated stuff showing how popular he was, climbing onto a desk and proclaiming the values of the BBC, being wildly applauded by the BBC hacks, was all a bit pathetic. He still seemed to have no inkling of how badly he had fucked up. Their strategy now was to show themselves as the wronged party, me as the bogeyman. They would use their own outlets, as before, to promote their own case rather than cover it. TB said it was like living in the reverse of a police state, where anyone who attacked the government was right, but any government successes had to be thought to be undeserved or the work of someone else. He felt on balance, my diaries were probably a net gain because they showed Hutton the efforts we had to go to in dealing with these tossers the whole time. I said that was not what you said when you were trying to get me to persuade Sumption to argue they shouldn't be asking for them. 'Hindsight is a wonderful thing, is it not?' he said. And then he was on to asking me about stuff he was up to next week.

Friday 30 January

The papers were full of Dyke, the sense of a backlash growing. The media were starting to go into overdrive on the idea that the report was too one-sided. TB was a bit exercised that it was all coming over as me intimidating the BBC, based on the tone and nature of my interviews. Rebekah Wade suggested, based on something I'd said at the triathlon event last night, where I had said I was not anti-BBC but felt these had been allegations so serious they could not be ignored, that I do a pro-BBC piece for *The Sun*, pointing out that it wasn't about attacking the BBC but about upholding the reputation of the Prime Minister and the government. It was a good idea, a bit counter intuitive, especially if it was in *The Sun*, which hated the Beeb, so I drafted something very quickly, called TB on the drive to South Shields and he agreed it, but then it seemed the rest of the office weren't happy, and wanted me to pull it, which I did. I actually felt that was a mistake, but I didn't want to cut across what David [Hill] and co. were doing, which was trying to lower the temperature a bit. The BBC coverage was a total disgrace, constantly promoting their own agenda through their own programmes and bulletins.

Mark Bennett [researcher and assistant] came round after one and he and I headed north with Mickey the driver. I had decided it would be easier to get driven up there rather than go by train, and it would give me the chance to drop in on Dad. I listened to Dacre on *Desert Island Discs*, which was absolutely puke-making, trying to present himself as warm and cuddly, and getting a soft ride as he went. John Sergeant [former ITN political editor] called to give his advice re tonight, having done some of these 'Audience With' events. He said don't do a lecture, be light and funny, take questions in groups. He said there were more journos on my side than it might seem, and he seemed as bemused as I was at the reaction to Dyke. We stopped halfway up the A1 so that I could drop in on Dad, who seemed a bit better but his eyes were failing and he wanted me to read some of the coverage to him. I was glad he had survived long enough to know I had been cleared. I think he and Mum both found it hard to understand why I seemed to have so many people really out to get me. 'It's a good job you have a thick skin,' he said. 'I'm not sure I could have put up with it.' He said he hoped Mum would be able to sleep better now. He asked me what I thought the public thought and I told him what Mickey the driver had said, mainly that the BBC had talked bollocks and should take the hit and stop whingeing.

I rewrote the speech for tonight to take out a few of the anti-media sections. We stopped just off the A1 so that I could go for a run, having checked beforehand there were showers at the venue, the Custom House in South Shields. It turned out though that although my dressing room had a shower, it was clearly designed for someone in a wheelchair, as the head only went halfway up the wall and I couldn't remove it. So the only way I could wash my hair was to get down on my hands and knees and jiggle about under the water. I got a fit of the giggles and ended up lying on the floor with the water spraying all over the place, just laughing at the ridiculousness of it all. Wendy Bailey and the Custom House could hardly believe their luck at the timing of it all. They said there were touts outside trying to buy and sell tickets, and they were having to turn media away because they were out of space. I did a few interviews, a mix of questions about the event, and why I was doing it – God knows, that I had quite enjoyed getting my thoughts and experiences down on paper – plus the Hutton fallout.

David Miliband [South Shields MP] and Chris Lennie [Labour deputy general secretary] came in and we did some local media, which was fine. There was a nice atmosphere building up and a fairly warm reception when I went out. The format was my opening spiel, then a break, then Q&A. Most of the jokes and anecdotes went fine, some a bit flatter than others. Funnily enough, the anecdotes about my time as a journalist in some ways worked best. I felt at my best defending TB in particular and politics in general. During the first half, I looked around for a few friendly faces and clocked one bloke who seemed to laugh and nod at all the right places and decided if he wanted to ask a question he could go first. He did, and I called him. It turned out he was the theatre critic of the *Daily Telegraph* [Charles Spencer], who asked me if I was a dry drunk. Although Iraq and Hutton took up a few questions, there was a much broader range than I had expected. I quite enjoyed it. At one point, Mark B, who was standing to the side, flashed me a card saying 'Gilligan has resigned.' I was tempted to say something but didn't. Brendan Foster had come over with Sue and said afterwards he thought it was brilliant, that more people should do that kind of event. DM had been sitting in the front and had scribbled a few thoughts. He felt it needed more stories that lifted the veil on government. I felt I was probably too much in briefing mode, at times not human or personal enough about the job.

There were a few dossier obsessives in there, one even asked on Alison Blackshaw's role. Otherwise fairly obvious stuff, what's Bush like, why are the government doing tuition fees, how to deal with the press, best bits and worst bits of the job, what was the [London] Marathon like? The *News of the World* were apparently offering £750 for a ticket. The theatre people were thrilled with it, and we did a little fundraising event for them afterwards, where a very funny auctioneer raised some money flogging off my running shirt. Out for dinner with Brendan, Sue, David, Mark etc. As I left for the car, the media were still chasing me for a comment about Gilligan's departure. I ignored them, not least to avoid seeming triumphalist. Jonathan Beale [BBC reporter] shouted out, 'Surely you could say you are happy?' I still ignored him, before he added under his breath, 'I am, it's a great day for the BBC.' I laughed but said, 'I'm still not commenting.'

Saturday 31 January

The reviews of last night were not as bad as they might have been. The *Mail* wittering on about the 'Campbellisation of politics'. Newcastle's *Journal* going off on one claiming I compared TB with Mandela, when I had done no such thing, Simon Hoggart [*Guardian*] saying it was a surprisingly nice event. I chatted to TB a couple of times, who wanted to calm everything down with the BBC, ditto Tessa. I could tell they were both worried I would keep the thing going, but in truth I wanted it to go away. It would be difficult though because they [the BBC] were determined to keep it going, and the rest of the media determined to help them generate a sense of backlash, and the Sundays would be driving that for all they could. I stayed over at David M's little place in the constituency. He was generally positive about the South Shields event but felt for the next ones, more anecdotage, and that was right. He thought I had a role to play in trying to be a kind of insider-outsider who knew all sides of the political game and who was able to stand up for politics and politicians, not just Labour. We chatted a bit about

TB–GB and the usual blah, but actually just as much about family and it was nice to be there with him.

I met up with Calum at Wigan, then did a photocall with Dave Edmundson re the 500 Mile Club, BFC's latest fundraising idea. I chatted to him and Barry Kilby re the idea of renaming BFC 'Burnley Football and Community Club'. Dave loved it, Barry a lot less sure. Good 0–0 draw. Alex called, said the United team were poor today, though they won 3–2, but the fans had been terrific, really making clear their absolute support for him. He said he was grateful for the help I had given, especially given everything else I had to deal with this week. The Magnier–JP McManus camp had written a letter to the board. They had put in ninety-nine questions about all sorts of things, transfer deals especially, including Jaap Stam and [Cristiano] Ronaldo [former and current Man Utd players], not just related to the horse row directly. He sounded exhausted with it all. He knew he had to get it resolved. David Gill had gone on MUTV last night and said it was damaging the club, and he knew that. But the fans and the players had been great today, he said. It was pretty clear they were not backing down. He would struggle in the claim for half of the stud fees. It was a lot of money but was it worth the grief?

Sunday 1 February

Reams and reams in the press post-Hutton, still all over the airwaves too, lots of 'backlash/whitewash' and goalposts being moved all over the place. I took a lot from the Burnley fans yesterday, who had been really good. 'You won, they lost and they can't fucking stand it,' one of them had said. I flicked through the papers and then went out on a long bike ride. I saw Ed Victor later, and was clear I did not want to commit to any kind of deal re books, that I wanted to get through the 'cashing in' timezone, whatever that was. I liked him, thought he was an interesting man, and capable of subtlety. He realised this was going to be complicated and long.

Monday 2 February

Cathy Gilman was round first thing to do letters re LRF. Later with Grace and Fiona to the Commons for the PLP farewell for me. Really nice do, good turnout and nice mood. Did a funny speech which also made a few serious points re where politics was going with all the shit surrounding it now. No doubt that of the two careers and the people in them, these were the people I had more respect for. Siobhan McDonagh [Labour MP for Mitcham and Morden] was organising them all to have pictures taken with me, which she wanted to make into an album. She and Margaret [McDonagh, former Labour general secretary, sister of Siobhan] just could not stop organising and they were brilliant at it. Margaret Beckett [Secretary of State for the Environment], Tessa, Hilary A, Tony Lloyd [MP for Manchester Central], Fraser Kemp [MP for Houghton and Washington East], Kim Howells, Rose Winterton [MP for Doncaster Central], Lorna Fitzsimons [MP for Rochdale], Adam Ingram [Armed Forces Minister], Clive Soley [former PLP chair], Jean Corston [PLP chair], Ann Taylor, Keith Bradley [MP for Manchester Withington], Phil Woolas [Commons deputy leader], Martin Linton [MP for Battersea], Alan Johnson [Higher Education Minister], Dale Campbell-Savours [MP for Workington], Alun Michael [MP for Cardiff South and Penarth], [Lord] John Evans [former MP] etc. etc., loads of them.

I said thanks to all of them in the speech but did special tribute to Bruce, as sound a citizen as exists, to Dennis Skinner, for being able to be both way to the left of me and TB, but totally dedicated to Labour winning everywhere, and having been the source of lots of good advice down the years, and to Peter Pike [MP for Burnley], for being a Burnley fan. I said I would always be around to help if people wanted me to. Really nice do. Martin Salter [MP for Reading West] presented me with a very funny spoof *Mail* front page of them apologising for getting everything wrong about everything, with a hilarious bit on the top on Dacre dismissing *Mein Kampf* as 'liberal tosh'. They'd had a whipround for a present but decided to give it all to LRF which was terrific.

Tuesday 3 February

Amid the beginnings of a backlash against the backlash, the big news was the Butler Inquiry into intelligence [on weapons of mass destruction], though of course the media were trying to undermine it from the word go. Judith Dawson [broadcaster], who was making the triathlon documentary, came round with the Channel 5 crew and we set off for [journalist] Catherine McLeod's boys' school in Hertford where I was doing a Q&A. Took ages to get there, with the traffic dire. Alex called on the way, getting really worried at the effect of the whole Magnier business on Cathy and the kids. He said it felt very nasty. Some of the United fans' groups were talking about organising protests for him at race meetings. AF really beginning to sound exasperated by it all. I said there is no way you can be focusing on the job with all this going on. Also, I had watched David Gill's MUTV interview with AF and though I know they are close, he was clearly reflecting a lot of pressure from the board to get this thing sorted. I did a couple of sessions at the school with different groups. Nice school, good head, and the kids seemed pretty bright. Quite enjoyed it. 'What do you really think of Bush?' plus top-up fees were the most asked area for questions.

Wednesday 4 February

Pulse 54. Meeting with Michael Lynch [CEO South Bank Centre] re the speech at the Royal Festival Hall, which was going to be one of the big events in the theatre tour. Nice guy. Aussie Republican campaigner. He was confident it would sell well as an event and he seemed to know what he was doing. I noticed he had the cuttings from South Shields. Pat and Sally both called to ask if I had any interest in standing for the NEC. I think until I work out whether I actually want to stay centrally involved, I had better say no. I was working on a piece on John Smith [late Labour Party leader] for Labour Party news, and writing up the interview with Gebrselassie for *The Times*. I was enjoying the sports stuff but couldn't see it as anything like a full-time thing. I signed off the Five press release on the stuff I was going to be doing with them. Again, I thought it would fill a gap, but of time rather than of purpose. Stuart Prebble [TV producer/director] came round with his team to discuss the documentary and asked what I envisaged for it. I wanted something that linked past, present and future, with the triathlon giving the sense of journey, and the charity getting a big hit out of it. Beyond that, I hadn't really thought that much about it.

They seemed a pretty good bunch. He said they would have to go over a lot of the obvious political stuff, but they didn't want that to dominate. They wanted something new and fresh and different and that would require me to be open and trusting. We went through the forward diary to go over the kind of event they might want to film. They would love to have been able to go to the first thing in the diary, today, which was the little TB reception in No. 10 for the people involved in the Hutton Inquiry. Scarlett on good form, said he felt very relieved it was all over and they could get back to doing their jobs. Catherine said she felt a big gap, because the whole thing had pretty much taken over her life for so long. Butler's inquiry into the intelligence issues was needless to say being rubbished by the media.

Thursday 5 February

Pulse 54, ran for an hour. The 45 minutes issue was still running out of the coverage of Butler and with TB in the debate, he was still to get closure. The media were determined to keep going in a way that would just park the idea we were cleared by Hutton and reframe the issues as best they could. I was barely reading the papers now, nor following things on the news, and could not be bothered listening to the *Today* programme. I spent a bit of time transcribing the diaries. God, I wish I had typed it all. This was going to take for ever. But maybe actually writing it, pen on paper, had been an important part of it. It was weird at times, felt like living in different time zones, dealing with issues of several years ago, then suddenly thinking, today, that it didn't feel like the right time of year, or mixing up thoughts about events then and now. In for a meeting at LRF, then to No. 10 to give Alison some work, and I stayed for [press officer] John Shields' farewell. Already, it felt very different when I went in there. I still sensed people looking to me for ideas and what have you, but I wasn't in the swim. Also, there will have been some, rightly, who just thought you were either in or out but there can't be a halfway house. It would take a bit of time to settle down, but I was surprised at how quickly I had got used to the idea of not really knowing what was going on, at the micro level, even if I also felt a bit discombobulated and drifting.

I went to play football at Talacre, which all ended terribly. I picked a bit of a fight with Iain Hutchison [surgeon, family friend] over Helena [Kennedy, his wife] putting Blunkett and Mugabe in the same breath.* We were arguing quite loudly when Tim, one of the kids who had been on our team, came over and thought Iain was just some bloke just having a go at me. 'Leave him alone, he just wants to have a night out and play football.' Then it escalated into a proper fight when Roland [Iain and Helena's son] piled in. I thought it best just to get away from it before it got totally out of control. I could tell Calum was really upset

---

* Blunkett's plan to tighten anti-terror laws prompted Baroness Kennedy to comment on TV that it was as if the Home Secretary 'takes his lessons in jurisprudence from Robert Mugabe'.

with me that I had allowed a situation to develop where his friend, Roland, felt compelled to get involved like that.

Iain came round later and wanted to talk about it, why it was important people could stay friends even if they disagreed about things. After he left, Fiona and I had a dreadful row, her needless to say failing to see any merit in any argument I put. Later I went round with Calum to the Kennedys and apologised, and we ended up having a very nice chat about it all. I think Iain understood some of the issues I was dealing with here, trying to make this transition. Fiona felt I had left and just had to stop feeling I had to defend the government the whole time. Our argument earlier had been pretty vicious. Trouble was we both had a point.

Friday 6 February

The media still raging away about 45 minutes and what TB did or didn't know, Howard pushing it all he could. *The Times* were saying Gavyn Davies intended to sue me for defamation. I went out on the bike, and came off pretty spectacularly in Swains Lane. I was pretty shaken up and went down to the playground on the Heath, where I knew they had first aid stuff and got patched up a bit. Calum and I set off to see Dad at the nursing home in Worksop. He was really weak and I think Calum was a bit shocked at how badly he had deteriorated. He still had his marbles and we could talk about this and that, but it was an effort, and his breathing wasn't great. He found it hard to keep his eyes open, and one of the lids seemed to be just about permanently closed. We popped into the pub on the way back to Mum's, and a couple of the regulars came over, saying they were sorry I had been through such a hard time recently.

Saturday 7 February

Rest day, pulse 55. I took Calum, Graeme and Jamie [Naish, nephews] in to see Dad who was really tired, though a bit stronger than yesterday. He was being given a bed bath which just underlined how frail he was, and again I think Calum was a bit shocked. Graeme was doing his usual trying to make everyone laugh, but I could tell Dad was just in need of rest. We set off for Burnley, the only little media flurry coming from a *Telegraph* splash on an interview with Tessa which they spun up as her attacking me over 'testosterone politics' and saying my 'gloating/triumphalism' post-Hutton had backfired. She called Fiona in a terrible state, really distressed, close to tears, said she had not said it, that she had made a few general observations about the political debate and she couldn't believe they had done it like this. It is kind of what I imagined and I can't say I was too bothered. I got Fiona to speak to her again and suggest she put something out to that effect. She put out a statement saying the article was a total misrepresentation, that she had always liked and respected me and I was someone who put Labour values into practice. It died down pretty quickly.

The 45-minute thing was still rumbling on. TB called, sounded quite down about things, really quite fed up for him. There had clearly not been the 'Hutton moment' we had hoped for, when vindication saw a change in mood. The media were determined not to give any sense we were cleared, and would just keep going as if nothing happened. He said even after all our experience of them, even he was quite shocked at how totally unreasonable they were. He said he didn't really know how to deal with them. 'Black is white.' He wanted me to think about what he could do to deal with it. Peter M and PG both called about the same thing. Philip felt No. 10 were not showing enough fight, not fighting back against the wave of criticism, which had such an obvious vested interest attached to it but which nobody was articulating. Peter M was due to do a speech on Thursday and was keen for me to put some thought into that too. It was a dire match and I got a bit of grief at half-time from some twat trying to tell me all the problems of the world were caused by 'the Pakis' and what was Blair gonna do about it? 'I'm not racist but' preceded virtually every statement, before I said I'm afraid he was racist and I couldn't be bothered listening any more.

On the drive back home, I started to think about how to put together a strategy that dealt with the fact that Tories, the right-wing media and the left media now all had an interest in keeping the debate focused on Iraq, and on us failing. The answer had to be back-rooted in domestic policy, and government making a real difference to people's lives. That was where we had to keep things focused, and expose the fact the Tory strategy remained one of avoiding policy. I did a two-page note and sent it through. I'd not heard TB so down for a long time. Then when I went upstairs to the fax I saw he had done a note too, echoing the things he had been saying earlier. 'We remain mired.' His problem was that the public just keep hearing the allegation about lying, and the findings of the Inquiry just get rubbished by all those who had expected something else. And they do not get any explanation as to why our opponents are acting as they do. He was worried though – this echoed what PG said – that there was not enough fight in the operation, and said that while my departure had helped in terms of relations with the press, there was no driving through of big message with confidence, and the lack of that was leaving people in the party feeling confused and bewildered, including supporters. He sounded like he had almost given up thinking a sensible debate on Iraq was ever possible. It meant he had to focus even more on economy, living standards, public services.

Sunday 8 February

Pulse 52, 90-minute run. I ran out by the canal, into a biting wind, which was hellish but coming back was wonderful, and for the first time in a while, I really felt like I was running. Did another note just for TB's eyes after David Hill called to discuss tomorrow's meeting on how to get out of the current feeling of malaise. It is going to be a hard slog and I was worried TB just felt the old answers would do. I don't think so. I think he needs a different sort of approach for himself and for the operation, and me not being there can be a help in that. He still goes over all these issues as though two sides are having a rational argument. Most of the media have gone beyond, they just see their job now as making his difficult. His communications has to be totally focused on getting through and round them, to the public, who have their own handle on this. David felt TB was just ground down at the moment.

We went out for dinner with the Kennedys [Ian and Andrea, personal friends] and I was quite shocked by Ian's view that TB was basically now just done for – shocked because he is normally very commonsensical and never just inhales a media line. He felt there had just come a point where the weight of the baggage and the problems became too heavy and the same person couldn't keep lifting it. It was the old 'tides come in, tides go out' thought. Ian also felt I should make a move to draw the sting from Gavyn Davies' apparent claim re defamation, possibly making clear I had not questioned his personal honesty or integrity.

Monday 9 February

Pulse 54, swam 1,500 metres in just over 40 minutes. Felt I could go a lot faster once I got my head around the length. The *Mail* ran some balls about my appearance at the FAC again, suggesting I hadn't been honest with them. Fraser [Kemp] called to say it was nonsense, the Tories on the committee trying to get something going, and no worry. A photographer came round to do publicity pictures for Five, and said he had done a 2 hours 30 triathlon, which was pretty impressive. Then a Danish journalist who was interviewing me pre my trip there. Helle [Thorning-Schmidt, MEP and wife of Stephen Kinnock, Neil and Glenys's son] had said he (the journalist) was fine, but he was obsessed with spin and so I found myself coming out with the same old same old, all a bit tedious. A rash of calls from the media because John Humphrys had had a go in the *Radio Times*. Said nothing.

Tuesday 10 February

Humphrys's attack got a bit of play. I was also checking out with lawyers how to play the Gavyn Davies defamation claim if it came to anything, and with Anji [Hunter, special advisor] to check with Sue Nye whether there was anything in it at all. Wendy Bailey and the Royal Festival Hall were putting together a media plan to promote the event there. I suspected it was going to take a fair bit to fill it out, but they seemed confident. A meeting with the Manchester Chamber of Commerce crowd to plan the event I was doing for them. All women, good crowd, bit more energy than most. They wanted a basic funny after-dinner speech with the odd serious point thrown in.

Philip filled me in on the meetings in No. 10 post the flurry of notes. He said it was fine, but very different without me, and he was worried there wasn't enough muscle in there to see things followed through within the system. He was worried at how down TB seemed to be. I think he had genuinely felt on seeing the clarity with which Hutton came to his conclusion, that it would provide closure. In fact, it had made things worse in terms of the media mood around TB and Iraq. TB called later, said, 'It is incredible, these are people who said Hutton was a model of his kind when he was grilling us and giving them story after story to make us look dreadful; then when he comes out and says what actually happened, he is a silly old establishment fart taking everything down at dictation speech from you and me. It is fucking incredible the way they have moved the goalposts on virtually everything.' True, but the only way through now was to get back to focusing on a policy agenda that actually made a difference to people.

Ed Victor called, said Gail seemed to think Greg Dyke had signed up with Harper Collins, and that being so, there was no way that I could. I didn't see the logic but in any event, as Ed said to her, I hadn't signed up to do anything. This whole thing was going to be incredibly slow. I had a call from John Lloyd [*FT* journalist] who was doing a book on the press, and whose views matched my own in some respects, re their role in politics. I was happy enough to help him, but it was interesting how quickly I had moved from a position of feeling all this mattered so much, to one where I didn't want to have much to do with it.

Wednesday 11 February

Good swim session. Dad was supposed to see the consultant but wasn't well enough to travel. Mum sounded very down about it all, like we were in last lap territory. I was working on the football sections of my *Times* series (re greatest sportsmen of all time) and bounced a few thoughts off Alex, who was very pro-Puskas and Di Stefano. I was beginning to feel a bit bombarded with all the speech offers coming in, and felt it might be best to do a few and see if I actually enjoyed it or not before committing to too many down the track. I was definitely up for doing the Murdoch conference in Mexico. Les [Hinton] said they were pretty much up for me saying whatever I felt about the media and not holding back. I had a chat with Rebekah who said she felt No. 10 was weakened without me and was it too late to go back? She was under orders from Murdoch to get right behind the Olympic bid and wanted some ideas on that. I was hoping to get Murdoch as one of my interviewees for the Five interviews I was doing. Mark Bennett and Mark Lucas [Labour film-maker] came round to get some pictures to put into a short film to trail my Festival Hall event. It was nice seeing them, and getting a reminder of that amazing enthusiasm that Labour people had when they were in a kind of campaign/deadline mode.

Thursday 12 February

Pretty wacky start to the day's media programme to promote the RFH event. BBC London with Danny Baker [radio show host], whose studio is done out in all manner of weird and wonderful stuff and who does the interview standing up behind his desk, blaring out the questions. Nice guy though. Not too heavy or political, probed a bit on drink and madness, what TB was like, all fairly straightforward. Also there a very odd but charming American woman who said she was a

Burnley fan and was on some kind of sponsored weight loss to raise money for the club. She seemed genuine enough, certainly knew what was what player wise. Did LBC by phone, again very straightforward, Nick Ferrari [breakfast show presenter] plus phone-in, chatted with Nick about his dad and brother, who were at the *Mirror* when I was there. Then left for XFM breakfast show with Christian O'Connell, again fairly straightforward and easy. I was beginning to understand better why TB didn't much like when he did interview after interview on the same subject. No matter how hard you tried, it wasn't always easy to say the same thing again and again and make it sound interesting every time. To the Festival Hall, who told me they had sold 800 tickets so far, so they were confident it would sell out. Met Stuart Prebble and Judith Dawson to go over filming opportunities for the planned documentary.

Then the *Ham and High* [*Hampstead and Highgate Express*] and the young guy interviewing me had never heard of [West Indian cricketer] Gary Sobers, which stunned me. He hadn't done much research and I was getting pretty irritated by the whole thing. The guy from 'What's On?' [listings magazine] was altogether more switched on and I felt a bit more engaged by it all. Then *South London Press*, a very nice guy called Cedric with a lovely smiley photographer who kept chipping in with views that made it very clear she was a supporter. A few more, then pictures for the locals and for the paper from Denmark, then home to what must have been the longest answering machine message I had ever heard – it must have been five minutes or more – Alex on my piece on the greatest ever footballers. He went over the various factors that you'd have to put in the mix, at one point comparing the dribbling skills of Pelé and Maradona. He would take a look at Cruyff, Neeskens, Muller but he reckoned Di Stefano was probably the best he ever saw. 'Anyway, I'm just rambling now,' he said, but it was all good stuff. Mark Lucas was round when I was listening to it. 'This is like getting a lesson on the economy from the Governor of the Bank of England,' he said.

I was speaking to the Ham and High Labour Party at Queen's Crescent. Good turnout but a pretty tired bunch and lots of cases of the left inhaling the right's propaganda. The mood wasn't hostile so much as sour. A few hecklers on Iraq, and one or two of the upper-middle-class Trot types that I really can't stomach. Really miserable, some of them.

They clearly saw TB as the problem, and that his going would solve all problems. The idea that he had helped create the strong position in the first place sort of passed them by. Iraq was the poison in the debate with tuition fees not far behind. I won some of them round but not many. If these were the local foot soldiers then we didn't stand much of a chance. Too old, too miserable, too prone to believe the worst. New blood most definitely needed. Mick Farrant [local party organiser] said it was the biggest turnout they'd had for a meeting, and there were definitely some good people there, but they didn't strike me as strong on the campaign capability front.

Friday 13 February

Had the Five film people around a good part of the day. First reading at Gospel Oak school. Swimming lesson with Claire and Sam at LA Fitness. Not easy. Not yet feeling I have even mastered the basics. Then a spinning class, which was really good. At the end I felt absolutely shagged out. News from RFH was pretty good, tickets really shifting now and they were pretty sure it was going to sell out. Working on diaries but I couldn't believe how many interruptions there were the whole time, emails and calls and what have you, and without the shield of someone there the whole time sifting them, it was all a bit irritating.

Sunday 15 February

Pulse 52, good long run on the Heath. Went out to the Barbican, Mozart Requiem, then out with David M and Louise for dinner. David said he had been wondering when watching me at South Shields why I had never done what he and the others had done in going for a seat, because it was so clear I was higher quality politics wise than virtually anyone else. I said I felt I had been a round peg in a round hole doing the job I had done, and the way I felt now I needed time out from all of it. I actually hated going near SW1 at the moment and was slightly dreading getting drawn in even more as the election neared. He felt TB was in major drifting mode. Also that GB was inevitably going to be next leader but it might not be the right thing.

Monday 16 February

Up at 5.30 and off to the Midlands for a bike session with Steve [Loraine]. Kate Garvey called to say so far as she could ascertain from Sue Nye, Gavyn D was serious about mounting a case for defamation. Fiona's view was that if he did, I would have to say the only way I could afford to deal with it would be to do a book deal now, and that would be bad news for GB, which might make Davies think again. Good bike session, fairly hilly in parts, 37k in 1 hr 37, legs a bit jelly like at the end but good advice from Steve re gear changes, style on hills etc. Did a phone interview with the *Manchester Evening News* to promote the event up there, a bit ratty. With Steve to the pool at Tamworth, good session and felt technique improving a bit.

Tuesday 17 February

John Lloyd came round to talk about his book on the press, which was going to be based on the argument in his recent article, very negative about the media's role in political debate. He was one of the few people in the media prepared to take on the argument in a serious way. He and I were not that far apart in terms of our basic view of what was going on. He was appalled at the general decline in standards. TB called halfway though and said inter alia that if John wanted to talk to him, he would give some interesting background on the way they now operated vis-à-vis him and other top-flight politicians. TB felt I should respond to the Richard Eyre article in *The Guardian*, preferably without it becoming big news, but he felt this was the way these myths took hold, because we had stopped challenging them.* We also discussed the Gavyn Davies threat and TB felt there was a case for me writing to him and making clear there was certainly no intention to suggest he lied.

Re the general scene, he felt there was a definition problem and the question was whether it was recoverable. He felt it was. He did not feel people wanted the Tories back. He also felt that those who used them knew there had been improvements in public services. He sounded at various points up, at other points down. He felt I should try to find ways of being more engaged, but I knew in myself I had to do it full on or not at all. At the moment, I was working around the edges and it wasn't great for anyone. He knew that lack of WMD was a real problem for us, but said also that part of our problem was simply the baggage that goes with time in power. I drafted a letter to Gavyn but

* Theatre and film director Eyre, a former BBC governor, wrote in *The Guardian* that 'Campbell bullied and taunted the BBC' during the Iraq War, arguing that Greg Dyke and David Kelly were martyrs and the government and Andrew Gilligan 'villains'.

then read it to Charlie Falconer, who was en passant very nice about my *Times* column, and to Gavin [Millar, QC, Fiona's brother.] Both felt that it would be a mistake to send it. Gavin felt strongly I should do nothing unless or until they came for me. Charlie said he had heard from several people that Gavyn was blaming anyone but himself, and especially me, and he could not see how he had done anything wrong. The Festival Hall sales were going well, and the RFH put out a line that tickets were going faster than for Woody Allen [the film director/actor played there with his New Orleans Jazz Band]! I did Steve Wright's [BBC Radio 2] show on the way to a couple of Manchester interviews to promote 16 March ('An Audience With'). Got word that Lance Armstrong would see me on Monday for the *Times* series, so I started to think about the best approach for that. Exciting, and the excitement shared by the boys.

Wednesday 18 February

Up early working on speeches for Denmark, then to the gym to do some triathlon photos. Did a spinning session while I was there, which really got the heart pumping. Shagged out. Festival Hall confident of sell out. Sales in Birmingham slow and the local papers seemed to be on for negative coverage. I got Gail to send me round Lance Armstrong books and was reading up on him. Genuinely looking forward to it. Definitely in the top three of sportsmen I wanted to get for the series. Got an absurd email from Tess Alps re the WACL [Women in Advertising and Communications] dinner in May. She said that because of the 'pain and sensitivity' at the BBC, and because there were some BBC people among their clients, it might not be appropriate for me to speak as advertised. Then Deborah Mattinson [pollster] got involved and agreed with me that it was an absurd decision. Tess said she took it alone. I emailed saying how absurd it was, and did she think it was inappropriate that I did a BBC interview yesterday and they asked me on their programmes the whole time? Eventually I settled for a donation to the charity but it didn't half show how silly people got about all this.

I worked with Bradders on a response to the Eyre article but David shared my doubts about doing it. Tom Baldwin called re *Private Eye* on some of Dacre's private files being leaked. 'It is so nice to see your enemies floating down the river,' he said. Dick Caborn came round. Wants me to take over the Football Foundation. I love Dick dearly but I'm not sure I need this right now. The politics of it all sounded very confused, because the power structures in football are so confused. It sounded good on one level, and grassroots sport is definitely worth getting involved in, but the combination of Premier League, FA and the government on the edge of it didn't feel great. Dick wanted me to inject a sense of real hard strategy into the whole thing. I said I would think about it and meet the decision makers. Dick felt eventually I should aim to run UK Sport. He is such an enthusiast and so obviously loves his job and is determined to use it to make a difference. He said whatever some people thought about me, nobody questioned my ability or my credibility in sport and football would like the idea of a big hitter getting involved in the grassroots. We had a really good natter, and I sensed if he got the backing he needed he could drive through a good overall sports strategy. We had a bit of a reminisce about Maxwell and the Mandela concert, and wondered if the money ever got paid. [When at the *Mirror*, Campbell had at Caborn's behest persuaded Robert Maxwell to sponsor the 1990 Nelson Mandela tribute concert at Wembley Stadium.]

Thursday 19 February
Up for a run then we set off for Copenhagen. First time I had taken the whole family on a speech trip, and it would be great to see Helle. Staying at a hotel linked to the Danish Sports Institute, and it had a superb pool which was designed like a running track, 100 metres per lap, so brilliant for swim training.

Friday 20 February
Pulse 52, 1,500m swim. Loved the pool. Felt like it was meant for horses rather than humans, but it was great for training to be able to swim round and round, into a good rhythm, without the usual turns at the end of every length. Helle and her fixer Simon Pihl Sørensen [strategist] came round. We got the kids sorted then I did a couple of Danish interviews and got very ratty with one of them, going on endlessly re 45 minutes and whether I thought it was battlefield or strategic weapons. The UK Ambassador [Sir Nicholas Browne] came round, having said he wanted to go with me to the event I was speaking at, where the audience came mainly from trade unions. The speech went fine, pretty strong modernising message and the Q&A was OK. They were not quite as old Labour as Neil [Kinnock] had suggested

February '04: AC pondering bids from the world of sport

they would be, though one or two were pretty antsy. Neil had been announced as the new head of the British Council and I sensed Steve was maybe feeling he would never escape his dad's shadow, never just get established in his own right.

Then to the event organised by some of the main papers, packed out, a lot less on Iraq than I thought there would be, loads on spin but they pretty much bought my line that they would do well to resist becoming like the UK media. Helle was looking great and though clearly there were one or two image problems caused by the way she was covered, I got the sense they took her seriously and that she was making progress. We had dinner with her and Steve and went over how they would live if she really made it to the top. She was going to go for a seat back in Denmark rather than the European Parliament and was already being seen as a possible leader. She definitely had something a bit special and was bang on the New Labour pitch politics wise. The kids were really enjoying themselves and Grace loved seeing Johanna and Camilla [Helle and Steve's children] again.

Saturday 21 February

Big coverage for the speech yesterday, several news stories, *Berlingske* newspaper's magazine front cover, and Helle said it was fair to positive. There was a trail for a Sunday paper editorial saying my speech should be required reading for young journalists. Clearly the centre of gravity in the media here is very very different to the UK and they do not want their own media going like ours. It was interesting how in several of the EU countries, not least France and Germany, the worries about the UK-US media trends were shared not just by the politicians but by the journalists as well, at least a fair few of them. Jon Sopel [BBC reporter] was in Copenhagen seeing an old friend and we met up with him to find a pub to watch Man U v Leeds, then out skating, then to see Jon's friends in a very nice part of town, before dinner and home. The kids were loving the sporty theme to the hotel. Helle was really fixed on a big career for herself. When the kids were skating around she asked me about the kind of team we built for TB, and what all the various needs of a campaign were. Steve seemed totally up for her going for Danish politics, but he was also clear he couldn't imagine living there all the time. Fiona said it must be hard for him, first of all people knowing him as son of, and if Helle gets into a big role, as everyone seems to think she will, as husband of.

But Steve seems to have a pretty good temperament for it all. They both felt I came out well from the last few days, but Steve made the point the media would never let go of the idea we had been as much in the wrong as the Beeb. We talked a bit about what it had been like when his dad was getting monstered by the media. He said it probably got to him more than he let on, but he and Rachel were both conscious of the need not to add to their problems in a way. I sometimes felt ours had done the same, but maybe it got to them more than I realised when I was under the cosh. Mum was the only one who just kept coming straight out with it, that it made her ill.

Sunday 22 February

For the third day running, a really long swim, then off to the airport, goodbye to the family and off to Barcelona. I had been reading up over the weekend, books and cuttings, and was really looking forward to meeting Lance Armstrong. I got the kids to suggest a few questions too, e.g. Rory saying ask him if he is able to endure more pain than the others. He was a real one-off. I landed in Spain and there were a couple of messages from him making sure I knew where I was going and when etc. He sounded very friendly, not at all like the image, and there was a real humour to the way he spoke too. We spoke later and he really laid into David Walsh, the *Sunday Times* guy [sports writer]. Mark Neale [personal friend] had fixed me a local driver/fixer, Dany Vivez, who had worked with Mark on films and was thrilled to be involved. TB called, sounded a bit fed up. He said the media was not that bad at the moment, but only by comparison with what we normally got. By comparison with the press in those countries with a sane media, it was still pretty awful. He said the problem was it had become like the elephant in the room, everyone knew the problem it was but everyone was too busy doing other stuff. He said he wanted me to keep doing notes on the domestic agenda, and I worked on something, but I was conscious of not being as plugged in as I used to be, partly because I didn't want to be.

Monday 23 February

They had sold almost 2,000 tickets for my 'Audience With' at the Festival Hall, which was pretty good, and they said after the media blitz tickets had gone faster than they had expected. We were thinking about who to get as a chair for it, maybe Ross Kemp [Labour-supporting actor]. They also wanted to talk about security because there was already stuff on the internet about demos and disruption. Dany and I drove to Girona Airport to collect John Cassidy, the *Times* photographer, and then headed to Lance's place. I could see why he wanted to live out here, not just the scenery, but some quality hills. Lance called while I was getting a haircut to check we were on time and also to say he preferred to do the chat first, then the pictures. We had a quick bite to eat over the road from his apartment then by 2.15 we were in there. We were greeted by Sheryl Crow [Armstrong's girlfriend, singer], who was really friendly and chatty, said she liked my haircut, but after a while she left us to it. Not that much small talk, straight in.

I liked him. Straight talking, really looked you in the eye. Much leaner than I expected, but he had a real presence. He was a good talker, terrific on the whole Tour de France thing [consecutive five-time winner] and what it meant to him, pretty passionate on the drugs allegations, and even though he must have been asked about doping hundreds of times, he didn't sound formulaic; interesting on politics, religion, Bush, keen to know about TB. Even a few minutes in, I knew it would be a good piece. I think it maybe helped that he didn't really see me as a journalist, kept bringing the chat back to politics and other stuff. We talked for ages, to the point I was worried I would have too much and have to ditch loads of good stuff, before I got John in to do the pictures, and though he didn't exactly enjoy it, again he was friendly enough with John and Dany and posed for some decent shots. The best snaps were in the little chapel kind of thing that was next to the main sitting room, with a picture of Christ on the cross. I could tell John was happy with it the moment he took it.

He, Sheryl and I had a cup of coffee and some fancy chocolate biscuits – though I noticed he only played around with one, didn't eat it – a chat in the kitchen and they were fascinated to know how TB had managed to develop the kind of relationship he had with Bush, having been so close to Clinton. They were keener on Bill than GWB. He knew a bit about the Hutton thing, knew I had been in the news a lot recently, and I think when asking about that, maybe thinking a bit about himself and cycling some of the storms he went through. They were grilling me about Clinton and Lewinsky* too and how he

---

* Monica Lewinsky, former White House intern with whom Clinton had what he described as an 'inappropriate relationship'.

got through all that and came out smelling of roses. He was majorly against the Iraq war, and taking the piss re WMD, came back to it three or four times. She was wearing a pair of jeans that looked like they had been handstitched up the side, and a low-cut blouse, and the whole effect was really sexy. She had a lovely speaking voice, drawly but also quite refined and soft. She had been working next door earlier for part of the time we were talking and all you could hear was occasional guitar, occasional words, and then she would settle on a line and seem to play it again and again. But they were both very friendly and approachable.

I sensed he was much more left-wing, in US terms, than people imagined. He clearly had the Texan thing with Bush, but was politically in a very different place, while she was very traditional music world Democrat. His kids meant a lot to him, that was clear enough, but his relationship with their mum [ex-wife Kristin Richard], and his mother-in-law, had clearly gone pretty badly wrong. It was hard to tell if this one would last, given who and what they were, but they seemed a genuine enough couple. They loved the story I told them about the woman on the treadmill in Waco who wanted me to join the Bush email prayer group. He was not big into God, far from it. He was mildly obsessed with David Walsh, said he was one of the few people in the world he really hated, because he just pursued this vendetta against him, when he was the most drug-tested athlete in the world. He was really fed up with him following him around all over the place.

John Cassidy was thrilled with the pictures, said he had more than enough but then afterwards he got some more when Lance took us down to his bike shed, where he told us the stories behind the bikes in there and then gave me one of his Tour de France winning shoes to auction for Leukaemia Research. It was raining by now and we were getting worried about getting back to the airport, but he seemed keen to keep on talking and was also showing me a few tips on how to use a BlackBerry. He said we ought to do some cancer stuff together and also if ever I wanted to go for a ride, he would slow down for me! Dany took us to the airport, where I had my first Ryanair experience, which wasn't great, but I managed to listen to and transcribe most of the interview on the plane. It was even stronger second time around. Some great stuff in there, especially his line that losing was the same thing as dying, that losing the Tour this year would be the same as if he had been killed by cancer. Sounded like he meant it. He must have talked about the cancer thing hundreds of times but there was a passion and a humanity there that I had only really felt in his books, not in the interviews he had done. I felt he opened up a lot.

On the drugs stuff, I don't know if I could have pushed him harder, but I felt he had all the answers off pat anyway. What was compelling was the emotion in there, how he talked about what it was like to be so tested, and so the one people wanted to bring down. Cassidy and Dany were both surprised what he was like, far more human, friendlier than they expected. I got home and worked away till 2 a.m. to get it cracked while it was all still fresh in my mind. I loved his line that 'dying and losing – they're the same thing'! Wow. I wondered if a straight Q&A might actually work better, but that would set a precedent and not all the interviews would be so strong. Also, it would kind of defeat the point re it being sportsmen and women talking more broadly about what makes certain people great not just very good.

Tuesday 24 February

I honed the Lance interview, then sent it through to Keith Blackmore. Half an hour later, he called, said he liked it a lot, found it breathtaking at points, one of the best sportsmen interviews he had ever read. I sent it to Lance to make sure he was happy with the way the quotes were used, given some of them came from when we were just chatting, rather than the formal sit-down interview. He made a couple of factual changes and that was that. He also agreed to do another interview for the Five series I was doing, and said he would put in a word with Tiger Woods.

Wednesday 25 February

Email from Lance saying he had thought about whether he should be quoted using the 'f' word, but on reflection he felt fine because it showed he felt strongly. Keith Blackmore and Tim Rice [sports executive] both came on after I filed and said it was as good an interview as they had read. Keith was totally raving about it, said he was really going to give it a huge show. He had also got Robert Thomson [*Times* editor] interested and engaged on account of the fact he was amazed Lance lived with Sheryl Crow! Keith was hoping to get all 4,000 words in with the chapel/Jesus picture on the front. TB had a big speech coming up for the conference in Inverness and Matthew Taylor sent me through the draft asking for a few ideas, but I was struggling to get enthused. Mark Malloch Brown [diplomat] called from the UN asking if I could go to New York to do a week analysing the UNDP [United Nations Development Programme] and then advising them on a comms strategy. I quite fancied it but it would be hard to fit in at one go. I did the James Whale show on LBC to plug the theatre tour and I didn't like him at first. The whole thing felt a bit shambolic and he was far too deep into conspiracy theories, and big on Iraq. But he grew on me as we went on and I ended up staying longer than planned.

Thursday 26 February

Pulse 54, 45-minute run. Out to head to the M25 and meet up with Nick Faldo's PR. We met at a hotel just off the motorway, collected milk for Faldo on the way to his house, a really nice place overlooking the grounds of Windsor Castle. Very plush without being over the top. Found him a lot more relaxed and funnier than I thought he would be; from the word go, when he took the milk, said thanks, 'You've bought the milk, now fuck off.' Easy to talk to and even though some of the stories felt like he had told them dozens of times, he was a good talker and lively and engaging. We did the pictures outside and he showed me a few tips. Long-term he had a lot of business interests, plus broadcasting, but also desperate to be captain of the Ryder Cup team. I sensed that he was fine with the business stuff, made shedloads of money, but getting back into the game via the Ryder Cup captaincy would wipe out any of it. I sensed that was probably the main reason he was doing the interview. Wouldn't harm him I guess to be in a *Times* series on the greatest of all time. He was dressed all in black, and I sensed his wife had decided how he would look. He was a little bit self-obsessed but told his story well and I liked him more than I had anticipated.

The main news when I got home was Clare Short [former Labour minister] claiming she had seen transcripts of bugged conversations involving Kofi Annan.* TB was doing a press conference where he went for her as being irresponsible. Philip was trying to get me engaged in the Inverness speech but I was not really getting into it, other than at the margins, reading the drafts, feeding in a few thoughts but not really getting the towel round the head. To be fair though, he sent over a brilliant note about what TB needs to do with the speech. It was one

---

* Clare Short claimed reading transcripts of conversations obtained by British spies listening into the UN Secretary-General's office during the run-up to the Iraq War.

of Philip's best, in terms of analysing the problem and making a few suggestions. He reckoned there are several 'layers of public opinion'. One, the top layer, where people are drawing a general conclusion somewhere between disappointment with us and real deep wariness about the Tories coming back. Two, where the big issues play out – economy which people think is strong but do not want to credit us; public services which people feel are better locally but worse generally; and the populist issues which damage us.

Next, the layer with what he called 'the hidden issue of the war' – not that it felt very hidden to me, but his point was it was not always front of mind or top of agenda but it was there, always troubling and difficult. And then the final layer was what he called 'deep drivers', namely trust (lack of – because of high cynicism); connection (lack of – because people think we do not listen); and purpose (lack of – because people are not sure what we stand for.) His idea for Inverness was to take all of those points, and turn them. Easier said than done, and it will take time, but he said if TB could aim just to take on one or two at this stage, it would begin the fightback properly. He felt the best areas for immediate action were economy, and purpose/values. He said we needed a 'fighting and confident speech', and I knew where that was heading. 'You'll have to write it.' I said I am pleased that even though I feel sadly lacking in fight and confidence, I remain the go-to man for fight and confidence.

Friday 27 February

Pulse 55. Went to LA Fitness, started in the pool, in 15 minutes when suddenly they announced all out for an aqua aerobics class. I did a bit of bike and treadmill instead. Lunch with Ed Balls at Livebait. We always circled a bit with each other at first, made not very convincing effort at small talk but were actually better when we got straight down to the tricky stuff. I could never really work out whether he wanted a good relationship or not. I had seen so many times a near contempt for TB but with me he was very different. He talked a good game re the need to get them working together better though often TB's view was that Ed was the problem between them because of the nature of the advice he gave. He indicated that GB accepted TB would go at a time of his choosing and they wanted to work for a smooth transition 'some time after the election'. I said I always felt GB's best interests were served by him being close in. Division between them was lethal.

He said they knew that and there would be no pressure on TB to go early. He confirmed he was going for Wakefield [parliamentary constituency], he felt the time was right to get a seat for himself, not just be the GB guy. He said he had always assumed I would do it at some stage. Me too, I said, but right now I was pretty sick of politics. I admitted that the idea of being brought back in to try to sort TB–GB didn't appeal. 'Not surprised,' he said.

We reminisced a bit re the whole story of the euro, those crazy days, and basically agreed that however badly the route had been taken we got to the right position. He felt if we had pushed for it, as at times TB wanted to, we would have been in a political disaster area by now. He said the No. 10 operation had weakened since I left, that he had always known how to get into No. 10 to resolve an argument or get things moving but it was all less clear now. There were lots of people but few who could decide or get others to. He was very down on the Department of Health, felt the money was going in but there were real problems in there not being addressed. We nattered about Clare [Short] and wondered what more havoc she could wreak. He was on good form, more likeable in a way. I know TB was very down on him just now, felt he was the one who fed the worst stuff into GB's mind, but I sensed a real desire to get things on a better footing, maybe because he felt TB was nearing the end. It was interesting how a little bit of distance was making me look at people in a slightly different light.

We discussed what if anything I should do for the next election and he felt the question was getting the right balance between public and private. I felt I would be able to do a different kind of job, helping and advising, but also be out there publicly. I said it was interesting how things that really seemed to matter a lot when you were inside the bubble seemed to matter a lot less when out. He said if I did come back for the campaign, he for one would welcome it and more importantly so would GB. I told him about the rather odd message I got from GB's secretary on the day I resigned. He laughed, said, 'He's not great at the touchy feely is he?' But he said GB had said just yesterday he was worried the operation had weakened since I went, so he had no doubt he would be happy if I went back. A bit of football, actually quite a lot of football talk, then I headed home. I sensed his Norwich supporter thing was real, though perhaps not quite as mad as my Burnley thing. Fiona was out at the ballet later. Mark Lucas and Mark Bennett came round and showed me the latest edition of the film to trail my theatre events. They'd done a terrific job.

Saturday 28 February

Clare Short was now saying that [Hans] Blix [chairman, Weapons of Mass Destruction Committee] was bugged by us too. *The Times* did a terrific job on the Lance piece, the main picture was great, and I got a stack of messages, including one from Roger Alton [editor, *The Observer*] saying it was one of the best things he'd read in ages and why didn't I work with them? Did an hour on the bike then with Calum to Millwall v Burnley. Met up with Dave Edmundson to plan the fundraiser I'd agreed to do for the club. Dave had the idea of raffling sponsorship for fifty quid a head. Nice guy, really good with Calum. We went round to the away end. Dire match (Millwall 2, Burnley 0) and the racism was revolting, including by some of our lot, but the really bad stuff was aimed at Mo Camara [Guinea-born Burnley defender], just about every time he got the ball. It was back to the bad old days stuff, and pretty obvious where it was being directed. Really felt depressed about it. Glad to get away from there.

Fiona and I went out for dinner at Neil and Glenys's. Neil was in a bit of a rage, not helped when I said that I thought Steve was worried he would never be able to escape his shadow. He also seemed worried about the fact Helle wanted to head back to Denmark, felt there was no way Steve would want to live there the whole time. Glenys [Member of European Parliament, Labour International Development spokesperson in the EU] very down on TB's Africa Commission, perhaps felt she should have been on it, but felt TB didn't spend as much time listening to the right people as he needed to. It was all a bit depressing all in all. When I was on a downer, I tended to shut up and sit in the corner. When Neil was on a downer, he just raged against the world. So it was me in the corner shutting down, him in a bit of a rage, Fiona and Glenys chatting away as best they could.

Sunday 29 February

I spoke to *The Times* about doing a piece on the racist undertones at Millwall and the way they went for Mo Camara. I drafted something and ran it by Dave Edmundson. He said they had raised complaints after the (previous) FA Cup game. He was OK re the content but said the club would probably keep distant from it. I said there were one or two of our people at it but it was basically the Millwall lot. I wondered about suggesting to Stan he make Mo Camara captain for the Preston game and maybe get a couple of Asian mascots. I called him and we discussed it. He said he had told Theo Paphitis [Millwall chairman] after the Cup game that it had been pretty awful. He felt he should maybe have made a proper complaint but in the end didn't. He said Mo C was pretty distraught after the game. I finished the *Times* piece, felt it was strong. Then out for a run before going to see *Cheaper by the Dozen* with Grace. Loved it. Really soppy comedy and a couple of father–kid bits that moved me to tears. Really funny too, and uplifting in a way.

TB called re the Lance piece, said he thought it was awesome. What a guy he said. He said he had been thinking about me a lot, imagining the scale of my explosions re Clare. I said I did warn you. He said yes, I know, but maybe it is better to have someone like her as your main enemy because she is so clearly just bitter about things. Nobody really takes her seriously, he said. So why had he kept her in the Cabinet for so long? Oh, he said, I have my little ways. He was pretty chipper about things. Economy strong, public services moving in the right direction, felt if we could just get a bit of mood purchase and get Iraq in a better place things would be fine. He was pleased, as was I, that Fiona had met up with CB and that they seemed to get on OK. He said we should try to get the four of us together because it was so pointless people ending up feeling hurt and bitter. He asked how Fiona was. I said we were getting on better on one level, and had had a good time in Denmark, but the undercurrents were still there and unlikely to disappear quickly. I think she had felt I would just vanish from the political scene once we left No. 10, and had been surprised how much of my time was still going on Labour and on him.

I filled him in on the Balls lunch. He said GB was definitely trying harder but it was still tough. He thought it was a good sign that Balls was reaching out to me, and trying to see the extent to which I would come back in, felt he would not have done that without GB's say so. He said Scotland had been interesting because the party had clearly wanted him to go for Clare. He said he had some advice for my Festival Hall event – keep it light and humorous, be charming, don't look like you are going to hit someone. He said there was clearly a lot of interest and it would be good to take people by surprise, not let them do the caricature. You want the people who turn up because they like you to have their views confirmed and you want the ones who turn up because they don't like you to have their own views challenged.

Monday 1 March

Pulse 50. 1,700m swim session. Working at home on the script for the Festival Hall. Wendy called to say it had now totally sold out, and the RFH were saying it was the best response to a speech event they could recall. I got there after 2 and it was kind of odd, seeing all the posters of the people who normally perform there. Musicians in the main, and much more conventional performers. Ross Kemp came down to do the sound check. Nice guy and good of him to chair it. He said he felt nervous for me. It's a lot of people, and a lot of them will be hoping to have a go. I said I didn't feel nervous. Just a bit bemused. South Shields – which was one of a very few, if not the only seat always to have been Labour, had been broadly friendly, whereas a London crowd would have a lot of the antis out. Wendy was fretting and fussing a bit too much around me but basically being nice and helpful. We had the idea of giving out signed T-shirts and free tickets for future events for good questions. Fiona and the kids arrived about an hour or so before and Grace was enjoying the whole backstage thing. There were quite a few visitors in the final build-up, and I felt more nervous now, hearing the audience arriving on the sound feed. Ross and I were taken to the side of the stage. He introduced the film which went down really well. It was a snappy three-minute thing with lots of highlights from time with TB. Simon and Garfunkel singing 'You Can Call Me Al' as the soundtrack and a huge cheer for the JP punch, which came as S and G were talking about incidents and accidents.*

The format was the same as South Shields, me speaking for the first half, then Q&A after an interval. Nice welcome. I swallowed a few lines and was gabbling at times but the stories went down well, lots of laughter, then into a more serious analysis re the relationship between politics and media and then half-time. As we walked off, Ross said, 'They're eating out of your hands, mate.' I felt it had gone well. The film had made a difference in settling things down and getting them in the right place. The Q&A was fine. There hadn't been any heckling in the first half. One woman stormed out re Iraq and Grace said afterwards she had been really scared. The boys were sitting behind Rod Liddle [journalist]. Rory said he abused him roundly. Best laugh of the night came when I was asked where I was when JP punched the bloke on election manifesto day in 2001 and I did a long, detailed and funny answer.

---

* John Prescott's bruising encounter with a protestor who threw an egg at him in Rhyl, north Wales.

One or two questions re Clare which I used to broaden out and stress the difference with Robin Cook in terms of how they handled the Iraq issue. Tuition fees. Someone raised my Millwall article which had caused a bit of a furore. Paphitis, possibly helped by Liddle [Millwall supporter], had put out something saying it was bollocks, I was a prawn sandwich [hospitality] merchant and asked for his helicopter once to get to a match! I rubbished it with a couple of hacks during the day and also got a question raised on it. When Iraq, Hutton and Kelly came up, I tried to be more reflective. Good range of questions – hunting, fees, Iraq, BFC, all over the place. The heckler yelled out, 'Lying scumbag' but it didn't really catch on. Ross was pretty heavy in the chair, didn't let people go on too long. I felt I handled it all better than at South Shields.

The size of the audience was not a problem. I was maybe a bit too cagey and could have opened up more but that was because I kept seeing media people in there. Spotted Michael Portillo [former Tory minister] at one point. Anji said that she was impressed, and Portillo had told her he was. She felt if I had stayed on at the end a bit longer, there would have been a standing ovation. She felt there was a real warmth there and the hacks would have been taken aback. I probably overdid the *Mail* stuff. Afterwards there was a little Labour Party private reception and I spoke re LRF [charity], did a few warm words and again seemed fine. Kids enjoying it. Me too now it was over. It all felt a bit weird though. Briefing the media was one thing. But this was the public and it felt odd them listening to me in the way I had usually watched people listening to TB.

Tuesday 2 March

Pretty good response re last night. Generally felt I did OK plus some constructive criticism, especially a good written analysis by Matthew Doyle [TB advisor]. His big point was that sometimes I talked to people as though they were lobby journalists. I was so trained to see something behind a question that I didn't answer questions as directly as I could, including the friendly ones. But he felt the big argument was clear and compelling and I had definitely won over a few waverers. Off to Bart's with Iain Hutchinson who was very kindly taking out a bad tooth for me. Felt sore but relieved afterwards. Good news on the Audience front – Mick Hucknall was keen to chair the Manchester event. Barry Kilby called re the *Mail* and the *Telegraph* coverage of the Millwall fallout. Paphitis had decided attack was the best form of defence and had been pushing the prawn sandwich helicopter freebie line. Barry was keen to help me push back. The helicopter came out of the time I was worried if we had got through a Cup game I would have struggled to do the match and the marathon on the same day – semi-final, I think. Barry was happy enough to hit back on my behalf re the freeloading stuff. Sally called, said TB was planning to make a speech on Iraq, basically saying we were right even if we were wrong!

Wednesday 3 March

Resting post the tooth op, which felt worse today than yesterday. The right-wing papers had a bit of poison on the Festival Hall event. PG, Alan Milburn and Steve Byers came round at 9. All very down re the general scene, felt we were lacking drive and direction. Philip felt it would be difficult to lose the election, but we could see a small majority. Alan pointed out that we had so many rebels that a small majority made some things impossible. GB was being a bit of a nightmare. We discussed how we get Alan and Steve back in the general mix but they both felt GB did not want them anywhere near the place. They both felt Ian McCartney was doing fine. I wondered about a group headed by JP that did campaigns etc. and that we could get Steve on to. JP effectively party chair. We knew that 1. We had somehow to get Iraq in a much better place. 2. Get the best people into the operation and so strengthen No. 10 and Old Queen Street [Labour Party HQ]. 3. Get a manifesto team working properly on policy. 4. JP in a position where a broader team can work under him.

Alan said the big gap I had left was that people were unsure who to go to to make things happen and get stuff driven through the system. He felt the civil servants were retrenching subtly but successfully. Steve said many of them combined uselessness with hostility. PG felt Iraq was totally contaminating people's view of TB. They felt I had to get back in there sooner rather than later. Steve was warning against the plans afoot to have five-year plans submitted to the PLP for review. He said it would lead to strangulation. Nothing radical would happen. I spent most of the day working on the Burnley speech for Friday night and also transcribing Faldo. I had too many speeches coming up in the diary. Ross Kemp called to say he was up for doing more events. He said he had enjoyed it and it was good for his profile to be involved in stuff like that. Jokey email from Lance A saying he had not replied earlier because he was so busy following the Kofi bugging scandal. Blackmore called asking if I would do an email exchange with Rod Liddle on Millwall for *The Times*. No ta. Long interview with Ian Katz of *The Guardian*. He had said he wanted it to be Crampton-style but he got too bogged down in Iraq and Hutton stuff. I got irritable and closed down as a result. Chatted to Stan, who said he had got some stick from the local BNP councillor re what he had said post-Millwall.

Thursday 4 March

To Gospel Oak Primary School to read. Lance was enjoying himself re Kofi, more emails, 'Is Tony still bugging Kofi?' 'Who is Tony bugging now?' 'Does he bug Bush?', also whacking [Jacques] Chirac [President of France] for trying to ban Muslim women from wearing headscarves. The reason for the exchanges was me trying to get his views on UK cyclists so that I had another piece out of it all. He knew all about Graeme Obree [world champion Scottish cyclist]. To Rory's parents' evening. Absolutely brilliant. Felt so proud of him. Out to a Clifford Chance [international law firm] dinner. Basic speech and Q&A but I felt tired. Lots of them rank Tories. The driver who took me home was really depressed because his wife had left him and taken his two kids, aged seven and eight. Hard to know what to say. I didn't know the full circumstances so just platitudes really but he seemed on the edge. Doesn't bear thinking about. Fiona was asleep when I got in so I went up and worked on the note TB had asked me to do, setting out how I saw things. Economy strong. Worries on tax. Jobs story good. Personal living standards/optimism – OK. Public services – a grudging sense that things are getting better in health and education; crime and anti-social behaviour stuck; transport not great, welfare reform stalled. Constitution bogged down. Europe stalled, everything clouded by Iraq and Blair/Bush; but TB established as statesman despite the difficulties.

On the political front, near invisibility of the party as a voice or a campaigning machine. Party members not sure about direction. No sense of council or Euro elections. TB–GB better but not that much. Some want a change of leader. Howard is making an impact at a certain level but in his busy-ness and frantic-ness, he is exposing his weaknesses, which TB correctly identified at the time of Hutton – nasty, opportunist, unprincipled. Add to that the fact that he is the past and that he has no clear agenda for the future, and he becomes a great target. Vulnerable on patriotism, because he has inhaled the Dacre strategy – destroy trust in the word of the PM and say everything in Britain is crap.

So the challenges: handle Iraq as best he can, underline leadership and ability to do the hard things. Improve TB–GB. Energise ministers and party machine. Strengthen No. 10 and HQ. Find proper role for Milburn, work out how to use me, David M, Peter M, others who have moved on. Find roles for the good campaigning MPs, George Foulkes [UK delegate to Council of Europe and Western European Union], Brian Wilson [MP for Cunninghame North] etc., and for those who are good when asked, the Jack Cunninghams, Ann Taylors, Helen Liddells [former Secretary of State for Scotland] of this world and the others, down to whip level, who have lost jobs. Work to bring back in to some kind of role some of the ministers turned rebels, Robin Cook, John Denham [chairman, Home Affairs Select Committee], Nick Brown. Sort party chairmanship soon. JP/Ian have to be properly involved. Proper new role for MMcD [Margaret McDonagh, former Labour general secretary]. Also advised on a team to defend and promote TB. Hardly anyone does it. Improve attack capacity on Howard. On policy/manifesto we had to turn the Big Conversation [consultation initiative], which was good PR, into Big Policy.

When we discussed it earlier, I said the '01 election was less exciting than '97 and we had to be careful we didn't just lapse into something even less so. It has to be stronger, but despite AA etc. having some great process ideas, was the policy debate really happening in a way that led to a good manifesto? Couldn't we get David M back to help more? Also we had to make sure the '05 campaign was more interesting than '01, which was dull, safety first, which meant that when a JP punch or a Sharon Storer handbagging came along, a vacuum was filled, and they were the only things anyone could remember.* So on both policy and campaigns, we need new energy and freshness. I was also worried that TB felt we could just hammer home 'achievements and delivery' through people banging out lists. In the note I suggested a reverse side pledge card which had achievements in the same areas as the pledges. Well past 1 a.m. when I finished it.

* In 2001, Ms Storer had ambushed Tony Blair outside Queen Elizabeth Hospital, Birmingham, to complain there was no bed for her cancer patient partner on the bone marrow ward.

Friday 5 March

Left at 6.45 and got to Burnley by 11. Alison called to say Thomas Cook were faffing around, claiming people were pulling out because I was doing the North-West Chamber of Commerce. Likely to be bullshit. Long chat with *Liverpool Daily Post* for interview piece. I was emailing rather testily with Ian Katz on the interview he had done, angry that he said I had not been candid about the Hutton aftermath. Just after I arrived, Alex called, with bad news. He was our star speaker for the Burnley fundraiser tonight, but he was going to have to pull out. He was really apologetic, promised to do another one at another time, but he had finally had a pacemaker fitted last night, and had been told he had to rest up a bit. He was confident it wouldn't necessarily get out, which would amaze me, but we agreed I would just say he was feeling under the weather. He felt bad letting us down at short notice. He asked if he could help get someone to stand in. I said there were only two people I could think of, and one of them, David Beckham [England captain], he had sold to Madrid. The other was Bobby Charlton [former Man Utd and England star]. Leave it with me, he said.

Bobby called a few minutes later and was fantastic about it. He did say he got very nervous about public speaking, but he was fond of Burnley, fond of Alex of course and keen to help out. He was a pretty good get out of jail card for all those who would be feeling let down by Alex not doing it. I decided I wouldn't tell many people until nearer the time as it would only freak them out. I did a fundraising lunch with businessmen at the Club. Derek Hatton [former Militant Liverpool council leader] was there, and did a long, very funny question, going over some of our past encounters and finishing by saying that he was now way to the right of me. Then he went off on one on Iraq. Did a couple of Granada TV interviews, one on sport and the need for clubs like Burnley to raise money, and the other on politics with a really irritating interviewer going on about psychological flaws and whether GB would go for the IMF job. Over to Radio Lancashire in Blackburn, which was a good laugh, and a couple more sports interviews.

I was staying with Stan Ternent. Lovely house up at Cliviger [southeast Burnley]. I went for a little run with the Channel 5 documentary film people and then did an interview with Judith Dawson in Stan's garden. All very soft focus at this stage. At the dinner, though people were disappointed about Alex, they were pleased with his replacement and also that Alex promised to do another event later. Those at the top table were held back and there were special-mention entries for Bobby, me, Dick Caborn, Peter Pike, and also Kitty Ussher [Labour candidate in Burnley], which raised a few eyebrows as clearly quite a lot of people didn't know who she was, but based on the brief chat I had with her, I thought she was doing fine. Bobby was totally supportive of Alex, said he was brilliant at his job and brave in some of the big decisions he took. I was genuinely surprised at how nervous he was before speaking, but he told some fabulous stories, all without notes. He was very funny about the rivalry with Jack [brother, also a former England player], telling a funny story about when Billy Bremner [Leeds player] flattened Bobby to the sound of support from Big Jack. Also a hilarious story about [former World Cup-winning England manager] Alf Ramsay's absolute dedication. They went on a long, long successful tour, at the end of which Bobby thanked him, and then said he was looking forward to getting home to see his wife, to which Ramsay said, 'If I'd known that was your attitude, I wouldn't have brought you.' He told another story about Bill Shankly [legendary former Liverpool manager], as relayed to him by Roger Hunt [former Liverpool and England player], about a Shankly team talk, in which he rubbished the United team, at the end of which Ian Callaghan [Liverpool and England player] said, 'You never mentioned Best, Law [George and Denis, Man Utd star players] or Charlton,' to which Shankly said, 'Can you lot not beat three people?' He said Roger Hunt had said it was the nearest Shankly ever got to a compliment for a non-Liverpool player.

There was a fabulous atmosphere and my speech went fine, so did the auction, where we raised £23,000. I also picked Bobby's brains for the *Times* series. He felt [Alfredo] Di Stefano [Argentine football legend], because of his ability to control all aspects of the game, was the greatest footballer. He singled out Michael Jordan [basketball player] and Wayne Gretzky [ice hockey star] as the best outside football. It was a fantastic evening. Made loads of money for a cause I believed in, great audience, all fine. TB was making a speech on Iraq/WMD. Godric called later and said No. 10 was in a bit of a state.

Saturday 6 March

Up early, chat with Stan and Kath [wife], and a guy called Charlie, who was chief scout for Newcastle. Stan was pretty down, felt that Burnley would never have the money to make the next step up. Even though some of the players were on silly money, it was still a lot less than clubs around the same place in the league were paying. The two of us went out for a run by the reservoir, fantastic scenery. We did a little interview together for Judith. Both he and Charlie were interested in TB's style of management, how he took decisions, how he handled the pressure. Charlie said TB had sent Bobby Robson [former England, now Newcastle United manager] a really nice private letter when he was going through a difficult period, and that kind of thing meant a lot to people. Did a long interview with Judith, lots on Iraq, my temper, and obsessiveness. To the match (Burnley v Preston North End, 1–1), met Calum. On the drive home, I was working on a note to TB. Chatted to Alex after the Fulham match. He said he felt a lot better after winning and also at having sorted out the heart and the horse situations.

Sunday 7 March

Ninety minutes on the bike. Cinema with Grace to see *Cheaper by the Dozen* again. Coming out of the cinema, a woman shouted out, 'You are horrible, sorry but you are.' Grace looked really angry and the woman saw it and left it at that. I sat down to read 'The Plan', a 50–60-page paper that had been done up out of a lot of the work on the five-year plans, and in part married to a political strategy. It was a pretty good piece of work, if a bit dense at times, perhaps trying to pack in too much. But the outlines of a strategy were all in there, and there was obviously some decent work being done across pretty much all of the policy areas. There was enough progress made to be able to point to, and tied to the promises of further progress provided we pressed on with reform and modernisation. The Big Conversation to bind in party and public was going to have to be real to make it effective. But all in all, I think anyone reading it ought to get a lot of confidence about where the political debate lay. I tried to imagine an equivalent Tory document at this stage. I couldn't see them having anything near as strong. Also what it did was take the really difficult things TB had done and turn them into strengths via tough choices, difficult decisions beginning to pay off, against Tories who were either desperate to lurch back to Thatcher, or just go all-out negative. I sent TB a note saying all this, and above all saying he should be confident. Some of the key delivery facts were really good if we could make sure people knew them.

Monday 8 March

The Ian Katz interview worked out OK in the end, big piece on the front and five pages in G2. Worked most of the day on planning out a few speeches. I had five speeches coming up, all different. I got an interesting email from Mike Forde [Bolton Wanderers FC analyst], who had been at the lunchtime event at Burnley on Friday and done his own presentation on how they motivated and managed players at Bolton. He said he was inspired by the stuff I had talked about, especially about leadership and team-building, and thought I should do something with Sam Allardyce [manager] at Bolton.

Tuesday 9 March

Cab to the airport, and the driver was a Pakistani who was genuinely trying to persuade me to convert to Islam. At points, he was so passionate, he seemed to be driving along without paying any attention to the road at all, switching his gaze between the mirror and looking directly back at me. He was quoting whole chunks of the Koran at me. Up to Edinburgh, and to the RSE [Royal Society of Edinburgh] conference, where I was speaking about the impact of devolution, with special regard to the media. There was a small demo, which I managed to avoid. David Steel [former Liberal leader] was very friendly, Tam Dalyell [Labour MP] growling at me but was later very nice about the speech, which I had put a lot into, but then had a go about Iraq. Back to the hotel, and then to the Institute of Directors dinner, nice enough crowd and the Q&A was more interesting than most, with two or three of them genuinely worried about the way the media was changing so quickly for the worse.

Wednesday 10 March

The main story from the RSE speech was something out of the Q&A, me saying we got things wrong. It kind of proved the point I had made yesterday – how hard it was to have a serious debate. Flew to Manchester, the air hostess wanted to pick me up on something I had said on the James Whale show. Arrived at the Lowry to do an interview with some students about apathy. The Thomas Cook lunch seemed to be a mixture of business, politics, media and ladies who lunch. Did another media round to flog tickets for the Bridgewater Hall ['Audience With'] event. Then a radio phone-in, astonishing how many people were into conspiracy theories. Bumped into Martin Ferguson [Alex's brother] and Alex McLeish [Glasgow Rangers manager], who were there for the match. Both very supportive.

Thursday 11 March

I seemed to be doing interviews the whole bloody time. It was probably the only way to get the interest up for these theatre events, but it was a bit of a pain. Phone-in at BBC GMR [local radio], largely on Iraq. Tessa pressing me to do more on her speech for the weekend. Off to Liverpool, more media, then up to meet Phil Redmond [TV producer], did a tour at the studios. Lunch in his office. Nice guy, totally on my side re the BBC row. He had an interesting take on TB, thought that maybe there was just a shelf life for politicians and that no matter how good you were, that was that. Then to John Moores University, interviews, then speech and Q&A, generally friendly, including some good Labour members, but one or two really vile on Iraq. Back to Manchester, students, really good and lively. Up to Old Trafford for the Chamber of Commerce dinner, VIP reception, more interviews. Alex arrived. He and I were at the top table together. He was looking a bit tired, which was hardly surprising, but said he felt the problems re the horse were subsiding. I asked him why he had even bothered to get into all that, and he said it was an area he was interested in, good money when it went well, and he had honestly thought they were a partnership on it. At least the fans had stuck by him 100 per cent.

Good crowd at the dinner. Speech was fine, really good reception. Derek Hatton won the raffle. I said he was clearly following me around. Back to the hotel for a meeting with Mark Bennett and Tim Carter [Labour Party official] re the Bridgewater on Tuesday. TB called a couple of times during the day. He was worried about his spring conference speech, and asked me to work on it. He was sounding very defensive, not confident at all. The draft was a bit same old, same old. The news was totally wiped out by the Madrid bombing.*

Friday 12 March

TB called while I was having breakfast, and really didn't sound in great shape. I did a long passage on the general picture, hard choices, dividing lines, no complacency for the country or party. I can't say it felt that great but he just needed basic message stuff. In terms of impact, the media would only take the Madrid bombing stuff anyway, so it was

---

* Co-ordinated bombings on Madrid's commuter train system killed 192 people and injured around 2,000. A Spanish judiciary investigation found an al-Qaeda-inspired terrorist cell had directed the attacks.

March '04: Derek Hatton surprise winner at Manchester dinner

much more important that we gave out a broader message for the party. Into the *Manchester Evening News* for a webchat with readers and then an interview. Good questions and one of the journos there spotted that the public often asked very different questions to the ones she heard asked again and again by journalists. On the train back, working on a piece on Bobby Charlton for *The Times*. Back for a meeting with Clive Conway and Wendy Bailey. I told them I'd taken on too many of these theatre events and as they didn't really have marketing budgets, I was having to spend too much time doing media.

Saturday 13 March
I might as well still be there, the calls I was getting re speeches, not just from TB, who had been in fret mode, but from JP today re his own speech in Manchester tomorrow. He had been to Madrid yesterday to represent the government in the big protest against terrorism, which he said had been incredibly moving. He wanted to express that, but couldn't find the words. Interestingly, he had a very different take on TB at the moment, felt he was in good shape and on form, but it was probably because he felt good about being asked to go to Madrid. I drove to Maidstone to watch Rory in the English Schools cross-country. He didn't run well and was pissed off on the way home. TB only got covered for the terrorism part of the speech, as expected, though he was reasonably happy with the political argument in the other sections of the speech. He still sounded a bit anxious though. Something or someone was sapping his confidence. Did 1 hr 20 on the bike.

Sunday 14 March
Twelve-mile run. Then working on the speeches coming up for Manchester, the Murdoch do in Cancun, and Yorkshire Forward, which I would doing straight after getting back from Mexico. JP called, said his speech had gone fine and he wanted to have dinner soon. He said he thought it was important I stayed plugged in. Louise Plank [publicist] was putting out stuff about the deal with Five, and told me there was a lot of interest. Peter Hyman and family came round. He was clearly enjoying his new life as a teacher, said that it felt very different, the difference being that we work on ideas and policy, and how that all fits together, and it just felt very different being at the other end of the policy process, trying to do the job that we all thought we understood.

He was such a decent guy, very honourable and would throw himself into the teaching with the same commitment he had shown in No. 10.

Monday 15 March

1,500-metre swim. I went to St Paul's for [businessman and Manchester United director, Sir] Roland Smith's memorial. Dreadful acoustics. I finished several speech drafts, then one of the Birmingham papers came round to do an interview. I was beginning to understand why TB used to rage at me, Anji and Hilary when we kept fitting in regional interviews on the campaign trail. Nice enough guy, accompanied by a very old-fashioned looking photographer.

Tuesday 16 March

Finished the various speeches I had to get done, including for the evening in Manchester, Yorkshire Forward and Cancun. Micky and Wendy set off for Mick Hucknall [singer] in Surrey and before long he was into the running joke re a driver who couldn't navigate. Mick had to direct Micky through North London and was thankfully in good humour about it. Mick etc. arrived and we set off for Manchester. MH very Labour, very supportive of TB on the war, worried as everyone else was about the way people were gunning so much for TB. He regaled us about the time he went to Chequers with a girl-friend – I remember her, all dressed in white and she sat next to GB, the evening I had a go at Sarah Brown [GB's wife] and suggested trust wouldn't be rebuilt till Gordon got rid of Ed and Charlie. Mick and I had a good laugh talking over how we would deal with hecklers etc., and about his crumpled suit. I had told him about the role 'Money Too Tight To Mention' played when I went mad, when I listened to it again and again when I got home drunk at night, and he was telling me he was re-recording all his old records so he could stop being ripped off by the record company. I was constantly singing 'Holding Back the Years' and reading him some of the better jokes in the speech. There was a problem with the promotional film because they had to hire in equipment to show it at a cost of 1,300 quid.

Earlier another chat with TB, who had wanted me to be more descriptive and less judgemental in the media part of the Murdoch speech, so made more changes there too. We arrived at the Lowry, checked in then off to the theatre for sound check etc. They seemed a nice crowd

March '04: TB urges toning down attacks on media

but not as on the ball as Festival Hall. The Labour Party guys were a great help. The first questions were about whether there was really any difference between the parties and whether I had had too much power. Mick's manager Ian Grenfell arrived and having done marathons agreed to sign up for triathlon team. The crowd was about 1,000, not as many as London, and they felt more cerebral than before so I junked some of the jokes and gave a more political argument.

Questions OK, and Mick dealt well with hecklers, saying the mic should go to them and then when it did they went quiet. Quite a lot of aggro re Iraq and a guy saying we all lied and I went back to him and felt I moved him a bit. Did the T-shirts at the end, throwing them out to the people who asked the best questions. The one with the 'Hated by the *Daily Mail*' logo went down best. I gave it to a guy in a wheelchair whose carer asked if TB saw himself as Bush's carer. But everyone seemed to think it went fine and there was a good mood at the reception afterwards and then when we were having a drink in the bar. Mick came back with a nightclub owner friend, Leroy, and then headed out on the town while I went to bed. Before that a couple of women had been chatting us up, and after they went Mick said: 'I guess the difference between my world and yours is that I am expected to go and shag them; but if you did you'd be all over the News of the Screws.' He said: 'I might be, but that's what people expect of rock stars!'

Wednesday 17 March

It was Budget Day and weird not to be involved. At breakfast with Wendy in the hotel, a massive six-feet-ten-tall lawyer who had been there the night before came over and said he really enjoyed it. He wanted advice re how to deal with hecklers. We then set off for Birmingham, working on Cancun speech. Did *Oxford Mail* interview on the way. *Birmingham Post* had done the interview in the kitchen on page 1 and 2 with a cross ref to a big interview at the weekend, and it was a fair piece with nice pictures. Did a tedious interview with *Wolverhampton Express and Star*, the guy was obsessed with Iraq. Did Saga radio and BRMB [local radio] – with a Burnley fan – then Central TV. Kate G called and said how weird it was that I was going to all these different places the same as TB did. Symphony Hall was where G8 was, and the CBI, so big moments there. Auditorium amazing when empty, fantastic acoustics. Jean [Templeton, relative] came up for a chat then we headed for Nottingham to do the BBC then get Calum from the station and go to

Forest v Burnley. Good game, we should have won but drew 1–1. I gave Ray Ingleby [Burnley director] a lift back and he was as ever trying to press me into doing stuff with him. Back knackered and then packed for tomorrow. Budget went well if low-key.

Thursday 18 March

Early out and car to Heathrow. Budget got a good press so far as I could tell. I bumped into Michael Howard as he was wandering round duty free. He was also going to Cancun but thankfully he was on a different flight with his wife Sandra and Trevor Kavanagh [*Sun* journalist], who was clearly going to try to use the trip to persuade Rupert M to switch *The Sun*'s allegiance. I was bumping into lots of News International people, including Keith Blackmore and he and I chatted over future interviews on the plane. Brent Hansen [president and CEO, MTV Europe] was on the flight and I briefed him on a thing I was doing with BBC Radio 2 re snobbery in pop music. The Tory candidate from Milton Keynes North [Mark Lancaster] came up and asked me for an autograph for his wife Katie. Trevor Beattie also there, also heading out to Cancun. Chaotic time in Miami then on to Cancun and I got Trevor to read the speech. He said he was setting up his own company with Andrew McGuinness [advertising executive] and did I want to be involved? He and I were met as VIPs and taken off ahead on arrival, having a laugh at the lack of traffic and the idea that we were going to be the token lefties in a very right-wing world. Checked in and then went to the reception party by the fountain at the Ritz Carlton. Lachlan [Murdoch] seemed OK but was duller and seemed a bit more robotic than his brother James, who was very full of himself. Jane Friedman of Harper Collins gave me a very heavy sell re the book, saying they could make it fly in publicity terms in the US and elsewhere in a way that Gail could not. She said she had briefed Rupert and he was very keen to do it as a major project. I said I was not rushing. Rebekah was her usual cat on a hot tin roof, more nervy than usual. Nice to see John Hartigan [CEO, News Limited] and also [Richard] Littlejohn [*Sun* columnist] and Colin Myler [executive editor, *New York Post*]. The Americans there were very low-key, the Aussies were nice and the Brits the most noticeable. It hit me in the face that there was not a single non-white, though one of them told me there was a Mexican woman coming tomorrow! Bed fairly early but I couldn't really sleep. Les [Hinton] and Rebekah were both hoping that I wouldn't kick off with Howard. I think some of the hacks were hoping I would.

Friday 19 March

I went out for a run on the beach, which was beautiful but tough on the legs. I was struggling after half an hour. On the way back, I bumped into RW and Andy Coulson [editor, *News of the World*] who were out on the beach together, and looked surprised to see me. They said they were planning one of the morning sessions together. I was working on the speech on and off in between the sessions. I bumped into RM [Rupert Murdoch] and we were chatting re Bush/Kerry when Les took him off to see Howard. Lachlan kicked off, said he didn't want to compete with the sessions or the RM speech. It was all a bit humourless but there were some interesting bits, for example a discussion on youth, and John Witherow [editor, *Sunday Times*] did an interesting presentation on *The Month*, the *Sunday Times* CD-Rom. As I said to RM and Les, and later in my speech, there was a lot of crossover in the issues they and we were concerned about – diminished brand loyalty, problems attracting youth, technology, demography etc. I fiddled with the speech all day. Steve Morris [No. 10 official] texted me that Howard pre-spin was all re Europe referendum etc. and so I wrote in some stuff re that.

Rebekah's presentation was on campaigns, and was really low grade. I had to decide whether to go for them on it. She did the Sarah's Law campaign as though it was some wonderful success story, totally skipping the paediatrician who was attacked because people felt it meant paedophile.* They also did the Europe campaign, where she showed a film of Jacques Delors [former President, European Commission] being attacked with custard pies, which fell flat. An Aussie journo on the same subject was more witty and clever and human. Re Europe these people were passionately anti-European. At lunch Howard was next to RM and I was with John Hartigan, who I liked a lot, and I was telling him stories re my sports column and did he fancy having it for one of the Aussie titles? As for the speech John told me to be myself and have a go and not worry about what Les and RW thought.

---

* In 2001, plans for the *News of the World* to reveal the names of proven child-sex offenders were curtailed after innocent people were mistakenly attacked. The paper's campaign to allow parents to ask police if someone with access to their child had been convicted or suspected of child abuse was named in memory of murdered child Sarah Payne.

There was then another corporate session before Howard who was given the big build-up by Trevor K, clever, respected, part of the brave government that allowed RM to break the unions, and deliver an enterprise economy opposed by Labour etc. etc. Howard did OK but as Paul Kelly [Australian journalist] said, it was not as impressive a speech as TB in Hayman Island. He hit all the RM buttons – Iraq/Bush/Europe/tax/regulation/ – but in too obvious a way and although he was well received and there were people nodding to each other a bit, the glow didn't last. I felt I could respond and rebut without being too heavy and above all, after a fairly humourless day, I wanted to make them laugh and then give them a serious message.

RW introduced me by reading stuff from the *Mail* about me being a poison etc., then nicer stuff from *The Sun* and I went on and did *Mail* poll, Hampstead Heath story, Maxwell, money for old rope, and all went well. The speech itself felt strong though I cut it down towards the end when I saw RM starting to do his paper work. Also I resisted being too heavy on RW though I did point out it was interesting the Aussie campaigns were fun and positive as well as serious. I felt it went well and got lots of nice plaudits afterwards, especially from Hartigan and the Aussies. Jeni Cooper [editor, Australian *Sunday Telegraph*] came up to me while I was talking to Trevor and said it was brilliant. Howard's reception was polite rather than impressed, e.g. foreign correspondents Bronwen Maddox [*The Times*] and Marie Colvin [*Sunday Times*] both said he had not made many new friends or admirers. The exact opposite of the TB impact at Hayman Island. I also had to stay on the panel for a session chaired by Witherow on war reporting and I felt that went fine too.

Then out to the gym, level 15 on exercise bike with Lachlan on seven I noticed. OK workout then on to a bus and out to another hotel for a rather noisy dinner. Howard was on the Les and Kelly/RW table, I was with RM, Robert Thomson and [businessman] Jack Welch and his new glam wife who he ran off with after she interviewed him for *Harvard Business Review*. RM spoke so softly it was hard to hear him but I sensed he was only superficially taken with Howard. What was clear, however, was that the Europe thing ran deep. He felt the commissioners were anti-American and anti-him. He hated [Romano] Prodi and [Mario] Monti [European Commissioner for Competition]. Welch was out of the same school, very right-wing, talked about the communist media – in the US! – and loathed Kerry.

RM said he felt TB had lost his authority somewhat, but used an odd example – that he had to get a committee to pick the new BBC chairman. He felt we had been very restrained re the BBC on the war. Christ, not sure the Beeb would agree with that analysis given what happened post-Hutton. I suppose maybe he had a point in that the personnel changed but the attitudes didn't. He was also pressing, as Paul Kelly and Witherow had been, on what TB would say re how long he would stay if he won a third term. RM, according to Maddox, liked GB – and that GB worked Robert Thomson very hard – but wasn't sure he would be a good for business PM. He also felt TB was not as strong in the party. And I sensed Murdoch was tired of hearing from TB that he was winning all the arguments in Europe, said he would never trust Chirac not to stuff us etc. He felt GWB was a shoo-in because the country understood there was a war on terror and he had handled it OK, and also because the economy was doing well. I was struck by how dark and hairy RM's hands were, how often he banged the table even when he was not emphasising a point.

Jack Welch was OK in small doses but I couldn't quite go for RM's view that he was the most charismatic businessman alive. OK chat with Witherow and others and I was trying to talk down Howard's speech, helped by Paul Kelly who I reminded wrote a piece with my favourite ever headline re TB, namely 'Nice kind of bastard'. Bus back and a rather cynical and jaded Bronwen Maddox was saying she felt RM was toying with GB but not sure, he wanted to support Howard but he didn't offer enough today, he just hadn't risen to the mark really. Re the speech, I think the main point was that media and political and cultural change had come together to give us an unhealthy political debate and we had to work together to improve it. Bed and slept a bit better than last night. But even though I had worked on it fairly hard, done well, I couldn't help reflecting it just didn't matter as much as before.

The other issue of the day had been the *Mail*'s splash, based on a claim by [Labour MP] Kate Hoey, that I fixed Alex's knighthood. The News Int people could not believe they splashed on it as it was so obvious he would have got a K for the treble [Man Utd had won the Premier League, FA Cup and UEFA Champions League in 1999]. RM said to me he agreed re the *Mail*, felt it took its hatred of TB to extremes and Dacre was obsessed. Alex called me and said they were getting calls. The thing that upset him most was Hoey saying he was not a role model. I told him not to worry, and we were saying – ie Godric – that all the processes were followed. Nobody followed up but then the *Mail* were chasing a story that I went to the Champions League final as Man U guest and I got GS to explain that I went with Victor Blank [businessman] and paid the fare. Lots of the Murdoch people were on at me re the diaries.

Saturday 20 March

Swim, breakfast with Aussies and then listened to Jack Welch and the beginning of Robert Thomson before doing a few letters and then headed for the airport. It had been quite a nice little break, though as at Hayman Island, just a bit weird to see how they all operated around Murdoch. He was so evidently all-powerful, and all of them just operated in their different ways in his orbit. Rebekah was like a different person around him. I was pleased though that Howard, while not having flopped, had not really impressed.

Sunday 21 March

I went round to Philip's, ostensibly for a chat, but I knew we would end up going over the polling, which he had been gathering and analysing in recent days. He had been in Doncaster doing some groups himself and said they had been the most racist and unpleasant he had ever done. The report he had prepared was not exactly happy reading, but not disastrous either, especially when you dug. Support overall was down, and we had slipped further on tax and living standards. There was a real paradox in there though, because the quantitative numbers were pretty bad on things like economic optimism for the country, and right direction/wrong direction, but the groups were broadly good on their own sense of optimism about their own lives and public services. The Tories were also massively vulnerable on cuts and charges. It had been done between 9 and 17 March, and though we were just ahead, by two, among all voters, the Tories were ahead among people certain to vote.

On living standards and tax, we had gone from being ahead in February to behind now, in the case of tax 7 per cent behind. Positive leads on NHS and education had slipped a little. Crime was not great. Economy overall was still holding up. But the link between asylum and immigration and public services was definitely harming us. PG said the worrying thing from the post-Budget focus groups was that asylum and immigration had become living standards and public service issues,

March '04: PG on 'racist, unpleasant' focus groups

which created more space for the Tories to go on it without attracting the usual opprobrium. The Madrid bombings had also really broken through to people, and people were sure London would be next.

On the Budget, the spending for education got through. People were really not sure about the extra payment for pensioners, thinking it was too gimmicky, and that it conflicted with the idea of the focus being hard-working families. Despite it all, we were both reasonably cheery about the general feel of it all. True, there was a lot of grunge around and people didn't want to give the government much credit for anything, but the fundamentals on which a campaign would be based were all pretty good considering. If it had not been for Madrid, I reckon the Budget would have had a positive impact. And a pretty traditional 'investment v cuts' dividing line was definitely potent. Interestingly people felt far more persuaded of the impact of schools spending than health.

Fiona came over and we had dinner with Philip and Gail. TB called to discuss the polling and I also filled him in on Cancun, re what Murdoch was saying, how Trevor was greeting Howard. TB said Howard's problem was that fundamentally, he just wasn't a very big or impressive figure. But he still believed Europe could shift Murdoch. He thought the Budget went fine. GB was behaving better but in part he knew it was because the media were building him up again on the back of the Budget, weakening TB a bit. He had a bit of a cold, but said apart from that he felt good and up for the fight. Having spent so much of the day talking politics, for once it was PG and I who didn't particularly want to, and Fiona and Gail who were asking what was going on. I felt the one part of the analysis we did not really know how to deal with at the moment was the security issues and how they were linking to asylum, immigration, Iraq, economy, public services. We had lost the bigger picture on security, and needed to get back to some of those arguments TB made post-9/11.

Monday 22 March

Working on a couple of *Times* columns. Did an 8-mile run with Jon Sopel, who had been banned by the Beeb from chairing any of my 'Audience With' events. He had been quite keen and couldn't really see why they stopped him, as Beeb people did stuff outside their day jobs the whole time, but they were insistent. Later I did a couple of tour promotion radio interviews, basically on autopilot.

Tuesday 23 March

1,200-metre swim. Central TV to promote the Oxford 'Audience With'. TB off to Northern Ireland. He said it was going backwards again. I left at ten for the speech to Yorkshire Forward at the QEII Centre. It went fine and Huw Edwards [BBC newsreader] did a good job chairing. It kind of made the point about the inconsistency of the Beeb's approach re Sopel. Quite a cold audience, though not totally unfriendly. The Q&A was the best bit. Eddie George [former Bank of England Governor] was also speaking, and afterwards I had a little chat with him. He said he was enjoying a much quieter life. He said he had got to know and respect GB more with time, but the early days had been tricky. I told him of the time Maggie [Margaret Thatcher] had come in to say to TB that Gordon needed to show the governor more respect. 'I'm not sure it had much effect.'

He said the problem with GB was that he did tend to split people to enemies and friends and he didn't see that it was possible to be neither. People at the Bank had a lot of respect for his abilities, and he was able to analyse and make difficult decisions, but he tended to have it in for anyone at any part of the process who did not agree with him there and then. He also tended to the view that if you made it in a traditional Establishment job it meant you must be a traditional Establishment sort. He had sat in for my session, said he enjoyed it, that he sensed people were getting a real sense of life close to power, which not many people ever really experienced. Laughing, he said he thought I did a good job of not answering a question on the euro. I had basically said that I bowed to GB's wisdom on the subject.

The money was good for these speeches but they weren't terribly satisfying. The truth was people might be interested in what you had to say, but it didn't much matter. I went out to meet James Murdoch at the Langham. Really bright guy. He had really followed my sports series in *The Times* and quizzed about Armstrong in particular, and what made these guys tick. He thought I should really immerse myself in baseball, become an expert and do something on the great baseball players. He thought I should go to interview the coach of the New York Yankees to kick it all off. He said he would arrange to send me copies of an amazing TV series there had been on the history of baseball. He was a fairly open character, for example telling me without prompting that he had voted for Al Gore and would certainly support us. He believed TB was just about the most interesting person he had met. He was very funny, if slightly embarrassed and apologetic, about the time he effed and blinded in front of TB and RM at No. 10. He said TB should call a snap election, win, clear up all the rubbish and the day after he should shoot GB and say he was there for the full term. He was very anti-the European constitution, though not as virulent as his dad. He said he had spoken to him this evening and got good reports about my speech in Cancun. He felt Howard was just not a big enough figure whereas TB consistently blew them away. He felt Bush had it [the second term as President] sewn up and yet had screwed up a lot on domestic policy as well. He was very confident, quite charming, said he would like me to do stuff with him, though not sure what. Re Madrid, he said he had been reduced to tears both by the human stories and also the political reaction. He felt [José Maria] Aznar [Prime Minister] had been good for Spain and [José Luis] Zapatero [Spanish Socialist Workers' Party] was an idiot.

Wednesday 24 March
I was getting really quite fed up with the amount of media I was having to do to shift tickets for these theatre events. They weren't selling well in Birmingham so I did a whole round of stuff and agreed to go there if necessary. JP was doing PMQs with TB away and called a couple of times. I gave him a few lines on Howard and opportunism. He was clearly not very happy that TB was going to see Gaddafi without it really having been discussed or debated. I didn't see PMQs but he called afterwards, said he felt it had gone well and the PLP had reacted well, but needless to say the media were very iffy. TB was in Northern Ireland, where he said it was all a bit of a struggle, then Madrid for the memorial, then to Lisbon for his speech on terrorism, and explaining why he was going off to Libya. He was looking tired.

Thursday 25 March
1,500-metre swim. I was losing it with Wendy over the amount of PR I was having to do myself to flog tickets. I felt I could go up to Birmingham tomorrow on the way to Oxford and do some publicity. Also fixing a free ticket competition for the Sunday Mercury. Ian Riley [regional party official] and Tom Watson [Labour MP] had some good ideas. Tom thought I should do a visit and emphasise the good side of Birmingham, which he said was being transformed. I spoke to Ron Atkinson [former football manager] about chairing it but he was going

to be away. He recommended Gary Newbon [TV presenter], who leapt at it. He also told me of a Birmingham Press Club lunch tomorrow, which would help push tickets too. It meant I wasn't really focusing enough on [upcoming BBC interview with Michael] Parkinson, which was one of the interviews that kind of mattered, or at least one where it was possible to cut through. Parky's researchers had asked me to play the pipes at the end. Mine weren't up to it, because I had not played enough in recent weeks, so I got them to organise a set. I tuned them up in the dressing room. They were pretty shit but I was probably just going to have to go with it. Not exactly scripted, but certainly they knew what stories they wanted.

I got a text to say Dacre went for me at the Select Committee. Agreed to do an interview responding. Ross Kemp and Jimmy Carr [comedian] were the other guests and Nora Jones was singing. Michael Parkinson said the most important thing was to understand it was a chat not a tough interview, and just relax into it. Nora Jones was incredibly shy and nervous, while Jimmy Carr was fascinating. He and I were waiting in a kind of tent while Ross was on, and he said he couldn't live with not being laughed at every few minutes. I could tell he was trying out a few lines on me. Fiona thought he was terrible but I thought he was genuinely funny, on and off camera. Fiona thought I was maybe too political but generally the reaction was pretty good. Quite a lot on my breakdown, maybe too much on David Kelly. But it was impossible not to like Parky. We had a long chat afterwards, mainly about how journalism had changed. He said he was just as enthusiastic as ever, and still loved what he did. He agreed to chair my Old Vic event provided he was in the country.

Friday 26 March
Up at 7 and off with Wendy and Mickey to Birmingham, and working on the speech for tonight. Lost it with Mickey because we missed the M6 turnoff. I said to Wendy the whole thing was too wing and a prayer and I was going to pull out if things didn't improve. She was quite upset but I felt I had to say so. I did Ed Doolan [BBC West Midlands radio presenter] and called Kate Garvey to have a laugh about how I was now following in TB's footsteps again on the regional media strategy. I wasn't on form. Too much about the BBC and Kelly, as there was on Radio Derby. The BBC people in particular felt they just had to do it and I was conscious of being on autopilot. The Birmingham

March '04: AC on Parkinson; lots on Kelly, and nervous breakdown press lunch event was a bit low grade. Richard Whiteley [TV presenter] was the main speaker. An acquired taste. I was told that he had had more TV face time than any other TV presenter. Tom Watson's visit idea went well. I did a tour of the Bullring as the backdrop for some pictures and interviews. The theatre thought it would all drive sales.

Then to Oxford, met up at the Parsonage with John Sergeant and his wife for a quick dinner pre-event. John was the best chair yet. Gently piss-taking the whole way through, e.g. at the end when he said 'Alastair will now close with a few words to lead us all into the next stage of our lives.' I thought we were a pretty good double act. Beautiful theatre [the Sheldonian]. Sold out. Security a bit heavy, including a couple of guys right behind me. I did a much shorter, tighter introduction. John chaired the Q&A so that it flowed a lot more and the reception at the end was easily the best. Richard and Penny [Stott, AC's former editor at the *Mirror* and wife] had come along and loved it. I went for dinner with them and a few people who had been there came up to say how much they had enjoyed it. The key had been the venue and John's chairing, which just created the right atmosphere. Less on Iraq than I had expected.

Tony Wright [Labour MP, chair of the Public Administration Select Committee] called. He said they were going to write to me formally, asking me to reconsider my saying I did not want to go to PASC. He said that *The Guardian* had already been briefed by the Tories and were likely to make a thing of it. It was a bit of a pain, but I said I would.

Saturday 27 March

Off to Bradford with Calum. Fabulous atmosphere. Met up with Stan [Ternent, Burnley manager] and for some reason ended up pitchside. One-nil, then one-one, then disallowed goal, then Ian Moore winner in injury time. Absolute bedlam. Best for ages. OK journey back apart from a couple of hooligan twats on the train.

Sunday 28 March

TB called first thing. He had seen Parkinson and thought I came over well. He felt I should do more telly, particularly talking about media culture, and its impact on the country. TB thought that if the public could get to see more of Dacre, it would help our case against the *Mail*. He also thought I should do the Select Committee. David Hill and JoP were not keen, because the plan at the moment was to try to play down the whole spin thing, but TB thought I could move it to a different place, by talking dispassionately about what happened at Hutton, about the general trends and the big changes taking place, and the fact that everyone in public life hated the *Mail* both for what it was and for its influence on the rest of the media.

He was very funny about his meeting with Gaddafi. I said it was the first time since I had left that I'd really wished I was back there, because it looked completely surreal. He said it was like talking to someone like Keith Richards [Rolling Stones guitarist]; there were times when he couldn't hold back from laughing. He said Gaddafi was shrewd but a bit crazy. His first words were apparently, 'Hello Tony, you're tired, but not exhausted like they say you are, but you have been very very busy.' The tent thing was a bit weird, and there were camels wandering around outside, plus he had his gorgeous women bodyguards around the place and staff who were clearly on edge, never quite knowing what he was going to say or do next. There were one or two moments where TB really didn't know what he was talking about. But he definitely wanted to get into a difference place with the rest of the world, he was sure of that, and he was looking for help on how to do it.

On the general scene, he said he felt there was no appetite for Howard and the Tories but the mood was tough and it was largely the media doing it. Most people were happy in the main with their own lives but they were conflicted and confused because of all the negativity. I said he needed more people out there, region by region, being more positive about him and the government. He said what was annoying was that there was no policy agenda being put to counter ours, so it was just a general negativity that filled the gap. He said he thought I could still do a lot to put out a strong voice for party and government. I said he needed more people out there, that ministers just weren't political enough in the way they were communicating. There wasn't enough connection being made between politics and the decisions government made, and what was happening for the better in people's living standards and public services. He wanted to meet up soonish and find a way of me continuing to feed in on the strategic front.

I went to Arsenal v Man U in [boxing promoter] Frank Warren's box. I like Frank, a lot cleverer than the image, and he has a good grasp of politics. He said he was a big Labour man, very pro-TB, that history would judge him as one of the great PMs. He was very keen to know about Bush, and also what the pressures had been like. We talked a bit about boxing, which he said was the hardest sport in the world to reach the top, which is why Ali was the greatest sportsman of all time, though Sugar Ray Leonard was in some ways the better fighter technically. He said people would think I was mad if I concluded in *The Times* that Lance Armstrong was the greatest of all time.

Monday 29 March

Did a column, then train to Retford with Audrey and Rory. Dad not too bad, actually a bit better than the last time. I managed to work on speeches, mine and TB's, on the train, then back for dinner with Ross Kemp and Rebekah Wade. We had a nice enough time, and I liked them both but I was giving her a very hard time on the tone of their coverage on asylum and Europe in particular. I thought some of it was just nasty and bigoted. We were at the Wolseley, which I quite liked, but I still wasn't that keen on going out to this kind of place, though it was nice to bump into Anna Ford. PG, I told Rebekah, was strongly of the view that the media coverage on immigration was fuelling racism. He had done some groups in Doncaster which he said were terrible, truly vile, and something of an echo chamber for the way the media was covering it, especially the right-wing tabs. She didn't really engage on it, said they were reflecting readers' concerns. I said they were also creating them, through some of the myths. It was interesting how some of the strongest feelings came in areas of low immigration. Ross was on our side, and seemed pretty sceptical about the press more generally, and did not share her admiration for Rupert. I couldn't quite work them out as a couple.

Wednesday 31 March

Early train to Coventry. Four speeches to get through. First at Coventry Chamber of Commerce, where it was great to meet Paul Fletcher and Alan Stevenson [former Burnley footballers involved in building new stadium at Coventry City]. I told Alan [goalkeeper] the story of when I had been yelling at him from the crowd after he had dropped the ball and given away a penalty, and the woman next to me said, 'Excuse me, but that is my son you are talking to.' I had often thought about that listening to Mum talking about how she felt when I was under the cosh. And of course Fletch scored one of the greatest goals I ever saw, away at Leeds, overhead kick when we beat them 4–1, when

I was sixteen or seventeen. Then to Birmingham, KPMG [professional services company] event, all men apart from a very bright head teacher. Then to the Belfry, crisis management seminar. I can't imagine doing this stuff for too long, though they did seem to get something out of it. Then the after-dinner speech, which was fine, though I didn't feel that on form. Overnight at the Belfry. Nice place, nice room, felt quite rested though I had been running around all day. At three of the events I was asked why I didn't stand as an MP. I had noticed just going around the place, and on the train this morning with a guy from Stafford, the same question getting asked more. I couldn't see it right now.

Thursday 1 April

Bev[erley] Hughes resigned [as Immigration Minister] which really annoyed me. I had been following it off and on and it just struck me as one of those that could have been toughed out. It was a hoo-ha rather than a real scandal, and she shouldn't have been sacrificed like that. It was all about some kind of visa scam, but as ever with these things it was less about the issue than the handling of it. So she had said she had been unaware of the issue to do with Eastern Europeans, but then it emerged that Bob Ainsworth [deputy chief whip] had mentioned it to her a year ago.* I said to TB he should have toughed it out, but he felt it had gone beyond.

Off with Steve [Loraine] for a swimming lesson, then to his for lunch and a load of interviews by phone to promote ['Audience With'] ticket sales in Guildford. He was giving me a lift in to the Symphony Hall for the event in Birmingham. There was a dreadful crash on the M42. We just sat there for ages, and it was obvious something pretty bad had happened up ahead. We listened to the radio, and they said there were miles of tailbacks. Eventually, I got out and walked, then ran, just following the signs to Birmingham. Then a school bus pulled up alongside me, the door opened and the driver shouted out, in a thick Brummie accent, 'Oi, Alastair Campbell, hop on board.' He gave me a lift to the outskirts of town, and I jumped in a cab and was there on time. Steve made it in time for me to change into a suit, just as we were trying to find out where we could buy one.

* Hughes resigned when it became known that she had been informed of irregularities concerning visas for certain categories of Eastern Europeans and had taken no action. She subsequently said that she had not intentionally misled anyone.

Fabulous acoustics, nice atmosphere, maybe 700 people there, including Ian McCartney. Questions could have gone on all night. Usual stuff. 'What's Bush like?' or, usually, 'Is Bush as stupid as he looks?' was coming up pretty much everywhere. Ditto Iraq, spin, my breakdown and what it taught me. I found myself enjoying talking about that, and when people came up afterwards, that was maybe number 1 or 2 in terms of follow-up. Good reception though there was one lone heckler who at one point started to walk towards the stage, and I worked out quicker than the audience, who were shouting at him, that he was a bit disturbed, so I ended up calming him down and giving him a T-shirt.

There was a party reception afterwards, where Peter Snape [former Labour MP] made a funny speech taking the piss. Fiona Gordon [party official] said the party felt really enthused by it all, and I should do more of these events for them. She was another one who felt I should get a seat and, if I really put my mind to it, should have the leadership in mind. That left me feeling a mix of being overwhelmed at the thought, but also guilt at not wanting to do more right now than I already was. She said apart from Tony, Gordon, one or two others on a good day, how many people did we have who could get a crowd like that, have them hanging on every word, make an argument and take any and all questions in their stride? Steve had said something similar, which made me feel bad too. Got driven home, and now, just getting into bed, doing diary, I got a message from No. 10 asking if I could come in in the morning to see TB.

Friday 2 April

Tired, but I had a whole load more interviews to do to promote different events. A very nice girl from the *Western Daily Press*, and a photographer who snapped pretty much the whole time. I took them upstairs at one point to dig up cuttings from when I was on the *Western Daily Press*. I had only been there a few weeks, which they hadn't known. Didn't feel much like going in, but went and TB was up in the flat with Godric, DH, SM, going over what needed to be done. I said I felt we should have kept Bev Hughes, but TB said it was a tough one for him, because not only was there the letter from Bob Ainsworth, but also he had warned her in the lobby ten days earlier that it was there. So even though yes, it was a case of a frenzy, and she got caught out on detail, the fact was it was not really tenable and she had to go. It was odd being back in the kind of discussion I'd had so many times before.

The need for a clearer plan, the need for the grid to be more strategic, the need for stronger co-ordination, more politics from the ministers.

I was very conscious of the need not to speak in a way that anybody could analyse as saying that things were being done, or possibly not done, as I would. The truth was there was an upside as well as a downside to me not being there, and what TB was trying to find was a way of keeping some of the upside. If anything, he was the one who seemed to be saying the problem was the weakness in systems at the centre. He felt they had a good enough overall plan, but they lacked short-term strategic capacity and a system to drive things through.

He thought it would be sensible for me to try to see GB when I was up in Scotland over Easter. He said GB was not at all reconciled to TB standing at the next election. As the others left, he asked me to stay behind. He said the central question which he had to resolve in the next fortnight was whether he was going to stand. I said I thought, from a recent conversation with Balls, that GB was reconciled to TB being there at the election, that was the impression I got. TB said far from it. He said I've not told anyone this, but the truth is that the only way I was able to get him to come into line last November – tuition fees, foundation hospitals etc. – was to say that I wasn't sure whether I was going to stand next time. He did that thing he does, to indicate he may have been devious, when he appears to raise both eyebrows, the left one slightly more than the right, and smile.

In other words he may have given a signal, and Gordon may have picked it up, but he did not spell it out in so many words. He said GB was probably of the view that he would go. He said GB was very worried about me because I had been a big figure on the inside, and I was a big figure on the outside now, and he knew I could damage him if I chose to. I still had a role to play here, he said. I clearly looked a bit downcast at that, because he said 'Look, I know you're not keen to get dragged back in like before, but I am going to need you. I am not as strong as I was, I have more enemies in the PLP than I did, he has a stack of them working it the whole time now, and even though I still have more popular support than most do at this stage, it is not what it was.' He shrugged, said, 'There it is.'

He knew I would help, but I also said, 'Listen, you know I will help. But you also know not that long ago, we all agreed it was time for me to go, and to be honest if I hadn't, I am not sure I could have held things together at home.' But that was the relentlessness of it all, and the fact you were taking so much of the shit, he said. We can find a different way of doing this. I don't want you doing everything as before. I want you helping me on the big stuff and the big people, 'especially our friend next door', and JP. He said he didn't have anyone else who both of them would talk to reasonably honestly, and he didn't have anyone else that Gordon took seriously and remotely feared. 'I am not flannelling you here. If I am going to get over the line for another term, I need you to help me get there.' He said JP was very keen for me to be involved in election planning; that JP was going to be important in sorting out whatever happened between them, and so was I. He knew I was going to Scotland for a few days soon and he said he felt it was important I tried to spend a bit of time with GB, really get to where we thought he was on all this. He said that if there was a secret ballot in the PLP, he would win by two or three to one, but politics does not always work like that.

I asked him where his gut feeling was. He said if he had to make the decision, right here, right now, it was probably towards going, standing down before the election and letting GB fight it. He had never felt he would do three terms. He was not worried about legacy because there was a lot that people could point to as success. His worry was GB and whether he was up to it, whether he could actually do the job, also whether he really was a moderniser. He said, 'The difference between me and him was that I really feel it. New Labour. I feel the middle classes because I'm of them. GB is an intellectual, who thinks he understands working-class people and middle-class people alike, but he doesn't. I am not sure he really understands either.' He said he was also worried about how the chatterati would eventually turn on GB. He said there seemed to be quite a lot of Tory talk, including from Murdoch people, about 'Vote Blair, get Brown' as a viable strategy. That suggested the Tories had the research that showed GB was a negative if people thought he was PM. In other words, build up TB as the good one, GB as a risk.

Leo [the Blairs' three-year-old son] came in, and we had a little chat. He was looking more and more like Euan. TB was looking pretty chilled considering what he was thinking about. He was wearing blue suede shoes with no socks, and a pair of jeans that were a bit tight. He said there were times recently he had felt like throwing it in. He said his hatred for the *Mail* had grown, that they were evil. But he knew how to do the job, better than when he started, and there was still a lot that he wanted to do. He said I want your best brain on this. 'Is there any way of standing in the next election without being clear about how long I would stay? Could I stand but say it would not be for a full term, or if I did that was I so weakening myself I might as well go before?' He said he was going to decide in the next two weeks and he would then know whether he had to put together a fightback strategy, or he had to get out. He seemed a bit more down than usual. He said David [Hill] was finding it hard because of the comparisons with me, but he was a good firefighter. He would be fine about me being more involved. As I left, he said again he really wanted me to think about it.

He said on one level, GB had been behaving better, but that made him think it was because he was sure TB was going to topple over before the election. He said would it be possible to say he was going some time in the future, go for whatever he wanted in a reshuffle – including moving GB – or does power move away as soon as you say there is a time when you are leaving it? My instinct was that there was a lame duck element to all that, but I said I would think about it. I popped in to see Sally M on the way out. She said she was more worried than she had been for a while. I said he was giving me the hard sell/a bit of emotional blackmail. She said she thinks he had underestimated how different things would be if I wasn't there, and that it wasn't the same just being on the end of the phone. She also said that GB was motoring more than before, and that on the political level, the lines in had weakened. She was totally down on GB. She had said that he felt he was deliberately doing a bad European elections campaign, hoping for a sense of panic after it, a recognition around the place that TB was no longer a vote winner.

Saturday 3 April

Philip called, and said it really was time for me to get involved now. I also heard from JP that he had told Gordon that he wanted me, Peter M and Philip centrally involved in election planning because we knew how to win elections, and we had to go for it properly now. Philip said TB had been pretty ambivalent about his own future when he spoke to him. My instinct was that he was torn, but ultimately he would stick with staying. Philip thought the same but knew he was feeling the pressure. I got a message to GB that I was going to be in Scotland next week, with Philip, and we could meet up if he wanted. I got a message from his secretary that he was tied up in meetings all day, but he would get back to me. TB sent through a note which was basically a more detailed response to 'The Plan' document, which he reckoned was good, and wanted to put into action, but he was worried we didn't have the short-term strategic and tactical ability to match what was definitely a decent piece of long-term work.

All the research PG was sending me was confirming that our best strengths were economy, health, education, and the worst negatives crime, immigration, Europe, which were all becoming linked anyway. I had to talk PG out of a rather wanky slogan he felt could bring it all together, on the lines of 'Britain is doing a lot better than people say.' I said, 'Stick to the day job.' 'What's wrong with it?' 'It is defensive, apologetic, lacks edge, has no sense of the future in it. Forget it.' But he was right that the negatives had to be neutralised and part of that was about making sure people knew the difference between the country as it is and the country as portrayed by Tories and press.

In his note, he was back to micro-managing the grid [monitoring media coverage of government policy], even counting how many items from each department/issue were on there. Twenty-two from the Home Office, twelve on health, half that on education, just two on the economy. I said, 'Did you sit down and count them all, or get Leo to do it?' He laughed, but said he had a bloody point because the grid was not reflecting the strategy. I said I feared there was another reason why there was so little on the economy on there, namely that there was another grid in HMT [Treasury] and not all of its contents were shared. TB's note also suggested a whole load of straplines for different policy areas. I said, 'Are you worried I am not going to help you? Is this not a bit below your pay grade?' My favourite was 'NHS – on the road to redemption with Labour.' He also had this idea that someone in government should open a new school or school facility every day till the summer break. Fat chance.

Sunday 4 April

Keith Blackmore [*Times*] told me that at Cancun, when he had mentioned that I might wait till there was no Labour government before doing a book, the general reaction was that the value would fall pretty fast. That much was obvious, but I didn't feel the time was right, and even more so if I was now going to be drawn into helping try to sort the TB–GB stuff again.

I lost it with Tom Bostock when I went for a repeat prescription, and he said I was letting myself down in continuing to stand up for TB. He got really quite angry, said I was jeopardising my own position in history for God's sake, by failing to distance myself now I had the chance. 'You have managed to get out with a lot of integrity, a lot of people like you, and loyalty is a good thing. But you are out now, don't keep seeing yourself as his spokesman. You are better than that. You are better than him.' He went off on one about the NHS again, also Iraq, said he felt deep down I had been against the whole thing but had got myself into a place where I couldn't say what I really thought. I said I do say what I really think, and I think it is bad that so many people seem to be going negative on TB just because he hasn't met everyone's different expectations of what they want him to be and do. And it is a bit much having a GP who spends more time whacking me for politics than sorting out my various ailments. 'I know, I know, but I think this is part of it. I don't think you will ever be fully well while you are still this Blair figure.' He said he hadn't liked the Festival Hall event because again, he felt, 'You are better than that, telling funny stories and then defending the government and politicians and going for journalists. Was it politics or was it entertainment? Why are you doing it? What are you trying to achieve?' We ended up having a bit of a laugh about other stuff but I came out with my head reeling a bit.

Out for dinner with Catherine McLeod [journalist friend] and family, during which Fiona was saying the usual stuff about party and government being out of touch and not listening, and not understanding what was actually happening on the ground. I lost it a bit, said if we ever lost, a lot of it would be down to people talking the government down the whole time when there was a lot to talk up.

Monday 5 April
Out for a swim with Grace, watched *Love Actually* with her, did a couple of local papers then in for a meeting at 4.30 in the Cabinet Room. TB, JP, Joan Hamill [special advisor to John Prescott], Pat McFadden, Sally, DH on one side of the table, and on the other GB, Spencer Livermore [strategy advisor], Matt Carter, Douglas, Ian McCartney, Peter M, PG, AC. I was trying to think of the last time TB, JP, GB, PM, PG and I had been in the same room. Quite a while ago. The mood wasn't great. GB plonked himself down, noisily put his papers on the table, and generally looked dischuffed to be there. Philip and I tried to jolly things up a bit. JP was looking grumpy too. TB said there were two things we needed. Harder strategy, and better systems. There were three good policy areas for us in particular – economy, health and education.

Our opponents were trying to replace that agenda with three perceived negatives – crime, asylum/immigration and Europe. They were getting their act together. We were no longer dealing with opponents quite as weak as the ones we were used to. We had to get back to systems and a message that get us back on track, starting with the locals.

GB's big point was that we had to get up a sense of the choice. There was still no big interest in the Tories, so they were able to move position without paying a political price, but they were attacking us better. Peter M said that the Tories were not that good, but we really did have to get our act together, both in going after them and in promoting ourselves. I proposed a very simple 'Who's better?' dividing line as a way of framing the policy debate around economy, living standards, jobs, schools, hospitals, fight on terror. I explained how I thought we could use it. TB and JP immediately liked it, but GB tried to find fault in it, and said it needed more research on dividing lines. It reminded me of some of the discussions of the past, where very simple ideas, not complicated, were immediately made complicated by the nature of the analysis. The 'Who's better for your schools, your jobs, your hospitals etc.?' idea was so clearly made for what he was suggesting but because it had not come from one of 'his people', he immediately sought to find fault in it.

The general discussion felt a bit tired, Douglas going on about the need to make certain admissions of failure before 'getting permission' from the electorate to talk about the future. I said I was simply proposing an umbrella phrase that would allow you to get a simple strategy and dividing lines in place in a way that at the moment we didn't have them. TB said he wanted it put together on that theme. Peter M got it, said that what we were talking about was not difficult, it was a basic message device, plus TB had to get out and about more and be more confident, and we all needed to get after the Tories with far more conviction. GB said we had been trying to go after the Tories but the press weren't interested. They were only interested in using them to attack us. I said they would get interested if we kept at it, and did it more intelligently.

JP said the truth was that economically people had never had it so good, and we weren't doing a good enough job at getting over the fact that a lot of that was down to what the government had done. I had thought Ian [McCartney] looked pretty ground down when I saw him in Birmingham. He said he was really alarmed by the way immigration had picked up as an issue. It was THE thing that was coming back from the phone canvassing, and people were just melting away on it. Peter felt it was a mirror of the press, but agreed it was a problem. TB said they wanted to know we got it. Outside of the meeting itself, GB was far more friendly than the last few times I had seen him. He and JP were both joking about me being in a tracksuit, because I was planning to run home, but also perhaps subconsciously I was saying I didn't really want to be there.

We arranged future meetings, though I was feeling a bit queasy about how much I was being sucked back in. It was not a great feeling at all. I felt very ambivalent. I didn't think it was that great a meeting, but TB said afterwards he had found it a lot more useful than previous meetings, so clearly they had got to a low base. I felt confidence was low. They had bought too much into the idea of trust being a huge problem, which was making them nervous about really pushing on delivery. I felt the arguments were there to be made but GB didn't seem that keen to be making them. We agreed to work up a 'Who's better for you – your future?' plan.

Tessa called later and said the problem was that until TB was clear he was staying, there was instability and people would exploit it. I had been in there for a couple of hours, 70 minutes in that meeting, and was quite glad to get out. I got a lift home as far as Philip's, then ran from there. Spoke to Peter later, who felt we had made a bit of progress but not much. He said we were back to trying to make people work together who for some reason resisted doing so. TB called and said he felt more confident after that. At least we had got everyone in the room and started a proper process. I could feel that I was going to have to lift a lot of this, and it left me feeling a bit down. I was glad we were leaving for a break up in Scotland but also knew I was going to get more sucked in up there.

6–13 April, holiday, Pitlochry

The No. 10 meeting had reminded me of both the good and the bad about the job. On the one hand, as PG said later, it was the same old faces coming together and throwing around the same old problems with the same old perspectives. He said it was like one of those old rock bands that thought they should do just one more big tour. On the other there was still sufficient energy and drive there and it was important that with the Tories slowly getting their act together that we did likewise and started to get the party focused on the coming fight. But equally it was nice just to head off with the family and not feel that I was going to be drawn into work the whole time.

TB was about to head off to Bermuda. When I'd asked him why all the bags were packed and where they were going, he said you're not going to like this. He didn't want to tell me, then I pressed him and he said, 'Oh, all right, Bermuda.' I sighed but said oh well I'm not sure it matters that much. It indicated how my instincts and perspective had changed, as with the statement I made in the interview with *The Herald* at the Belfry when I said most of what I did didn't matter. The frenzies didn't matter. All that mattered were the big policy decisions. I'm not sure if I thought that really or not, but I'd left the flat thankful it wasn't me that was going to have to deal with the mini-frenzy in some of the papers when it emerged he was going to Bermuda and then seeing Bush, at a time Iraq was looking a mess and that was going to bring its own pressures too.

One year on from the fall of Saddam, and there were killings and hostage-takings, increased pressure on Bush, and a clear sense that things had not progressed as planned. We set off, then a relatively painless flight north, relatively painless car hire, though it took us ages to fit the bags in and work out how to use the new credit card type key, then off to a cold but lovely house in the Borders (with the Goulds), and though I wasn't sleeping as well as I should considering how quiet it was, we had a good and largely restful time. Right old Tories who owned the place we were renting, tweed and Barbours and funny-coloured-trouser types. Fiona had made the booking and when they saw me, they looked like they had had a lemon squeezed down their throats. I did a few phone interviews for Cambridge, Bristol and Guildford. I'd taken a decision to pull Glasgow but then they lobbied me and said it was going well, so I decided to reinstate. I did a *Times* column on the next two athletes and chatted endlessly with Philip, who like me seemed a bit down and subdued, but apart from that we did little. His and our kids were getting on great as ever, which always cheered us up.

The first full day I did a long interview for the Channel 5 documentary, over at the Atholl Palace Hotel, Pitlochry, lots about Alex, the *Mail*, the job, and a lot about my breakdown, which Judith [Dawson] seemed to like because she sent me a message later saying please could I not talk about it again between now and transmission? We did lots of running, cycling and swimming, filming in and around Loch Tay. Running OK, but on the bike I was struggling to get over 18mph. Then open-water swimming, with two rescue divers alongside in water that never got deeper than four feet (health and safety, said Judith) and it was absolutely freezing. She asked me about my 'funerals to attend' list which in a jokey chat can sound funny but in a TV interview could sound a bit lu-lu so I tried to play it down.

The house was called Baledmond and owned by landed gentry named Mackenzie. There were Old Etonian pictures on the loo walls, landowner mags and books. But around the place all week, people were nice. Some were broadly supportive of TB, and of the executive. Others, including one guy called Campbell who said his son had seen my speech at St James's Place, felt TB was a goner because of the war. Jack McConnell [First Minister of Scotland] was at the centre of a modest frenzy because of a designer kilt he wore in New York. TB's future was the main focus of our political discussions. He had basically said to me that he was going to decide when away whether he was going to fight next time round; or whether there was any way of standing but not staying for the full term. PG had got much the same message and he was moving to the view that even though we would not get a lift out of GB replacing him, things were not going to get better for TB.

PG was strongly of the view that the war had fundamentally altered the position for TB, that there was a sense he misled the country and therefore he got no credit re leadership and instead Iraq was now just part of the swirl that made immigration, asylum and crime so difficult for us. He said he was shocked by the mounting overt racism in focus groups now; recently a group of Labour voters all openly discussed voting for the BNP and he felt some would. And the Tories, for all that we thought Howard was the past, were making inroads. The press were still giving them an easy time but there is no doubt they were doing better on the political and presentational side and they were creating room for themselves.

TB had admitted to me that until he had resolved in his own mind what he intended to do, then it would be hard properly to fight back. Over the week, PG and I were both moving towards a managed transition with a proper legacy/exit strategy. Both of us felt this would be our last campaign but equally we felt we owed it to the party to get properly engaged. It wasn't clear what exactly I would do in that. I had sent GB a note at the No. 10 meeting re PG and I being in Scotland and maybe meeting up and he had seemed resistant, but Gail had liaised with Sarah [Brown] and we agreed to meet up on the Monday before we left, the day the Goulds were heading back. Fiona and the kids didn't want to come but the meeting having been my idea, I felt

I had to go, so we set off and after getting lost in South Queensferry, pitched up around eleven. GB, dressed in white shirt and filthy jeans, was holding the baby on the steps. Sarah was looking a bit stressed for her, but they were friendly enough, solicitous re Gail, Grace [Gould] and Helena [friend], and though we never really got to the point, we had a proper discussion of sorts.

I always found myself agreeing with a lot of Gordon's analysis, but when you pressed him on what we should do, he tended to move to another area of analysis. He said we needed a single argument and we needed to push it through with ruthlessness and focus. So what is it? He said it was in the area of standing up for Britain. But then he would say that you'd never get away with it at the moment because of asylum and the constitution.* When you pushed on any structural changes he would say well you could do this or do that but I'm not sure it would make much difference. He was scathing re Charles Clarke, said that we had got more money than ever but he let the NUT away with an attack that we were cutting spending, because Charles saw the Treasury not them or the Tories as the enemy. He said he didn't know why we bothered with the teaching unions. He thought JR was pushing the wrong message, that he was focused on reform rather than progress through investment and technology etc.

TB was barely mentioned. I was about to ask the central question – was TB a problem and did he think he would be there at the election? – but Gail and Sarah came back with the baby, now wearing a Harvard hat given to him by Ed Miliband [chairman, Treasury's Council of Economic Advisers] – and the moment went. He was spot on about Howard; said he was unprincipled, opportunist, the classic do-one-thing, say-another politician. I said we weren't hitting him hard enough. GB sort of agreed but then said if you're going to attack him, you have to make it work, and that was that. PG and I both found it frustrating because we never really moved to a point where we properly discussed what we needed to do, but at least we had had a civilised and reasonable chat about things. It was a start. It had been cagey but that was probably no bad thing. He had been sussing out what we were up to, and we were doing the same. We never got to the point but it didn't matter for now, we would get to it later.

* It was feared that government bills concerning the rights of asylum-seekers, and constitutional reform involving judicial changes might not conform with the European Convention on Human Rights.

Fiona was concerned that I was getting myself into a position where I would continue to be beholden to the government even post-TB. I suspect Gail had that worry too in relation to the book, which I had pushed further on to the backburner on account of Ed Victor being ill. GB and Gail discussed what books were coming out, we swapped a few stories re Clinton, had a superficial chat re Bush/Kerry then that was pretty much it. He was impressive in many ways, but in others not. He was an intellectual which was a good thing on one level but not so good when it came to putting in place what he said was needed – a ruthlessly focused strategy. PG said afterwards he was not sure he was a real leader. I also noticed more than before how he looked his age. The hair was still thick but greying. He was overweight and he had a very fleshy lower chin. But the dynamic had definitely moved towards TB going sooner rather than later. PG felt we should be thinking of a strategy for him leaving after ten years as leader. That was soon. It would all depend on TB's frame of mind when he came back. What was extraordinary was that we were having these thoughts and these discussions and there was no real sense of this issue in the media.

Meanwhile I'd decided to extend the holiday. Auntie Nan [AC's mother's eldest sister, Nancy Caldwell] had died on Thursday and I thought I should stay up for the funeral on Wednesday, having also finally made contact with Graeme Obree, who lived in Irvine, just a few miles from where the funeral would be. So after the Goulds had gone, and we'd had Alex and Sheena [Downie, relatives] round for dinner, Fiona dropped me at Pitlochry station on the Tuesday morning before they all headed home and I headed to Glasgow. I sat opposite a Tory TV scriptwriter who was a friend of Gregor Mackay [former Tory spokesman]. I was met by the *Sun* snapper and did some pictures there before heading to the theatre for a full day of interviews. Then out to do the Real Radio football phone-in with Alan Rough [former Scottish international] and Ewen Cameron [broadcaster], which was fun, Ewen taking the mick out of Rough for always agreeing with me. Then a pre-record for their Sunday programme which was too much re Iraq/Hutton. But of all the theatre publicity days, easily the busiest and most productive.

Sometimes I found myself getting tired of what I was saying, and it was tiring anyway, but I felt it would help make it a success and it was a nice old-fashioned theatre. They had published their brochure for the season today and had broken records, so felt confident about this one. Planning visit to Cardiff now for BFC/Neil [Kinnock]. Did OK with running training but I was falling behind on swimming and cycling. Last night out with Donald [brother] at his work at Glasgow University and then for dinner. Lots of students coming up to talk. Bizarre that our lives took such different courses.

Wednesday 14 April

Staying at Donald's, up really early for an interview with the BBC Arts programme, Claire English [presenter] and producer. Surreal, she said, with me on the bed and her in the chair, but it would help shift tickets. Also doing (telephone) interviews for Cambridge including two student mags. James Dacre, editor of *Varsity*. He sounded like a chinless wonder. I said are you related to the most poisonous man in public life? To which he said yes, he's my father. I went ahead anyway and actually later felt a bit bad that I had hammered him a bit over his dad, knowing how sometimes our kids got whacked because of me. I quite liked the events themselves, but not all the interviews I had to do to promote them. But these theatres were operating on such tight margins and had no real marketing budgets at all. Pretty big coverage in the Scottish papers, two page spread in *The Sun*, big piece in *The Scotsman*, lots on the radio, but it was hard grind.

Donald and I drove over to Irvine where I had fixed to interview Graeme Obree, who had held the world record for distance travelled in a single hour. We got lost, asked someone for Irvine Cycles and found we were right outside it. Obree was a very bouncy but chaotic character. The house was tidy enough but certainly not luxurious, and he hadn't done as well out of the sport as he deserved. Very open about his mental problems, the depressions, the low self-esteem, the suicide attempts. He said he couldn't believe I had been so positive about his book. He really had no sense of his own special-ness at all. He and I then went out on bikes through some really pretty country roads with the *Times* photographer following us. We had a fantastic chat. He was so open, and then we re-ran it when we got back to the house so that I could take notes. He was odd but nice and he and Donald got on. He said he was happy for me to make up any quotes so long as they roughly reflected what he had said. He was going to do creative writing, said he would love to write a novel like *The Great Gatsby*.

There were people from the local papers outside when I left and I could tell he was anxious that I thought he might have tipped them off, which I didn't. I thought there was something crazy about them being more interested in me than him, but I guess as he had lived there for so long he was part of the furniture. Nice running round the place with Donald for the day. Did a few calls as we headed to the Lang Kirk in Kilmarnock for Auntie Nan's funeral. Really good service, fabulous turnout. Mum was looking pretty stressed out. I noticed that she couldn't look at the coffin, either in the church or later. Off to the burial, chatting with Sheena and Ann [Caldwell, cousins] then off to Burnhouses Farm at Galston. Chatting away to all the relatives. The farm had changed quite a lot since I spent my summers there. I was glad I'd stayed up for the funeral. Also, lots of them wanted to come to the event in Glasgow. Got a lift with Donald to the airport and flew home, working on the Obree piece, then to the Vine [Kentish Town pub] for a do for Christine Garbutt [former *Mirror* colleague], lots of the old *Mirror* crowd.

Thursday 15 April
Up really early to work on a foreword for [Burnley specialist author] Dave Thomas's latest book on Burnley. Surprised to hear his view that a lot of the players didn't get on with Leighton James [Welsh former player]. Finished the piece on athletics for *The Times* and then working on the Obree column but had to break off to go up to Hampstead to do some telly for Meriden and Anglia, ticket flogging. Lunch with Nigel Bennett, the lawyer Ed had put me in touch with who was looking over all the contracts with Channel 5 etc. PG called. He said Douglas had told him that GB had said he was touched that I went all that way to see him, and that despite everything I was still trying to be constructive between him and TB. He said he had been positively enthusiastic about the meeting, which is not how it had felt at the time.

The big news was Bush going back on the Middle East Road Map [US-backed peace proposal] with Ariel Sharon [Prime Minister of Israel]. Dreadful, and bad for TB, given how much we had emphasised that he had managed to get Bush to a more positive and proactive place on MEPP [Middle East Peace Process]. TB was heading there and it was all looking a bit ropey, and the sense of setback adding to a feel of decay. Both *The Sun* and *The Times* ran stories – and it wasn't immediately clear to me whether it was wishful thinking or inspired from somewhere – that we were going to go for a referendum on the constitution, which would be a pretty monumental U-turn. Crazy. Derek Hatton called, seeing whether I thought there was any point in him trying to get his internet firm plugged into the Labour Party. It struck me as maybe being a bit difficult, and I didn't really understand what they did.

Friday 16 April

Off to Bristol to do media. Met by Kwame [Kwei-Amah, actor and playwright] who was going to chair the event and we did several interviews together. Liked him a lot, and felt he'd be a good chair. Got a lift to the station and linked up with Fiona and Grace on the train to Cardiff. Got to Neil's in Wales. Judith and her team were there, wanting to film the four of us talking, but there was always something terribly unnatural about it. Eventually Neil and I both opened up a bit, particularly on the press, the nature of the modern media and why Neil's experience had been such an influence on the way I did the job. Over dinner though, I felt Neil was still too angry about things, and Fiona still way too negative. He thought that I should try to get myself into a position to be the next European Commissioner from the UK. He said he was not against Peter M per se, but worried that he wouldn't be able to manage all the relationships he needed to deal with.* Neil was pretty keen himself to get out of things, clearly found it frustrating as well as fulfilling and challenging. Re TB–GB, he felt TB had probably won over all the people he could at various stages in the past, but it was unlikely he was going to win over extra support, but he could lose some of what we had gained. He felt GB was still his own worst enemy. He felt it was probably right, and the best thing, that he took over at some point, but still felt it was possible it wouldn't happen.

Glenys was very down on TB, mainly Iraq, but now also because of the shift on the referendum [on ratification of the European Constitution Treaty]. She and Fiona seemed to be much more negative about TB and the government than Neil, who although angry about one or two specific things was at least understanding of the problems TB was having to deal with.

Saturday 17 April

I couldn't sleep and got up halfway through the night to read. I finished the book on Obree and did the piece for *The Times*. Found an

---

* Mandelson had expressed interest in becoming the UK's European Commissioner when Kinnock and former Governor of Hong Kong Chris Patten were due to step down.

interesting book on the shelves about Welsh rugby legends, and had a read of that. I had a long chat with Glenys before Neil was up. She said no matter how much time passed, he would never fully get over defeat [in the 1992 general election]. The anger, some of it with himself, some with others who he felt had let him down, was always near the surface. He had put everything into it, and it was taken away very late. I did an 8-mile run, and after stepping out of the shower later, I could hear Neil being interviewed by Judith outside, very warm about me, none of the anger or the angst about TB apparent. We set off for the Cardiff-Burnley game. Sam Hamman [then owner of Cardiff FC] doing the usual joking around. Terrible game. I thought at one point Neil was going to lose it completely with the referee. We played for a draw and got punished (2–0). Relegation looming.

Sunday 18 April

The referendum story was picking up pace, without any real sense of where it was meant to be heading. Off to the [London] Marathon. Rory did pretty well in the junior race, came in fourteenth. Nice atmosphere despite the rain. Bumped into Cherie at the main grandstand and she was pretty chilly. I asked her how Bush and Laura had been and she said 'I'm not going to talk about any of that to a journalist.' Suit yourself, I said. Probably a good job that Fiona had already left. Cherie was nice enough to Rory and Grace, though Rory said he really thought she had changed a lot, that she was a lot less friendly. Had a nice chat with David Davis [Tory MP], who said he wanted to sponsor my next event. Also said he felt sorry for Bev Hughes, that even though they had been putting the boot in, he thought she was a good minister and it was a pity she went. He asked my view on the referendum and though I tried to be nuanced, he laughed and said he would put it around that I thought it was a dreadful idea. Roger Bannister [doctor and athlete, first man to run a mile in under 4 minutes] was there and had seen the piece yesterday and we had a nice chat, recalling the time Fiona asked him what his event was. [Lord] Seb Coe [politician and former athlete] agreed to do an interview for the *Times* series on great sportsmen and also asked if I would give him some help re strategy and comms on the Olympic bid. I met Barbara Cassani [chair of London bid to host 2012 Summer Olympics] who seemed a lot nicer than I had been led to believe she was, though she definitely had a thing about equestrian sports ahead of others.

April '04: Cherie doesn't want to talk to 'journalist' AC

Set off for Guildford, meeting Mick Hucknall at his place in the middle of a golf course, great house with his studios inbuilt. He said he had a girlfriend moving in next month and that it was settling down time. His one condition for chairing the event was that we arrive at the front of the theatre in his Ferrari and do pictures together sitting on the bonnet. It was at the Yvonne Arnaud, which was more atmospheric than most of them and Mick felt it was better than it had been in Manchester, that it flowed better and that the Q&A was livelier. Kwame was there and said he was now looking forward to Bristol. Got quite lively with a guy who called me a hypocrite. I asked at one point who read the *Daily Mail* and when only two hands went up suggested Guildford had its fair share of liars. One of the two with their hands up said I was too sensitive, because though she read it she didn't believe a word it said but she loved the horoscope.

Monday 19 April

All the leaks and briefing were leading to the confirmation that TB was doing a statement tomorrow setting out the need for a referendum on the European constitution. I felt really fed up and worried about it. I had been asked about it at Guildford last night and said that though the current position was difficult, it was tenable, that while people could see the sense in holding off till after the election, this looked weak and it was the wrong move for the wrong reasons. Peter M sent me a copy of the email he had sent to TB, saying that it was a mistake and that it would not have the effect he thought it would. He argued that our enemies would make hay with it, and exploit the sense of weakness it displayed. I totally agreed. Philip said the same. But it seemed both GB and JP supported it. I texted JoP, saying simply, 'Is this wise?' He replied, at our best when at our boldest, after the election.

Met Syd Young [former *Mirror* colleague] after getting the train to Bristol and he drove me to the BBC. Very soft and quite enjoyable interview with John Turner, who said to me he thought Richard Sambrook was a wanker and Gilligan should have gone on day one. Nonetheless, I could feel there was a fair bit of angst among the BBC staff re me being there. Did a few more interviews at the theatre, then a session at the *Western Daily Press*, where Terry Manners [editor] presented me with a really nice photo album of pictures they had taken of my various visits there. He was a real pro-us kind of guy, but said down in their patch people were very worried about getting GB. He said he worried that TB would lack the same energy and direction if I wasn't there. Back to Syd's for dinner, did a bit of work.

Tuesday 20 April

Two days of talking bollocks ahead, and I can't say I was looking forward to it that much. Syd was joking about him being my spin doctor, because his phone kept going with local and regional media wanting to talk to me. TB's statement on the referendum was going big. I spoke to David Miliband who said there was a lot of unease about it, and a sense that TB was being pushed around, and it would create a sense of weakness. I was doing a session with students at Bristol College, probably a bit unwise given it was where Tony once got hit with a load of tomatoes. We got a message in advance that there was a small demo. I arrived and walked through them but what was clear was that there was no control or security at all. One of the lecturers struck me as a bit of a Trot, while another of them was using the whole thing to push her own views. The students were more measured than they were but all in all it was a bit of a pain and Syd wondered why I put up with it. We then heard that eggs were being given out to the students as they left so we decided to use a different exit and a different car. Someone must have told them because the ringleaders found out where we were and lobbed a few eggs at the car. Syd seemed a lot more upset about it than I was, but I did agree to cancel the university event in the afternoon, and instead he and I went for a long lunch.

The demos certainly jacked up the coverage, and I did a live spot with HTV from the venue, and there were more police than there had been at any of the venues apart from the first one so far. At one point, it was possible to hear the demos outside as I spoke. I spotted a couple of the ringleaders from the morning in the audience and drew attention to them, so they left to join their friends outside who were now banging on all the doors and windows. Kwame handled it really well and inside the mood was pretty good. One of the best rounds of applause came when I pointed out Syd in the audience and said it was possible to be a good journalist and a good human being, and he had shown it all his career.

TB called during the interval. He said today had gone OK, but he admitted he would rather not to have had to do it, but he had felt he had little option. He said he was keen to see me soon because it was difficult knowing who he could talk to at the moment. He sounded pretty fed up. There was less strength in his voice than usual. He said Bush had asked for me and had said the Blair visits weren't the same without my irreverence. We talked for ten minutes or so but I had to go out for the second half. Kwame referred to the call. I didn't go into any detail, and I suspected they would all be a bit alarmed if they knew how down he had sounded. What he really wanted was to get to a position on Europe where the question was in or out. Where they were with it was not a healthy position. He said Howard had really gone for him on trust, saying people would never believe him on anything again. OTT. But the reality was TB had been pushed into something he didn't really want to do, and even though he said it was about smoking out the sceptics, I don't think it worked. At the end of the event I did an interview with five students, nice bunch, one of them absolutely gorgeous. They were pissed off at the demos but felt it had gone fine. Syd was touched by the tribute but said he found it hard to come to terms with the kind of life I led. I said I was now, to quote Rory, talking bollocks for a living.

Wednesday 21 April
Off to Dublin. Wrote a piece for *Pro Cycling* on Lance on the way. TB called again, clearly fretting a bit post-statement, and fearing it had hit him on the strength front. Paul Allen [Dublin PR] had done a brilliant job setting up the visit, interviews like clockwork. Did a round table at the Merrion Hotel with a few hacks, good bunch. Then to the Institute of PR, spoke to the students then off to see Bertie [Ahern]. They left us one on one, and he said he had been really surprised at TB changing the line on the referendum. His main preoccupation was the presidency of the EU, which was a massive job for any country that did it, but probably magnified for the smaller ones. Ireland punched above their weight though in these negotiations, and he had pretty good relations with most of them. He reckoned on 'the North' that they were going to have a few more ups and downs, but that the broad framework was solid. He just could not see the Provos going back from where they were. There were still a few out there who would never stop, but they didn't have the weight or the muscle.

He was looking OK, but said he had to pretend to be celibate most of the time because the press made things so difficult for Celia [Larkin, Ahern's former companion]. He felt that TB and Jonathan were both having to carry too much of the burden since I left. Like TB, he was still thinking about whether to go for another term. If his kids had their way, he probably wouldn't, but he thought he could win and he thought he still had a lot to give. He reckoned TB would and should stay for another term, but felt he had dipped a bit in energy and confidence the last time he saw him. 'It can't be easy having Gordon growling at you the whole time.' He quizzed me a bit on whether there were any actual differences between them or whether it was about personality and ambition.

Lovely man, nice to see him and talk probably a lot more reflectively than we were used to when surrounded by the intensity of a negotiation. He and TB were still working pretty well as a double act. He walked me out, said keep in touch and then I set off for Belfast. Hilary Coffman called and said there was a rumour that the *Daily Express* was switching its support to the Tories. She asked if I could call [Richard] Desmond. I spoke to him and he said it was not going to happen, which turned out to be utter bollocks. He said he was not interfering, that there was no way they would back the Tories at the election. I passed that back but it was duff information. I had a stack more media to do in Belfast, the best of which was Gerry Kelly [broadcaster and journalist]. He also agreed to chair the event at the Waterfront.

Thursday 22 April
Up to do a blast of radio in the hotel then headed to the BBC to do [radio presenter] Stephen Nolan's show. Quite spiky, obviously a man trying to get himself noticed, but OK and I was able to say re the *Express* that it was nothing to do with political principle and everything to do with gaining attention in a competitive marketplace. He had seen the interview with Kelly last night and was keen to talk about my breakdown. Also lots on TB–GB. The big story of the day was Ron Atkinson calling Marcel Desailly [Chelsea footballer] a lazy nigger when he thought the mic was off. Did half a dozen interviews, lots about the peace process, and you really got a sense of things changing for the better, not least at the Waterfront itself. The theatre seemed to think the media blitz would shift enough tickets. Flew home, dealt with backlog of emails. There was a sense politically that both the referendum plan and Iraq were unravelling a bit for TB.

PG sent through an interesting note on some groups in Enfield – it was hilarious how often Enfield and Edgware featured in his focus groups. They had been shown a number of possible attack films on

April '04: TB should stay on, says Ahern

Howard, and it was amazing how little they knew about him, and it led quite a few to say he was better than Hague or IDS. It was almost like he had never existed in government. But when they were reminded of his role in the poll tax, it was quite a powerful reaction.* Immigration was still running big and bad, lots of talk of 'swamped, over-run, out for themselves' and a lot of the anti-feeling linked to the war, but there was far more openness to the idea of controlled immigration when it was of clear and direct benefit to the economy. The good news was that almost all of them said they felt better off, living standards wise, but their big worry was how their kids would ever be able to afford their own home.

Friday 23 April

One of those days where I feel I should write things down straight away because of the sense of having been involved in a conversation that will be one of those the historians will want to know every little detail about. TB had called a few times in the past few days and had been anxious about the referendum, not sure if he had done the right thing, pretty clear that even if he had, he had done it for the wrong reasons. He also felt that GB was still diddling around. He had mentioned it during the chat we had when I was in Bristol, then again last night after I got back from Belfast. He said things were pretty grim at the moment and he would really welcome a chat. He asked if I could go and see him today.

I cycled in, parked the bike in Catherine Rimmer's office, saw the press office team briefly, lots of ribbing re eggs in Bristol, and also the story saying I was still in charge of No. 10. TB was held up with a call to Chirac re referendum/justice and home affairs stuff. When he was finished, I went up and joined him and Cherie in the kitchen. I knew something had gone on with the PCC yesterday because I had got calls about it. I asked Cherie what had happened and she said, 'Why should I tell you when you are now a member of the press?' Pretty much the same as she had said at the marathon. I said, 'Well why start talking to me about it in the first place?' TB raised his eyebrows.

He made a cup of tea and we went through to the lounge. He looked relaxed enough, wearing jeans and a shirt and trainers, quite tanned,

* Howard personally supported the introduction of Margaret Thatcher's Community Charge local taxation, which provoked public protests against the 'poll tax' in 1990.

but he said some days he'd just had enough. He thought if he wanted to he could fight another general election, and win it. But it would mean really getting himself up for it and totally changing his operation. He said he had good people, nice people as well but he worried whether they were good enough or big enough really to get things going again. He said he had lost me, Anji and Peter M and it was like Alex losing Roy Keane, Ryan Giggs and Paul Scholes [Man Utd star players] and getting Nicky Butt, Diego Forlan and Darren Fletcher. Good, but not as good. He said a lot of days at the moment, he found it a real struggle. The upside was he thought he could win. The downside was all that he would need to do to make that happen and also that he would hate the campaign. Also, he felt if he stayed to fight another term, GB would go into total destruct mode and it would do real long-term damage. He felt there was a chance GB would grow into it. He was crazy and difficult in many ways but he was at least able, capable of devising and delivering strategy.

He was worried though that a lot of people who still supported us did so because of TB and that support would end with him if he left. I said maybe but there are also people we have lost who might come back to us, some more traditional voters. TB said they didn't have many other places to go to. So far as I could tell, he had basically decided because his list of downsides was definitely longer than the upsides, though clearly some of this was driven by a rare down mood in general. He then said there was another complication. He wondered whether he shouldn't go for the European President's job, because he felt he could do it well and he would be doing it at a very important time. I said I would be amazed if the French wouldn't try to block him because of his basic pro-Americanism. He was not so sure. He felt the key people would be Bertie, who was not only the current President but also someone he could trust, plus [Gerhard] Schroeder [German Chancellor], who could maybe keep the French in line. I reminded him of some of his previous run-ins with Schroeder, who even though he might not like the French that much, was probably not agin siding with them on something like this. There was a push at the moment for Guy Verhofstadt [Belgian PM] but he felt he would be a disaster.

I said it looked to me like he had made his mind up not to fight the next election and he said yes, 'What do you think?' I said I thought that's what he would do, based on recent signals, but wondered if it wasn't driven by mood and events. I thought it would lose us some votes but gain us others. I said that he had done the job well, in difficult

April '04: TB thinking of going for EU President job

times as well as more straightforward times, and part of his consideration could justifiably be what was good for him as well as others. I told him in more detail of my conversations with GB in Scotland, said that basically TB barely figured in GB's script these days and I felt there was a chance that if TB stayed he would go right offside. He said it might not be possible to get the European job and it would definitely be bad for him if he went for it and then failed because of a French veto. But he said that even if that happened, he could always make a bit of money for two or three years and then do what he really wanted to do, namely focus on religion, all the faith stuff. He seemed pretty settled on it, felt he had a strong legacy and he had to move on at the election. I said it sounded like he was feeling how I had felt towards the end, too many days when you wake up and wonder whether it's the right thing to be doing this any longer. He said he had always been of the view that two terms was probably about right.

He was confident on the legacy front, economy, investment, constitution, Ireland and so on, but some days he was just fucked off with it. He said he thought he commanded a certain amount of respect because of his sheer resilience, but said it's not really a reason for going on. He said he had discussed this with Anji but felt he couldn't really discuss it with anyone else at the moment. He asked me direct whether I thought he should keep going. I said I could see it both ways. I had no doubt he could win again but equally I wasn't that convinced things were going to get much better for him. He had done well on any fair and reasonable analysis, but partly because there had been a backlash against what people thought was image, and partly because of Iraq, there was very little fair and reasonable analysis around.

He had just seen Les Hinton who gave no hint whatever that Murdoch was even thinking of shifting to the Tories. I said nor did Desmond, and he said, 'He sat here three weeks ago and said there was no way they would do that.' We were interrupted by Stephen Wall [foreign policy advisor] and Matthew Rycroft who popped in for a chat re the French. TB showed me a UK analysis of the French analysis re the referendum plan, rightly saying it was necessity born of virtue. They felt it showed TB's genuine commitment to Europe. He felt Europe needed a big figure heading the Commission right now. After they had left, he asked me to think about how he might start planning a campaign to become European President quite soon. He said he had the idea of doing a big reshuffle, totally New Labour, bring back Peter M and Alan Milburn, really go for it, then the next day say that he would not be leading the party into the next election. I said he was more popular than the polls indicated and more popular than it probably felt to him, and he would be a lot more so when he left, so it was important he wasn't exaggerating because of the relentlessly negative media. I said of course there were people who hated him, and there were people who disagreed fundamentally with his politics and with individual policies like Iraq. Some of them would never vote for him again. But some of them never did.

I said I got a very different feel from people these days, maybe because I was out of the front line, but the mood I picked up, even if it wasn't great, always contained a lot of respect, and that was because people knew he could do the job. And there was a bigger constituency out there than he imagined of people who positively responded to him and his leadership. He said, incidentally, that he had picked up rave reviews for my theatre stuff and speeches and he felt I should do more and more of it.

He had to leave because he was heading off to Chequers for a meeting with Sinn Féin and a call with GWB. How many more of those were there going to be? Who knows, he said. He said re GB that on one level he will be able to do it, but I worry that he won't be able to cope with all the personal pressure, because he'll feel it's all so unfair. He'll feel that he shouldn't have to put up with it all. It'll be classic Clinton–Gore, politician followed by intellectual. He over-intellectualises and therefore sometimes misses the point. In the Treasury, he can disappear for weeks on end and then re-emerge. You can't do that in this job. Here, there's nowhere to disappear to, the pressure is always on. I asked him what CB thought. He said she was happy either way, marginally probably hoping that he stayed but she would be fine if he didn't. I said she seemed a bit mixed up at the moment. She definitely had it in for me again. I said I'd think about things and get back to him. He looked settled and calm, but it might be he was just going through a bad patch.

I cycled home, belatedly doing an interview with the *Cambridge Evening News* on the mobile. They asked me if I still saw TB, and what kind of things we talked about. I waffled on, conscious of the fact I was now in possession of a story that would blow their minds, that TB was thinking of leaving, possibly announcing it in a matter of weeks. It was quite something to be one of a minuscule group of people who he felt able to share that with, knowing I would share it with nobody. I got the train up north, reading Seb Coe's book, and working on the speech for Ireland. Train delayed two hours, but I got there in time for the start of the [Labour Party] fundraiser in Bury. Good event, organised by David Chaytor and Ivan Lewis [MPs]. Good reception, nice event, definitely a feeling in the party that even if things felt a bit ragged at the moment, we had the record and the message for the future to put together a winning campaign. I also sensed they were getting sick of the TB–GB thing and blaming GB for most of it. I got a lift late on to Stan Ternent's.

Saturday 24 April

Dreadful hay fever. Stan close to the end of his tether. He said lack of money was making it impossible to do the job. Barry Kilby wanted him to stay but there were clearly others who felt we needed a bigger name, maybe George Graham or Glenn Hoddle [prominent managers], and it would be tough. He talked me through all the wage bills and felt it would be impossible to keep our better players, who could get more money elsewhere, as could some of the less good ones. The difference between clubs in and around us even, in terms of overall wage bill and the kind of salaries individual players could get, was big and getting bigger. I had invited Geoff Hoon and his son Chris and it was interesting that the Derby County board didn't really know him, even though he went there a lot. I went over with Calum to sit on the far side and got into a bit of a ruck with a couple of twats singing about how Derby 'have Paki fans'. I went to find a steward to sort them out but needless to say he was Asian, so I thought it would probably just make things kick off more and embarrass him, so I left it. We won 1–0. I did an event for the party in Burnley at the ground afterwards. Terrible organisation, really poor, no grip whatever. Frank Teasdale [former Burnley chairman] was there as a guest and said he couldn't believe how shambolic they were, said it was a totally wasted opportunity.

Sunday 25 April

Paul Allen called, said I was wall-to-wall in the Irish press and the Dublin event was selling out. Re the political scene, the referendum U-turn had taken its toll, TB was getting hit all over the place and looking a bit fragile again. The question marks about his future were starting to pick up a bit, but there was no sense anywhere of what we had discussed and what he was thinking. I hadn't mentioned to anyone and didn't get a sense from the others that he had been talking to them about it. I worried that he saw the Europe job as a possible replacement for where he was now. I just couldn't see the big guys wanting a big country leader in there, and certainly not one like TB.

Monday 26 April

David Mannion and Lauren Taylor [both ITV News] came round to discuss ideas on political engagement, and wanted me to do authored pieces for the campaign coverage. They felt that even if I was working directly inside the campaign, that was fine provided they got someone similar from the other parties. I was slowly getting used to the volume of emails that seem to come in. Bad hay fever. TB/referendum still boiling away, and pretty negatively.

Tuesday 27 April

Visited Lilian Baylis School [Kennington, south London] with Fiona. The head, Gary Phillips, was clearly a good guy, but admitted he got the job in part because nobody else would do it.* I spoke to the citizenship class, who were terrific. One particularly bright and inquisitive girl who had a brilliant natural political mind. She asked me afterwards if I thought 'someone like me' could ever get into politics, and I said, '"Someone like you" has to, or else politics is in trouble.' Gary was big on the little things, and there was a sense of good discipline and, even though loads of them had tough backgrounds, there was a lot of aspiration in there.

I was feeling tired though, had too much stuff going on at the moment, and all a bit bitty. I needed to sort out a bit of clarity in it all – charity, media, speeches, party stuff, TB, and making sense of all the ideas and offers that were coming in which I was just pushing into a growing file on my desk. PG was calling me the whole time, pressing me to get more and more involved again, and I felt I wasn't contributing much at the moment. He felt David Hill was good at killing stories but not at pushing strategies through the media, and TB needed more of that. I felt buoyed up a bit by the visit to the school, where the head

---

* Fiona Millar was to write in praise of the school, situated in an area referred to by shadow Chancellor and local resident Oliver Letwin when he claimed he would rather be a beggar than send his children to a state school.

April '04: Hard to see major EU leaders backing TB for top role

admitted the government had made a difference, and where so many of the kids, whatever their backgrounds, were clearly nice and bright.

Off with Cathy Gilman and the documentary team to Hainault to get new gear from the triathlon shop. Good set of blokes, fanatical about triathlon. Again, I was amazed at how hard it was to get inside a wetsuit. They had some fantastic bikes in there, and once we decided which one I was going for, I rode with cleats for the first time, and fell off once, but fairly quickly got the hang of it. Home to change then off to a party gala dinner at the Park Lane Hilton. Chris Lennie [deputy general secretary] was keen to get me schmoozing around the place. My speech was mainly based around some of the best funnies from the ['Audience With'] shows, plus a bit of ra-ra about TB and delivery. TB agreed to do a brief chat for the benefit of the documentary, just the two of us talking, reasonably natural, but he wasn't relaxed. His own speech was a bit tired and defensive and he was still a bit fed up, I could tell. I asked him if he had decided yet and he said no, he was still thinking. What did I think? I said he shouldn't rush. I doubted the European job was a runner. And he certainly shouldn't make a decision as big as this when he wasn't feeling his usual self. It was nice being back at a party event, and the speech seemed to go down fine, especially the story about JP and the punch, which I had turned from the answer at the Festival Hall into a fullscale rolling anecdote. Richard Wilson [actor and Labour supporter] said he thought I was a lot better than the last time he saw me, that my timing was better but I had to watch the cough. He felt there might be something wrong with my vocal chords. June Sarpong [TV presenter] agreed to do the Old Vic event.

PG sent me another note from the groups, Hemel Hempstead, economy still our biggest strength, and a weakness for the Tories. When people were reminded of the Tory record, negative equity etc., it resonated, and when you played Howard into that, it carried some weight. But people always had to be reminded Howard had been there. On schools and hospitals also, we are stronger than the Tories, but they are unpersuaded all the money is delivering as it should. Again, there is a real 'short memory syndrome' at work here. On the referendum, broad support for the change of tack, but more evidence this was real Westminster/media bubble stuff compared to economy, NHS, immigration. PG said they tried out lots of attack lines and dividing lines. The one I had been pushing for – 'Who's better for...' – was better received here than in previous groups, but it still required too big a leap for some.

'Britain's getting better, don't let the Tories wreck it (again)' worked better. 'There is only one choice' was seen as arrogant.

I sent a note back to PG, saying what was becoming clear was that we had to do a much better job of definition on Howard, who was like a blank canvas and in some ways moving from neutral to positive; we had to link him to Tory record and to being the risk to the progress we had made. PG felt we already had the shape for the PEBs [party election broadcasts] structure for the campaign – Howard definition; their record on the economy v ours; their record on cuts v ours; charges for public services, NHS in particular.

Wednesday 28 April
Cambridge interviews, then Jon Smith [First Artist, football agent] came round for a chat. He said he was in charge of the biggest football agency in Europe but he was trying to broaden out. He thought I could really do something for his company and use it as a base to do something for sport more generally. It wasn't clear exactly what he wanted me for but he was clearly a fan and said if I could take some of the zeal I'd used for TB and Labour, and apply it to his world, he thought we could make a big difference. I also had a bid in to get involved with the Football Foundation, but I wasn't finding it easy to decide what of all this stuff I actually wanted to do. I could see that Jon Smith thought I was a bit odd, not biting when he went on about share options, but I wanted to be sure.

I ran to Battersea, where I was meeting Seb Coe to do a piece for *The Times*. He was with Tamsyn Lewis, the Aussie middle-distance runner he was coaching. We met at a little cafe by the track, got the interview out of the way and then had a really good chat. She was a big John Howard fan, so probably a Tory. She said she thought TB was more a spokesman than a leader. Though Seb had been a Tory MP, I had never thought he was that far away from us politically, and we always had a good relationship when he was with Hague. He had a very nice manner about him, some good stories to tell. Interesting on his relationship with his dad, more coach–athlete when that was what they were, but still close. Interesting too on the relationship between physical and mental. He admired Steve Ovett [rival athlete] a lot, much more than I had imagined from all the coverage I had read. Interesting on how for a top athlete, demeanour really matters too, off track as well as on. He was aware of the conversations I had been having with Tessa and said he was keen to involve me in the Olympic bid. I said, 'What about your lot, are they going to be OK with that?' and he thought yes. 'Might get you out of campaigning against them the whole time,' and he laughed. We chatted for a couple of hours and then did the pictures. The photographer had the idea of trying to recreate the famous picture of him winning gold, arms outstretched, with me just behind him in the Steve Ovett role. I thought it was a bit wanky, but Seb went for it and to be fair, it sort of worked.

I was feeling a bit mega stressed out. Out for dinner at the Jays [Margaret and husband, AIDS specialist Mike Adler]. Bob Kiley [London commissioner of transport] and his wife were there. He was very well-informed, very clever but had maybe inhaled too much of the 'US transport guru' stuff and was therefore a little bit up himself. I wasn't entirely convinced listening to some of his arguments about the tube. He seemed to have struck up a pretty good relationship with Ken [Livingstone, Mayor of London], though. I didn't like the way he talked about GB, though I suspect it was just par for the course where he was.

Margaret was hilarious as ever. I got the feeling she hated the flummery of the Lords but she had a great feel for political argument, and was brilliant at the short put-down of some of her more ridiculous colleagues. Mike was more interested in my piece on Lance Armstrong. I don't think I'd ever written an article which had been mentioned to me by so many people. Mike was interested in the medical recovery side of things, and how much I thought Lance's success was about just having a tougher mind than everyone else. Neither he nor Kiley were wholly convinced about the drugs side of things, but I found I was becoming a bit of a true believer on that one. Home and then Alex, who was out in Monaco, called later for a long chat. He thought the Football Foundation would be good, but that I'd go mad with some of the people at most of the clubs. 'You'd be amazed how many of our clubs are actually run by people who probably couldn't run anything else.'

Thursday 29 April

Definitely on a bit of a dip. I did the Coe interview, which was fine, then another piece on the Dutch athlete Fanny Blankers-Koen [late Olympian and multi-world record holder]. Off to Cambridge at 4, to do the theatre event. Kwame chairing. Godric and family came in for a chat, also four Burnley fans who I'd seen at loads of games were in the second row. Then at the half-time interval, they brought in a card from Millie [Lay], who was the barmaid at the [Gonville and] Caius [Cambridge college] bar when I was there. She said she was still going strong after thirty-two years. I brought her into the Q&A, when she said she had followed my career with interest, she was very proud of me, and given how much I used to drink, amazed that I was alive. I had a nice natter with her and her daughter afterwards. I got more Hutton and Iraq than before. Also quite a lot on Cherie and Carole [Caplin]. I lost it a bit with a woman near the front who kept muttering at me all the time, but by and large it was OK, very friendly. Kwame was a top bloke, very up and upbeat, very religious. Nice to see Millie but maybe evidence I had not exactly set Cambridge alight academically that she was the only person from my student days that came along, at least so far as I could tell. The Burnley fans came backstage, which meant I had more Burnley Cambridge connections in the audience than from student days.

Friday 30 April

A real prostitution job, presenting the Britvic Awards in Soho. Quite a nice crowd, but not great for the soul. Alex had agreed to do one of my Channel 5 interviews, but was pissed off at the contract that had been sent through. Heaven knows why we needed one, but his lawyer was suspicious, thought it was too detailed, and it wasn't clear that it was to be a one-off. I told Stuart [Prebble] we would have been better not to have a contract at all. I wondered if Jason had stirred it up a bit, because he had been trying to get me to do telly stuff with him. It was a pity though, as Alex and Lance as the first two would have been good. The *Mirror* had a stack of pictures of UK soldiers mistreating Iraqis. There was something that didn't look quite right about them, and the MoD was casting doubt on them, but it was all a bit heavy and grim, and another sign that TB was just not able to get out of the Iraq shadow, and though he kept thinking better news would be round the corner, it was usually one step forward two steps back. Things weren't looking great for TB, and there wasn't much sign of them getting better.

We went out for Grace's birthday with the Goulds to Joe Allen's [Covent Garden restaurant]. Philip off to the Lords finally, but it didn't change the main diet of the conversation – TB–GB, and TB's future. I was pretty down at the moment, not making decisions well re the future, mainly because I was doing nothing that required a real sense of purpose. Philip was at me again to see someone about my depression as the gaps between the bouts seemed to be getting shorter. He felt I had been hoping for some miraculous improvement in my mental state after leaving, but it was never going to happen. It was like when I stopped drinking thinking that was going to make everything great and it sort of did for a while, but then the low times still came. Also, I think I had thought Fiona would mellow a bit after we left, but she was still pretty antsy on the political front and that was going to get worse not better the more I got dragged back in I guess.

I got home to another huge note from TB on the fax machine. He was at least really starting to motor (or get the system motoring) on thinking about the third-term agenda, not least as a contrast to the Tories who seemed determined to go negative and make it all about us, rather than a policy choice. He was obsessing on Europe, worrying about whether the CBI was in the right place. The referendum was going to happen. The danger he faced was that it was existing Treaties most of the antis hated, rather than this one, but the antis would make sure they were all mixed up together.

Saturday 1 May

My bike was nicked from the shed at the side of the house. Majorly pissed off. The Seb Coe interview looked good in *The Times*, despite my worries about the photo, and he came over really well. I went to see Rory running, and he won all three races. Calum went to see Burnley at Rotherham (3–0) on his own, then started his line that he was the only real supporter in the family.

Sunday 2 May

TB called after getting back from Dublin. He said he had discussed things with Bertie, who was totally up for it [TB becoming EU President], thought it was a good idea, and doable. I really wasn't sure. It also meant he was widening the circle of people who knew he was thinking of it. I totally trusted Bertie but couldn't always be sure he wouldn't mention to someone who mentioned to someone etc. And if it was going to be a runner, he might also think he had to start sounding out some of the other leaders, sooner rather than later. It was incredible that there was not even a whisper of it on the radar, even among the people close in.

Monday 3 May

TB still getting a very rough ride. I was doing some interviews, and in one came close to saying Piers Morgan [*Mirror* editor] must go if the pictures are shown to be false. I was running late but made it in time for the show at the Bloomsbury Theatre. Kirsty Young [broadcaster] was chairing it. I was surprised how nervous she seemed before we went on, but she was great. Nice woman, lovely manner. Given this was London again, I thought there would be much more anti-war aggro but apart from one guy who got a bit antsy, it was fine, and funny. We went out for dinner, Kirsty and her husband Nick Jones, who owns Soho House. Really funny guy, very laid-back, smart. They were clearly of the view that TB was the best thing we had going for us and we had to keep going with him. They would be amazed if they knew what had been going on inside his mind recently, and how much pressure he felt.

Stan Ternent called at 11.30 to say he had seen Barry Kilby, who was not renewing his contract and he wanted my advice on how to deal with it. He said he had not been given a reason. Barry was trying to say there was no one reason, it was just time for a change. Stan was refusing to put his name to a joint statement saying he was happy with the decision. Got home by 1.

Tuesday 4 May

Had a speech in the morning on B2B [business-to-business], which went fine, then saw Bruce Grocott. Like me, he was moving towards TB's thinking about going but Bruce felt he should wait for a better period to do it. He felt GB would be OK but we would definitely lose something that TB gave us and nobody else could. He felt that if GB was leader at the election, I should go back in as his campaign manager. He felt 'our Tone' was reaping something of a war whirlwind at the moment and also paying a bit of a price for bad man-management down the years, but he still felt that he was the best man for the job, if only for a bit longer. He agreed with TB that two terms was probably about right. But he had no truck with people who imagined that Tony going would lead to a sudden transformation. Bruce was still more Old Labour than New, but reckoned TB remained a lot more popular with people in his patch than the chattering classes or the GB crowd thought. I did an interview with Allan Brown [Scottish journalist and author], who felt the whole media obsession with me was erotic, including and especially homoerotic. Funny little chap.

Wednesday 5 May

I spoke to TB first thing and he asked me to go in to see him on my way out to the airport. I got a cab in, met by Felicity [Hatfield, former assistant to AC] at 70 Whitehall [Cabinet Office] and went up to the flat. He was sitting where he normally does when preparing for PMQs, eating a piece of toast and drinking a cup of tea. He was not his usual ebullient self, didn't get up, the smile a bit forced and he just said, 'Well then?' I said I had been thinking about it a lot and it all depended on how he felt. I said I didn't think things were as bad with the public as with the press but I could see why he was fed up. He said that it was a bit like what happened to me. He was waking up more days than not feeling just a bit ground down. He was also was pretty much clear that two terms was what you get these days. He asked me several times just to say what I really thought and he said at one point, 'Big doings isn't it?' and I was conscious once more of being there at what had the potential to lead, possibly quite quickly, to a moment of history.

I had kept a lot of secrets in my time with him but this was about as big as it got. The PM was on the point of resignation and for all the blather in the press, so far as I knew nobody but me, him, Cherie and Anji, and to a certain extent Bertie, were aware he was thinking in these terms and that this might, as he said, happen in weeks if not days. I recalled the questioner at Bloomsbury last night who said, 'When was the last time TB sought your counsel and what was the subject?' Here was the answer, and also the reason why it was so hard for him. It was a one-fact situation that he could trust very few people with.

I said that all that mattered was how he felt about it. That would guide the bigger issues like the succession, what it would mean for the country, because I could tell that was weighing on his mind, it wasn't just about whether he stayed in the job or not. So if he was waking up every day thinking that it didn't feel right, that the downsides were outweighing the up, then it was time to go, and the future would take care of itself. He said that he felt yesterday's local elections launch had been tired and he had thought to himself 'I would rather be anywhere than here.' He said if he had to, he could get up for an election fight but it would mean totally re-organising his operation, which was tired and which needed a lot more energy. It would mean getting his own juices flowing again and it would mean really focusing in a different kind of way. It was also about policy. He felt that there was sufficient coming through for the kind of election campaign we needed but he was not sure if GB was totally up for it. GB basically thought – accurately

– that TB had had enough and was thinking about exit strategies, and so helping to push in that direction. Also, TB said he had forced himself to think about whether in fact if the GB problem was not there, he would in any event feel the same. The truth is that if the GB problem was not there, it would be better but he was not sure that it would be enough for him positively to want to carry on.

He looked down, not his usual self and at several points stared at me intently but without the usual hint of a smile and I knew he was trying to read what I really thought, strip away any of the niceties. He had told Anji he was surprised that when he first raised the idea with me I had not been too averse, as he thought I would be the last one at the barricades, but I said I had been thinking for some time that it had been getting worse not better for him and that he would end up miserable and disappointed unless he organised his own exit on his own terms, at which point the dynamics surrounding him would change. I also said though that he had to be careful not to let my general mood at the moment affect him. I was pretty down. I said this, as he said, was big doings, and though my departure had caused a lot of waves, his had massive, massive ramifications and he had to be sure about it, and sure about the reasons. If after doing it he felt he had been pushed out by GB, aided and abetted by the media, he would resent and regret it.

I told him what Kwame had said, that he felt great when TB walked up the street in '97 and that though he hated our policy on Iraq he would feel really bad when he walked back down the street. I told him what Kirsty Young's husband Nick had said, that when TB was gone, people would quickly realise they had lost something very special. So I didn't feel he should be worrying too much about the legacy front or on the way he would be seen – provided it did not look either like he was running away or that he was thinking of himself ahead of the country.

He said he had met Bertie last weekend and had said to him what would people think if he put himself forward for the Europe job. Bertie's immediate reaction was just, 'So you're fed up with it all then?' TB had sworn him to secrecy and BA had gone straight to the tough question – would Chirac veto his appointment? TB said he could not be sure. I was pretty sure he would. I felt the flaw in the whole plan was that the big country leaders just would not want another big country leader in that job. They would far rather a safe Belgian or Luxembourger. On the one hand, as I said, there was a legitimate national interest argument JC could mount – why let the transatlantic friend who put US ahead of Europe take on such a big job? On the other hand, as TB said, it would amount to a declaration of war, and it was much bigger than Major blocking [former Belgian PM Jean-Luc] Dehaene.* He said he just could not be sure whether JC would do it, he was impossible to read. He was due to see him at the weekend and did I think he should raise it? I said you might as well tell PA, AFP and Reuters. He said the problem was that the decision was set for 16 June so it would have to be sorted before that. I said the local elections were 10 June so if he was going to announce anything about his intentions re giving up the PM job, he would have to do it in the next few weeks. We ran round in circles a bit and finally I said he struck me as being fairly settled, in that he was not enjoying the job, he was not feeling that it would get much better, and maybe it was just a fact that you get two terms in these jobs and that's that. What he could do was in the next few weeks, tell the Cabinet, then the public, that he intended to stand down at the election; that a leadership succession or contest would take place in the latter stage of the Parliament; that he would be around for that, and also to offer help and support re preparing the manifesto and re planning the campaign; that he would do a reshuffle, e.g. bring back Peter M; that Bertie etc. would start a process of identifying him for the Europe job.

There was a danger he ended up with nothing though, and he had to realise that. He could get his hat in the ring for Europe, but the minute that happened in any meaningful let alone formal way, he was signalling he was finished as PM. Then if he went a bit into the process, and JC put the kybosh on it – I was pretty sure he would – he would end up as former PM and former future EC President, with GB in No. 10 and someone like Guy Verhofstadt in Brussels.

I asked again what Cherie thought. He said she felt that he would take two months off and then feel re-energised and wonder why he had packed it in when he didn't need to. He was clear he wanted to end up doing stuff related to religion, that he would have lots of energy and lots to do, but he did worry about whether he would be seen by the party as running away from a fight, or by the public of leaving them in the lurch for Europe. He had continuing worries re GB. He had

---

* In 1994, Prime Minister John Major used the British veto to block the appointment of Dehaene as the next European Commission President, objecting to the manner in which his candidacy had been pursued and to Dehaene's 'interventionist' tendencies.

told GB he underestimated the problem he had with a large strand of opinion. He had great strengths. People saw him as Scottish and cautious and clever on the economy, but they felt he was interfering and also that he needed TB there to restrain his Old Labour tendencies. He had seen Les Hinton recently who made clear to TB it was TB, not Labour, not GB or JP or anyone else, who they backed and that could easily change. I said GB totally underestimated what it would take to get himself positioned properly as New Labour. On the other hand, I said GB might galvanise parts of the electorate who were drifting away.

These arguments cut both ways. I told him what Neil said – that TB had pulled in lots of new voters and some had gone away and he might get some back. He had lost other voters who GB might get back. But it was not clear where TB would get any new support from. TB felt, and this is something Bruce said to me yesterday too, that the party basically wanted TB and many would be shocked if they heard we were talking like we were. But I could tell that as things stood, he was not going to go beyond the election and that meant getting a plan in place. He said he had only talked to me and Anji about it, and he had mentioned Europe to Bertie too, but he had not felt able to discuss it fully even with JoP or Sally. SM was very down but in part because he was down. I saw Sally later and she said the morning meetings with GB were awful, even worse than before.

TB talked about legacy. He said I suppose there is a danger that people will just say it was a premiership that never fulfilled its full potential and I suppose that was possible. We had to stop because he had to get ready for PMQs and I had to get off to the airport. He said, 'Even PMQs now, I'm thinking it's a bit of a bore.' I said I don't say this lightly, but you actually might be depressed. He said no, he still had a basic optimism about the world, but he did feel more ground done than he ever had done. Cabinet meetings, visits, press conferences, maybe I'm just too familiar with it all, he said. We left as ever, just like that, down the stairs, him to the right, me to the left to see my old team, like we had done hundreds of times and I wondered if it might be the last time. He still looked fit and strong but there was a sense of loneliness far more stark than I'd seen it before, even those times when he was going to bed having sent troops in to places where he knew some might not come out alive.

I had a chat with GS and TK and then with JoP re N Ireland and what I should say. JoP said, 'What advice did you give him?' and I was vague, but it became clear JoP knew what was going on, as I had

May '04: TB 'sense of loneliness more stark than ever'

imagined. He said he would be mad to go now. He is letting things get to him too much and all this stuff will blow away like it has so many times before. He gave me a low down on NI and I set out for the airport. I got to Dublin, was met by Paul Allen, very dapper, very man about town, clearly plugged in to the whole Fianna Fail scene and also hardworking and funny. JoP had told me Joe Lennon [Ahern spokesman] was pissed off I had been to see Bertie and not him last week so I put in a call and he came back to me from Sweden and we had a long natter about things. He said Bertie had asked him to go back on the comms side for the EU presidency but he was keen to get out after that. I was also keen to get any sense of whether Bertie had mentioned TB's conversation re the Europe job, because I reckoned if he had, it might have been to Joe. The only hint he might have done was when Joe said Bertie was 'a bit worried about yer man', that he felt TB was tired and a bit beleaguered.

The other thing I was having to deal with was the collapsing interview with Alex. When I was at the golf range with Calum the other day he had said he was not happy with this big legal contract that had gone through and I could not understand why it needed one. Stuart Prebble said it was unknown for a major interview like that not to have such a contract but I explained that all we needed to do was turn up, do the interview, get him to sign a form, publicise and broadcast. They had over-complicated things, and they were in danger of fucking it up. I called Alex who said he had asked Les Dalgarno (lawyer) to have a look. Then when I was in Dublin I got a message from SP that Alex's lawyers had written to say he would not be able to do it. On the one hand, I was deeply pissed off because had they just left it to me, I think it would have happened fine. On the other, I was looking for more slack in the diary, and maybe thinking I should get a few more interviews lined up and agreed before going ahead. So it was a mixed bag, but Five were really disappointed.

I had a good swim session at the Merrion, got dressed and left for University College. Paul had organised everything brilliantly, different league; proper security, proper rehearsal with people who clearly knew what they were doing; every detail attended to. Paul had got John Bowman of RTE [presenter of *Questions and Answers*] as chair, and he was OK, but lacked the light touch of the better chairs I had had in the UK. There were 500 plus, lots of PR types, mainly the political class, and they were a good audience but the price, fifty euros, meant there were fewer punter types and the second half was heavier than usual. But it was fine, and Paul seemed to think it went well from his perspective too. I liked the Irish because they were far less cynical and far more informed about politics in the UK as well as Ireland. Paul was also on the case fixing a chat with Brian O'Driscoll [Ireland rugby union captain] for *The Times*. Back to the hotel for a drink with some Labour people and bed by 1.

Thursday 6 May

I had a terrible night because the air conditioning fan refused to be turned off. The switch said off but the hum went on and after hours of trying to sort it, eventually I moved rooms. New room, same fucking problem, so the bottom line was I barely slept. I had half an hour on the bike in the gym, then breakfast with Paul and a guy from the finance ministry who was filling me in on the plan to farm whole departments out to the regions. It was not dissimilar to what GB was looking at and I could see all manner of problems. We talked about civil service/ politics relationships, and he was with [Charlie] McCreevy [finance minister], who had no special advisor, and he was not convinced it worked. Like me, he felt the civil service had good people but not enough strength in depth. I was driven up to Belfast, having cancelled the Stephen Nolan phone-in because it would have meant *Talkback* [Radio Ulster] pulling the plug.

I got there, checked in, turned on the news and John Scarlett being named SIS chief was raging on. Excellent, really pleased for him. For once the right thing for the right reasons despite all the obvious pressures there would have been to do something different. There would be all the blah and the Tories were straight out the opportunistic trap, but it would blow over and I was pleased for John who had taken a lot of shit for doing the right thing. I called him and he said he was a bit disorientated by the whole thing. He went through all the hoops for it, and people obviously felt he was the best man for the job, but he knew there would be flak and he would just have to press on. I said I had been worried that the controversy would be held against him and I was so pleased that it wasn't. When I was asked about it at the Q&A later, I lacerated the Tories and said he was a man of real and genuine integrity.

Talkback was OK, first question 'What would you ask yourself?' and I found myself saying, 'I'd ask what I dreamed about,' probably because I had been having all sorts of weird and wonderful dreams

May '04: Scarlett named new head of MI6

recently, a lot of them involving violence and bloodshed between TB and GB, and in one of them me trying to drag Gordon to see Bostock and get some medication; in another Calum coming into a meeting with Chirac and saying in perfect French that it was time for my dad to leave now; all pretty obvious stuff I guess. But also I was constantly dreaming about being in situations where I was trying to do something and then I would suddenly forget what it was, and be asking people if they had seen what I had been trying to do. I guess that was obvious too. The only caller they put through was totally hostile but around the place, people were fine. I had a meeting with the Waterfront theatre people to sort detail and like Dublin they were very efficient and professional, and it felt fine. Ted Oliver [ex-*Mirror* colleague] came over for a chat and a cup of tea and we had a good old natter about the old days. He was doing fine, divorced now, not drinking as much, and seemed OK. He was hoping for Piers Morgan's demise. There were so many negatives on his copy book now and yet there was no sign of moves against him at the top. I was beginning to wonder if he had something on them.

Gerry Kelly was a good choice for chair. He was nice, warm, a big presence without wanting to be domineering, and really looking forward to it. He was positively raving about the improvements in Belfast over the last five years, and there was no comeback at all when I talked up the process of change and the improvements. There were more than 700 in, fantastic hall, good atmosphere, though we got off to a bad start when the DVD didn't work. But Gerry handled it fine and I just marched on, and made lots of jokes about it. First half good, second half excellent, went on to 10.45 and they would have taken more. I said Peter M should be back in government, and that provoked a bit of coverage on the lines that it meant it was probably happening, which I guess underlined that I was still seen as saying nothing unless TB wanted it said. Some of it was fairly light hearted, e.g. my Paisley impersonation which Kelly said wasn't bad, and describing the bike theft as the worst thing that had happened to me. Very few questions on Ireland which surprised me. I enjoyed it though, then dinner with Tom Kelly, Linda [his wife] and a friend of theirs, just chewing the fat. TK and I only briefly discussed TB. I felt a bit of a heel knowing what I did and yet basically discussing it as though there was no way he would be going. Tom actually felt TB had been OK of late, had the better of Howard already, and that the mood around No. 10 was picking up a little bit. Bed by 2, getting tired.

Friday 7 May

I had been speaking to Stan [Ternent] and helping him draft his statement for the press conference on Sunday. I was even more of the view
that he should go for the dignified route and while not saying he supported a change as manager, basically make clear he wished the club
all the best. He called me from training and said he agreed. But he had
told Barry he was going to get another job, and he was going to bring
his new side back to Burnley and win. He said there were only thirty
jobs he fancied and he felt confident he would get one of them. He was
still fond of Barry but he felt others had persuaded him they needed
someone more modern. I said he had the chance really to cement himself in Burnley's affections on Sunday.

Paul had fixed Brian O'Driscoll for 12 at a pub in Dublin so we had
breakfast and then set off in Paul's little sports car. He wanted me to
sign some memorabilia and we chatted all the way, not least re AF and
the horse, which he felt had all been a bit odd, and maybe Alex just
fell for the hail fellow well met thing without realising these guys are
as tough as they come. We also talked about Bertie and his manner –
Paul kept trying to get him to be a bit more presidential, but part of
Bertie's appeal was that he still went to the same old pub, didn't dress
too flashily, was still seen as a man of the people. It was a beautiful
sunny day and the pub where we were meeting BO'D was upmarket,
in a nice suburb of south Dublin. He arrived, casual, almost scruffy
but trendy clothes, shades in the slightly dyed hair, big smile, nice guy,
and we chatted outside for an hour or so before doing snaps. I liked
him but he was so different to the others I had done recently. Not so
much obsessive as obsessively laid-back.

Even when people came over for autographs and stuff he just took
it all in his stride. He was good fun, loved the craic. Modest too. He
thought it was ridiculous people putting him in the same bracket as
Mike Gibson [former Ireland and British Lions player]. He was also
adamant that Jonny Wilkinson is in a league of his own. 'The man
is different class. He is a unique human being, absolutely unique.
In world rugby today, there is Wilko, then there are a few more
below him a bit, and then there are the rest.' He was funny about the
way he would train hard, but then that was it, whereas Wilkinson
would train hard, and then go and do it again. Brian would think
for a while after a game but not that long. JW would relive it and
go over it again and again, trying to work out little things he could
have done better. He reckoned if Jonny had a machine scanning his

thoughts it would show he was thinking about rugby every minute of every day.

He was dismissive of the Lance idea that losing and dying are the same thing, and when I told him about Faldo's golfing dreams, he said most of his dreams were about women, and when he does dream about the game, he does well, he is not riddled with anxiety. I clearly had dreams on my mind, but his sounded nothing like mine. He said he had a dream recently where Jonah Lomu [New Zealand legend] was charging towards him and he tackled him to the ground, and the crowd roared its approval, then he got the ball, flung it out to Shane Horgan [Ireland international] and he was away and scored. Pretty amazing to have fifty caps at his age, and have the reputation he has. He said that because there was no top football in Ireland, the rugby players were closer to the English Premier League footballers in the way the press were into them. But he seemed to be handling it all fine. He was just twenty-five though, so when he said Pete Sampras was the best tennis player ever, and I said what about Björn Borg and John McEnroe?, he said he had never seen them. We went for a walk to do some pictures, said cheerio and I was off to the airport. At one of the shops airside, they were playing his tries against Italy again and again on a continuous loop, to advertise a DVD alongside a giant cardboard cut-out of him, and the guy watching alongside me just said, 'Is he not the dog's bollocks?'

I slept a bit on the flight back, and got home to a long note from Sally on forward plans. PG was nagging me relentlessly to get more and more involved, but I was still a bit resistant. TB called for a bit of a rant, said he had been pushing for departmental five-year plans but even getting some of them focused on what they needed to do with them was harder than it should be. He was also seized by the whole 'race hate clerics' issue and the difficulty of dealing with them.* He had a whole load of speeches coming up, starting to point in themes terms towards the manifesto and the election, and asked if I would take a look. He said the one he was most worried about was education, because there was such a gap between what he wanted to do and what the educational establishment/department felt was possible. He felt we hadn't done enough to use the argument that the changes we were making were about improving things for the consumer of the

* The support of some Muslim clerics for radical Islamist goals was causing great public disquiet.

service, not the provider. I asked how much he would be able to focus on all this given that foreign policy stuff was so dominant. He said he felt he had to launch and co-own all of the five-year plans, and have common narratives linking them together.

Saturday 8 May

I finished the BO'D piece, plus my speeches for tonight and Glasgow, then did a 15-mile run along the canal, longest for ages, and I felt pretty stiff. The US pictures scandal was raging, and really hurting Donald Rumsfeld [US Defense Secretary], and yet people by and large still felt the UK soldiers were not bad and that the *Mirror* pictures were probably fake.* Alan Barnard [Labour official] picked me up at 7 and we headed for Enfield North where I was doing a fundraiser/motivator for Joan Ryan [MP], who was a bit worried about the current state of play in her seat. 100 people there, old-fashioned Labour hall, a few younger ones, a few black people but not many considering the area. I did a mix of funny and heartfelt, including what would John Smith have thought, and then Q&A, and it went down really well. I wondered if this motivational stuff wasn't what I was better employed doing. Left at 9.30 to go to Chelsea, dinner with [film-maker] Hugh and Marianne [Hudson], NK, Glenys, PG, Gail and Fiona. Neil had been in one of his rages and PG had been fighting back but it was not exactly barrel of laughs time. Neil really had too much anger still in him and I think Marianne was a bit shocked by it. Hugh and Fiona kept trying to turn the chat to films and books and blahdiblah, but the politics was where it was at, and it wasn't a happy scene at all. Another late night before another early start.

Sunday 9 May

Up at 8 and off to Burnley v Sunderland. Calum was being a lot more teenagerish than usual, hating anyone coming up and talking to me. I worked on a few bits and bobs on the way up. The feeling re TB was not great at the moment, and the chatter about him going was beginning to pick up. He was emanating weakness and lack of

---

* Photographs of detainees in Abu Ghraib prison in Iraq being tortured resulted in eleven soldiers being charged with dereliction of duty, maltreatment, aggravated assault and battery. Sentences ranged from imprisonment to reprimand and demotion.

confidence and that was getting out there somehow. It was a good game played in a fairly surreal atmosphere because everyone knew Stan was going, and he was really emotional about it. I had to leave a bit before the end to meet the car and head to Glasgow. We made good time so I was able to stop and have a little run somewhere over the border, then made the King's Theatre. Donald [AC's brother] was there with two sets of pipes as we had agreed we would play at the end. Fred Macauley [broadcaster and comedian] was chairing and had a really good sardonic style. Great atmosphere and I would say it was one of the best so far. Lots of relatives there and I made a joke about them being ready to protect me if things got heavy but the mood was terrific. I joined some of the media guys who had been there at a restaurant for a quick dinner and then got driven back through the night, managed to sleep on and off and arrived home in the early hours pretty tired.

Monday 10 May

Monday basically resting, but I was starting to dip into another down swing. The TB scene was a bit grim. The sense I had was that it was going to be very hard for him now to escape all this. Of course knowing as I did that he was thinking of going, the timing of the current frenzy could not really be worse. When boiled down it was all about Iraq and Bush really. The controversy over the pictures showing abuse of detainees was just the latest example of his fate being in the hands of the Americans. The tragedy was that the domestic side was coming strong now, the last NHS report showing huge improvements being the latest example. I didn't feel there was much I could do and started to think about the Select Committee hearing tomorrow.

Tuesday 11 May

I had set aside all morning to prepare for the Select Committee but first went for a run. The cameras were outside again but it didn't feel as important or as tense as before. The theatre events had honed most of my arguments and I was intending to treat the whole thing like one of those but maybe with fewer jokes. I even wondered if I shouldn't go along with a few free tickets and hand them out to the MPs, but doubtless one or two might take it amiss. In the event Tony Wright [Public Administration Committee chairman] plugged the tour at the outset so I was able to plug away throughout, including the Old Vic and saying I did deals for Labour but Tories would have to pay full whack. I went in to No. 10 around ten and saw CR who was the only one who had really put in any effort on my behalf. She had been monitoring the *Mail* and had got me the basic lines on the Phillis Report. I wondered if I should say what I thought, which is that it was a pretty second rate piece of work – maybe not, but what I did say in the end was that it took insufficient regard of the media role in the diminution of trust and respect or understanding of the political debate.

CR was very good but I was not terribly psyched for it. The committee clerk called, said there was a lot of interest and maybe I would prefer to go over early. I read up then went over to Portcullis House and prepared in Boothroyd Room, which is where I had done the FAC. The hearing was in the Thatcher room. The clerk said they were using Boothroyd as overflow. He said that basically they had wanted me unashamedly for publicity reasons. The way these people talked about the MPs was extraordinary. 'Tony is OK and [Bridget] Prentice is quite sharp but they tend to waffle and we've done them a brief but not sure if they will stick to it much, you can never tell.'

I didn't feel tense or nervous and never really felt under pressure from the questions. The Tory, [Ian] Liddell-Grainger, waffled on, Tony asked some OK general questions, as did Prentice, but by and large it was easy. Anne Campbell re perceptions, Kevin Brennan re whether I thought TB missed me. The sketchwriters seemed to think they were over-respectful and one of them said I was like an exotic snake. I certainly did not feel they got anywhere near me. The one shift I made was to say I was now more in favour of Freedom of Information than before, in part because of Hutton. I went for the *Mail* fairly hard but I was deliberately being a bit calmer than they were expecting or hoping for. Basically I said Piers Morgan should quit though, and hammered home the culture of negativity point. Back to No. 10 to hear Mike White [*Guardian* political editor] and Michael Heseltine on the telly broadly agreeing with me. Meeting with Alison who said she could not really cope with the workload, didn't want to be a PA any more, and was going to go back into civil service full time, which was fair enough. She thought I would have slowed down more than I had and that basically I was a workaholic. I felt I had slowed a hell of a lot, but maybe not, I don't know.

I had a meeting with Peter M, who was warming to the idea of being one of my Five interviews, but wanted to see a proper treatment.

He also wanted to know what my personal strategy was. I felt I didn't have one at the moment. I was busy every day but it didn't really add up, and I had to work it out. It probably needed a big new project. I think people might be amazed I was thinking in those terms but it was a mix of depression and boredom probably. We met in GB's room in No. 11 and we were perfectly friendly. Peter M said he thought my attending GB meetings at HMT was a waste of time at the moment. They were not really trying to have a strategy. They were just hoping things would go wrong. He said he still didn't trust them at all and in any event it would become a big story if I pitched up and not necessarily a good one. He was really keen on the European Commission job and he felt GB might be OK on it too, as was JP.

I left for JP's flat at Ripley Building [part of the Admiralty complex facing Whitehall], very much on the lines of HMG residences, and he proudly showed me round. He said he was doing one hour exercise a day, and feeling better. He was in the kitchen cooking away and slightly lost it with Joan [Hammell] when Fiona turned up and said she was a vegetarian, and why had nobody told him etc.? But he was terribly proud to be cooking and serving and all that and he did well, Loch Fyne kippers bought on the way back from the John Smith ten-year memorial event on Iona, and coq au vin. Rosie Winterton and Dick Caborn were the other guests and Dick and I did a bit of Burnley business, as he was seeing Barry Kilby and Dave Edmundson tomorrow, and was keen to get something going, not least as a way of thwarting the BNP.* I liked Dick and his voice was one of calm as Fiona and Rosie worked themselves into a lather about the current scene. Dick said that hardly anyone in Sheffield was talking about the TB situation and they would be amazed to know anyone else was. They thought the government was doing fine, particularly re jobs and the public services were definitely improving. Everyone agreed Iraq was just a bad shadow but even that, like me, Dick felt we could get into a better perspective if we were not so bloody defensive. He had a right go at Fiona at one point, asking her what else the government should do, and she had not much to say beyond schools selection.

JP was fairly quiet until we got on to GB etc. He said TB had to decide what to do, and only he could or would, as the party just would not move against him. But he was in a pro-GB mood in so far as he was saying he was the only choice and he was doing a lot of good things.

---

* Racial tension in the town had seen the British National Party gain support.

We agreed if he did get the job then he would be totally the same re the US – a view underlined when it emerged he had seen Murdoch twice recently. There was a fair amount of discussion re Tessa who was apparently manoeuvring to be deputy leader. The general feeling was she lacked the profile or the party base, but as Fiona said she had done very well on networking etc. JP said I was solely responsible for getting Tessa in the Cabinet and he didn't think she was up to much. I said are you sure you're not just against her nice manners? He recalled the day she came round to our house bearing plums and apples.

Rosie was bright and very political but like Fiona was full of the problems and not the solutions. She also had severe doubts about GB. She said to JP, 'You used to say he was basically a bit mad and would not be right for it, but has he changed? I mean you are as mad as a hatter basically and that is why you couldn't do it, but what about him, has he changed?' Joan's view was that he was a dictator and would not be able to manage all the various sides of the job. Rosie said TB was basically a good bloke and that was why he was able to do all the various bits so well.

JP said GB was better at managing the media than the rest of them, because he worked at it all the time. I said that was because comparatively he was not actually that busy and he totally underestimated the change of gear that would be required for the top job. He had always viewed it as a slightly different job to his own, which he could do better. He had no idea what was going to hit him. We didn't really agree to do or seek to achieve anything because in reality it was down to TB to decide what he was going to do. JP said he would back him whatever. I got no sense that JP was even remotely aware of TB's current thinking, but the mood was definitely a bit fragile and of course the local and European elections were going to cause a few more problems. It was a nice evening but worrying I guess. Joan said that since I left, No. 10 had virtually collapsed as an operation. I think sometimes people said this to me as a way of making me feel better but in fact it always made me feel worse, and guilty at having left. We then meandered round a few policy areas, Fiona trotting out her liberal views on drug legalisation, JP raging at London liberals, Rosie saying dentistry was a disaster waiting to happen. All of them really down on JR. Joan said he was so ambitious he was evil, which I thought was ridiculous. Very down on Pat [McFadden, TB's political secretary] and Charles [Clarke], and the 'ideological outriders' Milburn and Byers. All a bit bitter and nasty but as always with JP we had a few laughs.

Wednesday 12 May

Most of the day dedicated to media stuff to promote the Old Vic. LBC, Heart with Jono Coleman [breakfast show presenter], *Telegraph*, Jeremy Vine, then BBC London and finally Richard and Judy. I was slightly on autopilot at these interviews but Jono and his sidekick Harriet were good fun and I enjoyed the chat with Robert Elms [presenter and writer] at BBC London, who was very down to earth and a good bloke. Big QPR fan. R and J were good. They played one of the Rory Bremner clips of me and TB singing 'The Way We Were' which was quite funny, did a few of the usual lines, e.g. gigolo, drink, future, but it was fine. Vine had been OK too and there was one very good caller who was really pro-TB. I got through a lot but as ever, at the end of it all, I felt what the fuck was all that about?

I had a bit of a spat with Chris Shaw, who called me as I was about to go on saying I should let them know when doing stuff like R and J so that his bosses didn't ask why I was always on telly apart from Five. I texted to say tell your bosses nobody owns me, you'll get your money's worth, don't take well to messages just before an interview and if someone hadn't fucked up re Alex F, I would not be doing R and J in the first place. He said OK. I went to get Calum from tennis then after dinner had a nice chat with Gerald Davies [former rugby player] about the best rugby players. He felt Gareth Edwards [former Welsh rugby union star player] was the way to go, plus maybe Ian Gibson. I was also keen on a League player.

Thursday 13 May

Telegraph interview OK-ish. Piece from Jackie Ashley [*Guardian* columnist] attacking my attack on the media. They love giving it but can't take even a bit of it back. Prebble called saying Murdoch was a yes for the Five series. Up to Mum and Dad's, working on the rugby pieces for *The Times* on the train up. Dad not so good, Mum bearing up.

Friday 14 May

Piers Morgan was sacked, though even now he was refusing to accept he had done anything wrong. The thing about Piers though is you can guarantee he'll be back doing something else pretty soon. Stuart Prebble came round for a chat about the interview we had got fixed for Murdoch.

Saturday 15 May

Busy with the kids all day, tennis with Calum, Grace to Anna Sher, and Rory won the 800 metres at the Middlesex Under 17s. TB called to say I should really think about whether there was anyone we should try to get in as *Mirror* editor. I wondered about Terry Manners [*Western Daily Press*] who was totally New Labour, really liked TB and because he was from Associated Newspapers he would not be seen as a poodle of ours. I was mentioned in a few places in relation to it but I couldn't see it really. One or two *Mirror* folk called me and said I should go for it, but I didn't feel the fire within. TB sounded pretty fed up with life. He said he felt OK but the mood was really shitty at the moment. The truth was the Americans did not really have a grip on things and the pictures of prisoner abuse had turned off a lot of people who were otherwise reasonably supportive on the war. He intended to get out and about more, and also wanted me to think about how we got better coverage below the radar, e.g. for improvements in the NHS.

Sunday 16 May

I did an interview with former Rugby League player Alex Murphy. A real bighead, but it was very hard not to like him. He was the first of the sportsmen I'd interviewed to name himself as the best in the business, without a hint of embarrassment.

Monday 17 May

Grace's sports day all morning, unbelievably hot, so I went for a swim in the lido afterwards, then wrote the *Times* piece. The media was going into real wank mode after a story in the *Sunday Herald* that GB and JP had sat talking in a car at Loch Fyne on the way back from the John Smith event. Clearly that was where JP had got the kippers we had the other night! I sent him a message – 'Historic kippers!' Iraq was still grim, and a lot of talk that TB would have to go. He called, asked me how I thought he should deal with it. I felt ignore it, carry on with the job and be seen to be carrying on. But he did sound very fed up.

Tuesday 18 May

I was writing up the interview with Gareth Edwards, while working on a speech for a school prizegiving later and doing media for King's

Lynn. I really liked Edwards. I hadn't realised English was his second language. He was brilliant about the PE teacher and coach who he credited with really making him see he could make it as a player, a guy named Bill Samuel. Lovely quote too... 'I had a talent and it flowered.' He ran for England at one point because he got a scholarship to Millfield. As I was writing an email came in from No. 10 saying I had to make a statement to the Butler Inquiry about who spoke to which journalist when re the WMD dossier. Jesus! I sometimes felt I was becoming a professional witness. The schools event was good, first a speech and then awarding certificates at Alexandra Park. Good school, good atmosphere.

Long chat with JP later. I was doing *GMTV* tomorrow and wanted to say, as a way of showing how ludicrous things had become, that he had cooked the Loch Fyne kippers for me, and he was up for that. I wasn't sure why, but he believed JR had briefed the stuff about him and GB. He was also raging at Milburn and Byers – he didn't even name them anymore, they were just 'the ideological outriders'. He said he had spoken to TB a few times and made clear his view that it was entirely up to him when he went and that even though things were difficult, the party was definitely up for him being there longer. He said he sensed TB was genuinely not sure. He said GB had met Peter recently but they had barely started when GB said something which provoked PM, who walked out. He felt the next round of elections were going to be really bad.

Wednesday 19 May

GMTV interview with Fiona Phillips, who was really nice and has the perfect manner for that market. I did a number on the kippers. It had become almost comic, the extent to which they had tried to blow this up into something really serious and important. Worked on the outlines of my draft statement for Butler, much of it based on previous statements and evidence. Given the way memories and goalposts were shifting on this, I made the point that at the time we published the dossier, the media were complaining because we were saying nothing in the build-up, including the same people who now claimed we had been leaking. I set out details of the conversation with Jack Straw which showed that even though we were worried the media would be filled with speculation, we agreed just to live with it, and not engage; and also that Jack having promised to give advance copies to some governments, I persuaded him not to, because of the risk of leaks. Instead we sent a talking points note for Ambassadors to use with trusted contacts. And I was absolutely clear we did no pre-briefing other than on logistics, and for the nth time made clear I had nothing to do with getting the *Standard* to headline on '45 minutes'. It was actually pretty remarkable how little active briefing we did. Godric reminded me we had actually decided not to do the usual lobby briefing because we wanted the dossier and TB's words to speak for themselves.

I felt totally confident in what I was saying, but pissed off that I was having to deal with these same questions again and again, inquiry after inquiry. Most of the media couldn't give a toss about the facts now, it was all about just keeping going with the same conspiracy theories and innuendo. I had a run then into Old Queen Street to talk to the Attack Team. PG had felt they could benefit from a bit of a gee-up. I had a proper chat with Matt Carter [general secretary] who seemed OK. Nice atmosphere in there. Matthew Doyle was worrying about a fuck-up on music rights for an election broadcast. Mick Hucknall had given us the go-ahead but Warner claimed it was theirs not his. I did a bit of a pep talk. Meanwhile TB was hit by a purple powder bomb in the Commons. It sparked a big frenzy and must have been shown hundreds of times during the day, but he was amazingly calm. He was about to deliver a line I'd given him – about kippers not being the only good thing to come out of Scotland, that it also gave us the best Chancellor in history and the wisest political judgement in making itself a Tory-free zone – when the 'bomb' landed. I had lunch with Clive Hollick at the People's Palace [Royal Festival Hall restaurant]. He was sounding me out re the *Mirror*, and ideas for Five. He said he was sick of all the peers who owed their place to TB or Neil and now spent all their time slagging us off and helping nobody but the Tories.

Milburn called and said things were terrible. He had tried to press on TB the need for greater clarity but he just didn't feel he was there at the moment. I said TB often let things drift like this for a while but then he would come back in with clarity and move things on. Alan said he felt TB had to face up to GB, or else it was death by attrition. I spoke to TB. He seemed a bit more himself. I said I was moving more to the view that he should tough it out. Things were not quite as bad out there as we sometimes thought. I sensed he was too, that the recent slough had been a bit out of character but he was not going to be pushed out yet. My worry was if the talk about the EU job got out.

May '04: Milburn – 'things are terrible'

Out to the Cafe Royal for a Leukaemia Research dinner. There was a *Question of Sport* event – Bill Beaumont [former England rugby captain], Bob Willis [former cricketer] and me against Ian Botham, Sam Torrance [golfer] and Gary Rhodes [singer]. I arrived to find Cathy Gilman in a panic, huddled away with Sue Barker [broadcaster, former tennis player], who was chairing. Piers was there so we indulged in a bit of the usual mutual abuse. He said I would live to regret saying his position had become untenable. He said he intended to bring out his memoirs at the same time as mine, and so bury them. I said, 'You've always been cocky and arrogant, but now you're delusional as well. There is nothing more ex than an ex-editor.' 'I am going to be a TV star,' he said.

Thursday 20 May

Cycled over to Ed Victor's to see him and John Witherow. I wasn't totally clear what we were trying to get out of it, but it was an opportunity to gauge the level of interest in the diaries, and kick around a few ideas. I explained that I hadn't decided what or when to publish, and also that I didn't particularly want to break the chronology, that I would start when I first began working for TB and publish in order, even if it meant the later stuff came out some time after the early days which, because they covered opposition, were perhaps less interesting. I set out the context and tried to give a flavour. He was desperate to read something, but we made clear that wasn't happening. Ed had not wanted to discuss money but Witherow said that if we went to Random House he was up for serialisation of £750k for three volumes [in the *Sunday Times*], which Ed told me basically meant a million, and he felt that when he saw the content it would be more. It was a perfectly civilised conversation but I didn't feel totally at ease about this.

I had lunch at the Camden Brasserie with Phil Webster and Tom Baldwin [journalists]. They were really pushing me on how long I thought TB would stay. It was really hard to bullshit on this one given I knew what I did. I said vaguely that you could not rule out before the election, but it was unlikely. I enjoyed seeing them, but I was still finding it hard to work out what I was and wasn't enjoying, what I did and did not want to do.

TB called. He said he, Anji and I had all, on the same day, independently come to the view that there maybe was a case for staying the course. I said I'd definitely come back to the idea that he could go for the long haul. He asked me why I'd hardened my view, because he had been quite surprised that I had not reacted violently against the idea of him going early. I said partly because I think we'd both allowed ourselves to be over affected by the current mood, much of which would pass. Also, because I still thought he could do it, and his extraordinarily calm response at the powder bombing yesterday had steadied the media frenzy. He said he had spoken to Schroeder but had not been able to raise the Europe situation on the phone. I felt that was probably a good thing. I felt in his voice that he had recovered some strength. Also it was perfectly clear, not least today from lunch and also the meeting with Ed and Witherow, that there were a lot of doubts out there about whether GB could do it. Ed for example said he felt that if TB left it would be an act, if not of political suicide, at least of serious self-harm by Labour, and having read the diaries he could not see how we could even consider GB as capable of taking over. Witherow said one of the reasons some of the papers talked up GB was because they felt he would not be nearly as effective as TB and so give the Tories a road back.

Friday 21 May

Pottering around most of the day. Then out to Sevenoaks, June Sarpong chairing the event. She got the audience going pretty well. More hostility than there had been at most of the others. But I felt when you got into deeper arguments it was possible to win most people round, at least to an understanding, if not always agreement. June had a lovely manner about her and was great fun as well.

Saturday 22 May

I was basically reading books on Murdoch most of the day, in between going for a swim, and watching Man U win the Cup Final (beating Millwall 3–0). Rebekah called about some story the *Mail on Sunday* were running, that I used to let her see the No. 10 grid. Complete rubbish.

Sunday 23 May

Long run. The *Mail on Sunday* ran four pages from the new Oborne–Walters [Peter Oborne and Simon Walters] book on me, but didn't seem to have much and I felt best to leave it. TB called, and he agreed,

May '04: AC also hardens his view for TB staying

said he had read it and thought it was annoying but undamaging and would only become a problem if we reacted too heavily. Old Vic in the evening, with June chairing again, looking absolutely fabulous. Really nice atmosphere, beautiful theatre of course, totally sold out. Alan Edwards [PR executive] was there and said we should have filmed it. The best moment was when I gave a long-winded, waffly, overly diplomatic answer to the question whether I could ever vote for Bush and the woman shouted out – 'So that's a no.'

Nice little do afterwards. Ed Victor had been there with Gail and he said he felt I really ought to think about a career in some kind of live TV, because I appeared able to handle any tricky situation. He loved the story about the guy I rescued on the Heath after he got mugged, who, when he realised it was me, just said, 'I fucking hate you.' The self-deprecating stories were definitely going down the best, and they were the way to get a hearing on the more serious stuff, and especially standing up for politics against the media culture. June said afterwards I would regret it for ever if I didn't go into elected politics myself. 'You have to do it,' she said. 'Apart from Tony on a good day, and Clinton for sure, I can't think of anyone else who can talk about politics like you do.' I said if you are trying to make me feel better, you're not succeeding. She was such a star though, and brilliant with Grace.

Monday 24 May
I took Calum into *The Times* to sort his work experience, then had lunch with Trevor Kavanagh. He told me he kept a diary. 'You're in it a lot.' I said he was in mine a bit! He was very down on GB, and I sensed that was the general mood in there, that they felt he had gone along with the New Labour thing for a while but had more and more tried to distance himself. It was also clear to me that once TB went, they would start to mark him up even more and that too would affect GB badly. Alan Rusbridger called and agreed to resolve my complaint about Jackie Ashley with a small apology.

Tuesday 25 May
47th birthday, and I was hoping that my resting pulse rate would be the same as, or lower than my age. I missed it by one – 48, which was still pretty bloody good. I spent most of the morning working on a speech for Qatar, and fixing to see Ian Botham at the Test Match in Leeds.

Wednesday 26 May

Doing Norfolk media. Loads of exercise. Seb Coe round for dinner, picking my brains on the message for the Olympic bid and also how to work some of the diplomatic stuff. He definitely looks the part, and I think sometimes because we know him so well we forget just how big a thing he is in world athletics. He was telling me how the whole process works, and it's bizarre in a way that they are not allowed to lobby directly, and that there are so many rules and restrictions, especially as it is so widely assumed they get broken by the others. He was great with Rory on his past and his running. Also about his relationship with his dad and what that was like, having a really tough coach who was also his dad. Barbara Casani had basically gone because of anti-Americanism and because it was a bit of a problem to have an American leading the London bid.

He said there was a lot of guesswork involved because it was never entirely clear what kind of thing moved votes from one city to another. I said I felt we needed to agree the one unique selling point that could put London ahead of all the others, and get the other points to flow from that. The technicalities of the bids were obviously important, but everyone knew how to do that bit. I felt that London's development, including recently, into an even more multiracial, multicultural city might be the place to start building an argument, that it was in some ways the capital of the world, so the most obvious place for the Games right now. Also we had to find a way of turning the underdog thing to our advantage. Rory noticed that Seb always called me 'Al', which very few people did. In fact I couldn't think of anyone apart from David Mills and Mike Stephens [university friend].

Thursday 27 May

TB out and about doing more on the domestic agenda. He had definitely rediscovered his equilibrium. UKIP were getting far too much attention though. Ed Victor called to say, as expected, that Witherow had moved up to one million for three volumes. Ed was clear that we should keep the serial rights, whatever the deal we did with Gail or anyone else. I don't know why though, but I found it very hard to get motivated and crack on with getting the diaries done. I was up to '96, but a lot of it seemed such a hard grind, so God knows how other people would look at it.

May '04: Seb Coe picking brains on Olympic strategy

Friday 28 May

Off to Paddington, working on the speech for Qatar on the train to Cardiff. Conference call with Chris Shaw and Stuart Prebble re the Five interviews which were coming on fine. Met by Glenys [Kinnock], did the local media, and the phone-in, then a good session at the school of journalism. Very bright bunch, Q&A excellent. There was more buy-in than I had expected for my basic thesis that the media were in large part to blame for disenchantment with public life, and for their own problems of circulation and reputation. Glenys said that today was the first time she'd been able to generate any real interest about the pro-euro campaign among the local media. Lance Armstrong called, agreed to do a TV interview on 14 June. He was taking the piss again re WMD, asking me to bring them with me.

Saturday 29 May

Out on the bike when TB called, said, 'How do you see things?' I felt, not least after yesterday in Wales, where both media and public had not been bad at all, that things were not nearly as bad as they had seemed. He said he had been out a fair bit and he felt the same. He felt in the party that given how much noise there had been in the media, there was actually very little pressure on him to go. He had always felt that if he became a liability, he would go, but he was not sure it was like that at all. He also felt that Howard was not really up to the top job. He was a good attack politician, but was poor on political leadership. He had spoken to IDS re Iraq and it was clear there were still real problems for the Tories, and divisions that could come up any time. *Der Spiegel* had run a piece saying TB had sounded out Bertie re the new European President job. I said I assumed that came from Schroeder. TB assumed so, because he had virtually told him. He was going to see Bertie about it again this week and what did I think? I said I had definitely moved to a position where I felt he should stay and fight and that if he did he would win. I also felt he had gone a bit wobbly recently and the rest of us had been affected by that, but he probably had moved back to where I now was. He had.

He was going on *Frost* tomorrow and I said if he basically had decided he was likely to stay and tough it out, he had to have a strategy based on that – that resilience and toughness, the ability to see things through, is what leadership is all about. He should make a virtue of recent unpopularity so-called. He said he was basically going to make clear he did not intend to move over. I said in which case, that had to be pretty clear. He said I had been very badly missed in recent weeks, because usually if he was down I was able to lift the operation. I said it was probably a pretty good job I hadn't been there, because I had been feeling pretty depressed about things, lacking drive, which was unusual and alarming me. He said I probably wouldn't have been like that had I been there. He talked through some of the stuff he was working on over the weekend and it was absolutely clear he had got through the frenzy and was feeling OK.

Sunday 30 May

Seb Coe was done over by the *Sunday Mirror* re a sex scandal story. I called him and said he should ignore it but be seen to be doing something sporting today. We were heading to Watford for Rory's 800m final. I suggested that I fix it for him to present some of the medals later. For a start, he'd get a great reaction and most of the people there wouldn't even know about the story. It would show he wasn't hiding away, carrying on doing the stuff that was important. It caused quite a stir that he was there, but also I was quite shocked that some of the younger ones didn't actually know who he was. He was definitely glad he went because of the warmth there was towards him. He told Rory that in 800m races, 600–700m is 'the killing zone', that races are won on lost on the back strait.

Monday 31 May

Vicky Barnsley told Ed she felt she was just being used by us to get Gail to go higher. David and Louise Miliband came round for dinner. Mainly talking kids and non-politics. I said re GB that there was a rational and an irrational part. When the rational part was motoring, he was still brilliant when he chose to be. When the irrational part kicked in, he was a nightmare. I said I felt sometimes I had those same two sides to me, but that when I was irrational I was more creative than destructive. Fiona pulled a face at that one. David felt TB was a lot weaker than I realised and that GB was incredibly strong in the party. He felt TB had to rediscover what he was for, because it wasn't clear at the moment. Politically and intellectually he was drifting. As for GB, he felt that his weakness was that if he identified a problem, he saw the solution only through his own eyes, or if he couldn't work it out, he tried to change the nature of the problem. It meant he didn't take the decisions that he should be taking.

Tuesday 1 June

Oil price was the big drama for the whole of the West because of the price of Saudi oil and OPEC not increasing production. Out for dinner with Tessa, David and Matthew [their son]. I was trying to talk to Matthew mainly because at the moment I couldn't be bothered talking about the political scene, and hearing the whole time how terrible things were. Tessa very pro-TB as ever, even more anti-GB than usual. People still talked to me as though I was there, able to move things and change things. David got the plot, said he thought I was well out of it and clearly wished that she was too. I said I found the whole thing depressing.

Wednesday 2 June

Mark Bennett came round, then we left for King's Lynn. Three hundred or so people. Mum and co. came down from the Midlands, and Grace with the Bridges [neighbours], who were on holiday in Norfolk. Protesters with quite a funny stunt outside, giving out cans of 'Campbell's Bullshit Soup'. There was a nice atmosphere though, and even the protesters were quite friendly, though Mum had been really worried when she saw them and gave them a piece of her mind according to Victoria [Bridge]. I felt a bit defensive on Iraq, for the first time, perhaps because the woman asking me did so without any anger or hostility, just very straight questions about motivation and what we thought of the Americans' motivations. Richard Park [broadcaster and businessman] chaired it pretty well. I really liked him and his wife. Mum was really chuffed at the reception I got at the end and Liz [AC's sister] felt it had worked better with a smaller audience in a smaller theatre.

Thursday 3 June

Up early to Leeds, working on the speech for Qatar. Home Office Central Unit said it was OK to go, and I got briefed on what was happening at Al Jazeera [Qatar-funded international broadcaster]. One of the security guys said Qatar was the size of Guildford, nobody moves without the top Qataris knowing about it, they need the American presence, they need stability and it's about as safe as anywhere in the Middle East right now. The main purpose of the trip to Leeds was to interview Ian Botham for the sports series. It meant going up to the little scaffolded village [at Headingley cricket ground] where all the TV people hang out in their portakabin studios, so I ended up talking to and picking the brains not just of Botham but a whole stack of former England players. David Lloyd, though we spent as much time talking about Burnley as cricket. Mike Atherton, who was really interesting on his experience of detoxing from the obsessiveness required to play modern sport at the top. I think this was one of the reasons I found myself gravitating so much to sports people, because they had been through this same kind of thing I was going through, but in a different context. I sensed Mike was as dedicated to the media work now as he had been to playing.

I also had a long session with Geoff Boycott [former Yorkshire and England cricketer], who was fascinating but hard work, full on in-your-face politically, said he felt TB had conned us and was finished. Really heavy about Europe and asylum. Every time I tried to change the subject, reminisce about watching him as a kid, remind him I had started a fan club for him at Bradford Grammar, he'd be straight back on with a fullthroated political rant, a lot of it just straight out of the papers but quite entertaining in an 'and another thing' kind of way. The others kept wandering by, rolling their eyes or giving me sympathetic looks. I ended up saying it was hard to work out who was more right-wing, him or Botham. We talked at length about his cancer. I also picked his brains on great cricketers and he went for Sobers, Viv Richards, Brian Lara, Graeme Pollock. I noticed no Brits and assumed that was because he considered himself to be the best.

Channel 4 asked me to do a clip on Michael Vaughan [England captain] opting to be at the birth of his child ahead of playing, anathema to Boycott of course. The interview with Botham himself went fine, less on cricket, a lot on him rampaging about hunting, countryside, saying we didn't understand, generally a bit dispiriting on the political front but good copy. Despite his politics, I liked him and he still had that same rumbustious spirit that he played with, and of course he was brilliant for Leukaemia Research. Atherton seemed very thoughtful. He said he liked TB personally but felt he was politically finished because of the war. Headingley didn't seem like it had changed that much since I was a kid, bit scruffy, but I really enjoyed the day, and had finished the piece by the time the train got in to King's Cross.

Saturday 5 June

Trying to get on top of the various different speeches coming up. Bit of diary work, long bike ride. Dinner with Chris and Shirley Boffey [personal friends]. In the car back, Fiona said it was the first time she could remember us having dinner without TB being discussed.

Sunday 6 June

Rory racing in St Albans. Won the 400m in 53.1. Listened to TB on *The World at One*. Really strong. He could still communicate well in tricky circumstances. Home to pack then off to the airport for the flight to Qatar for the travel trade conference I was speaking at, with the Five documentary team in tow.

Monday 7 June

Met at the airport in Doha by a nice man from Burnley, off to the Ritz-Carlton and up to the twenty-third floor to meet Steven Freudmann, chairman of ITT [Institute of Travel and Tourism] and Richard Carrick, CEO of Hoseasons who was going to compere the event in the absence of a delayed Nick Witchell [BBC royal correspondent]. Judith Dawson and the Channel 5 documentary team were coming along but got in a real state because their equipment was seized at the airport and we had to get the Qatari Tourism Authority to release it, amid all sorts of warnings about where they could and couldn't film. The speech was in a big venue, poor sound system but it seemed to go down fine, usual message on strategy but tailored to them. I was vile about the *Mail*, who had a team there. Bob Ayling [businessman] was very friendly, said the *Mail* was the worst thing about Britain. Michael Fish [BBC weatherman] said it was the only paper he hated. I gave them a pretty frank assessment of how poorly I thought they and most business organisations lobbied government. One of the delegates said I could do worse than take that message out to businesses, but I can't say it appealed much.

Lunch with the sponsors. Then out for a swim then left for a meeting at Al Jazeera to see the MD, a couple of their reporters and the wonderfully named PR man, Jihad Ballout. Fascinating place, not at all as I had imagined. Security not that heavy. Premises tiny and overcrowded compared to our media places. Jihad worked out of a cluttered Portakabin of the kind you saw on building sites. We had a chat there, then over to the main office and studio. All small and crowded, lively people. They were very different to what I expected. They felt beleaguered, under total attack by the US, especially Donald Rumsfeld. They felt that they were part of the kind of change and modernisation that the US said they wanted for the Middle East. They gave a voice to ordinary citizens. Yet they were branded as terrorists and treated with contempt. Re the bin Laden videos, which had led the West to label them as part of the AQ [Al Qaeda] propaganda machine, they were treated like the news events that they clearly were.* They treated them with care, they listened to people's concerns about them, but did anyone seriously think if they went to other media organisations, they would not be broadcast?

As they spoke, I did feel my mind opening to a different way of looking at them, that possibly we should be engaging more not less. I had tried at one point when in No. 10 to get the Americans to go down that route, but they were pretty closed up on it. They said of course they saw things through a Middle Eastern perspective, the same as the BBC saw things through a British perspective and the US networks saw things through an American perspective. But they were an Arab voice, not a terrorist voice. Of the two reporters, the one who was due to interview me was fairly measured and sensible, the other pretty contemptuous about TB, said he was Bush's poodle, not serious about doing anything for the Middle East peace process, may have achieved lots at home but nothing abroad. He had the same belief British Prime Ministers had had down the years, thinking they could shape the whole world. But Iraq was a disaster for everyone and TB would get a lot of the blame.

It was a good meeting though, in terms of getting inside their heads a bit and seeing things through their perspective, and I was glad that I went. The Channel 5 people filmed the whole thing and thought it was fascinating. I did feel that we had allowed ourselves to accept too much the US line against them. Dinner at the conference. The travel trade was quite a boozy lot. It felt a little bit like Fleet Street in the '80s. I had a chat with our Ambassador [David MacLennan], who felt the Americans complained too much to Al Jazeera, and lost sight of the big picture. Back to Al Jazeera to do a live interview, which was fairly chaotic. I had some guy down on the floor plugging in my interpreter, right up to the point where it began. I could barely hear

---

* The Qatar TV station was broadcasting videotapes recorded by Osama bin Laden and released by Al Qaeda.

the interpretation over the sound of the voice of the interviewer who spoke really loudly, and at points I was guessing some of his questions, which as most seemed to be on TB–GB, Iraq and MEPP was mainly no bad thing. Back to the hotel where the tourism people were even boozier than before. Good feedback on the speech.

Tuesday 8 June

Filming with Channel 5. Run on the beach in extraordinary heat, fabulous feeling collapsing in the water. We did a long sit down interview then back into the conference. Tim Hames [*Times* journalist] did a very funny speech without notes, comparing the relative peace, prosperity and stability of the world now with past periods of war, pestilence, disaster. I was part of a panel with Jihad and some whinger from France. We got into a pretty interesting debate about terrorism. Tim and I both made the point how poor they were at lobbying. The guy from the property industry said he had been at a similar event where Peter M had said exactly the same to their organisations. He said everyone felt hurt but then went away and thought about it. Then had another interview, half-hour sit-down, with Al Jazeera.

One of the production team took me aside as we walked in. She said she was Iraqi. She said please don't say anything to anyone because this is not the done thing, but I want you to tell TB, 'Thank you from the bottom of my heart.' She was a Kurd from the north of the country, said people would not believe the suffering Saddam had inflicted, nor the joy that he was gone. Even now though, it was interesting how scared she was at being seen to talk about it. She was almost crying. When the rest of the team came back in, she went very formal again. The interview was fine, usual stuff, no real problem. We were driven out to the desert to see the sunset at yet another booze-up. Channel 5 got some fantastic running shots through the sand with the sun setting. Jerry Bridge [neighbour, travel agent] introduced me to a very nice woman from the *Telegraph* called Sheryl who said I had been the star of the conference, but she thought I had to be careful not to come over as bitter about the press.

Wednesday 9 June

Quick session in the gym then up to the airport with Nick Witchell. He felt Gilligan should never have been hired and Dyke should never have been made Director-General. He felt sorry for Sambrook who was still under pressure. He felt Hutton let us off lightly. But for a BBC man, like a lot of them, he didn't in private fully take the BBC line. Tom Baldwin called. He felt somebody should be making something of John Humphrys' relationship with YouGov, that it was a conflict of interest that should be declared.* JP called, wanting some ideas for PMQs, as TB was at the G8. On the plane I was next to a very dull man who worked in car parks, and was endlessly going on about how they worked, and did I think the car park industry was properly understood? I did the cricket articles plus a piece *The Herald* had asked for on whether I was English or Scottish, then watched *Touching the Void*, which was terrific.

Thursday 10 June

Steve Loraine sent through a new schedule, a lot harder than I thought would be required. Out on the bike for 90 minutes, bit of speech work then to Windsor to speak to the Channel 5 press team awayday. Usual stuff on strategy, modern communications, OK Q&A. Local elections going on which were clearly going to be a bit of a problem. Calum was doing work experience at *The Times*, but he complained they didn't actually give him much to do. TB at the G8, and in all of the coverage, he seemed to be alongside Bush the whole time. It was hard to tell if that was because he was alongside Bush alphabetically – UK, US – or just that they were the only pictures the media wanted to use. Ed Victor called. Vicky Barnsley had made clear Les Hinton was angry that Witherow had committed to £1 million for serialisation even with Random House as the publisher. Ed said it was clear that from Murdoch down they really wanted to do the book, and were angry Witherow was only thinking about it from the paper's perspective, though he had said they were bound to promote it a lot more if I went with Harper Collins. Ed's view was that if I removed the element of friendship with Gail from the equation, then it was probably better to go for Harper Collins, but he knew that was unlikely.

---

* *Today* programme presenter Humphrys had been given shares in the polling company in exchange for writing a weekly internet column. He rejected criticism that his *Today* role and the shareholding could constitute a conflict of interest.

Friday 11 June

Local elections overnight, pretty bad, with worse to come during the day, e.g. Newcastle falling to the Lib Dems, which was grim. By 7 p.m., Ken Livingstone had won [re-elected Mayor of London], so that was at least something I guess, though maybe it was a sign of how bad things were that a win for Ken was the one thing to cheer us up. TB, GB, JP, DB and some of the other big guns were out saying the results were bad but we were confident of getting it back for the general election. TB called and said he felt for the Tories to be at 39 per cent was still not high enough for them. He was at [former US President Ronald] Reagan's funeral having left the G8. Thatcher had done a video for it. He said the whole thing had been very moving. I was saying that Reagan showed the importance of keeping smiling and keeping going. He had basically set out two big objectives, to make America feel better about being America and to bring down the Berlin Wall. Big goals, and he just kept going with them, whatever people were saying. Obviously America is a much bigger country and the President has greater reach, but I said to TB he had similar skill, in some ways greater, like his understanding of policy detail, and though he could have done with more of Reagan's calm, he was easily as good at the big picture and the big goals. This was just one of those periods when he had to get through it strong.

I was doing interviews to promote the event in Wycombe and was asked if I wished I was there in No. 10 today. I said I didn't and I'm pretty sure that was right. Lance Armstrong sent through an email confirming he would do one of my Five TV interviews. He wanted to do it in Belgium, where he was training for the Tour de France, and staying with Eddy Merckx [Belgian cycling legend], which was great. Then Sara Latham [communications advisor] came on to say that Clinton had agreed I could do him too when he was over promoting his book, so despite the fuck-up with Alex, the series was shaping up really well.

Saturday 12 June

One hour fifty-minute run. Papers not as bonkers as they might have been. The sense was of a bit of a crisis which would blow over. TB's interviews were strong and though DB said he was 'mortified' at the results, which was an overreaction, I felt it wouldn't be that hard to get through this. TB thought, as did I, that it wasn't great for him to be at the Reagan funeral while all this was going on, but I really did feel there were parallels we could draw from Reagan. When you think how he was often portrayed in the UK media in particular, as a bit of a dolt, yet here he was in death and the impression was of a big figure in history who stuck to a real plan on important issues that really mattered. I'd found it quite useful in some of the Q&As to pose that question about history and how it would judge TB and there was plenty to point to already, the elections, Bank of England, minimum wage after a hundred years of trying, Scottish Parliament, Ireland, Kosovo etcetera. Rory running in the London Schools, won the 800 metres. Home to watch the first Euro 2004 games. I watched Anthony Seldon's TB documentary on Channel 4. It lacked any real insights and as ever with these documentaries, there were too many pictures of the presenter rather than the participants. He ended by saying Cherie and God were the only relationships that really mattered to TB.

Sunday 13 June

Working on the diary for September 1996 – JP and I having a big argument. GB refusing to attack over tax. Robin diddling, Clare being difficult, Peter M worrying about his status. I read bits of it to TB when he phoned up just before the England–France game. Plus ça bloody change, he said. He said he had recovered his form and he was up for it again. He said he wanted me back on form. He said we really miss you in the operation and I miss you personally because I have nobody I can really go over the whole range of things with. He said he was having to micromanage Iraq. GWB was looking more troubled, lacked a bit of his confidence. TB felt the Butler Report would be difficult because he would be worried about being accused of a whitewash, especially after the attacks on Hutton. He thought we could get to a position where we said clearly some of the intelligence was wrong but it was still the right thing to do. He said it would be so much easier if the Tories had a sensible position, instead of which they were so short-termist they were happy to get out there and attack the security chiefs.

He felt I should be out there doing more media on the political scene, possibly in an official position. He said he and JP had discussed it. He felt there was nobody who could defend him, and what the government had done, with more conviction, and conviction was what we needed at the moment. He sounded pretty up for it all. He said he had gone through a moment of conversion, he had been very down, felt it was time to go but had decided there was still too much to do and that GB would not necessarily do it. Also, he feared if he did leave now and let Gordon in, he'd go in a very different direction. He felt despite the election results he was in a stronger position than for some time. He said he needed me back to help get the message developed and delivered in a disciplined way. He felt we had lost some of the oomph. He wanted me to go in later in the week and discuss what I could do. He knew I couldn't go back to anything like the old job, but he would like me in key meetings and thinking through positions. He said he was totally up for the battle ahead but needed more and better support, and especially from me. I felt a bit more up for the fight than of late, but not like before.

Monday 14 June

Up early and off to City Airport to head to Belgium to see Lance. As airports go, totally pain free. Post-election analysis pretty grim. UKIP doing far too well. It was being seen as a kick in the slats for all the main parties. I bumped into Stephen Timms [former Labour minister] and we had a brief chat while he was getting his shoes shined. Very New Labour, I said. Stuart Prebble came out with the rest of the team. We went over the interview structure re Lance. I was a bit worried it was so close to the Tour itself, that he wouldn't have as much time as before. We were doing the interview at Eddy Merckx's place. He also had a shop there and a little bike factory. I thought it would be bigger, with maybe more people around given what a legend he was. He met us himself, but he had lost so much weight I wasn't sure it was him at first. He seemed fine, showing us around and trying to decide the best place to do the interview.

Then Lance called to say he wasn't happy, that it was better to do it outside without us barging into their house. The problem was we were too close to the airport and there would be aeroplanes flying over the whole time and we'd be stopping and starting. He was out on the bike and I said he had to relax, be calm, but I could sense he wasn't relaxed at all. Sheryl Crow arrived, and I asked her to help us get him in the right frame of mind. She said the problem was once he was in full training, he got very focused. He would also want to watch the Tour de Suisse on TV. She said they loved the piece in *The Times*, which is why he had agreed to this, but he was definitely in a different mindzone right now, I knew that even before he arrived. She advised me not to push him too hard at the start, and just go with the flow. She said she had taken to cycling herself.

We hung around for ages but then eventually Lance, Viatcheslav

Ekimov [Russian Olympic triple gold-medallist] and Big George Hincapie [American cyclist] and the US Postal Service pro cycling team arrived along with Johan Bruyneel, the team manager. They had been out for a few hours, and Lance said he had been going steady not fast. They all had extraordinary physiques, barely an ounce of fat on them. Even when they were sorting out the bikes, Lance was straight away talking about David Walsh [*Sunday Times*], how he was going to sue him, the French papers and their follow-up on some of it, defamation was a criminal offence and he was going to go for them big time. He had hired Keith Schilling [privacy and reputation lawyer]. He seemed a bit distracted and I wondered if the whole media thing was getting in the way. We got Sheryl to do a little comment about him – she said, 'Sorry if I sound tired but I've been meditating.' Lance went off for a shower and a change, then seemed to take ages having lunch which was cooked by Mrs Merckx and served up by Eddy. Lance was so clearly the top dog among the whole team.

I hassled him along to get the interview done and it was OK though he was not nearly as relaxed and flowing as when I did him for *The Times*, partly I think it's because people get fed up with all the fuss and kerfuffle that goes with TV, but also he was just less relaxed, had more on his mind. Stuff that he'd been very open about in Spain, some of the personal stuff, marriage, religion, politics, he was less forthcoming about. So it all felt a bit flat. I felt I hadn't got him in the right zone and maybe that had allowed him to control the agenda at the interview. At one point, he just said he'd had enough, and he and his teammates were supposed to be going to see *Troy* at the cinema. As Sheryl had warned, as soon as the Tour de Suisse stage was reaching a climax, he wanted the TV on. Stuart and Judith felt they had enough to make the programme, but it really wasn't as good as the print interview. We did a nice interview with Merckx, who was incredibly welcoming considering we had taken over his house for the day and also full of good advice on the triathlon. I felt a bit down about it on the plane home. Chatted to Stuart. He said Dyke was convinced in his own mind that he was one of the ten most popular people in the country; he could not see that he was a twat, who had failed.

Tuesday 15 June·

I'd been asked to do a training day with Tim Don [international triathlete] at Windsor. The place was actually Eton Dorney, where kids from Eton, and a few internationals, did their rowing. I had a nice chat with James Cracknell [Olympic gold medallist rower]. I mentioned I had been to see Lance and I was surprised by the extent to which he said the sporting world felt cycling was now totally defined by drugs. I got a call from Nigel Sheinwald [No. 10 foreign policy advisor] re Al Jazeera. He was interested in my take on them and what we did, whether the government should take a different approach. I got a bit panicky at the open water swim. The bike ride was a bit slow and the run too short but it was definitely worth doing and quite interesting to train with somebody who really knows what they are doing. I would get a piece out of Don. One of the other people doing the day told me his dad had died of leukaemia. I definitely noticed an increase in people telling me they had a connection with leukaemia. Home, then out for a dinner that Ray Ingleby [Burnley FC director] had asked me to do for Leeds University. OK event.

Wednesday 16 June

1,200-metre swim then out to a conference at *Euromoney* [financial magazine]. Good audience, big international contingent. The speech went well I think. It was being chaired by [UK CEO, *The Independent*] Ivan Fallon's brother Padraig [*Euromoney* chairman]. At the end, a few people came over and said they thought it was a brilliant speech, at which Fallon said, 'I can assure you nobody said that to Michael Howard.' Another chat with Sheinwald who was clearly interested in whether and how to engage more deeply with Al Jazeera. I think he felt too that the Americans were too hard line on it, and wondered if I shouldn't head out there at some point to try to talk them round. Blunkett round for dinner. He seemed pretty down about the political scene, as we were, but I felt a bit bored having the same discussions about the same old stuff. At least TB somehow managed to get up for it most of the time. David was very down on the civil service, felt the Rolls-Royce machine was one of the great historical myths. He felt the good were buried by the bad and that the culture was one of complacency. He also believed that GB was holding back investment so that he would have more to spend if he became PM. He was still clearly hoping that TB could get rid of GB. 'I can't be Home Secretary for ever,' he said.

He had the same stomach complaint as mine, ulcerative colitis, so we had a little chat about medication. We were both on Asacol, I was on a bit more than he was. I was worrying a bit about Butler. I think TB was right, that he was the sort who would worry about people thinking he was whitewashing the issue, and would look for something to show that he hadn't. He was very much part of that out and about great and good chattering circuit and I suspect he would be getting loads of people from inside and outside the government saying he had to be tougher on TB than Hutton had been.

Thursday 17 June

I was beginning to get into the flow on the diary. Gail [Rebuck] called in a state about Clinton and the interviews for his book [*My Life*]. He had done a Dan Rather interview as part of the promotion, and there had been lots about Monica. David Dimbleby had done him and Bill said he was rude and disrespectful and they had broken all sorts of agreements about content. I suggested she had to get chapter and verse on content before making a complaint. There was also a danger of giving the thing legs you didn't want to give it with a complaint. Briefing meeting re the lawyers' conference for next week. Then a longer meeting with a woman who had come from Holland to discuss a conference I was doing there later in the year. She was wearing the most extraordinary micro skirt.

There was a big bust-up at the EU Summit, with TB against Chirac and to a lesser extent Schroeder, in saying he didn't want Verhofstadt as Commission President. He was hanging tough but it would make Chirac even worse. It was a bit of a rerun of Major–Dehaene. Out to Wandsworth to be interviewed on the *Fantasy Football* programme. Bit of a chaotic show, not as funny as I thought it was going to be, a few people in there booing me, not sure whether because of politics or because I said I supported Scotland not England and that I thought France and Croatia were better than England. I found David Baddiel more impressive than Frank Skinner [both comedian presenters]. We had a long chat about the press and he felt the government should legislate, that a privacy law was a minimum, but he felt politicians were frightened of Murdoch. He had not been against the war in Iraq at the start but felt the WMD argument was now absurd. He was much more thoughtful than I expected him to be, whereas I think Frank Skinner was closer to the TV/lads persona. Baddiel was also very supportive re my difficulties with the BBC. He felt the problem was a culture of journalists refusing ever to admit they could be wrong. Fiona had been out to the opera with Cherie, the first time she had seen her for a while. It was interesting timing, as *The Independent* was on day three of their serialisation of the Oborne/Walters book on me, after the *Mail on Sunday* threw it away, and they did me and Fiona falling out with TB and CB. More multiple timezone echo chambers.

Friday 18 June

Long swim session, 1,800 metres. The TV interviews were coming together well. Lance done, Clinton sorted, and today I went to see Peter M to go over how we might do it. He felt it was going to be difficult. He said TB was shocked we were even thinking of doing it. I said we had to agree a mutual purpose or interest. I said from my perspective, I wanted an interesting interview and a sense that he was communicating frankly. What he needed, I suggested, was the clear intimation from me that he should not have been made to resign the second time around. We went through it. He told all manner of long stories about him/GB, him/TB. He said GB had said to him TB was a weak man propped up by PM and AC, and once you removed the props, TB would fall over. I said I didn't imagine he would wish to say any of that on camera and he said no.

We went over other areas and he said he felt the need, and that this might be the place, to say something about being gay. He felt it was part of the reason for the demonisation. I felt it was more caused by the central tension in his life, the difficulty he and more importantly others had in seeing him as a politician rather than as a political operative. Also, because he was one of the more interesting characters on the political scene, and because of some of the lifestyle issues, Notting Hill, fancy friends, he copped a lot of the soap opera stuff. He was anxious about the interview but also up for it. He was clearly keen on the European job but felt the situation with Chirac would make it more difficult, especially if there was going to be a hoo-ha about Verhofstadt.

I had to leave for lunch with the Ethiopian Ambassador at the Embassy. He basically wanted advice on how to get Ethiopia a broader image that was not just based on war and famine. He said that the government did not really believe in PR and would I help? I gave him and his very nice press officer, Gail Warden, a few ideas but I was reluctant to get drawn in much deeper. I was happy to help with advice, but didn't want to take on any kind of hands-on role myself. They were very keen on me doing the Great Ethiopian Run again, as we managed to generate a fair bit of good publicity for them last time.

He was a nice man but clearly frustrated that the country was defined so narrowly for people here, an image rooted in the past. The Lance interview transcription came through and it was not nearly as bad as I feared, certainly enough in there for a half-decent programme.

Saturday 19 June
I did a couple of swimming articles, then diary work and a tough bike session which ended in a calf strain. The increase in the training programme was making me feel tired. The papers were full of the Europe deal and TB was clear he could win the argument on the constitution* but the propaganda against him was pretty bilious at the moment.

Sunday 20 June
TB was on *Frost* re the constitution. Did pretty well, certainly looking more confident. Nice letter from Blunkett re dinner and our continuing support for him. Took Calum to a tennis match and interestingly the other team was looked after by Adam Sharples [Treasury official, ex-Ugly Rumours, band co-founded by Tony Blair]. Peter M getting more nervous about the interview. Ed Victor came round. He said it was a unique situation because we were trying to sell a book while saying we could not be sure when it might be published. He said imagine if that was a car. He said obviously the value would fall after TB left and fall even more if we waited till Labour was out of power. Clinton's office came on, said he was really pissed off at the way the *Panorama* interview came out. But I warned them that the BBC would just use it to get more publicity for the programme, more focus on Monica and they were better to ignore it.

Monday 21 June
Pulse 52. 1,800-metre swim. Email exchanges with Peter M on the interview plans. Ben Wegg-Prosser [Peter M advisor] said he thought we were mad so I spent a bit of time trying to persuade him it was not such a bad idea. It would all depend on how we were and what we actually

---

* After long negotiation, EU leaders agreed a deal that met most of Blair's demands for a national veto to defend sovereignty but left divisions that would hinder the adoption of the EU's first ever constitution.

said. He felt if we unleashed a whole lot of TB–GB–PM-ery, TB would not be happy and we had to be careful. Fiona thought Peter was trying to put himself back at the centre of attention again. I was up to '96 conference in the diaries, so two years already done, but it was slow. I went to the tennis at Wimbledon, and was doorstepped about the European constitution going in. Julie Kirkbride [Tory MP] was at the lunch and said things had gone downhill since I left, and politics was less fun. She felt TB should stay for a long time and I should go back and once the fuss died down, it would be fine. She felt the Tories were in a better position but she still felt they were likely to lose. I spent a fair bit of time round the media centre talking to some of the former players for the *Times* piece on the best tennis stars. Very good chat with Fred Stolle [Australian former grand slams winner] and also went to the Roger Federer press conference. Got a few words with Martina Navratilova. Home to England 4, Croatia 2. The LTA [Lawn Tennis Association] were sounding me out about getting involved with them. They did seem to be doing some pretty good stuff on the grassroots front.

Tuesday 22 June

Vicky Barnsley wrote to Ed to say Murdoch was personally committed to getting the diaries, that they were the best firm for it, and they would pay more up front. Gail and I were not discussing the book at all. Best to leave it to Ed. I didn't feel the need to push for a deal right now, but Harper Collins were really pressing. I was doing the Lawyer of the Year awards at Grosvenor House. They wanted me in for a rehearsal, so I did that, then had a run round the park. Beautiful day. Peter M was definitely getting nervous. He was calling the whole time to have the same conversation about whether we were making a terrible mistake. I really didn't think so. I thought it would be good TV, and good for him if it became clear I was saying we got it wrong over the second resignation, and if he could just be a bit more his old self in his manner and demeanour.

The event was pretty well organised but as well as the speech I had to present twenty-eight awards. I played the speech mainly for laughs then did a serious point about the nature of the media and drew on Hutton and those events. James Dingemans [QC, counsel to the Hutton Inquiry] won the public sector legal award, but there was a bit of a fuss because he didn't want to have his picture taken with me, and though he was perfectly friendly it was all a bit obvious that he came up to accept it and it was the one time when the flashes didn't go off.

Wednesday 23 June

I got home too late last night and had a headache this morning. Nigel Farndale from the *Sunday Telegraph* was round to do an interview. Lots of Hutton, lots of personal stuff, God knows what will come of it. Out most of the day on a training day and chatting again to Peter M about the interview tomorrow. Into Soho to show the Lance interview to Chris Shaw, who said he liked it. I worked on a piece for *The Sun* to promote it. It certainly came out a lot better than it felt at the time. TB was out doing a speech about choice in healthcare while Howard was doing the same. Germany out of the Euros at group stage.

Thursday 24 June

In to do the Peter M interview at the RAC Club. It took a while to set up, then PM arrived looking a bit pale and nervous and now saying he wasn't so sure it was a great idea. But once he got going, he was terrific, about himself, his politics, his resignations, his support for GB! We got fairly spiky going over the second resignation and I think just about got the tone right and had a good laugh doing the stills. It was another example of where sometimes it pays to over-worry, because I felt it was much better than most of his interviews. He was still not totally convinced, but I felt it would do him good in the party at least, because his basic Labour tribalism came out well, how deep his roots went. We had agreed on how to do the gay question and it was fine, not too heavy, just there, enough for him to be able to say in the future that he has said all he needs to say. Stuart and team were happy with it. I headed back home to do a fair bit of writing. Diaries. I was doing the My Week slot in the *Independent on Sunday*, the quiz for *Time Out* and a big piece on Lance for *The Sun*. Then Gail called to ask if I could do a review of the Clinton book, because they weren't confident of getting too many good ones around the place. England v Portugal (Portugal winning on penalties). Interesting how the kids seem to have followed me in not really supporting England.

Friday 25 June

I whizzed through the Clinton book last night and this morning and started to work on a piece. Gail was hoping we could get it syndicated. It was not getting great reviews. I found the first half much more interesting than the second. His early life was the best bit, partly because it was full of things I didn't know, but also sounded more authentically him, his voice. Once he got into the presidency, it all felt a bit rushed, as if someone was filleting through lots of papers and documents, rather than relying on his big picture assessment.

Saturday 26 June

All day triathlon training day at Dairy Crest HQ in Esher for the Leukaemia Research team. I did opening remarks followed by a guy called Tim Swale who was a hypnotist and motivator and whose son had been diagnosed with leukaemia. In the swimming session, they simulated the start of a race with bodies clambering over each other. 5k run, lunch, session with the race organiser, some interviews then a 20k bike ride.

Sunday 27 June

Took Calum to tennis, long run. Chris Shaw called, saying they were really pleased with all the publicity for the first interview. It was 'choice of the day' in most of the papers. He also wanted my help in getting him out of an embarrassing situation, namely that Kirsty Young had gone her own way in trying to get an interview with Bill, not knowing I had already fixed one for Five. Things kicked off with Fiona, kind out of nowhere.

Monday 28 June

Pulse 51, 1,800-metre swim. Into W1 to do the voiceover for the Lance film. All fine, dead easy. Then went for a wander to avoid going home because Fiona and I had a huge great row last night, about nothing and everything, the usual bollocks. Met Natascha [McElhone] for lunch. She said she was not remotely surprised I had been getting down, because 1, I always did and 2, I had left something defining and definite for something vague and uncertain. But she said Fiona and the kids were the most important thing in my life and I had to focus on that, and forget the Labour people pulling me all over the place. So don't go back and help? 'Not if it is going to take you right back to where it was; only if you can manage it differently.' She felt that was probably what Fiona was saying.

Tuesday 29 June

Going through the Peter M transcripts. Fairly strong, quite edgy, funny in parts. I took the boys for lunch, then back to work on the diaries. Two consecutive days rowing with Peter!

Wednesday 30 June

Diary work. Ed Balls selected [as Labour candidate in Normanton]. Working on Peter M film. 2.45 had a session with Tim Swale, doing a piece for *The Times* on hypnotherapy in sport. Quite interesting. He made me a tape to listen to at home, and we worked on trigger words 'better, faster, stronger' for whenever I felt I was struggling. Screening of the Peter M film for Chris Shaw. He loved it. Really over the top about it. I felt Peter came out fine. I had an amazing energy crash after a swim session, and ended up guzzling down Magnums and Lucozade. Steve said it meant I needed rest. Watched Portugal v Holland (Euro 2004 semi-final, 2–1) with Grace but she really doesn't have the boys' interest.

Thursday 1 July

Ninety minutes on the bike. Working on the press strategy for the Peter M interview. He was getting nervous about it now. He had talked to TB about it who called me for one of his 'Is this wise?' chats. He obviously thought I had bamboozled Peter into thinking it could be good for him, but he could not see how it would be. But I honestly thought it was fine, fine for him and me and for GB/TB. Theatre event at Broxbourne; perhaps because of the football it was easily the smallest audience. Tony Robinson [actor and broadcaster] chairing it, did it well. It was really nice to see Helena Hopkins [No. 10 duty clerk], nice atmosphere and no real heat. Real Tory area but there were a few Labour supporters who came up at the end including a woman who said she may have been responsible for the purple flour bomb thrown at TB in the House. Not sure what she was on about. Greece beat Czech Republic [Euro 2004 semi-final].

Friday 2 July

First thing got a visit from the liaison guy from the Home Office Central Unit. He said the general security threat re individuals like me was being downgraded because of progress with the IRA and because

July '04: 'Is this wise?' asks TB of Peter M interview

Al Qaeda went for spectaculars rather than individuals. But he warned about going to the region. Ed Miliband came round. Usual old stuff. He felt GB had had a total understanding from TB that he was going to go, but he had now changed his mind. He said it was not going to help things if GB felt TB was reneging. I did the usual, of saying I was sure if TB had made some kind of real commitment on it, he would have told me. I felt the last signal was a wobble about his leadership in general, not least because GB, or certainly some of his people, were deliberately undermining. Ed M thought that it was best for the long-term interests of the party if TB went sooner rather than later, that if he was planning to stay for the whole term, or even a large part of it, he felt it would be disastrous. I said there was a bit of a problem with that, in that it was TB who was elected, and you could argue it was a breach of faith to go sooner rather than later.

It was interesting the extent to which we were so different on what had been going on for so long. There was no longer much pretence that things were anything other than pretty permanently tricky between GB and TB. I was of the view GB was much more to blame for the position they were in, whereas Ed was vehemently of the view it was the other way round. He said GB felt really hurt, he was sure in his mind he had a clear understanding that TB was going, and now was being fobbed off again. I said TB was in truth not sure that GB was delivering on his side, which was to help drive through some of the reforms, in the public service arena in particular. If anything, he felt he was blocking him more and more, just making them even more difficult changes which ought to be quite straightforward. That got Ed arguing not just for TB's departure, but for a radical shift away from what he had been doing, but to what, I was not exactly clear. He said several times I had to think about what the party should be doing in five years. 'Are you sure that more of the same is the way to go? I don't think so.' I asked him how on earth GB could defend the relationship he had with Dacre. He said it was the same as me wooing *The Sun*. I said the difference was we were wooing *The Sun*, as he put it, to try to level the media playing field and help the party and government as a whole. GB uses Dacre to get a better press for himself, often at the expense of TB and the rest of the government.

Saturday 3 July
Up at 6 and off out on the bike, trying to work out what to say at Lindsay and Mark's wedding. Just went on a general wander round London.

It's a fantastic way to see the place, and a great time to do it. Despite the lack of traffic though, I was shocked at how many people were still out, on the piss, in one place a great queue to get into a club on the road down to Tower Bridge. Did Wapping, London Bridge, headed south, round back near Victoria and home. The wedding was at St Bride's in Fleet Street and I was trying to work out whether I had been there since John's memorial. It was nice to see lots of the old *Mirror* crowd, also Tessa and David. It was quite a hard speech to do, hard to decide on how to get the balance between the reason for our friendship, which was John, what had happened to Lindsay in the past, with his and Ellie's death, but also make it an event about the future. In the end, I went much more on the future, and the fact that Mark had genuinely made her happy after all she had been through. As I was speaking, Lindsay was holding on to my arm, almost to the point where it was hurting. Fiona said afterwards she thought it was a way of not letting go of John and Ellie and the past, even while looking to the future.

Lots of people seemed to have seen the Lance interview which had got good previews and reviews. The *FT* and the *Telegraph* particularly went on the preview front, *The Times*, *Sunday Telegraph* and *Independent* the best reviews. The main point that seemed to come through them was that it was a good old-fashioned format based upon letting people speak and being genuinely interested in the answers. Played the bagpipes, and Grace was up dancing with friends and cousins, and gorging on one of those chocolate machines. It was a nice do though and Lindsay did seem really happy.

Sunday 4 July

Pulse rate 44. Absolutely brilliant. Lowest yet. Phoned Steve [triathlon coach] to tell him. I had been planning a one-hour run, but went longer. Took the boys to tennis, suddenly felt knackered. I'd briefed Kamal Ahmed about some of the lines from the interview with Peter, and it ran on the *Observer* front. I briefed the dailies on the line that Peter was backing GB to be the next PM. TB called at 6 and said, 'I thought you said this wouldn't play into the TB–GB, PM–AC soap opera.' I said if GB's people had responded positively it could have been good all round but they were basically saying who cares what Mandelson thinks? He said GB had been worse than ever recently. I told him about the conversation with Ed Miliband, and TB apparently saying he had promised back in November not to do the full term. TB said, 'What I actually said was that if GB worked with me very closely, as a team, I would stand down before the election.' He said he had done anything but work with him closely. 'I said the same thing as I've been saying for the past ten years, but the truth is he's being trying to fuck me over on the public services, winding up the unions the whole time.' He said he found GB's relationship with Dacre stomach churning. Also that Simon Heffer [*Telegraph* journalist] gave Anji a blow-by-blow of the lunch when GB went to the paper and talked about how he shared a lot of their assessment of British values. 'What do they actually have in common?' said TB – nothing, apart from the fact that they want me to fuck off.'

He sounded pretty fed up and steely about it, even suggested at one point someone should write a piece about GB's relationship with the right-wing media. I told him what Ed had said about it being the same as us going after *The Sun*, and he made the same point that I had, said that we were putting a case for the whole party while GB goes round putting a case against the government as a whole, 'against me in particular and for himself'. He was again asking me when I was going to start going in more and again I said I was fine about going in so long as I wasn't sucked into the day-to-day lunacy. He said there was going to come a point where he would like me in there pretty much full time, and we had to be clear about that. I said I had a few commitments, and he said he hoped I wouldn't take on too many more.

He felt Iraq was getting better and it was frankly idiotic this line being run against us that we had no influence there. He said he was worried about Robin Butler and his report on the intelligence. He felt it was liable to be a mixture of naughty and naive, said it was a dangerous mixture. His guess was that the report would say intelligence was wrong on 45 minutes, right about Niger and uranium [intelligence that Saddam Hussein had tried to buy uranium powder from Niger]. But the overwhelming message from the conversation was that he was really pissed off with GB. He said there was no way he could run the election campaign because he would effectively be putting in charge of the campaign someone who didn't want to work with the leader of the party. I said the thing sounded untenable and what was he going to do? He said get new people to do the campaign, get through the election and then deal with it.

Monday 5 July
Pulse back up to 52. I really liked it yesterday when it was below my

age. OK follow-ups to *The Observer*, including a fair bit on the BBC over the past day or so. To be fair to Five, they were promoting the Peter interview big time. I got a cab to Aldwych for the screening. Some of the lobby big cheeses turned out, Adam Boulton [Sky News political editor], Phil Webster and Tom Baldwin, Simon Hoggart doing a sketch. The best thing, given that as a bunch they tended to be a bit cynical, was that there was no sense of laughter during the screening. My worry had been if they had seen the whole thing as a bit of a parody, but I could tell they were pretty gripped by it. Setting it up as Peter backing GB was fine, but they quickly moved to our discussion on the second resignation, and also on the fact that he had been open about being gay. I did a session with them afterwards and was probably a bit too lukewarm about GB. I told them that not having regular contact with the press was without doubt one of the best parts of post-No. 10 life. Also told them I'd be doing Clinton later.

I had breakfast with Chris Shaw who said he could not have asked for more in terms of the profile the interviews had generated. He thought it was the first time Five had ever been on a Sunday broadsheet front page. He felt that what came through the reviews was that I was able to ask tough questions without being offensive. He wanted me to do more, possibly go full time with a weekly current affairs programme. I said I would think about it but was not sure I wanted to go for such a regular commitment. Peter texted me to say, 'You and I are on the back page of the *China Daily* [English-language newspaper based in Beijing], but I am not sure what it says.' He called later from China and I told him I thought the briefing came out fine. Jonathan was a bit pissed off that I hadn't specifically told them I was doing it, though I know Peter had told TB. Jonathan was worried too much would be read into it, whereas I just felt it was a quite interesting interview involving two people who knew each other very well. I was tired and spent a fair bit of time watching the cycling on TV while reading Bill Clinton's autobiography again, this time to prepare for the interview.

Tuesday 6 July

OK coverage from yesterday, big in *The Times*, usual piss-take in *The Guardian*, page leads mainly. TB was a bit worried it would come up at the Liaison Committee [umbrella committee for Commons select committees] and he would be expected to be on top of long-forgotten detail. Ed Victor had asked me to meet Philippa Harrison [publisher], who came round to take a look at some of the diary material. I reckoned I'd done about 440,000 words up to November '96 so we were on for 2 million words in total. She was sixty-one, nice enough but a bit too posh, and she smoked, but Ed was adamant she was the best. She felt the whole thing should be published at some stage, though I was pretty clear, particularly after some of the recent stuff, that I couldn't do the whole thing while we were still in power. Ed had said from some of the material he had read that he was quite shocked by some of the GB stuff. She felt it would need to be cut, possibly substantially, while accepting it was an absolutely faithful record which in some ways should all be published. Fiona and I were back to rowing again, which was getting me down and making me tired and when I went out for a run, I just couldn't get going. I was also totally unsure what if anything I wanted to do with all these fucking words.

Wednesday 7 July

Pretty vile piece from Alice Miles [*Times* journalist] about me and Peter, but overall I thought it went fine. The main news out of TB at yesterday's Liaison Committee was him saying we may never find WMD. Not a great scene. TB was really pushing on the choice message re public services, which would be another indicator to GB that he was digging in. I didn't have much in the diary for the day so I got through another twenty days of 1996, then an hour on the bike and a short run. I was feeling tired. Steve said it was normal to feel like this given a pick-up in training. Peter called a couple of times and seemed to think the interview came out OK. He felt No. 10 would feel he had gone too far in saying so unequivocally that GB would be the next leader, because it would play into the pressure on that now. He had spoken to JP beforehand and basically done a deal, him saying he would back GB, back him as New Labour, say he was TB's natural successor, and in return GB would work with him in the future. 'It'll never happen though,' he said.

Philip came round for a chat, ostensibly to talk about stepping up general election planning. He thought the interview was strong and did both of us a bit of good. Clinton was changing his schedule the whole time, which was proving to be a bit of a nightmare pinning down the interview. I did a bike session at the gym then Jerry Bridge brought round Sandra Nori, the New South Wales tourism minister, who was a typically ballsy Aussie. Nattered away a bit, mainly about how you deal with relentless negativity. It was only when you talked to people like her though that you realised just how big the whole New Labour thing was in politics around the world. She said Australia was full of wannabees pretending to be TB and me.

Thursday 8 July

Judith Dawson and team were filming again. Round to Simpson's bike shop (Kentish Town) to get a lesson on how to change a tyre. Very funny moment when I asked how you'd know if you had a puncture and Scott [Simpson, owner] said, 'It'd be flat.' Then to the lido to practise getting in and out of a wetsuit, which is a lot harder than I remembered. Later off with June Sarpong to High Wycombe. I filled her in on the triathlon on the way down. She said Jim O'Neill [Goldman Sachs] had asked if I would do an interview with Gavyn Davies. I said yes, for fifty grand for charity. Graeme [brother], Anya [sister-in-law] and Kate [niece] were there. Enjoyed it fine, nice enough atmosphere but I was beginning to feel I'd done enough of these theatre events now. The best question was a guy asking, and apparently in all seriousness, whether I really believed Maxwell was dead. Philip called. He felt TB had pulled through OK and was now in a stronger position and winning the arguments with the public on public services. He said as things stood GB was a real problem and not up to leading a campaign. Philip felt perhaps Alan Milburn was the person who should do it. Fiona and Grace were off to Majorca for Glenys's 60th birthday. I had decided to stay back and go with Rory to the English Schools Finals instead.

Friday 9 July

Up at 6, train to Newcastle, finished Clinton's book. Brendan Foster picked us up. He clearly felt the bad internal vibes inside the government were beginning to connect a bit too much. He said he was surprised that some of the people he knew were moving towards GB. He was horrified when I told him about GB's relationship with Dacre. Up to the stadium at Gateshead, which was a bit ramshackle these days. Amazing to think it was once state of the art. Got dragged in to meet all the VIPs, then out to watch Rory on the warm-up track. It was dreadful that an event like this couldn't attract proper sponsorship, given how much money was going in at the top end. Rory didn't run as well as he could have done, came fifth in the heat after being third on the last bend. I later found him face down on the warm-up track, really fed up. Out for dinner at the Baltic [Centre for Contemporary Art]. Brendan felt Stan, his old coach, thought Rory should move up to the 1,500.

Saturday 10 July

I did a long run while Rory watched the final (Portugal 0, Greece 1). Ed Miliband called. He said he was just back from Italy and there were lots of reports doing the rounds suggesting he had come to me as an emissary for GB complaining TB had reneged on a deal. I was trying to remember who I had mentioned it to, TB certainly, and Philip. But I considered both of them to be safe. I tried to remember if I had mentioned anything to Peter M during our various conversations about the Five film, but I don't think so. I said to Ed that this was the reason why I was so glad to be out of it, because there was just so much bad blood and suspicion flowing around. Up to the stadium and I was asked in for the lunch again. The chairwoman of the English Schools association made the same speech for the second day running. I was doing more reading up on Bill on the train back.

Sunday 11 July

Out early, hour and a half on the bike. Matthew Doyle called late last night with a message that some of the press were saying Gavyn Davies had said he may still sue me. He did a big interview in the *Sunday Times* Review saying the same. Fiona had a pretty brutal view of it, that if he did, I should do the diaries now, including all the GB stuff, as a way of raising the money to take it on. Certainly, it could get very messy vis-à-vis Sue Nye [GB aide, Davies's wife]. Ed Miliband called again, ostensibly to say the same as yesterday re how he was worried about rumours doing the rounds about our meeting. I said he should calm down. I had mentioned it to nobody but people I trusted and certainly not to journalists. There was a bit of a frenzy building about the Butler Report. It was due on Wednesday, but stuff had been leaking out for days and it was clearly not going to be good.

Doing the Clinton research, I was genuinely shocked about some of the detail re Kenneth Starr [independent counsel]. I had always thought Starr had just been gunning for BC but the more I read about the way the inquiry was done, the more I felt that the right-wing conspiracy charge occasionally made by Hillary and others was real.* Phil Webster was planning to do something re me seeing Ed, which somehow had got out there. I told him it was just two friends who have not seen each other for ages, but the TB–GB stuff was definitely building up again. Tessa called re yesterday's story by Andrew Marr about four ministers going to see TB to say he must not leave. Tessa denied having had anything to do with it. But we were definitely into another pretty febrile phase re the TB–GB mood stuff.

Monday 12 July

Pulse 52. Grace was off school ill. So she was lying down upstairs on the sofa in my office, where I was starting to hone questions for the interview with Bill. Stuart Prebble wanted me to focus more on stuff that was exclusive to me, e.g. re past meetings so-called. I felt it was a bit self-indulgent, but he was worried Clinton would just trot out the same lines as in other interviews. Latest TB–GB stuff was still going pretty big. Phil Webster weaved in a line about me and Ed. I was trying to get myself psyched up for the Clinton interview, but I was finding it hard. The rest of the team were really excited about it; the fact that I wasn't made me think this TV malarkey was not really my thing. It would be good to see him and have a chat, but I couldn't say I was hugely excited about doing the interview. Got to the Ritz. Bill late needless to say, having been out signing books. The Five board had apparently all asked if they could come and meet Bill. I put my foot down on that. Louise Plank from the press office turned up wearing a micro skirt and more make-up than I had ever seen her wearing before.

When Bill arrived, he was warm and friendly, but looked tired, and was clearly feeling a bit like he was on a conveyor belt, doing so many interviews wherever he went. His answers were a bit long and at times I felt he was defaulting to policy line-to-take positions. He was best, and most open, when I asked him if he ever feared Hillary would end the marriage, which he did, and talked about sleeping on the sofa when he was meant to be the most powerful man in the world. He was also good at Ireland and strong on how he got through the whole series of

---

* In his report after investigating Bill Clinton's relationship with Monica Lewinsky, Starr concluded that the President had lied about it in a sworn deposition. This led to Clinton being impeached, but subsequently he was acquitted in a Senate trial for perjury and obstruction of justice.

scandals and crises, but overall, he was not really firing, and nor was I. He still looked the part, still had that way of making words work, and using his face and hands to good effect. He was definitely tired, and not on as good form as I had seen him. He didn't really bite on the stuff that Stuart had wanted. Also the bloody light shield fell off the window, which lost us a bit of time. In the end, we got 35 minutes out of it and I felt it would be OK without being electric, in the way that some thought the one with Peter had been. I had a little chat with him afterwards and it was clear that off camera, he was worried about how to square a pro-TB, anti-Bush position on Iraq. I think he felt we had got way too close to the Bush crowd.

Off with Fiona to the Guildhall, where Clinton was making a speech. Big crowd, lots of the usual media lot. I was talking to Roger Alton and Kamal Ahmed when Robin Butler came over. He said he had been preparing for Wednesday's press conference today and said one of the tough questions was, 'Why didn't you specifically clear AC?' So why didn't you?, asked Roger. Butler said, 'Because after Hutton his integrity is beyond doubt.' Even though he was being quite jokey about it all, I also think he was being genuine in sending a signal to me and people he knew to be journalists, that he was not going to go for me. Elinor Goodman [Channel 4] said the lobby just wasn't the same, she missed me, and so did some of the others. The *Mail on Sunday* books editor asked if I would consider giving them my diaries. I said I was very grateful for the enquiry and I intended to see a lawyer tomorrow to get it written into my will that nothing I wrote would ever appear in the *Mail* papers. Martin Rowson [cartoonist] said he would really like to illustrate the diaries with cartoons. He said he felt at least I was a colourful human being and he'd love to do it as a professional challenge. It was a good enough do, and BC still had the old magic when he spoke and when he worked the room, but I would have thought given who was speaking there should have been more political figures and fewer media.

Tuesday 13 July

Editing Clinton, then a long chat with David Hill about how to handle Butler. Jonathan felt it was not going to be as bad as people were predicting. I was on the diaries for late '96 and told him I was at the point where he and I were against the Dome. Off to see Tim Smale re triathlon, and to do a piece for *The Times* about how he planted certain concepts in the mind – like the 'better, faster, stronger' mantra he had done for me, which I was using already, and found it worked – in the mind. On a couple of runs when I had started to hurt or feel breathless, I just did the 'better, faster, stronger' thing and it seemed to get me to push through. I bumped into Andrew Adonis as I was leaving. He said the GB lot were pushing back the whole time. Also bumped into Simon Kelner [*Independent* editor]. He said he thought I seemed a lot saner.

Wednesday 14 July

Butler Report day, media set up for a great wank. A few press outside. Went into the studios to do voiceovers for the Clinton interview. A bit like the Lance interview, it looked better and came across better than it had felt when I was doing it. There was actually some very strong stuff in there. Ran home, got back in time to watch Butler do his stuff. Jonathan had said it was all fine, David Hill that it was difficult but manageable, and I felt Butler's opening statement was harder than I had expected, even if he reined back a little in the Q&A. The BBC were clearly going to push hard on it. That much was pretty clear from Marr's reports from the off. The truth was it was mixed, on the one hand everyone acted in good faith, no deliberate misleading, on the other hand, key claims in the dossier were wrong, e.g. 45 minutes. Some support for Brian Jones [Defence Intelligence official], the JIC should not have done some of the things they did, but he was not into blaming people. TB's statement was pretty strong. He accepted the report, accepted there were no WMD but insisted it was still the right thing to go to war. Howard went at him over credibility and trust.

TB called later and said he felt it was mixed but not devastating. The vox pops from the media were relentlessly bad. I suspected it would hit us hard in the by-election tomorrow. Did about a week of diary transcribing. Jonathan called to ask if I thought TB should do TV. I felt the statement was strong enough. Out to Grace's choreography show, in which she was easily the best. Back to watch the Clinton interview, which was fine. John Sergeant called to say he thought it was brilliant. He said he was sure I was able to get more stuff out of people like Bill because I had been involved in some of the things we were talking about. TB called again at nine, said the Queen had welcomed him with open arms at some do or other. He felt things were going to be grim for a few days, but he was fine. He had been through a difficult few months and felt a lot stronger. It was now clear that he had to stay.

'Do you think I'm mad?' he asked. I said no, so long as you have the energy for it. He said GB was at it the whole time. He had no problem with his ambition, but the way he was going about it was madness. He felt if the two by-elections were really, really dreadful, there was an outside chance of a move against him, but he doubted it. He felt that only he could take the government and the country forward.

On Iraq, he said it was not great but they would get there. He was on good form but clearly worried about the next phase. He asked how I thought he should go about it. I said get his head above the shit, get out and about in the country with a proper agenda for the future that was rooted in people's lives. He needed to start doing the kind of communication Peter Hyman had been banging on about for years, emblems and stories in people's lives, get out there and draw attention to the changes for the better that were happening and that would be put at risk by the Tories. Re the manifesto, he said he was pretty confident in the process that was being put in place, said JP was largely on board at the moment.

Thursday 15 July

Out early, only ITN outside, and to the Hampstead Heath ponds for a swim. 1,400 metres, and the lifeguard timed the last 200 at 3.23 which wasn't bad, especially as I did a slight detour. Getting changed, the only other guy there was telling me in winter it was spiritual and he could not face the day without going in, even if just for a few moments. Back home to get Grace off, then work a bit on researching Michael Parkinson, and finally got to the end of 1996 in transcribing diaries. Then on the 24 bus and in to see TB. Jonathan was in his usual good form, said the press were bastards but we knew that. They had basically written the Butler report on their terms, as a total denunciation. TB thought Butler might actually be a bit shocked by the way they had done it.

He feared it was the end of any chance of winning the by-elections. He was seeing DB who came out arm in arm with Sally [Morgan], nice new suit, he looked thinner than usual and looked fit and well. We joked about me coming back, or maybe being in to do an interview with TB or even John Scarlett. TB made a joke about me sitting down on the sofa, saying obviously sofas are not really proper government furniture etc. But beneath the jokes he admitted he was pissed off at Butler, felt he could have made the same points without giving the press so much with which to skew it. Also he should have made the point that one of the difficulties throughout was the lack of any balance on either side of the debate.

He said he had basically decided to stop worrying about anything and just get on with it. GB was being more difficult than ever but he intended pretty much just to work around him. He was more open than ever about what he saw as 'the flaw' – a total self-obsession that meant he only saw things through the prism of his own position and ambition, so that the world was divided into people involved in a conspiracy for him, or a conspiracy against him. So the other day for example GB spoke of John Reid as being 'evil', and TB said he was a very good minister, and GB would have none of it. He said he had to own ministers or else they were useless, and currently the ones he felt he owned were AD and AS [Andrew Smith] but that was about it. He'd said JP was on board at the moment, and basically on his side. GB (through Ed coming to me) was putting it round that there had been a deal. JP was clear that TB's interpretation was right – he'd said if GB supported him 120 per cent, and worked with him 120 per cent, he would help him become leader and he did not actually want to fight another election, but there were no guarantees. JP had told GB that if he put out a different version, he would contradict it.

TB said when the IMF job came up, GB was in asking TB for his view on who it should be, clearly angling for TB to say, 'Why not you?' and he said nothing. 'He didn't raise it himself because he was worried that if he said he was thinking about going for it, I might have said go on and do it.' He was on about the Dacre relationship again, which he felt would damage GB if the party knew the extent of it. [Simon] Heffer had told Anji the full extent, and also that Dacre felt offended that he having decreed TB should not be PM, he still was. I said to TB he needed a few attack dogs more than me to unsettle Dacre and unsettle GB about the relationship. He also needed to get above the Iraq fray, get out and about and with fresher language.

TB expressed his first disquiet re my diaries, when he said, 'Presumably you could pretty much kill the lot of us?' I said I would do nothing while he was there and also that he came out of them pretty well. He said nobody came out well from those kind of things. He joked about a memoir that was published after someone died which was described as a 'posthumous suicide note'. But he kept coming back, again and again, to GB, the flaw, the difficulty of working with him. He said also he hoped to bring PM back in the reshuffle, maybe at defence, and PM wanted it done before the deadline on the Commissioner-ship ran out, because he was worried if TB waited till the summer – which is what he wanted to do – something would happen and he would go back on it. TB also wanted Milburn back as party chairman, though I was not sure if Alan was yet ready for that.

He was in good form on one level but did say a couple of times 'I feel I have the energy and the ideas. The only question is whether the public still want me after Iraq.' He said he had deliberately put his toe in the water with the briefing to *The Guardian* that he would go if he thought he was a liability, and the message that came back was stay. He said to Jean Corston [PLP chair], 'You must tell me if you think I should go.' She said she would but that if there was a secret ballot it would be three to one in his favour, even among those who disagreed with the direction of policy. He said the clear judgement he had reached was that it would be wrong to hand over to GB. GB just did not have all that it would take.

He said he did not actually like GB emphasising the sacking of civil servants, which was all about pleasing the *Mail* and sent out the message that we were anti-public service. Normally in these conversations, TB would always throw in that GB was brilliant if flawed, but any reference to brilliance had gone. He described him as a wild animal who had to be managed. He said in some ways he wished he had dealt with him a long time ago but heaven knows what damage he could have done working openly against him. He said that GB had actually told his staff TB had given him a date, and of course that percolated out and it was bollocks. Every time he cranked it up, it actually made it harder for TB to say anything other than he was going to stay. GB should have loved him to death, I said. TB agreed and said he had played it all wrong, constantly given him reasons to stay not go, above all the fear his behaviour aroused that he just wasn't up to it. He said GB complained about the way the press attacked him. 'What on earth does he think I get compared to the pinpricks he gets? Do you imagine he could remotely cope with the pressure from the media we have had to deal with?' And so it went on. I sensed a man who really had finally given up on a former friend, who was managing him a little while longer but then intended to see him off. But he still had political realities to deal with and we had to wait to see just how bad the by-elections were. I went to the press office and did the rounds a bit but it really wasn't the same any more and though everyone was very nice as ever, I was quite pleased to get out and go home.

Sunday 18 July

Mum phoned just as I was getting ready to leave for the London Bike-a-thon [Leukaemia Research charity event]. She sounded really worried and low. 'Dad's really not well today.' She said he was breathing but not awake and she thought this time it could be the end. I said, 'Shall I come up straight away?' She said, 'Do the bike race and then call me.' Cathy picked me up and we headed off. She was angry with Gary Lineker [former footballer, broadcaster] for pulling out. She said, 'Are you sure you shouldn't go up to see your dad?' I send Donald a text – 'Shall I pull out of the bike event and come up?' By the time the answer came through, I was on my way. As with all the LRF events, it was a bit chaotic but nice, and in a way I was glad to be doing it. I chatted to Michelle Lineker [Gary's ex-wife] then did my little speech about how much the charity meant to us all, and how they couldn't start until I was on my bike. Then off we went. My mind kept wandering from concentration on the race to thoughts about Dad. I kept wondering whether this, or this, or this was the moment he finally passed away, then imagining how Mum, Donald and the others would react. I had had years to think about this moment, and think about it I had, but it was as if every reaction now would be new, different, a succession of firsts and I was not sure how I would react.

Then something extraordinary happened which convinced me he was already dead. A young cyclist, in his twenties maybe, a member of my triathlon team but one I had not met before, told me how much he admired the work I did for the charity, how he had got involved after his dad died of leukaemia because he felt he ought to do something, and was now doing races like this. I said when did your dad die? He said funnily enough, a year ago today. I said do you know what, I think my dad is going to die today. It was an odd thing to say, and he looked at me and asked why and I told him of the conversation I had had with Mum earlier. He was very nice, said he hoped it would be OK. We parted company when he got a puncture.

I raced on to the end, did a few pictures, then phoned Mum. She was engaged and it took me several times to get through. By the time I did, we were in the car, Cathy taking me home. 'Ali, your dad's died,' she said, her voice tailing away at the end. I said nothing for a while, asked her how she was, and she described how she was popping in and out on him and one minute he was breathing, the next he had stopped. She called Donald and Graeme through and they all knew, he had gone. I said I would be up as soon as I could. I put the phone down and started sobbing. I couldn't bring myself to speak to anyone so texted Fiona to tell her and she called back and I couldn't speak. I just told her to tell the boys but don't tell Grace yet, as she was having a day out with Gavin [Fiona's brother] and his kids. I got home, and for all the rows we had been having of late, Fiona was really nice, and so were the boys, Calum crying his eyes out, Rory tougher but I could tell upset as well and I wished for him that he could let it out, and not feel he had to seem tougher than Calum. I found the kids a massive comfort. I said I would drive up as soon as I got changed and both the boys said they wanted to come.

We set off, talked a bit, though there was lots of silence and Calum and I cried from time to time. I talked to Donald, who was phoning round and sounded remarkably calm. I sensed he was a little bit in denial. He said Graeme had taken it hard. Liz was up in Keswick with the family and he said she had just wailed on hearing he had finally gone. We got there and Mum came to the door and as soon as I put my arms around her, we started sobbing. She seemed so small and vulnerable now, and we just stood there together for a few moments. Rory and Calum came across and she hugged them and we went inside. Donald was his usual self, joking with the boys within minutes. Mikey [AC's nephew] was cheering everyone up with his running around and his incessant inquisitiveness. 'Where is he? What is heaven? Who created God?' I could tell Graeme was bottling things up, and he later told Liz he felt bad that he had not been over more often, that he sometimes found Dad a bit difficult to deal with etc. but he too I think benefited from the boys being there and they were talking away about the cycling, Formula 1 etc.

George Mills, the minister who had been seeing Dad on and off for a while now, and who he had found a great comfort, came up and we went over some of the options for the funeral. After he left we agreed on a committal at the crematorium, for family only, then a service at George's church in Doncaster. It was odd in a way that the end should come in Doncaster rather than Tiree [island birthplace of AC's father] or West Yorkshire but Mum just wanted it all over and done with as soon as it could be done. George had to go on holiday on Thursday so we were going to have to push hard to get it all done and dusted by then. The death certificate would have to be done tomorrow, then a slot for the crematorium, and George said the church was available all day Thursday. Rory left for the late train, Calum and I stayed over and later on Liz and I worked through with Mum what we would do by way of order of service.

Mum wanted me to do the tribute, which at least gave me something to think about, and I read the little autobiographical note Dad had done years ago for his own parents, which gave me lots of material. My big worry was going to be holding it together. Syd [Young, former *Mirror* colleague, personal friend] called and said he remembered saying to me when Ellie died that it doesn't matter if they are young or old, it is always hard, hard, hard to deal with. I didn't sleep much and got up around 5 to start working on the tribute. I had it more or less done by half six, felt better for having done it and went for a run. What I had done with Mark Gault's funeral was weep as much as I possibly could and then hope that come the church service, I would hold it together for the tribute. At John's too, even though in the end I could not get through the last few sentences, it had pretty much worked. I ran out towards Leverton and within five or ten minutes was running with tears streaming down my face, barely able to see where I was going, and talking to Dad as if he was still there. I did 4 miles, and by the time I got back Mum was up and about and we had a little chat about how the others were reacting. We both felt Dad had been waiting for Graeme to come over from Poland so that he could see all of us before he went. Graeme was finding it hard, I could tell.

I went in with Liz to see the undertaker, Mr Bradley. at half eight and give him some trousers and Dad's favourite casual shirt. Mr Bradley said he would prefer to dress him and get him in a coffin before we saw him. Liz and I arranged to go and see him at 11.30. We gave the undertakers everything we wanted in the order of service, then back home to collect Calum, who wanted to see the body and say goodbye too. Some soft music was playing as we went into the chapel of rest. The coffin was angled in the corner of the room to our left, face and body covered by a sheet through which I could make out his features. I pulled back the sheet slowly and there he was. Liz came over beside me and we both burst into tears which fell over his face and Liz wiped them away with her hand and then stroked his face and hair as the tears continued to fall.

I was hanging on to Calum and he was hanging on to me and I was so grateful that he was there. I said to Liz I had lost count of the number of times I had thought I had seen him for the last time, but had somehow never imagined it would be like this. He looked serene. Though the face was yellowed, his eyes, closed, looked less pained than the last time I saw him. His hair had thinned even more in the last few days but the features were still strong, the nose bold and dignified, the lines from nose and lips looking as if they were shaping to smile. Calum said I keep thinking he's going to open his eyes. I said, 'See you, Dad,' and set myself off again.

I don't know how long we were in there. 20 maybe 30 minutes then we all agreed it was time to go, a brief chat with the undertaker's son to go over the final details and then back home. I was so glad I had been, and that Calum was with me, and wished Graeme would go too. I know he had seen Dad yesterday but I think it would be good if he went and saw him now, and talked to him, and said goodbye properly. By the time Calum and I left for home, things were pretty much on autopilot. I was finding it a lot harder than I thought I would. There were moments when I felt life was fine, because I was thinking of nothing, and then the reality would come into my mind, and I'd feel weak, legless, stomachless. Yet meantime I was having to do what seemed like meaningless things like fix up filming times or interviews or speaking engagements. I had assumed I would stay up for the duration but Mum felt I ought to go to Philip's party to celebrate his going to the Lords. Rory had gone with Fiona for the lunch, Audrey and Grace joined them for the ceremony itself and Calum and I made it for the party. It was odd to be talking normally with the people who were there, again as if nothing had happened.

Philip mentioned Dad's death when he introduced me and as I went through the funny speech I had written on Saturday I wondered if people thought it might be a bit odd for me to be cracking jokes etc. It went down well and it was probably OK and in some ways it was nice to be at a happy event but it all felt very weird. TB called via Kate Garvey and was really nice and warm, said it is always so hard because it is so much part of what we are. We chatted about the political scene and he felt a lot stronger though the GB thing had gone bad again. GB and his lot – Sarah virtually cut me dead at Philip's do – were absolutely clear – TB had promised he was going and were sulking all over the shop. PG did a presentation with Stan to GB, DA and Ed M and by accounts they listened in total silence. Especially the bit where they said TB ratings were rising.

Wednesday 21 July

First thing Calum, Grace and I set off and with the A1 closed because of an accident it was a bit of a nightmare journey, five hours plus, but it was nice when we got there. Grace was playing with Mikey. Jamie [nephew] was back from Keswick. The service was coming together. The Scots were coming in good numbers and Mum was coping OK. I had pretty much done my speech. I was worried about the last bit, and also the bit where I mentioned Robert Templeton [relative AC's age confined to bed]. I had been to tell him on Sunday and it was extraordinary how someone confined to bed, incapable of movement, was able to keep up the spirits of others far more lucky than he. I took Calum and Graeme and Jamie to play golf and while they played I practised the speech, forcing myself to cry some more, then trying to do it without crying, and just about managed it by the end. Yesterday I had wandered around town for a bit before the Philip thing, got a book on the Tour de France for Rory and Calum, bumped into June Sarpong and we went for a cup of tea, then saw Bostock and got a couple of Librium. He was less banging on about Iraq than usual, and we had a nice chat before I headed for home. I just wanted to sleep but couldn't.

Thursday 22 July

Despite it all I was managing to get some kind of exercise in every day. On the morning of the funeral, having shared a room with Grace down at the farm, I went for a run, and did the most difficult lines of the speech as I ran. I sort of felt it would be OK. Rory had run brilliantly at Watford last night, finally broken 2 mins – 1.57.63 – and I went to Retford to buy him a present. The man behind the counter couldn't believe I was in there and he asked me to sign an autograph for his dad, who was a supporter. He said he won't believe you've been here. I said I went there a fair bit, and told him about Dad, and we had a nice chat. I collected Fiona, Rory and Audrey from the station and once we got back it all kind of went into auto pilot. We did some pictures and I then went for a walk, found a quiet country lane and read my speech to a field. As I got back, the hearse was arriving and the sight of the coffin set me off again. I had done a car plan and Mum, Donald, Graeme, Liz, Grace, Kate and Aunt Jeanie got into the first one, the partners and Graeme and Mikey into the second one, then me and the boys, then Jamie and Rob [nephew and brother-in-law]. I was crying again. Calum was holding it together better than I thought he would. It was a fair distance to Doncaster and not an easy journey. I was glad Grace was in with Mum because I knew she would help her along.

As we arrived, the hearse stopped, Donald stepped out of the first

limo, got his pipes, began playing and slow marched to the crematorium. I was really impressed by the way he was holding it together. The
relatives were lined up outside and as we walked in, I was off again
and so was Rory. George did a great job, made it clear the service would
be fun as well as sad. It was hard though to see the curtains close as
the coffin went through and then just file out. Of my three, Rory was
now taking it the worst. Calum having seen the body he had kind of
let it all out already. Grace was just helping Mum. But Rory was in
floods now, came out and just wept on my shoulder and I was glad
that he did. Young Graeme [nephew] came with us to the church and
we got a bit lost, but somehow made it before the hearse. We filed
in together and by now I was just focusing on holding it together.
I decided not to look at any of the front rows as I spoke. The tranquilis-
ers were helping but the biggest help in a way came from George and
Mikey. I had suggested [Polish-born] Mikey sing the Polish national
anthem and he did so, with George making the most of it to lift the
mood and by the time I spoke, I was fine. Once I was over the Robert
Templeton moment, I felt fine.

Moira [cousin] and young Jean Templeton were leading in the floods
of tears stakes. Mum, as she had at Auntie Nan's, just kept looking
down, rubbing her hands and trying not to cry too much. I was pleased
how many people afterwards said they thought I had captured his personality. As it was Liz's birthday I got them all to sing Happy Birthday
at the end of my tribute. Donald played the pipes really well again.
Mikey got his Polish flag then we all set off to the do at Mount Pleasant hotel. They did it well. Aunt Jean, 2 Sheenas, Anne, Mrs Hamilton,
George from Tiree, all the remaining Clark cousins, some of the Kent
lot, Templetons, Jock from Hull, Astons from Leicester, Yorkshire farm-
ers, Mum's bridge friends, nice do and I felt a lot better after. Audrey
had to leave and then we all went back.

Mum was so nice to us all, thanking us individually for the support, saying she would never have got through it without us but now
she was looking forward to things quietening down. She would have
people to stay for a couple of nights but then wanted a night on her
own fairly soon to start getting used to it. Her whole life in the past
few years had revolved around looking after him and now he was
gone. I was sure she would find new things to do, a new sort of happiness. We were getting nice cards and letters. Mum was thrilled by
a nice handwritten note from TB which she showed around to everyone. Rory was trying some of his brain teasers on Moira and Jamie.

Eventually we left, said goodbye to Graeme etc., pouring with rain but it had all gone as well as it could have done.

Friday 23 July

I woke up feeling depressed, worse than yesterday. Philip was there talking to Fiona about the *Mail* and I could not engage, was fed up of hearing about TB, GB and all the rest of it and just wanted to be on my own or with the kids. I went upstairs and did some work. Keith Blackmore had asked me to go to Paris to do a piece on Lance for the end of the Tour and said why didn't I take the family? I fixed to stay with John Holmes [UK Ambassador] and so Grace was looking forward to seeing Bonnie [John's dog]. We were also going out as a family to a big table tennis event in Croydon. So things were getting back to normal. I worked on the Lance piece and talked to some of his people about seeing him at the end of the Tour. I sent out the funeral speech to a few people.

The big political story was Peter M going to be a Commissioner in Brussels. C5 gave out clips from our interview which ran on some of the bulletins. I texted Peter to say how you feeling – he said grim but good. I think he had persuaded himself that a Cabinet return was possible, and also persuaded himself that TB had promised it. So once it was 'only' the Commission, for a while he was a bit low again. He was going to be all over the media for a few days, and though there were the usual suspects out saying how terrible it was, everyone was saying that he was more than capable, and that it was a serious appointment.

I spoke to TB at various points over these days, he – and at one point CB – asking how things had been at the funeral etc., but of course we went over things. Clearly there had been opposition to Peter M getting any kind of return but he was clear he was the right guy for the Commission. We talked about his own worries about his dad, his certain knowledge that it would be a big blow. He said what death does is just underline how small we are, no matter how big the job we do. In the end, there is the end, and that is it. Even though he has his faith, it is still so final, and so very difficult to deal with. I told him Mum was really touched by his letter, as she had been by the phone calls during Hutton and my departure.

The table tennis was OK, good fun and Matthew Syed [journalist and former table tennis international] had organised it really well, though it was really hot. But it was nice to be out as a family, and then we had Paris and the Tour to look forward to as well.

Saturday 24 July

I worked on a Lance piece on the train to Paris and then we jumped into a cab and up to the residence, Grace thrilled to see Bonnie. Peter Jones, Sheffield family judge, there with his daughter Clare, plus Sarah and Emily [John Holmes's daughters]. Good time. John took us to a really nice, very Parisian restaurant. Usual chatter re TB, CB, GB etc. John such a lovely bloke, who had made a real difference at No. 10 [when TB's foreign affairs advisor]. He was another one who felt that TB had the temperament for the job in a way that GB didn't. He found it remarkable in a way that they had lasted so long. Lance won the final time trial, so it was all set for the coronation tomorrow. The people at the residence looked after us brilliantly, though someone had told the *Mail* we were there.

Sunday 25 July

Ran up to Le Meridien Etoile to see Jeremy Whittle [journalist] to get tickets for the finish. Met the Tour comms guy, who was really interesting on the way they ran the whole logistics side of things – which were huge – then back for breakfast after sampling some of Champs Elysees ambiance. More chat re usual stuff with John, then out with R and C to watch the race. OK atmosphere though the ride itself was very much just up and down, up and down. Mind you, Lance came right close by as he was twiddling around before dismounting pre the ceremony. The mood among the French was not that great towards him.

26 July–31 August

After Dad died, I didn't really look at the diary – either this one or the ones being transcribed – for ages. There is something of a blur surrounding events after he died. Though we had been expecting it for so long, the death itself hit me far harder than I thought it would. I have now settled seemingly into a pattern in which I have at least two hours a night just lying there awake. It is not that I am thinking about Dad the whole time – all sorts of things are coming in and out of my mind, but that must surely be the main reason for what is becoming a mild insomniac habit. We did not have the perfect father–son relationship but it was strong, and I know I owed him a lot and would miss him. Mum was very touched that TB, unbeknownst to me, had written to her. He said I should take comfort from the fact that he was so proud of what I achieved, and that so many of my strengths came from the two of them.

I was pleased with the speech I made, thought it captured him quite well and I had some nice letters about it amid all the tributes to him. Mum was doing fine. Graeme seemed a bit all over the place and Donald in denial. Liz, Calum and I had been to see the body and I felt it had really helped, even though it was so emotional and difficult on one level, and though Graeme had been there and seen Dad just after he died, I felt it would do him good to go and see him at peace, and looking better in many ways than he had been of late. We all talked late and the boys played nine holes of golf, and Mum was just keeping busy. On the morning, I went for a few walks and shed as many tears as I could. I knew I would cry at various points but didn't want to break down when speaking. I was out walking again when the hearse came and the sight of the coffin was pretty hard to bear. Young Graeme was in a terrible state. Rory was holding it all back but wept buckets after the brief service at the crematorium. I was so glad to be with the kids. Donald piped really well and I was impressed by the way he conducted himself throughout, apart from the odd outburst.

There was a good turnout from Scotland and after we made it to the church, I had a long chat with the Clark cousins before going in. The church was full and George again got it going on the right note. By the time I was on, I felt confident I would manage to get through with it all, even though everywhere I looked there were people weeping buckets. Funnily enough the bit that I was most worried about was mentioning Robert, and also reading the words Dad gave to me at Cambridge. But it was fine, though I was glad when it was over. The do afterwards was nice, and the hotel did a great job. It was just odd to have all these people talking about Dad, and him not being there. We stayed two or three hours, then back for a couple more hours at Mum's before heading back. There were lots of letters waiting, including one from Clinton which was nice. Mum was thrilled by her letter from Tony, which she showed to everyone and was keen to get a reply to him before he went on holiday. We sometimes underestimated just how much a letter from the PM could mean... I've just realised I wrote a lot of this already, when it was happening, but had forgotten doing so. Odd.

The next big thing was the triathlon, Sunday 1 August. The training had been fine and I was enjoying the rest days in the build-up. We were there all day Saturday for Fiona who was doing the relay, all a bit tense and stressful and we had a bit of a row before she went. But the organisation was great and it went OK and our team was easily the most visible. Horrible period when a man was dragged out of the water clearly having had a heart attack and he died later in hospital. Put a dampener on it for everyone. I had a bit of a scare in the car when the driver taking me to the event braked and I whacked my calf which went into spasm. Steve had to work on it till late and though I got through the day with it he said it could easily set me up for a summer of injury so be careful. The day itself was great. Steve had arrived the evening before, Fiona had done well, dinner at [special advisor] Jo Gibbons's then home to bed. I didn't sleep well but felt fine when we got there.

The TV people seemed to have an army covering the whole thing for the documentary. Went through the whole thing in the transition area, lots of nice people coming up, then through to the start, get the official swimming cap, got doorstepped on the way to the water, lovely pro-Labour woman steward at the pontoon. Got myself into position halfway in the pack (mixed 17–24 and over 45s!) and quickly got into a good rhythm. Calf got hit after the second turn and it went into spasm. Called up the 'better, faster, stronger' mantra and it was fine. Hypnosis had been worth doing I think. I didn't get out of the wetsuit as fast as I had practised but it was OK. At the bike transition, the Channel 5 team said I had done 31 minutes for the swim which was faster than I had predicted (in fact it was 30.37). On to the bike, and got up to a good speed straight away, and heart rate well into the 150s. I loved the bike section. Easily over 20mph on the flat. The family were out and about and Steve was in different places shouting encouragement. With a few miles to go, Steve said, 'You're murdering it. Under three hours easily.' Did the bike in 1.16, OK transition, and then off for the run, by now really hurting, and could not really get going properly, but managed to get into a kind of steady pace and managed 48 minutes for the run. Again, LRF people – participants and spectators – were great. 2.43.42, really felt good, on a par with the marathon.

I did a few interviews and then up to watch the rest after the others went home. Audrey stayed for a while. She, Steve and I set off for

Euston. Pretty knackered but it had gone well. Cathy thrilled. Judith pleased and as we set off for France on the 3rd, she said she would spend the whole summer editing the film.

Holiday – all getting on better than recently. We stayed in a lovely hotel on the way down. Getting genned up on Olympics after days on the Tour de France. The holiday so quiet compared with the horrors of last year. A couple of calls from TB, but we were recalling his attempts not to be panicking last year when we got the Hutton call for my diaries. He felt OK. God knows why he was going to spend time with [Silvio] Berlusconi [Prime Minister of Italy]. Iraq not great. John Kerry was ballsing up his response to the Republicans' attack on his Vietnam record. More anti-UK feeling in France than usual. Fiona and I were getting on a lot better. We had fewer visitors but once the Olympics started that was the main focus. I didn't read much. I wasn't sleeping well. And I couldn't run at all after my Achilles went. I'd got Brendan to fix me a proper pro running trainer in Lindsay Dunn who gave me a schedule and on the very first day my Achilles went. The calf hurt the whole time and at times the Achilles was agony. I did lots of swimming and weights but was really frustrated I couldn't run. I then got some sort of problem with my bloody ear and eventually went for treatment and got a whole load of stuff drained out. I saw a physio re the ankle and he said there was no chance me being ready for the GNR and I would need ten physio sessions.

I was genuinely having a holiday in that I was not doing much work and I felt fairly chilled. Georgia [Gould] had a load of her friends out and we ended up doing a kind of *Big Brother* thing, in which Rory and I got kicked out first. I had a few interviews to do that had been fixed up while I was away, but nothing too heavy. I was also trying to think about general direction. Chris Shaw and Stuart Prebble were very keen to sign me up for more TV work, but I wasn't convinced it was the main thing for me. I had fixed to do Michael Parkinson as one of my Five films, but it fell through because ITV banned him from doing me and he was very embarrassed about it, called me to say he was really up for it, they were dickheads but there was nothing he could do. He said he thought I should concentrate on telly because I was good at it and would enjoy it. He said he had had the perfect life, that he could not have dreamed when he started out as a young reporter it would work out as it did, and he reckoned I could go down much the same route if I wanted. He said I know politics is important to you, but there are so many interesting people out there and they are most of them nothing to do with politics. I did want someone from the entertainment world for the series and was pushing for Bono now.

Sara Latham was fixing for me, PG and Georgia to be going to the Olympics in Athens for the last few days which was fantastic, and even better towards the end of the holiday when we established that Rory could come too. We drove back in two days. Olympics not going great though we did well in cycling and sailing. Amir Khan [boxer] was making an impact. Lots of texting to and fro with Brendan Foster re us doing badly in Olympics. We went there as guests of *Sports Illustrated* and were treated to the kind of hospitality that would have been hard to accept when in government. Staying on a luxury boat docked alongside the one where the US basketball team were lodged, and we had transport everywhere and passes for pretty much everything we wanted. Carolyn Dailey was looking after us. We were there for the best night on the track – Kelly Holmes' second gold (800 and 1,500 metres), Rory's running hero Hicham El Guerrouf getting gold, Britain winning the 4 x 100. Fabulous night.

I fear that Time Inc's German guests thought we were a bit over the top. Great moment when El Gerrouj stopped on his victory lap and said well done to Kelly on the podium waiting for her medal. Georgia got lost and we missed our car to the party, instead going on a bus with car dealers, as the *Mail on Sunday* and *The Observer* dropped with details of the Greg Dyke book. The only new 'fact' was TB's letter to Dyke complaining re coverage and PG allegedly saying we got the right judge. I said to PG he must deny and we drafted a denial. The rest was just vitriol and I felt best ignore, which I did. The next day I got doorstepped at the boxing but ignored it.

Seb and Tessa were sending me messages saying I had to get more involved in the Olympic bid. TB was there and the bid presentation seemed to go well. I had had a dinner with Keith Mills, Alan Pascoe and others [bid supporters] just before and felt they had not yet got a clear central message. I felt it was in UK passion for sport and London being home to all nationalities already. France arrogant and racist and the Olympic village there would be split between different places. The US not safe and lots of fears re safety. Madrid too close to Barcelona having recently had it. Moscow no chance. So it was there for the taking. Seb did well. Ditto the athletes. The scale of the Athens Games was at times almost overwhelming. Stadia everywhere. Volunteers fantastic. A massive logistical exercise. Everyone nice. It was at times a bit annoying being part of a group, but we managed to break away most of the time.

On the night we arrived, we had wanted to stop in a bar en route to the hotel to see Kelly's semi but the Yanks weren't keen, so we listened down the phone instead. Our boat was over the water from *Queen Mary 2*, so dwarfed, but nice and Rory and Georgia were loving it. Because the US basketball team was across the way security was fairly tight.

Michael Phelps [swimmer] came onto our boat to do a Q&A which was interesting and also gave me another *Times* piece. He was fascinating about his diet, how much time he spent in the pool, also the mental side of his work, and how he sometimes struggled with his success. He somehow managed to be both charismatic and non-charismatic. We took in some of the sports we knew nothing about, like handball, which was interesting if only to see how passionate people got about it. Brendan called to fix lunch and while we were on the phone Paula announced she was running. He thought it was crazy as she clearly wasn't fit. Rory did brilliantly in his GCSEs, eight A*s and two As so he deserved the treat he was getting. As Brendan said, he will never see a better day of track and field than the day Kelly did her stuff. The Paula story was exciting but ultimately her race was a bit of a disaster. We had tickets for anything we wanted. Got our own driver and went for nice open air dinner after the track events. The stadium was made for TV but the whole area impressive. Still not sleeping. Next day Rory slept in and didn't want to go to football so we messed around a bit more and then went for nice lunch with Brendan and his Aussie fixer.

Good chat re the whole sporting and media scene. Michael Johnson and Colin Jackson [former athletes, now commentators] at loggerheads with Darren Campbell [GB sprinter]. The *Sports Illustrated* party was pretty wild. Lots of young athletes off the leash after weeks under the cosh. Maurice Greene [US sprinter] grinding with some French athlete. They might as well just have had sex in public. PG and I flirting with the US synchronised swimmers. Long chat with James Cracknell and wife Beverley Turner [TV presenter]. Cracknell said he was in the same position as me, working out what do next. He was more political than I had realised, basically a Tory, but likeable. We had spent lots of holiday joking about how PG would get off with Merlene Ottey [Jamaican athlete] and Polish weightlifter Agata [Wróbel]. Loads of gorgeous women, mainly in their early twenties. Wild by the end of the evening. Long chat with Michael Payne [marketing director] of the IOC [International Olympic Committee] who was about to leave to work for Bernie Ecclestone. He invited me to the Games' TV centre which we could not fit in. I met him again the next day to get his take on the bid and he felt we were not in a bad position. Pretty impenetrable electoral system though.

The party was too loud and not as great as it should have been because you couldn't actually talk to these people. A few drunk UK rowers having a go but fine. We left around 5 a.m. I was up at 10 to see a masseuse about my heel which was still bad. Then we had to move from a boat into a hotel on the way to boxing. Steve Cram, Sally Gunnell, Allison Curbishley [athletes turned media] all there to cheer on Amir Khan in his final. Dick Caborn too, who wanted me still to do Football Foundation and also get more involved in the bid. Darren Campbell came over for a chat, remembered we met at the Olympic reception four years ago and was nice but saying he was going to sue Michael Johnson.* He said it was affecting his sponsors as well as upsetting his family. The boxing was fine, good atmosphere in a rather tinny pop-up arena, but Khan lost [claiming silver]. Ticketing bad. Back to hotel, rest, out to the closing ceremony after hospitality, watched the end of the marathon. Greece as a country was getting a fantastic press now, especially given all the talk in the build-up that they were heading for a fiasco. Rory was really tired and we were a bit bored with the ceremony. TB called during it re Dyke. He wondered if I should write something. I felt not. It was not going anywhere.

We came back on the Monday. Met Seb, Brendan, Cram, Steve Rider [broadcaster], Steve Redgrave [Olympic rower]. I had a long chat with Seb on the flight back re the bid. He went through what they did well, what we could do better, where the French were going wrong. He said he needed me to help as wordsmith but also come on in some near official capacity. I said if getting the UK media universally on board was part of the plan, that might not be a great idea as me having a big public role would alienate some further. But I was definitely up for helping as much as I could. The *Panorama* programme did some damage† and there was a chance, according to Michael Payne, that it would all be played out again in Singapore [next IOC meeting] because the main

---

* Former Olympics and World Championships gold medallist Johnson, now a commentator, had criticised Campbell after he had failed to make the finals of the Athens 100m and 200m events, citing a hamstring injury suffered in training. Johnson insisted a pulled hamstring would take six weeks to heal. Campbell went on to run in the 100x4 relay, winning a gold medal.

† Nine days before the opening of the Athens Olympics, *Panorama* had revealed how some 'agents' had been offering bribes to members of the IOC in efforts to get votes in the bidding for the 2012 Games.

guy they did over would have his case heard. Seb wanted me to write for him. He felt we could get transport sorted, venues sorted, athletes deal good, but the media was a real problem. A lot of the people we needed to win over just didn't like our media and worried about the damage they could do.

Seb did inspire a certain amount of confidence but he did also need help. Brendan clearly a bit jaded with it and maybe thinking of packing in. Half an hour with Seb, said I would help with words, strategy and foreigners. He seemed to think that was OK. Rory was having the time of his life, talking to Seb about his races against Ovett, and Brendan talking to him re his training and his times. I was worrying re not being able to do the GNR. I was still no clearer re my future plans. Home tired, but having had a terrific time.

Wednesday 1 September

I had spoken a couple of times to TB over the holiday and his mind was beginning to whirr towards conference and beyond. He now made next to no effort to conceal his feelings about GB. When he had phoned me in France, I asked when he last spoke to him. He said he couldn't remember. Today, he asked me to go in to No. 10 to see him and, out on the terrace, nice weather, I asked what GB was up to. 'Plotting or mithering, or maybe a mixture of the two,' he said. He wanted to discuss the long note he had done over the weekend. It was twelve pages long, an assessment of the situation, reasonably accurate if less gloomy than Philip's, and an attempt to map out a way forward. There was a bit of a groundhog feel to it though. When you boiled it down, we were back to the economic/social/political/international template. Iraq hung over it all, or more particularly, Bush. TB alarmed me at first by asking me to think about going out to Iraq to help Dr [Ayad] Allawi [interim Prime Minister]. He seemed dead serious. People keep telling him what he should be doing but they are not giving him the capability to do it, he said. He is only going to be able to do it if he has someone who knows how to get people and systems to work, 'and that is you'.

He had just been seeing Jack Straw, with his new look via contact lenses who came out and ostentatiously gave me a big kiss. TB was nice about Rory and his results. He was wearing a Paul Smith shirt with lurid flowered inside cuffs. I asked how he was and to my surprise he looked worried and then said what I am about to tell you I don't want you to mention to anyone. I am actually a bit worried about my ticker. He said he was seeing someone next week. The problem was that if for example he bounded up the stairs, he would feel it fluttering a bit. He looked genuinely concerned. I said it would be fine. He just needed to get it seen to, and not worry if it came out he had seen someone. He said it was not a heart attack he feared but a stroke like his dad's. He had always worried he would go the same way, and the heart thing had been bothering him a lot over the summer. We were out on the terrace, interrupted by a succession of people, Andrew Adonis ('worth his weight in gold'), Sally (doing really well) etc. Jonathan was in Northern Ireland again. I really felt for him, still there, still doing Ireland, still absorbing a lot of the TB angst that I used to take.

TB said he was thinking in the next week or two making clear that he would fight the next election, say he would stay for a full term, but not fight the one after that. I said my instinct was that was doable. He said it might actually disarm GB though DH and Peter M were worried about 'lame duckery'. I said he just had to make the explicit connection with US/Spain, fixed terms, limited etc. He said he felt totally up for the campaign, and felt he would be able to get into a better third term rhythm if he were freed from concerns about his future. He then said there was something else which was potentially a bit trickier. He was buying a very expensive house from which he would also be able to work when he left. How much? I guessed at £1.5m. It was £3.5m. His aunt had left him some money but he was actually taking out a huge mortgage on the assumption that he would be able to earn well when he left office, which of course he would certainly be able to do. Again, he seemed nervous but I felt he could do it, provided it was linked to a sense that he would be carrying on with some kind of public service work when he stopped the job.

We then got on to political strategy. He was really keen for me to get engaged as close as possible to full time, and wanted me permanently inside campaign HQ once the campaign really got underway. He was going to appoint Milburn as party chairman. JP was not that keen but more because he was worried about GB's reaction than because he thought it was a bad idea. He was not sure Douglas Alexander was ready to provide the political direction for the whole campaign. He felt our policy programme was developing fine, but he was thinking of putting Ruth Kelly [Financial Secretary to the Treasury] in charge of the Policy Unit. The press side was OK on day-to-day handling but lacked the strategic sense we had when I was there. But he seemed by and large pretty confident.

I said he had to start connecting better. His speech should be really earthy and rooted, less the stuff about choice, less conceptual, more the real difference we would continue to make. And painted in pictures, not concepts. He agreed with that. He said he thought PG was too pessimistic about the public mood. He felt fine yesterday in Harlow, felt people were coming back to us. I said in some ways Bush was his problem, not Iraq. He agreed but said it would be a huge mistake to distance. GWB had called him yesterday to ask whether he would mind him mentioning him in his Convention speech in New York. TB laughed and said he told him 'I'd be honoured, George.' Real in for a penny, in for a pound stuff.

I said Berlusconi and the coverage around his visit were pretty disastrous. He was adamant he had to do it. Silvio had been desperate for it to happen. It was almost part of the deal to get his backing for [José Manuel] Barroso [former Portuguese PM] as Commission President in the face of Chirac–Schroeder opposition. TB had clearly just about had it with Schroeder. He said he was very friendly to his face but at it the whole time with Chirac. He had been to Silvio and suggested France–Germany–Italian trilateralism. Berlusconi had said no. TB said he would much prefer to deal with left-minded people but these guys are weak. The new Greek, he said, was a right-winger but far more reliable than [Costas] Simitis [Prime Minister, succeeded by Constantine Karamanlis]. Aznar had gone and the new guy, [José Luis Rodriguez] Zapatero, was hopeless by comparison. He was generally in good form, definitely up for it, but feeling the need to boost organisational capability. I said I would do him a note on strategy at the weekend.

I went round to the press office, David a little bit distant, nice chat with GS re things generally. We were in a better place than a few weeks ago and the feeling was a good conference season would get things back on track. PG and I both felt that was a bit too optimistic. PG felt there was a real disconnection problem and that TB was at the heart of that. His note, he felt, was not really a big enough response. We needed a big negative attack campaign focused on the Tories/dividing lines, but we also needed a big positive inspirational campaign centred around specific policy proposals and focused on the future.

Thursday 2 September
Off to Brussels to interview Hicham El Guerrouf for the *Times* series. He was there for a race at one of the big meets, the hotel was full of

top athletes, but there was definitely a certain aura around him. Very impressive, humble, quite amusing at times. Clearly very religious, with Allah seeming to work his way into most answers. He was great on the theme of pain and suffering as part of training. He named Seb as his best ever athlete. TB had a meeting at Chequers with the usual team plus Milburn and then word started to get out that Alan was going to go back to the Cabinet as party chairman, which would fuel a whole load more TB–GB-ery. I worked on the note I had promised TB. I used the OST [Objective, Strategy, Tactics] formula, Objective win with a decent majority, Strategy setting terms for debate around dividing lines on economy, jobs, public services, social advance and international strength, in such a way that we play to our strengths and expose their weaknesses, and reconnect. Tactics were important in that we had to make it all interesting and exciting again, and break through the media negativity. The frustrating thing is that objectively, we are in a strong position. But years of grind and attack have undermined confidence and political boldness. That is what had to come back and conference was where it had to start. And the best, simplest message, was that the country had improved, could improve more, whereas the Tories would wreck it.

We had to make it an optimistic message though, and TB in particular had to get his head above the media grunge. A good economic narrative has to become a strong narrative about past, present and future. How we learned from our past, changed our approach but stayed true to our values, how we have delivered, how we can deliver more in the future. I was clear with TB that if GB does not do this in his speech, TB must make it a major part of his. If GB DOES do it, TB should do it too. BLAIR PUTS ECONOMY AT HEART OF ELECTION BATTLEGROUND may be prosaic, but it is where we need to be. From it flows jobs and trade, investment in schools and hospitals, transport and crime, help to pensioners, children and the poor, hard working families better off, and what the Tories did with economic success – tax cuts for the rich, privatisation, waste. That is a portent of what Howard would do. This is the road in to the 'Don't let the Tories wreck it' mantra. The great thing about Howard is that he gives us the excuse to focus on Tory past policy as a bridge to their current policy. We have not properly executed the strategy to make him suffer for the Tories' past, but it is there for the taking. Conference gives us another chance. Blair is still the future. Howard is still the past.

On public services, I was trying to persuade TB to move away from conceptual language which has not connected – choice, personalisation, new names in the system – to a more prosaic communication. Better local schools. Better local hospitals. A celebration of the great teachers and doctors and police officers who have made it possible. Give THEM the credit. We made it possible. But they did it.

On the international agenda, the feelings about Iraq were still raw and opposition widespread, and we had to show we understand why, but equally people are ready to respect TB's leadership, and can see the contrast with Howard as an unprincipled opportunist who would sacrifice the national interest for a good headline and who is therefore unfit to lead one of the most powerful countries on earth. Added to all this we still had some of the best songs to sing – future not the past, many not few, leadership not drift, investment v cuts, full employment v mass unemployment – Howard had not diluted any of those. Far from it. And having delivered on the pledges in '97 and '01, we needed another pledge card and we needed to make sure people understood we had delivered on the past ones to signal we would do the same next time. It was not a bad piece of work, if a bit dull, and I could see the fundamentals becoming stronger.

Friday 3 September

TB was having another session at Chequers, but Philip said he feels nobody really tells him how things are, that if he says something now, he's very definitive, not really listening to everything that's being put to him, but in part because he senses that not being hard and strategic. He felt I had to get more involved, whether I wanted to or not, because at least I could get through to TB if we felt he was not going in the right direction. TB's note was fine in so far as it went, but very much running along lines we had been on for a long time. We could do with some fresh eyes around the place, not the same old same old crew, but they were hard to find.

Saturday 4 September

OK run, then did a long strategy note to TB, taking his thoughts and trying to harden and distil them into actual speeches and an actual campaign. He was right to want to focus on improving public services, and always being the reformer, but we had to be careful that he was not just seen as brewing up a stack of ideas that internally could be defined

September '04: Strategy needs fresh eyes, says PG

as centre right rather than centre left. He was definitely in better shape psychologically than before the holiday though, had recovered a bit of zeal and energy and seemed less spooked by the friend next door. I sent the note over, chatted it through, and then worked on another one for Seb Coe re Olympic positioning. I actually felt they were in good nick, though the politics of the decision were well nigh unfathomable. All we could do was have the right team, the right messages, the right access wherever we needed it, and hope Paris did not do as well on all fronts. The truth is though it is not one of those where you can be guaranteed the better bid wins.

Monday 6 September

Andrew Smith resigned [as Secretary of State for Work and Pensions] so off we went into another TB–GB soap operatic row, with Milburn's future thrown into the mix. Most of the day I was at the BBC with Rory and his mates to do *They Think It's All Over* [TV sports comedy show]. Jonathan Ross [panellist] was very funny pretty much all the time, nicer than I thought he'd be. He said he used to be a Labour Party member but not now. Phil Tufnell [former cricketer] and Ian Wright [former footballer] were both real working-class characters. They seemed genuinely pleased I was on the programme. Quite a lot of rehearsal, and some indication of the questions which gives you plenty of time to think, but it was probably best to let the funny men do the funnies. We knew that the synchronised diving team was the mystery guest. I did really well on the pictures, and got Leighton James [former Burnley player] from his shirt alone. Ian Wright was really nice to the boys. I suppose it was worth doing, though not totally convinced. I needed to get back on track. Also the *Radio Times* put out a press release saying I was going to be an MP and that started a whole lot of angst from Fiona when I said I was not sure I would ever do anything meaningful or significant again, which she took as an attack on her/family.

Tuesday 7 September

Keith Blackmore was very nice about last week's column. I had a discussion with him and Tim Rice to work out how to bring the whole series to an end. TB did his monthly press conference and the reshuffle questions were becoming more and more difficult. In the afternoon I did a couple of *Times* interviews by phone, first Nadia Comaneci, the Romanian gymnast, and Jan-Ove Waldner, the Swedish table tennis player who had been suggested to me by Matthew Syed. Comaneci was a real character and fascinating about the need never to imagine perfection exists, even when she got the perfect ten. Waldner seemed a nice bloke and I banged out the piece fairly quickly. He was massive in China, apparently on a par with Clinton in terms of being a famous Westerner, and clearly intending to spend a lot of his time there when he finally stopped playing. I sent to Matthew Syed to get his take on it. He was thrilled I was including Waldner in the series.

I had a big bust-up with Fiona over her article on Cherie which made some fair points but which gratuitously went for Anji, and had far too much about me in it. I said you keep saying you want us out of the soap opera but this gets us right back in. Ed Victor came round. We were discussing whether there was any way of doing the book earlier. At the moment, he said, we were asking for money up front for something none of us knew when it would appear. I was not sure if I could do anything before TB went, but it was worth thinking about.

Wednesday 8 September
The TB–GB stuff was rumbling on and TB was looking a bit weak and vulnerable again. He eventually got round to the reshuffle. Alan Johnson was moved up [to Work and Pensions Secretary]. I had been speaking to him last night about my visit to speak for him in Hull. Alan is such a good guy, would be able to do pretty much any job he offered him, and he was also becoming one of our best communicators. He could definitely move into that John Reid/Jack Cunningham type place of being someone who could talk across all areas. It wasn't just the working-class, former postman thing, it was that his nice, positive personality always came through, and he spoke like a human being.

In terms of the media take on the reshuffle, it was becoming yet another botched operation, seen as JP and GB uniting to stop Alan Milburn becoming party chairman. Ian McCartney clearly had JP protecting him and GB was looking more menacing. Ian had a big interview in *The Guardian* defending himself. Margaret McDonagh called and said if TB does not stand up for Alan he really will look weak and people will make the judgement he doesn't protect his own supporters. It was a bad, bad scene, she said. Christ, TB had come back ready to fire on all cylinders but was getting ground down and dragged back straight away. AJ said something interesting though, that for all the talk of GB, most people if they were forced to make a real choice would still want TB – as in 1994. 'Things have not really changed in the fundamental question of who people think is a better leader.'

Friday 10 September

Long chat with Alan Milburn before I went for a run with Jon Sopel. Alan clearly felt both vulnerable, and emboldened. Vulnerable because he knew he was in GB's sights a bit more now, and also that JP had been standing up for Ian to make sure Alan didn't get in as party chairman. But emboldened in that TB had made clear he wanted him in there with a big role in the campaign. Alan clearly felt the TB–GB situation was beyond repair and that it would be a disaster if GB was even nominally in charge of the campaign. Had lunch with Rebekah Wade at Chez Gerard. She seemed very down, not just about us but about everything, including what was happening at her place. I sensed Murdoch had his mind and his time elsewhere, also that *The Sun* had hit something of a plateau.

Saturday 11 September

Up to Burnley v Crewe, then spoke at the launch of the Clarets Trust [supporters' group], which was a bit of a ramshackle do. Then over to do a fundraiser for James Purnell [MP] and the party at Hyde. James seemed popular. Speech went pretty well. I found no difficulty in defending TB and the government and it was a bit alarming the extent to which party activists said how refreshing it was to hear somebody defend Tony and the government with confidence. Truth be told, there just wasn't enough of it going on. We were so quick to take for granted the idea that we are in government, and bound to win. But if we didn't speak up for him and for what we did as a government, the media were not going to do it for us – au contraire – and the Tories and other parties also had a vested interest in talking down the record, and in doing in TB as our best asset. I didn't detect any great yearning for GB. But people rate and respect him and they just want us all working as a team.

Sunday 12 September

Lunch at the Kinnocks with Michael Foot, Geoffrey [journalist] and Margit Goodman, Ian Aitken [journalist], Dick Clements [former Labour official] and Bridget [Clements' wife]. Nice enough do, but Dick was really quite ill. Michael was on extraordinary form, clearly losing it physically, really struggling with stairs for example, his bodily jerks even more pronounced and his eyes a bit wandering, but mentally completely on top of things and recalling meetings of fifty or sixty years ago as though they had just happened. He was very supportive; after an hour or so of people being a bit down on everything, he said, 'Well, we have a Labour government, we have a Labour Prime Minister doing a good job and lots of good things that are changing the country, and we have Alastair in there making sure everyone knows it, so I think we should all be happy.' I ran home from Ealing, much of it on the North Circular, which has to be one of the most depressing stretches of road on earth, only you notice it more when you are running than when you are driving.

Dinner with Seb Coe, Tessa and David [Mills], mainly to talk about the bid. Both Tessa and Seb seemed on top of it, and fairly confident, despite all the pro-Paris stuff that was around. Kicked around a few thoughts on basic strategy and agreed it had to be in the area of London effectively being a global capital because every nation on earth was here, and also major focus on youth, legacy and regeneration. I think sometimes Seb was a bit awestruck at the amount of work and travel it was going to entail, but they both seemed to think it was doable. Tessa said that one day the full story would be told about all GB's efforts to block and resist. Seb was due to be making a presentation to the Cabinet so we worked a bit on that. He had a pretty good feel for the politics of it, but again he knew that his best card, politically, was TB's total support.

Monday 13 September

Seb had asked me to meet up with Mike Lee [Olympic bid communications director] so we had breakfast at the Renaissance Hotel. We had a pretty good chat but he had a bit of a reputation for talking up his own role in all these bid processes, and I had an instinct he didn't want me to get too involved with Seb. Meanwhile Seb asked me to help with his speech to the TUC and I banged out something on the kind of basic message we were discussing yesterday, plus something he could point to as a trailer at his Cabinet presentation.

TB called as I was in the gym. He was on his way to the TUC. He said did I think he could say something like, 'Even though I've not been away, it's time to come back.' I felt he could, though it was a bit convoluted. He got a very lukewarm response from the brothers, another reminder that I was glad I wasn't there.

Tuesday 14 September
Paul McGuinness [U2 manager] had agreed I could do Bono as one of the Five interviews in the week of the Labour Party conference, which was good news.

Wednesday 15 September
Syd Young called to say he had heard the *Mail* were planning some story about me and the talk in the paper was that it had come via some text messages. He felt I should at least get legal advice. Hunting vote in the Commons. Massive demos, bit of trouble.* Went to Judith Dawson's with Grace and Sissy, to watch the actual screening of the triathlon documentary. They had done a pretty good job, using the story of the triathlon as a kind of storyline spine but along the way talking about all the obvious stuff. Grace liked it and thought I came over well.

Thursday 16 September
Meeting in Piccadilly with Dave Edmundson, Peter Salmon [BBC sport executive and Burnley supporter], and Stuart Binns [broadcaster and Burnley fan]. Dave wanted to pick our brains on ideas both about fundraising for the club, and general repositioning. We were still not out of the woods financially and we knocked around some OK ideas. Afternoon doing a load of interviews for future events and in the evening doing an event Rodney Bickerstaffe [union leader] for Geoffrey Goodman's book [*From Bevan to Blair*]. A majority probably against the war, and a few hostile but generally OK. Then to Victoria for the Leukaemia Research Triathlon awards party.

Friday 17 September
I was doing a note on message to TB and while we were talking about

---

* Five protestors burst into the House of Commons chamber during debate on hunting with dogs. MPs then backed the ban, 339 votes to 155.

it he asked if I could help write his next speech. Wednesday saw violent scenes from pro-hunt protesters at Westminster, so there was a huge story raging re security, particularly after the Buck House protest in which 'Batman' got onto the front of the Palace.* The scenes were pretty violent but of course because these were basically right-wing protesters they got a far fairer hearing than e.g. poll tax, miners, environmentalists etc. But it was pretty ugly and I knew that TB would be really worried about it. His instinct had always been that this hunting ban wasn't really worth doing because of the anger it would stir up, and these people were clearly capable of doing a lot of disruption during an election. He called me first thing Friday morning. I said, 'How's your hunting bill?' He said that's why I'm calling. Do you think I could say – as early as today – that I have always felt the Alun Michael [minister presiding over enactment of the Hunting Act] compromise position has a lot of merit, and challenge the Lords to back it. His concern was that moderate opinion would think we were being disproportionate about this. He still felt it was cruel, but these people really felt strongly about it, and it was not worth this kind of confrontation.

The Michael compromise would set a pest control test which would actually see a lot of hunts fade away, and would allow independent judgement etc.† I said the main problem was one of being seen to cave in to violence but not enough of an understanding out there meant he was not really keen on this. The other thing was whether he would end up with a bloody nose from our side because it looked like he was siding with our opponents again. He asked me to think about it hard. He said his instinct was strongly to do it, which meant almost certainly he would. The other thing that has been going on is the huge coverage for CB's book [*The Goldfish Bowl*, written with Cate Haste], [broadcaster and author] Melvyn Bragg's silly remarks that TB had thought about quitting because of family pressures, and Fiona's article for G2 on CB. CB called her after and she said they had a nice conversation but she clammed up when Fiona said I was helping Seb (e.g. wrote his TUC speech). Yet on Thursday night when she did *Richard and Judy* she said I was lovely and cuddly – Judy had asked if I was a big thug – and

---

* A Fathers 4 Justice (fathers' group protesting about being treated unfairly by the courts) campaigner dressed as Batman climbed onto a ledge by the Buckingham Palace balcony.
† Hunts would have to show that their hunting was undertaken for pest control purposes and would cause less suffering to the fox than any other form of control.

Fiona and I were among her closest friends. As several of the papers pointed out, she wasn't asked why we hadn't been at her 50th party, though in fact Fiona was invited to the No. 10 version.

CB was coming out of it all fine, but I was fed up hearing all the soap opera droning on stuff. I was even asked about Melvyn's remarks – by Ian Aitken [former *Guardian* political editor] of all people – at the *London Review of Books*, where I was helping promote Geoffrey Goodman's book. Good reaction to the documentary. Reviews sniffier than previews but lots of them fine.

After TB called Friday am, JP came on and said Pauline [JP's wife] wants a word. She came on and said she didn't care what Judy said, she knew I wasn't a thug, and we had a good laugh about that. JP chatted through recent events. He said re Ian McCartney losing the chairmanship that it would have been bad politics and he did say to TB that if he did it, he would publicly denounce it. It wasn't just because he was his mate. It was silly politics and Milburn would have been a disaster as chairman. He wasn't against Alan but it would not have worked. He said he had told GB he was going to stop it and GB had said he should get McCartney to get the unions to brief on his side. JP said 'I'm not playing that game, Gordon, and I have to say it hasn't done you any good in the long run.' He sounded very down on GB, said that even he had been amazed how once the Ian McC decision was reversed, GB briefed it in such a way as to get credit from within the party. He said he had been there with TB when TB 'gave it to him between the eyeballs', meaning that TB had finally made clear to him he was intending to stay. He said GB had spent months thinking TB was finally going to go, but he now knew.

JP said he had said to TB he must make it clear, because it was debilitating for everyone. TB was worried GB would 'bring the temple down' but 'I said it was his temple too and I didn't think he would do that.' He said the Milburn job could be made to work but TB had to understand there were others he had to listen to. We had a chat re his and TB's speeches – at least John had a draft – and also the idea of him and Pauline coming to my show at the Brighton Dome. He told me that at political Cabinet yesterday, John Reid said he had been reading R. H. Tawney [economic historian] that morning. JP said, 'Did you say Tawney or Tony?' He sounded on good form, felt TB was in OK frame of mind but shared his worries re hunting. I gently sounded out whether he was aware of TB's current thinking, which I don't think he was, and he didn't bite when I threw out the compromise idea.

Saturday 18 September

TB called. Asked straight out, can I get away with not doing hunting? JP called re the same, asking if TB was trying to dump it. I told TB I thought it was too far gone. TB had always been uncomfortable about it. He said I hate doing things when my instincts are screaming at me. It just isn't worth all the grief it has given us. Off to Leicester v Burnley. Reading up re Bono.

Monday 20 September

Long run, probably the last before the Great North Run. Good session at TBWA [advertising agency]. Trevor Beattie on great form. They did a presentation on connection, achievements, future and Tory attack. It was very much work in progress but it was very good work in progress. It also helped focus me for another section of TB's speech. Bono called, asking to reschedule our interview by a couple of weeks. Quite an interesting chat about religion, which hopefully we could explore a bit more. He is not your average rock star I would say. Most of the chat was political.

Tuesday 21 September

Bruce round for a chat. He said Dennis Turner's seat in Wolverhampton was there for the asking if I wanted it. He really felt I should go for it. He thought I needed a new challenge, that I'd be a good MP, and would be in the government in no time anyway. I felt it was a few years late, but he rejected that, said it was actually a very good time to do it. He felt TB was getting more and more isolated, and it was a good way of getting me back in, but properly, and also he reckoned I would quickly become a contender. He felt there were just too many people in the party worried at the moment that TB was not of them. Dumping the pledge on hunting was not a runner, he said.

Wednesday 22 September

I was working on the Olympics section of Tessa's conference speech. The first draft was a bit defensive, and needed more uplift. TB called when I was out on a run. He bought the idea of setting out the outlines of the new pledge card towards the end of his speech. He asked me to redo a couple of the sections. On Iraq, he felt he had to go into it in some detail, set it in the context of there being two world views, and that he genuinely feared the consequences of inaction. Re GB, despite the sadness at his mother's death, he felt it was unlikely to change anything. 'God knows what he's planning for conference.' His speech draft was pretty strong, but he was obviously going into that phase where he just questioned every aspect of it. Out to the Leukaemia Research reception at Renaissance Chancery Court Hotel in Holborn. Speech went well.

Thursday 23 September

Alan Milburn called. He was working up lines to brief on the need for TB's speech to be more focused on the third term and the future, and the choice re the Tories. Out for a meeting with Jon Smith at the Landmark Hotel. Made his money as a football agent but was now branching out into other aspects of the sports industry. Thought that we could work together to position me as a kind of sports commissioner, self-styled, bringing together government, local authorities, the sports governing bodies. He admitted it wasn't totally thought through, but was keen to get me involved. Not a hundred per cent sure.

24–29 September

Writing after a fairly long gap, having been away at the Great North Run and then down to Brighton for my final theatre show and more important to help TB with his speech. The build-up was pretty nasty. Ken Bigley [British civil engineer] was taken hostage in Baghdad, a video appeal made to TB pleading for help, Iraq very difficult and GB, having buried his mother a few days earlier, really gearing up for trouble. I'd done a few sections – on trust/delivery in particular and TB had done a full draft himself with a good personal section on Iraq. But he was more nervous than in previous years and no longer making any attempt to deny how bad things were with GB. The media prism being framed was TB–GB with Iraq as a shadow and according to Milburn, SM, Jonathan and the rest, it was shaped by a vicious briefing operation. Their latest nonsense argument was that Alan wanted to dump on our record as a way of framing radical forward policy as the heart of the manifesto. As if you could only do past as well as future. TB was convinced Ed Balls was at the heart of it. I had a brief and not very friendly chat with Charlie Whelan [former press officer for GB] before I did Radio 5 from the start of the Great North Run on the Sunday with Matthew Pinsent [rower]. The mood was very febrile down there.

On Friday after the kids were out of school we set off for the train to Newcastle. I worked on an article re Ken Bigley for the *NotW* and then on the speech. TB didn't add to it much over the weekend so apart from constant messages from PG to say how grim it was I was able to cut out and focus on the weekend. Met up with Brendan [Foster] on Friday night and tried out the line about TB admitting fallibility and not knowing for sure if he was right or wrong about certain issues. Brendan felt he did need to 'give a bit', but also said he was still popular in the North East and most people would want him to stay. Grace and Sissy were going round collecting autographs while we had a drink with Prince Charles's chef, who was doing the dinner on the Saturday.

On the Saturday Rory came fifth in the junior race, which was pretty good, and he seemed chuffed. I had a meeting with the team putting together the campaign for the North East Assembly [devolution referendum] campaign and they seemed in good shape. Brendan totally behind it now, Steve Cram not keen. My big worry was whether there would be the interest in it that it was going to need. Kelly Holmes was the star attraction of the weekend and at the dinner I was sitting next to her. She had an unusual but very attractive face, deep brown eyes and nice skin. She looked smaller than on TV. She was wearing a smart suit and the only thing that made her stand out as a top athlete amid the crowd were the veins bulging out of her legs.

She was still flying high, talking at length, how she felt now and then, really going over it all in detail, really wanting to share it. She was very one-track – and said most people would never understand her relationship with athletics, how deep it went – and I wondered whether she might make a good Five interview. She and her agent Jane Cowmeadow were both keen and so was I. She was good on what it was like overcoming injury, and how to be at your strongest on the day itself. She had family and friends there and asked to do a little speech so that she could say thanks to her physio and UK athletics. I was struck by her down to earthness and as with El Guerrouf just how much it all meant. She said she used to cry herself to sleep at failure. She never thought she would win the 800, thought she might win the 1,500 but the whole thing had clearly overwhelmed her. Now she was having to adapt to being known by everyone. I liked her though as with many top athletes she was very self-focused.

I wasn't totally sure about Charles's chef's cooking. Nor was Gordon

Ramsay, who was scathing. A massive starter – deer – that everyone thought was the main course. A fish course that was OK. But it was a really nice evening and Fiona and I got back to find the kids exhausted and Grace and the girls fast asleep. The dog issue was continuing to be incredibly divisive. Grace was desperate for one and the boys and I were totally opposed. Fiona was not keen either. The boys were sure I would cave in to Grace, Fiona was piling it all on me to decide. I was up early on the Sunday and luckily a charity physio had a look at my heel and seemed to fix it. Out to the start and then off with the same pacer as last year. We started well below 7-minute-mile pace settled into 7.30 and then slowed after 7 or 8 miles. I found it harder this year but almost caught Ramsay on the line. Couple of hours in the VIP tent and then off by helicopter to Newcastle. I was pretty knackered by the time I got home.

PG and Jonathan were anxious I went to see TB asap. They said he was getting a bit more worried about GB and the unions and also was not clear on the central speech argument. They sent through a new draft including a new policy section. I said it was strong but we needed a better opening, a better ending and much stronger use of pledges etc. I finally set off for conference on the Monday. On the platform at Victoria the ticket seller said she loved TB and would vote for him because she and her mates had jobs. A hundred yards on an anti-war harridan was giving it to me on Iraq. I travelled down with Patrick Wintour [*Guardian* journalist] who said the GB briefing never stopped and was always done through what they saw as their tame people. He and Mike White felt like lone voices at the paper sometimes. GB was speaking as I arrived and got a terrific reception though TB and JP felt he milked it too much. JP said to me he had to laugh listening to GB talking about getting consensus around the world. 'I can't get a bloody consensus between the two of them!' he said.

Most of the day PG and I were working on new sections. The best work I did was at 3 a.m. when I wrote a new bridge between the Iraq section and the end and also wrote a new ending. It was a strong speech and ought to do the job OK. We didn't really want an apology over Iraq to be the main thing, but he got close to it. I did a section trying to build a third term narrative. It was very different to previous years when I was so close to it and became totally driven on it. I could stand back a bit. I found myself advising removal of all references to the press and trying to be less defensive. I was struck by how little I was now engrossed in gossip and blather but also just how much of it went on. I felt a bit sorry for Alan Milburn who was being done in. He said that we could not just go 'screaming about our record' and it was taken as a declaration of war. Ridiculous but that was the media mood. GB was also playing in the sidelined victim angle. TB and he now barely spoke. We had a couple of hours writing then a line-by-line session and it was definitely coming together.

I had to leave for the Brighton Dome and the last of my 'Audience With' theatre shows. JP came up at the interval and walked on after I told the story about him punching the guy in 2001. We had a bit of banter then off he went having told the story of the Burnley National Front hooligans he met at Doncaster station who said I was their mate. We both got a good reception, there were no dreadful questions and I set off back to the hotel and the speech. TB was having a mild twitter but it was OK on argument, good on forward policy and powerful on Iraq. I did a new ending and finally got to bed by 4. By the morning we were doing tone and hone. We made a few cuts and additions and got it in shape for the run through far earlier than usual. Milburn got whacked in the press a fair bit and was a bit low about it. He said GB had come with the aim of causing 48 hours of division and had succeeded. TB said if the party knew how he operated they would be horrified.

PG felt I was able to give a better perspective from having been out but then close in for the last few days, and TB was profuse in his thanks. So was CB who said thanks for coming down. She said he really needed help and she threw her arms around me and gave me a big kiss. I just never knew what kind of mood she was going to be in with me, from one day to the next. I had a nice chat with [TB's sons] Euan and Nicky who were incredibly supportive of their dad. We had to go through the speech with an eye to GB points, e.g. the line 'Every change will be fought over', in the current mad atmosphere would be taken as reference to him rather than people we knew to be opponents outside the party. But it was fine. I stayed to watch it at the hotel. I was a bit alarmed that David Hill did not seem terribly involved in the speech writing process, but maybe it was possible to be remote from the process but still do the briefing OK. I guess that was the way with a lot of leaders. One of the longest discussions was how to do the GB and JP lines. I wrote a draft and then rewrote so that we ended on John not Gordon. Media seemed to go OK but we'll see. TB came back for a little chat with Leo who was incredibly sweet and very funny. Euan said he was really proud of his dad. I asked Leo the best part of the speech. He said the bit where he said that thing.

Afterwards TB, Jonathan and I had a chat re GWB/Iraq. We had been joking through the last couple of days about how TB was the last to believe unequivocally we did the right thing. More seriously I said that I felt they had pretty much decided early on and they used us a bit, and we got caught up in their propaganda from time to time. I felt Cheney and Rumsfeld didn't have much time for us at all and were perfectly happy to use TB as a better presenter of the case than any of them were. Bush genuinely liked him and understood the risk he was taking but ultimately that would not weigh that heavily with him. TB said he always asked after me and asked if I was kicking ass. I said I thought at a personal level he was a lot better than most people imagined but I was less convinced than I was before about whether we did the right thing; or maybe I felt we did the right thing but not in the right way. TB said there was something in it but he still felt it was the right thing to do. I said I would always defend him, and defend the way the decision was made, but that was the one thing I worried about, the extent to which we were played by the Americans. But again, he repeated that regardless of Bush, Cheney or anyone else, he felt we did the right thing.

I left at four, decided it was a bit risky to get the train because of all the hunt protests, and got driven back. Seb Coe was down there, and got a great response. Ditto Amir Khan. On the Wednesday I did a speech to Sanford Bernstein [investment research firm] and the New York boss, Lisa Shalett, agreed to help set up an American branch to support our bid for London 2012. I was now working on JP's speech – at least I could do it from home.

Thursday 30 September

Working at home. Sally called from Brighton. She said the *Standard* were on to the story of TB buying a house, though they thought it was a flat. Clearly it was all coming out from somewhere. Added to which he was due to be going to hospital tomorrow to have the thing done on his heart, so now was maybe the time to say something about his future plans. He was thinking he would say he was fine, the op was straightforward, he continued to enjoy the job, that he was going to fight the next election, stay for a full term if we won. But that would be it. As to what GB would do with that, we would have to wait and see. I felt he should simply say he didn't contemplate a fourth term, but not go beyond that. He called later and we had a long chat. He sounded

quite nervous, but felt he had to say something because of the risk people would put two and two together and make up any number they
thought of. We had been talking about these issues for some time and
agreed perhaps now was the time to say something fairly clear.

We agreed maybe three broadcast interviews, then PA and put up
JP tomorrow to steady the ship a bit. TB said he felt strong and totally
up for the challenge ahead, but he did feel nervous about the heart. He
said it's not nice having people poking around your vital organs. The
worry about his dad's stroke, and whether he would follow suit, was
also in there somewhere. But I felt the combination of end of conference, rumours re the house, fact re heart, and constant speculation re GB
made it the right time to instil a bit more clarity.

He said I had made a big difference to the speech, and felt better
if I stayed around a bit more. But truth be told, I had got home a bit
depressed, and I think it was because I was not really being allowed
to disengage at all. There were not many days when at least a fairly
substantial part of my time was not going on political stuff I had tried
to leave behind. It was fine to be wanted, I suppose, and TB knew how
to press the duty button, especially vis-à-vis keeping out the Tories,
but I hadn't felt the same sense either of tension or of ownership re the
speech. I was happy to help, but happy to get away from it. I asked if he
intended to tell GB about the house/heart/staying on announcement.
He said he would get Anji to talk to Sue Nye, but he really couldn't be
bothered having the conversation himself.

I went out for a run and got a phone call out of the blue from Clive
Woodward [England and British Lions rugby coach], asking if I wanted
to go on the Lions tour of New Zealand. He said he had got my number from Tessa. The rugby hacks all complained that on the last tour
the media operation was a bit of a shambles, and they needed a heavy
hitter. 'I thought I'd go to the heaviest,' he said. I was quite tempted,
though it would mean a fair amount of time away from home. He
sounded pretty determined about it. He said it would be a very tough
tour, the All Blacks were sensational at the moment, but he was determined to give it a go, and he wanted excellence in all departments,
and that included communications. He said I know you love sport,
and also he reckoned there were bound to be situations where the
unexpected happened and my experience of dealing with big crisis
moments would come in handy. He said the fact I was out running
and out of breath when he called was an omen – it meant I should be
heading down the sporting route. I asked him the dates, which would

actually work out in terms of when I thought the election would be. I said I would think about it and get back to him. 'I reckon we would have a lot of fun working together. We will get a lot out of you being there, and hopefully you will too.'

Friday 1 October

The media was massive on the various TB statements on his health, his house, but above all staying on. It had all been a bit high wire but it just about worked. The health issue did not provoke as big a frenzy as I had expected. I thought some of them would have tried to push the idea he was becoming a spent force, or that he was going to keel over one day like his dad. The house coverage was also less incendiary than I imagined it would be. I guess the reason was they reckoned there was a better story in what it all said re him and GB. The GB situation really was pretty bad at the moment. On the back of the briefing re TB's intentions and the other developments, GB put out words of support and sympathy re the heart issue, but then one of his people briefed that it was 'like an African coup' – that TB's people had waited till GB was out of the country, and promoted JP. GB really had to get a grip of his people; though I guess he could have authorised it himself. African coup! TB was the PM, so how could he be the one doing a coup? What it indicated was their mindset that it was his entitlement, sooner rather than later. I had a chat with JP who said it was hard to want to support GB sometimes, given the operation he ran.

Saturday 2 October

Forty minute run, hoping I'd feel better at the end, but I didn't. I was still very down. I wasn't feeling suicidal, in that I wasn't actively thinking of killing myself, but I was thinking a lot about death, and not feeling that bothered about it, other than how it would affect the family. I went to Reading v Burnley, which got me out of myself for a while, but I was feeling totally empty and hollow inside, and though people were nice, I just wasn't in the mood for the small talk, the banter, or the questions about conference. I got home and knew I had to be on my own so I went upstairs and worked on a speech for Holland. Fiona asked me if I was OK, and I said yes, and she said no you're not, I can tell, and when I told her I felt really shit, depressed to the core, she asked what had triggered it, which I didn't know. It just is. I worked till late.

Sunday 3 October

TB called to get my view on how it had all gone. OK-ish, I thought. Medically, he said he felt fine. It had not been that complicated and though they advised a bit of rest, he had been pretty much straight back into things. Politically and media wise, I felt there were two problems – they were not going to let go on Iraq, and they were not going to let go on TB–GB, not least because it was being fed the whole time, mainly but not exclusively by GB's people. He felt that if he had not said he was staying on, there would have been no end to the speculation. All he would have got from now to the election was whether he was staying and so it was as well to be clear. I agreed with that but said it would be a while before the ramifications were clear. The unions were out speaking up for GB. 'Does he really think that helps him?' he asked. He said JP had spoken to GB and told him to get a grip, that he had to understand it was TB's right to fight another term, and his duty to support him. It had not gone down terribly well.

TB had seen GB on Wednesday. You'd have loved it, he said. It was a collector's item. GB – You wanted to see me. TB – Yes. GB – Here I am. TB – I wanted to say that we give it one last go to work together. GB – What is your proposal? TB – My proposal is that we work together, and you co-operate with me, and then one day I help you take over. GB – That is not a proposal. TB – Yes it is. GB – No it's not. TB – Are you saying that unless I give you a date for my departure you won't work with me? GB – I need a proposal so that I know what the future holds. TB said he used the word proposal in virtually every sentence, and he would not engage beyond that. 'I'm afraid it felt like talking to a lunatic.' He said he had been more worried than he let on about his heart, and felt relieved the doctors had done what they had done. Grace came in as we were speaking and I put her on to him so she could explain to him as well that she wanted a dog. 'There you are,' he said, 'the Prime Minister is supporting your campaign for a dog. I hope this helps, and I hope you win.'

Monday 4 October

Got a lift in with Michael Farthing [neighbour and AC's gastroenterologist]. He felt I should have another examination so had a colonoscopy then home to work on various speeches. This latest bout of depression has gone on close to two weeks now. I could tell Fiona was trying hard to be sympathetic but when Grace told me to snap out of it, I wondered if she had heard that from Fiona. I said it is not so easy. Grace said it was making everyone feel sad. I said I'm sorry, I know that, but it is hard. I don't choose to be like this, it just happens. It will pass.

Tuesday 5 October

I had agreed to do the BBC commentary on Michael Howard's speech for [BBC broadcaster] Andrew Neil's programme with Tim Bell. I had a lot of time for Tim, he was clever and had a real grasp of Tory weaknesses. He was very down on them off-camera but had clearly been given the script and was putting over at least some of it. I just felt Howard lacked both the strategic skills and the empathy that he was going to need to take out TB. *The Guardian* had run a story that I was going back for the campaign and I had to dance around that a bit. TB was off to Africa.

Wednesday 6 October

It was obvious the Holland event was meant to be quite a big speech so I worked on that a bit more, plus the last article for the *Times* series. Also, Bono had agreed a date for the Five interview so I started proper research on that.

Thursday 7 October

I was working at home then out to do the prizegiving at Islington Green school, where Peter Hyman is now a teacher, and loving it. The event was at Sadler's Wells theatre and there was a good buzz to it, though the kids were pretty wild. I had to cut short the speech bit of my presentation, as I wasn't convinced it was what they wanted. Good event though, and nice to see Peter clearly taking to his new life. He really had made a go of it, and was very teacherly with the kids, but in a nice way. I suppose my main message was that none of them could possibly know where their life would turn but they should aim high and really go for it. If someone had said to me when I was their age that I would end up working for a Prime Minister or meeting people like Nelson Mandela, or being seconded to run NATO comms, or been part of the talks for peace in Northern Ireland, or met and had a laugh with Diana, I'd have said they were mad. But I did. A lot is down to luck, but mostly stuff comes from hard work etc.

They were a bright lot in many ways but a lot of them would face an uphill struggle.

Friday 8 October

Working on the diaries. Reached 1 May '97 – 95,000 words since the start of the year. When the hell did I find the time to write it all? PG called. He said that at the Frankfurt book fair, publishers had been asked what their favourite piece of fiction of the past year had been, and Caroline Michel [publisher and agent] named the Hutton Report.

Saturday 9 October

I had written to Gordon about his bereavement, and today came a letter from him about Dad's death. It was a nice enough letter, albeit belated and written because I had written to him about his mother. He had a nice passage about how he saw his dad looming over him every day, but these personal letters from him were always rather marred by the messy writing. There was one bit I really couldn't read at all.

Sunday 10 October

I did the *Frost* programme. David seemed really tired, and I asked him over breakfast afterwards if he was OK. He said he did feel a bit tired. But he said he would never stop working. He just loved it too much. Ming [Menzies] Campbell [Lib Dem MP] was on and I thought did OK. Ewan McGregor [actor] and Charley Boorman [TV presenter and McGregor's co-writer] were in there and we had a good chat about Mark Neale [mutual friend]. Dinner with the Goulds. I was still feeling very low, not really getting into the conversation. Philip did his best to chivvy me along but I was not having it. I just wanted to get to bed. Georgia and Rory were reminiscing about the Olympics which suddenly felt a long time ago. It would be so much easier when I felt like this if I could just hide away, but I know that has an impact on other people too. PG was at me again to get proper help, not just struggle on and use sleeping pills.

Tuesday 12 October

Off to Holland. I was met by the event organisers at Schiphol and then taken to the hotel. I had a fair bit of time before my speech so went for a long run through a little forest with some nice trails, then had a meeting with Leo Van Der Kant, a speakers' agent who was keen for me to do stuff out there. Out to the venue which was fine. Ditto the event, well-organised, nice people. Jack de Vries from Prime Minister [Jan Peter] Balkenende's office was there, and we had a little chat. It was interesting the extent to which, even though they did not feel they had anything like the press we did, they could learn from how we handled them. I did the usual spiel on change in media age, and the need for strategic, proactive comms to deal with it. It probably did me a bit of good to get away for the day, and would be easier for Fiona and the kids too. I managed to leave the dinner fairly early and get to bed, hoping a decent sleep would help lift me.

Wednesday 13 October

Alan Milburn called while I was waiting for the plane back. He and Philip and I had been talking about the need to inject more optimism into TB's politics and message. Ironic given how down I felt. Alan was putting together a note for TB, but he wanted to run it by me before he sent it. He felt TB needed a real injection of fresh ideas and energy, and also that he had to break out of the prison in which GB and his ways kept him. The clarity about staying for another term ought to help him do that. I was now pretty resigned to going back full time for the build-up and the campaign itself. Alan said he felt I needed some kind of title that ensured everyone understood I was essentially directing things with him. I felt I couldn't do more than a couple of days a week, then build up slowly to full time. I didn't feel I needed a title, certainly not yet. The main things he wanted out of me was the work I did with PG on message and strategic development, with Fraser [Kemp, MP, election co-ordinator] on attack, TBWA on advertising, and giving strategic direction to the media team. But I was also going to be doing a lot of the scripts and speeches for TB etc. Added to which according to Carol Linforth [conference and event team] I was down to do more motivational and fundraising speeches for party events than most if not all of the shadow Cabinet. I sat down and wrote a bit of an audit of what I was up to, *The Times*, the Lions, a stack of speeches in the diary already, a load of charity events, reading at Gospel Oak. It all felt a bit overwhelming right now, but only because of the political stuff.

Thursday 14 October

I was doing a bit of research on Bono then out to speak to a law firm, Dundas & Wilson, at the Banqueting House. It was well organised and the speech went down fine. It shouldn't be the case that a few jokes transform a speech, but truth be told they do, especially if speaking to a bigger point you go on to make. Still, no matter how lucrative, I'm not sure I could go on doing this kind of thing for ever. I need to start seeing it as the financial base of other stuff, especially the charity stuff. Some guy from Northern Ireland had a pop over me saying things were better there now, which to most reasonable people was a statement of fact, but he clearly didn't like it. When the phrase 'Queen and country' popped out, I knew where he was coming from and went off on one about how 'some people' might think it was OK to treat Catholics like an inferior form of human life, but that kind of hatred had no place in a civilised country and I was proud to have been part of the process that has helped reduce it, even if some want to keep the hatreds as they were. His face was going redder and redder as I spoke, but I got a nice round of applause for saying it. I was also going to have to get used to the fact that at events like this, some people just like the idea of saying they'd had a go.

Ed Victor called. Vicky Barnsley at Harper Collins had said her offer was not on the table for ever. He had said fine. He was keen that I move towards a deal, almost certainly with Gail, but I wanted to keep options open a while longer. When I said to him it was not impossible I would end up working with GB, he said he thought I was mad. 'How can you after all you have seen and all you know? And all you have written?' I know, I said, but one day TB is going to go, and I think it is in our interest that whoever follows does well. I will always work for Labour rather than Tory governments to be in power. Fiona heard my side of the call. I said perhaps it was the prospect that I'd never actually get away from all this that was depressing me. She said on the contrary, it might be that I was out of it and had felt forced out, not least by her, and it was actually the only thing I really wanted to do.

Friday 15 October

Just couldn't sleep. Gave up about 4 a.m. and got up to do some work upstairs. Feeling a bit edgy. I was working on optimism stuff for Alan M. It could become a good way of getting up delivery, the old glass half full not half empty approach. Also, a way of getting over the sense of utter negativity in the media. I did a general strategy note for him and the outline of an article. I also suggested the idea of a cheer-up launch with a quiz for the hacks to check out their happiness. We needed a bit of fun in the fucking campaign. As I got into it, I was a bit worried I was going a bit manic, but at least some of the ideas ought to work. I ended up doing a nine/ten page note, which I sent to TB, AM, PG, which went over pretty much every aspect of the campaign. The main point was the need for a big change in style, tone and gear. We had to get interesting again, and bold. Scrap the battlebus and dragging the media around with us everywhere, scrap the daily press conferences to give us more flexibility, get going now on direct mail, decide once and for all on TV debates – my recommendation was just say No – get the broadcasters to broaden the list of 'must do' programmes, sort localised planning, boost the regional operations, get my and GB roles for the campaign properly sorted and announced, show that we are ahead in thinking and planning.

I also wanted to brief out the research from TBWA on the way media coverage was fuelling the cynicism, alongside the fact that unmediated TB still gets the highest thermometer rating of any politician, by a mile. For this stage of the pre-campaign, PG and I were recommending 'Britain is working, don't let the Tories wreck it' as a campaign strapline, and the optimism/pessimism approach was an important part of that. And it was time to make a big thing of the 'conditional support' idea on Iraq. I suggested a rally of pro-Labour/anti-war people who could say to TB's face: 'I didn't support you on Iraq, I hated what you did in Iraq, but I'm still voting Labour.'

Then I did a riff on the idea that TB and the UK were in a 'relationship, it didn't always run smoothly but let's stick together'. By the end of it I sketched out a single briefing with a stack of possible stories, the idea being to swarm the press and spoil them for choice. New approach – a campaign aimed directly at people, not media. TB says new mindset for politicians needed. Key campaigners get battle plan with numbers of people they have to hit. TB demands more spontaneity, go to critics not just the faithful. New HQ. Boost for regions. Boost for resources on direct mail/phone/internet. New website. Scrapping daily press conferences. Scrapping leader's battlebus. Rule out TV debate. Call on the broadcasters to broaden the list of interviews that all leaders agree to do. Focus groups show TB still most popular. Ad agency advises... JP role. GB role. AC role. Campaign structures. Optimism strategy. Poster on leapfrogging France's economy. Africa piece in election campaign. 'Conditional support' concept. I was now totally motoring, but knew I was heading into the manic zone when I started to script a long briefing on the optimism strategy, and was laughing at my own ideas, and it was not yet half six. But there was definitely something in it. The Tories and the press wanted us all to be pessimistic, well fuck that, optimism is the way. So we send out a calling notice to the media for a 'Cheer up you lot' event. They arrive to street music, happy dancers and very pretty women giving them directions and being very jolly. On the way to the venue poster-sized pix of a smiling TB and a miserable looking Howard. Then in the media room a split screen video is playing happy shots of Labour people on the left, miserable shots of old Tories on the right. The Labour shots are interspersed with pictures of delivery and captions on screen re economic and public services progress. The Tory shots are similarly interspersed with captions of e.g. employment and economic figures under them, with Howard smiling above pix of the poll tax riots. When our people go to start the press conference, they press the Billy Bass [an animatronic fish presented by JP to TB which plays 'Don't Worry, Be Happy' every time a button is pressed]. On the media seats envelopes. On the cover pix of TB and Howard. Beneath TB the words 'Happy Days'. Beneath Howard – 'I could be back in power'.

Inside is a survey for the press to fill in. 'How much did you earn in '97? How much did you earn in '01? How much do you earn now? Concerning your own economic prospects, do you feel confident or pessimistic? Do you have children? In your estimation are they happy or unhappy? Do they attend state schools? If yes, are they happy there? In your estimation is their school improving or worsening? Does it have more teachers than in 1997? Has the school had money for a building programme? Have standards risen?

When was your last contact with the NHS? Would you describe it as positive or negative? On your last hospital visit did you notice whether there were more nurses than in 1997? Have you ever been to Brixton? Did you see any police officers? Do you go to restaurants? How often? How many holidays do you have? Do you own a car? How old is it? Do you have a computer in your home? If so, how many? Do you go to the theatre or concerts? How often? Do you agree with any or all of the following statements? The UK economy is performing well. Britain's employment record is good. Investment in public services is rising. Britain has led the world on development issues and in writing off debt for the poorest countries. Britain has some of the best companies in the world. Britain has some of the best writers, musicians and sportsmen and women in the world. Britain has some of the best hotels and leisure sites in the world. Finally, does this questionnaire fill you with the urge to do a pompous editorial or po-faced two-way? If so – cheer up and get a life.'

Fiona was by now up and about and asking why I was up and what was so funny? She didn't exactly bust her sides when I told her, but she did seem relieved I seemed to be emerging out of the total plunge. I said we would then use our own channels to get the survey out more widely, alongside the survey on the shift from positive to negative in media. Big point that optimism v pessimism is a new dividing line. And the reason for Tory pessimism is the belief they must break the link between government and delivery. End the presser with a goodie bag handout and 'Always Look on the Bright Side of Life' playing. Try and get one of the Monty Python team involved. I thought the party would love it. I tried it on PG who loved it. Later on TB thought I had gone mad. But we needed a bit of life in all this stuff. I said we should get a young whizzkid to come in and launch 'reasonstobecheerful. com', a website where people could register their own accounts of great things happening in their areas. Use them to send weekly updates to the hacks, and once the idea was well established, TB could make a big, serious speech on the economic and social and cultural value of optimism.

I had to leave for the Riverside Studios in Hammersmith for the interview with Bono. I'd read lots of stuff including all the briefing from Lucy Matthews at DATA [Debt, AIDS, Trade, Africa], Bono's campaign. Sara Latham had said she was gorgeous and indeed she was. Tall, willowy, very clever. Paul McGuinness popped in for a chat, really warm and friendly, then Bono arrived. We had a little natter about the party conference before doing the interview. He was open, very articulate, got out good stuff on the serious issues, but also on himself and his background, his dad etc. Very nice about me on film, saying I'd helped their campaign by getting TB and GB on the same page. Very funny about Geldof getting TB in an armlock and lots of good stuff on his own ego, himself, how he did it. Southan [director] said he thought it was the best interview yet. It certainly felt very relaxed and it helped that he was so clever and articulate, but also with a good deal of self-awareness and humour so he wasn't as pop starrish and pompous as he might be.

We did some publicity pictures together. Had a good laugh about the meeting in Cologne at the G8; he said he remembered me telling Geldof he was a wanker in the way he was talking to TB. He said off-camera that the country would only realise just how good TB was once he was gone. I felt it went well, he had been so open and fresh. I also bounced my optimism idea off him and he loved it. I told him TB thought I was going a bit loopy with some of it. 'You've just got to persuade him,' he said, and I said I would, inspired by that brilliant line we had just discussed, when he told TB, who was saying we couldn't get everything, and we had a mountain to climb 'that if you see Everest you don't say, "Gee what a big mountain," you fucking climb it'. Really enjoyed seeing him and later he faxed through a very funny little cartoon about our meeting.

Then I headed off up the M1 to London Gateway service station to meet Clive Woodward and his wife Jayne. Odd place to meet. Reminded me of football managers in the old days when they were forever meeting to do deals with players in motorway services. It was quite clear that Jayne was more than just a wife, and when he was pitching the role he envisaged me doing, she was chipping in a fair bit about why they needed someone like me. He said that last time the media had basically seen the media operation as a shambles, that he wanted to take it to a new level, in which we really developed a proper strategic focus. He felt that both he and the players would learn a good deal about how to use the media and deal with the media from having me along. I went over some of the difficulties, not least the general election, but also my baggage, and the fact that the media would not necessarily want it to work, so though he thought he was doing something they asked for, they might see this as a step too far. He said they had asked for a big hitter, so he was determined to get one. He said he really wanted me to do it. I was very tempted, but also said if in the end I didn't do it, I hoped I'd be able to help him find someone.

I was impressed by his focus and professionalism, and he was clearly someone who was always looking to do things differently and stir things up. He agreed that ultimately what happened on the field would dictate whether the tour was a success or failure, but he was convinced that how they handled themselves off the field, not least in their dealings with and through the media, could have an important impact on morale, teambuilding, professionalism. He said there was still a very amateur ethos about the Lions. They wouldn't have that long together, so the preparations were vital. But he really felt I could make

October '04: Meeting Woodward to discuss Lions job

a difference, helping him to build a team. He felt that the recent success of Europe in the Ryder Cup was obviously largely about performance, but he felt they had worked out all the other stuff too, that the confidence they all showed in part came from things that were happening outside the golf itself, not least how they came over on the media. He said it would also give him real confidence if I was involved as there would be no crisis or difficulty I couldn't help him deal with. He also wanted me to put together a proactive plan for the players to go out into the community. He said on the last tour there had been a breakdown of discipline and players had ended up attacking coaches and each other and it was all a bit of a disaster. Again, hopefully, I could help ensure that kind of thing couldn't happen.

We were spotted by a few people, some of whom came over for autographs, but one guy who worked there asked if he could take our picture. I insisted he take the pictures separately, just in case he flogged one of us together to a paper. As the guy walked away, Jayne said 'That's why we need someone like you. We'd never have thought of that.' They were both very good fun and I felt he was much warmer than the public image, and there was no doubt her view mattered a lot to him. He said it really didn't matter that I wasn't a rugby expert. There would be plenty of rugby experts, he wanted a communications and strategy expert. Fiona and the kids seemed reasonably OK about it, though I was a bit worried about being away for so long.

Saturday 16 October

Iraq and problems with some of the troops were the main news focus until Boris Johnson and his clownish remarks re Liverpool took over.* Ed talking to Gail about various ways in which we might do a deal on the diaries. Maybe we should be looking at a far longer timescale. I was having real ethical turmoil re the GB problem. I didn't want to be someone who caused the party trouble, but it would be hard, with GB in charge, for publication not to be used against him in some way or other. Ed said it was a statement of the obvious that the longer I waited, the lower the value, but he said he knew me well enough now to know I wouldn't or shouldn't do anything I felt uncomfortable with.

* Johnson published in *The Spectator* an editorial that said Liverpool was wallowing in 'disproportionate' grief for hostage Ken Bigley, who had been killed in Iraq. Michael Howard ordered him to go to the city and apologise, which he did.

Monday 18 October

Worked on future speeches then ran to Wapping for lunch with Keith Blackmore. He was also at me again re the book, while also saying no pressure. He was keen for me to do more for *The Times*, including on politics. He also had the idea of a regular slot 'AC runs a mile with...' I said I'd think about it. He said everyone had been pleased with the sport series and Robert Thomson [editor] was keen I do more. I went to meet Godric, thinking he might fancy the Lions job. I could see he was tempted, but later he came on to say no.

Tuesday 19 October

Train to Runcorn, working on a piece for *The Times* about the Tories, and today's speech to north-west businessmen. I was met by Paul Smith [former *Mirror* colleague now with own PR company] who had managed to coincide the speech at the Heath [Business Park] with a Burnley home game. Really nice crowd, mainly small and medium-sized businesses and a real feeling of get up and go. The Q&A in particular went well, really nice atmosphere. Burnley 2, Coventry 2, good game then off to Bolton with Mike Forde [performance director], who had approached me with a view to doing a bit of work for Sam Allardyce. Mike was twenty-nine, ex-cyclist, background in psychology, interesting guy, clearly quite important to Sam and thinking through everything for him. He told me on the drive over that Sam had been offered the Newcastle job but said no, that the money wasn't as good as you might think, and that Alan Shearer [Newcastle player] was too powerful. I was staying in the hotel at the Bolton ground, so with a reasonably late start tomorrow hoping to get a decent night's sleep. I felt a day or two away from the depression lifting fully.

Wednesday 20 October

I met Sam in one of the executive boxes overlooking the ground. Very much as per the image – big, bluff, jacket without tie, gold necklace. Very nice guy but obviously worried a bit about his media profile. He obviously had in mind going for the England job at some point in the future, possibly soon, and knew he perhaps had to get his profile in a different place. I gave him my usual spiel on strategy, clarity, really deciding what you want to put over and then just do it. I said I thought Arsene Wenger [Arsenal manager] was in some way the

October '04: Advising Allardyce on going for England job

best on media because he was superior without being arrogant. José Mourinho [Chelsea manager] was arrogant without being superior and Alex F was very testy, and his contempt for them came through a fair bit. In a way, he had reached a different position where it didn't matter that much, but if Sam really wanted to go for it, he really did need to get to a different place. He should take his authenticity and his Englishness as a base, and build on it by becoming a serious analyst of the game and its development, not just in relation to Bolton but of football generally. For example, the way he had to go to Africa to get cheaper players, the way transfer systems were changing, the impact of changes to wage structures, people were fascinated by it, but it needed people to make sense of it.

He clearly had issues with his chairman, and I sensed he worried he wouldn't be able to build the club up that much more. He was clearly good with the players. We chatted for a couple of hours or so and though I wasn't sure if it was of that much use to either of us, he seemed to get something out of it, and he said he would like to keep in touch. Mike was definitely an innovative thinker. He had been a cyclist but I could see when he was with the players and the coaches they took him seriously. We had a bit of a political chat. Sam had been raised as Labour, went for Thatcher, but supported TB, but he wasn't convinced we had done that much for sport. Interesting how sports people seemed to be gravitating towards me. I got a long email from Clive Woodward saying he was more convinced than ever that I could make a difference, that he understood the point about me being too high-profile a figure and the media might react, but he felt he and the players could get a lot out of me being there and 'Please do it.'

Thursday 21 October

To St George's Hospital in Tooting with Michael Farthing to see a chest specialist. Twenty-five per cent more lung capacity. More drugs for nose and throat. He thought I was doing OK. TB had said he wanted to see me but needed to clear some time in the diary, so I hung around for a bit waiting to hear when I should go in. I went to a little cafe close to the hospital. The owner came over for a chat. He said I was getting a much better press since I left, and the same would happen to TB. I went in to see TB. He had just come from a meeting with GB, Ruth Kelly, Charles Clarke and Patricia [Hewitt, Trade and Industry Secretary].

He said GB had been 'at it again'. They had been talking about child-care and GB kept saying there would be no room for major expansion till 2008. TB said it became comical, and he kept pressing GB as to why there couldn't be more before and what was the significance of 2008? He said the others found it as bizarre as he did.

He was looking OK and said that his heart felt a lot better, that he was totally up for it, but Iraq was a nightmare. He said the MoD had spilled out the request from the US re troop movements and something that shouldn't have been a big deal had become one. I said he just had to get his head firmly fixed in the real world and not get driven down the media/real world disconnect. Although you could see how the media would parody Alan M's stuff on optimism, it was actually the perfect place for TB to be, because it spoke to his personality and was a non-whingey way of getting over what a total fucking pain the media is. He asked what I would do and I said help Alan establish himself as a bigger political force and get out there with some big speeches delivering big messages about optimism/delivery and I had confidence we were still winning the arguments. He said lots of people had mentioned my *Frost* appearance and he thought I should get out and do more TV and radio, particularly talking positively about him, because so much of the attack fell on him personally, and too few people felt comfortable being absolutely out there in his defence.

I told TB about the approach from Clive Woodward and he thought I should go for it, thought it would be a great thing to do, but said we would need to have systems for keeping plugged in. Jonathan was looking his old bouncy self and Liz [Lloyd] looked like she was doing fine. I went to Old Queen Street, saw first Matt Carter, then Philip. PG was very up, felt that given how much we had taken, TB and the party were in pretty good shape. The Tories had fallen again, and the little rise Howard had had in the focus groups a while back was not being sustained. He said Alan had made a big difference already in election planning, and would do even better if we could get GB out of his head. To Peter M's party. Gavyn Davies there, so I avoided him. I had a nice chat with Margaret Beckett about what she might do after the election. Quite a few media people. Martin Kettle [*Guardian*] said that Rusbridger had said that nothing positive should be said about TB in the leaders. Cherie came over and made a point of being very nice in front of Grace. Didn't stay long. Had dipped badly again after having a couple of blips upward.

Saturday 23 October

Rory's birthday, but I was really depressed all day. I just could not lift myself above a sense of emptiness and gloom. Actually felt almost sick with it too. Fucking horrible, and especially as Fiona wanted us all to be really chirpy for Rory. I did next to nothing apart from a long run, and at one point I found myself crying as I ran. This couldn't go on like this. Most of my depressions have been a few days. This seemed to be going on for weeks. A woman walking her dog on the canal saw me, recognised me and I could see she was using her body language to get me to stop, and I did, and she could see I had tears on my face and I made some crack about the wind, then we just had a brief chat about politics and off I went. I got back, had a bath and went to bed pm, just hoping it would pass. The Gambling Bill was becoming a real problem.*

Sunday 24 October

TB called a few times. He was thinking about doing a press conference tomorrow. He felt that not just gaming, but one or two other issues as well were looking ragged. He felt he ought to get out there with a message. The main event was Manchester United against Arsenal. Really hard game, all sorts of trouble and niggling going on. Alex and Wenger barely looked at each other at the end. Alex called later and said it had led to amazing scenes in the tunnel. Wenger was laying into Ruud van Nistelrooy [United striker]. Alex told him to stick to looking after his own players and leave his alone. Then things really kicked off, with soup, pizza and water flying all over the place. He reckoned the pizza came from Cesc Fabregas [Arsenal player]. There was a little gaggle of them at the door of their dressing room and when the food was flying he was the one who looked as if he had chucked it. He said to tell TB he still had his total support. He worried sometimes that GB was too emotional, that he made it all too much about himself. He had seen the 'African coup' comment. 'Fucking incredible.' I asked him how long it took to come down from a game like that one today. He said he was actually pretty good at putting it behind him quickly, but today had been weird. He said he thought he had seen everything in terms of rows and arguments after the match, but this one was something special.

* The provision in the original draft of the Bill for eight 'super casinos' in the regions caused controversy.

Monday 25 October

Finding life real hard pounding at the moment. Just cannot get my head into gear at all. Negative about everything, down about everything, only the kids get near to getting me out of it, though I felt bad about not being upbeat on Rory's birthday. I think in part it was the lack of any big purpose, and Fiona seems to have accepted that in a way she forced me out. Yet in terms of the way I was spending my time, a lot of it was doing stuff I used to do for TB, for JP to a lesser extent too, and just keeping an eye on things for them, but I did it in a different way, better in some ways, worse in others. Fiona could tell I was on a major down and varied between over-asking what was wrong, and then just ignoring it, which was probably better. I tried to persuade myself it was the right thing to have left and even if it was, it was a pain to have days like this. My feeling was I had had more depressed days since I left than when I was there. Maybe I was totally depressed a lot of the time I was there but work drove it out.

Trevor Beattie sent me a documentary about Fox News. Amazing stuff, real inside story on how its right-wing messages are promulgated, and which the guy who made it couldn't get screened anywhere. I watched TB's press conference and then did a note for him. It was too bitty, not enough narrative and he looked like he was lacking confidence on the big arguments. I also felt he should stop asking the political editors of the three broadcasters to have the first three questions as they had always worked out their clever-clever exchanges and that was all that would ever get on the bulletins. Normally he would rise right above them, but today I felt they had managed to needle him a bit.

Tuesday 26 October

Into Old Queen Street for a meeting on the next stages of the ad campaign. They had done some really good work. I could see why Philip still liked going in here, because despite all the crap, there was still a fair bit of energy and creativity and commitment. Despite capacity for mockery, I felt the optimism argument was already beginning to have an effect. The regional press guys said they felt things were turning a bit. Milburn was in the chair and did fine, though sometimes I felt he tried too hard to look and sound authoritative, which indicated a concern in himself about whether he lacked authority. He was excellent though when he was relaxed and just setting out stuff he wanted done. We agreed TB had lacked narrative and needed to get back to big picture. Philip had a meeting with Spencer Livermore and it was pretty clear that whatever we did, the GB lot were likely to do the opposite. It was a pretty hopeless situation. The main meeting was a good meeting though and I still felt we had the people in there who could turn it round. I recorded the voiceover for the Bono film. Then to the City for a speech and Q&A. All fine. Even better, Burnley beat Villa 2–1.

Wednesday 27 October

Alan Milburn called. He liked my analysis in *The Times* of the Tories. But he felt our current problem was the lack of a clear narrative and he wanted me to help him get something down on paper and around the system. I said nothing much would fly before the American elections but he was keen to get something moving over this weekend. Pat McFadden called. He too felt TB had not been at his best on Monday. He had spoken to him and TB agreed that with the current mood maybe there was no point trying too hard. But he certainly had to raise his game from that kind of performance.

Thursday 28 October

Spent part of the morning working on a piece for the *News of the World* on the American elections. Ran it by Jonathan. Clive Woodward came round at lunchtime after doing a launch of the Lions kit. He has a very strong face and is really clear minded. He said the note I had sent over to him made him more convinced than ever that I had to get involved. I had done a fairly standard five-pager about how comms can be used in various environments in different ways, and suggested different systems we could use to implement an agreed strategy. He was dead keen, kept saying that nobody had ever tried to bring this kind of thinking to rugby and it would help him create a winning environment. He had spoken to Louisa Cheetham, who was down to be doing the PR. He said he had lifted the ideas from my note, taken them in and presented them as his own and told her we were going to need more people to do what he wanted. He said she was a bit defensive at first but then OK, but then he hadn't mentioned my name.

He said he had definitely lined up a job at Southampton FC and was currently doing his coaching badges. 'You should see the looks of some of the other guys when I turn up.' He was pretty scathing about football management in England, that it was like a small circle run by similar types of ex-footballers. He felt that Alex and Wenger were the only ones who really took it to a different level, that they were way ahead of the rest. He felt that in some ways rugby was ahead, like the fact he relied on an eye coach because the eye muscles were so important to awareness, observation and everything that flowed. Grace and her friends were in and out serving us cake and other stuff to eat. He was here one and a half hours or so and in the end I agreed to do it as a consultant, help devise a strategy, perhaps try to get Martin Sheehan or Ben Wilson [No. 10 press officers] on sabbatical or as a secondment. He said he had mentioned me to Bill Beaumont, who was the tour manager, who had said I was a good bloke, not at all like the press said. He said they would have to add to the initial budget to do all this but he was confident he could do that. He agreed I ought to be able to do pieces for *The Times* and maybe some speeches while I was out there.

He was clearly one of those guys who just decided what he wanted and went for it. I had my doubts, but overall, felt it would be interesting to see a group of elite sportsmen up close, also fun, but hopefully I'd be able to make a difference in the way he was suggesting. He was determined it should be the most professional tour there had ever been. He said he would only have the players together for a week or so before departure and he wanted me involved in all of that. He wanted me to bind them in to a different approach. He felt most of the players would be fine, but the more I was around the better. They all needed to think it was worth doing. I agreed to go out in some shape or form, even if it was only for the three Test matches. He said his ultimate ambition was the England football job. He said he was confident he could do it but there was a hell of a lot of politics to go through first. He thought it would be fascinating to see how coaching differed across different sports. It was a good meeting, and I felt he was the kind of guy I would enjoy working with. Liz Lloyd called, saying they urgently needed a fresh narrative script for TB.

Friday 29 October
Working on the diaries am. Finished the *NotW* piece on US elections, then off to the Belvedere in Holland Park for lunch with David Frost. He was doing a series for Sky on the greatest ever sportsmen, not dissimilar to the stuff I'd done for *The Times*, and wanted me to promote

Ali as the best ever. He said TB was absolutely safe, because whatever people thought of him, they recognised he was a top quality modern politician, who understood what made people tick. It was a really nice lunch, no agenda either side really, just a chat about various people we knew and, in the main, liked. I loved David's ability to stay enthused about what he did, even after so many years and so many big events.

Saturday 30 October
Long bike ride then off to QPR v Burnley with Philip and Georgia, Calum and Charlie [Enstone-Watts, friend of Calum]. Up to the directors' box for lunch. Barry Kilby, half in jest, asked me if I wanted to go on the board. Clive Holt [director] asked me why I didn't want to be an MP. He said you don't want people in five years' time asking ask ing, 'Whatever happened to Alastair Campbell?' like they do with old footballers. One or two of them said that Kitty Ussher [Burnley Labour parliamentary candidate] was not going down too well because she came across as so not Burnley. I said she had a talent that would come through. Lost 3–0, bit of a comedy of errors. Home to a row because I had forgotten we were going out to the Hodges' [Margaret and Sir Henry] party. I really didn't feel like going out at all, not up for it, tired and fed up. It turned out to be not too bad, talked mainly to Sally and Pat McFadden. Hilary Armstrong said we were going to get hammered in the devolution referendum in the [north-east] assembly. DM, who incidentally asked if I was depressed, said that it was because we had used bogus arguments about the Assembly being a job creator rather than just a voice. Jackie Ashley gave me a big number about her basically being a loyalist and really wanting us to go for lunch.

I was sick of the whole game though, didn't want to be thinking about it, talking about it, getting dragged back into it. I really liked Margaret, and Henry made a lovely little speech, but I just so didn't want to be back in this kind of politico-media mix, other than on my own terms 100 per cent. And when I was going through a depressive period, as now, it was just a fucking nightmare. Fiona had said we would only stay for an hour but we ended up staying way longer until at one point I just said I would see her at the car, and went out and waited. I think she underestimated how hard this was for me when I was as depressed as this.

Sunday 31 October

Went for a two-hour run, hoping it would clear my head, but it didn't. Felt no enthusiasm for anything. TB called, said he had spoken to Bush yesterday who was on good form and felt he was probably going to win. It was pretty clear to me that TB wanted him to. I said 'I won't brief that you are backing George.' He said even by their standards, the press were pretty vile at the moment, but he still felt he had to get some of them back on board. Out for dinner with the Goulds at Bacchus. PG said the latest groups were not great. He had found TB a bit deflated in recent conversations, as had I. He said he felt really up for it, but he wasn't sure he could go the whole mile unless I was there too. I was totally conflicted about all this. Part of me just didn't want to know. But the other part felt bad about that, felt I had to get engaged and involved, and make sure we won again. Philip was laying it on with a trowel, saying, 'Imagine how you'd feel if the Tories got back and you hadn't help stop it? We know how to do this stuff but I also know if I am in there and you're not I won't be so effective and the same would go if you were there without me. It's only for a short time and then you get your life back again.' I was wondering if I ever would.

Monday 1 November

Really fed up at sudden weight increase up to 15st 3lb. Working on a piece for *The Guardian* defending TB re what they were calling 'sitting on the fence'. I went to see Bostock, said I was thinking I probably needed anti-depressants. He was not so sure. He said there was a big difference between being unhappy and being depressed and that I needed to be more patient. He went off on his kick that I should never have left the job in the first place, that I needed total full-on activity, and this was inevitable. He said he'd felt watching my profile change that I was trying to recast myself as a nice guy but I wasn't really and I should accept what I was. 'So are you saying I'm a complete bastard?' Not at all, he said, but your strength is your strength. He was very keen that I try to resist going back on the drugs, which was a bit of a role reversal. I just felt I needed to get my head a bit above where it was now. He felt the problem was I was a big person driven by big projects that mattered and I wasn't currently doing that. He said the real you is a bruiser in politics, not the nice man going round the world raising money for good causes. Bottom line is he talked me out of going back on medication.

Tuesday 2 November

Lots of calls on the *Guardian* piece, where I had supported TB not getting involved in the US elections. Did bits and bobs of radio in between an interview with Phil Whalley for the Burnley London Supporters' Club magazine. He clearly felt I was not nearly aggressive enough about the way money and the markets were changing the game. He got quite agitated but I was keen not to say anything that could be taken as slagging off the club. It got me thinking though, that he might have more of a point than I was prepared to concede, that the game was changing fast and not all for the good, and though Burnley FC were better than most, unless people like me argued against some of the things happening more generally, we would get hit badly down the line too. Jonathan sent through a brief note setting out how TB would react to a Kerry win. It was far too much a tribute to Bush and not enough a message to and about Kerry. I put in stuff re the need to refocus on MEPP, new relations with Europe, and a broader message re the future. Then working through the day on the general narrative note they had asked for which needed to be a bit more personal and less nerdy. Chris Shaw came round for a chat re possible future Channel 5 projects. Life would be a lot easier if I could get more enthusiastic about doing more media stuff, but I can't.

Out to the CNN party at the National Portrait Gallery for the US elections. Did a Q&A with Christiane Amanpour, mainly about how TB would deal with whatever outcome. Everyone seemed to think Bush had lost, but having spoken to TB, I got the sense he was going to win. I think Christiane thought so too, though she was saying that life might change if the Democrats won and Jamie [Rubin] got involved. Nice chat with Elisabeth Murdoch [daughter of Rupert], who said she wanted me to work with her on TV projects. David Frost called, said he had been approached by Al Jazeera and did I think it was a good idea? It slightly took me aback, but I did. If CNN was the big TV story of the last decade, it was probably Al Jazeera that was the big media story now. It would be an interesting and different way of him using all his old contacts. We had a brief chat about whether we might do something like that as a double act.

The buzz was now all Kerry because of the exit polls. I was being very 'wait and see', partly because of what had happened the last time, partly because of what TB had said. But there was a lot of excitement around. David and Ed Miliband both had a real go at me for not whacking Bush harder in the media stuff I had done. It was an odd event,

Hugh Grant looking a bit out of place, ditto Renée Zellweger and what looked like a minder. David Davis [MP] and David Davies [FA] under the same roof. All Kerry, Kerry, Kerry, but it was just rumour fuelling rumour. Then Sara Latham got a message that Bush had called in the removal vans, which went round like wildfire but turned out to be nonsense. Mark Seddon [journalist and NEC member] very funny, saying how my exact role at a general election would have to be debated and agreed by the NEC. I stayed till about two, then home to watch the rest of it with Rory, but the situation was all still a bit confused.

Wednesday 3 November

Up at six, and it was pretty clear that Bush was going to win. It cut both ways. Indeed, it was an indication of how tortuous the whole US/ UK thing had become that in some ways a Bush defeat would have been seen as more difficult for TB, especially re Iraq. All the pro-Kerry stuff last night really had had the feel of wishful thinking driving out rational analysis. TB would have got on fine with Kerry but it would definitely have created a new kaleidoscope. I went in to do Andrew Neil's show and there really seemed to be a deep gloom around the place that Bush had won. The first part of the programme was with Shirley Williams [Lib Dem peer], IDS and Armando Iannucci [writer and satirist], then Marr and I. It was extraordinary to think that IDS had been Tory leader. He just didn't have it. Neil was very bright but way too right-wing. I thought Marr's analysis was superficial and I also noticed that he and Neil were chatting away about their agents. Marr complained that there was 'never a story' from PMQs and so he couldn't get it on the ten o'clock bulletins. I said it would help if they gave less time to journalists talking to other journalists and more coverage of politicians actually speaking.

The main argument I was pushing was that TB was right to have stayed neutral and that he was now in a strong position and had to use his access and influence to get real progress on MEPP. I sent over a note to Jonathan saying once it was clear GWB was going to win, he should use it for a new start in the Middle East and a better alliance between US and Europe. TB was up for it. Jonathan did a second draft which I rewrote to take in a bit more subtle pressure. Then did the media rounds. There was no end to bids on a day like this because they had so much space to fill. Met Fraser Kemp for a cup of tea in a cafe near Old Queen Street. He was trying to persuade me to stand for Parliament, at which point an Algerian who was working there came over and said the same. Then 'The Winner Takes It All' by Abba came on the radio. Weird. Over to No. 10 for a meeting with Alan, PG, Liz, Sally, David Hill to go over message for the weekend. Popped in to see TB who was putting together his response to GWB's election, based on the draft Jonathan and I had done. We asked him to put in a bit more re MEPP. He was clearly perfectly happy that Bush had won, felt that sensible people would see this was the best outcome for him.

Liz was trying to get him to be less pro- and Sally felt he should put in more to praise Kerry, but TB wasn't that keen. He did though want to use the next day or two to make clear to Bush that there had to be change and he was confident GWB would listen. He's not stupid, he said. There wouldn't be that long during which he could use changed circumstances to make progress on MEPP. He asked me to stay back for a chat with him and Sally about what I might do in the election. He said Alan was good but inexperienced at the very top level, and sometimes lacking in confidence. He said he wanted me to stay very close to him and as the campaign neared, just be around so he could call on me. Then out again to do loads more media, both radio and telly. I didn't think Kerry's speech was up to much. Bush did OK. TB looked a bit tired. I did *Newsnight* with Portillo who told me TB's colour co-ordination had gone to pot since I left. I assured him colour co-ordination was never my thing.

Thursday 4 November
God knows how many interviews I'd done yesterday and the thing about the media was that if you're reasonably good at it, the more you did, the more people seemed to want you, so there were more bids today, most of which I turned down. I agreed to do a piece for *The Times* on Bush's re-election. I included an account of a row I had with Cheney at Camp David when I said they should be more careful in how they talked about 'democratisation' because all people heard was 'Americanisation'. It had been quite a moment and he looked appalled. 'Are you saying we shouldn't be proud of our democracy?' 'No, I am saying the same words mean different things to different people.' I ran it by TB, who asked me to take it out. Reluctantly, I did.

Mick Hucknall called and said he felt that oddly, people might soften to TB a little over Iraq now. We discussed the concept of conditional voting, welcoming people who would say they were against the war, but still voting Labour. Trevor Beattie had been on to this for a while, and compared it to dating – you don't have to like everything about someone to want to go out with them. Clive Woodward called, said he was making progress on getting things squared through the Lions. He said the chief exec, John Feehan, would come to see me next week.

TB called, said he had appreciated the notes I'd done recently and wanted me to do more on general message, learning lessons, economic message, radical reform, international agenda. In to a TBWA campaign brainstorm. Quite an interesting exercise. They were going for what they called the disruption approach, trying to work out new ways of doing the campaign. They went round the table asking us all to select words we would like to describe the campaign after it finished. I went for optimistic and energised. Then they asked, if the campaign was a person, who would we want it to be? I said Kelly Holmes or Jeff Stelling, the guy who did Sky's soccer programme on Saturday afternoons. Most of them had never heard of him. I said he was solid but also exciting, optimistic, totally on top of the subject, passionate about what he did, good with people, and they ought to take a look.

Two good sessions, and the thing we were heading to was devising a campaign that relied much less on working through the press and media. They had largely bought into the idea that we didn't need press conferences every day, and there was no need having all the media with TB all the time. Far better that we decide the events and messages we want to promote and then the means by which we want to promote them. The web was also, hopefully, going to come into its own for this campaign. There was also a big argument to be made about building up democracy and participation as a way of dealing with the media's spreading of apathy. TB would of course be central to the campaign, out and about promoting the main messages, but there was a case for us having our own TV crews following him around, video diaries etc. It was a good meeting with some good ideas and an approach that was new and different, but it wasn't quite the leap of ambition we needed. We still had a long way to go and wondered even if there was a case for organising some kind of big event like a concert that was anti-war, pro-Blair, pro-Labour. Then a more formal presentation of some of the ad ideas in development, which were strong. I liked these TBWA guys.

Friday 5 November
I was getting back into the rhythm of transcribing a few days of diary

at a time. Now into June '97, and it was extraordinary how quickly we seemed to have settled down into dealing with all the big things government has to deal with. Finished the piece for *The Times*, said no to the *News of the World* re [Yasser] Arafat [Palestine leader, in a coma at a Paris hospital]. I had to watch over-exposure. TB sent through a draft of a piece he had done for *The Observer* on lessons we could learn from [John] Howard and Bush victories. He said it was important the left learns the right lessons, most important of all that while the right can win from the right, we have to win from the centre, and that the economy and leadership are always key. Also, that terrorism does hold sway. When it came to it, the Americans thought Bush was better placed to deal with these problems than Kerry. Round to Tessa's, then out to the Casalinga [St John's Wood restaurant] for dinner. David [Mills] said he had seen some of our stuff on the TV and I should really start to go for the media. Tessa was really down about things.

Saturday 6 November

I'd been thinking a fair bit about the nature and style of the campaign and started to work on another note. I think TB had been a bit dismissive of the earlier one on optimism because of all the mad stuff I put in there, but I was sure the campaign had to feel and look different, and if we just let the old media ways dictate its rhythms, there was no chance of that. So no press conferences, except when we wanted them tactically, no battle bus because all that did was give you a couple of busloads of second-stringers with nothing to do but cause trouble, no leadership debates, and go for new and different sorts of programmes as well as the ones you had to do. Went to [personal friend] Pete Bond's fireworks party. They had effigies of GWB, TB and Alex for the bonfire. 'All your best pals are getting it tonight,' he said.

Sunday 7 November

I did a new version of the two notes on the campaign, bringing it all together and then turned it into a briefing note, full of a whole raft of new stories we could use to shape the terms of the campaign. Philip thought it was brilliant, TB said it was good but he wasn't sure we could actually go as far as to scrap the daily press conferences. Alan M felt it would be great if we could make it all happen but he was worried we had a capacity problem, that only he, PG and I really took pressure on the planning. He felt Matt Carter was too defensive and we needed new people with real imagination. Philip said Alan was really working at the moment and the nuts and bolts were coming together, but he felt it wouldn't really fly until I went in there full time. TB wanted to make an announcement soon that I had some formal position, e.g. campaign co-ordinator, or something that effectively meant that.

Monday 8 November

Lunch with Jeremy Heywood [former civil servant] at Frederick's in Islington. He had gone into the private sector, and was doubtless making loads of money, but it was obvious he was going through much of the same stuff that I was. He was even thinking of going back. Like me, he clearly needed that sense of purpose. He was very pro-TB, even more so than when we were there, as he felt being outside had given him another perspective on just how well he did such a big job. He thought Fiona had been very badly treated, especially by CB, and felt it was sad that even with all that she couldn't look back on it all as a net positive experience. Jeremy had been around for years, had worked in difficult circumstances for all sorts of people, and had been one of the best in terms of the job he did for us, so maybe it would be good if he went back. It was certainly nice to see him.

I went to Old Queen Street for Alan's general election planning meeting, where we went through the note I'd done on the idea of a new style of campaign. I was still not motoring but at least we were beginning to generate some new ideas. I saw what TB meant about Alan sometimes lacking confidence. It came out in odd ways, like his exaggerated hand movements. He also had a very odd way of pronouncing Bush, the u as in bus, rather than boosh. But he was clearly getting a grip of the place, though joining the TB–PG clamour to get me in there more. I said at one point 'Philip, I am much more likely to come in more often if you stop telling me to come in more often.' 'That's good. I won't say it any more.' Then after a pause, he said 'I'll pick you up at 7 tomorrow.' The place fell about.

Tuesday 9 November

Clive Woodward called, and said he was confident they could raise the money to pay me and a team. He said Bill Beaumont was fine, John Feehan was fine, Wales and Scotland were fine. The Irish rep, Noel

Murphy, was a bit iffy about it because of what he called my baggage, but he felt confident John Feehan would square him. I drove up with Calum for the Burnley–Spurs game (0–3). A minute's silence for Emlyn Hughes [former Liverpool and England footballer]. Games without a minute's silence were becoming a rarity. Such a long trek, home 2 a.m.

Wednesday 10 November

Working on odds and ends. I got a call from June Sarpong who had seen TB yesterday with some arts people. She said he was in fantastic form and they loved him. She totally bought the idea of trying to have a strategy for anti-war people who would still rather have a Labour than a Tory government, and felt she could help find more. Out to ITN for a meeting on the media charity quiz.

Thursday 11 November

TB off to the US. John Feehan came round at twelve. Big guy, charming. He told me, as Clive had warned, that Noel Murphy, the Irish member of the main committee, had been very iffy because he was worried it would become the Alastair Campbell roadshow. I said people knew what baggage I carried, not least me, but I was confident I could do a good job for them as a consultant. There was no need for me formally to be part of the management team. He said he wanted me to work with the existing people, which I said was fine, but I still felt we needed one more person from the HMG side of things, hopefully seconded. He seemed to buy into Clive's line that the whole thing needed to be on a more professional footing. He was up for a basic fee of £30k and ten say for Martin or Ben. The money wasn't really the thing, and I would probably make more than that in speeches. What was interesting was seeing whether actually this comms stuff could be taken into that world and make any sort of difference. I liked him. He was clearly growing used to Clive wanting to do things differently, but I did not sense he was hostile. Clive was a proven winner and if he came up with new ideas it was important to listen to them. Also, rugby was constantly talking about getting to new levels in terms of public support and maybe I could help with new ideas on that too.

TBWA dinner at which I was speaking to some of their key clients. Sitting opposite Stephen Marks [founder of French Connection], who struck me as a total twat, one of those 'Why do we need politicians anyway?' kind of people. Also some guy from Weetabix who was total Tory and quite irritating, throw in the boss of Dixons and it felt a bit like an away game. I wasn't on great form but the TBWA guys seemed OK with it. Generally though, I was worried I was drifting.

Friday 12 November

Worked on the diaries for a while then set off for Hull. Crap journey sitting next to a woman who just never stopped talking, no matter how strong the signals. It wasn't that what she said was terrible, just that it was like several hours of small talk. I felt exhausted by the time I got there. I was met by Alan Johnson [new Work and Pensions Secretary] and his assistant Sally Waters. We had a cup of tea at the Holiday Inn. He was asking me whether I thought the TB–GB relationship really was creating nothing but tension, or whether there was still some good, some creativity, in there. I said there certainly used to be at least some positive read-across from the tensions between them, but I thought we had gone beyond that and everyone spent far too much time thinking about it and how to deal with it.

Coincidentally, Steve [Loraine] was at the same hotel as he was doing a big project advising Hull Council, so I had a session with him before heading off to the fundraiser for Alan at Hull City's ground. Impressive new stadium. Adam Pearson, the young chief exec, was lobbying re the government holding firm on allowing more casinos. As party fundraisers go, it was one of the best. Well organised, made painless by Alan and Sally, nice mood. Alan took me round the tables and we chatted away and I got a sense of why he was so popular up there. He had a lovely manner and I think together we were a pretty good double act. The speech went fine, ditto the Q&A. I also did the auction and Alan seemed to think that it raised enough money for his entire campaign.

Saturday 13 November

Breakfast with Steve. [Lord] Robert Armstrong [former Cabinet Secretary] and his wife were there, having been up for some function. I had a little chat with them and he was keen to know whether I preferred life out or in. I said both. I got a lift over to Burnley, and met up with Stan Ternent and Kath. He was still very angry about the way the club had treated him, said he couldn't stand watching what was going on there now. It must be so weird to have your whole existence determined by one club, and still be part of that area but now, with home games on Saturday, he was just busy tending his trees. The match was poor (0–0) and I was amazed how much Steve Cotterill [new manager] swore on the touchline. I was picked up at the end by Mark Taylor [Keighley CLP] and driven over to Haworth. I was doing a fundraiser for Ann Cryer [Keighley MP]. As last night, seemed to go OK. John Bailey [primary school friend] was there and bizarrely, I realised it was him as soon as he spoke, though I had not seen him for decades. I sensed the mood was OK but people were quite down on TB, largely because of Bush. The do was at Steeton Hall Hotel and it was nice going round so many of the places I grew up with. No real tough questions in the Q&A – Bush, press, Iraq, how to deal with the BNP, and all the 'any regrets' type questions.

Sunday 14 November
I went out for a long run on Haworth Moor. Freezing but absolutely beautiful. Boris Johnson was all over the papers, having finally been sacked.* I got a lift up to Newcastle, picked up Rory on the way and headed to St James's Park. I was waiting for Alex [Ferguson] when Graeme Souness [Newcastle manager] came over and said, 'What are you doing here, you're a Burnley man?' I said you're a Blackburn man, but we had a little chat. Went up to the lounge for a bite to eat with Alex and met Sammy Lee [former footballer, now coach]. He said the press were still into me because they knew I was still a player. They'll always be into you, he said, because they know leaders will always be needing you. On the train back, I was being lobbied ferociously by United fans about standing, and the need to bring it back to the terraces. Good laugh on the train. I felt Alex had looked a bit tired.

Monday 15 November
I was working on July '97 diary, mainly Northern Ireland, fuelling the sense that there was no real credit for TB and Bertie for the scale of the achievement. Recalling those meetings, what a fucking achievement

---

* Despite dismissing them as 'an inverted pyramid of piffle', and assuring Michael Howard that they were untrue, lurid claims about his extramarital love life resulted in Johnson being relieved of his roles as arts spokesman and party vice-chairman.

to have got from there to here. I ran in for a strategy meeting at 1 p.m. As I was running in, TB's convoy drove past me on its way to a meeting with party staff. He got back and we met in the Cabinet room, the usual lot plus Alan. TB seemed tired and disengaged, and lacking in confidence. When Philip said that we must get GB more engaged and that we were unable to get figures done and JP was having to chair meetings of special advisors to get anything done, TB looked pained. His tie went over his mouth.

The purpose of the meeting was to agree to the new campaign stuff in my note and he had said yes on the phone but was now back to worrying whether it looked like running away. I said we had to understand it required a new mindset. It was not about what the papers thought. It was about how we reach the public directly. When Alan said we had to take more risks, learn something from the fact JP's punch was the only thing people could remember from the last election, he said, 'Ah, back to the masochism strategy.' No. He did not want the Cabinet briefed yet that we would be making all these changes but when Alan said we were intending to do a briefing after Cabinet on Thursday, he said no, I don't think we should brief. Alan said that was all in Alastair's note and he said OK then. He was not in great shape though and at the end of the meeting he asked me to go through with him. He said 'God it's pretty hellish at the moment.' Iraq was just there the whole time, difficult and he feared it would get worse. GB was a nightmare. We were getting no credit for the good things we'd done. I said he had to get his head above it, practise what we preached. He said I should get as involved as possible. He was looking a bit vulnerable and lonely and I felt bad that I was not going to be in a position to help that much in the short term. He said Bush asked for me and asked if I was staying on message.

I still didn't feel like going back full time. I was still in need of a lot of sleep and struggling with the depression and also wanting to be at home, even though things were hard at the moment. I had finally caved in on Grace's demand for a dog, as the boys predicted I would, and when I got home I set off with her for Bristol to meet Fiona, who had gone ahead, and collect the puppy. On the train as yesterday it was noticeable how people were staring at me, not in an unfriendly way but it was annoying. I could not quite understand why I seemed to be recognised more than when I was there and in the press and media the whole time. On the train down Grace was very sweet and on the way back of course ecstatic. The boys less so when we got home.

Tuesday 16 November

I left fairly early for Old Queen Street, bumped into Sally on the way who said TB was still pretty down. The meeting chaired by Alan was not good, as yesterday's with TB had not been good. This is what happens when leadership goes weak at the top. It works its way down. There was a lack of ambition and direction in OQS. E.g. when Sally Dobson said she didn't think we could get ten Cabinet ministers to do a launch. Matt Carter was quite defensive and rightly obsessed with budgets. Compared with the agency meeting the other day, yesterday and today left me deflated so when Alan called later saying he didn't think he had ducks in a row necessary to do the post-Cabinet launch on Thursday as planned, I was pissed off. He said he had seen TB and told him very clearly that he had to get more engaged. He just wasn't at the moment. It was Iraq and GB combining to get him down. PG and Jo Gibbons were still keen on going for tomorrow. Alan didn't know that the British hostage had been killed and when I told him that, it was the final straw. He really didn't think it was the right thing to do.

I left there to meet Margaret McDonagh and discuss her and [media entrepreneur] Waheed Alli's impending visit to Iraq. I was not sure how much help I was but I felt [Ali] Allawi needed to build a message around the theme of security in all its guises and accept systems to deliver it. She said Iraq was now a huge problem on the doorstep and she was not sure how to counter it. I ran the idea of conditional voting by her, the comparison with a marriage or friendship – no such thing as perfection but on balance etc. – and she said she would try that.

I did a half-hour interview at Al Jazeera, all the usual stuff, but OK. Steve Clark, who was setting up their English language service, asked me to present a programme. Not sure about it. Left there for a meeting at LRF where Douglas [Osborne, chief executive] and Cathy [Gilman] asked me to take on a job, as chairman of fundraising. He said he saw it basically as a door opening job. Of course it was impossible to say no though the prospect of yet another unpaid time consuming task left me not exactly jumping for joy. But they were good people and it would basically just mean being more proactive and staying in touch with Cathy. She said the triathlon had been a huge hit and we needed to look for more interesting opportunities like that. I left for home and loads of the boys' friends came round to see the puppy. Calum still very pissed off about it. I ran for half an hour. Anne Shevas [No. 10 press officer] said HMG could not fund secondments for PR for the Lions. I told John Feehan and Clive Woodward, who said he would press for the cash to pay for it if we wanted to continue with the idea of me taking a Ben or a Martin.

Wednesday 17 November

Alan M on first thing on whether to do or not to do the briefing tomorrow. PG called, still keen. Alan still opposed. I agreed with him he should do a press gallery lunch in two weeks and go for it then after Cabinet. Fiona took me to Euston and I worked on the speech on the train, met and did half an hour with Association of Colleges leadership, then half an hour with five principals, then speech. Young students were OK but I was worried they knew very little about politics or how to find out. The speech went fine, well in fact, helped by the briefing on [Michael] Tomlinson's working group [for secondary education reform] from Fiona. Q&A OK, chaired by Mike Brunson. Nice to see him and we had a warm, friendly chat. Home for England v Spain and the Spanish monkey chanting at Ashley Cole and Shaun Wright-Phillips [black players] and Wayne Rooney behaving like a twat [substituted after being booked and clashing with several Spain players].

Thursday 18 November

Alan had decided we were not in a position to do the briefing on 'new campaigning' because 'the ducks are still not in a row'. PG, Jo G and I all felt it was doable not least because of the *Guardian* poll showing us 8 points ahead, and the Tories really in a state. But the truth was if he didn't feel confident he was right not to do it. Also, the Cabinet discussion, it transpired, was awful and he felt vindicated. TB had not really pushed it. GB was agitating throughout and PG, who did a polling presentation, was challenged on his polling – which was upbeat and confident – by DB and JS, both being wound up the whole time by GB. Jo said it was the first time she had ever been to Cabinet; she was really excited about it, and it was dire. 'I couldn't believe it. There was no camaraderie, no respect, just awful.' She felt they were bad to TB, and GB was at it big style. She said at this rate we will be running the campaign with TB and Alan alone.

TB called me and said it had been pretty grim but we were used to it – the truth is we have to do everything, he said. Where Alan was right was in saying it was hard to project confidence when they didn't feel it. They were spineless a lot of them, and DB and JS were diddling.

Apparently JP barely spoke. TB was also having to deal with Chirac (who later kept the Queen waiting at Windsor), Iraq grim, Charles Clarke attacking Prince Charles over his views on education and the Parliament Act being used on hunting so that it would be banned before the election. Worst of all worlds for TB – authority defied and it would be more of a focus now. We had David Davies and Susan [wife] for dinner. Nice time chatting re Sven [Göran Eriksson, England team manager], Nancy [Dell'Olio, his girlfriend] etc. Lots of rolling eyes. DD thinking about doing a book. He really felt that the FA was not fit for purpose, but that it was incapable of the modernisation it needed, and felt it would never really change. He wanted out asap. He is clearly close to Sven, but I said he reminded me a bit of Chauncey Gardner [character in the film *Being There*]; he sometimes seems bemused to be there. Fiona doing Andrew Neil late show.

Friday 19 November
Read at Gospel Oak Primary, then to ITN for a news quiz meeting – they wanted me to take part in a charity news quiz thing with loads of the main media people. Then to a meeting with Louisa Cheetham re the Lions tour. Nice enough, though she was bound to feel I was treading on her toes, and I was not yet totally convinced I could provide added value without major change. Ran home.

Sunday 21 November
TB was starting to call more regularly, twice over the weekend and both times saying much the same thing. There had been a political Cabinet which had been grim, as both PG and Jo, and later Tessa, had told me. TB said David [Blunkett] was always sceptical on polling, and liked to give that sense even if it meant it looked like he was undermining what we were trying to do; he was also worried about his own position the whole time. Jack [Straw] just liked to give the impression he knew what was going on. Also he felt that PG did rather overcook things. He sounded totally resigned re GB. He could try to bring him on board and he would try but he did not hold out much hope. He said he had challenged him over his 'disgusting' relationship with Dacre. GB said it was important someone talked up the government to the *Mail*. TB said to GB, 'You don't talk up the government. You talk it down. You don't say what a good government this is, what a good PM I am, you say you

buy the *Mail* analysis. It's disgusting.' TB, as did Fraser when I spoke to him Monday, felt the party would judge harshly the lack of respect. TB really wanted me back in full time but I wasn't ready. He sounded a bit down. His only positive observation was that he felt Chirac had genuinely been trying to be helpful, he was more hopeful Iraq elections would go ahead, and he felt the press's impact was diminishing.

The Goulds came round to see Molly [the new puppy] and PG and I ended up going round in circles as ever. But both of us felt there was a fairly clear strategic path. Deal with crime, terror and asylum. Root optimistic message – Britain is working – in the economy. Work started to develop the forward offer for voters, positive reasons to give us another go. All of it contrasting with Tory record, pessimism and lack of forward agenda.

Monday 22 November
Went to King's Cross and on the train worked on a piece to trail the news quiz and analyse Andrew Marr, Adam Boulton and Nick Robinson [broadcast political editors]. The most interesting point was that they were neither friends nor enemies, that once we could not really see a life without each other, and now we could. I was heading to Stoke Rochford [near Grantham] for the party staff training day, working on case studies for the regional press officer seminar, and my after-dinner speech. I was also trying to sort Lions stuff re Ben and Martin. We were also in the endgame re the election broadcast, which I saw after arriving at Stoke Rochford. It was good, if not musically pacy enough, with a couple of good new endorsers, though Dickie Bird [cricket umpire] went on too long already and then insisted he had been cut and over-edited. The hall was owned by the NUT and a great place for a conference. On arrival I did a clip for a BBC profile of Alex on his thousandth game. Then saw PG and Fraser before going for a run, then back for the regional press seminar which was OK. At dinner with Alicia Kennedy, Matt Carter, Matthew Doyle, Fraser [Labour officials] et al. – good laugh and felt totally at home. I got a fantastic reception when Matt introduced me and was really touched. I did my usual stock of jokes and then a serious section re political strategy and then really tried to fire them up, including the great quote from Vince Lombardi [American football coach] about the finest hour for anyone being 'that moment when he has worked his heart out in a good cause and lies exhausted on the field of battle – victorious'.

It was nice to see Georgia [Gould] so in her element among the team of organisers. Fraser gave me a lift to Mum's and was saying he thought I should be election director of strategy, open, up front, and doing media. He came in to see Mum and had a cup of tea before heading back at midnight. Great bloke.

Tuesday 23 November

Mum was looking and sounding pretty good. Kate [niece] came up to see us. I was talking to *The Times* and writing the piece on political editors. Also preparing four speeches in coming days. Calum was ill so I came back early. On the train, opposite talking ever more loudly as the morning booze went down, were two sisters, one of whom was going on *GMTV* tomorrow to talk about being the only female demolition expert in the country, and a porn star, real name Helen, film name Alexis. She was regaling them with stories of her work. I got back, did a bit of work and then out to the motor trade dinner at the Hilton. The event was OK but over-ran. TB called during the dinner to say Man U had won and I should congratulate Alex for him. He felt the Queen's Speech had gone OK but it was ridiculous the way they presented the whole thing in terms solely of politics not the actual issues. He said he was really grateful I'd gone to the Stoke Rochford do. The speech went OK but after the jokes went down a storm one or two felt I got too political and I got one or two heckles when I really spoke up for TB. I also took on Evan Davis of the BBC [economics editor] because he looked sceptical but he told me afterwards he agreed with every word I said about media negativity and the culture of cynicism and he spoke out about it all the time. The top table all genuinely seemed to think it was a good speech and that I was right to lay into the media but one or two complained it was too political. Meanwhile PG and I had had to talk Alan M into doing a briefing on the PPB and make it a good antidote story to the security theme of the Queen's Speech. Alan was very loath to go and do briefings where there was risk or his ducks were not in a row.

Wednesday 24 November

PG called to say he still thought a PPB briefing was worth doing. The security message certainly got through from the Queen's Speech. I was doing the first day of my SoVA [Safeguarding of Vulnerable

Adults] mentoring training at the Hampstead Britannia hotel. I had been approached to ask if I would train as a mentor and make a film about the experience and of the TV offers so far it struck me as the most interesting. The TV people came to film me leaving the house then arriving at the young offenders' institution session in the basement, a bit dingy but OK. A woman called Clare was leading the session with a nicely dressed black woman Marcia, mum of two, psychology graduate. The other volunteers were Dean, Isha, Maria – all black – an American named Chris and a middle-aged woman called Edith. They were a nice bunch though Edith was a bit textbook intense. Boy's haircut, said she worked at Feltham. Talked of how she was a classic second child.

After introduction we went through ground rules for the discussion – confidentiality (a bit ironic with TV crews there), respect etc. In pairs – I was with Maria – we discussed what dreams and aspirations we had. I said mine were through the children – e.g. sporting success, personal fulfilment. And I said I wanted to be part of a third election win. We went through what we expected. What we hoped for. Using flip charts we went over reasons we thought led people to offend. Then what we thought mentors should do and be. Then the difference between mentor and friend, during which the whole issue of boundaries came out strongly. It was clear if we followed the rules – e.g. no family involvement, very structured, don't make them part of your life – it would make for dull TV in the eyes of the ITV people. Also I could see Edith didn't like the whole thing and suggested it was about me not the mentee or client as we were meant to call them. I felt the boundaries were over-restrictive.

I chatted to Clare over lunch and some of the budgetary and funding issues. Then, in different pairs, we went over case studies to analyse appropriate behaviour and then go over what we would do to empower or disempower in various circumstances – helping with CV, find a home, deal with debt and help with a troubled relationship. Interesting stuff but I still felt the restrictions were too tight. We ended the day by listing the potential benefits to the mentee. I went home and did an interview with Fiona Foster. I was a bit worried the TV people would overly present it as me wanting to do it rather than doing it like an ad for the charity. It was OK I think. Meanwhile Alan M was chasing me for more meetings. I worked on LRF speech for tomorrow and Scottish speeches for Friday. I had a really good run – 40 minutes with good tempo. Calum off school.

Thursday 25 November

I spent the first part of the morning working on '97 diary and after the kids left for school set off for mentoring training. I was still worrying about how to get the balance between good TV and meaningful mentoring. My worry was the TV people would present it as though I had woken up one day and decided to be a mentor. Rory made me laugh earlier on – and I passed it on – when he said, 'You're not going to embarrass yourself like Portillo' and then, 'Who do you think you are, Mother Teresa?' I was last to arrive and there were two others, a counsellor and psychiatrist named Rebecca and an Asian woman called Bav. We went through some of the legal issues to do with health and safety etc. We also had a long session on the difference between stereotyping, prejudice and discrimination and in groups produced a long list of all of them. We then worked towards case studies and role modelling after an interesting discussion on good and bad listening. I sensed one or two of the unmellow ones softening and by the end of the day, when everyone had to write down something about everyone else, I had a nicer set of testimonies than I'd seen since school.

The role modelling was interesting. First Isha and I, playing mentee and mentor, had to read a script in which the mentor was clearly a bad listener. Then I played a mentor opposite a difficult and stroppy mentee, with Maria, then vice versa with Dean. Then we worked through a particularly difficult case study and they warned us it was the kind of case we should expect. Claire and Marcia were nice, clearly compassionate and good at the job. Isha and I had a discussion about whether swearing was unchristian as part of yet another session on how to break down barriers of fear, mistrust, insecurity, language etc.

There was a great laugh when we worked on the difference between closed and open questions. I said closed was, 'Was that good?'' Open was, 'How was that for you?' Edith had mellowed a bit, Rebecca was a very cool addition. Chris appeared to be the most natural mentor judging by the judgement of the others. I was glad I'd done it and felt I'd learned something too re looking after the kids. Meanwhile in between times I was fixing a Blunkett interview with Five wetting themselves re whether we would do the current paternity issue etc.*

---

* *The News of the World* had revealed Blunkett's affair with Kimberly Quinn, publisher of *The Spectator*. The parentage of Mrs Quinn's first son was disputed, but DNA testing showed that Blunkett was the father.

I was also fixing to see Richard Curtis [screenwriter and director] and Emma Freud [broadcaster, Curtis's partner] re Make Poverty History [coalition of aid and development agencies working to raise awareness of global poverty].

I got home in time for a conference call on the new campaign briefing. PG said there was another bad poll for the Tories tomorrow and we agreed we needed to do it soon but make sure we had positive things to say and ensure it did not become a media whinge story. The meeting was at Old Queen Street and I was phoning in. Jo Gibbons chaired it well and yet as PG said later there was a lot of timidity around the place. I had another fundraising dinner, for LRF, but Cathy had organised it well so that I could just turn up, speak to Ian Robertson [rugby commentator], who was compering, a brief word with the Anthony Nolan Trust [charity] people and then in to do jokes plus John [Merritt] etc., lots of plugs for LRF, then home.

Friday 26 November
I was up at half six and off to the airport, where I bumped into first David Campbell from the [Ulster] Unionists, who said how well I looked and 'Are you rich yet?' And then Martin McGuinness, Gerry Adams and Gerry Kelly [Sinn Féin leaders]. They were all in good form and like David C said how much fitter and more relaxed I looked. They said they were pissed off at things but kept going. I said I'd read a story the other day re GA and MM laughing uproariously in a hotel over breakfast. Kelly said they start every day like that. Kelly spoke so rarely in meetings, and always looked so hard-faced, that it was almost disconcerting to have him smiling and joking. Gerry and Martin both said they hoped I was sticking with TB and continuing to help and support him. 'There is a long way to go,' said Adams. 'Tony will have his work cut out yet.' On the plane to Glasgow, amid a muddle over two O'Haras, one of whom was on the wrong flight, Rory Bremner tapped me on the shoulder and gave me a copy of his new book. We had a chat towards the end of the flight about Howard. He felt – and Paxman's recent profile was the latest evidence – that he had no chance. 'So you'll still have me as opposition.'

I was picked up in Scotland by a very nice driver, Leo Metzstein, who had been moved to Kilmarnock as a six-year-old German Jew to escape the Holocaust. He was telling me stories re his family tree and was a very nice bloke. I told him the last time I'd been to Hamilton was when I had the final collapse in my nervous breakdown in '86, little realising I was going back to the scene.* I'd always thought it was Hamilton council building but it was South Lanarkshire and though there had been a lot of rebuilding and refurbishment, and my mind had been scrambled at the time, I recognised the place as soon as we got there. 'Are you sure it's here?' I asked Leo. 'Well, this is what they gave me.' 'This is where I flipped my lid,' I said. I went in, and was met by council officials. I told them what had happened there, and said I would love to have a look around. They took me up to the chief executive's office. That was where I finally tipped over I think, when I had been phoning anyone whose number I could remember, to ask for help, and nobody replied – because I wasn't dialling 9 for an outside line and so was going straight to an unmanned switchboard on a Friday night. We walked down to the foyer where finally I was arrested. I think they were a little taken aback by how open I was about it all. I said what are the statistical probabilities of this? I felt fine but had some pretty powerful flashbacks.

I did the speech to eighty or so middle managers and it went fine, and the questions flowed OK. Leo then took me to the Bruce hotel in East Kilbride where I had tea with Adam Ingram [MP and Armed Forces Minister of State], his agent Michael McCann and a friend from Inverness. I had a nice run out of the town which was all a bit concrete and roundabouts and then through a country park. I got back for a meeting with Adam and two sets of party members who were really nice, up for it, wanting not to whinge but asking the best way to win arguments. The second group was more male and more political but they were nice good people up for the fight. They were pissed off at the PR for local government changes which would slash their control. The reception and dinner were good events. Nice chat with Helen Liddell [Labour MP about to become High Commissioner to Australia], who was taking her dad when she went to Australia and, expensively, her dog, who would have to get there via a series of short-hop flights. She was dead keen for us to go there.

We were piped in and when it came for me to speak, I was effusively introduced by Adam and got a terrific reception. The jokes started working slowly but they went well and by the time I got to the serious

* In 1986, AC, then working for *Today* newspaper, flew to Scotland to cover a visit by then opposition leader Neil Kinnock. He suffered a psychotic episode brought on by stress and alcohol, was arrested for his own safety and then hospitalised.

bit, using the device of what would John Smith have made of it all, I totally had them. I produced a Rangers shirt for auction at the end and got a great reception. I was struck at these fundraisers how many people urged me to stand for Parliament and even, in a few cases, to think about going for the leadership after a few years in the House. There were a couple of thirty-something blondes, said to be the daughters of a wealthy night club owner whose wealth sources were unclear, who were raving afterwards. Ditto the wife of the health minister Andy Kerr. It was the best of the recent ones I'd say and then Andy Cameron did the comedy and the auction which went fine. I eventually got to bed around 1. Earlier I had a bit of a text spat with PG. He said, 'When are you coming in for your two days a week?' I said 'when I stop having to go round the country unpaid fundraising because too few politicians are up to doing it.' He said we need you more here because there is so much timidity.

Saturday 27 November

Breakfast with [brother] Donald and then a lift to the airport for the delayed flight south. I worked on the Cardiff speech and a piece on TV debates. Just before leaving I got a call from Kamal Ahmed saying their [*Observer*] sports guy Denis Campbell had got the story re me working for the Lions. I didn't deny but insisted he make clear I was approached by Clive and that it was not replacing the existing team. I was keen for it not to go too big but as Stephen Jones [*Sunday Times*] had been one of the people pressing for a heavy hitter, I suggested to Louisa she tip him off. It all went fine. Meanwhile England lost to Australia and GB were thrashed by the Aussies in rugby league. I was tired after all the running around.

The big story about to break was Blunkett's ex-woman who had clearly gone to the *Sunday Telegraph* and a whole stack of new allegations were about to break around him. The most 'serious' was that he had intervened to fast-track her nanny's visa. Huw Evans [Blunkett special advisor] called a few times both to try to get me to talk to people and really push his line – namely a father trying to do what's right, public/private separate – and also for advice on how to handle. I felt he had to calm it down, because even if people felt he was in some way wronged, she was pregnant and the whole thing was just so messy and the more it looked like he was fuelling it the worse it would be for him.

Sunday 28 November

There was a fair bit of follow-up to the *Observer* piece on the Lions but it was all fairly straight. Huw called re Blunkett, which was leading the news all day. I emphasised the need for DB to be seen focusing on his public duties, and not get too drawn into the emotional brief and counter brief. I could see they had to hit back on specifics, but should not go too hard on the emotional side. Then as I was in the car I heard the headlines that DB had called for an independent inquiry into the nanny visa situation. I'm not sure that was needed but it emerged he himself had insisted. TB was standing right by him. He had his press conference tomorrow and I sent through a note, saying he should back him but also get above it and make clear he and DB are working on the things the public would want them to.

Monday 29 November

I was surprised how straight the reporting was on the Lions job, and how little snideness there was. CW thought it went fine, and I agreed with Louisa I should go on the little tour of the four nations with Clive next week. I ran in and saw the party press people for half an hour or so, promising to meet weekly and try to go over things from a strategic viewpoint and give them stuff that they could brief out more effectively. I had a meeting there with Richard Curtis, Emma Freud, Kevin Cahill of Comic Relief and Siobhan Hawthorne who wanted my advice on the Make Poverty History campaign. They did a little, and very effective, presentation. I said I thought what I could bring to them was political advice re the leaders and the G8 governments, how to operate as a pressure group on governments used to being pressured. Emma asked me to get very involved and I said I was happy to do that. They had seen the Bono interview and liked it.

I had lunch with Bradders and Steve Morris [Downing Street Europe advisor] and then to Milburn's meeting on election planning, without PG who was making his maiden speech in the Lords. We agreed to put the bulk of posters into marginals. We discussed security after the Peter Hain [Secretary of State for Wales] Welsh gala dinner 'riot' from hunt supporters.* There is no doubt there will be hunt demos stalking the campaign. Also how to keep 'Britain Is Working' going.

---

* Four police officers were injured and three people arrested after pro-hunting demonstrators protested outside a hotel in Cardiff where a Labour Party dinner was taking place.

Things were OK but we still needed to move up another gear. It was so hard to get motoring though with GB in paralysis mode, and the Tories considered totally hopeless. I ran home and did a bit of work before going to football with the boys at the school.

Tuesday 30 November

I worked on diary '97 – Diana's death. Incredible week. I had a meeting with the ITV quiz people and went to the school Ofsted parents meeting but otherwise a quiet day. Doing the diaries was so tedious. Why the hell hadn't I typed them at the time? It would have been quicker, easier and I would not now have this ballsaching task. Even when it was fascinating, as with the Diana stuff, a lot of which I had forgotten, there were just so many words, and it was all so slow, and I have no idea what I will do with it anyway.

Wednesday 1 December

The Times presented my piece on the charity news quiz really well. I was working away on the diaries and also planning ahead for the speeches to come, and placing a few calls for the Make Poverty History campaign. I went in late pm for a rehearsal at a club in town for the charity quiz. Edwina Currie [former Tory minister] was there and pretty eccentric. She made it clear she would be pushing her own agenda and making the scores up as she went along. We went through the scripts which were better but we had a fair few technical problems, e.g. the buzzers didn't work and I was worried the drink and smoke would be a problem. The team started to arrive and some of them were pretty nervous. Anji told me Adam Boulton had been revising and swotting for days.

The crowd was pretty raucous but I just about got them under control. The women did OK, especially Julie Etchingham [Sky News presenter] on US elections and Fiona Bruce [BBC] – who was very competitive – on everyday life. Edwina's scoring was so eccentric that she didn't really keep track at all and for the political editors' round, God knows who won. But it seemed to zip along OK and lots of people afterwards said they would want to televise it next year, though I'm not sure the contestants would want it. Afterwards there were loads of the younger TV women wanting pictures and autographs etc. and one – I think an ITV news channel presenter – incredibly forward. It was nice to see Jeremy Thompson [Sky presenter], who was very relaxed about it all,

Mark Austin [ITN presenter], who said he was just wanting to be at home and seeing his kids grow up.

I had a nice chat with Fiona Bruce about the time I cried in Sedgefield on election night '97. She said she was really emotional that night too, that it had felt really special. There was a very intense BBC editor who wanted to talk about the election. But these people did not really get their own role in turning people off. The DB stuff was now in total frenzy mode. If only they gave a tenth as much coverage to the policy stuff and to delivery, the public might not be so cynical.

Thursday 2 December

I went for a long run with Jon Sopel who was amazed at how badly the political editors had done last night. I caught a train early afternoon, having finished the speech at home. The first-class compartment was heaving and I sat next to a woman who worked for HBOS, who was showing me the way 'spin' was used in company reports etc. I got there and was driven to Cardiff University Business School, and to Dean Roger Mansfield's really smoky office. I did a Welsh TV interview, then to the reception where I mainly talked to Ian Hargreaves [academic and former editor]. I was spared all the mingling and then through to the lecture theatre. It was more or less packed out and though they were 25 per cent media students, I felt it went down really well. If only we had a few more politicians making this case, the public was ready to hear it. The speech carried messages re devolution but the main thing was the impact the national media was having on politics and it went down well. The guy who gave the vote of thanks told of a PR exam paper which started with Question 1: To what extent did Hitler use PR and communications skills in his rise to power? And 2: What is the significance of Alastair Campbell? Funny. I did a fair few jokes, then on to the main message and they seemed to like it.

At dinner I was next to a woman – Sylvia Sheridan – who had built up a company which specialised in subtitling for the deaf, and wanted to make a large donation to the party. I had a very nice chat with her about all sorts of things. She was really grilling me on my breakdown, which was still front of mind after the trip to Scotland. She was a friend of Revel Barker [former *Sunday Mirror* colleague] and got me to sign the programme for him. I then got changed and was driven to Bristol ready for tomorrow's business breakfast. GB's PBR [Pre-Budget Report] seemed to go fine. I had missed the speech but caught lots on the late news and it seemed OK, though it was still more about childcare than the economy. He had at least seemed to have avoided the worst of the TB–GB excesses of the build-up, though TB said it had not been easy getting everything agreed and properly pinned down.

Friday 3 December

I used my basic script on why business should prepare for a Labour third term, for 135 businessmen at the launch of the *Western Daily Press* business guide. It went down pretty well and in the Q&A I felt under very little pressure. Hunting was clearly a problem and there was anti-Europeanism there too, but no basic challenge to our economic and strategic pitch. If the Tories were recovering fully, this should have been the kind of audience totally up for them, and they weren't. If anything I felt quite a few were asking for reasons to vote for us. After a swim I was picked up by the Labour regional staff and taken to Southville and a meeting with seventy or so members. I did something similar to the East Kilbride speech plus tried out again the 'dating agency' approach on Iraq – make the analogy between people in personal relationships not expecting perfection so why so in political relationships? – and it seemed to go down well.

Greg Cook [Labour pollster] was there, having done some groups in Gloucester last night, where he said there was real ignorance about the Queen's Speech and the economy, and huge knowledge re the DB soap, where they felt broadly sympathetic. I didn't know whether it was a fault of the media or the public that the serious stuff did not break through in the way the personal and often trivial did. I was asked about it and said sure there were questions but it had gone from story to frenzy, as if there was nothing else happening in the world. But the mood was good and I was now just trying to inject some fight into activists. On leaving I was surprised to see a van load of stand-by cops waiting for trouble but I guess after the last visit to Bristol it was sensible enough.

Saturday 4 December

I was liaising with Louisa W about an announcement on my Lions role tomorrow, so that it was out before we did the little mini tour with Clive on Monday. With the PBR out of the way, the media agenda was swinging back to DB, with stuff spilling out all day and no doubt the Sundays set to be pretty grim. I called John Holmes [former No. 10 foreign affairs advisor, now with UN] about the Make Poverty History campaign, and later Peter Torry [UK Ambassador to Germany], and got them both on the page for it. David and Louise [Miliband] came round for dinner to celebrate their news that they were finally about to adopt a baby, out in Kansas on 8 December. They were mega happy but re politics, DM felt we were heading for a total conflagration post-election. He felt GB was just going to move in for the kill, whatever TB did to handle him. Tim Allan had a very good piece on Paxman's profile of Howard, and the need for politicians to fight back against the media priesthood.

Sunday 5 December
PG had called me for help on some patriotic lines I was working on, and also to agree when and if we could do the Leapfrogged poster. TB called twice during the day, said he was amazed at Dacre's capacity for evil. Not just the DB stuff today but Anji done over re cannabis,* and the occasional comparison between him [TB] and Hitler. He said DB was strong because he knew he was getting strong support. The problem was the frenzy was just drowning out everything else. He was also alarmed how few of our people seemed able to put up a proper fight for a case. He said in Scotland on Friday he really pushed back on the Black Watch decisions† and it was clear they had not heard the case properly. He said GB had been worse than ever in the run up to the PBR. He [GB] told him last week that once the election was over, he was just going to go for him [TB] and try to get him out. He asked me to think about how he handled it. His instincts said, as always, he should try to bring him in. Indeed he had offered him the chance to do everything he did last time round, but GB said he would only do it if Alan Milburn was sacked. TB said he was thinking that it might be better to win without him, to get his own legacy rather than one that GB claimed as his. He said we all had to listen to this guff that GB won the two elections and maybe there was a case for TB going for it alone. He felt fairly confident we were on for another big majority or so and all the better, you might think, if he did it without GB. DM

* A businessman former friend had alleged that he had smoked the illegal drug with Tony Blair's political assistant.
† Blair decided to modify plans to merge Scottish regiments, including the Black Watch, in a reorganisation of the army.

yesterday was convinced GB was unmoveable and was going to get his way. TB felt a lot could happen. He was confident that the third term could be liberating, but especially if it was seen very much as his victory. GB had made it clear as far as he was concerned, the succession battle began the day the election was over.

Bill Beaumont returned my call of yesterday and was very nice about things but did say there were some senior people who were sceptical about my presence on the tour. He said I should work closely to him and Clive and go softly softly and win them over. He said rugby was conservative large and small c and though some of the people he spoke to were enthusiastic, others were not. It was up to me to show I could bring added value. He said he was looking forward to advice on how they build bridges with the community out there, and the travelling fans, and also what he could do to show that he and Clive were working together. He said what people out there would do would be try to catch me out on rugby and I was best to admit I was primarily a football man, but I could hopefully bring my expertise to bear on a very different situation. I was also finalising the press statement and Q&A which was delayed because Louisa had not cleared it with John Feehan. Half in jest, I said I never used to clear statements with my last boss, unless they were really important.

Monday 6 December

The DB saga was still not abating but at least it wasn't leading the news. I went for a short run before heading into Old Queen Street and lost it a bit with PG because I was hanging around for half an hour waiting for the agency people to arrive. He rightly said things didn't revolve around me but I was pissed off to have juggled things and then just hang around. The meeting itself was to go over the upcoming poster campaign. They had done the Leapfrogged poster on the Union Jack to get over the point that we had overtaken France in the world economic league. For once I was on the unbold end of the market, unconvinced we would get so much out of it against the potential diplomatic row. The 'frog' reference just seemed a bit silly, and risky without any real guarantee we would get much out of it. The agency said recent groups were really grim, Labour switchers feeling let down and only planning to vote on the basis of who they hate less. TB had made the point yesterday that we lacked people who could go up and fight and put over a big argument in a difficult or challenging environment.

December '04: Risking upsetting the French with silly poster

Also at the meeting I did with the party press people I sensed they were a bit down and undirected. Matthew [Doyle] said they didn't really get the big picture. I volunteered to start doing regular strategic notes but was conscious of possibly treading on DH's toes. It was ridiculous that we were in such a strong position and yet people were feeling down the whole time. They had to get lift but there was so little inspiration out there.

I left for the airport, first met Louisa who was on an earlier flight [to Edinburgh] and then Clive. It was interesting how few people clocked him. Given how high-profile he had been that was a bit of a surprise. Also he had quite a self-effacing manner, always offering to carry things, pay for things etc. He was quite nervy in lots of ways, very confident in others. I had done him a note on what to say at the start of the three briefings we were doing – unity through strength being the main thing, the need to be the best prepared tour ever and pace of change in the game. He was quite intense. He was taking loads of calls from Rupert Lowe [Southampton FC chairman], who was about to announce Harry Redknapp as manager tomorrow. He was scathing about preparation and attention to detail in football and at the way players and agents had taken up so much of the cash out of the game.

We chatted about the media on the way up and the need to create more space around the team and the coaches. I was keen to show strategic communications could apply to sport and gave him the three main message lines to hit. He was clearly keen to do it and desperate to do things differently to how they had been done before. He felt that traditional sport PR was limited and he clearly felt the game's old fart tendencies were still fairly strong. He had folders on the Scottish players and was trying to memorise a few names beyond the handful he thought had a chance of being selected.

He had spoken yesterday to Jonny Wilkinson and was worried that he knew in himself he had maybe been doing too much of the extra curricular stuff and that was why he kept giving interviews saying he was obsessed with rugby. That being said, he said he 'truly is obsessed'. He said I would love working with Jonny, if he made the tour, because he is a total perfectionist, his own biggest critic, and would be hurting that he had not been as strong since winning the World Cup last year. Clive also felt he was not being brilliantly managed, was taking on commitments ad hoc rather than strategically. He went over the recent troubles when someone falsely put round a tip he [CW] was involved in a relationship he should not have been and had all the tabloids chasing him. It was noteworthy that he thought and talked about the press as much as, if not more, than the politicians. He was not sure why he was doing this little briefing tour and as soon as we arrived – a bit late – at Murrayfield, Louise gave a very downbeat assessment of where the Scottish media were – cynical like the political hacks – and Ian McGeechan [coach] was very down, said his role with the Lions had gone down like a lead balloon.

Bill Beaumont had come up from Lancashire and was OK re things but I sensed a bit of tension with CW at times. Bill was a good committee man, whereas Clive was very much an individualist. CW was OK but it was a bit bitty and I did him a note later saying there was no clear message or story, and he tended to be a bit commentator rather than leader. I was pretty frank about what was good and what was bad and he took it all fine, and agreed to do opening remarks tomorrow and lay down those themes right at the start. There were maybe a dozen or so reporters and a handful of snappers who were split between pictures of the top table and me at the back. It was OK as an event but felt a bit old-fashioned. I had a chat with Peter Jackson [*Daily Mail*] and Mick Cleary [*Daily Telegraph*] and one or two of the Jocks afterwards. As to whether it was my scene, it was hard to know yet. Louisa was very chatty and open but I sensed she was not totally over the moon at me being involved. Equally I was not sure whether I really could make a big difference though CW was in no doubt and said he had never had feedback like that about how to do things better. So my note pointed up a few things he could do differently. Chief among them was the promotion of key messages, but he did at least give a lot of yes, no answers. We headed off to the airport taking the mick out of Louisa's huge bags carrying a portable backdrop of the Lions' logo.

In the car to the airport I went over the need for some kind of bigger context in every answer as a means of rooting answers and showing that there was a bigger picture only he could communicate. We had a drink at the airport, where he was on the phone to Rupert Lowe again, and were then crammed in at the back of the plane. I was trying to define new ways of doing things when they were out there but Louisa, with some justification, was emphasising that the hacks were spending lots of money to get out to New Zealand and would need fairly traditional access e.g. press conferences pretty much the staple diet. It was reasonably interesting to be seeing inside a new world, and CW was very open about it all, but I'd be lying if I said it got the juices going in the same way as politics. We got to the hotel in Dublin around half eleven and had a snack in the bar. The barman reminded CW of the time they stayed there before losing a match against Ireland.

Tuesday 7 December

I went for a run over the golf course in the dark and then down for breakfast with CW and Eddie O'Sullivan [Irish coach]. Yesterday seemed to go OK and today was better, first because CW was doing the big message stuff but also because he was facing a far friendlier press corps. They were a reflection of the political press, the Scots a bit jaded and cynical, the Irish sharp but basically hoping things worked out OK. CW was a lot sharper and hitting key messages, especially re this being the best prepared tour ever, sufficient for that to be the first questions in the one-on-ones. Eddie O'S was a nice bloke, fairly quiet but tough minded. CW said the Irish had the best set-up because they could control appearances and manage injuries from the centre. I texted Brian O'Driscoll to say I was looking forward to working with him and got a nice reply. I mentioned to John Feehan an offer from the Irish government to provide a press officer and he was happy either way, provided that Louisa was happy. We had a chat about how to match media demand to the desire of CW not to have to devote too much time to it, and the need to rest the players. He and I were keen to think outside the box a bit and do stuff that was new and innovative. Louisa felt the press would expect things to be press conference-based.

I wondered e.g. about releasing some of the video analysis, press pools in the medical room, platform Q&A, maybe a daily video diary or morning interview that was syndicated out. We chatted away on the way to the airport and then hung around for a while pre-flight. I was thinking how in government days there never seemed to be a moment to stop. On the flight I read a copy of *Rugby World* and was amazed at the extent of marketing and merchandising. It was a pretty professional product. We landed at Bristol and were then driven to a very nice place, Lakewood, where the English and Welsh press had gathered. I met Andy Robinson [coach] and we waxed lyrical about the view and he said he could never leave Bath. His ears were something else. Gareth Jenkins, the coach from Wales, was also a nice bloke and confided to me in the loo that he was a lifelong socialist. 'You won't be meeting too many of those!' he said. The coaches were all welcoming. Louisa was fine considering she was bound to feel a bit undermined and by and large the press were OK. CW was OK in questioning, though he seemed to have cocked up in going into too much detail on the process for agreeing to who refereed. I did a round of one-on-ones and they seemed fine – all asking how it came about, what I thought I could achieve, similarities and differences with politics, and between TB and CW.

Louise Ramsey, tour manager, who had been built up to me by just about everyone, was there and afterwards the four of us plus John Feehan met to go over some of the issues. CW wanted to do things in new and interesting ways and John and Louisa were a bit on the conservative end. We agreed Clive and Louise would agree what they needed by way of space and time and what we had actually happening and then we could overlay a media plan. A woman at the conference centre was a big fan having been at the Bristol Q&A, and another big Labour supporter. I said to Gareth [Jenkins] one of the best signals I was picking up at the moment was going into non-Labour areas and having loads of them tell me they were 'the only real Labour man/woman here'.

Wednesday 8 December

I went in for a meeting with PG etc. plus the ad agency re New Year plans which started late and I got really bad tempered. The stuff for the New Year was fine but the poster launch would require a big hitter, preferably GB, and he was pretty disengaged. The agency guys said the groups were dreadful, really just 'Who do you hate least?' I had lunch with Jamie Rubin, who was scathing about John Kerry. No charm. No inspiring of loyalty. Didn't motivate his own people. He said they were worried at one point that while they understood why TB had to stay out, we actually wanted Bush to win. I said I just railed at the PC view that said he was a moron and you couldn't say anything good about him or anything bad about Kerry. I thought Kerry was a hopeless campaigner. Jamie was also scathing re Bob Shrum [US political advisor who advised GB], said he was just not a strategist. Cristiane [Amanpour] really good re me and what I should do. Jamie said he had just two speeches in his diary. He was doing *Hardtalk* [BBC news programme] as a stand-in and they might want him to go full time. He was also keen we try to think of some project to do together. In the evening I did a fundraiser for Mitcham and Morden CLP. Really good mood. Qs quite tough but good event.

Thursday 9 December

Old Queen Street at 12 for a brainstorm on the Tories. Met Fraser Kemp first who was pretty down about the state of the operation. There was a good presentation from a podgy looking Shaun Woodward [Tory defector MP]. Having been a Tory for so long, and plugged into their ways of working and thinking, he still had a good feel for where they would be. He went through his paper on them, which was pretty good. They were going to depress the vote, not worry whether they could win, just create noise re us not related to policy agenda. Tax. Trust. TB. I worked up a couple of notes on a plan for dealing with the Tory strategy, plus a draft of TB's New Year message. Meetings were a bit directionless and I was not sufficiently on top of the detail of everything to grip it all. It was all a bit groundhoggish. I was really feeling the pressure to be more involved but not really wanting to be. Ran home.

Friday 10 December

I had lunch with Danny Finkelstein [*Times* journalist]. He said GB was really working *The Times* but they were developing the view that he was basically at it, in an undermining TB kind of way, which ultimately went down badly. They also knew he was giving them a very different message to the one he gave to *The Guardian* or the *Mirror*. He felt TB ought to be 'more Blairite', that he was not really being himself at the moment. He was quizzing re TV debates, which I still felt were unlikely to happen. We probably spent as much time talking about football as politics. He was big into data. I had a long chat with Alan M re GB. It was clearly getting to him a bit that GB was in the position of being outside, but he knew that he could come in any time and would create chaos. I said there was a danger he would just have Gordon inside his head all the time, and it stopped you thinking the right thoughts. Ignore it. Do what you need to do. He felt TB was veering towards getting GB back in properly. He may well be, I said, and in a way we had to go with what he wanted but in the meantime AM should try to branch out a bit and get things going on the planning front.

TB had always wanted a world in which all his key people got on and even though it had rarely happened, he always seemed to live in hope that it could yet do so. I could tell he was feeling a bit vulnerable, like was being set up, just there as an interim. I didn't hide the fact TB would like GB back on board if he could make it happen. Alan said he underestimates just how much of GB's mind goes on trying to do him in. He had seen it when he was at the Treasury and he did not for one second think he had changed. If anything he was worse, because GB would see every day TB stayed in the job as a day too long, and a personal slight.

Saturday 11 December

Took Rory to Stowe private school where he was doing a cross-country race. Really brought out the class war in me. Unbelievable facilities. He ran OK, and came 13th. We went to Tessa's. She was seething about comments Blunkett had made to Stephen Pollard [journalist and author] for his book on Blunkett. She said she was not going to do any more briefing on his behalf. It was not going to help David. Dinner ended with a row over Iraq – me and Tessa v David and Fiona, usual old stuff, and it got a bit angry. David had had a few and was not holding back, catastrophic disaster, bullied by the Americans, no understanding of history and the region. Then on to public services and it was just as bad, with Fiona leading the charge. Tessa going on re new politics and lack of strategic narrative. She asked if I would go back. No.

Monday 13 December

Went to see Alex before the Fulham match. The dressing rooms were under the Cottage in the corner of the ground, and he came out to give us the tickets, and then just hung around. He said there was not much space in the away dressing room, and he had no need to be in there. He was incredibly relaxed and feeling pretty good about stuff, though he said it was getting harder and harder to keep on top of the players. Too many of them had too much stuff going on outside. I told him I was feeling pretty torn about being sucked ever more into the election planning, and he said he knew himself how hard it was to get people alongside you that you trusted totally and felt added something, so he understood why TB was pushing, and I ought to do it. 'It's just a few months and then you're out again.' Rory chipped in 'You know you're not going to say no when push comes to shove so you might as well get on with it.'

Alex was a bit sniffy about the Woodward approach, but that was partly because he didn't like rugby. Rory was with the fans, I went to the directors' box, where I had a chat with Sven [Göran Eriksson]. I liked him, but he was quite hard to penetrate at times. Martin

Edwards [former Man Utd chairman] was quizzing me about the election and what I thought would happen. I was always a bit wary because of his attempts to get Alex to tone down the political profile, which I assumed may have had a pro-Tory political angle to them. Des Lynam [broadcaster] was on good form, asking about Burnley more than Labour.

TB called just before the game started. He sounded a bit ratty and nervy. He said he really needed me engaged now. There was something missing badly and it had to be sorted. He felt the policy operation was getting stronger now but there were major dysfunctionalities elsewhere and we could not just blame GB for everything. It was true everything was a struggle with him, but he had to get other problems sorted. He sounded a bit down. He was really laying it on re how much he needed me back there. I told him I was very ambivalent, so don't count on me coming in as a saviour. Mmm, he said, in that way he has of saying he is listening when in fact he's not, and he is determined to get his way. I told him I was at the football, and he sounded irritated. I said the game was starting but I would speak to him tomorrow.

Tuesday 14 December
The Home Office were suddenly being difficult about the mentoring project because of confidentiality issues and I was livid it hadn't been sorted as ITV had claimed it had been fixed right from the start. I was beginning to think about pulling it and sensed there were people at the Home Office ready to cause trouble on it. I got a cab in and pre-recorded a Christmas interview with Adam Boulton in a freezing cold studio. It was OK until Iraq when I went into autopilot mode. I had a meeting with Nick Pollard [Sky News] who asked me to do a daily current affairs show early evening. He said I could have major control over content, minimum pay package 200 to 250k. Gave me a big spiel about how they were trying to keep developing and staying ahead of the BBC who were picking up against them. He didn't think Richard Littlejohn [right-wing commentator] worked because it was all his agenda and monotonous and he was keen for me to take on that slot, felt I could do more light and shade.

Another big project to think about which did not immediately fire me with enthusiasm. I was beginning to wonder if anything ever would. As I left, walking through the mini newsroom where all the journos were working away, I felt a bit of a heel, in that they worked their balls off for a lot less money, some of them would give their right arm to have their own show every night, as I might have done one day, but right now it just didn't get the juices flowing. There was another problem though: it would also become impossible to do something full on like this and be involved closely in the election.

I got home, did a bit of work and then went to meet Alex and Cathy to head to meet Mick Hucknall and his girlfriend Gabriela at their house out in Surrey. Cathy was giving AF gyp as we went, very funny and clearly the one able to keep his feet on the ground. She was ticking him off when he was complaining about anything, and also suggesting he needed to cut down on things that had nothing to do with his job. Mick had cooked some really nice food but she would only eat plain fish or chicken. Then he served her salmon and she said as he left the room it was the only fish she did not eat. Alex regaling us with stories of the players and their wealth, not just the basics but the huge deals they were doing outside, six- and seven-figure stuff to do next to nothing. It was getting harder to have control over their lives, and they were harder to mesh as a squad. He was always happier when talking re the old days particularly in Scotland. He filled us in on all the gangsterism around football in Liverpool. In one of the transfer deals the Adams family [north London gang] got involved.

Long chat re DB. I said it was vanity and vulnerability coming together lethally. Mick felt the blindness must be a factor. Alex was very down on GB. He felt he was too emotional, self-obsessed, only seeing things as they affected him. He wasn't sure it could go on for ever. Mick was very pro-TB still, felt he was way above any of the others, not just in UK politics, but most of the big figures around the world too. He felt he was a Prime Minister who made all generations feel good about being British. Most just manage to speak to one class or one or two generations. He seemed very struck on Gabriela who was nice, funny, and not afraid to put him in his place. He and Alex slightly veered to the wine snob category but it was a fun evening. We drove back and just nattered. Alex was doing a celebrity charity version of *Who Wants to Be a Millionaire?* with Eamonn Holmes [broadcaster], and was really up for it. Mick and I were both nominated as phone-a-friends. I was firing quiz questions at him for part of the journey, the rest of the time just the usual mix of soccer and politics. Mick had mentioned to Anji that we were going there, and he was working on me on TB's behalf too. Alex asked Fiona what she thought of me going back in full time. She said as long as it is only for the

December '04: Alex Ferguson down on GB

campaign, it's fine, but I don't think he would be happy getting drawn in afterwards.

Wednesday 15 December

DB had asked me to have lunch with him, but then his office called as I was leaving to meet him, to say something had come up and it was cancelled. Bad vibes. I then watched PMQs and he looked pretty wretched on the frontbench. Then I started to get calls asking if I knew he had resigned. All over what? Fast-tracking a visa for someone's nanny where someone had scribbled 'No favours but quicker' on the application and even though it clearly wasn't DB, and he had almost certainly not known about it, off he went. Really good minister and good man, career fucked over this. Bloody visas. Peter M. Bev Hughes.* Now David. Charles Clarke taking over. David Davies [FA] called re some weird things going on at the moment, e.g. Faria Alam, his PA, saying he sexually harassed her, Max Clifford was involved.† A woman had turned up asking him for money at a car door near his home. He wanted advice. I said do nothing and be prepared. He thought about telling police, having alerted them about the woman. It sounded pretty awful, but I sensed from his voice he was totally telling me the truth and there was some kind of set-up going on. With Sven also involved it would be massive news, and tricky to handle.

I did a bit more work then heard DB was definitely going so I switched on to the live news. It was all very sad, and he looked awful, absolutely wretched. I felt he should never have had an inquiry and he should not have resigned. But he had got too emotional and obsessive and now he was suffering. Crucially the political support eroded because of his comments about colleagues to Stephen Pollard for his book. Why on earth was he doing a book at this stage? Vanity. Why was he involved with that bloody woman? Vulnerability and loneliness. Why was he so determined re the child? The two coming together in obsession. I felt desperately sad for him and after a while people

---

* The Immigration Minister resigned after accusations that the Home Office had approved visa claims from Eastern Europe despite warnings that they were supported by forged documents.

† Alam had hired publicity agent Clifford, who brokered a deal with Sunday newspapers for her to tell of affairs with FA chief executive Mark Palios and Sven-Göran Eriksson. She made claims against the FA of sexual harassment, unfair dismissal and breach of contract, but all claims were rejected by an industrial tribunal.

would forget why he resigned as they had with others like Steve Byers. Nobody could remember why he went. I'm not sure I could, not in any detail, and I had been totally involved in dealing with it.*

I went to the TB 1994 staff reunion dinner. It was a nice enough event and we had a few good laughs but a fair few absentees. TB called me, said he was really sad for DB, a good man. I said I wasn't sure whether Home Secretary was right for Charles C. He said he knew Charles could be difficult but he was a big figure, the cops liked him and though David was terrific there is a case for doing it a bit differently, being less in your face the whole time. So he was happy with that while knowing the risks, e.g. CC did not really believe in campaigning in the way we did, and was not always a team player. He had been impressed with Ruth Kelly and was confident in her taking over from Charles at Education. DM had just taken delivery of his baby in Kansas and he was not keen on the move to replace Ruth as minister of state at the Cabinet Office. TB was having none of it, said these people just had to learn to get on with it, and David would be able to work on the manifesto. We agreed to meet for a long session tomorrow. The GB people were needless to say seeing it all as a whack at him.

Thursday 16 December

I went into No. 10, where the staff made a presentation of the things they had done for my farewell that had never happened because I had put it off several times. Some of them thought, I'm sure, that it was because I didn't really believe I was leaving. In fact it was also because I was looking for reasons not to be going in all the time. But I knew that I would be going back in a lot as the campaign neared, and it was a bit weird to think about having a big farewell bash in those circumstances. Added to which I am not sure Fiona would have gone. This was much lower key, mainly my own team, and some of the regulars from around the building who were always on trips etc. They had made a really nice book in which they had put all their little tributes and messages. I did a little speech saying how much I missed

---

* Transport Secretary Byers had come under attack when his political advisor, Jo Moore, sent an email suggesting the 11 September 2001 terrorist outrages in New York was 'a very good day to get out anything we want to bury'. In February 2002, there was a similar incident when the Department of Transport's head of news, Martin Sixsmith, appeared to warn Moore not to bury any more bad news. Both resigned, as did Byers the following year.

them and how proud I was of the team we built, and would be even prouder if they could carry on and do well without me.

I went round to see TB. He was obviously getting a bit tired of all my mithering and dithering, and was playing a bit harder ball. He said he knew I had reservations but the time had come to push them to one side. He said he wanted me more welded in to the campaign and the strategy. He wanted me at his key political meetings and he wanted me to oversee development and implementation of strategy. He said he was more confident of the policy agenda than ever and sure a third term agenda would be good. He felt Alan had made a difference but he had a bit of a confidence issue sometimes and he needed support. Alan was a bit spooked by GB. He said GB was worse than ever, basically on strike, constantly raising problems and saying all the strategy was crap, constantly feeding the media his lines and TB felt he still wanted to push him before an election but it was getting harder.

He had seen Robert Thomson, who said *The Times* would support a Blair policy agenda but not Brown. Yet GB worked them the whole time. He said when he saw Alan Rusbridger recently Alan had said trust was in part about how TB dealt with GB; in other words he had bought the line that TB promised to move over. TB said what GB never wanted anyone to know about was the other side of the deal – that he would hand over if GB worked with him, which he has never done, not properly, for ten years, and on which now there was no support at all.

TB said JP and Ian McCartney were totally fed up with GB; he had overplayed his hand with them. He had told the PLP the economy would be central but was now refusing to lead the economic campaign. He said the last strategy meeting was 'dreadful'. In fact 'I don't want to flatter it with the word strategy. It was awful.' At least Ian had got stuck in. Ian said to Gordon, 'All we were asking was for you to do what you told the PLP you would, namely run an economic campaign.' GB just brooded silently. I said to TB, 'You are not exactly making this an attractive proposition.' No, he replied, but 'I know you can help us sort it, and we have to, or else we are fucked, and the Tories are back.' Now he really was pressing the buttons. I said I was sorry, but I really did not want to come in full time, I did not want to be ground down by grind and I wanted to avoid the internecine stuff taking over my life again. He said what about a couple of days a week for the first part of the year and then full time for the campaign? I said that might be fine, but please don't pretend that is what you really mean. He laughed. 'OK, seven days a week, no time off.' No, he said, 'we can make it work, and it does not have to be all-consuming, but it is not a bad thing if GB, the Tories and the media think you are with us the whole time.' He said he had pretty much given up on GB helping. 'He has realised I am not going before the election, so his approach now is basically to wait for the majority to be cut, and go for me from day one.'

I told him I felt like I was living in different time zones at the moment, but with some constants. I was transcribing the diaries and some days back then we were having exactly the same kind of conversations as now. At the weekend for example I had come across an absolute belter of a row between the two of them over who was getting promoted, why not Douglas, Nigel Griffiths, Andrew Smith, all GB's people. And now here we were again, the papers full of Blair–Brownery because he dared to put David M in a central job. He asked – not for the first time – if the diaries were a disaster area for everyone. I said he came out OK, though we had our moments. At least he was broadly sane throughout. I am not sure the same can be said for me, GB, JP, Peter.

I said there might be a case for me doing part of them while he was still there, e.g. if there was a plan re GB. He said he would mull. All in all it was a good chat, I think we both knew where we were coming from and both wanted to make it work somehow. He said 'I know this can be a screaming pain in the ass, and you don't need it. But I do, I really do.' He had to leave to head to Brussels to see [Recep Tayyip] Erdoğan [Turkish Prime Minister]. But before he did he got Sally and Pat in and asked them to pin me down on times etc. He really wanted me to work up a strategy and then ensure it rolled out properly. I said fine but not full time.

I spoke to Sally and JR who were planning the political Cabinet for Monday when GB would be away 'taking his fight' on Africa to the States. They all talked about him all the time. I said it had to stop. They had to work out the campaign and do it with or without him but there was a danger they were going to be spooked into inertia. JR said with Cabinet signed up to an overall plan it would be far harder for GB to fuck around though he would. It was wasting so much energy. TB said earlier that GB would be worried about the reaction in the party and would feel he was running out of time. He was also giving TB an excuse. Later I spoke to AM re me. He rightly said we were both unresolved about what I did and how I did it and what we said about it. He said he was relaxed indeed happy for me to be up front and do media. He was planning to do the briefing on Monday. He said he was determined not to get spooked by GB but it was hard. He said it made a massive difference if PG and I were around and the more I could do the better. He also felt it was important I was paid something. Even if not what I could get doing other things, he thought it would send a signal that I was really in there.

Friday 17 December

Train to Leeds, working on a Burnley article and the speech to the Yorkshire Forward [regional development agency] event. As I came out of the station a very posh woman stopped me and said 'Is it fantastic being recognised all the time? I would absolutely love it.' Then she said, 'By the way I know more about your life than you do. I know absolutely everything. Good luck.' And off she went. Really weird, but she was quite funny, in a posh Northern kind of way. Leeds was looking good. We did not make nearly enough of the way our big regional cities had improved since '97. The Yorkshire Forward event was in a marquee opposite Elland Road Stadium and as it was running late, I just did the speech, no Q&A and got back for the 12.50 train. I was rushing back for the Lions management two-day meeting. I read all the Lions papers on the way back and though for a rugby person it must be the most fantastic thing imaginable, I could not stop thinking about seven weeks away from the kids and how it would affect them and me. I called PG who said he had spent a whole day persuading GB to get involved in the economic launch. 'He just says the same things repeatedly.' But PG said it was not sensible to play Alan's game which was just not engaging with GB, and allowing people to use him as an excuse. We had to bind him in and if he refused to do it properly, well, there we are.

I got to the Marriott at County Hall for the Lions' management meeting as they were halfway through the session following up [leadership consultant] Humphrey Walters's pre-work. He was a former round the world sailor who now worked with businesses and other organisations to build objectives, morale etc. Clive had used him with England before. We had all done the definition of our jobs, what irritated us and how we thought others could get the best out of us. I knew a few of them and slowly got to know the others, more northern and less middle-class than I expected, and with a good smattering of Rugby League people, like Phil Larder [defence coach]. I was best able to make a contribution when we thrashed out the seven rules of leadership, teamship and partnership. I was trying to explain strategic communications but also felt some of the leadership rules translated from politics. CW asked if we did this kind of exercise, assessing ourselves and each other's roles like this, in politics. I said only through the newspapers. People were not as open, honest and trusting as this because the pressures were so intense media wise. I found it useful and there were definitely things to pick up. I wished we had done this for the party at various points.

On the Friday evening we met in the bar, I chatted to Tony Biscombe [video analyst] re security and video analysis etc. Fiona came down for the social part, and we were all taken up on the London Eye – the last time Fiona was up there was with the kids and [Vladimir, President of Russia] Putin's kids. We were with Jayne [Woodward] who was really warm, effusive re me saying yes. I said I hope I can make a difference. You already have, she said. She said Clive had shown her the paper I had sent him on how a communications strategy works, and what one might look like for them and 'it was the kind of thing we have never seen in rugby'. Then with Andy Robinson and wife Sam, both really friendly, Dave 'Otis' Reddin [fitness coach], one of the five Daves on the trip, with a stunning girlfriend. Beautiful light, fantastic view from the Eye, good atmosphere, then we walked over to the House where one of the old messengers recognised me and took us for a little tour before the dinner that was being thrown for them. They loved it. Slightly embarrassing moment when my phone went off in the chamber.

Lots of them were asking me if I missed it all, and the truth was part of me did and part of me didn't. I didn't much miss the House of Commons food, but the mood at the dinner was really good. Tessa Jowell and Bill Beaumont made nice little speeches. Derek Wyatt [Labour MP] was good, on sport generally and the need for Lions to get involved in the London bid. I texted Seb about that. We strolled over to the hotel, back to the bar and I was chatting mainly with the physios, and Ian McGeechan who was really friendly. I was telling them stories about some of the people I had done for the *Times* series. As ever, Lance seemed to be the one they were more interested in.

Saturday 18 December

We spent the first session recapping from yesterday then putting the agreed rules together, first in small then large groups. There was a good mood to the whole thing and at times I got a real sense of how big this could be and how inspiring it could be and also how much difference maybe I could make after all, not just on the media and comms but on some of these leadership and management issues. I noticed CW asking my opinion on things that were not just media. I did the presentation on what we expected from the players and told the story of Dad and Keighley, when he stood in for the team doctor, despite being a vet. I went through the need for them to get a sense of history. Great Lions and All Blacks. The Scots physio, Stuart Barton, said he was in awe to be in the same operation as people like CW, Ian and me – and I don't think he was joking. The Scots were much quieter in general. Gareth the only Welshman in tow.

Sunday 19 December

I had a long chat with DB, who sounded really really down. He said he had never been so low in his life. It felt like a bereavement, and that same thing you get with a bereavement when life goes on all around you and you are having to cope with a new normality. He said the kids had been great. I said that was the starting point for his recovery. He had to rebuild out of family, Sheffield and politics – in that order, although as ever all mixed up – and then get a role in the campaign. There would be a lot of sympathy for him and there was still a lot of regard for his abilities. There was no need to engage re Budd Report, I said, but I could tell he was going to engage.* I said I had been through the experience of full on intense to something less so, and he needed to be careful. He should take a bit of time to reflect, but do not allow yourself to get dragged down to the depths.

GB did a note to TB re strategy, the usual capital letters and no real clear sense of what it was about. If you had to distil the strategy in a word or two, you'd be struggling. It was more a piece of positioning to defend his role last time in 2001, and to make out he was the one who delivered victory according to his strategy. It was self-serving rubbish, though there was something in the criticisms he made generally, about the lack of cohesion, the lack of energy and new ideas, though the irony appeared to be absent re any possible role he might be playing in all that. The problem was he had no solution and was, as TB said earlier in the week, basically working to rule, if not on strike. The note was all

* Sir Alan Budd had been asked to investigate the circumstances of the issue of a visa to the nanny of Kimberly Quinn, Blunkett's lover.

about how the campaign plan didn't work but it was based on some spurious themes. E.g. he didn't like the posters because they went on interest rates not inflation. TB did a detailed response and said he was dismayed if not surprised at what he had sent over, that he had asked GB to take central role but he did not want to co-operate. It was not really a strategy, it was an explanation that it wasn't his fault that we didn't have one. There was a tacit hint that if he didn't he would have to do it without him. For once he was preparing properly for a political Cabinet though it was a problem GB was not there, as he had gone to America 'taking his fight for the poor and destitute of the world'.

The *Sunday Times* and *Mail* had pieces about my role in the election and, worryingly, Simon Walters [*Mail on Sunday* political editor] had been briefed on my note about the changed nature of campaigning, though he did not seem to have the note itself. We had dinner with Gail and the kids, but without PG who was in with TB to go through polling in advance of tomorrow. TB had asked me to join them but I felt it was better if Philip gave it straight, and then agreed a plan about how we presented it. It was neither great nor terrible. There was definitely the makings of a decent win if we could get our act together. Big if the way things were. Gail and Fiona were both a bit jaded by it all. 'How many of our weekend dinners have either been hijacked or dominated by what essentially is just the story of Tony and Gordon?' Gail said.

Monday 20 December

I ran in first thing and met the party press team. They were OK, but a lack of adventure was a problem. I guess most of these guys had only really known working for us, and they felt it would always work the same way. But I was worried we were going to be fighting the campaign with techniques and methods that were already outdated. Patrick Loughran [special advisor] in attack was good and there were plenty there who were fine if led. It was the leadership that had been a bit missing, partly because of the dysfunctions elsewhere. I took them through what Alan would be saying, as the Cabinet was going on. Philip had given what he told me was a 'realistic but rosy' presentation. I said, 'How can it be both realistic and rosy?' 'When I present it,' he said, laughing. Alan said it had gone well and when he set out where we were in terms of campaign structures and planning, they seemed to take a bit of confidence. TB did a piece then on strategy to come, and apparently said I would be writing it, to which JR said, 'Thank God for that.' There were a few cracks re GB not being there when the last Cabinet pre an election year was meeting. But David Hanson [TB's PPS] pointed out how much better the atmosphere was when GB was not there. AM did his media briefing but he feared they did not really get what he was saying. I didn't think it mattered too much. What mattered was the party people knowing we were starting to motor as the New Year came.

Thursday 23 December

I worked on a piece for *The Times* about working for the Lions. I was keen to establish the principle I should write for them during the tour so it was as well to get started now, and the main message was the extent of their professionalism. Clive was keen for me to get out there and sell that message, but there were bound to be a few discordant voices in the media about me writing for one title. Fiona, Calum and Grace went to [family friend, QC peer who had been critical of New Labour] Helena Kennedy's but I was worried I would lose it with her after some of her recent votes and statement so Rory and I stayed at home. I was also going at a good rate in getting the '97 diary transcribed. Hard to imagine 2005 would have the same outcome, but the same problems were there, just in different form and at different stages.

Friday 24 December

Clive called re the Lions wristband, with the colours of the four countries woven in together. After my initial reservations I thought they were pretty good, not naff at all as shown by the fact the kids wanted one. He said he had done it totally off his own back and without John Feehan knowing, so he'd only done a limited number for players and management but if the Lions wanted to market it, fine. TB called, back from the Middle East. He said re Iraq that on the way in to Baghdad what was amazing was how much from the air it looked like an ordinary bustling city. They were talking about 50 per cent turnout plus in the election. Re Middle East, he was convinced that we had to get the Palestinian reform programme moving before it could get the whole process on track. Re political Cabinet [meeting], it was the best they had ever had, and it can be no coincidence that GB was not there. He said they were all making sensible contributions and for once he had prepared properly, as had AM and PG. I filled him in on the Lions sessions with Humphrey and we had a laugh about what it would be like if we had a Cabinet session on the same lines – all writing down and then saying what irritates you about the others? How do you get best out of self? etc. GB would make it impossible but a version of it might be worth doing.

Re the New Year message we agreed it had to be about facing the future with confidence and also injecting some politics to get up the idea of the election being a choice between us and them, him and Howard, not a referendum on whether we had a perfect government. PG was heading off to Jamaica for Christmas but he had done a very down-beat note in advance about where we wanted the consensus to fall for the electorate and I sent one back saying whatever the groups said, we had to get them to a more positive mindset, seeing that a third term was deserved for what we had done, and necessary because of the threat from the Tories to the changes we had made, which had to be taken forward.

Tuesday 28 December

Burnley v Wigan with the Channel 5 team. The Indian Ocean earth-quake and tsunami was overwhelming the news agenda. I recorded the track for the BFC film I was involved in.

Thursday 30 December

To the Kinnocks. NK the usual mix of merriment and suppressed anger and long stories. He had done an interview with Julia Langdon [political journalist] for *The Spectator* – God knows why. He said she had been pestering him. Glenys was angry he'd done it and thought he was lacking good advice and doing things for the sake of it. She was very nice about Peter M, thought he was doing well settling in and making a good impression (as EU Commissioner for Trade). Neil talked of the British Council as being particularly important because Britain was lacking in respect overseas because of TB, much as it used to be because of Thatcher. I couldn't be bothered engaging on it. There were only the six of us and PG chivvied him along while I was feeling very anti-social and wanting out of it. Fiona and I were not getting on great at the moment. Calum asked me earlier if we had ever thought of splitting up. I said we never used to row at all, for years and years, including when I was drinking and out of control. Then when we had kids we rowed a bit more, but I think it was the combination of the kids and the job together that made it a bit toxic. But I could never see us splitting up, and I knew that deep down she was driven by a real care for me and the family. I think we were both frustrated that leaving No. 10 had not been a miraculous transformation. Anyway, I said, you guys wouldn't like it if we split.

Saturday 1 January 2005

Up to fifteen and a half stone. Jesus. In the evening F and I went out to try to work through my various work situations. I was still really conflicted about the campaign, felt it was the right thing to do but that I would get more frustrated at not really being able to move things on. I was not totally motivated by anything. I was pulling out of the SoVA mentor situation because there were still hurdles, the organisation in charge had not produced suitable mentees and the whole thing felt half-baked. Nick Pollard's offer of a daily programme had superficial appeal but if I was going to do anything full time, is telly really what I wanted to be doing? *The Times* and the Lions and above all the speeches made sure we didn't have to worry too much about money, but maybe what I needed was a proper structured role re the campaign. It was nice just the two of us going out for once, and being able to talk things over in a calm, civilised manner, though re the Lions the only thing holding me back was the thought of two months without the kids.

Sunday 2 January

I had been managing to motor through the '97 diaries over the Christmas period and was almost up to the end of the year. We took the dog out, then did Fiona's [birthday] presents and later Carmel [Fitzsimons, FM sister-in-law] and kids plus the Bridges [next door neighbours] came round. The news was overwhelmed by the tsunami in Indonesia and amid it a bit of a feeling TB should have come back from his holiday in Egypt. The mood generally was a bit grungy. GB was more visible than usual, and not only for good reasons. He was on the move again.

Monday 3 January

I was not sleeping well, and felt a mix of demotivation and lack of clarity about things. Alan M called as I arrived at Stoke v Burnley and I was frank with him, said I was really conflicted about going back and felt he, TB and PG had very different but equally unclear ideas of what I should be doing. TB felt we could just get back to where we had been before. PG just needed to have me around to make happen the stuff he wanted to happen, and because we could always make it more fun. I felt he [Alan] wanted me as a bulwark to GB but if the campaign was going to motor we had to have all the different engines firing. I felt I could not make a contribution without getting into it full on, which I didn't want to. I said he must not take it personally. I needed to be motivated to be at my best, and every time I went in there I did not feel a spring in my step, I felt my legs getting tired and heavy. I said I wanted to help but it had to be on my terms, otherwise it wouldn't work. TB wanted too much of me right now.

We agreed I should write down how I thought I could work with them. He also said again we should put it on a proper professional footing, that he get some money from Matt Carter and agree a role, fees etc. Took Calum and Florence [Bridge, neighbour] to the match, good win (0–1). Saw Bruce [Grocott] who was pressing me to go back to No. 10 for TB's last bit. He said you were there at the beginning, you've been an important part of the wins and you have to be part of this one.

Tuesday 4 January

Howard on the radio, not that impressive, certainly not the form you need at the start of an election year. Very negative, no real message about the future. GB was on with his tsunami initiative, impressive but everyone in the know could sense he was indicating he was taking charge while TB had been away. All it would take to deflect that was a few words re TB being in constant touch, or something positive, but he just couldn't do it. I sent Jonathan an email saying I thought TB should be visible today. But he decided to wait till tomorrow and do the *Today* programme then. I set off early for Lakeside [Country Club, Camberley] and the darts, having been asked out by the organisers. Interesting enough day. All very working-class. A bit circus-y. I played a leg with Bobby George [former darts player turned commentator] for the TV coverage. For some reason I decided to play left handed. I did interviews with several players. Raymond van Barneveld [Dutch former world champion] was easily the most impressive, especially on how he prepared and took care of himself. The crowd was interesting. Just loved being able to be raucous.

Milburn called to take forward chat re me going full time. PG was also calling the whole time at the moment, saying the problem is with GB just doing his own thing, PM out of it, you and I are the only loonies in here and you're a bit out of it at times. He didn't feel we would get energy unless I was in there the whole time and people felt I was there the whole time. He really felt we had to energise and move up through the gears quickly. He said I was the only one who had the reach to energise the place, but I had to do it soon. GB was all over the media on Africa, tsunami and a piece for tomorrow's *Guardian* on what the manifesto 'should' include. I stayed for two matches, did a couple of interviews, had a bit of an argument with Bobby George about whether it was a sport on a par with football or boxing, say, then set off home. On the way back I actually came to think it was a sport. They had great skill and dedication, the best obviously had something the rest didn't, and if rifle shooting was a sport, so was darts.

Wednesday 5 January

AM had sent through a note on various things he wanted done in advance of a dinner with TB tomorrow night. He wanted a narrative note from me and I revised the piece I did pre-conference which tried to use a humbler and more connecting tone. I was writing stacks today – the *Times* piece on darts, a script for TB's press conference tomorrow, a speech for the launch of a new campaign promoting Britain etc. PG was complaining it was a never-ending battle to get things moving, that there was a torpor around the place, and that No. 10 was unsure what to do and not keen for TB to be up and about. As Jo Gibbons said, TB is a great communicator and yet for some reason at the moment they don't let him communicate. I told JoP TB should start to connect with people, less the Westminster village, and start to look like he meant it on domestic message.

Mark Neale came to say goodbye before going back to the US, then Bob Geldof with Paul Vallely [writer and consultant on international development] and Andrew Jackson [Commission for Africa, a Tony Blair initiative to work towards a strong and prosperous Africa]. After lots of small talk re him winning the people's peer contest on *Today*, BG said he was really worried about two things – the fact nobody was in charge of overall presentational strategy, and the fact GB (a Commission member) was basically laying out the stall before the stall was built. He swore massively but was intelligent and political. I said for it to work the leaders had to be seen to be under pressure, then respond to it. The feeling I know in e.g. JoP and others was that GB was deliberately trying to set us up for a fall and the Commission to be seen as a failure, with GB getting brownie points along the way. He was no automatic fan of GB but felt on the issue both were doing good and should be supported.

He and Vallely were full of stories of non-joined-up stuff in government and I told them it was one of the reasons I left – you spent so much time sorting things and so many did not get even the basics when it came to the media. There was a real sense of them feeling this was a great opportunity – for them, the politicians but above all for the Africans but BG said GB could blow it. I advised him to have a very frank word and say he would not be forgiven if this became part of the TB–GB game playing. I said he might take it from him. Bob had a very direct way of speaking, and enormous passion, and clearly got really frustrated at the way politics often got hijacked by personality stuff. They stayed for a couple of hours after which I chased up the need for a comms director for them with Jonathan and Liz. I spoke to Bono after they responded and we agreed Justin Forsyth [No. 10 development advisor] might be the man, with proper support on PR. Bob was worried about the Germans, thought that [Chancellor Gerhard] Schroeder would really milk the tsunami and then say there was nothing for Africa. He said the French and Germans saw it as TB trying to be a good boy after Iraq and he should fuck off. The Germans virtually said as much. Bob didn't imagine Chirac would want to help TB either.

Alan called re Monday's poster launch and whether he could do a *Times* interview in advance or would it all be about GB and what he was up to. PG's latest obsession was the spring conference and the need for it to be whizzbang. I went out with him to do some groups, the usual lower middle house in Edgware, and I sat at the back and watched. They were recruited as likely to vote Labour, but swithering a bit. There was a lot of moaning about political correctness, and also immigration, especially with the women. We were strong on the economy, but they were still finding it tough financially. Also it was pretty heartening to hear a whole load of the men talk about their recent experience of the NHS and say it is definitely getting better. Schools was for once behind health. Several had moved house to live near a better school, and worries about discipline went across both groups. When Philip got them on to the Tories, and Howard, they didn't like

him too much, and the 'something of the night' line came up sponta-
neously in both groups – thank you, Ms Widdecombe.*

One of the men said Howard's role in Thatcher's government was
also a big problem for him, and others then started asking about that.
PG smiled at that one. It looked like all the reminders about his role
in the poll tax was getting through and then someone raised unemployment going up when he did employment, police numbers being
cut when he was in charge of police, and then a bit of boom and
bust and double-digit interest rates too. PG was positively beaming
now and gave me a discreet little thumbs up by the side of his leg.
Then, when they were shown the clip of him saying he had an 'aspiration to cut taxes', they howled. The women in particular thought
it was nonsense to claim they could cut taxes by cutting waste and
red tape. When he showed them dividing lines, by far the best was
the idea of Labour prosperity v Tory economic risk, and GB was
seen as a big strength in both groups, even if one or two made dis-
paraging comments about his appearance and one was blatantly
anti-Scots racist.

Where I took real heart was from the general mood which was part
'better the devil you know', but also worries about the Tories, and a
couple of Thatcher voters said they had been worried about whether
Labour could run the economy but now felt totally assured. One of
them said, 'All Labour needs to do is say safer economy with them
and they'll win again.' Where we had to be careful was in the 'for all'
messaging. In the anti-immigration/asylum mood, there was a ten-
dency not to see it as fairness for people like those in the groups, but
immigrants. It was tricky stuff. But when they came to saying how
they would probably vote, almost all said Labour, a couple of LDs, a
couple of not sures, no Tories. And even those who weren't sure said
they were sure Labour would win. For once, PG and I were reasonably cheery in the car home.

Thursday 6 January

The TB–GB thing was getting ridiculous. TB had brought forward the
monthly press conference because he had to do a tsunami statement
on Monday. The only time he could do it was 10 a.m. today – the same

---

* Ann Widdecombe, a former Tory minister, was considered to have damaged Michael Howard's general election prospects when she said he had 'something of the night' about him.

time GB was doing his 'Marshall Plan' in Edinburgh.* So the Ed Balls briefing was cranked up and the latest victim game played out. It was all fucking crazy. Ed Victor came round and we agreed next steps, including possibly getting Richard [Stott] to edit. We had the TV on in the background so I could follow what was going on. TB came on at 10 and then GB a few minutes later. Sky did split screens, with a message saying GB was on news active. The BBC said press red to see GB. The whole thing was ridiculous. The split screen image was dire, a symbol of a divided government. Ed, who said he had no idea things were quite so bad until he had read some of the stuff I sent him, just whistled through his teeth. 'This does not say unity.'

TB did OK but was asked repeatedly about it and was a bit frustrated. What worried me a little was that DH was telling him it was not too bad. I thought it was dire. Ed said it was dreadful, and was right. Fiona came in and just laughed. 'Are they both on live? What on earth is going on?' she said. 'Isn't it time someone sorted them out?' It was not good at all. I did some work and then ran in, on the way digesting some OK groups from last night. TB not coming back from his holiday had been fine, people seemed to understand he needed a break and also that there was a limit to what he could do. But they were negative in other ways, the sense being he had been ground down to become an ordinary sort of politician, when they wanted him to be special.

AM chaired a two-hour session and we got through a fair bit. PG and I both had a sense of No. 10 not being as coherent or as confident as they should be. We went over a stack of areas that had to be covered. I took away the task of narrative and script and also dealing with RC on how he might come back to do more on the Iraq/conditional voting stuff, the idea that people could be openly critical on Iraq but say that on balance they still preferred Labour to the other parties. We were still struggling to settle on a central message and that missing element would also dominate the dinner later with TB. I saw Matt Carter to agree a modus operandi and then ran home, worked on some messages before heading back to No. 10.

TB arrived back from Yorkshire as I was driving into Downing Street and we went up to the flat. He said he felt fine and the visit up north had been good. He looked taken aback when I said how awful the GB situation was, that today it went from paper talk to TV mainstream

---

* Brown called for a 'modern Marshall Plan' for Africa that would include 100 per cent debt relief and international immunisation funding.

and there was a danger the public would turn on them for thinking this was what they cared about, not getting problems sorted. He said, 'What do I do? This is all stirred by them all the time and the press know that but of course it takes their story away to say so. GB is just impossible at the moment.' He said he had said to him about his so-called strategy note: 'This is not a strategy; it is an emotion. It is a sense of grievance.'

JP was now convinced GB was at it and was seeing him on Monday and if things carried on he said he would tell him he was putting the black spot upon him. TB felt shackled and ground down. For example GB, without consultation, had announced IFF [International Finance Facility] changes and debt write-off plans which he now expected TB to deliver. 'I can't write the aid budgets of the US, Germany and Japan.' The Australians are furious. So are the Americans. But he is crazy. TB said that it was untenable and they could not go on like this. I said someone, maybe JP, maybe an outsider, needed to say publicly that they would lose the election if this carried on. He said it was now totally impossible to speak to him. He only asked 'what proposals' he had, by which he meant when was he going to go. We went upstairs while he got changed and I saw CB and we had a chat about the non-sense requests coming in re Freedom of Information, like how many toilet rolls got used at Chequers or in the flat. She seemed in good form though. Leo had had his first day at school, and had enjoyed it.

The others came up – Jonathan, Pat [McFadden], Liz, PG, DH and HC, PH and Alan five minutes later. We had half an hour on GB during which TB said maybe the only thing to do is put him out and say he will have to challenge me and get it cleared up that way. But even though most of the people in the room had thought at some point that might be the best way, there were not many takers for it today. We were getting too close to the election. He said, and I agreed, that it was untenable because the sense of division was going through to the public. As that came back through the party, maybe it would scare GB into shaping up a bit, but it wasn't certain.

On general message we could not really get clarity on what the third term was for and what message we should put centre stage. The options were in the area of the future, modernisation, our values. He said what he really wanted to do was to give a sense of being New Labour unshackled, that he had felt shackled by political timidity and by the GB problem and that in the public services, more big change was needed, like an openly mixed NHS economy, freed-up education sector and more big criminal justice change. We agreed he had ceded too much to GB. As JR had said to TB, he had allowed him to build a sense of being his equal. With any other minister, if the PM wanted to do a press conference and it screwed up their plans, so what, nobody argued, they just did it and found another time? But he had made GB feel unsackable and he had allowed him too much sway.

We agreed he should write a totally frank single page on what he wanted to achieve in the third term. As he set it out – New Labour with the shackles off – that spoke to doing it without GB, but I sensed that just wasn't going to happen. He clearly wanted to be able to say the first two terms were frustrating and now he wanted to go for broke to get the job done. Re GB he said earlier the wisdom was he [TB] would be a lame duck after the election. In fact he would have more power, a third mandate and the clear sense it was the last, and he and would be able to sack GB if he chose to. GB even at his most enraged probably knew that.

The two massive majorities meant that even a reasonably big majority could look like a massive diminishing of his stature. He looked worried and strained. He was not fizzing and we were not getting clarity. It was a nice enough evening and through the day I at least felt we were getting towards shaping the argument but we were a long way from it and the GB problem was now of fairly nightmarish proportions. The thing I still felt was that of all of them, for all his foibles and occasional blind spot, TB was head and shoulders above the rest and easily the most human. PG said that is what the public sensed but they wanted him to be him and get on with it. The Miliband adoption story was kicking on with Theresa May [Tory MP] piling in in a really horrible way.* I spoke to DM to agree I would do a piece for *The Times* on it.

Friday 7 January
The groups tested the various messages I had banged out for Philip yesterday and the ones that worked best had a mix of economy, on your side, and an admission things needed speeding up. What they didn't want was TB to apologise or say all was woe is us. It was clear the mood at the centre, probably in large part because of GB, was worse

---

* Tory spokesperson on family policy Mrs May questioned whether David and Louise Miliband had received preferential treatment from the Department of Education in approving its own minister's adoption application.

than how it felt out among the public. Even though the media had been banging on about it for so long, they did not have a real sense of how it was affecting the government as a whole. What was clear was that they did feel disappointed that the TB they saw in '97 was not the TB of today but there was still a lot of potential support in there and no real desire to move him out. Reading between the lines, I think they would have been surprised by the nature of some of the internal discussions being held.

I worked on a narrative note for the launch of the posters next week, which GB had finally agreed to take part in. AM had secured his agreement to do it and I wrote a long briefing note and I finally persuaded them we should do something with it to try to get a more positive element into the Sunday mix which would be dire. It was the first wave of advertising for the election year and would make clear the relentless focus on the economy, with each poster putting over one key economic fact, the lowest unemployment for twenty-nine years, the lowest inflation since the '60s, the lowest mortgage rates for forty years, the longest period of sustained economic growth for 200 years, and joined together with 'Britain is working. Don't let the Tories wreck it.'

I used JP saying nobody would have believed us if we had promised that kind of record back in 1997, and Alan saying that us replacing the Tories as the party of the economy and economic stability is the single most important strategic change in British politics in recent years. I threw in a bit of the polling on Howard showing a rise in people linking him to the last government's excesses and failings. Calum and I left for Burnley v Liverpool and the nightmare of a postponement just as we arrived. There are few more annoying things than the drive back after a game has been postponed just as you arrive there.

Saturday 8 January

TB was doing *Frost* tomorrow and called early on, thinking about what to say re GB. He felt it was no longer credible to say it was all tittle tattle got up by the press. I did feel he could signal to the [Ed] Balls of this world the potential damage they were doing and focus on economic message generally. He was clearly moving towards something more dramatic. He said it was untenable, you could not have a situation where there were two messages, two policy agendas, two campaigns. I said it wasn't sensible to have raised the prospect of moving him out – even in jest – in front of people as on Thursday. He said he trusted them but he really had to think this through. I had had a chat with Joan Hammell [JP aide] yesterday, who said JP, due to see him on Monday, was pretty exasperated. TB felt GB now either had to pull back or press on and if he pressed on, he would have to do something about him. He was trying to dress up personal ambition as policy difference and because we can't really hit back, and have to play this game of saying he's doing a good job etc., he sounded pretty fed up but also steely.

The other thing coming up was [associate editor, *Sunday Telegraph*] Robert Peston's book on GB, done with GB's and Balls's help, which would fuel the theory of grievance. 'What is sick and obscene is the fact this is a never-ending operation. It is all they do. Yesterday I was dealing with a big policy away day, the IRA, the tsunami etc. All he does is work the media on his own activity and his own grievance.' He felt that this time it had got through to the public who would not understand that we were squabbling when we should be working to resolve people's problems. Matt Doyle said GB had done an article with *The Observer* alongside a briefing that he had big differences with AM on policy. The whole thing was a disgrace.

Sunday 9 January

The Sunday papers were dire, led as we feared by Robert Peston's book, *Brown's Britain*, and the story that TB reneged on a deal to make way. It was the usual stuff but rehashed with more detail than usual and though some of it read like a fairly standard cuttings job, it was damaging to both of them. The most damaging line was GB saying that he could never again trust anything TB said. It had also gone to being a regular broadcast story, not just print. TB felt he could not just dismiss it as tittle tattle so instead just refused to engage on it and instead did a very powerful New Labour message re the manifesto on education, health and crime. It was an OK interview but with two problems – he looked annoyed and frustrated and he did not really answer the question about whether he had said he would go, as was reported. The book was just the latest chapter but in part because it was election year, and also because relations were so bad in reality, and the press knew it, this was worse than ever. PG sent me a text – 'GB should be shot, publish your diaries now!' DH said they were going to be pushing the New Labour message out of the interview but we needed something more than that. This was going to open up a whole new barrel-load for the press to gorge on.

January '05: Peston book revives grievance over TB–GB 'deal'

I called JP. He agreed it was worse than ever. 'What's your analysis?' he said. I said it was bad, and these were the only options – JP to knock heads together or, a variant, to sort out Balls and anyone else who was at it. Get them to stare into the abyss together and start working. Or TB to sack him either before, or after the election. JP said he had spoken to both today, was seeing TB at 6 and GB either tonight or tomorrow. He said he had asked TB outright if he wanted to get rid of Gordon and he said no. He asked GB if he would ever challenge Tony and he said no. So they had to work together and this was now bad enough to put the future at risk. He agreed that TB was more sinned against than sinning, that he had tried to work with GB, but it had not worked. GB did feel he had welched on a couple of deals but that is politics. This is too close to an election and he wants to pull back.

JP wondered about them doing the poster launch together and even though it was contrived, and people would say so, it might work. His overall analysis was that TB was getting more and more frustrated at the lack of planning for the election and got AM in to do the planning job. But because they had the kerfuffle about Ian, and AM did not get that part of the job [party chairman], TB had to give him something else to make it worthwhile and let him into the policy area. There was a lot of stuff being put out by what he called the outriders, e.g. Byers, and we had to rein it in. What he intended to say to TB was that he was no longer going to be a go-between negotiator. What he was going to do was say to TB right, let me see what the manifesto policy stuff is, let's agree it or not and if we do I'm on board for it and I tell GB he has to be. He really felt he was beyond negotiating but felt it was worth trying to get them to work together. This was damaging because the public would think they were squabbling about a job, and working through old enmities, not dealing with the country's challenges. I said the other thing that had to be established was a sense that TB was the top man, that this duumvirate was nonsense.

JP felt the PLP would give them a hard time. He sounded pretty hacked off but as ever glad to be at the centre of things. The worry was if GB was now so beyond things that he really didn't care about the impact. It sounded ridiculous but if he was just angry and bitter why should he? I said also he should make clear to him that on his Africa trip he should not be fuelling this TB–GB stuff but focusing totally on Africa. JP and I agreed to stay in touch and try to get on an even footing. I said I didn't think you could rule out TB getting so frustrated at being unable to get going and deliver a strategy that he thought about putting him out. I was just dropping a hint but he was clearly not keen.

Monday 10 January

The TB–GB scene was bad, the media monitoring report grim reading, though given just how bad it was in reality you could make the case the media were actually underplaying it. We definitely, to find a silver lining, now had the chance to get up the poster launch tomorrow. I worked on words and choreography for tomorrow. I had been talking to Clive W and asked him what he thought. He just felt TB was so obviously a PM and Gordon so obviously a Chancellor. He sent me one serious email, saying the problem was everyone thought we would win so the only debate was who would be the better leader? We should take credit for the state of the opposition and they should both show they're just happy to be winning for Labour. A humorous one, from Bangkok, said we should photograph them shaking hands wearing the Lions wristband. I went in to see TB at half twelve as he was finishing the tsunami statement. He then settled down to eat a disgusting-looking lunch of soup from a flask and a sad cheese roll. I wondered if any PM in the world had such crap food for lunch.

We were back to the old subject. What do we do with him? There were only three options – get rid of him and face the prospect of a leadership fight, get a genuine new modus operandi, muddle along. The third was untenable because it was debilitating. The Peston book didn't take things much further forward but we had the direct allegation, with words, of GB saying he could never trust anything TB said and neither of them denying it properly. As Dale Campbell-Savours [Labour MP] said at the PLP later, unless GB disowned that comment, it would be used relentlessly against us by the Tories. JP and I were talking the whole time and he was clear that we needed to use this turbulence to get back on firmer ground for the campaign ahead.

TB was pretty down. He had not spoken to GB over the weekend but he felt GB would be recoiling from this because it was damaging to him personally. I said it was also damaging to TB because it got us back on to the trust issue in a different way. He said, 'He won't mind the damage to me but he won't like the damage to himself.' Also it showed weakness that he couldn't control things. He said the problem is not his ambition, it is the madness attached to it, and the hatred. At the broader meeting to go over the coming days, they were talking about a health speech. PG and I both said it was crazy. With the economy up, we should keep going on that. Of course TB, as on *Frost*, wanted to do a big New Labour policy thing, saying where we had made change we had been bold and signalling big change, bolder change, in the third term. DM was there and saying the message ought to be prosperity and what it is we're trying to do to extend it, in a New Labour way. TB was not on form and too prone to accept e.g. my and PG's judgement without challenging it. I was arguing yet again for a different sort of dialogue and communications style – candour, openness, 'people talk' – but he always said you need an angle for the press, which missed the point. We agreed a speech on prosperity.

Then with Matt Carter and PG to the new HQ in Victoria Street. It was small but OK and had the feel of a campaign centre. We had a meeting to review the decisions of last week and then went over the choreography for tomorrow and I did words for the launch. There was a pretty edgy mood around and AM's meeting full of the usual black humour you get at these times. MC, PG and I agreed that there just was not the sense of urgency there should be this close. And we were going to have to waste so much time and energy going through hoops the whole time to get them to agree to do anything. The PLP was pretty bloody, with around ten MPs from different parts of the party saying they had to get their act together. Dale C-S was the only one to go direct at GB but though JP said it was plague on both your houses, the balance of blame was definitely tilted at GB. AM said TB had not been so good in his opening remarks though he recovered when he summed up and said they had got the message.

Then to Lions work – I left for the rugby writers' dinner at the Cafe Royal and Louisa Cheetham and I went through all the plans for the tour. She told me her mum was a Tory councillor who was wondering what she was doing with me. I think we worked up some good ideas for the trip including the use of video. The dinner was OK. I was next to Gavin Hastings [former Scotland international] and we had this spooky moment when I was talking about the dinner I was doing for Susan [Law, AC cousin] in Edinburgh when she sent me through an email saying she was approaching Gavin Hastings to MC it. [England player] Jason Leonard said he really enjoyed my *Times* stuff. Amazing ears. Fergus Slattery [former Ireland international] did the main speech and was OK, though probably overdid the crude stuff. Too many after-dinner speakers assumed everyone laughed at swearing. I probably overdid the swearing sometimes but in the stories where I swore, the swearing was usually relevant. This was overdone, though he was quite funny. A few of the guests were sniffy and they were certainly more right than left but by and large they were friendly. Francis Baron [RFU chief executive], who had struck me as a bit of a wanker when he came to No. 10, did nothing to change my view. He was lobbying me about getting GB to go to Twickenham.

Jayne W was on our table and really warm as ever and afterwards she and I went to a bar full of young snoggers and loud music. She was clearly as much a colleague as a wife and we chatted over Clive's football ambitions. He had never wanted to leave the England job but found it incredible that we could win the World Cup and then they did not really want to do it again, or assumed we were now always going to be the best. I liked Jayne. She was bright and warm and far prettier than she photographed. She was also very good with people. She said Clive really enjoyed our discussions and the fact he felt he could have high-level strategic advice on tap.

Tuesday 11 January

I was trying to get in every day this week but also do at least some other work. It was typical and rather depressing that, as I went through '98 diaries, it was all TB–GB. I even had dinner with DM 'last night' in '98 to talk about what we might do to resolve their differences, and Neil [Kinnock] was on *Frost* re the factions – today he's on Radio 5 talking about the same thing. I went in to Victoria St and was busy with PG and TBWA brain storming on lines and message. It was a struggle because we lacked clarity from the top about where we intended to go in the third term. I had a nice lunch with [Lord] Dennis Stevenson [businessman] who though a bit of a name-dropper was a nice man and clever. He advised me to set myself up post-election as an independent power base, making money to provide a base to make changes to things I cared about, especially mental health. He was, in common with other serious people I had spoken to, very down on GB, felt TB was head and shoulders above him. He said TB trusts you because he knows you're not interested in credit or blame because you've had bucketloads of both. He had been to China and was pressing for TB really to invest time and energy in the Chinese and the Indians. He felt the US just did not understand how much change was upon us.

The poster launch went OK. AM introduced, GB and JP words were OK and the posters got good TV coverage. Even though the media all had the body language experts out in force, it went fine. GB did door-steps and clips to say yes, he trusted TB but stopped short of denying the quotes from the Peston book. But there was no doubt he was shaken. TB, who called to discuss Thursday's speech, said that the mask had slipped and a lot of our troops saw for the first time the extent of the GB operation, how far it went and how ruthless it was.

I was working on a reconnection speech and helpfully, coincidentally had a meeting with Promise, a brand management company brought in by Shaun Woodward. The main guy was a bit over the top with flattery about the brilliance of New Labour as branding, the focus group guy was good though, and on to this idea of the relationship between TB and the public being a bit different to the usual politician–voter relationship; that they felt like a jilted lover but they wanted him back at some point and wanted reasons to be back. At least some did. The problems were becoming clear – lack of clarity on message because there was lack of clarity on the forward agenda. Lack of unity. Lack of connection. I ran home and though still conflicted was feeling glad to have a project. The worry was whether we had the time to turn it around. Stan Greenberg [US pollster] was over and said the polls in the marginals were dismal.

Wednesday 12 January

We did just about OK with the posters and now GB was off to Africa with his press entourage. Both had been damaged by recent events, him more than TB. But TB said he did not expect him to lie down for long. There was a steel there and I couldn't see much of a future for GB under TB. The party had shown maturity and that helped close it down. But we had PMQs to get through and the Tories were getting up a poster saying how can they fight crime if they fight each other? I went in with PG and we had a big AM meeting on spring conference which I might not be able to go to because of Leukaemia Research commitments. We sorted a schedule – TB pledge tour up to Newcastle. Interactive Saturday plus GB/TB Sunday.

Robert Jackson [Tory MP] had decided to defect. I kicked myself because that was the purpose of the call I forgot to return a while back. Undeterred he had worked through Jonathan and Andrew Adonis and was now ready to do it. I went to see him at his flat in Covent Garden and we went over his letter, injecting a little more into it re TB and Howard and his worries that he would lead Britain out of Europe.

I told him to watch the 'Tory Tony' charge v TB and also not get caught into the TB–GB so-called policy battle. He was a bit worried about his wife because she was staying as a Tory MEP. I said I couldn't imagine me and F staying together if one of us defected. He said he did feel really bad about this but there was a logic to it. I said we would organise a good welcome for him and he was particularly keen on JP saying something positive – just the same as Alan Howarth and Shaun Woodward when they had come over.

Re GB he didn't buy the 'It's all about policy' line. He felt it was all a bit weird. I was there for an hour or so. He wanted to do it with the *Sunday Telegraph* and didn't want to do *Frost*. He had to do it now because there was an anniversary dinner in his seat coming up and he felt it would be wrong to do it after that. He was writing lots of individual letters to people he was close to. He reckoned Ken Baker [former Cabinet minister] suspected it already. We agreed *Sunday Telegraph* exclusive but if it did not go big we would put it out on the Saturday afternoon all round. PG urged me to take control of it. We worked on the letter. Earlier did RTE on TB–GB. TBWA brainstorm. New party building a bit morgue-like. Left at 6 for Chelsea and met up with Alex in the tunnel. He was on good form and looked like he had lost a bit of weight. We just stood at the door of the dressing room as the players came in from their warm-up, talking about the books we were reading, films we had seen, and the state of the campaign. The match was OK (Chelsea 0, Man Utd 0) and Rory had a good time. On the way home I spoke to Andrew Adonis and we agreed a conclusion for the speech tomorrow in Kent. We were all slowly getting to the same position. Economy. Future. New Labour the key. And TB reconnection. Clive called from NZ, said it was all going fine.

Thursday 13 January

I finished the connection speech draft, worked with Andrew to finalise tomorrow's speech, did some '98 diary work, chatted over with Robert Jackson a plan for weekend media and made a few more changes to his letter. He rightly said there would be cynicism e.g. re whether he'd been offered a peerage. I said he simply said No to that. I don't know if he was fishing for hints, but that route lay disaster. But he had a strong argument about the reasons for defection and would put it fine. I got the bus in for the 1.30 meeting I was chairing for Mark Penn [American pollster] to present his poll. Stan was really pissed off we had got him in but he had come with Bill and Hillary [Clinton] backing and though he and his sidekick Scott were a bit odd, they had a good strong poll and they read it well. We were not in great shape, and they didn't varnish it overly. We'd gone up a little after the conference but had since been embroiled in muck in various forms, or just been mired in foreign stuff. The Lib Dems were getting far too much out of it all for my liking, particularly on public services.

It was not all doom and gloom though, and there was a lot of strength in the fundamentals. The war had slipped down the agenda and what came through clearly was our strength on the economy and jobs. That was where we needed to be rooted but we also needed to be New Labour, and TB had to reconnect. For the other thing that came through was that we were winning back working-class support but slipping in the middle classes. TB felt on crime for example there was a danger CC [Charles Clarke] was so keen to differentiate from DB that we could lose the plot on law and order. It was a good meeting which later we took to TB who agreed with the basic analysis and also that he needed to be out in the country far more, making the case. He looked better, had enjoyed his visit to Kent but said he was a bit worried that the party audience didn't quite get it. New Labour had to be the way.

Of all the various thoughts kicking around as slogan 'Forward not back' was Penn's favoured one. I liked it too. Simple, but with the capacity to have a lot built around it. Penn also polled the GB row and GB came out very much second best. Tories thought it mattered. Our people didn't. Tories backed GB against TB. Our people didn't. Penn briefed TB and though he looked odd, and was near Ralph Coates [ex-Burnley player with a comb-over] hair wise, he was clear and drew sensible conclusions. His main message was get back on the domestic and keep TB out there giving people reasons to come back. Fight on the economy. Sort asylum and the other negatives. Forward not back. TB wanted to go off at a tangent re Iraq, said he could see positives in the polling on that. I said please Tony, don't fight on Iraq. He said no I won't, but the arguments are bound to come up and I want to have the best arguments possible. He said it was a God's send I was back. Penn said afterwards he didn't know of many aides who spoke so directly to their boss.

Friday 14 January
Robert Jackson had done his interview and it seemed to go fine. TB told JP and I got words from him and Alan Johnson to put out when

the story broke. I was working through a few Lions issues with Louisa. The Jonny Wilkinson injury (medial knee ligament) was looking bad. Clive had been too open with a Sunday reporter re the NZ game and we were trying to establish exactly what he said. *Who Wants to Be a Millionaire?* called, wanting me and Fiona for a Valentine's Day special, for LRF. Maybe. Fiona was totally opposed, said she hated that kind of thing. But what if we won it? I was working on a few different speech ideas for TB.

Saturday 15 January

Rory won the Middlesex under 17s and ran really well. The Jackson operation went totally according to plan. He called me a few times through the day, including when he was with his chairman, wanting the number for PA. He sounded a bit hyper but OK. He was a very good explainer and the timing was perfect with the James Report [the Conservatives had asked 'company doctor' David James to do an analysis of public spending and efficiency] coming on Monday and Howard on *Frost* tomorrow. I went on the No. 10 conference call but there were too many people and too much talking and it was a shambles so I dropped out.

Sunday 16 January

The *Sunday Telegraph* did Jackson big and straight though they also had a big number from Peston's GB book. GB had been chugging round Africa getting OK coverage but there had been a definite shift in the party's perception of him. TB said he had definitely changed his view for good as a result of the book. Today's instalment on their discussions on EMU [Economic and Monetary Union] was a total outrage, he said. It managed to be both true and false at the same time, accurate enough to seem believable, inaccurate where it damaged him most. I said Balls needed to know there was a cost to this. JP should murmur the reselection word. TB had done another long note – he wanted a totally New Labour policy agenda and better systems for connection. I said he needed to fire a few rockets because with one or two exceptions the operation was not working well. There was no energy and very little politics in his Cabinet and they had to be shaken out of their complacency.

Howard was OK on *Frost*, but the Jackson defection blew it news wise and we had [Alistair] Darling up doing an OK job torpedoing

January '05: Jackson defection goes according to plan

the content of David James. We had them on cuts and we had them on going back and sums not adding up. Gerald Kaufman [former Labour shadow minister] suggested we try to get David Faber [writer and former Tory MP] over. After meeting Tom Baldwin at a lunch I called Phil Webster, who put me in touch with him. He had actually joined the party a year ago but wanted to wait to announce it because he was finishing a book. It was the connection with his grandfather [former PM Harold Macmillan] though that would connect if and when we did it. I had AM on several times. He needed a lot of reassurance when he was micro managing, and it could be a bit wearing. PG was calling the whole time as well.

Monday 17 January

I woke up early, couldn't get back to sleep and felt depressed. I was not into the election role and although the Jackson operation went well, I was feeling frustrated at several levels. First I was conflicted about whether I wanted to be there at all, because it felt so much like going backwards. Second, TB and others looked to me for the same kind of influence I had before but I had neither my hands on the levers nor the sway with the media I once did. Added to which DH was there, doing the job in his way, which had upsides but downsides too. I worked on a speech for the Policy Forum on the way in, then wrote reaction words on James for the press conference AM, PG and I had agreed to last night. But DH's meeting seemingly spent half an hour unpicking the decision. Plus JP, having first said he would do it, then said he wouldn't and later made clear to Alan he was pissed off at the 'unremittingly New Labour' line from TB last week. Meanwhile we were faced with the main Tory tax and spend day and GB was still swanning round Africa with his media fan club, led by Mark Mardell [BBC reporter]. It was not a good scene.

I went to the TB 1 p.m. strategy meeting and after a desultory start – TB saying, 'What shall we talk about?' – I said there was a real lack of cohesion. We had a Jonathan zone, SM zone, DH, plus the party situation, and worst of all the GB shadow operation. There were too many people of similar clout, having discussions in different places about the same thing and we had to grip it. TB kept saying, 'Well what's the solution?' I said again I did not want to be totally immersed again and it needed someone with 24/7 grip. TB said the gap was strategic communications and the only people who could do it across the whole place were me or GB. He was laying on the emotional blackmail. He then took me through with Sally and said the gap was clear and he wanted me to fill it. It was a very specialist thing and not AM's skill. He was not even sure he – TB – could do it.

I was a bit worried about upsetting DH but TB said David knew there was a gap here. He was a good defensive press officer but he knew he was not a strategic communicator in the way I was. TB said the only alternative was GB and he didn't really want him in that role. The Peston book had changed things totally. It was part of an attempted coup in effect. They had been hoping to use it both to knock him over and also to destroy any legacy. He said he was reluctant to bring him centrally into the campaign because he would then either want Alan out, or it would be harder to boot him out later if he had to, if people felt he had put together the campaign that secured the win. He felt the extent of co-operation by GB and his team on that book was obscene.

SM said that in the call on Friday TB tried to get him up on the Tories' James Review and he came up with excuse after excuse as to why he shouldn't. TB definitely seemed to have developed a greater steel about it. Meanwhile GB was giving interviews about how he was only interested in making change, not the position, and how he was so moved by Africa that it put personality politics in perspective. All with a straight face. We left it that basically we would streamline meetings so that we had a sharper decision-making structure. I said we spent too much time picking and unpicking decisions.

I got TBWA going on viral stuff re James but Matt Carter – probably rightly – held them back so that we could discuss clearance. AM came to Victoria St after his press conference. SM told him of the TB meeting and he said he felt we had to move things over here. He felt he should chair them, and DH and I should both be there and SM then take an implementation meeting to drive through the government machine. Alan said he knew how I felt because he felt the same ambivalence but we just had to go for it. He felt re GB that we should offer him all the opportunities to come back in but not run the show. I called a few of the hacks but didn't really feel back into it. There was a bit of a fuck-up when it turned out there was something factually wrong in our rebuttal [of the claim that the James Review would generate £13 billion worth of savings]. Howard looked OK at his presser, using autocue, crap backdrop, Oliver Letwin [shadow Chancellor] a bit weak, but the press were going to give them a lift, especially as we had successfully rained on the parade yesterday with the Jackson defection.

PG and I went to see the new campaign media centre in Victoria and the very loud pink-purple set which was really striking. Both of us felt it was maybe too loud but it grew on me. Matt C called later re whether he thought we should change it. I felt not. The news was giving the Tories quite a lift re James and without HMT input it was hard to fight back properly. AM however said we had shown in the last few days that we were able to organise without him. I was feeling down, and Gracie crying later at the idea of me going to NZ for seven weeks made it even worse. I was back to being at the beck and call of others. CW called, back from NZ, felt things went OK, wanted to meet up to go over it all.

Tuesday 18 January

I went in to Vic St for meetings and tried to keep them focused on keeping James going. We were surprised at how some of the Tory messages were getting through pretty well. We had assumed our cuts attack would go home but their waste argument had played OK. Even though Howard was weak in many ways I felt his *Frost* interview plus this had got them into a much better place. Also there just wasn't the sense of urgency in our campaign. PG and I were joking about it but Vic St was fairly dead, and the politicians by and large were hopeless. GB was as disengaged as ever. We got a JP letter to Howard re publishing James in full. I did a Wenger–Fergie piece for *The Times*, which I read over to him before he left for Exeter, where United had a Cup game tomorrow. I was making the point that these rows between managers were now an important part of the spectacle, and we shouldn't knock them. AF was totally vituperative re Wenger, said he had lost respect for him. I sensed he was getting under his skin more than he was letting on. They were actually quite similar in their obsession about winning, though I think Wenger took defeat worse and for longer.

We were planning a New Deal event for tomorrow which would be the first time using our new media centre. I wanted TB to do clips from Airbus in Toulouse. DH was against so later I wrote to him to work out how we were going to work together. Letwin was going on the black hole in Tories' public spending estimates. Calum and I set off for the re-arranged Liverpool match at Turf Moor. The weather was still dreadful but we left and survived some dire storms, snow, the lot. The atmosphere at the match was terrific though I had no idea the cameras were on me when I was going mad at the end as we held on to our lead to win (1–0) after they scored an own goal. Loads of people were calling to say how mad I was including AF, who was in hysterics. He said Gary Neville and Ryan Giggs [Man Utd players] had said to him, 'Your mate is going mad on telly.' Six of them had big bets on us to win.

I'd had the phone on mute and in the car back went through a stack of calls and messages I'd missed. Fergie, Mick Hucknall, Jack McConnell, Paul Allen. I did a couple of interviews on the way back, TB called having watched last 20 minutes and said it was hilarious. People would have been worried for my sanity, he said. He said to Euan, 'I hope he's nothing to do with me.' Euan said at least it showed I was a proper fan. Re the campaign he still felt something was missing, a grip on the centre and strategic communications. He basically wanted me to take over. Home by 1.40. It had been a great night.

Wednesday 19 January

I was tired and the phone started early with a stack of interviews re Burnley's win v Liverpool, and my madness. I hadn't quite realised the pictures had gone as big as they did. The Sky cameras had gone back to me several times as I was going mad. I was even the bong on *News at Ten*. I did stacks of telly at Millbank. AM was doing a New Deal presser with Jane Kennedy [Work and Pensions Minister] and Alan Johnson. I noted how good AJ looks on telly. It went OK. Penn was over with a new message poll which made things pretty clear. Economy. Forward not back. Plus we needed TB to reconnect via on your side values connection. The messages that tested best were all in that area. 'Britain working' was not quite right. After PMQs we trooped through for TB's Penn meeting where first he regaled them with stories of me on the telly last night. I asked them to stop polling GB. They had also polled [Prince] Harry and we asked that to stop. I had a couple of chats with Seb and was worried on the Olympics front – combination of Queen, Harry being photographed wearing a Nazi uniform to a fancy dress party and Iraq army brutality pictures was a real problem. He sounded a lot more down than before, though his meeting with Sepp Blatter [FIFA president] went well.

GB was back and seemingly not in a much better mood than before. Also the groups were still very grungy and difficult. We were not lifting them at all, numbers wise or spirit. I also felt the No. 10 operation was a bit shaky. The Stan line on hard-working families went well.

Man U beat Exeter. AF called to say he hadn't had such a good laugh watching football in ages as seeing me have a meltdown live on Sky. I did a Burnley piece for *The Times*.

Thursday 20 January

Clive W early call. I'd been helping him with a speech he made at the FCO [Foreign and Commonwealth Office] and he said it went fine. PG had a good idea re TB doing a whole day interaction with TV and press ads etc. PG, Matt Carter and I were feeling that they just did not have the sense of urgency throughout the government or party. MC said that he and Ian had been at a dreadful dinner with the unions last night and they were very negative. Then I heard TB did not even do a pep talk to the Cabinet as promised, which didn't help my mood. They did the ODPM [Office of the Deputy Prime Minister] plan then DWP [Department for Work and Pensions], a couple of minutes on spring conference. Nothing about the need for them to do more politics and point out who had been crap helping re James. I left with Matthew Doyle for the BBC seminar on their election coverage which went fine. Nick Wood [Tory Party] was quite factual, Jackie Rowley [Lib Dems] too obviously pleading for more Lib Dem space. I pushed on better mutual understanding, less two-way mediation etc., stop the trend to politics without politicians. Q&A OK.

Philip called after he sent through a note on an interesting set of groups he had done in Wandsworth. He reckoned there was still a lot of goodwill towards HMG but that we were stuck, and that a PM they liked and admired for the way he shook up things at home was spending too much time working on war and foreign policy. They were not as angry as other groups had been, just felt he was stuck. Also Howard was reckoned to be doing OK at PMQs, and starting to make an impact. But when he showed them his interview on *Frost*, they recoiled away from him, thought he was a bit slippery, didn't like the way he pretended he hadn't really called TB a liar [in parliamentary statements over the existence of WMDs]. Also his attack on tuition fees while not really having a policy himself was seen as totally lame. On Hutton, likewise they felt if TB was shown he had lied, he had to go, yet the feeling was if the final decision was that he 'misled people', they didn't think he should go. I am not sure of the logic of that one, but PG's point was that they were much more reasonable than the media and the Tories might expect.

Friday 21 January

I was working on TB's speech for the Policy Forum, which was OK but lacked a bit of drive. He had a session with GB and then rewrote it to make it more New Labour. To school to do some reading with Jeremy, then back to do a bit of work. Lunch at Camden Brasserie with Louisa, Ben Wilson and Marcus Jansa [Lions media team]. Nice time and I felt pretty confident we would be able to work well together. I went home and worked on my Lions speech for the April get-together. Humphrey Walters sent me the book bringing together some of the ideas from our awaydays, which I skimread. It was interesting how you could learn about the characters involved re how they expressed their own priorities. The differences between politics and sport were becoming clearer all the time. GB would be rooted out of a sports team in days. Reading Clive's book I kept seeing negative things they did which we would not be able to because of disunity. Neil called re meeting tomorrow pre-Burnley at Cardiff and told me Glenys had not been too well and had been told to take a month's rest. He sounded worried.

Saturday 22 January

TB called a couple of times before his Policy Forum speech. Overnight it was running as a TB–GB attack on the Tory cuts. But he wanted to hit the message about fighting the campaign in the centre ground as New Labour too. He said he had another extraordinary meeting yesterday, in which despite everything GB did not even apologise for the Peston book. I told him of the lines Peston was running and TB said they were allowed to tell these monstrous lies, and GB may even believe them, e.g. that GB did not think much about becoming PM when in truth he spent the whole time trying to 'topple the bastard'. TB still lacked fire and energy though and when I asked a few who saw it how the speech went, 'fine' was the best they could do. We had somehow to get back to people saying 'great'. He felt it was OK, and we had to keep going at the middle ground. I had another flare-up with Calum which was probably my fault and a lot about my frustration and anger at being back in there and not really motoring. We had a nice time on the train though and with Neil. A horrible day weather wise and we lost 2–0. Neil was a bit more worried about Glenys than he was letting on I think. I asked what he thought we should do re TB–GB. He said he had said to Gordon before, and would say again, that he was the only man in history who basically knew he was going to be PM. He alone could blow it.

TB's note came through, longer than usual, more compendious, leading on education and the continuing rows and difficulties over academies, selection etc. He was going big on the need to tackle what he called the NK [Neil Kinnock] line on schools (of which I heard plenty yesterday), saying the core question was who has the power to decide – school or LEA – whether a school becomes self-governing? He went through the whole thing in detail, saying the problem is that the proposals were part evolutionary and part revolutionary. He was also singing the praises of city academies [state-maintained, independently run with the help of outside sponsors]. But he felt he was not winning the arguments because opponents were successfully distorting them. He was setting a lot of store on his speech tomorrow, said he needed to describe the evidence on school improvement and the lessons from it and make it clear it was all about levelling up not down.

On ID cards, as ever he was banging on about the need for proper costings. He was asking about SOCA [Serious Organised Crime Agency], and wanting a plan to make its launch a big part of the crime agenda. And on terrorist deportations, he was warning that this was going to come and hurt us, not from the civil liberties end of the argument, but how the law was stopping us from dealing with terrorists properly. He had a long section on the white paper on community health and was clearly unimpressed with the draft, said all the buzzwords were there but there was no coherence. Was it about competition among GPs, diversity of supply, incentivising treatment in the community, putting money into the hands of the patient, people taking more control over their own health and if so, how? On Iraq, he was stressing the need to keep the outreach going to the Sunni, saying we would help them but needed help in return. If they were going to be part of government they would have to urge an end to the insurgency. He had decided [Adil Abdut] Mahdi [Vice-President of Iraq] was probably best bet as PM, but only just. He was also looking to go to the US again soon, namely as soon as he could after an Iraqi government was formed.

On Afghanistan, 'as ever' the PR war was being lost. He wanted [Hamid] Karzai [President] out on the airwaves more, and more done to emphasise the positive progress there had been. As with Iraq, there had to be the constant communication that if bad people are fighting against us and against the ordinary people, Afghan and Iraqi, who want democracy, then our response should not be to give up; or say it's all our fault; but to fight still harder. Then he went into a big thing on

Europe, effectively a speech outline, which we later discussed. He said he reckoned it was possible to be more reflective, about what he had learned about Europe since becoming PM and what Britain had gained from membership of the EU. His basic argument seemed to be that all the difficulties pre-joining meant that we never really engaged as we should have done, and it had damaged us fundamentally.

Even after joining we were uneasy and lacking in confidence, and part of the country had never really accepted it anyway, whereas he did. He reckoned it was as much about culture as politics. And because we were late, a more continental style and a more integrationist approach always seemed to have the upper hand so it looked like it was being done to us rather than us doing it. Even on the euro, the politics always seem to come ahead of the economics. Then throw in an unreasonable media and mix it with reasonable concerns and you end up with the parody of a debate we have had.

As a result, the British PM is put in a nightmare position. To co-operate with Europe is betrayal. To fail to co-operate is to risk isolation and ineffectiveness. He felt – though I am not sure why – that there was the chance now to change all this. Globalisation forcing economic reform; enlargement; and the public being more realistic than the sceptic media. His line of argument seemed to me very similar to what we were saying back in 1997, that Europe finally had the chance to set out a clear political direction for the future; that the priority was to reconnect people in Europe with the European ideal and that is done by showing people what Europe can do, together, for them. The main policy areas were economic reform, security, terrorism and illegal immigration, defence and foreign policy, and energy and the environment. It was all pretty optimistic stuff, as was his analysis of how the other leaders were placed in this. You had to hand it to him. He was good at getting back on the big picture, and relentlessly confident about his ability to persuade other leaders. I'm not so sure.

Monday 24 January

JP sent me through his housing statement and asked me to help rewrite it. I rewrote and also did a briefing note but then discovered they were already briefing on slightly different lines. I was getting more and more frustrated at being expected to deliver and then not having the levers to pull. JP called a couple of times and was going through his usual agonies before a big event. He was also furious with AM, felt he was overcoming the policy on extending Thatcher's right to buy. The news was being dominated by an ad Howard did in the *Sunday Telegraph* on asylum and immigration and people could sense that we were cautious in our response.* It was classic Howard stuff. We spent a fair bit of the morning discussing with TB whether he should do clips or would that blow out housing? He did it in the end but we lacked clarity on the line and we lacked real force and firepower.

I told PG tonight any more days like today and I was not going to stay around for long. AM chaired the first of the new morning meetings but it lacked focus and meandered. Spencer Livermore was there from the Treasury and AM clearly felt constrained. Everything that we asked for from HMT was basically met by resistance. PG felt resistance at every level – from Matt who was very defensive re the ground campaign, from No. 10. The meeting rolled straight into another one, mainly on longer term, but both PG and I got a sense of panic because there was drift and directionlessness. I was getting angry at being there. I said to AM afterwards this was not working. I felt for him because he had been put against his will into a nightmare situation. GB had withdrawn his labour and was hoping for him to fail. He was expected by TB to deliver across the board and it was tough. But we had to get sharper focus. The meeting with TB was worse than usual. PG had sent lots of stuff on strategy but it was the meandering 'What shall we talk about?' approach. We ended up on the Libs with me and AM arguing we needed a clearer national message on it, and TB saying he was sure if we did big attacks it would help them and the Tories, and so it had to be done locally. In so far as it was a national campaign the message had to be that the Tories had a backdoor strategy. Vote Lib Dem, get a Tory government. I felt that risked being totally dismissive of a big swathe of opinion.

I had to go out to speak to Charles Clarke and try to get him on to James and cuts. He said he thought it was a third order issue. He would do a bit of it because he was communitaire. But the main thing was explain the context. Charles was doing his own thing a bit too much. Cabinet had basically had politics removed from them. It was pretty hopeless. And depressing. Then to a meeting on the leader's tour, a good presentation by TBWA then a ragged discussion in which

---

* The full-page newspaper advertisement was an open letter in which Howard promised that if elected the Tories would impose quotas on asylum seekers, put 24-hour guards on Britain's ports and introduce an Australian-style points system for economic migrants.

again I felt everyone either contributing nothing or raising problems and looking to me for solutions. I was getting pretty depressed about it and dreading the months ahead.

Tuesday 25 January

I got in early and Vic St was like a morgue. Media monitoring were in, and that was it. PG and I were joking about it but we were also getting quite panicky. I was not sleeping well because I felt ministerial complacency and campaign torpor. I was alarmed at how low the capacity and confidence seemed to be, in No. 10 and at the party. I chaired the morning meeting, got the usual non-stuff from Spencer Livermore who was clearly just there to help GB plan his counter attacks the whole time. The days were rolling into mush. Meeting then meeting then another. Sally and Pat were doing their best but it was tough. Pat said they were incapable of getting stories into the press. The best meeting of the day was on advertising. They totally got the plot. Trevor Beattie felt the Tories had just about alienated every non-white but I was not so sure. They had done a few things for viral and tactical use too. I also did a session with the regional press officers who were a good lot, and set them a talking-point task. I was finding though that I was very bitty in there. Never-ending email and phone interruption and it was hard to work in any sustained way. The crime figures coverage was dire. Grace was really pulling the heart strings re going to NZ.

Wednesday 26 January

Alex was interesting on the Howard stuff. He felt he had a point but that every foreigner would hate it. I said he and Wenger should do a joint presser saying they would have to send all their players back to their own countries under a Tory immigration policy. I sent JoP, Sally and PG a note saying TB had to get a grip, and a proper understanding of the scale of the problem. E.g. was he really going to deliver this new kind of campaign? Did he get the stuff about what he needed to do re seeing his relationship with the country like a human relationship? Did he have the energy and drive? I felt he was sitting there, spooked by GB and still too foreign focused. He was not connecting. Still refusing to admit doubt which led to anger and guilt and so rebuttal and a very defensive mindset. I said to Milburn I was beginning to get angry at what I was having to do, today for example the strategy for a Home

Office asylum plan. Yet CC apparently said to AM why was he having to deal with me? I had a good chat with JP about his sustainable communities stuff. He was up for stuff at the weekend.

I was working on a script, then left to see NZ high commissioner Russell Marshall, nice enough rugby fanatic who thought the Tories just were not credible. He had wanted to meet up before I went off with the Lions, and to say any help I needed from government out there I just had to ask. I went to AM's office where Promise, Shaun Woodward's brand management friends, did a second presentation. The main stuff was fairly pedestrian but a real colourful character called Roy [Langmaid] was terrific. He presented the whole thing in the same context as I had done the speech for spring conference. He said it was a love affair and the country was a jilted lover. TB spent too much time abroad because he was no longer interested. Bush was his new friend. They were looking to GB just as a way of sending him a signal. They didn't really want to go off with him. They actually still felt we were modern, the future etc., but there was so much resistance to the brand – media, non-delivery, war etc. He said Tony had to get it at the emotional level. It was on exactly the same lines as the speech I sent through a while back, which some of the No. 10 team felt was a bit mad, and there was a compelling argument there. Everyone felt it was strong. It was back to the idea about conditional support etc.

Lots of MPs came round Vic St. It was too late to change TB's Davos speech which was dire. Too pro-Bush and no real big-picture stuff. At the campaign meeting I said to PG it was a sign of failure that he and I were still in charge; we had not brought on the people who could replace us, we had not found and developed talent. Pat told me that for his NPF [National Policy Forum] speech TB actually wrote the briefing note himself. At Vic St I was working with Darren Murphy on his cities report then to Deloitte's for an LRF event. Home to see Man U lose to Chelsea in the Carling cup (1–2). I got a message that TB wanted to see me for dinner with JoP, SM, AM and really work through all our problems. It was not just GB. A lot of this was about him and he had to get it. I said to Alex that it was like a football team being run without players. We had good coaches and masseurs and physios but no players. We had TB losing the plot. GB sulking and on strike and basically screwing us over the whole time, e.g. without consultation announcing an extra billion for vaccines (as Howard was successfully doing immigration and the polls were saying we only cared about abroad).

I ran in at half six to the morgue. Only media monitoring in there again. I finally did the 'Forward not back' script. Spencer was not there for the first meeting because he felt 8 a.m. was too early. So we had a more frank discussion than usual. We were again saying we needed a proper rebuttal document on James and the truth was we were getting nowhere because GB was on strike. We had to go ahead whatever and start doing things. We had a situation where some of the attack team were basically working for Spencer. It was hopeless, really hopeless. It was AM's birthday and there was a fair bit of black humour around. We had an excellent meeting on the spring conference and the pledges and I had a good session with Matthew Doyle, Hilary Coffman, Jo Gibbons re the bus tour accreditation etc.

I had a cup of tea with Hilary [DH's partner], skirting round the DH issue but agreeing we had a problem with TB. PG and I suggested we go on strike. TB hopeless. GB trouble. CC a liberal and a non-team player. JP raging. AM understandably finding it tough. JP called me p.m. to say he was worried there was another TB–GB clash on the grid on Wednesday. He was pissed off at AM's policy speeches and another one from JR today. I was in agreement with him that we had a more basic job to do than emphasise reform. We had to reconnect as on your side/capable/realistic/progressive people. I gave him my assessment of how bad things were. We could not go into a campaign with this dysfunction between them. It was not possible. He agreed. He asked if I thought anything could be done about it pre-election. Or were we just storing up for after, because the bitterness was such everyone now assumed there would be war? He said he was sick to fucking death of trying to resolve it. We had a bit of a laugh saying, 'No, I am more fucking sick to death than you are', 'No, I am, I am so sick to fucking death I could not be more sick to fucking to death...' etc.

But he was clear GB had to do his bit for the election. He would tell him he just had to get on and do it. He went into one of his great tirades, saying they were as bad as each other sometimes. I said we were operating with GB on strike. TB could not raise his head above it and was failing to connect as a result. The Cabinet was depoliticised. The press were killing TB day in day out. The Tories had had a lift. He said GB either stops pissing in the tent or he pisses outside. But as well as getting GB in check he felt we had to stop the ultra modernisers from talking up reform etc. We had to get back as a team. We agreed to meet next week and try to work it through.

I drew up a plan with PG and SD to use the three days a week we were to get from TB. A Talk to Tony weekly event, a regional economy event every week, and a team event. We needed to get motoring though. We were stuck. JP got the point and was clear it couldn't go on. He said is there any chance of a war before the election because there will be one after? I'm fed up with it and it either gets sorted or we're fucked. If the party is going to get hurt by this then I'll adopt the position that hurts least. He was moving, I sensed, to a position of backing TB if he decided to deal with it. I left for No. 10, meeting a tearful Kate Garvey on the way in because she had told JoP she was going [to work for Make Poverty History]. I went up with JoP and Pat. Sally was already there. JoP said we really must try not to talk about GB the whole time. They were laughing about Roy Langmaid's presentation to TB. He had done the full works about it all being a story of love and how the public wanted him back. TB seemingly thought he was terrific, as we all did.

I went to open the door to Alan who was almost shaking in rage. He had just seen GB to try to get his agreement to the economic pledge and to his role at the spring conference. He was more mad than he had ever seen him, said Alan. He had raged at the pledge, then demanded to see the others. AM said they were with the other ministers. He said what the pledges were. GB said we could not commit to eighteen-week waiting times. It wasn't costed. He said childcare was Treasury not education. He was at his most bullying and angry. AM said he got very close to lamping him. TB came in, wearing casual gear and slippers and looking exhausted after his Davos and Holocaust [Memorial Day ceremony] events. He looked pained as Alan went through it again. TB said, 'You guys' are getting what I've had for ten years. We went round some of the problems we were facing. They all went back to GB and the basic dysfunction of his relationship with TB. I said it was not possible to mount a proper campaign in this mode. He said what do we do? I said is it too late to sack him? JoP, Pat and AM all felt that was impossible though they moved as the evening wore on.

TB said he felt we had gone on as though there was no problem whatever we did because we had been coasting, in part because the Tories were so weak. But now this split stuff was getting through to the public and would really hurt us. JoP said, rightly, there were only three options – sack, work with or work around. TB said bringing him in would mean AM humiliated ritually and with GB probably demanding a written guarantee of his departure. 'And the rest,' I said.

Working round was possible but totally debilitating. He felt it had to be brought to a head. That meant sacking him and giving the PLP a vote on whether they wanted a contest. GB could of course challenge but I felt he lacked the bottle to do it. Pat felt if push came to shove we had the MPs three to one. TB would make clear it was not a loyalty test, that people should back who they felt was best placed to do the job, and also that if he did not get a clear mandate he would go.

He would make clear he was staying as New Labour, that we had been living a lie in pretending they worked together well. He said he hated saying on camera to Marr today that they worked well because everyone knew it was not true. I was pretty clear that despite it all serious people wanted TB. The PLP would be fine. So would members probably. GB would walk it in the unions. That was not a good position for him to be in. I suggested we start to brief 'GB on strike' stories, how he was basically blocking a campaign etc. AM was strongly against going down that route. I told TB what JP felt. He said he would have to come out totally for TB. Most of the Cabinet would be fine. Pat said Cabinet had been grim with GB leading off a series of whacks at CC over yesterday's plans on house arrest [of terror suspects].

TB looked drained and grey and he clearly looked like he might be moving to do this. He said he wanted to see JP tomorrow and think about it all day Sunday. He may need to move quickly. He asked JoP when the World Bank top job was sorted and whether it might be an option for GB to be president. It was high-risk stuff. But he said if he could not do the last few years without the ball and chain around his neck and his ankles, he didn't want to do the job at all. AM and he were both a bit down on JP and his attempt to water down New Labour. I argued it was less important what they said than what they did and they were unnecessarily provocative sometimes. JP was basically onside and definitely more on TB's side than GB's right now, so it was stupid to push him away just by cranking up a bit of New Labour rhetoric. We had a more basic job of connection. Not bad food, brought in from outside. Seafood starter. Duck and rice. Cheese and grapes. Between all the agony and the agonising, there were a few laughs.

We went through to the sitting room for tea. He wrote down what we had agreed. He would see JP tomorrow. John Reid and Shaun Woodward would be asked to work together on Tory attack. He wanted help with how he looked, how to get less tired, better clothes. Then he said to me, in a way that was almost embarrassing, 'I don't know how to say this and it sounds a bit pathetic but Ali, I really think I need you close in, around every day.' He said he'd like me to work in No. 10. As a joke, I said why can't you come to Victoria St, and he took it seriously. OK, I will some days. It was nice to be wanted I suppose but it was just another big layer of pressure going back on. If we went ahead with the route we had been discussing, we were essentially looking at a primary followed by election situation. Done right it could galvanise and energise. Done badly, it could be the end of him. I liked the boldness but had to watch I wasn't pushing too hard for it for that reason. Building on the relationship theme, I said he would have to say we had been living a lie and it had to stop. He would be liberated and the campaign would be liberated from paralysis.

We agreed he would take care of strategic command from post-spring conference. It was going to get busy. Sack GB, then force a contest partial or full. Then election. As TB went through how he would argue it, as a policy argument rather than personality, it sounded sensible. JoP started nodding. AM was still not sure. I had no doubt. It was odd how TB and I often reached the same unspoken point at the same time. There was no point going on in these circumstances. So he looked like he was going for it. He had said earlier, 'I feel like I am in a small three-roomed flat with two lunatics in each room either side of me, the media in one, and the guy next door in the other.' It was an intolerable situation, and was going to kill us if we did not resolve it.

Friday 28 January

I worked at home most of the day. I'd done a flying pig poster about Howard and Letwin which was causing a row, with some Jewish groups calling them anti-Semitic for putting Howard's and Letwin's heads on pigs. The fact both were Jewish had not crossed my mind, it was more designed to show they could not deliver on what they promised, namely increase spending and cut taxes at the same time – 'and pigs might fly'. AM and I agreed we had to keep firm. Matthew Doyle stopped us going further and doing a 'Which animals are they then?' At least we were getting a bit of edge into it but even Trevor Beattie eventually bought the line that it was anti-Semitic. Ridiculous. We got Gerald Kaufman [Jewish Labour MP] out on it and he was fine. I managed to plough on but there was growing nervousness around the place.

Mum came down and Fiona and I went to Tessa and David's. Ross and Rebekah, Charlie [Falconer] and Mariana there. Rebekah was clearly fairly sympathetic to GB, but was also asking why didn't TB sack him ages ago. She was a bit tense and edgy when we were ribbing her about Fox News claiming to fair and balanced. I was also winding her up re the *Sun* line being dictated by Trevor Kavanagh. After she and Ross left, we had a pretty frank discussion. Mariana thought we could lose because people had gone off TB. I was arguing for my emotional reconnection strategy. CF was worried it would show weakness. Tessa was totally on my side. David felt it was about distancing from Bush and getting key facts communicated. We ran round in circles. But what was clear was we could not have a campaign on this basis. I didn't fill them in on TB's thinking re sacking GB and going for a contest. I think even these guys might be shocked to know how close he was to it.

Saturday 29 January

I called TB. The phones were down at Chequers which meant he was on a mobile and so a bit circumspect. But he said he had decided. I asked if that meant what I thought. He said yes. He was now in no doubt. He had tolerated it for too long. He intended to move in short order. I assumed we were talking Thursday. He felt the public did not want him out but they were confused, because they heard so much negativity about him. This stuff was pumped out against him the whole time and he had to decide whether he could fight back. He could. He said you sound down. I said I was angry and frustrated but at least this would energise things, even if it was high risk. He felt it was the thing that would allow him to reconnect. When push came to shove, he was the only one the public wanted up there. People didn't want or rate Howard, they knew Charlie Kennedy wouldn't ever be in the position to do it, and GB conflicted people. They wanted to be clear what they were getting and he had to give the clarity. PG and I discussed the next two weeks and what we needed to do and I felt bad not telling him what was going on but TB wanted a detailed plan drawn up first which he would do over the weekend. The pig poster was everywhere but fairly low-key. We had a dinner for Audrey's 80th which was nice, though apart from her I reckoned most of the others were pretty much flaking off. Lots of little speeches. Burnley into the fifth round of the Cup.

Sunday 30 January

I woke up in the middle of a terrible dream in which JoP, Jo Gibbons and I were involved in a dreadful car accident – inside the Cabinet

Office – and as we were being dragged out of the wreckage, we were put in another car, but it was going round in circles inside 70 Whitehall. A messenger was shouting at the driver just to smash his way through the walls. Ambulance sirens were going outside but I could hear people shouting they couldn't get in and we were saying we couldn't get out. Jo said she thought Jonathan had stopped breathing.

Back in the real world, TB had decided re GB that he would square JP then have a meeting with both before political Cabinet. He would ask GB to deny the reports that he intended to challenge him for the leadership after the election. We reckoned GB would probably say, 'What about a guarantee of being Chancellor?' TB felt they were different issues, and would say for him to give such a guarantee would require a total change of operation and that he alone would be judge of whether it had changed. So no guarantee. If he messed around he would be out. TB would then say to Cabinet we were actually in a strong position because we had a record to point to, and plans for the future far better than anything the Tories could come up with. But the public was confused by the lack of clarity created because two different strategies and two different sets of messages were being put out. He would make clear the direction was New Labour and he was staying for a full term. If anyone disagreed with that, he wanted them to say so now. I said it lacked clarity. But he felt if he just put him out it would be a big problem. He could not really do that. But he felt the public would understand we could not go into an election with people not sure who would be PM.

He kept saying I sounded down. He said he knew I was conflicted about being back but he was asking me out of friendship and said he really needed me to be strong. I said I would try to be there for him but I had a lot else going on. He said he needed total focus. I said I would try. He did sound a bit more energised but this could still go wrong. Alan M called while we were on the Heath with the grannies and Molly. He said Greville Janner [Jewish Labour MP] was threatening to make a public statement attacking us over the flying pigs and Fagin posters.* He knew no offence had been meant but it had been taken and we had to remove them. I said if we did a big public thing on it it would be a mistake, and we should just let it blow over.

---

* Like the flying pigs image, the 'Fagin' poster, showing Michael Howard hypnotising people with a pocket watch and saying 'I can spend the same money twice' was criticised by some as being anti-Semitic.

Monday 31 January

The posters row was carrying on and there were mixed views as to how to take it forward. After my discussions with Greville we were on for saying two plus two sometimes equals five, and as they had been misinterpreted, we wouldn't be pursuing them. But they would take that as us dropping them, and I didn't want them to be able to say we had climbed down. I said we should get a whole load of new ones to keep the thing going partly using a series of new ideas. The reality is they were not even posters in that none of them would ever get up on a billboard. It had been a device to float a message via the internet, and went way bigger than we expected, not because they were particularly good, but because of the reaction. Trevor Beattie had actually had nothing to do with them and was pissed off, felt we had a problem with it, and felt the ads were not that good, and he was getting dug into by the press. But even though this was all a bit uncomfortable, we had a new device now for getting up images and message, and coverage for them, in the internet age. These had not been put up as posters. We had just put them out there.

I commissioned the agency to work on a new set and we got them out late Monday with a plan for them to run through Tuesday and into Wednesday's papers. The newspaper cartoonists were going on it now too, including a few I fancied buying. I wonder if the Tories were wondering if they had overreacted. At the morning meeting I slightly lost it with Spencer Livermore because he was doing his usual non-communicative thing and we were trying to extract a plan on James. He suggested a different way of doing things which was department by department and then a big hit pre-Budget. It was not a bad approach but in reality an excuse to stall. At one point he sat back and said nothing and I shouted at him to say what he thought. SM said afterwards there was no point having meetings with him there and we had to work round it probably with another meeting.

I was glad to leave at lunchtime and head for Birmingham, where I was due to interview Kelly Holmes for *The Times*. On the train I worked on a briefing note based on Mark Penn's superb message map – forward not back, then the three areas, economy, crime and asylum, modernising public services, plus dividing lines and negatives. I drafted a possible briefing to do on it and suggested I do it, basically going through the strategic map for the election. AM liked it but was worried about me doing it. He felt that would be the story. But I was getting frustrated that there was no real operation. Burnley v Blackburn in the Cup draw. Fantastic. I did Kelly Holmes in the press room at the indoor arena and felt it went fine, including the run round the track together for the photographs. The obvious theme was whether she was now athlete or icon. She was much better looking than I had remembered her, and though she tended to repeat herself a lot, I liked her and the piece would work.

Tuesday 1 February

The *Mail* doing 'Rattled Blair drops posters' made me feel it was tipping our way. And we had another wave of posters to get up which would make the same central points re Howard again. We just had to hold our nerve. Now we were planning an 'I believe' press ad Howard spoof which was strong and would generate more controversy. PG and I were getting really fed up with the long meetings which AM did not just decide and move on. He wanted us to brand together Ruth Kelly's school discipline plans (urging a 'zero-tolerance' policy for classroom disruption), Alan Johnson's new Incapacity Benefit (removing disincentives to return to work), and asylum and immigration next week, as a big rights and responsibilities thing. We were starting to use 'Fair deal not a raw deal.' I bumped into James Blitz and Cathy Newman of the *FT* and they nodded along to it when I started to try to shape it into a message. I tried to place a *Sun* article on rights and responsibilities but Trevor K resisted after we supplied the draft. He said there was nothing new in it. Trevor was definitely trying to get the paper to turn. We tried to push the line of TB saying 'I get the message' but then DH said TB didn't actually like that line because he would get hit with it at Questions. So we ended up postponing for 24 hours though I suspected TK would find another reason not to do the piece. I had lunch with Bradders to go over it.

Earlier TB did a pretty dire *GMTV* interview. The setting was crap, content was poor and he did not punch message. I felt he was having to decide for himself what to say. His draft speech was wordy and poor and again lacked a driving message. I called him and said he should say we will reward work and learning, build respect, tackle abuse. He kind of delivered it. But there was something very ragged and rushed about the whole thing. ACPO [Association of Chief Police Officers] were publishing the new guidelines on defence of burglary victims and that got us into a slightly better place. Ruth Kelly was doing well and TB running fine. I called Alan Johnson to go over the next bit and said we would like him to do more. He said OK but without enthusiasm.

I left at half three for home to collect the family then to Elstree for *Who Wants to Be a Millionaire?* Fiona was dreading it. The kids seemed quite excited by it. Rehearsal was fine and we got all the questions right. Met Greg [tennis player] and Lucy Rusedski and then up to the green room with family, neighbours, people from the charity etc. We had to wait ages because Greg and Lucy took so long. They were given ages to think about the answers and actually did OK. I felt pretty confident because between us Fiona and I got all their questions straight away. We sailed through our early ones, though we needed a lifeline – ask the audience – on a question about whose catchphrase was 'Knowing me, knowing you' – Alan Partridge – and then got to 8k, and the question was 'Which country launched Skylab space station, US, UK, France, Russia?' I said straight away, 'Not France because they wouldn't give it an English name.' We didn't have a clue though. We called Ian Kennedy [academic and legal/medical expert] as a phone-a-friend lifeline and he said he didn't know but he thought France. We went to the 50/50 lifeline, and it was that or US. We went for France and we were out. Fuck it. How could I go from saying it would definitely not be France to saying it was France? So much for Clive W's T-Cup mantra – think correctly under pressure. Fiona was convinced it had been a mistake to do the programme but it could have been OK. Our other phone-a-friends were Charlie F and Mick Hucknall, and when we spoke afterwards they both said they knew the answer. We watched the end of Arsenal 2, Man U 4 at the studios and Alex called later from the bus where after my text he was trying out Skylab on the players. None of them got it. I suppose at least it wasn't a question I would be expected to get but even so I felt a bit down about it. It would have been great to have won a million for the charity. How the hell that was an 8k question – ridiculous.

Philip, Mark Penn and I had been whacking off different versions of the long 'Forward not back' message script, and it was getting really strong, though Penn was still worrying we were not strong on the immigration/asylum message. What I liked best about it was its simplicity, the fact it took you to future, but also record, and big choices, the biggest of which, as Penn put it, 'keep on modernising for all or go back to the Tories fucking up again.' The economic strength of the message was clear, ditto public services. And we were coming to an agreement around the idea of 'forward on this strong economy, or back to boom and bust; forward to better public services, or back to Tory cuts; forward to a modern Britain with prosperity for all or back to a failed course that worked only for a few.'

Then a whole series of sub-messages with record and future policy messages built into them:

Forward to prosperity for the many, not back to an economy for the few.

Forward to opportunity for the many, not back to privilege for a few.

Forward to quality modern public services for all, not back to services run for a few.

Forward to security, not back to insecurity and a raw deal. (weak)

Forward to a Britain strong in the world, not back to weakness and isolation.

Penn was adding a fair amount on message, and was now planning to poll on big message and also on alternatives. I tried to bring it all together with a new conclusion which we settled on after a series of email exchanges. 'We are proud of our achievements, but we know there is much more to do. We learn from our past, but we focus on the future, because that is how we create a better life for hard-working Britain. So the choice we offer is **forward to a better future, not back to a failed past**.' PG and I went through the last manifesto to make sure that we felt every policy area could be touched by the same message and by having record, future and values.

Wednesday 2 February

I was able to laugh a bit more about last night but still felt pretty down about it. Hardly anyone got the right answer, including TB who felt it was probably an OK thing to do and Sally M who thought it showed empathy. The morning meeting turned into a much longer forward planning meeting, with policy, after having a kind of non-meeting first with Spencer. Everyone seemed to think yesterday was our best day for ages. I felt that was only by comparison with so many bad days before. We had a discussion on what areas would require their own mini manifestos, more on TB visits and interaction, then a long argument about whether to use Howard's signature on the spoof 'I believe' poster, where we were going to put his name to values and beliefs he would actually claim to be opposed to, but wasn't. I was keen to use his signature but AM and PG bottled it. TB was OK with the concept later.

I went to see RC at Portcullis House, met by Joyce who used to work for JP and was now with Robin, up to his very tidy and horsey office, where I noticed a photo of the Queen on his table. We did a bit of small talk and then he said, 'How can I be of help?' I went through my spiel on all the various problems we faced, and got to the point of conditional voting, and said he was uniquely placed to do a 'Disagree on Iraq but... Vote Labour.' I could tell he was pleased to be asked. He said he thought it was an interesting idea and – classic Robin – 'I think you are right I am probably the best person to do this.' He asked if I felt it should be done as a speech, a press conference or interviews. 'All of the above.' He liked the idea of being used. He said he felt sure he could get others to echo the approach. He said his stance on Iraq had made him particularly liked in the Muslim community and that might be a place to target this message. The chattering classes too.

I asked him how he felt things were going. He was pretty damning about TB and the scene generally. He said Iraq was huge out there and it was not just chatterers. TB had lost a lot of support among our core vote because they felt he was too remote and with too many fancy friends. GB was respected. 'Be careful,' he said, 'because he has a lot of support and respect.' He believed that GB would win a secret ballot of MPs. I said I didn't agree with that, but I accepted TB was not as strong as he had been. He felt the Tories were doing better than people thought, which I agreed with.

The last time we had had a one-on-one discussion like this was to plan his departure from government, and I reminded him he had said he hoped it did not all go horribly wrong for TB and me. I said we were still in with a shout for a third election. Yes, he said, but 'I was right about Iraq. It is a disaster getting worse.' It was not an unfriendly meeting and we agreed to have further discussions about how to bring him in. We needed some kind of umbrella label and organisation for his campaign activities. Even if 'conditional voting' was not the phrase, it was in that area. He liked the idea of talking about it as a relationship with the country, that as with a relationship between any two humans, there were agreements and disagreements, ups and downs, but ultimately people could stay together.

I had been trying to push an argument that we should be saying the election choice is not Labour or Perfection, but Labour or Tory, Blair or Howard, and if we could get that it was a way of saying both that we had made mistakes, we were not perfect, but also that we were always going to be better than the other lot. The politicians were too nervous about the mistakes/not perfect bit, but RC might be a good voice for that. He did say as I left that he thought there would be problems for TB after the election, and not just from GB. I went to No. 10 and watched PMQs before going over for a meeting with TB, JoP, SM, Pat and David Hanson [TB's PPS]. TB wanted properly to plan tomorrow's political Cabinet. PG to do polling. AM on organisation and then TB with the main forward not back message. But the main question, which we would also do over dinner (TB, AM, DH, PG, SM Pat and I) and later when TB, JP and I had two hours in the flat, was still about GB.

I was late after going home and to William Ellis [School] for Rory's (excellent) parents' evening. When I arrived back at No. 10, they were going through the polling, taking out one or two things that GB might use against us. Then a discussion over dinner of the message we wanted out of tomorrow. TB wanted it to be New Labour message, clear direction, policy and organisation. I was less convinced we wanted a policy story and felt we would be better doing a campaign story. Forward not back etc. TB was a bit unconfident but that was largely because he had not settled on the plan for GB tomorrow. JP had been up at his (Delivering Sustainable Communities) conference in Manchester and so only just got back this evening.

TB asked me and, for the first bit Sally, to stay behind. He wanted to get to a position where either GB was bound in, helped to deliver a big majority, which would mean he could not challenge; or that it became clear he would not co-operate, in which case if he went for it after an election, his failure to help and his constant undermining could be properly exposed. JP arrived a bit grumpy and was complaining at the way his conference speech up north had been overshadowed by incapacity benefit changes. Sally left and the three of us went into the sitting room, and JP was not in a great mood as we kicked off, but he mellowed a bit as we went on. TB asked him what he thought of the GB situation. He was hoping JP would say something on the lines he had been saying to me, that GB had to get into line or go, but JP didn't operate like that. He started by saying he was in listening mode, and above all he was in listening mode on policy for the third term. He knew how TB felt at the fact he was still buggering about but there were policy issues to do with the manifesto and the pledges and TB had said it was a coalition and he [JP] was part of that and had to be listened to.

He wanted to get a proper manifesto process and he didn't want all this unremitting New Labour pushed down their throats the whole time. He felt we had to take care of the core vote too. TB said polling showed we had less of a problem with the core vote, that the problem was the other part of the coalition. 'You mean the Tories you got to vote for us in '97 and '01,' said JP. TB said, 'Bluntly – yes.' JP said he understood why we won so big because he made Tories feel comfortable with Labour. He was also signed up now to some of the New Labour ideas he at first resisted. TB said he wanted to keep stressing New Labour as a way of signalling he was still there for those people, not weakened. He said he had hoped the GB operation against him would stop after the Peston book, and all the grief it caused, but it had gone on, he was not co-operating with the campaign and we had to bring it to a head. JP agreed with that but went back into policy. He did come round as the evening wore on and said he accepted TB was more aggressed than aggressing and he knew he had to bring it to a head. TB said it was not much to ask that the Chancellor supports the PM and makes clear he won't challenge. He said to JP, 'I really need you there, making clear that if Gordon refuses to rule out a challenge, you would not support him.'

JP took some time to come round but by the end was fine, and pretty much on board for the approach we had been discussing. He said, 'You should bare your chest and see if he stabs you.' They both felt he would not challenge now. TB said he felt there was a strong streak of cowardice in there and so probably he wouldn't. JP said TB should spell out to him where he was coming from, say he wanted him running the economic campaign and hitting James and getting engaged. If he refused or buggered about JP would say he had had enough of it and we would have to work around him. I raised sacking, saying, 'The other option is he just asks him to leave the government, and challenges him to challenge him now, rather than after the election.' He said that would be a big step, maybe too big. I said you could not have a campaign without your Chancellor. He agreed with that but said the aim must be to keep him in. TB said despite everything he wanted GB to take over but to get his help he had to co-operate for the rest of Tony's time in office. He wanted JP to take the same position. JP was pretty much up for that but unsure about TB thinking he would stay for another four years, and whether we were intending to keep up on the notion that GB would take over earlier.

TB said that when the three of them had had dinner at JP's flat in Admiralty House, when JP had left the two of them together TB had said to GB 'I will go, if you work with me meanwhile.' I said the trouble with that is GB only hears 'I will go.' TB said he had told him if the GB lot put it out there that TB was thinking of going, he would deny it and say he was staying on. But they put it straight into the press as they always do. By the end of the night JP was fine. I felt a bit odd, no longer being in the job but TB asking me to be there because JP was a lot easier if I was. He was fine about the posters and I showed him the Howard 'I Believe' ad which he liked. TB was unsure after it all exactly what they had agreed but when JoP and SM came back in I summed it up as follows – we try to keep him in. TB puts cards clearly on the table with a demand that GB runs the economic campaign without, as JP put it, 'hanging Milburn from a lamppost'. GB has to make clear he will help the fight to deliver a big majority and make clear there will be no challenge after the election, however reduced the majority.

What was interesting was that though JP bought some of the GB analysis – e.g. TB making half deals, using outsiders to undermine him etc., he bought more into the TB thesis. He could not let it go on and it had to be brought to a head. 'I would never have put up with it like you have. His feet should never have touched the ground.' TB told him he [JP] had never let him down and did not feel that he would. He knew he was primarily motivated by the party holding together and he needed to know TB also felt an obligation to ensure it remained in strong shape. He felt if JP made clear to GB he would not support a challenge then he felt there was no way he would go for it. We ended up in better mood than when we started, JP joking that the whole thing went back to TB guilt at the original decision in '94 and it had been a nightmare for everyone since. 'Longest guilt trip in history,' I said. 'And longest sulk,' said JP.

JP asked him how GB leading an economic campaign would fit with our current structures under Alan. He said provided we had someone at the morning meetings who was au fait with GB and able to deliver him doing things, and provided GB and I [AC] had some kind of ongoing dialogue, there should not be a problem. TB said AM's confidence was getting hit because they were constantly briefing against him. It was a good evening though and JP was in an OK place. But as to what tomorrow would bring it was impossible to tell.

Thursday 3 February
I was out of the house before seven, and for the first time in ages, as I was going to the political Cabinet, I was in a suit and tie, which

I hated. I got the bus in for a meeting on the design for the pledge cards which had to be signed off today if we were to be ready for the launch next Friday. The designers had done a good job. We agreed that we would go for six pledges not five and that we should launch the asylum one [introducing a points system] separately. TB disagreed later, felt economy should go first. It kind of missed the point, which was to make clear the economy was the bedrock of the campaign, but we needed to isolate asylum and immigration to show we 'got it'. I went off to write AM's post-Cabinet briefing words while they went to the ordinary Cabinet. But before that TB saw GB with JP. He left it to JP to give the very clear message, later communicated to the entire Cabinet (though with GB not there because he had Treasury questions), that there was only one leader, one team and we stood together. TB said JP was pretty clear that he would not support him in a challenge. GB left the meeting 'almost tearful', according to JoP.

I sat around with PG, Matt Carter and Matthew Doyle waiting for the Cabinet to arrive in the state dining room for the political Cabinet. With the exception of GB, who said not a word apart from a look that could kill, they were all very warm and friendly. I suspect GB is thinking I had brought the whole thing to a head, and he knew I had a better relationship with JP than anyone else in No. 10. I said, 'Hiya Gordon,' as he walked past, and he just glowered, first at the floor, then at me, then at the floor again. The others, especially CC and JS, who was in a flap about all the media stuff re GB becoming Foreign Secretary, were very warm and welcoming, lots of 'Good to see you back.' Both *The Sun* and *Times* had stories today saying GB would be happy to be Foreign Secretary. We assumed GB had briefed it out as part of an effort publicly to show good grace. But then we heard his people were briefing that the story came direct from TB to Rupert M.

PG kicked off the polling and did a terrific job. Not too downbeat but realistic. It was all from the marginal polls and showed that we were strong on the economy, getting stronger on public services, but weak on crime and asylum. He hammered asylum the whole way through. He did the message polling stuff well too, taking them through all the different messages and sub-messages we had tested, and led them to 'Forward not back'. TB did an excellent overview up at his flip chart, based on the note on messaging I did at the weekend. Forward not back. Going through the three areas. Economy. Modernising public services. Then dealing with crime and asylum. Any highlighting of progress made only as a signal of more change and reform to come.

He stressed New Labour not as a kick in the teeth for the old but as a way of signalling more change and also showing we were still reaching out. He did a very good job and was well received.

He said he had asked GB to come back with an economic and James campaign next week. The other thing he hammered, as did others, was the team and the need to kill division. When it came to the comments around the table, I would say the dominant themes were a sense of relief that there appeared to be a campaign plan and a fairly simple strategic message and plan; but also again and again that the division was damaging and had to stop. There were the usual anecdotes from the usual suspects to underline the point.

TB emphasised the whole New Labour agenda and said if people would not sign up to that, now was the time to say so, and he left it hanging in the air just long enough for a bit of tension. It felt like the moment in a wedding when the minister asks if anyone has any reason why the couple shouldn't get married, and even though the stats suggest it hardly ever happens, there is a tiny part of you thinks it might, and there is a bit of tension until the minister carries on. I was looking at GB, as were others, and he was just staring at his pad, scribbling something. The discussion was fairly desultory but some good points came up.

Pat [Hewitt] said it was intolerable to have the kind of discussion we had last week and then find it recorded in the press. CC said he had all of the main negatives in his brief – crime, anti-social behaviour, asylum, immigration – and he needed to do it as a team. MB [Margaret Beckett] was good. AD minor tactical points though both he and GB made the point the media would not cover issues like the economy unless we made them controversial. GB's contribution was to say it was not a typical campaign because as well as the Tories we had the Lib Dems and apathy as enemies. He said he would do a campaign on the economy but he didn't sound convincing, and there was very little detail. He looked bad, jowly and with big bags under his eyes and kept looking up to the ceiling. Shaking head. Sighing. Stroking the side of his face. Looking at JP and smiling if TB said anything overly New Labour. JR was fairly provocative both on the division and also on policy.

JP though was the star. He did a rambling but powerful speech saying how well we had done, how he had his doubts about New Labour but TB had proved him wrong, how we would have rows on policy but let's have them and then agree and get on with it. He had everyone in hysterics when he said, 'Come on Tony, it's about Tories innit? We've got our vote basically coming back but you're worried about the Tories we had yeah? You want them back. I'm not daft. And I know we need them and of course you said your aim was to destroy the Tories and you've done it. You've replaced them.' Laughter. 'They think you're a better Tory than Howard.' More laughter. Then he got serious again.

On discipline he apologised to Milburn for getting into the papers as saying he was a jumped up backbencher. He actually meant Byers – laughter – but that's not the point. He should never have said it and allowed people to use it against him. Likewise all the gossip and briefing had to stop. We have a great leader, a great team, we're a good government so let's stick together and get out and fight the Tories not each other. He talked directly of the 'Blair–Brown thing' and the need not to feed it. 'It has helped nobody but our enemies, and it has to stop. We all know it and we all have to do what we can to make it happen. Time to stop fighting and start winning again.' It was a powerful end to a good meeting. Also TB had slipped GB a note saying he wanted him to meet him and me to go over the economic campaign. Fat chance.

I went off with AM and the briefing went fine though there had been a lack of communication which meant there were no cameras in for it. But it went OK and though his answers were a bit long and he was a bit too laddish it was fine. I had a perfectly civilised chat with Andrew Marr. I had in my pocket a personalised pledge card addressed to him, which was one of the ideas we had brainstormed, and which would be part of targeted direct mail. I went to a series of meetings in No. 10 re TB's diary and forward events. We gave KG [Kate Garvey] a stack of ideas to work on. This week had certainly been better than last and we were working hard to get the message right on asylum now too. I had been a bit wary about going to Cabinet but it was the right move and TB made clear if anyone at Vic St – me, Alan or Matt e.g. – asked for something, it was a priority. AM did an OK presentation too. I was home fairly early but it was becoming too much like the old days with phone and email going too often. Fiona seemed fine about things but that may not hold if the pressures keep mounting, which they will.

Friday 4 February
TB called to go over media strategy on asylum and immigration and we agreed he should do [*Observer* journalist Andrew] Rawnsley's radio

February '05: Stirring words from JP

show on Sunday night. The lines had all been tested – tough but workable, alongside a message about the need to welcome genuine asylum cases and also the migrants the economy needed. I worked on the pledges – long and short – before heading for the train to Euston, heading north to do another fundraiser for Burnley FC. I did some Lions work and also, with Trevor B getting very upset at media intrusion – for example, the MoS had been getting into his 85-year-old mum – I briefed Tom Baldwin about the flying pig posters having been more us than TBWA as a way of taking some of the heat off Trevor. Alex had had to pull out of the last fundraiser because of his heart scare, but as agreed he was coming back, and I also had Brendan [Foster], and Ray Stubbs and John Motson [broadcasters] lined up to support us too. I got to the Oaks Hotel in time to meet Brendan for a cup of tea before we headed to Turf Moor. He felt we were actually in not bad shape, but of course his patch was always better disposed towards us.

The mood at the club was a lot better than last time. We were on the Cup run, and had more money in. Alex was terrific both beforehand in chatting to people, signing autographs and then made a terrific speech. He got them laughing telling the story of me on Sky celebrating the Liverpool win and how he called Fiona to ask if she had ever thought of getting me locked up, and she said she was ashamed of me. He told a couple of great stories about Roy Keane, like when he asked the fitness coach if he could take on Roy at kick boxing and the coach said, 'Are you not well?' He was also brilliant on the Arsenal match and what it meant, and as Bobby Charlton had been, really good on why football people liked clubs like Burnley.

Motty wavered between off the wall and totally brilliant, with the mention of anyone or anywhere unleashing a torrent of memories, and he was very funny when he and I did Q&A and he said Blackburn was the worst ground to work at, and the tea was much better here. He also told the story of how when he was commentating on the Euro 2004 Final last year, the first text that came through when he turned on his phone at the end was from me, asking why he had failed to mention when he came on that Dimitris Papadopolous [Greece substitute] had played for Burnley? Brendan was terrific and Stubbs threw in an extra auction prize – reading final scores on interactive grandstand. I auctioned and got Sonya Kilby [chairman's wife] up to £4,200.

We must have signed hundreds of autographs and the atmosphere was terrific. AM called and said he thought I was going to be the story over the weekend after being pictured going into No. 10. The *Standard* splashed on a memo Fraser [Kemp] was involved in re us trying to use FoI [Freedom of Information] to dig up stuff on Howard in office. Fraser was worried but I said we had to be firm – not knowing that tomorrow's papers would blame me for it anyway.

Saturday 5 February

Fiona was upset about the papers, which were starting to get into me again, and said I should think long and hard about whether I want my reputation trashed again. 'You are just about getting your head above water again and now you are diving straight back in. Nobody will thank you for it if you take all the shit again.' I said they did it because they wanted to stop us being effective and also give cover for what they would do by way of negative campaigning v TB. But her take was I was just a useful foil and lightning conductor for the politicians, and they used me. Tom Baldwin did me proud re Beattie and PG and Trev both texted to say it was a big thing to do, to take the blame as a way of helping him. I was now copping it for posters, FoI and all round bad guy-ism. John Major went on to do a poodle interview with John Humphrys and got going a story that I was involved in getting up the Black Wednesday story again [fresh details of the Black Wednesday financial crisis under John Major in 1992 had been released following a Freedom of Information request]. In fact, as Andrew Turnbull [Cabinet Secretary] said to me – calling to dispute a report in the *Sunday Telegraph* of bad blood between us over Hutton – it was an *FT* request over which the Treasury got a bit over excited.

TB, AM and I had a conference call and agreed we needed to deny the JM allegations but also get up the Tory strategy which with the help of the *Mail* was to delegitimise legitimate inquiry and attack. We had to hold firm. Meanwhile the important thing was getting the asylum message right. The Burnley match was dire, 1–0 to Leeds and a missed penalty. I also had a dreadful cold and had to do a Rossendale and Darwen [Labour Party] members' meeting, then to Liverpool for Jane Kennedy's CLP dinner which went really well. I told all the old jokes which seemed to go fine. Jane was really nice and I said we should use her and AJ much more. I sang a song to Traore to the tune of Yesterday which went down well, re the own goal he [Liverpool defender Djimi Traore] scored when we beat Liverpool. And they gave me a replica '60s Burnley shirt, which was great. I was driven back and was home by 1.30. Matthew was texting me endlessly with what was in the papers and loads re me including two or three splashes and stuff on salary, posters, Major having a pop (what Mike White called revenge of the Y-fronts).*

Sunday 6 February

I watched CC on *Frost*, who was good. John Sergeant did me proud on the review of the papers suggesting it was all fuss over not much and the press loved the fact I was back. I did a letter to the *Telegraph* denying Major's stuff and spoke to TB re how to expose the broader Tory strategy. He said it was classic – they accuse us of dirty tricks so that they can then indulge in them. I drafted a statement from AM for the web defending me and defending our attacks on Howard's record and policies and exposing the Tory–*Mail* strategy. Clive W called from Rome, said he had enjoyed reading the front pages. I said he might get a bit of blowback from his people. He said he thought it was great. It would put the wind up people. He was really disappointed at England (9–11 losers to Wales in Six Nations championship), felt it was a mistake to play [Matthew] Tait, but the great thing he took out of the weekend was Gavin Henson who was awesome at centre. He felt with him, Gordon D'Arcy and Brian O'Driscoll we had amazing choice at centre. We agreed we would brief a few background words on Henson as being a real contender now.

I spoke to a few hacks re the AM statement on the Tory strategy and also to TB to plan his Rawnsley interview. I watched Italy v Ireland while briefing Louisa on what to brief out of Clive. I tried to get a bit of work done and talked a couple of times to TB. There was far too much re me in the Sundays. Fraser called to say he was doing the *Today* 0730 slot and we went over various lines. Rory texted a couple of times from Russia (school trip) but I hated it when they were away and was dreading him leaving for university.

Monday 7 February

The commentariat were having a field day re my so-called return. Fraser did well, as did Peter M, who was on about something else and defending me as under attack because the Tories knew how effective

---

* Cartoonist Steve Bell of *The Guardian* had famously lampooned then Prime Minister John Major as a grey superhero wearing his Y-front briefs on the outside of his trousers.

I was at campaigning. Rachel Sylvester [*Telegraph*] had a piece about me and Alan being macho and how GB was preparing an alternative campaign. I drew it to JP's attention when he came over to Vic St later. I did a piece on the BBC on the way in and then took the meeting, going through the week, asylum today, Liaison Committee plus Jack [Straw] presser on Europe, AM and Hazel Blears [Home Office minister] on internet and pledges Wednesday, 'reform works' Thursday, pledges Friday. TB had suggested that Ian McC write to meet Liam Fox to discuss agreed legitimate parameters of campaigning. We agreed a poster of Howard facing both ways. There was nobody from HMT at the meeting so we probably got more done. There was plenty of briefing against us going on but things feeling a bit better.

I left for Euston and got the train to Wolverhampton. Worked on various scripts, spoke to TB re asylum message etc. and also forward stuff. He was seeing JP again before JP came down to see the team at HQ. Mike Ion [candidate] is a lovely guy but the first part of the visit was a bit grim. Lib Dem and anti-war demonstrators, kids with attitude, a Trot teacher saying all politicians were corrupt and people yelling and bawling outside. A few eggs. Protests during and after. Police having to help us out. Then to a hospice where I was really moved by the dedication of the people working there. Two-thirds raised through charitable donations. No media at their request but they wanted me to mention them in interviews. We went then to the *Shrewsbury Chronicle*, editor John Butterworth, the interviewer named Alex Ferguson, then to the Lion Hotel, a couple of very strong interviews who seemed less interested in protests than the fact I was there to support Mike.

Leo [TB's father] and Olwen Blair [Leo's wife] came to the members' meeting and Leo seemed to be speaking a little better than last time I saw him. I did my usual pitch then Q&A had some great moments, a woman going at me re Iraq and then a guy laying into her, saying he used to live there and he knows the reality of Saddam and if people can't say anything good about the government, they should shut up. Applause.

Mike gave me a lift to Wolverhampton and due to a multitasking malfunction I did the daftest thing. I was talking to Mike while going through emails and there was one from BBC *Newsnight* about a *Standard* story that I was behind flying pigs and TBWA saying Trevor had nothing to do with them. Trevor called and said he was also being harassed by *Newsnight* now and what should he say/do? Then I sent an email to Andrew McGuinness [TBWA] – so I thought – setting out what TBWA should say to *Newsnight*, then ending, 'Now fuck off and cover something important, you twats.' It went not to Andrew McGuinness but to Andrew McFadden of *Newsnight*, as on the BlackBerry 'Andrew Mc' was all that came up. I chatted to MD, PG and Trevor, all of whom felt I should send another humorous one, to show that I was non-phased. But it was bound to be the latest AC brouhaha. Tim Allan called and was in hysterics when I briefed him. It was ridiculous. *Newsnight* went big on the email. Fiona not amused, said it was all part of the way the politicians let me take all the shit for them. This one however had been entirely my own making.

Tuesday 8 February

The AC story was going far too big and the email fuck-up was not going to help. MD called to say the *Standard* were splashing on it and I had stacks of calls through the day. All we could do was keep saying it was about the media trying to help the Tories take me out of the game because I was an asset, plus all part of the trivia agenda. But I could do without it. We also had Lynton Crosby [Australian strategist working for the Tories] and CCO [Conservative Central Office] suing *The Times*, which was suggesting they were losing the plot in there. At the morning meeting there was some frustration that we were not really following through on asylum. We had TB at the Liaison Committee but that could go anywhere. The morning meetings were getting too long and crowded and HMT presence, while necessary on one level, was stopping openness. Also Alan tended to make decisions and then unpick them. But there was a bit more energy around and a bit more zip. I did an interview with *Rugby World* and found myself again feeling keener about the Lions than the election.

Then to a meeting with Alan and Greville Janner, David Triesman and Jonny Mendelsohn [leading Jewish figures in the Labour Party]. They really laid it on the line about pigs and especially the poster of Howard looking like Fagin, and then went into other demands e.g. to do with Ken Livingstone, Muslim clerics. They were real chisellers as JoP would say, getting us to agree with one complaint and then raising another. Greville was adamant there had been real rumblings. He said Andrew Dismore [MP for Hendon] said he could lose his seat on the back of it. AM said he had heard stuff like that for eight years. But it was OK and we agreed we would give Jon Mendelsohn advance sight of anything that might be a bit tricky with the Jewish community.

Alan did a big W [for wanker] sign as they left, and said he found having to toady to Greville particularly awful. But it was worth doing.

I went to see TB, whose Liaison Committee meeting had gone fine but was low-key. He was not thrilled at the BlackBerry malarkey but didn't dwell on it. He knew the press would make me the story but felt it was worth the price. Even I was a bit taken aback just how big it had all gone. AM told me JS said to him he had to 'get AC under control' – not the first time JS had been at it. I had still not forgotten his dropping me in it over the Iraq second dossier at the FAC. TB said we had three issues – lack of real edge to policy, GB, and lack of strategic communications. He felt things were improving on all three, but we were still not exactly where we wanted it all to be. PG and I did a presentation on polling and strategy to No. 10 spads. We went through the polling and then I did a very upbeat run through of the message map and I said it was all designed for TB's strengths and we had to keep it focused, get his energy levels up and keep him motoring on that. OK Q&A, good mood considering, and then to the political strategy meeting attended by TB, GB, JP, AM, MC, Pat McF, SM, PG, AC and aides.

TB was speaking to Bush on the secure phone and was delayed. As we waited there were little chats but JP and GB were totally disengaged. GB scribbling, JP scowling and the atmosphere bad. TB came in and was fairly defensive, asked PG re polling then asked GB for his economic campaign plan. GB set off into circular non-conversation mark ten, ten years on. In short – it was very difficult to fight on the economy because we didn't know what would happen; difficult to sustain the attack on the Tories because with BoE [Bank of England] independence people didn't really think that interest rates would soar. Then he did his diversion – we should do public services first but health and education were not doing the business in terms of communication. It was hopeless he said. We were getting hammered and we did not have the killer facts up. He was right on one level but it was all a means of avoiding the subject. When we persisted and asked for the solution he prevaricated.

I said I felt we had to do economy and James first before we got to cuts. We had a good record and had to put it out there, allied to the future agenda. It quickly became a circular conversation at the end of which TB said we had to integrate GB into the campaign grid and work together but he was not really engaged at all. He reinvented past campaigns and suggested we had always planned 'schools and hospitals first' in 2001 which was not the case. According to the others

February '05: Jack Straw urges TB to get AC 'under control'

it was the best meeting we had had for ages but that was real 'I have stopped banging my head against a wall' mentality. I made the point that there was a real sense we only cared about Iraq and Africa – he smarted at that. He was due to go to China and said he would do a big number on globalisation and that was the place to do it. I said we should try to build it into our grid and operation.

The email story was going far too big, second lead on ITN after Ellen MacArthur [sailor] setting a new round-the-world record. Ridiculous. I got a couple of funny messages from Clive in Scotland who seemed fine. Ditto Louisa but they would almost certainly get a bit of blow-back. *Mail* total scum, ditto *Standard* doing Dacre bidding. I went back and we got a good story to the *Mirror* out of a document used at a Tory training event which showed them explaining how to deal with angry voters. Then a cup of tea with Andrew Mitchell [Tory MP] and David Davis's chief of staff. It was a nice enough chat and I was surprised by how much they had given up on thinking they could win. Andrew felt that for all our problems, TB was seen as head and shoulders above anyone else, the economy was doing fine, and Howard was not really cutting it. 'I don't know what you're worrying about!'

Wednesday 9 February

Pages and columns galore about my BlackBerry. Cartoons all over the place. Most of the feedback was that it was funny but that didn't stop all the sanctimoniousness around the place, trying to make it all about me bullying the media, even though it was blindingly obvious it was just mis-sent. The morning meeting went on too long. There was a general bottling out on the Howard 'I believe' poster because we were trying to go positive with the pledges. What we didn't realise was TB had agreed to do an apology to the Guildford Four because Bertie [Ahern] wanted him to and also to show nationalist opinion he could.* It blew us out for the day. Then a real problem – the families were expecting TB to do it in the House but it having been fixed with the Speaker the SDLP [Social Democratic and Labour Party in Ireland] briefed it was happening, the UUs [Ulster Unionists] got angry and

---

* The group of four whose convictions for the Guildford pub bombings of October 1974 were quashed in 1989 after long campaigns. Their confessions to Provisional IRA outrages were obtained by intense coercion and they served fifteen to sixteen years in prison after their original convictions.

the Speaker decided against calling Eddie McGrady [SDLP MP], who was due to ask it. So TB had to do it to camera in his Commons office.

I had a good meeting with Ed Miliband, who seemed to accept there was a new mood around the TB–GB question right now, and we agreed to try to get GB in China up politically. I did a note to that effect. PMQs OK and he hammered Howard pretty well. I got a message from JoP that TB had agreed with GB he would not do interactive stuff on Saturday so we had to persuade him again. I had a long session with Seb at a new Scots bar which was run by a bloke with a black kilt. Seb looking good, very expensive suit, getting ready for the IOC evaluation team. Also he said he thought I should get close to Kelly [Holmes] and advise her how to deal with things if and when the press decided to get into her. He felt sure they would at some point. Got some decent stuff for a decent piece about him and politics. Back to see TB first with Rebekah, him trying to get her back on board, her describing the right-wingers trying to get the paper back to the Tories. We gave her the story of the asylum pledge.

Then a meeting with TB, AM, SM, JoP and Pat to go over the situation. TB saying it was all about strategic comms, me saying it went deeper than that and beyond GB. E.g. we couldn't get proper strategic comms when Irish apologies popped up unplanned, or him changing his mind when we agreed he would do more interactive stuff, but we got him round on that one as well. He asked me to do him more sections for the speech. I ran home and on the way, just this side of Hyde Park, I was stopped by a bloke who said 'I don't care what they say, you are a star and you should punch the Tories and the papers into the middle of next week.' Fiona was anxious about me being up in lights again, ditto Mum who called and sounded really hurt by it all. 'But I thought you were leaving?' I have left, but I am helping for the election. 'They are just attacking you all the time again though.' It's fine, I said, and won't be for ever, but she wasn't happy.

Thursday 10 February

The stuff re me was dying down but was now spawning the cartoons and I tried to land some of them for LRF. G2 cover was me and the BlackBerry. Sara Latham jokingly asked if I would do BlackBerry ads. According to Pat, GB did an OK presentation on the economy to Cabinet, TB did fine on *Richard and Judy* and I worked at home and finally put together a complete draft. The news was totally dominated by the announcement Charles and Camilla were marrying but we did manage to get the pledges up overnight. I felt TB's speech was fairly straightforward but he was in danger of complicating it. He needed to reconnect, show hunger for the job, do 'Forward not back' and the pledges and yet I could sense he was as ever looking for a mythical big new argument. I sent the draft to JP because he was doing *Today* and he was worried about 'I'm back' because it felt almost like an apology, that he had stopped doing the job properly. He felt we just had to do record and delivery as symbol of credibility that we would do it again. He was getting agitated in particular because Tony Woodley had been given a slot to whack us at conference.

Richard Curtis, Emma Freud and Siobhan Hawthorne [Comic Relief] came round pm and we reviewed where they were on the diplomatic strategy front. I suggested they see DM and make a real effort with Condi [Condoleezza] Rice [US Secretary of State] who, as her Europe tour was showing, would make a real effort for distinction from the rest of the Bush crowd. The pledges briefing was going OK but was all pretty overwhelmed by Charles and Camilla. Clive called after his trip to Scotland and was enjoying my brouhaha. He said he was going to ask BlackBerry for free BlackBerries for the players. I managed to break the back of the TB speech I was trying to do, and enjoyed writing it, though worried whether he would go for it. The idea was to do 'Forward not back', but in the context we had been discussing on and off for ages, where he reflected on lessons learned in doing the job, was honest about what we did badly as well as what we did well, how sometimes he felt powerless to make change, that 'the real deliverers' were the businesses and the people who worked in public services; also talked about openly using the idea of him having a 'relationship' with the country and like any relationship there had been ups and downs, and maybe they worried he had floated off abroad instead of focusing on them at home. But now he was back. I think partly I was writing about myself, and Fiona, but I thought done properly, and at the right time, it could be a big connecting moment for him, and the presentation by the guys Shaun W had brought in had got him in a better position on this.

The truth is he does have a relationship with the country and a lot of his problems at the moment are caused by the fact loads of people loved him when he first came on the scene, and won, and now they don't so much because of the tough stuff he has had to do, and because – another point in the speech – no person and no government is ever going to be perfect. I liked the line about 'the only miracles being in the Bible,' and also the idea of describing himself and the country as a couple in the kitchen having a shouting match, throwing a bit of crockery – now I was definitely channelling me and Fiona – but then making up and deciding to stick with each other. 'You can run off with Mr Howard if you like, but is that what you really want?' What a thought. I sent it to PG before TB to check out if it wasn't all a bit manic and mad, but Philip loved it. The timing would be important though.

Friday 11 February

I set off with PG for Newcastle, Elinor Goodman [political editor, *Channel 4 News*] asking for a briefing on the way. We were launching the pledges one by one through the day. I'd caught the launch of the economic pledge on TV at King's Cross and it looked fine. Then saw the health one and the party had set it up fine. But as the day went on it became clear that nobody had actually briefed the hacks on the real policy content of the pledges. We did not really recover from the 'policy light – detail light' attack. They seemed to think the headline 'Your family better off' was it. Alan and I were both livid that the briefing operation hadn't been done properly. On the way up we talked over various forward plans. PG said that only he and I seemed to have campaign ideas. A woman reading every word of the *Mail* was sitting next to me, making me feel ill. Graeme Davis, ex-Glasgow University principal, came over and introduced himself. Very nice about Donald [AC brother, university piper]. We got to the Sage [Gateshead venue] and watched TB's arrival then chatted over what he needed to do as he launched the last pledge with JP, Patricia and Ruth Kelly. Ian and JP spoke for too long. TB did fine and we definitely scored a hit but the policy vacuity charge was going to hurt for a day or two.

We got back to Myrobella [TB constituency home] and I was struck again that there was no real proactive briefing operation going on for the speech but I didn't feel it was my place to be doing it. My worry was TB would start totally to rewrite the speech. I had given him some of the new stuff I did last night, but not the whole thing as it needed its own moment. In fact he was on for it being simple. Like JP, he was now worried about 'I'm back' as being a bit like saying he had not been doing the job. JP also didn't like it because he thought people would say it was because things didn't work when he was supposedly in charge. TB rewrote the policy section, cut down the personal stuff without taking out too much but it was basically OK. We had dinner bought in for me, him and PG and went over it all again. He was keen on a line about partnership. We moved on from 'All things to all men' to 'I know best' to 'We can only do it together', which worked fine. TB enjoying being back on the trail. It was odd being back at Myrobella. Liz Lloyd was there because she was going for nomination in Bishop Auckland. TB was on OK form but did ask at one point, 'Can we get my numbers up?' We were only four ahead in the marginals. He said he was struck whenever he was with the media that they didn't really want him to succeed. It was the jealousy of the same generation.

Saturday 12 February

TB was up before seven but when I went down a bit later he was at the kitchen table staring at a blank piece of paper. He was worrying about the policy bit. I drafted a piece on the different phases of leadership, then started to stitch together the whole thing. He said he didn't think he could improve on the stuff I had done about the relationship with the country, but he was worried someone would brief it was done by me with Roy's [Langmaid's] help. I was a bit worried about that, thought Roy was fine but was not totally sure re others. We basically got the speech cracked by the time I left. He said 'I can't tell you how glad I am you are back.' I said we had to get a better media operation in place. Pat and Darren could do more in that area, let David do the firefighting and maybe Pat and Darren the more strategic stuff. Parna [Basu, party advisor] came up to take me to the airport and go over what she might do in the election. I did the briefing note, spoke to the briefers and set off. Long chat with Rory, who said he reckoned quite a few of his teachers were Tories. I got to Sandown Park, where I was doing a race tomorrow, did a few interviews on the triathlon, swam in the 'swim for tri' tank, then did the triathlon seminar for first-timers. Toby Baxendale [entrepreneur] was trying to get me into the Ironman series [long-distance triathlon races].

Sunday 13 February

TB had got through a late wobble on the personal stuff. PM and AH [Anji Hunter] both liked it. Oddly, given he had always been pushing for more connecting language, Peter Hyman – who was getting a fair bit of publicity for his book about education – did not. TB also cranked up the attack on Howard. It was a good speech and as soon as it was finished I got a stack of positive feedback messages. The overnight briefing on no complacency had gone pretty well.

After the race I set off for Twickenham, England v France. I was in the royal box party and it was pretty high Tory. Francis Baron looked like something out of the Countryside Alliance with a red waistcoat and check jacket. There were one or two others straight out of the pinkie ring brigade. Clive and Jayne arrived just after me and CW said it was really weird being there. These were the people he held responsible for the game being held back. Lunch was OK, with a couple of Lancastrian friends of Bill B and two very French rugby board people. The welcome was fairly warm though. The game was poor (17–18). I was also surprised at the lack of real atmosphere and passion in the crowd, just the occasional 'Swing Low Sweet Chariot', which I hated. England should have walked it by half-time but missed half a dozen kicks while the French kicked theirs. I went with Richard Prescott [RFU media liaison] to the Andy Robinson [England coach] and co. presser. They tried too hard to say it was OK. [Coach] Phil Larder said he felt bad as he walked out. The speech coverage was going OK. Working on Burnley speech.

Monday 14 February

The press fairly sniffy but TB's speech did an OK job. At the morning meeting we tried to grip the pledge roll-out. We learned TB was visiting the Midlands. I worked on a script for overnight which Darren [Murphy] did. TB called and felt he had done OK. It was getting ridiculous the extent to which they would only cover us on their terms or if something OTT or weird happened. We joked about the idea of me and Alan doing a press conference in women's clothes. His attacks on Howard were being described as partisan. So they could go round saying he was a liar but he could not attack MH. He felt we were in better shape but needed to maintain momentum. Alan wanted to do reconnection, policy and third term mission. I was worried it would just end up in a stack of rows. TB said we had to watch GB because he will not have enjoyed the weekend and will be looking to cause trouble. We immediately had two e.g.s – a story in the *Standard* that he felt we would need to harden the pledge card because it was too vague. And then we learned he was doing a Sure Start visit tomorrow.

I saw George Jones [*Telegraph* political editor] to get a couple of

February '05: Media 'sniffy' about TB speech

cartoons and then saw June Sarpong who put me in touch with [comedian] Matt Lucas's agent as we were hoping to get him involved. Later we heard Howard was doing immigration tomorrow, saying that all would-be immigrants would be screened for HIV and tuberculosis. Classic nasty Howard stuff, but we didn't quite get our act together re the response. The Tories had clearly decided they were going to hammer this for all they could. I could see some short-term gain for them but it all felt a bit desperate. I got home and Joan Hammell sent me a text asking if I could have breakfast with JP before he set off for Chequers. Instead we ended up having dinner at La Casalinga with Fiona, Rory and Joan.

JP had virtually lost his voice. He was keen, tonight and then when we drove down to Chequers on Tuesday morning, to get in the right place but he also had a stack of concerns. He was not happy at the way Gateshead went, the fact there was so little reference to the party or local government. He was angry he had not been able to get hold of a proper plan. He had taken till Saturday night to establish what his role would be re TB's speech, which he felt was too skewed to 'getting his Tories back'. He was angry at what he thought were deals going on to get safe seats for 'mekons'. I assume he meant people like Liz, and said that was a bit harsh. 'You know what I mean, all these Spads thinking they can waltz in.' He was scathing re e.g. Jean Corston and Derek Foster [MPs] clearly signalling help for a TB candidate if they went to the Lords. He was also, as ever, tired of the TB–GB stuff. GB had bent his ear about the Q&A scenario at Gateshead. He had got GB into the frame of mind for doing a proper presentation on the economy last week, then just before he did it TB passed him a note saying he was doing the Q&A Saturday p.m. JP rather bought the GB line that TB kept upstaging him. But equally he said he had no illusions re GB and he had never given JP support when he needed it.

Tuesday 15 February

The Times did me – and Seb – proud re my piece on the IOC evaluation team. Seb was chuffed with it. I ran in to SW1 to meet JP and drive down to Chequers with him. He went over much the same ground. First at length on his negotiations with the unions on our pensions changes which were proving difficult. Then the whole New Labour thing, Milburn, mekons, lots of little complaints building up. He was down about Ian, said he regretted having put up such a fight to get him to stay as party chairman. He said Ian was now doing a lot less and Alan was party chairman in all but name. He had his usual beef about not being involved enough. He didn't feel Matt Carter was tough enough to stand up for the party interest all the time. By the time we got there, TB was waiting to do a [Hosni] Mubarak [Egyptian President] call about the Lebanon bombing.

JP said he had a real concern about the party, and said to TB 'You've never much bothered about it but I have to and I'm not happy. You've got your team and they do what you want but you've totally taken over the party and what you want is not always necessarily in the party's interest.' He was pissed off there was not a proper manifesto process and re the strategy committee, he said it was obvious from the reaction at the last meeting that everything always depended on whether GB was co-operating. He said he is a miserable git and we cannot be stymied by his moods. 'You have to have the strategy committee meeting regularly, making decisions, giving direction to the operational people, and then get on with it. We cannot be hanging around for Gordon.' He said he felt there was a Sally M list of candidates she was trying to get selected. He was not happy about that either.

We agreed maybe Joan should come to the morning meetings. Re the manifesto he did not think we should go beyond the five-year plans. He was worried AM would over crank it all as a way of stressing his role in policy choices going forward, and that TB would encourage him. He was OK by the time he left, and said to TB he had asked for the meeting and maybe it didn't justify a trip to Chequers but he wanted to be able to watch his back from a party point of view. TB made a joke about it – said next time I send GB a note we will convene a NEC meeting to discuss how I do it. JP laughed but emphasised he did not want to be pushed into a situation where he felt he had to criticise and disagree because that is what the media wanted.

TB then had meetings on future government structures with JoP, Ivan Rogers [civil servant] and John Birt, later joined by Andrew Turnbull. Then AM, DM, DH, SM, MC and Pat came down. We sorted the grid for the next month. In between we were trying to work out the best way to deal with the Tories promising HIV and TB screening for all immigrants, their latest way of keeping asylum and immigration in lights. The TB strategy meeting was poor, going through the grid so that we were like a sub group to Paul Brown [No. 10 grid co-ordinator]. Where were the big forward steps towards the Budget? Where was the boldness we were going to need? We meandered around.

I said we had to stop being so spooked by the press and the Tories and start staying ahead and make the weather more. We were too cautious. Over lunch we went back to the same themes – why the Tories seemed better at getting up stories, how we didn't provide edge that communicated policy. I said we were trapped in old ways of doing it and had to stay constantly ahead of the game.

I got a lift back with a rather unimpressed DM who was currently writing a draft of the manifesto. He felt we lacked clarity about what it was we were going forward to. He like me felt the meeting lacked drive and strategy. He was a bit down. I was also talking to Ed Miliband to try to bind in GB to a weekend briefing leading to NMW [a higher national minimum wage], Tomlinson [school reform], skills etc. But GB was arguing we should not do the NMW while he was in China. DB came round for dinner and seemed fitter and happier. He had had interim access to William [son] which basically meant he would get full access later. The second son was not his and he said he felt betrayed and sad he had fallen for her. He wanted my help because he felt the only obstacle to him returning to Cabinet was JP. TB, GB and most of Cabinet wanted him back. Party and public were fine. But JP was not happy. DB was scathing re the pledges but admitted that was because he 'consumed' the media as an ordinary person. He had done a visit to Keighley [supporting MP Ann Cryer] and felt good to be back on the trail. I said he should rebuild by campaigning, being pro-TB in a very personal way, and not talking about the child situation. Fairly surreal meeting earlier with a caravan company who wanted me to do a speech linking the theme of trust in government to caravans!

Wednesday 16 February

The Tories having successfully got up immigration/health screening yesterday they were now up on health. We got together AM, John Hutton and Jacqui Smith [ministers] to respond. We were going on the end of the NHS, deadweight cost etc., but there was no doubt the Tories were better at getting up stories than we were at the moment. The main thing in TB's day was an interactive public thing with Five [TV] and it went OK, though the press would get all the people who went for him. I could sense he was worried but still felt it was the best way to communicate through all the media blah. One of the problems was some of his people didn't really buy into it and were probably looking for things to go wrong.

The main story out of the morning was him saying Ken [Living-stone] should apologise for his remarks to a Jewish *Standard* reporter he compared to a concentration camp guard, which was getting in the way of the otherwise excellent Olympic bid coverage.* Later the story was more the people ganging up on him but he came out of it fine. We were now briefing ahead to the talk to candidates tomorrow. It was all feeling a bit tired though. Apart from PG and I, very few people had ideas. The Cabinet were either depoliticised or waiting to be told. AM was getting cautious. He did a briefing for women journos which got nothing but sneering. We went round later to PG–Gail's new house but I was beginning to go down with some kind of cold or infection and felt rough.

Thursday 17 February
I went in early for a pre-meeting with TB, SM and Pat before the 9 a.m. JP, GB, AM strategy meeting. TB, I was pleased to hear, thought that despite the mauling and the inevitable press presentation of it as a disaster, Five had been a good thing to do and we needed to do more. He was as ever dreading the meeting but felt we had to try to get GB's China visit into the overall comms framework. If that meant not doing the NMW on Monday, fine, no problem. PG started the meeting with a short presentation saying we had a bounce post-Gateshead, even though awareness had been fairly low. The press were giving the Tories a free run but it was not yet breaking through, though we had to be vigilant. He and I were arguing constantly that we needed to be doing surprising things and keeping ahead of them. I wanted to put today's *Mail* front page, with a 'Blair meets real people' headline, and lots of pictures of the people who went for him, on the website, with a thank you. But the forces of conservatism bottled out. Alan was starting to listen too much to some of the complaints, e.g. about it all being too macho and not enough women involved. I wanted MB [Margaret Beck-ett] brought in centre stage, not as a token but as a message carrier.

The IOC visit was going fine, though the Ken 'apologise or not' row was rumbling on loudly. TB asked GB how he intended to use

---

* Referring to the pre-war support for the Nazis by the *Daily Mail*, the *Standard*'s sister paper, Livingstone was said to have baited reporter Oliver Finegold by asking if he was a 'German war criminal' and adding, 'You are just like a concentration camp guard, just doing it because you are paid to.'

China to help promote the economic message, and GB looked at the grid and said it will be hard, because there is all this competing stuff. He didn't think we should do the NMW on Monday – that should be the end of the argument, not the beginning. TB said we would move it. Then you had Bush at NATO on Tuesday and on Wednesday we were planning Tomlinson and he was signing major agreements with the Chinese. What GB didn't do was give us a plan. I said nobody was better than him at getting up a message through a visit and that was all we wanted, with stuff we could dovetail back here. He said you and I are meeting later and we can discuss it then. He was just not engaging. When PG mentioned the next wave of posters, GB said it was the first he knew of them, though Spencer had been in the loop. We went back to Vic St. PG said it was almost comic. If people had seen that they would have been appalled.

I then set off for the Treasury, my first visit to the new offices, and better than the old ones by far. GB arrived a couple of minutes late and we went into a kind of waiting room, just the two of us, me on a sofa, him on a comfy armchair. He was more relaxed and friendly than usual. He asked if I was now full time, and what was I going to do afterwards. I said I didn't know but I could only get up for this if I saw it as a short-term project, I didn't want to think beyond that – election, Lions, holiday, think about the future. He didn't ask directly if I would do a book, but I think it is what he was thinking. He didn't ask directly either whether I would support him in a leadership battle in the near or distant future, but that was the unspoken part of it. I asked what he was going to do. 'It would be good to see some of my philosophy implemented. Do you not feel the same?' I said that I was not thinking beyond the election. He said you have to, anyone who cares about the direction of the party has to, and I know you do, and I know you agree with a lot of what I think, even if you can't say. You didn't come into politics for education policies that are creeping us closer and closer to 11-plus-style nonsense. You didn't come into politics to see hospitals borrow out of control, or private companies take it all over. You came into politics to help change the world and we're not doing it as much as we could.

He said Bush was dominating world politics, a right-wing ideologue. But he was pretty down about Clinton, with obvious resonances to TB. 'He won two elections, he did some good things, and was popular at times, but he didn't change the country's direction for good.' I argued that we had done a lot to change the country, not least thanks to him, but he said, 'Come on, you don't think it's enough and nor do I. We have not changed the country as much as we could and should.' Look at the media – 80 per cent come at politics from a right-wing agenda, and we haven't changed that. Look at how easy it is for the Tories to make immigration the issue, and we help them. And we have all these barmy policies being made by Adonis and crew. And what is Ruth Kelly up to? I don't know. What is Charles playing at?

He was scathing about them all. Milburn knew nothing about campaigns and I was having to carry him. It was a joke to listen to him twittering away at those meetings, he said, not knowing what he was on about. TB should never have lost Douglas [Alexander] from the central strategy team. I said that was all now by the by, all I wanted was for him to get the economy centre stage. He said I think Tony thought I was going to come back begging to do morning meetings and conference calls and press conferences. Why do I want to do that? That's what I've been doing for ten years. I said tell me about it. 'Exactly, so why would I want to do the same thing?' I said this is not the same thing. How do we make what he is doing fit with the campaign? He then got on to the substance of his China trip and it was classic GB at his best – a big message about the threats and opportunities of globalisation; arresting facts about China's coming dominance; fascinating stuff about how we could make education services one of our big exports; the areas he would be doing agreements on, and how that would shape the Budget.

It reminded me of the old days when his restless inquiry was working with my media management skills and we were dominating the agenda week after week. I said it was brilliant, and we needed it to dominate the political debate. We had the right dividing line on economic management, and this was about who best could shape the future. He read out parts of the speech, and was deliberately I think trying to show the contrast between TB – big picture, waiting to be told – and him in charge of an argument he had really thought about. He had the line 'Adapt or die', which I thought was a bit apocalyptic, but he had a strong package, around which I could change the briefing note for Sunday.

He kept coming back to the general situation. I asked if I was wasting my time trying to get him and TB in some kind of campaign operation together. 'It's gone way beyond – way, way beyond. You can only take so many lies from someone.' So what will you do in the campaign? 'Whatever you want, I'm happy to do whatever you want.' I laughed

– Gordon, I don't think anyone can say you are happy to do whatever we want. 'I am,' he said. 'I wanted to travel the country, but he doesn't want me doing that. You decide what you want me to do, and I'll do it.' I showed him the posters but he said, 'No, no, no, I don't want to see them. I haven't been consulted. I know the sites are booked and I don't want you saying I have agreed to them.' I said well at least tell me what you think. No, I'm not seeing them, he said, while looking at them. He said Spencer being consulted is not the same – I should have seen them. I said I thought he had but there we are.

We ended on a friendly note and he walked me out, talking about his son, showing off new parts of the building, then saying 'I'm serious – you can change things, you're one of the few people who can, and you should think about it. Otherwise we are just paving the way for the right to come back. I despair for progressive politics and so do you, I'm sure of it.' And with that he walked back, slouched, less angry but beneath it all seething at TB the whole time, even when his name was so rarely mentioned. Rory was in town and we met to buy some running shoes and get lunch, before I left for home, feeling flu-ey and my voice going, and wanting to do anything but the speech and Q&A I was down to do in Hampstead. It went fine, but by the end of it I was shattered.

Ed M sent me a series of emails with comments on my briefing script for AM, then said GB felt our meeting went well, and he hopes I did too. Indeed I did. I just wished he could be like that all the time, and any time with TB. The communication between them was close to non-existent. I mean real communication. Ed said GB felt he and I should work together more closely, both within and outside the structures we had. As ever, it was not totally clear what he was up to, but if he had set out to lodge doubts about the direction of the party and the campaign, he was successful. JP called later to discuss the council tax, next area of the Tory media blitz over the weekend.

Friday 18 February

I felt grim, and couldn't get through much work, beyond a bit of speech writing and trying to get up a proper economic briefing for the Sundays, liaising with Ed M. I worked on a speech for Bourne Leisure [holidays company] on the train to Mum's with Grace who was doing her diary and being very sweet and funny. Alan did the Sundays but it didn't seem to fly. GB was not building up China.

Saturday 19 February

I did a talkSport interview re BFC v Blackburn tomorrow. The Tories were beginning to motor on council tax and we were chasing around. TB called and was worrying about all the hunting protests and whether there was still time to work up a compromise. Impossible. Too far gone. He was getting more and more angry about the grid, and the way 'stuff just spills out of departments'. Train home pm to watch Everton v Man U. Fiona was determined not to watch *Who Wants to Be a Millionaire?*, which was on tonight, but I did and it was fine, and she looked great, it was just a shame we made so little. The general feedback was fairly positive, especially re interaction etc. and it was amazing how many people saw it.

Sunday 20 February

Off early with Calum to Burnley v Blackburn, both really excited about it. The Tories were up on council tax getting away with murder. Couple of chats with TB re things on the way up. He had spoken to GB about him doing more work on James. 'I'm not your researcher,' said GB. The China visit led to us cancelling TB's press conference on the minimum wage tomorrow yet GB was getting very little out of the trip, certainly nothing like he could have done if we had really organised it properly. The match was dull after all the hype, though the crowd was intense. I got taken to the away end at half-time to do an interview with Jack [Straw] for *Match of the Day*, in the boot room in the tunnel, followed by Alan Hansen [TV pundit] sneering, 'Who are they?' – which Alex felt was revenge for me having had a pop at their coverage of the World Cup.

I suppose a draw (0–0) was not a bad result but I feared the worst for the replay. The traffic was dire on the way back. TB called then Alan going on about the lack of a message rooted in third term mission. But my bigger worry was that we had basic operational problems not being addressed. TB was worried re the Sundays talking of tough interviews being a clever strategy rather than a desire to engage. He was definitely in mithering mode, which usually meant he was anxious and irritable.

Home late and TB's note was a rant about the grid lacking strategy. It was all 'This report, that report, what about this point, that point?' Very little big picture. He was getting pretty agitato. He did however do a very good analysis of 'The Plan', the big document being put

February '05: TB's note a rant at lack of strategy on grid

together to gather in one place record, values, progress, next steps, big message, right across the piece. I had seen a draft last time I was in and felt there was a lot of good material but it needed to be shaped better and more clearly. TB felt the same and had some pretty good specific ideas about how. He was worried that people were being too defensive in seeking only to 'neutralise' e.g. crime, asylum, immigration, because in truth we did have coherent policy and the Tories did not.

His big problem was that the government and the party had been expecting the mood to change if Hutton was positive for us, and if anything the opposite had happened. And the media negativity on public services was also having a big impact on morale. It was ridiculous when in truth on virtually every indicator we had set for ourselves, we were delivering. The public are led to think the opposite of the truth – that public services are not improving when they are; that we have broken promises which in fact have been kept; that we are all-powerful and centralising despite the biggest programme of devolution in a century. This explained this constant paradox in the polls between personal optimism and national pessimism. We had to somehow change that dynamic.

Monday 21 February

The Tories were getting away with the kind of media management murder we used to. Ads in the Sundays, briefing through Sunday plus Howard words on a Sunday programme then through Monday with interviews and speech. Their media team would definitely have started the week with a bit of a spring in their step. We were slow and hopeless by comparison. Also today was the day we were due to do TB's press conference which we cancelled because GB did not want to clash with his speech – so important (not) that when he delivered it he did not even have the TV cameras there. It was becoming ridiculous. We had taken TB out of the grid, what could have been a major thing to kick off one of the few remaining Mondays, for a GB event which had so little energy behind it it might as well not have happened. Whatever happened to all that oomph he had in our meeting the other day?

We got JP on to the *Today* programme but after that had nobody but Fraser to get going. AM was late down from the NE, I was away in Leicester all day, with the consequence, said PG, of a total shambles. Every time the Tories did anything the scale of our strategic failure to get a proper campaign going on James was becoming clear. We had not landed a blow which meant they could get away with making claims of tax cuts to come etc. They were in near perpetual free hit territory. We were flat footed and TB's interaction apart looking a bit behind the times.

Pat and PG called with regular updates of how awful it was. I'd said to Pat it was like being part of a football team with physios, dieticians, masseurs – and no players. Leicester was enjoyable. Keith Vaz [Leicester East MP] had finally worn me down into visiting my old school [City of Leicester Boys']. He had been badgering me for ages. He picked me up and we set off, there bang on time to do a turf-cutting ground breaking for a new sports hall. Otherwise the school and the area were very much as I remembered them. Better kept maybe but much the same. My old rugby teacher Dave Sarson was there with new head Mike Taylor, the mayor and deputy mayor and director of education etc. I did a little speech at the site, fairly obvious stuff about the school having been good for me, also about how I hadn't had a clue what I wanted to do with my life, and if you had said I would go on to work for a PM and meet people like Clinton and Mandela then I would have thought you were mad. I then chatted to some of the kids at the school council. They were mainly Asian and a really nice crowd, who had taken votes on what questions to ask. Fairly standard stuff about the job, ups and downs, Iraq, Diana.

I enjoyed it and was able to say thanks to the school. Dave Sarson and I did a Radio Leicester interview together. He was very nice about Dad, who he clearly remembered well. Keith had a portrait photographer there who took an age but clearly did nice pictures, then after an informal session and autographs and another chat with the kids, we set off for De Montfort University. The racism conference was fine and actually I sensed things were moving pretty well. We paused for a few minutes for the Cup draw and inevitably we got Leicester. I spoke for five minutes to launch the event then a short Q&A before heading off after a couple of interviews. Keith did an interview with me in the back of the car for *Asian Voice*. He was full of flattery and general bonhomie. Leicester struck me as much more affluent than I recalled it. We went through an area of large detached houses which he said were all Asian owned. Adie Russell [schoolfriend] had popped up too and it was great to see him. I actually felt a lot better in myself having got away from the campaign bubble for the day. Keith felt we were in OK shape.

Tuesday 22 February

I barely slept and was really getting alarmed about the situation, even before I learned of the *Guardian* poll with our lead down to 3. We had a stack of problems. The Tories were getting their act together. The press were basically anti. TB–GB was dysfunctional and GB was on strike. The spin thing was back a bit – Major had a pathetic Majoresque piece about it today in the *Telegraph*. I got into Vic St and was variously briefed on the apparent shambles of yesterday. People just weren't up for it enough. We had to sort it soon. But we were dealing with e.g. JP not letting other Cabinet ministers do things on his patch. Nick Raynsford [Minister for London] had been doing interviews wearing some dire pullover that looked like he had just been gardening. The whole media team all over the place without direction. Then the a.m. meeting with AM who was beginning to unsettle me because he was finding it hard to chair meetings that reached decisions and then drove them through. We were in there in three rolling meetings to 11.15, they just seemed to roll into each other. And apart from one or two minor issues we sorted nothing. We did not activate. We did not get agreed lines. We did not empower.

Mark Lucas presented re PEBs which was OK, some good ideas, planning advanced. AM and I met John Denham [minister who resigned over the Iraq War] to go over conditional voter-Iraq strategy which again was OK but there was a lack of drive to make things happen. We agreed maybe RC/JD plus more would do an event at the media centre, on the lines that they opposed the war but supported everything else. I had lunch with George Pascoe-Watson [*The Sun*] who gave me a pretty damning verdict of the media operation, said we were invisible in the gallery while the Tories were beginning to genuinely get their act together. And we were not shipping out stories and a narrative. He said the *Sun* meeting with TB etc. yesterday had been fine but they also saw Howard and his team. He gave the impression they were OK but Rebekah told me later she thought they were a bunch of freaks. I was going to have to do more of the hands-on briefing. I fear for example that nobody was talking to Robert Thomson, apart from GB and EB. We were not properly doing the commentators, and making sure they were all across our basic thinking. I was feeling mega stressed again.

I went to No. 10 for a meeting on TB's tour and PG and I suggested doing separate pledge cards on all of the pledges. It was unbelievable to think how close we were to a possible election. To a meeting with AM, JR, SM, PG and staff to go over how health fitted in the coming weeks. JR seemed a bit more down than usual. He and Alan were in a different place on how much new policy we needed. JR felt we should focus on dealing with MRSA ['superbug' bacteria] and eighteen weeks maximum waiting times. AM wanted more forward policy stuff done. JR felt we needed more talking points not policy. JR said we had vacated the economy and vacated James. We knew that. There was a bit of a tussle going on between them about who knew most re health I would say. JR said it was obvious TB must do the economic message and we should turn James into public service cuts and the health and education ministers should do it with him. In other words on the most economic parts of the campaign, we had to find ways of working round GB.

I spoke to Ruth K re topline message on Tomlinson. At least I felt the meeting had ironed out a few things and at the end of it AM, PG, Jo and I discussed the media problem. We just were not firing the bullets. I went to the MPs' researchers' meeting as a favour for Carol Linforth [Labour official] which was in the room where I did the Select Committee attack on the BBC. Loads of MPs there too. Did forward not back. Q&A fine. It was not rocket science but we lacked urgency and passion. And we had just weeks to go. I went to Peter Hyman's book launch where he made a nice little speech. He was really on to something in having been part of the team devising policy change for public services and then being on the other side of the fence. It was changing the way he thought about government and delivery. Nice do. Home bad tempered and feeling if I spent several hours a day in meetings like today I would lose the will to live. TB called from Brussels, fretting how the asylum stats were covered. He was being very small picture at the moment. We had someone up in Cleethorpes doing groups, who reported back that 'we are screwed up here'.

Wednesday 23 February

I had another sleepless night, plus I could not shake off my cough. CC was getting hammered after his tough line on house arrest. Ruth Kelly did OK with the Tomlinson briefing but it was not crystal clear. I went in early for a breakfast with AM, SM, PG and Jo [Gibbons]. Alan and I had a chat and I went through why I felt so low and pessimistic. We were not firing on all cylinders. TB–GB was debilitating, especially given not long ago TB had decided he was going to fix it and then, when he didn't, I felt I had got GB to a better place. TB was

February '05: Campaign cylinders not firing

not showing drive and purpose and not giving strong reasons why he needed the third term. Too much was expected of me and PG re creativity. We had no real media capacity. PG did a good note setting out how we needed mini manifestos to get up policy with a political edge. It seemed clear enough to us. But TB was in a bother when we went over to see him afterwards.

We all made the case that we only broke through when we did big things properly planned outwith the government mush. This was a way of creating a new policy narrative around political lines. But he was still exhausted looking and in micro managing mode. He was obsessing about the grid and the failure to manage difficult reports. He was really hooked on the idea our problem was a lack of management of strategic communications. He felt we had to grip the day-to-day. I felt we had to create and shape a new narrative above the day-to-day. I said the media thought we were hopeless – there was even a hint of it in *The Times* today – while the Tories were getting their act together.

He said he was unsure re timing. He also said he had no idea what to do about GB and the lack of an economic campaign plan. I feared he was finding reasons not to do it because he was dreading a fresh round of policy arguments with GB and JP in the final run up. He looked tired and fretful and kept coming back to the capability problem rather than the strategy problem. It was a pretty depressing meeting. He ended up with virtually all of us arguing for one thing and him saying he was not sure and suggesting we were panicking. I said a bit of panic would not go amiss because there was so much complacency. He felt things were not so bad but I was really not so sure. He got himself up for PMQs and he and Howard really locked horns on terror laws. He held his own fine. Howard could never resist just going a little too far.

I worked at home then went in for dinner with TB, AM, PG, SM, JoP, Pat, DH. He was still obsessing about the grid, rebuttal and even media monitoring. He was right in lots of ways but I reckon there was a bit of wood for trees displacement going on. He was really getting into the detail and, e.g., not focusing till the end of the discussion on whether we should go ahead with the mini manifesto idea we had been pushing. I felt we had to, and so did PG and AM, to shape a new narrative that got us above the day-to-day government grid. I had heard enough from Pascoe-Watson and others to know that we had to get a better media operation running. We needed far better rebuttal. We needed to shift the balance between party and government in the grid. We tried hard not to talk about GB but it kept coming back

to him. We had an economic campaign without an economic campaigner. TB was adamant he could only do so much. He could not do
the whole thing. He needed to be more strategic though and rise above
all this.

We went through people we needed to bring in, though a lot were
just more medium level people who would not necessarily fill the gap.
I was pushing for Pat McFadden and Darren Murphy to be the gallery
people, DH having decided he could not do that in the same way as
he was now in No. 10. TB felt we were overreacting a bit re how bad
things were but we had another poll tonight – Mori – and we were
down to a two-point lead. We went round and round in circles. It was
all being judged on day-to-day media. We had to provide the big stuff
that broke through. We kind of got there in the end but reached more
decisions which may not all be implemented. E.g. we agreed again
JR and MB should be in and around Vic St in order to be available as
general message hitters, but would it happen? Also I had been a bit
worried that even JR, normally cheery and ebullient, seemed a bit
beleaguered earlier, less up for it than usual.

We won the terror vote which had TB in a better mood.* He raised
the idea of 'one last chance' (again) for GB to come in and felt we should
offer the idea of a morning media call with him, and maybe control
of campaign press conferences. AM and just about everyone else was
against, feeling he would then continue to sabotage from a position
where he could really get stuff stopped, and that he would only use
his people. By the end of the evening we were having a laugh, as when
he was saying to AM sorry for ruining his quiet life and I said I could
add that to the long list of occasions where I have seen him flannelling
ministers without them realising they were being flannelled.

Thursday 24 February

I got the bus in, working on a draft of the Dundee speech and trying
to make it connect at the more human level but also connecting on
ambitions and the economy. AM's morning meeting was at the Cabinet Office and we tried to plan the weekend around new proposals on

---

* Commons vote enabling passage of the Prevention of Terrorism Act, allowing the Home
Secretary to impose 'control orders' on people suspected of involvement in terrorism.
A substantial rebellion by Labour backbenchers failed to prevent the Bill progressing to
the House of Lords.

parental leave while I did TB words for the NMW presser tomorrow. The *Mirror* did NMW on page 2 and weirdly Kevin Maguire [*Mirror*] had filed from China after Oonagh Blackman [*Daily Mirror* political editor] had filed on the same story here, and DH had the Treasury on the rampage about it, like they were the only ones who could talk on the NMW and it had to be to one of their poodles. To the Cabinet room for Mark Penn's presentation. The figures were narrowing a bit but the strategic needs were clearer than ever. It was all about the economy, both what people worried about most, and where they saw us as much stronger than the Tories. Yet we could not make the most of it because GB had vacated the field. Penn was saying at least it was obvious what we needed to do, which indeed it was – economy, public services, reconnect, and 'stay off abroad'. I slightly lost it at one point when I said it is so fucking obvious what we need to do and yet we are not doing it, and we do not yet have a campaign built around those themes.

TB called in me and Sal [SM] afterwards and said, 'I really don't know what to do. I don't see how we can do this properly if GB doesn't engage. But he won't or if he does it will be as part of a deal, minimum requirement the job after the election, and maybe more. And he won't really deliver anyway.' I said the strategy was clear enough. We just had to keep articulating it with or without him and, if TB was not going to put him out, we had to keep trying to cajole him back in. TB nodded and rolled his eyes at the same time. It was all so obvious, yet with GB in his current mode, pretty much impossible. TB had bought into the idea of mini manifestos and the need for big connecting stuff, which at least gave us a couple of big themes with which to start populating the campaign grid and the build-up.

We had a meeting on the final stages of the campaign chaired by AM which was helped by Penn and co. being there and sharing my / PG clarity re what needed to be done. We reached some good ideas on how to do the launch. Then to a long meeting with Ruth Kelly who was totally taken aback by the idea of doing a mini manifesto as early as next Thursday, saying that she had so much on and was not ready with the forward policy yet. We explained the thinking, that only big and political was connecting, and by the end she was in better shape, and realised she had most of the makings of what she needed already in place. She had done OK on Tomlinson but she was looking a bit worn. How she did all this with four young kids was amazing. She had a very attractive look, a mix of conventionally strong but also a bit vulnerable, she held your eye when she spoke and she was not afraid to express self-doubt. She signed up by the end, provided some of her parental stuff was sorted. I went home early again to try to work on the speech. These set pieces were going to be important.

Friday 25 February

We were swimming through treacle again, with MRSA big in the papers, terror kicking on as a problem inside and outside the party, and NMW struggling to get on the radar. At last we had agreed on some changes to the operation which we were due to put into practice on Monday. AM got Matt Carter signed up and later he spoke to the other key people in there. I went in for the AM meeting to plan the weekend and today's events and then to see TB pre his press conference. He was in a rage – this time at a Home Office report on rape that was coming out badly. He said 'I'm not sure if anyone has ever won an election with virtually every paper against you.' We were having the same old discussions, again and again. We went through all the various lines to take, but after he, Adair Turner [chairman, Low Pay Commission] and Pat Hewitt did NMW, most of the questions were about terror and legal advice on Iraq, which was back in lights again. Apparently this was all about an inaccurate transcript of a tape of [Attorney General Lord Peter] Goldsmith's evidence but because of the ludicrous line that we don't comment on leaked documents, we couldn't rebut it properly. Madness. So Iraq was running as a negative yet again.

We had a strategy meeting which was pretty lackadaisical. TB was totally obsessing about the grid which I'm sure was a kind of displacement therapy. I said so, that there was no way he was going to have his head in the right place if he obsessed every morning about some relatively minor issue on the grid. He said it wasn't minor. Usually it was, I said. But he was focusing on these things to avoid focusing on the harder stuff, like how to win a campaign on the economy if GB stayed on strike. I said to AM and PG later he had to be clear what he wanted to do, why he wanted a third term. I was even wondering, I said, whether the nuclear option was a runner. In fact there were two nuclear options. Sack GB. Or make way for him. Both were fraught. We had a fun kind of session with loads of black humour coming in but it was feeling pretty rocky to me. I went back to Victoria St and talked things through with Matt. The place was lacking drive and direction because that wasn't coming from the top. The drift was creeping in

February '05: 'Has anyone won an election with press so anti?' – TB

everywhere. I sent TB a note saying so, that we had to get clarity and then go for it, and stop all the fannying around.

Saturday 26 February

We didn't get enough out of the minimum wage. There was stuff around about GB sulking – they had clearly briefed that he was supposed to do NMW but we had done it instead – but more stuff about how we needed to bring him into the campaign. PG called to say there was a poll at the weekend that had us up to a seven-point lead. But they had also asked 'if GB were leader' and that option showed a much bigger lead for us. I was beginning to wonder if that was not an option, not just for the party, but also I could see ways it could help TB on the legacy question. PG and I were laughing at TB's grid note that came through as we were talking, which was ludicrous. He was normally able to get on to the big picture when he sat down to write a note at the weekend, but he was going through the smallest things – asking about the topline from little NAO [National Audit Office] reports, he was asking about some item from the NHS halfway down the grid about something called 'body part operations', which, whatever it was, was so below his pay grade it was ridiculous. I couldn't work out whether it was a genuine help, or displacement therapy.

I had been planning to go with Calum to Preston v Burnley but I was feeling a bit overwhelmed by the workload and so stayed behind and worked most of the day. We were having to think of ways of getting up delivery in a way that was not too pleading but also challenging the conventional wisdoms. TB called a couple of times to go over things. The problem was the feeling that we were stuck. Also, in days gone by he would be seen as the solution to our problems, now he was part of the problem in a way – he and GB were both solution and problem. The Sundays were wall to wall TB–GB madness. The *Sunday Times* splash was the opposite of the truth – namely that we stole the NMW announcement from the Budget. This was all part of the latest line the GB people were running – the idea that he was excluded from the centre, when the reality was we were desperately trying to get him back in. Several of them had stories about an alternative real Labour manifesto, some pamphlet Ed Balls was editing. PG and I had a long chat re the polling, and the fact that GB could deliver a bigger majority. I said surely there was a case for TB at least thinking about going if there was no apparent third term mission reason to stay

– which was not readily apparent from recent meetings. PG said the way GB behaved always led him to conclude it wasn't an option. The polling was probably reflecting the mood in the media, which in turn was reflecting an ill-defined and not-thought-through mood in parts of the party. But if people saw how GB was behaving at the moment, they might change their view. Added to which, it gave an indication of what he would be like if he did get there.

I said we needed to go a bit deeper in focus groups and find out what people really thought about TB and GB and their relative merits/demerits. PG said the tragedy was that basically they thought TB was the right guy to be PM and Gordon was the right guy to be Chancellor, and they couldn't understand all the division. I was worried about the latest GB line though, that it would appear TB was fighting to stay out of ambition and vanity, and because he wanted to stop GB, than because he had a burning zeal for further change to the country in a third term.

Sunday 27 February

Alan M called on his way to *Frost*. He wanted to have a real go, at least at the people doing all the on the side briefing. I was worried that no matter how much he said it was being done by 'people on the margins', it would just be seen as a whack at GB, and in addition to that producing a bad outcome per se, it would feed the victim thing they were clearly trying to engender. TB felt we just had to rise above it and talk up GB. Alan did fine. We didn't get much out of the briefing to the Sundays on plans to increase maternity pay and parental leave but just had to keep going with it. TB was in major micro managing mode again. He called me later and when I said I was getting more and more pissed off, he said 'nil desperandum'. I said it wasn't desperandum but angerandum. He was thinking about what kind of speech to do for Dundee and was worrying about whether it was big picture or a more political message rooted in the closing of the race, which was feeling real for the first time.

Monday 28 February

I ran in, my first decent run for ages. I was literally the only person in there apart from media monitoring. Pat came in for his first day and I got him and Darren working on words for an afternoon press conference for AM re dividing lines on childcare. The papers were not as bad as they might have been and TB did fine on *Woman's Hour* [BBC Radio], though, as Audrey and Fiona both said later, he could have defended me a bit more vigorously when the presenter said I was reviled or some such! His tone was pretty good though and he was building up one or two arguments, e.g. on the impossibility of a rounded conversation, or on the sense that delivery was never admitted because of one or two bad things. We went over for a strategy meeting. TB was late because he was seeing the delivery ministers about the grid.

We had an argument about Friday's speech, with PG and AM arguing it had to be big picture forward agenda third term stuff and me and Pat saying we needed something more prosaic, focused on the economy. TB was keener to do something simpler. He was obsessed at the moment with working out the headline and moving on from that. He had done a note saying what we needed to do in various areas – briefing, rebuttal, my role, other areas for everyone else, and he wanted weekly reporting back on it all. Matt did a report on the levels of voter contact being fed back from the marginals, which looked OK on paper but others were not convinced we had everything we needed yet, or that we had the operation required. We also had to think how postal voting was going to affect the shape of the campaign.

Back for a Stan Greenberg presentation on the marginals which was pretty depressing. Some of them we may as well give up. Iraq was still a problem. TB/trust was not improving in a lot of them. In London/SE it was more lack of public service delivery. But whichever way you looked at things, it was not a pretty picture. Also the Tories were definitely getting a bit of breakthrough and punch. The Tories had successfully created a new media prism for their stories and were doing it well. We were on the back foot again and we lacked the big forward message. Added to which I was feeling demotivated. When AM was arguing for the big forward mission statement I realised part of my problem was feeling TB was not clear what it was.

Tuesday 1 March

I was doing a paid speaking gig in Scotland and flew up from Luton with Ann Warner from Bourne Leisure, on a small company jet, while simultaneously trying to work on the education document. Richard Darlington [Ruth Kelly's special advisor] called to say AM had yelled abuse at RK and she was really upset and really didn't want to do the launch before Friday, or with an Academy launch as the backdrop. AM called and said we needed more policy crunch. He denied he had been rude, but I suspect he was just getting frustrated that plans and approaches we agreed were being stymied all over the place. TB had taken his first morning meeting which by all accounts had not been that brilliant, said PG, very bitty and piecemeal. We were not going hard enough on terror. The issue had become our concessions rather than the Tories' opposition to security measures. Plus the size of the rebellion was feeding a sense that TB didn't have control of the PLP. At St Andrews Bay Hotel, the manager said he had seen my name on a list and I was due back there on Thursday with TB. Talk about being sucked in. Now I was back on the No. 10 advance list, it would seem.

Gym, swim, then did the speech and Q&A. It wasn't easy to get the insider/outsider balance right, as I didn't particularly want them to know just how involved I was. Equally they were looking for an informed view of things. I got lobbied on red tape by some of the company top brass who said Paul Boateng – their MP as well as Chief Secretary to the Treasury – would not see them. They were mainly Tories, I would reckon, but the event seemed to be OK. Then to Edinburgh, working on various speeches, later rowing with Fiona when I expressed concern about her doing a BBC film around the time of Calum's GCSEs. The truth was that being back in the fray was just bringing out all the old tensions between us. I worked on the Dundee speech for TB before heading for Murrayfield, where I was doing an event for Susan's [Law, AC cousin] charity, Riding for the Disabled. Good event though loads of Tories. Gavin Hastings chaired well, speech went fine, auction a bit slow but really got them going when Donald, Gavin [Susan's son] and I played the pipes. I was beginning to worry about being away so long on the Lions tour – and whether I would be bored for large periods of time – and also starting to dream about the bloody election.

Wednesday 2 March
I had a breakfast speech and Q&A at McGrigors law firm in Edinburgh, which went fine. Alan Cochrane [*Daily Telegraph*] was there and came back hard at my usual whack at the media and its impact on politics. He gave me a bit of a hard time in a jocular way, reminding me of some of the stuff I used to get up to, but all in all it went well, and I do think the message about the media being as responsible for the

public turning off politics as much as politicians was getting through. The speech was a mix of my RSE [Royal Society of Edinburgh] on the Scottish media plus driving through strategy. Q&A OK though one or two tricky ones on GB – one who wanted to know when he was taking over, another who wondered why it was even thought possible. But they seemed fine. The guy who chaired it was the father of a sixteen-year-old killed after a football match by someone with UDA connections, and I remembered we had got involved when the murderer was trying to move to a NI jail.

I talked to Pat McF about the briefing operation needed overnight and we had to get going on it. But Ruth was still very resistant to doing it the way we wanted to. I felt strong on the arguments, and also that there was no comeback when we talked about our economic success and their failure. I caught a bit of PMQs at the airport, Howard going on a woman who had had her op cancelled seven times, TB strong on the Tories' record on health. As I was watching it, a woman came over and said 'I bet you're glad you're away from all that now then?' I didn't even know what to say. I just nodded and then asked her what she thought of Howard. 'Nae chance,' she said. But the feedback from marginals was still worrying. I got in for an election tour planning meeting with AM etc. which was a bit all over the place, and then a Group of Death [TB, GB, JP, AM, AC, DA, PG]. TB was not on form. GB, wearing black tie, was resistant to engaging and asked PG what the polling showed, even though P had just taken him through it. He was a little bit more communicative but not much and then only when PG and I spoke to him. JP meanwhile was reading the education document for tomorrow, getting more and more grim-faced as he went through it. He then complained – fairly gently for him – that he had only just seen it, and wanted to know the point, and did not want a whole load of new New Labour reforms. Alan looked pretty sheepish. GB said he thought these documents were for dividing lines and this one didn't do that. I said it was to show policy richness and establish us as the only party with a serious policy agenda. We needed to be able to undermine their eleven words.* We needed to play to our strengths – economy and public services.

We had another discussion about James. GB now wanted just to focus on £35 billion Tory cuts. TB wanted them to do a massive hit

* The Tory manifesto listed the party's six key policy headings as 'More police, cleaner hospitals, lower taxes, school discipline, controlled immigration, accountability'.

just after the Budget. There was also a little spiky exchange over Balls briefing the women's lobby that an interest rate rise might not be a bad thing for us. GB said he thought that was a good thing to do, TB muttered something about the MPC [Monetary Policy Committee] not being happy at public advice and commentary. As the meeting ended TB called GB through. Gordon looked pained, threw his head back, really didn't want to be there. PG and I wondered whether he could be clinically depressed. TB called later, after PG told him of some grim polling from Peterborough, and sounded pretty subdued. He said he would have another go at getting GB engaged. He asked how Alan was doing. I said OK but this is not an easy set-up. He said he thought we could click into gear. Not so sure.

Thursday 3 March

Andy Robinson was getting a real kicking because he had criticised the ref after the Irish match and he was not getting much backing from the RFU. I called CW who was doing a press conference later about a match being put on to raise funds for victims of the tsunami, and suggested he did a big defence of Andy as a way of showing he stands by people. TB and Ruth Kelly were due to do a press conference and visit on the schools document which had turned out OK but the news was focused on small group tuition when I had been hoping for better and bigger talking point stuff. On the bus in I wrote a passage on TB defending young kids and saying they were better than painted. The day started shambolically, with the TB meeting cancelled then people in different places for the Alan meeting which focused mainly on the health row which had been started by the Tories yesterday, about the woman with the cancelled op. JR decided to go up to Warrington to visit the hospital while the woman was being paraded by the Tories. We were running the line that it was clever tactically but stupid strategically because it got them off MRSA – the subject of one of their campaigns – and on to investment, where we were strong and they were weak. Also there was enough collective memory about the dangers of using real cases that meant there were a few Tories out there a bit alarmed at the way it was going.

TB was late from his visit and we agreed to cut the words and also just do one general investment message plus whack the Tories for talking down Britain etc. It was OK though the Tories were still dominating the agenda. At one point we had Tim Collins and Andrew Lansley

[Tory MPs] both on live on different channels on pretty much the same message. The presser went OK but we were not firing on all cylinders, and it really didn't help that they had been so late back from the visit. I had a chat with Ruth afterwards who was a bit frazzled but had a serenity about her eyes that presumably comes from her faith. She said she was worried we would spring new policy on her the whole time. I said we needed to see as much of her as possible the whole way up to and through the campaign.

I got a call from Sue Nye saying GB had seen TB this morning. GB wanted to see me and PG to go over the polling. We went over just before 2. I commented to Philip how much more modern and energetic the other government buildings were compared with No. 10. There was something much more dynamic about the new parts of the Treasury. We went in. GB, Spencer and Sue were there. The surprise was a very tired-looking Bob Shrum [US advisor]. Ed Balls arrived about 20 minutes into the meeting. PG had sent a note to GB last night saying that he knew he felt he had let him down (meaning re working with AM, and not fighting for Douglas to get the central election position etc.) but wanted to help him in any way he could. GB had the latest polling and wanted to start with asylum and immigration. He did his usual thing about why did we go on to their ground and now they/we had made asylum the issue, how did we put together a strategy to deal with it? He really pressed on it and we had to admit we were relying on CC. We made the point that we were not playing to our strengths, particularly the economy. He said it was hard to make the economy controversial. I said it was not about controversy but big driving message and a determination to make our issues the issues for the election.

I said Howard was doing better than before but they were not that good. We had big hitters like him and TB, a good record on the economy, improving public services and if we put our minds to it, we could do it. He said the polls showed we were slipping back on health. He felt it was because the sense was of rows between old and new Labour which worked for us in the early days but not any more. I said things had moved on from that. Nobody was provoking a row but we could not just stand still on policy. He said we had to get a proper dividing line with the Tories. I agreed. We agreed we had to get to investment v cuts, but with reform in there too. He asked me what the overall strategy was. I said the economy was central to it. Growing prosperity at risk. A budget for hard working families, an election starting and finishing on the economy, neutralising our negatives.

He wasn't convinced. He felt we needed a strategy for health which we didn't have; felt the message from the schools document was not clear – was it reform and parent power or was it investment v cuts? I said we needed to think through how we won back lapsed Labour supporters. He asked why they were lapsed and we said a number of things – Iraq, tuition fees, division at the top... 'Ah, tuition fees, another bad policy.' I said we'd had to do something. 'Yes, but not the wrong thing.' On James he was not convinced we should focus on it so much. Letwin had said £35 billion of cuts and that was enough for us to go on and campaign on. He felt people did not believe us on NHS waiting times but we could win the argument. TB was barely mentioned.

Ed asked why, in the interactive stuff, we were putting TB so on the defensive. I said it was a separate strategy. TB or Howard was a big part of the choice. To get to the choice between him and Howard, TB had first to get into a better position and this was part of it, showing that he could handle any difficult question or situation. It was having at least some effect, and that was coming through in the groups. That being said, I had said to Pat earlier – though I didn't mention this to GB – we were still assuming TB was solution not problem. I had spelled out, and made the comparison with what a football team would do if it was losing form, that maybe one option was that TB went, and GB led the campaign. Pat was genuinely shocked we even had it on the radar. I didn't get much sense of why GB had particularly wanted this meeting now, but took it as a good sign. It was pretty clear that no matter how often we discussed it, TB was not going to put him out, and so it was vital we brought him into the centre of the campaign.

As we left I said, 'The solution is easy, Gordon. Get involved, get engaged and take the thing over.' I felt bad that I was effectively setting him at odds with Alan M, but I couldn't see any other way. He had to be involved in the campaign, and the only way to get him in was to let him have more not less action at the centre. Bob Shrum said afterwards he was 95 per cent there. What was so bloody annoying was that when GB applied his restless mind, he was terrific. But fuck me the effort required to get there. We had to get him properly engaged from now in, without doing in TB or AM. Otherwise we had a four wheel campaign with three working wheels.

I got a car to the airport and TB called as I arrived. He felt the presser went OK. He was confident being on health was OK for us, and felt the Tories had made a mistake. He still didn't know what to do for the speech tomorrow and he was not clear yet what the answer to third term mission was. He was in listening mode. The fact was though that if he moved over we could get fresh energy and direction and momentum. He would be appalled to think I was even thinking it. But I was. I was reminded of all the times he said two terms is all anyone gets these days. I flew up to Dundee, sat next to [Labour MP] John McFall's son Gerry on the way up, straight to St Andrews, did an hour in the gym and waited for TB. He came up from Dumbarton and was in the bath when I half-heartedly raised the point with Kate [Garvey] in the corridor that it was obvious what we should do – TB goes, GB takes over and we get a 150 majority. TB, I could tell, was stunned I was thinking it let alone articulating it. I said I'm not even sure I am saying what I think but we have not thought through how to deal with the fact that you are problem as well as solution. Added to which the relationship with GB was not working properly, and we had not fixed it, not by a long way.

TB said he had seen him today and although he was still asking for a 'proposal' re TB's departure he felt the meeting was better, that GB did want to get more involved, and that had explained why he had asked for me and PG to see him. Coincidentally Phil Webster called me today and said he was doing a piece, part briefed by GB people, that he and I were coming together to try to get the campaign going properly. TB was staying in the Kingdom of Fife suite at St Andrews, like a really nice luxury flat, and he and I had dinner to go over things. He said he knew he was part of the problem but also felt that if GB took over there would be short-term lift but that he felt long-term it would be a problem. The business community would go fairly quickly. He asked if I actually thought he should go. I said I thought it at times. At other times I thought it was madness. I felt he was not on form but I thought he could refind his form if we could get a proper campaign with proper momentum going.

He asked how GB had been in our meeting, and I told him it had actually been productive and we were on the same page on a lot of things, but it was a bit of a problem that he could barely bring himself to say your name. He felt GB was finally up for it though, not least out of self-interest in that he didn't want to be blamed for a bad result. Also, though TB knew GB was out to replace him asap, he knew we had to work together if we were going to run a half-decent campaign.

He said he knew trust was an issue, and not just over Iraq, but felt the country did not want to go back to the Tories and if we could get the arguments right we would be fine. But he found the mood unsettling.

There were people who just would not come back to us but with others he felt confident they would. But I could tell he was unsettled. On Iraq he felt it was possible to win a different kind of argument, about the way change was happening in the Middle East. He felt fairly confident still, but knew we were in a very different position. How we won our way back was what mattered now. He felt we should major on health tomorrow and really start to take apart the Tory health plan, particularly on vouchers.

PG arrived about ten and by now TB was able to joke about it. 'Ah here comes my other strategist. Now I have the whole strategy team to tell me their defection plans.' PG laughed, but said it was best to get it all out in the open if only to analyse it. He was slightly less frank about the nuclear option discussions we had been having. TB felt confident we could win all the arguments but it was hard with the press so against you and with the sense that anything we said or did was not new. He said if he really felt making way was the right thing, he would not rule it out. But he wasn't sure it was. We were a bit tired and jaded and didn't have much time. He quizzed me on organisational weakness and what else we needed to bring in. I had been pretty hard with him, said there was no doubt there were people who saw him totally as the problem and we were stuck. We needed a change of dynamic and the change was him and GB getting their act together. Strategy was fairly clear. Operational capability was what we needed and they were the key. We just had to get going. But the mood was fairly volatile and the press were almost universally offside, which meant problems would get all the attention unless we were able to shape a bigger and better campaign narrative on our own terms. It was too late to push GB out now, so he had to be brought in, and if that meant signalling something pretty clear about the future, then so be it.

He had a glass of Scotch and called me back after PG had gone. 'I really need to know if you think this is the right way forward. I would honestly go if I thought it would help. But I don't, and I'm not sure you do.' I said I just knew that if we were going to fight a campaign on the economy – and it is blindingly obvious we have to – then we cannot do it without GB right in there.

Friday 4 March
I went for a swim and came back to find TB on the bed making notes and mapping out the speech. He sat down and wrote the health section

March '05: 'I'd honestly go if I thought it would help' – TB

while I worked on clips and arguments for briefing. We were in OK shape though I felt the Tories were getting too much out of the Mrs [Margaret] Dixon [Warrington Hospital] stuff still. Most of the morning was just toing and froing on the speech and fact checking. We got it done by lunchtime, then straight to the rather old-fashioned hall. The speech felt OK and TB seemed a bit more energised. George Foulkes [Labour MP] did the speech before and was very good re TB. The acoustics were difficult and the Scottish audience probably thought he was focusing too much on English stuff given health was a devolved issue but it went fine, if not brilliantly. I briefed one or two afterwards and we were trying to get up that the Tories had erred in moving on to our territory etc. Trevor K was pretty tricky and was trying to get a line going that it was a big personal attack on Howard – ludicrous – and saying it showed TB was rattled etc. But at least we had an argument on policy, dividing lines on health, and a strategy of sorts to get GB back engaged.

TB did *The Observer* on the flight back and was in good mood, felt the speech went fine. It was odd being back on the RAF flight. The magazines were the same, ditto the scones and cakes and the uniformed steward. 'I honestly thought I would never go on one of these planes again,' I said. 'Ah, wait till your friend Gordon is in charge. You'll never be off them.'

Saturday 5 March

I took Rory to Nottingham for the cross-country. TB called and was OK about the speech coverage but felt *The Sun* was basically offside and he was not sure we would win them back. He felt that Murdoch had either not given instructions, which meant Trevor would be pushing hard for Howard, or he had given instructions not to back us. I said it was not important and should not faze him. He was not really confident or strong on basic arguments and was moving more to a position where he said we had to defend the record, and communicate minimum delivery whereas I felt, as did PG and AM, that we had to do much more on the future and country direction. Phil Webster did a story today, started by GB's people, to which I added, re the two of them coming together and it came out OK, not a screaming splash or anything, but it would be a problem for Alan. It was fairly obvious GB was going to be coming back and would want Alan's nose out of joint a bit, if not more.

We had the [David] Milibands round for dinner and Louise was totally in the Fiona position – TB had lost too much support and credibility and integrity and she felt he could not win people back. I talked to DM re the GB situation and I could see he was torn, did not want to be disloyal, but he could see a lot of problems ahead. He felt TB did not have a sense of what the third term was for, why he needed it, what he wanted to do. He was curiously disengaged, even though he was doing the manifesto. I got no calls re the Sundays though there was plenty of TB–GB–Alan-ery in them, needless to say. PG and I worked on a '60 days to go, message overview' paper, which Mark Penn had drafted, partly to de-Americanise some of the language, but also to bring home how close we were. It brought together everything already done rather than mapped out new ground. Economy. Public services. Forward not back. Values. Leadership. But also with a focus on how we bring over fence-sitting working-class and lower middle-class women, and bring back people who are angry about Iraq but still want to back us. We still hadn't settled on the right approach on how to handle anti-Iraq people who were shifting to the Lib Dems. I felt the best way was a simple message that they were the Tories' secret hope of a backdoor win. But we were so focused on Howard and the Tories, I'm not sure we have done enough on this yet. That being said, the overview note was a pretty good case, especially on the economy and public services. The Tories had nothing by comparison.

Sunday 6 March

The morning conference call was largely about terror, and the house arrest debate.* John Stevens [Met Police Commissioner] had written a piece in the *News of the World* attacking the critics and warning there were 100 or more Al Qaeda-trained people out there. TB felt it was of benefit but I had a sneaking fear it would just lead to process-ology, ie who put him up to it kind of bollocks, which indeed is where it ended in some of the media. JR was doing OK on health and the Sundays were not that great for the Tories though there was a growing sense they were driving the news agenda, which was annoying and worrying TB. We still hadn't decided whether we were going for a new kind of

---

* Home Secretary Charles Clarke decided to amend the Prevention of Terrorism Bill at its House of Lords stage so he would have to apply to a judge for any house arrest 'control orders'. Fears that peers would derail the Bill grew as the Lords debate began.

March '05: David M worried TB unclear re what third term for

campaign re the media or basically just trying to get people over. Roy Greenslade called about a piece he was doing for *The Guardian* saying that *The Sun* had all but switched and was only not saying so because of RM on Iraq. TB felt sure they would come back to us, because he felt Murdoch would know GWB would make him pay in some way if he didn't, but I was less sure. Apart from the *Mirror* we had pretty much nobody really backing us at the moment and that was having a big impact on the mood.

I took Grace to the cinema while working on a briefing note to try to get up the science presser tomorrow with Robert Jackson. Jackson said he had done his first campaigning for us recently and found two or three switching to the Tories but they came back when you took them through the £35 billion cuts. We had dinner with Tessa and David, who was very down about the Italian court case.* Tessa said she had a pretty bad weekend canvassing. I said I seemed to be the only person who thought we could lose. She said she was the second. She felt we ought to win but it was far from certain. We agreed it was a tipping point election and could go either way – a big win for us or slide away to them. It seemed unthinkable till not long ago but now it was looking a bit more shaky. I tried Tessa out with a milder version of my GB option. She was aghast, said he was mad, recounted the story of him refusing to acknowledge TB at a Palace reception. I had a chat with JR re his MRSA figures and plan for tomorrow.

Monday 7 March

MRSA was going OK. I ran in then did a call with Alan and JR and agreed John should motor on the figures and then later in the day announce the plan for legislation and then into the health mini manifesto tomorrow. Meantime we were doing the science presser with Jackson. They then announced they would have at their press conference the autistic child's mum who berated TB on Channel 5 [Maria Hutchings interrupted a television debate, claiming her son's special school was to be closed], making us wonder if the whole thing was a

---

* Corporate lawyer David Mills, husband of Tessa Jowell, had acted for Italy's Prime Minister Silvio Berlusconi in the 1990s and was subsequently investigated for alleged money laundering and tax fraud. Some papers termed the affair 'Jowellgate' as Mills faced possible prosecution and trial. His subsequent conviction was later reversed by the Supreme Court.

Tory set-up from the start. She did a big emotional number but we did manage to disrupt by getting a letter from the *EDP [Eastern Daily Press]* to Tom Baldwin, from ex-Tory MP now [Norfolk and Norwich University Hospital] NHS trust chairman David Prior attacking Howard as cynical and irresponsible for using one case to undermine the whole of the NHS. He got right under their skins too, with Howard coming to the mic for the first time to take a question. The woman was probably a bit OTT but again the press were giving them something for making the weather.

To TB's 12.30 strategy meeting which was circular and grim. The circle was around whether we were basically more of the same, or unremittingly New Labour, or only concerned re outcome. I feared TB, in the absence of the compelling narrative, was moving to a delivery referendum position which would not be great. AM wanted means and ends, with a strong New Labour element. PG wanted the big vision. I just wanted clarity and then we could build around it. I could tell AM was worried about all the weekend stuff and after he left I asked TB what was happening about all that. He said he was going to see GB again to make the same proposal as before. It was pretty clear Alan was being set up to be humiliated. TB said he was in an OK position because he had made clear way back that AM was really replacing Douglas not GB. I said he had to handle it properly because he would have more than AM pissed off in the Cabinet.

After the p.m. organisation meeting, Alan asked me to see him. What is going on? he asked. I said he had to assume TB was trying to get GB on board. He said he has done a dirty deal, I can tell. He was clear he would not be staying on if he was to be humiliated. I'm not just going to be a glorified Alicia Kennedy [senior party official] doing key seats. He and I both bemoaned the fact we had rather been brought back against our will, with partners totally opposed, and set up to get no credit if it went well and all the blame if it didn't. I said he should ask him outright what he was planning. He said he might. He felt really badly let down. TB had brought him in when he didn't really want to come in and was now going to conspire to rub his face in the dirt. He was pretty calm on the surface but was clearly angry and upset. He asked if I had been trying to get GB back in. I said I had, that we could not possibly base a campaign on the economy if the Chancellor was on strike. But I would do all I could to make sure he was not humiliated. I said I would always level with him. He said Tessa had once said to him that he had to understand there were only three people TB ever really listened to – GB, AC, PM – and the rest had to fit in with that. He got that, he said, but he was not going to be humiliated. I said I understood. He said he felt he had replaced Peter M as the hate figure in GB's eyes. TB needed GB's strength, fair enough, but there would be a very big price.

I said it may not feel like it at times but we have to win this as a team. GB is not a team player for sure. But he is an important part of the team. And those of us who are team players have to put to one side any animosity we feel to get him involved. He looked a little bit crestfallen. Meanwhile Mrs Hutchins was leading ITN (though with a lot of doubt about whether it was playing well for the Tories) and we lost the terror vote in the Lords.

Tuesday 8 March

We managed to get health up much more on our terms, though we got very little coverage for the eighteen-week pledge. JR was on ferocious form at the press conference, though he interrupted TB a bit too much. TB was OK, and geed up by a good reaction when he went to a hospital in Tooting, but some of the stuff from the focus groups was grim for him at the moment. Trust, looking tired, not being as good as he used to, loads of negatives. The Tories looked on the defensive and I was still not convinced their strategy of using real people to make big claims about poor service was working for them, even if the media kept saying they were doing well. PG and I were both joking about nuclear options the whole time.

Wednesday 9 March

The debate was still being dominated by terrorism, with Howard getting more and more slippery but of course with loads of focus on our own rebels. TB was a bit spooked by it all, as he was by the GB business still rumbling on. Trevor K had a story that Milburn was being dumped to make way for GB, but also that TB would not keep GB after the election. So both AM and GB would be annoyed about it, for different reasons. I had no idea where it came from. I suspected someone on GB's side had told him about the Alan bit, and someone in our set-up had said the second bit. Either way it was a problem. I ran in and was in Alan's office before he was. He hadn't seen *The Sun* but knew about it. Someone found the paper, he had a quick read and said it was pretty much curtains if true. 'I'm not going to hang around to be humiliated.' He felt it would be bad for TB if this was indeed how things panned out. He would feel he had him on the run.

Sally arrived, said she was sure 'the bastard' had done it, as a way of doing in Alan, who asked whether TB had anything worth staying on for if GB was to take over. He said you should also understand that if we win, he will take the credit, and say we had to grovel to get him to come in and rescue things, while if the majority is slashed, he will say that was because TB hung around too long. Whatever credit is going, GB takes, whatever blame, we get. It was probably an over frank discussion, and I was a bit surprised to learn SM was pretty much in the same position as me, feeling Alan was going to end up being cut to shreds so why not take control of his own fate etc. To be fair to AM, he wanted to work out what was best for the campaign, and if there was a way of working together they would do that. But he also knew, and TB later confirmed, GB would want Alan out of the whole show. I was wondering whether I wouldn't take that opportunity to get back on the outside too. I wasn't really motoring, certainly not enjoying it, and confident I would take loads of shit, none of the credit or joy of the whole thing. Alan ended the meeting more upbeat than he started but he said he was pretty much hating every day.

I met Trevor K for a cup of coffee at a nearby café and we had 80 minutes or so of actually quite lively and interesting discussion. He denied, implausibly, that he was really a Tory, or campaigning for a change of line, but said he had to reflect Murdoch – small state, value for money, pro-US etc. – but also reflect the readers who were not convinced we had delivered enough in eight years. I pressed him on the notion that given Iraq TB should get much more credit on the leadership stakes, and that they should stop taking the 'GB excluded' line. He was clear, as was Irwin Stelzer [American economic and business journalist] with SM, that they did not want GB as leader and that after TB politics would all change again. I pressed mainly for at least a semblance of balance on public services, and also more benefit of the doubt for TB. It was a fairly civil conversation and I think we both got each other thinking a bit. I was in and out of various planning meetings, also working up lines on Howard who had now bounced from STDs [sexually transmitted diseases] to development. Ridiculous piece from Polly Toynbee [*Guardian*] about the Tory campaign being good and ours crap.

Lunch with Adam Boulton, who talked mainly about TV issues, but

March '05: GB 'takes credit, gives blame' – Sally Morgan

interestingly said he didn't think Howard thought he would win, and was doing it to set himself up to be rich. He was clearly on TB's side in the briefing nonsense from GB but clearly felt constrained because of his relationship with Anji [Hunter, former advisor to TB, and Boulton's partner] in the reporting of it. Back for an election grid meeting and also a brainstorm on Tony tour ideas. I saw TB and SM around 6.30 and he was really pretty fretful about things. He said he hadn't gone for Howard at PMQs over terrorism – though Howard had really gone for him – because he wanted to be firm and reasonable. Peter H walked in and asked how he was. 'Pretty fucked off if you want to know the truth,' he said. He went off to vote and said he intended to do interviews afterwards to hammer them harder. Nick Robinson was doing a two-way in the background with the sound off and TB suddenly said, 'These fuckers get more air time than any of the politicians on these stories now.' Chat with NK who was in seeing him and said he had seen GB and told him to get engaged with the idea of GB as manager and AM as coach. I said that was an interesting analogy because I had said to GB that PG and I felt like two ageing physios with no players.

Thursday 10 March

Mark Penn was over with the latest poll which had us fairly steady with a small lead. Mrs Dixon had 91 per cent name recognition after a few days of being in the news, but with interesting impact – health up the agenda, Howard ratings down, ours up on health. Howard's problem was that even when he was raising people's issues, they just didn't believe he was really on their side. So as I had suspected and hoped, them using a real case story had helped us more than them. I hoped they had polling showing the same thing. Penn seemed fairly upbeat, he felt we were withstanding a pretty ferocious onslaught, and had to keep going with TB interactive, forward not back the message, get the focus on the economy around the Budget. Terrorism was becoming more and more bitter and though Howard slithered around from one position to another, he did not get sufficiently hit as he did so, so keen were the media to give him a lift. Andy Marr started to run a ludicrous line that if we lost the vote we would go for a snap election. We were in for a game of parliamentary ping pong and needed just to keep going, but CC and Charlie Falconer were clearly pretty keen to make concessions.

Then to a Group of Death, which was better than before but still pretty dysfunctional, e.g. when TB asked GB to say something about next week, and GB just said 'I had not been asked to prepare anything.' JP snorted. TB looked sad. I said, 'Where are we going with the economy campaign?' He said, 'We can discuss that later.' He also rather took our breath away when he said the first roll-out post the Budget would be from AD and when I asked him if there was any health debate in the days after he just said no. JP meanwhile was consumed with the pretty disgusting campaign being got up by the *Mail*, *Sun* and *Express* re gypsies [demanding the removal of illegal gypsy camps]. It was the usual circular conversation.

I thought we were going on till 10 and was waiting to raise the issue of people briefing against the campaign, but then Cabinet was due to start at half nine and so in the end I didn't, but it was hard to get the campaign functioning properly with the constant briefing against it by GB acolytes. He was also refusing to engage in the clearing of the posters. PG had a ridiculous conversation with Spencer who said he didn't mind them but that did not mean he was clearing them because he was not in a position to clear them because he did not have a proper position. Mindblowing stuff. They wanted to be in a position to say they hadn't cleared them, so they could feed this nonsense line about GB being excluded and not properly involved. To be fair to Alan M, he was just keeping going. Home to work on a MB speech re leadership for Saturday. We needed to start landing blows on Howard as an opportunist whose opportunism would damage the country.

Friday 11 March

I'd been hoping to stay at home but was called in for a meeting at the House where the ping pong of the Terror Bill had been going on all night. We agreed we needed a clearer tougher political line out there, and JR did the rounds and as ever did it well. I felt the public were probably thinking it was all just silly though I could not help thinking what the media would have done to us had we stood in the way of a Bill wanted by the police and security services. Pat and I worked up a tough line and circulated it, while I was also sorting MB's speech for tomorrow. Both she and JR seemed glad to be involved. TB called and asked whether I thought he would be accused of caving in if we said that the planned new legislation next year would be an opportunity for amendments from either side and therefore no need for a sunset clause.* It was OK but because we had allowed the focus to settle on sunset clause rather than balance of probability, there was a risk of it being seen as a climbdown. As soon as Mark Fisher [Labour MP] in the House said it was a sunset clause in all but name Howard was out saying the same and accepting it and the thing was settled. It was a bit of a mess, probably a draw, but the press would give it to Howard because at the moment that is what they are doing about pretty much everything.

I went with Kate to Soho House to see the advance team, and just chat around what we were hoping for from events and visits, and then to a meeting with Louisa Cheetham and Ben Wilson re the Lions launch. It was likely to be on the same day as the start of the campaign proper. It might get a bit tricky trying to ride the two horses at once.

Saturday 12 March
Fiona was in Wigan at a conference so I spent most of the day looking after Grace and the dog. Howard was at his spring conference and lacked a real policy or political story but paraded his family and got all manner of half-decent coverage for that. MB's speech did well against it, and at least had the merit of chiming with what people thought about Howard, but come the Sundays they were still in better shape than us.

Sunday 13 March
The *Sunday Telegraph* had an interview with the Notts Police Chief Constable [Steve Green] saying they could not cope with murders and rising violent crime. Like the BMA [British Medical Association] attack on A&E planned for tomorrow, everyone sensed some Tory involvement but of course nobody could say that. It was going to run big though, with Howard coming in on the back of both. They were certainly getting their act together. TB was doing Jonathan Dimbleby [broadcaster] with a group of lapsed Labour women and though he did OK, the coverage wouldn't be great and would lead to more pressure on him to give up the so-called masochism strategy. He was standing by it though he felt there was a risk of him being weakened by it. He was clearly agitating at the state of the campaign, and GB was setting

---

* Sunset clauses are included in legislation when it is felt Parliament should have the chance to revisit it to decide its merits after a fixed period.

the whole thing up as him coming to the rescue. We were not firing on the necessary cylinders. Penn and PG were putting through notes that said the same things again and again but we were not really doing them. Fiona lost it with Rory when the dog jumped on him while he was asleep and he lost it with the dog. For some reason it sparked a furious row between us, with lots of the old stuff pouring out, and her basically feeling I should not be back helping, which I was feeling more and more myself, but of course I didn't say that, and we just went round and round in circles until eventually I went upstairs and did some work.

Monday 14 March

TB had done an overnight note which was a mix of big picture and micro management and the main strategy meeting went through it painstakingly. He rightly assessed the problems in the campaign but we were still no nearer resolution on the issue of the GB role. The feeling I got was GB was happy to come in only if Milburn's head was on a stake. I was getting very down and failing to hide it. I was also worried that where we had a situation where we felt TB would win by 50 and GB could deliver something twice as big and more, we had to say so. I had been raising it less and less subtly with TB. But he said he was clear – that it would get a short-term lift but it would go as the middle classes' fears about GB came more to the fore. Business liked him as Chancellor but didn't want him as PM. He also felt we had to go lower in the polls to come back up.

What has happened is the Tories have for the first time been allowed into the room for a conversation with the public. But the minute we get the conversation to £35 billion cuts, they are put back out of the room. Over the next two days we had a series of conversations. He was sure the dynamic was this – that we were going down because people wanted a choice but we would come back as they faced the choice. I feared a different dynamic – the economy was a given but we had not transformed the public services, TB–GB was a fundamental faultline, while the Iraq–trust issue weighed more heavily than we thought and got worse not better with the passage of time.

The TB meetings were depressing people because we were not being inspired or given real leadership. He meanwhile was blaming us for not gripping the campaign and for sending out messages of something near to panic. He called me later to say I really had to not let my head drop because it influenced the others to drop theirs and I was there to rally them and lift them to fight. I said we were fighting but with the faultline running through it all, it was like punching air. There was a new prism and we had not responded to it at all. We were tired, fighting an old campaign in an old way. AM was getting demoralised, as was I. Even PG was saying he was down. Through the day we were just doing hand to mouth responses on crime and health, which was OK but they were doing better. TB was getting more and more frustrated. So were we. Pat and Darren were losing heart and I was not exactly motivating them upwards.

I was hosting a high-value donor dinner at [entertainment entrepreneur] Sally Greene's Cheyne Walk brasserie. The donors were a mix of total complacency alongside one Jewish businessman who felt we were in a bit of trouble because the whole of the media was now ranged against us and the other side were running a better campaign. At one point twenty Countryside Alliance protestors turned up, thinking TB was there. Nice enough time, good food. I hope it helped but I sensed they realised at the end we were pushing uphill for now.

Tuesday 15 March

I went in for TB's 9 a.m. meeting and saw him first thing with JoP. I didn't quite say I thought he should go, but did say if he went we would get a big lift. He said it would not be sustained. He had seen the *FT* yesterday who just felt the two of them should work together. The morning meeting went on twice as long as planned and ended with him basically giving us a bollocking for not getting a grip e.g. on story development and rebuttal, and he said he didn't want discussion endlessly but action to take forward everything we agreed. He was convinced we needed an Iraq political strategy pre the campaign and Pat was in charge of putting one together with Ann Clwyd [Labour MP]. He was right on one level but on the other we could not get going properly with the campaign constantly being briefed against. I was demoralised because I couldn't give a damn what these wretched press people thought, or what their ridiculous definitions of stories were. TB could tell I was down and called three times during the day, at the end of the day saying he needed me to find the energy and drive and enthusiasm to motivate the others. He was confident we would go down to come up again. I was not sure. I felt the negative dynamic was too powerful at the moment and we had nothing to shift it. He had seen the *Sunday Times*, who he said were friendly. He saw Les Hinton afterwards who said they were deciding what to do with *The Sun* but he felt they would back us. I felt they were hoping it would get close enough for them to say go back to the Tories. TB was convinced RM would not have that but I felt the TB–GB dynamic and the Tory uplift were basically just good stories and that is what they wanted. He said that is the pessimistic view. I said I felt very pessimistic. He said I had to lift myself out of the gloom. It may be the country has decided they want a change, he said, but I really doubt that. It is just that they are listening to the Tories for the first time in years. Now we have to make sure they hear the truth about them. He said he was hoping to have the '97 structure – GB and me in charge of strategy, AM and me implementation, but he felt we had to raise our game and get a grip.

Meanwhile Cardinal [Cormac] Murphy O'Connor [RC Archbishop of Westminster], following the *Cosmo* spread on abortion, had stepped in, making basically supportive noises re Howard's comments on lowering the legal time limit, so that was their latest talking point extravaganza. TB said he was confident GB would come back on board, said he had the sense of being a worried man etc. But Spencer told PG he had not even put to him a proposal re structures. It was as though he was willing them into being. TB could tell, judging by the volume of calls he was making to me, that I was getting pretty low. He was full of 'We have to do it and we will' kind of talk but I had lost the appetite for it. I so didn't care what these papers thought about us. I got home to watch the David Kelly film [*The Government Inspector*, Channel 4] which I'd agreed to review for *The Times* and which was better than I expected. Grace watched it with me and was riveted. I wrote a piece that tried to get the balance between review and analysis and a bit of what it had been like back then.

Wednesday 16 March

I did the *Times* piece, sent it over to them, but also sent a copy to No. 10 so they were aware, and JoP came back concerned it would set off a great hoo ha and could I pull it? I had felt the film went beyond the usual one dimensional anti-us angle, and also felt it important to show we had at least reflected hugely on what had happened. But he felt no matter how reasonable the piece was, it would get spun against us. He said that was the feeling among all who had read it. Danny Finkelstein [*Times*] was great about it when I called and asked to pull

March '05: Catholic Archbishop fuels abortion row

it, and very understanding, but I was even more fed up. I had basically signed everything over again and for what? Endless grind and grief. The Budget was well set up and when the focus of the general debate was on the economy it felt better. There was always a soap opera undercurrent now though, re the TBGBs. I worked on TB's Welsh speech, trying to get up the economy as the story, then watched GB in the House. He did pretty well, good on the big picture, and the moves on council tax and pensioners were strong. Ditto no NHS charges. The Tories looked pretty floored as GB reached the end but Howard did OK and his side liked it.

The best thing about GB was that he stuck to big messages he had been pushing for years. He had a breadth and a determination and was steady, at least in public. I still wondered whether he would be able to deal with a less benign media environment though. TB called straight after to ask what I thought but was quickly on to the need to keep the right-wing papers more on board and how we could maintain momentum. He was irritating me now and the GB performance added to that. I just wish he operated like we said he did. GB came out fine on the TV but there would be more and more TB–GB undercurrents in the press. The message that we had to get the economy centre stage was there but whether we could maintain it was another matter.

I had a meeting with Ed Victor. He said he found it extraordinary, having read the diaries, that I was even willing to help GB, let alone to a position where he might take over. But today had perhaps shown the answer to that, namely that when he had to deliver big strategy and big message, he could. Ed said he found it incredible that I could push to one side all the badness and the madness and the angst he had caused, pretty much from day one.

Thursday 17 March

The Tory papers had totally bought Howard's 'Vote now, pay later' message on the Budget but overall GB came out pretty well. The poster launch was a bit shambolic, first because it was unveiled before TB GB got there, second because they didn't speak in front of it and then TB got into a rather unseemly argument with Nick Robinson. The media didn't really want to give us anything at the moment so even though the £35 billion words were Letwin's the fact we described future cuts as cuts at all had them all in a dreadful tizz. I did an OK meeting on story development at which Shaun Woodward gave a rather alarming list of areas he thought the Tories would go on as easy hit territory. E.g. fly-tipping, dentistry, cannabis review and half a dozen others. AD, AJ and AM were doing the £35 billion cuts press conference at 11 but HMT had not agreed to making sure there was a woman on the panel. The dysfunctionality problem was highlighted later when TB said he wanted DM totally on top of the £35 billion cuts argument. But he had not even seen the paper for the AD press conference.

The presser did not go too well with the hacks determined to say we could not say cuts because we were talking about cuts in the future. Andy Marr was apparently going round later briefing on it, and saying we could not be believed. These fucking broadcasters now valued their own views more than anyone else's. We just had to hold our nerve on this, engage in the row and really keep going on it. A leading Tory had talked of them spending £35 billion less under a Tory government than we would and we were entitled to call that cuts, but the media seemed not to agree. We had nobody on *World at One* so eventually Alan was up for it and did a discussion with Liam Fox who sounded nervous. We had to keep going.

I got Ed Balls and AD to do the rounds but we were clearly going to have to adapt to a different kind of media prism. I did a note to all briefers saying we hold fire and keep focused on public not media. Let them win plaudits from commentators. We need to win votes from people. I missed the presser because TB called a strategy meeting. The GB thing was nowhere near sorted. He said just leave it to me. He was fine re engaging on £35 billion but was also hammering away re micro personnel issues and so on. The more exposed to these discussions I was the more irritated I became at the moment. It was back the whole time to where the papers were, or some of them, and I had pretty much lost the appetite for all that. The launch had not been smooth though. At the end of the AM noon planning meeting I asked Spencer what structures GB wanted and he said a rerun of '97 would probably be OK, GB strategy, AM implementation. But he claimed TB never really raised it properly. He needed a diagram. PG said DA would be a step too far, effective humiliation for TB and AM. I did a bit of writing then left for the train. The £35 billion was running OK on the broadcasts but the papers were preparing to give us a kicking. TB spoke to GB who though fretting said we just had to hold firm. Phil Webster told me the general feeling among the media was that we were being disingenuous, and some were up in arms but he felt we did the right thing and the central point was well made. The Tories would spend £35 billion less than us. Fact. That means cuts to our planned expenditure. Trevor K was very tricky on it.

TB flew down via Gloucester and after my meandering journey around Wales we got to the [Fairyhill] hotel around the same time. But he didn't want to work on the speech. He wanted a relaxing dinner that included Robert Crampton and Nick Danziger [photographer]. I think he was avoiding a real discussion about things. Pat told me he was going for a seat in Wolverhampton, which was good news, but would be a loss to the campaign team if he got it. TB was recording a dummy run video diary slot in his room. I went through and could tell he was a bit frosty. He always knew when I was feeling offside. But after the others left we had a good chat about things. He asked where I thought we were. I said too close in the marginals. The media were determined to do us down. The Tories had their tails up. The campaign was still not firing well enough. He said he was trying to get GB fully engaged. I said it had to happen and the story of the campaign had to be the two of them coming together and with the sense of one day GB taking over.

He said just be careful about that – there are people out there who vote for us because of me and who would go because they don't think he is the real thing, not as a leader, not as New Labour. He said that GB brought back some groups of people but he was not convinced it was clear-cut. I told him what Ed Victor had said, namely that anyone who had the full story of how GB operated could not understand how we still felt he could make it to the top. TB said he had taken so much shit from GB but there was still part of him that liked and admired him and felt he should take over. But he didn't believe he would be a better Prime Minister. Having done the job for as long as he now had, he felt he knew better than at the beginning what it entailed, what skills and temperament were needed, and though GB had a lot of the skills, he was not sure about the temperament. He did feel GB would have to get the job to prevent the theme of betrayal being with us for ever more. He would try to get him into the campaign properly but clearly they had not agreed anything.

I said I wanted them to do an election broadcast together and TB agreed to that. He said he knew it was going to be tough. This was the last hurrah and we had to show we had the guts to go for it and win big. PG later gave him a pretty gloomy assessment from the marginals which were showing a 3.8 per cent swing to the Tories. He felt that Iraq and immigration were still big problems. TB's own numbers were not good. TB said he felt the masochism strategy had been fine but now he had to go back to strength. He felt we should take Iraqis with him on the road. We had dinner with Crampton et al. Chatted with CR re the David Kelly film. Good dinner, lots of laughter and TB relaxed. He said we had to stick to £35 billion and really go for it now, major explanation. Less fretting more doing, he said.

Friday 18 March

I went out for a hill run around the village [Reynoldston, Wales]. TB was up at 7 doing the £35 billion section at length and then rewriting my draft to round off the speech. Howard was in Scotland doing human rights review and wrapping in gypsies, asylum seekers etc. It was pretty nasty stuff. He is a pretty nasty man, which is why ultimately I don't think he can win. People sense it and now he is helping give more reasons. But there will be short-term resonance, and more support from the papers who are as nasty as he is. There was also a new poster popping up everywhere – 'How would you feel if a bloke on early release attacked your daughter?' The opportunism charge could be made to hurt but the current prism was positive for them and their agenda, negative for us and ours. PG and I had a long session going over everything. We had not really advanced and not really implemented. The Budget had come and gone and though TB was speaking more to GB he was not back on board and the post-Budget follow-through was not happening.

We had another session with TB in which I asked if it bothered him that GB would get a bigger majority. He was sticking to his line that he would lose support on the other end and lose media support – of which we had next to none. It had definitely got worse. At one point, as he was eating an enormous breakfast, he said, 'So what are you saying, I should fuck off? My polling strategist says I have to campaign with GB and my spin doctor says just make way.' He did a hilarious account of what they would be like on the road, TB transmuting from PM to GB's butler. But I could tell he was worried and annoyed I had raised it. I was trying to be honest without undermining him but failed. I said as leader of the party he had to think through what was best. He was going to be going anyway. GB was almost certainly the next leader, so I was just saying does it help to indicate it happens sooner? He was adamant that the public had the measure of GB, admired him as Chancellor but they were unsure about him in the top job.

We got the speech done and inserted a line from Howard's speech re him not mentioning the £35 billion big lie at all. PG thought the speech was the best of the three recent ones but broadcasters did not even take it live. We had the usual last-minute rush, then off to Swansea. It went down fine and was a good text but was not going to keep £35 billion at the top of the agenda. I was struck by how much more security there was around TB at the moment. Hundreds of cops involved in these visits now. The warm weather was bringing on early hay fever. He was doing a piece for *The Observer* including on school meals which I thought odd and off the pace. It is not an unimportant issue, but was it really what he should be focusing on right now? It felt like displacement again.

Saturday 19 March

The speech didn't really fly. The Sundays were all over the place. Anti-war march in London. We set out to Essex with Audrey for a farewell party for Brian Wilson [Labour MP] at Catherine McLeod's. Nice do, very Scottish. Brian was very emotional, broke down a couple of times, was very nice about me in his second speech, saying the media never bothered with unsuccessful Labour governments because the public would do that but they had to denigrate and attack people who helped make Labour successful. Don Macintyre [*Independent* journalist] was there saying we needed heroic things for the campaign. It was a nice do. I played the pipes and played a lament I had written which got me thinking about Dad, and which I could tell was moving them. AD the only other politician there, further sign he was able to straddle all camps. I had a chat with Brian, said thanks for being so kind and so supportive. He was vile about GB, said he was totally unfit to lead, and was doing all the damage that was undermining everyone. Maggie, AD's wife [former journalist], was really nice, good fun and full of flattery, saying she was worried the whole show would come crumbling down if I left again. Ditto Brian's wife. Funny speeches from Jim Innes [Labour press officer] and Tom Shields [*Herald* journalist], a lot of it about Brian's Celtic FC and Scottish cultural devotions.

Brian was probably emotional because he had not quite fulfilled all his promise. He said he had wanted to help the Highlands and Islands get a fair share from government and help Labour win and he had done both. But I recalled the times he had asked me what stopped TB from promoting him beyond the middle ranks, and our shared view that it was probably because of GB knowing what he thought of him, and TB not wanting to provoke any more than he did. Out for dinner with the Goulds at La Casalinga. Usual stuff chatting about the campaign, and even PG was getting down about it all. It felt like we were carrying twice as many bags as we needed to, so we didn't have the energy and creativity that we had back in '97 and even in '01.

Sunday 20 March

TB called and said he could not understand why we were unable to get stories up e.g. school dinners. He had written a piece in *The Observer*, but there was not much pick up. I actually felt the piece was a bit thin, too much about [celebrity chef] Jamie Oliver's campaign [for better school meals], not enough about where the issue fitted into our strategy, though they did trail the mini manifesto [separate condensed manifestos for specific policies] ideas. He felt the problem was organisational. I felt it was the construct of the new prism. He said what does everyone do at Party HQ apart from talk to each other? The problem with just waiting for GB was that it might not happen and in any event it weakened him that people knew that was the reality, waiting for Gordon. But GB was making clear he would only fully come in if AM was out and DA in.

He rejected the idea there was no big message or vision but the fact we spent the subsequent conference call talking mainly about the Tories pushing hard on gypsies and us pushing on school dinners pretty much said it all. We had to decide if we were just going to keep trying to work a better message through the media. We were briefing children's manifesto stuff, which broadened out from school meals into other issues affecting young kids and young adults, but I doubted it would fly.

JP called me later to say he wanted to do Channel 4 on gypsies. I wasn't sure, and knew that TB would not be, but he felt strongly he had to rebut some of the lies about the policy, so we agreed that provided he took it to the issue of Howard's and the Tories' opportunism, it was fine. We discussed the campaign generally. He felt it was stalling, as did I. He had opted out a bit from the TB–GB scene because they had 'gone bilateral on it all', but he felt they had to get their act together, and if they didn't we were heading for a car crash. He was not sure Alan had the capacity to hold the centre. I defended him, said the issue was not his ability, but the lack of clarity re who was doing what, and whether GB was going to play a central role or not. 'Bet you're glad you're back,' he said, and laughed.

I said it was weird because at the moment I was going through diaries from almost ten years ago, and the same bloody issues were playing out the whole time, especially the TB–GB stuff. The *Sunday Times* said we were changing the pledge card and I explained it was about different cards for different groups. It made me think the mini-manifesto approach was the right one. He said he would get out and campaign on whatever. 'I know where we are now. We just have to get on and do it.' He felt GB was beginning to worry the party and both of them would be blamed, not just TB, if he didn't get stuck in and get involved. But he was clearly down on TB too, felt he had never resolved this whole thing, was riddled with a daft kind of guilt, let the emotions of the whole thing take up too much time and space.

TB called a couple of times through the day to go over systems and work out whether we really had the systems to meet the needs we were facing. He was still pushing on this school dinner stuff which I thought was a bit tiddly, even if the media went on about it so much. It should not be consuming him so much so close to the campaign with so many key issues unresolved. David Hill got Ruth Kelly out on it but some of the broadcasters were saying her line was contradicting TB in *The Observer*. I took Rory to see Geoffrey Goodman [former *Mirror* industrial editor] for his essay on the role of trade unions in the creation of the party, and he was very nice to him. I called JP before his interview. He said TB had been at him, saying he should not be pushing on gypsies because it played into their agenda. But JP was adamant this could just go away. 'You can't just ignore it when Howard is up on it and the press are giving him such a hit.'

Monday 21 March

Howard had done an ad in the Sundays about his stance on travellers, and now had his press conference, preceded by a visit in Essex. It felt wrong to me, a step too far that could become a tipping point for the campaign. Here was a man who had to persuade the public he could be Prime Minister and he was making a massive thing out of gypsies. I spoke to MB first thing and got her to agree to the line that he was 'opportunastic', opportunist and nasty in equal measure. Our school dinners stuff was running OK but it looked a bit bandwagony and we were not clear enough about the money needed and where what was needed would come from. TB was pressing RK to be clearer but she felt the sums we were talking about still sounded pretty piddling and insignificant. The press conference with her, Alan and Margaret Hodge was again a bit scratchy. The media were desperate to give the Tories a lift and do us in. The polls were closing a bit but not as much as the recent torrent might have led us to expect. But Kevin Maguire [*Mirror* executive] told me *Sun* readers were moving to the Tories, the *Mirror* having polled on it. *Mirror* support was hardening a bit. Parna Basu brought over a Letwin newsletter with a survey showing huge satisfaction with the NHS and CCTV. We got going on that. The media were going big time on the Tories setting the agenda and doing dog-whistle issue politics,* with Marr saying the Budget had had no effect and the polls were closing. ICM arrived in due course showing the opposite. Our lead up. Ahead on all the big issues.

We had a long and rather meandering AM meeting about the next few days. We were not really hitting the mark on mini manifestos. I did another third party endorsement meeting to try to get Huw Evans [special advisor] and co. integrated, then AM before heading over to TB strategy meeting. He was in a foul mood re DfES [Department for Education and Skills] not having done what he asked for on school dinners. His weekend note was a bit meandering but he went through it with more energy and vigour than before. He had laid out that we do central dividing lines on all policy areas but was clear that the government machine was still not operating properly on this. He wanted edge to policy. AM felt we didn't have it and kept compromising too much.

We were all feeling a bit happier that the Tory stuff was so OTT and Howard's opportunism was beginning to break through as a given. TB was much more up for the fight than in recent days but had still not resolved GB, who had gone back on strike and was communicating absolutely nothing. I spoke to Ed Balls and Ed Miliband during the day, and both said GB was really trying but TB was being difficult. Mark Lucas [film-maker] did say that at the poster launch last week GB had been making more of an effort than TB so maybe he was to blame and did not want GB's help.

TB was very torn I think, in that he knew we needed GB to help power up the campaign but given the way he had treated him maybe wanted to do it alone. I left the meeting early to head for Marlow for a

---

* Dog-whistle politics: messaging that appears to mean one thing to the general public but has a different or more specific resonance for a target audience.

Lions planning meeting with CW and media team. Ed Balls called again as I was on the way, felt we should meet up. He said GB really wanted to make it work. I said it could easily work, we just had to get their act together and start campaigning. If he took over a strategy group it would be obvious he was in charge and he could drive the thing. But we could not have Alan humiliated. It would be bad for Alan and bad for Tony who had clearly staked a fair bit of authority in having Alan take over at the centre. Ed said that whatever had happened with the two of them back in 1994 – re a deal – and any of the bad blood since was history and we just had to get it together. I agreed, and I did feel they were currently reaching out. But whenever I said AM had to be part of whatever we decided for the centre, he backed off a little. I said if GB came back into the centre, then given he and TB were the only ones who could really drive message, it would be perfectly obvious who the big hitters were. The rest of us just had to make it all happen.

Good Lions meeting, Clive happy with the plans we had made. He said he had still not signed a contract and was obviously not happy at some of the commercial pressures being applied, for example there was to be a special behind the scenes DVD which he was totally opposed to. I joked that if we lost the election, I may not be able to come because I would be locked away depressed for a year. He said don't worry. If you lose we won't want you because we don't want losers. He then added – 'By the way, there is no way in the world you are going to lose. Blair v Howard is a no brainer.'

He confirmed Brian O'Driscoll would be captain and said he was determined that the story did not become who was left out. He was on good form but very spiky. When Louise said the All Blacks wanted to go first on press conferences post-Test matches he said no way – losers first. Then winners. He also said he was not having B-list refs for the non-Test matches. I got a lift back with Louisa and Marcus Jansa. I was looking forward to it now. It felt real and I was sure it would be interesting and challenging in a very different kind of way to the election. Clive was happy with the idea I go out for the start, then back for a bit, but there for all the Tests.

Tuesday 22 March

There was definitely a sense that Howard's whack at gypsies was a step too far, despite the *Mail* claiming we were saying he was a Nazi. The *Mail* was hysterical these days, worse than ever. My only hope was that it was so OTT it would echo and ventilate the feeling among their readers that Howard was too. I ran in, drafting JR words for the press conference, texting to myself as I ran. PG did a polling presentation to the NEC which I later briefed out quite extensively, given there were a lot of positives in there at the moment. We definitely had a different approach to polling than previous elections, especially '97, when we had basically played down how far ahead we were and how well we were doing as a way of killing any complacency. But this time the mood was less confident and positive and we needed to raise morale a bit. There was certainly enough stuff in the polling to do that. It wasn't just the state of the parties, but we were well ahead on leadership and economy, and on public services.

Philip had also been speaking to Andrew Cooper [pollster], who reckoned there was a 3.8 per cent swing in the marginals and the maximum majority we could hope for was 90. I imagined the Tories would also be getting the message through from focus groups that even if they didn't much care for gypsies, they did not like the way Howard exploited it. So I did a 'Howard bandwagon watch' item for the website with ten possible next bandwagons for him to go on. It was partly driven by a call from John O'Farrell [comedy scriptwriter] yesterday who said he felt we had to use more humour, that we were coming over as being a bit too earnest.

We had JR and Rosie Winterton [MP] in to do a number on health workforce figures, which were good. But there were also figures out on baby deaths from MRSA so that was clearly going to take over. I chaired the morning meeting and had an extraordinary exchange with Spencer. I asked what GB would be doing at the Treasury Select Committee. 'Economy.' What's the outcome? 'Depends what they ask?' I said my experience of GB is if he does something he decides the outcome first and then brings it out. Silence, not a word, looking into middle distance. 'Will he do media on the Tory economic plan?' No, it will be Paul Boateng or Balls. 'Why not Gordon?' He has other things to do? 'Like what?' Don't know. It was ludicrous. 'Thanks for turning up,' I said, and then said I would get JR and AD to go up.

To an agency meeting on the next steps on posters. TB had done a speech to an event called Faithworks [conference to propagate the 'intelligent' church] which was going OK. At the Q&A he was asked re my 'We don't do God' stuff. Along with bog-standard comprehensive, People's Princess and New Labour New Britain, it was probably the soundbite most quoted alongside my name. Yesterday I had a letter from an American faith college who were doing a module based on it. It was obvious to me they totally misunderstood what I had meant. TB said that he had never hidden his faith but that I had always felt there was a risk attached to UK politicians – unlike those in the US where it was impossible not to do God – talking about religion because it made people think they were trying to ally religion and politics. That being said, I was thinking we should be doing more of the faith stuff. He clearly liked the people and they liked him, and it was authentically him. We spent loads of the day umming and aahing about whether to do the pensioners' mini manifesto tomorrow. AM felt the care package was new enough – even though JR did it on Monday. But he was keen to do it so we just had to work it up. TB's faith speech was playing fine.

Parna had started her role as essentially a general support/PA/organiser and was making a real difference and helping to get a grip, not least of my diary and all the different people trying to get into me. She was also really nice and incredibly helpful. I did a JP tribute clip for his 40th anniversary dinner. Then home to meet David Faber [former Tory MP], who was coming over to us. We went through his life story and agreed we should do it some time between 4 to 12 April with Phil Webster, then a press conference, do the tabloids, a full media round and maybe a few visits. I said we could make no promises but we had to make sure he had some kind of longer term attachment. I liked him and he was full of good lines though he did not want to attack Howard personally, having worked with him when he was shadow Foreign Secretary. He was keen to say it wasn't just about TB, he felt he had more in common with the whole Labour movement. It would not be like Shaun W (who earlier asked me if he should come back from his holiday) and who was full of good ideas about how to deal with the Tories.

We worked up a plan for a JR speech which was meant to be a Fabians' third term vision event but in which we wanted to include a major attack on Howard. Though the MRSA baby story was grim today,* campaign wise things felt better, and there is no doubt we were benefiting from Howard being seen as both unpleasant and opportunistic. One was giving rise to the sense of the other. Maybe we just had to get TB out there as he was and we had to drive it behind him with or without GB. He went off to Brussels. We agreed that after Howard's gypsy stuff

---

* A baby died 36 hours after his birth as a result of contracting the superbug. Staff at Ipswich Hospital had missed signs showing he was ill.

we could not do the Leapfrogged poster re UK having jumped ahead of the French on various indicators as it would be branded racist. A nice bit of cheering mininews as I left the office – the picture on the front of the Tories' economic plan was from a Kansas car dealership brochure.

Wednesday 23 March

I'd briefed some of the private polling now which went well and settled people down a bit. I got together all of our staff from press, attack and policy to do a polling briefing and a pep talk, and tell them they were better than the other lot, also to bind them in a bit more to the general message and strategy. They were young in the main but there was a lot of energy and a lot of passion there. I did my usual thing about drinking water not alcohol, eating fruit not sweets and making sure everyone top to bottom felt part of the team. We did the usual meetings plus the Agency to go over posters. They liked 'If you value it, vote for it', which I wasn't so keen on. We didn't really have a killer last five-day hit, on the lines of the Hague–Thatcher wig [then Tory leader William Hague wearing a Thatcher wig] in 2001, and I arranged to meet Trevor B tomorrow to go over it all. We needed something that said stability and continuity v risk. We also needed to make sure people were reminded of Howard's past. Around half of the women in the groups had no idea he had even been in power.

PG had been to some groups himself and wrote TB and me a note to the effect that they wanted 'continuity plus a fresh start'. They wanted a change but not to the Tories. They wanted to bring us down but not kick us out. The trouble with that of course is that people cannot vote for the outcome, they can only use the one vote they have. We had a strategy meeting with TB, who, when I said we were not getting much out of the politicians, said, 'You'll wait for ever if you wait for politicians to do a campaign. They're hopeless.' I said, 'Do you mean we?' He laughed, but said – not unreasonably – that the one thing you couldn't say about him and GB was that they lacked energy for a campaign. We had another press conference with AJ – who is a very natural communicator. Pensions ran OK but low-key. We weren't really breaking through but the sense of a good solid campaign against their opportunism was fine.

TB got back from Brussels after another up and downer with Chirac and was at least more fired up but was still obsessing about process rather than gripping politics. No. 10 had cancelled a meeting with

March '05: Private polling boosts party morale a little

Anthony Minghella [Academy Award-winning film-maker] who was willing to make the TB–GB film we were planning as one of our main election broadcasts. I got TB to reinstate it but it was a real struggle at the moment. He did have a point about some of the weaknesses in the operation but his micro management was getting way too low down in the weeds. He was frustrated as we all were but so much was in the hands of him and his colleagues. I got JP to agree to strong words on TB/Howard for tomorrow. We had to make the choice more explicit – in terms of competence, likeability, what they had delivered, character. JP said, 'Shall I just cross out TB and put GB?' But he seemed on OK form, though No. 10 people were getting fed up with the policy mush problem.

I did a dinner for Mike Craven [Labour-supporting businessman] and some of his clients, a general speech plus Q&A and I was surprised at how nobody – including a woman on secondment to CCO – felt the Tories had a chance. I felt on form and really strong on the arguments, but the trouble was with our media as it is the public hardly ever heard them. It was infuriating. [Former Tory minister John] Gummer's brother [Lord] Peter Chadlington [businessman] was there and said Mori were saying another landslide but Andrew Cooper was on about 90. Andrew was the one PG believed ahead of the others. TB asked me to work on stuff re marginals and how we could organise and use ministerial visits more strategically.

Thursday 24 March

I ran in, soaked, but had a couple of decent ideas on the way in. But quickly, after a decent day yesterday, I felt dragged down. AM's rather meandering meeting style, his odd swagger, his thumping the table was all getting a bit much. We had so many meetings that went round in circles, ideas driven by anecdote not strategy. Tim Allan came in and was on good form but I could tell he thought it all a bit shambolic. The extent was underlined when we heard a Group of Death was cancelled, then it was back on again, off again, on again, so over we trooped, to hear in fact it was off after all. I had a brief chat with a grumpy GB who like me had thought it was on. He asked how 'Milburn' was doing? I said fine, but we had the same problems of dysfunctionality, not helped by the fact he and TB were not working together and he was not motoring on the economy. He said he would do more, but it had to be part of broader change. I think I know what that meant.

I bumped into JS who was looking nervous because he was having to do his emergency statement on the leaked resignation letter of the FCO lawyer.* We were getting one or two half-decent ideas but struggling a bit on policy storylines. Fraser Kemp was going for Mark Textor and Lynton Crosby [Australian strategists working for the Tories] over the dog-whistle nature of the campaign. I saw Crosby leaving their building, thought about saying hi but then decided against. AM was beginning to get a bit down, and it was beginning to show. He learned GB had a load of stuff planned with JP and was worried there was a separate grid operation. He was also fed up with TB's failure to sort out the situation, as were we all. I lost it a bit when Ian McC said they didn't have a message note and AM asked me to do one. I said what – like all the others that go into the fucking ether because ministers do not communicate message or implement strategy.

It was an extraordinary state of affairs – TB not on form, GB on strike, JP opting out if it involved contact with media, CC invisible and asylum and immigration still growing as a problem, the others apart from JR doing next to nothing unless asked. Hardly surprising Alan was as pissed off as I was. Also, having been pissed off at the refusal of anyone to see the political upside of doing sports recognition for darts, as an easy hit for a certain working-class constituency, I was even more pissed off when the Libs' Bob Russell [MP] did it today. Iraq was running too big still and though the Tory hits were stalled Howard was being allowed a change of tack without taking a hit. They were so desperate to lift him.

The attack team had landed a good one though – a tape of Howard Flight [Tory deputy chairman] at a dinner making clear their cuts plan went beyond James. I got on to Baldwin, got him to get on to Michael Crick [BBC *Newsnight*] to alert him once he knew it stacked up. It looked like a good one. Flight also said council tax cut for pensioners was nakedly political and he made clear thresholds and inheritance tax were next. We had to get it going. It was great having Parna helping me but really hard to write anything because people were just into me the whole time so I waited till we got on the train to do a direct mail shot for TB, message note and give handling instructions about all the Tory stuff. Baldwin loved it and we were trying to crank up.

---

* The resignation letter of Foreign Office lawyer Elizabeth Wilmshurst, obtained by *Channel 4 News*, claimed Attorney General Lord Goldsmith changed his mind about the legality of the Iraq War just before it began.

He wanted GB words but I assumed the Treasury would do their usual buggering about so suggested JR so that we could tie it in with the pre-promotion of the poster launch tomorrow.

I was trying to orchestrate it all from the train to Carlisle. Eventually we settled on Boateng to try to get it up. Then at about half seven, when I was in the cab to Hawick from Carlisle station, Tom called to say the Tories had sacked Flight. They were intending to announce it at nine to give *The Times* the first-edition exclusive. I was desperate to tell everyone at the office but my phone went dead on me. I tried to email but we were in a no signal area.

We got to the house Fiona had booked for Easter and I did a quick conference call with AM, Matthew Doyle and Patrick Loughran. They were ecstatic. It was going to get cuts right up in lights. We agreed AM should go to Millbank the second it broke. It was particularly good because Iraq/AG advice was still around. I felt great, for the first time in ages. I got on to Parna and got her to get a note to John Woodcock [attack unit researcher] who had been the one who had got into the meeting and taped it – 'I told you we were better than them and you proved it.' The news was gold dust – Tory turmoil, cuts, secret agenda, we could not have scripted it better ourselves. The Tories were trying to make it all about Flight, suggest he was a bit off the wall, but it wouldn't wash. I went to bed feeling good that the Tory momentum was well and truly stalled. Still I didn't sleep well though.

Friday 25 March
The house, just outside Pitlochry, was fabulous and the setting even better than last year's house. I went for a run up behind the house, then came back to join the morning meeting in Vic St by phone. We agreed to postpone the NHS poster launch till tomorrow and go for a big hit on Flight fallout today with JR, AM and RK. The lines of attack were easy, plus we had Flight on health, saying things that would also damage them, and we had Letwin making similar arguments in the past. We also needed to press again for the full James report and get up 'Where's Letwin?' and 'Where's Redwood [John, shadow secretary for deregulation]?' search parties. I spent part of the morning dictating notes for background briefing for the Sundays, including strategy v tactics, leadership v opportunism. Howard was a gift. I also gave out focus group stuff on women in particular not knowing what Howard did when in government.

TB called and we agreed he should go up and do a clip on Flight just to keep it going. He also wanted DB or AD to do a speech on how the Tories have not changed as we did, which I was fine about as it played into the differences we were trying to highlight. He felt it was going to be tough for them and Flight was a big name in the campaign overnight, with everyone following it up. But none of us expected what happened next – Howard did a clip from his kitchen of all places saying Flight was not only being sacked from his job but also as a candidate. Howard had clearly decided looking tough was all he could salvage from this. But it was probably another mistake. We had another round of conference calls and agreed the main line was that nothing Howard did could disguise the reality of the Tory Party today.

TB said he thought we should also say it was a vindictive misjudgement. But I felt it better we say he was pushed into it, blowing in the wind and that they couldn't disguise their beliefs. They had obviously told Howard all he could get out of it was toughness but it was backfiring almost immediately. Then Flight popped up and said Howard could not sack him as a candidate, that was a matter for his local party, and he expected to stand. Even better. Eventually the local Tory executive backed Howard but it kept ramping up higher and higher.

We had a JR, AM and co. conference call and agreed, against AM's wishes, to stick with the health poster tomorrow now. Alan felt it would let them off the hook on Flight but I felt we could link them – cuts leading to charges leading to extremism. Plus we had Liam Fox on tape on this policy as we had Flight on the other one. When they said 'charges' was a Labour lie we could say they said that about the last one, re cuts. We could hit them hard and JR would do the media rounds. Added to which we had to hope for the Sundays to be largely focused on Tory turmoil. On verra. We had a late night conference call and AM – I think spooked by TB saying GB thought we were going OTT in saying charges rather than vouchers as the attack on the Tories on health – was arguing to put the poster off again tomorrow so we could keep going on Flight. JR, PG and I were pushing hard in saying it worked to go from cuts to charges as a route to extremism and an unchanged Tory party. It also helped that we had a letter from Flight to Howard arguing for charges. If we handled this right, it could shape the campaign.

Saturday 26 March
The papers were dire for the Tories and we had to pile on the pressure.

AM was still worried that we would drive the story off Flight and cuts and into 'another Labour lie'. I was surer than ever it was right to pile on the pressure and take the argument to another point of policy vulnerability for them. JR was in agreement and totally up for it, to lead on cuts and Flight and move to NHS charges. I warned JR he would be asked re the provenance of the tape and he pushed it off with a bit of bluster at first, and later said he was not aware of Labour involvement. I did a note saying we should link it to the unchanged Tory party – that they were obsessed with me, Peter M, spin etc. because they felt they were cheated out of power and beaten by spin, but on policy and values they just had not changed. We also agreed to bring forward the NMW leak from the campaign guide as there would be added interest in the idea there was a leak. In between runs and swims and hanging around with Fiona and the kids, I was chatting to AM and JR. JR called afterwards and said the briefing by 'the Bear' [GB] was getting Alan down.

Meanwhile Ed Balls called me and said GB was keen to meet up if we could while I was up with the family in Scotland. I emailed GB who obviously discussed it with TB who asked me later if we were meeting up. There was a totally changed mood in the media re the Tories, though they were trying hard to get it all linked to me and some of the papers of course would help them. But when JR called with the papers at 11 it was OK, plus there was a bad new story for them re Tony Baldry [Tory MP] making loads of money out of business in Africa despite being chair of the International Development Select Committee.*

Then news came through that [former Labour Prime Minister] Jim Callaghan had died. Just eleven days after Audrey [his wife]. Really sad. The last time I spoke to him, a few months ago, he was talking about how even though she was in so many ways not the same person, he just liked to sit with her and talk to her, though she couldn't really understand. He obviously had been waiting for her to go before going himself. I think the time before that he had been a bit agitated with TB because he felt he didn't pay sufficient attention to previous Labour

---

* Baldry wrote to Hilary Benn, Secretary for International Development, asking if his department could endorse a British diamond mining company in Sierra Leone without revealing that the company had paid $75,000 to a company in which Baldry owned shares. The Parliamentary Standards and Privileges Committee observed that 'Baldry did not comply with the House's requirements in respect of the declarations of interest'.

leaders, and seemed more interested in getting Thatcher's views on foreign policy than his. We sat and watched the tributes, ruined by all the rentaquote hacks who knew nothing. The pre-packaged biogs were pretty good.

Sunday 27 March

I got the office motoring on NMW plus Patrick Loughran had good stuff to debunk Howard's new childcare offer which was less than before. He and Woodcock and the attack team were proving to be the stars of the campaign so far. Baldry was rumbling on and there was the build-up to tomorrow's Bank Holiday and moves on the social chapter [protocol attached to the Maastricht Treaty, setting out broad social policy]. TB called, said he was sure Howard would get a counter reaction for going so hard on Flight – Norman Tebbit [ex-Tory chairman] was already saying it was a question of judgement, and of course because of a lot of people's gut feeling about Howard, there were plenty of people saying it was unpleasant and nasty rather than decisive and tough. TB and I were both developing quite good impersonations of Howard, and imagining him doing 'terriboule ebserlootly awfull theengs to peepull'. He said he had slept 22 hours in two days and felt a lot better. He was not sure about the extent of the engagement strategy, felt that getting out and about in direct engagement with the voters had its place but also they did want him to be prime ministerial.

DH and Hilary C had called re the interview with Sky on Wednesday, Emily Hands [Downing Street press officer] having learned the Tories were setting up the MRSA mother whose baby died to be there. I said to David we had to get heavy, accuse them of bad faith and warn we would pull out unless we had guarantees about knowing the make-up of the audience. TB said he felt he should be doing big challenging speeches now, as well as the interactive stuff. I raised Little Ant and Dec – two young kids we had fixed to interview him – and briefed him on the Beckham interview. 'Oh God.' He did say though that the important thing was the ability to make adjustments as you went.

He sounded a lot chirpier, as did the people calling from the office. We were planning Social Chapter. Later I went into Hawick to get an Indian takeaway and had a long chat with Phil Webster, who felt the dynamic had definitely shifted our way. I was also toing and froing on plans for meeting GB. I kept emailing our phone number and suggested he call, but he replied by email. We eventually got it sorted for

Tuesday a.m. I was probably doing between five and six hours' work a day and in between times doing amazing walks and runs and bike rides. I had a long chat with Patricia [Hewitt], who was doing the morning rounds. I suddenly got a depression hit mid-evening, came right up out of nowhere and landed in minutes, full-on emptiness almost immediately after it started. I went to bed and switched off the phone.

Monday 28 March

Last full day at Hawick. I slept not bad considering the plunge last night and went out for an OK run. Mum and Donald arrived and then in the afternoon Sue and Brendan Foster. I did a couple of long conference calls after my run, first before the press conference. The Tories were using their papers to get up the dirty tricks angle, the idea we were up to bad stuff in getting material on them, and they were briefing that they were sweeping their HQ for bugs. Classic Aussie bollocks. They probably weren't doing it, but it was a way of making people – or the press at least – think that we might, and that was how we were getting these stories. We agreed Ian McCartney just had to go on the offensive and say it was a diversion away from substance. I watched on BBC live and both he and Patricia were pretty good. Pat Hewitt was excellent when she wasn't patronising or defensive and today she was neither. She did really well. They were both pressed hard but did fine in taking it all back to big stuff not the detritus of campaigning. Meanwhile happily Flight was still fighting away, added to which David Mellor [former Tory minister] had joined Tebbit in attacking Howard's judgement for trying to sack him as a candidate.

The later call was more about planning the next few days which were going to be pretty hectic up to calling the election, which is what everyone is waiting for now. Alan was sounding chirpier, and I took advantage to warn him I was planning to see GB. He was happy enough for me to see him but didn't want major structural change to the campaign and HQ and felt we had to get him engaged without him coming in the whole time. PG meanwhile felt we had to get him doing day-to-day stuff, and getting up the fight head to head v Howard. I was not sure that press conferences were the best use of GB's time. He was only good at them when he had something he really wanted to push, less so when he was just fielding all comers. Last time round they had not been a success. I felt maybe two pressers, two big speeches, a major TV event and something with TB was the way to go.

The cab came for me at 7.45 and I set off for GB's. I felt really sad leaving Fiona and the kids. Even though I had been on the phone a lot, and had a mini-blip on the head front, we had been getting on OK. Fiona seemed resigned to me being involved pretty full on up to the election, and the boys were pretty clear they felt I should be doing it. I was beginning to wonder though how I would cope with weeks away from them, election followed by NZ. Grace was pulling very hard at the heart strings at the moment about me going on the NZ trip at all. It had been a nice little break, Mum and Donald had enjoyed it, it had been great seeing Brendan who always had such a sound view of things, but we were not far away from the campaign proper now. I wasn't sure what I wanted to get out of the GB meeting, and hadn't really discussed it with TB but it was a good sign he wanted to meet up.

I got there about half nine, so we would have a couple of hours before I had to leave for the plane. I noticed he had had the security service doorbell system fitted since the last time we were here, the same one we had. Through the door I could see the clutter that goes with a young child, toys littering the floor. Sarah came to the door and was welcoming without being overly warm. She hadn't looked happy for the last few times I saw her. The boy was sweet. He was sitting on top of a pile of boxes which contained typed versions of all the sermons GB's father [Church of Scotland minister] had ever given. I said to GB, 'You should publish those.' It was a bit cold and misty but after Sarah made a cup of tea he and I went out to the little conservatory at the top of the garden. We didn't bother with much small talk, a bit of rugby and the Lions, and what I would do, and what was Clive like, how was Fiona, how was Alex, a bit of Raith Rovers and Scotland and Burnley and then we were into it.

He said he had seen the campaign grid, but what was the strategy? I said the grid was a bit of a shell because a lot depended on what he and TB agreed, and what they would do together. So it could not yet be filled out as we wished. I said the shape of the campaign should be economy, public services, then back to economy, with our record and future plans up against their risk and unchanged values. I wanted them to campaign together as much as possible, to do the Minghella film together and also to have a sense of them coming together as a team. I said there had been so much coverage of them falling apart there would be massive interest in them coming together. 'We might as well get some good out of all the shitty water that has gone under the bridge.' He laughed.

He was pretty scathing re TB and the agenda. He felt the promise to be 'unremittingly New Labour' had been a big mistake, Ruth had had a terrible start by doing all the parents' champion stuff and getting on the wrong side of teachers, the choice agenda (re social services) was meaningless as it stood and we were in danger of the dividing lines being in the wrong place, namely internal rather than with the Tories. DM should have done education but TB wanted someone 'that madman Adonis' could control. He was sympathetic to TB on Iraq because he felt he did the right thing, and it would have been hard not to act as he did, but trust was a nightmare – 'You know that better than anyone' – and out there it was very hard to see how TB could rebuild. He reminded me that the last time I was there was exactly a year ago 'when TB was thinking of going'. Another laugh, this time less hearty. 'I have gone beyond feeling betrayed.' He said it was odd me saying TB needed him to help get a good win, 'because a few months ago he was confident he could do it without me'. Another gentle laugh. He was scathing re Milburn, said, 'He fucked up everything until you got in there to rescue him.' He felt we were beyond structural change but felt if he went back in, he would need Douglas and Ed Balls there with him.

I said we needed him as engaged as soon as possible. People want continuity with change. He laughed – 'How can you get that if TB says he is staying the whole term?' I said you get it through Vote Blair, get Blair then the likelihood is Brown takes over. 'Don't forget that though Tony is not as popular as he was, he is still seen as a pretty good PM even by non-supporters.' I said, 'There has to be a sense of the two of you coming together and a sense TB will make way at some point. But surely you understand that cannot be fully articulated or else people just wonder why he is going to be there at all. This needs to be a coming together and around it rebuilding the sense of inevitability about who takes over. When can take care of itself.' He was listening intently, his face not unfriendly, and he at least understood – and said he appreciated – that I was trying to help.

He was troubled by an Irwin Seltzer piece saying he was not right for the top job, and pressed me on what I thought Murdoch was up to. He felt it was all about him being solely interested in America, that he felt we had to be subservient to the States on anything. He went through his difficulties with the Yanks on debt relief, and it was clear they just expected to get their way on everything. I said it might be that Murdoch just doesn't take the interest he did. But there is definitely a view among some in his papers that they can live with TB but are less sure about you. That is why I want a campaign that is built on the considerable strengths of both of you.

We went round for a while on the various policy issues and I said I didn't think TB was that far away from where he was on the nature of campaign – it had to be a fairly traditional left–right, investment v cuts public services election. The way to make the economy interesting was to have the TB–GB story developing through the campaign. Flight was a gift. If I did God I would have said it came from above, at a time we were struggling a bit and the Tories getting their act together a bit, and we had to keep going with it. I said Howard was not that good and we could knock him over easily if they could work together. He was scathing again re Milburn but I said TB felt it was a bit much to rub his nose in the dirt. He had to work with him. We could surely all work together.

I agreed to do a note on how I thought the TB–GB storyline could be developed in a way that benefited them and the campaign. He asked me to work it up on the plane and send it to him tonight. It basically meant TB committing not only to him staying as Chancellor but also to him being his chosen successor, but I felt that was a price worth paying to get this campaign functioning properly. What was infuriating was that – as he kept reminding me – I didn't disagree with a lot of the things he said. But it was so hard to pin him down. I said if he wasn't going back to the 1997 model, taking all the morning meetings, we needed him to do at least two pressers a week, two big events, one with TB, per week, him doing some of the big interviews, and regular input via me. I said I wish I had called him myself with the Flight stuff because it was made for him. It went well but if he had been there we would have got booster rockets on it. He said he only got a garbled version through his office. I said sometimes your office was obstructive, sometimes they were fine, but I always assumed he gave the orders and sometimes I couldn't be bothered with the aggro of getting him involved. As it happened the Flight story had flown without him, but we will get more out of future events if we can call him. 'I understand, I understand.'

And I really felt it was not worth him demanding some kind of ritual humiliation for Alan. One, he did have something to contribute. Two, it would just create another TB–GB faultline at a time we were

March '05: Howard Flight 'a gift from God'

trying to put an end to all that. Re TB he was less vituperative than the last few times I saw him, but he felt he was weakened. He said he should have gone when he first thought about it. It is all going to be so messy now, from now on in, to the end. TB was worrying about legacy but this choice agenda in public services leads one of two ways – to the next Labour leader rolling it back as the only way of holding the party together, or the next Tory government going full steam ahead to genuine privatisation.

We got up, had a little wander around the garden. He said TB was wrong to hate Ed Balls. I said he doesn't hate him, but he sometimes feels he gives you bad advice, and plays to a sense of grievance. 'He understands politics and he understands the economy, and those kind of people are not falling off trees.' How do you get on with Ed Miliband? he asked. I said fine, but ultimately they all took their lead from you, and I could always tell whether you were onside or not through them. I recalled some of the Spencer exchanges at morning meetings. 'Ed is better than David. He always knows where the dividing lines are.' I said I was happy to work with both of the Eds but that meant him telling them to be fully engaged, and it meant me and him staying on the same page, and him and Tony showing they could work together again.

We then went in for another cup of tea, more chat with Sarah, then through to the lounge where, despite the mist, he tried to show me the views out across the Forth. We did the US and his worries about their agenda. He thought the appointment of Paul Wolfowitz [US deputy Defense Secretary about to begin new role as president of the World Bank] was silly, and wrong, and showed how beholden Bush was to the right. He quizzed me a bit on what Bush was like in private, asked if he was the kind of person who made relationships across divides. I said he had done it with Tony, and his smile suggested he didn't think there was that much of a divide.

Then we were back to the domestic, and whether there was anything to get pulses racing. He felt it had to be fairly traditional – full employment, save the NHS, rebuild community schools. He was angry, he said, that we had had so much opportunity and not done enough with it because we went for these diversions all the time. 'We have not recalibrated the debate as we should. We still have the right-wing setting the terms of the debate, and that was one of the things we used to talk about changing when you were at the *Mirror* and I was writing for the [*Daily*] *Record*,' he said. 'We have not shifted the country leftward when we had the chance. We raised tax for the NHS but we then wasted the opportunity the debate gave us. We still let the right dictate terms of the debate.' He looked sad, and shook his head.

I said I felt it was changing – that's why they had to sack Flight for saying what he thought, even though for many Tories that was exactly the agenda they wanted to be on; why they had to pretend to support the minimum wage, which Howard used to say would cost a million jobs; why they felt they had to express support for Africa etc., or a Scottish Parliament. So they were being forced to change, and that suggested we had changed the terms of debate. But he felt we had not engaged in let alone won the debate on public services. They would use what we were doing to shift back the dial, because they would feel what we were doing went with the grain of what they would do, but they would go much much further.

As time wore on, I kept trying to go back to where he would be able to help in the campaign and by the end of it he was enthusiastically setting out what he would do by way of economic campaign, starting with JP on Friday. He was then motoring with argument and ideas and it was strong stuff. I said 'Gordon, this is why we need you to get engaged.' He asked me a few times what I would do in the future, suggested I take over the *Mirror*, for example. He said the Lions would be fun, but he wondered if I wasn't just finding a reason to be away, make sure I wasn't dragged back in after the election. I said I had certainly been dragged in now, that today had been real 'plus ça change' territory, sorting out him and TB and whether you can work together. He said he was glad I had been dragged in to Vic St because it had been going nowhere. I said the basics were there but ultimately all the best talents had to work to their full potential, and I could move things in there, but we needed him and TB properly motoring out on the road, out in public, and with proper engagement with the centre. Otherwise we risk handing things back to a nasty right-wing party that really will undo the things we had fought for. 'I understand,' he said. 'We will get there.'

We had a final chat on the steps. He said 'I don't expect you to reply but I think you are disappointed too, that we haven't reshaped things as we hoped. But if we get full employment, the best value for money NHS in the world, state schools as good as anything in the private sector, that will be worth the fight. We can still do that but it means remaking and winning the argument for the public realm. I am worried we are losing that argument because we are playing to their

March '05: GB's disappointment at Labour record

agenda and their philosophy, not our own.' I agreed to do him a note and then set off for the airport. TB called and asked me how it went. I said fine. He seemed to be up for being in the campaign. We covered all the bases. I said we should speak when I get back. The plane was delayed and I was able to get the note done on the BlackBerry by the time we landed.

Note written by AC, Tuesday 29 March
TB–GB AS KEY CAMPAIGN DRIVER

The key elements would be:
– Joint campaigning, including at the beginning and end of short campaign. That means shared visits, interviews and phone-ins, party events focused on marginals with occasional heartland events.
– Communication through briefing of constant consultation when in different parts of the country, with GB regular presence in London, including at least three press conferences a week, making clear central role in strategy.
– TB played into GB press conferences and vice versa.
– Weekly joint event in middle parts of campaign. These should not be routine but e.g. GB takes TB to Kirkcaldy (plus Scottish marginal). GB in Sedgefield. GB introduces TB at rally. TB brings GB back on stage after his own speech for joint Q&A.
– A joint PEB as our first, briefed as TB knows leadership does not just mean him, GB knows economic success not all his.
– A narrative weaved into all TB and GB communications thereafter, based on standard tabloid articles, TB on GB, GB on TB.

<u>Why?</u>
The relationship is now widely perceived by the media as negative. The media no longer accepts protestations of working properly together. They sense mistrust even loathing. They believe differences are ideological as well as personal. In defining TB negatively they go to trust, spin, Bush, only cares re legacy. In defining GB negatively they go to ambition thwarted, not a team player, old Labour, will want to undo TB legacy. The combination clouds out the pluses – for the media at least. Worse, it conveys us as soap opera not progressive politics.

Yet for the public there remain strengths in the relationship and what it says about Labour past and future. We can make it a strength for the campaign.

They fell for TB in a big way. Though time, experience and above all Iraq have taken their toll, there remains a reservoir of goodwill. The majority still want him to succeed. He has been tested and they do not doubt he has what it takes to be PM. What they sometimes worry about is whether he has the passion and energy for the job, and whether he is still focused on their concerns. If they could get the old TB back, they would be happy enough. But time moves on. The TB they get has the same beliefs and values but is more experienced. He has also made clear that this is his last election. So the public mind will inevitably focus in part of what will follow him.

That takes us to a strength. **Labour is not a one man band.** The changes in the party are deep. At some point there will be a change of leader without a change of party and the many good things that Labour are doing. That is the continuity plus change people are bound to look towards if we win.

TB was the right man at the right time because in a sense it was the New element of the New Labour equation that had to be stressed, to show we had changed and were committed to modernisation. He has shown he can lead and that Labour can govern. But GB was always a moderniser too. Yes, he is more rooted in Labour's heritage and proud of it, but some of the biggest, boldest acts of modernisation were his.

Stability, the most important element of continuity, is in a large part about him.

The party has changed. The country has changed. Labour is shaping a post-Thatcherite Britain that is very different to the one we inherited. That is the achievement of this team. The fact the Tories are going into this election pretending to be committed to investment, jobs, NMW, Africa – all shows how deep the change is going.

The feelings of the public re GB relate far more to the economy than anything else. They do not share the media obsession with the relationship. They know the two of them have their moments but it doesn't bother them.

On the contrary, it is seen in some parts as a good check. It is certainly not 'division' on a par with that caused under Major on Europe, for example. Most important, the public still think both know how to do their jobs. They know TB has taken a lot of hits and it is inevitable that he has changed in the eyes of some. GB is hugely respected. He has done what they most expect of him – met the challenge to keep the economy strong. He has embodied stability in part through longevity. He keeps going. He has shown strategy – budget nine contained many of the exact same basic arguments as budget one. All have shown government can make a difference re jobs, living standards, investment in public services.

GB is clearly the favourite to take over when TB stands down. The sense of that happening should be part of the unfolding narrative of this campaign. We must take the media fascination with the bad side of the relationship and get the public interested in it for different, positive reasons.

How?

We take the media by surprise at the outset, by TB and GB campaigning together, and by the first PEB being about the two of them. This is more than just being together in the same place. They campaign together because they intend to communicate a shared agenda and shared beliefs, but as two very different individuals who together have helped change Labour and are helping to change Britain, in which Labour not Tory values are in the ascendant. We brief around this at various levels.

It is the best, most visible way of putting the economy and public services centre-stage. It will be interesting because it will be unexpected.

It allows us to set out our basic narrative at the most important part of the campaign. It contrasts with Howard as a one man band. It says leadership and delivery. It speaks to stability. It makes clear the confidence of each in the other, whatever the differences between them.

Both will need to freshen up language – verbal and body – re how they speak of each other and interact.

This requires frankness as well as friendship. The phrases currently used are formulaic. We need to connect with edge, but in ways that help TB, GB and the campaign.

What has to be delivered is a real sense of what unites them and what makes them different. Part of this will be how they talk about each other in public, and about why they are in politics.

E.g. GB says TB was the right choice in 1997 because he symbolised more the change that was happening. In opposition, what you say is all you have. Where we were then played to his strengths.

TB praises GB's restless, probing intellect and deep sense of civic duty.

Asked re who will follow him, TB says 'Best ever Chancellor not a bad thing on your CV and he would be a great PM.'

Both can say GB would not be human if he did not imagine one day being PM.

TB talks up the importance of the team. Says it matters that we win not just now, but in the future with a new leader because we are trying to make lasting, irreversible change. Make this a Labour century in the way the last one was Tory.

GB says 'It is almost impossible to imagine the level of pressure on a PM, and TB is brilliant at dealing with it.' Describe the juggling that goes on.

GB says TB did the right thing on Iraq, leadership is about tough decisions, not easy ones.

GB on TB legacy secure. TB has changed politics and if I do ever become PM, I will be proud to build on that.

These are just examples. There will be many more, that get people interested, talking about this in a different way. What I am trying to say is we need more than routine formulaic responses. We need edge, statements that allow us to talk values and which take us to dividing lines.

Then build in texture, actually talk of some of the rows. E.g. 'Politics is about belief and passion. We do it because we care about making a difference. We are not automatons. We have the same basic beliefs but then policy is about how you put them into practice. So on x, I was worried re y, he was worried re z. But the aim is the same, a Labour Britain, not a Tory Britain.'

In other words, give a sense of the way you argue, about principle not ambition. You disagree on detail from time to time but not on direction, and you always come together. I'm sure we can find half a dozen points of difference that tell a positive story leading to the big themes, full employment, NHS restored, good schools for all, Britain playing a positive role in the world. In the end, headlines are forgotten, substance is not.

Use humour. Find a way of joking about the split screen press conference, the menu at Granita [Islington restaurant where TB and GB had famously forged a pact re succession to the Labour leadership] etc. Tell jokes at each other's expense, e.g. in joint *Mirror* or *Sun* interview. At the moment, as soon as the other is raised in interviews, you button up and go into politician speak. That has to change. There has to be a sense of being relaxed about each other's role, proud of each other's success and commitment.

Above all, this is about showing there is more that unites that divides. New Labour has been built together. Upon values. In government with the economy as its bedrock. Great noble causes remain.

TB leads well and has a lot left to give. Then the time comes for GB to take over. Every leader is different. History will judge Labour fortunate to have had two such figures in one short period of time.

At various points, I have exaggerated to make the point. But there is such a compelling narrative to be told here, and one which plays to our strengths, TB and GB as best campaigners, economy as strongest asset, public services investment as best dividing line, Labour as a team, Labour as the future not the past, many not few, leadership not drift.

I got back to London, then called TB to go over what I had written. He said he was pleased I saw him, and pleased he had wanted to talk. I said he had been more open than in a long time and though not exactly warm about you, not horrific. TB remained of the view the best thing was of course for them to come together but it meant him committing to the reform agenda rather than blocking it. I said he did refer to AA as a madman, but apart from that! TB said if we did not go forward with this agenda, we risked the opposite of what GB was saying. We actually risked gifting the Tories the space to come back as defenders of public services, absurd though that sounds. He said if GB was happy to fight on the same public services agenda, he was happy to keep him and later endorse him. His worry, and this was what kept coming back from the Murdoch people for example, was that he was the genuine old Labour article, and he had to disabuse them of that, which meant stopping Balls and DA going round saying he was so much more progressive than TB – for which they read tax-raising and anti-enterprise.

I sent my note through and though when he came back his first words were, 'OK, when do I go? Can I stay till the Friday afternoon after the election maybe?' But at least he could joke about it. 'Maybe I could fly back from the count, go and see the Queen to get re-appointed, head to No. 10, have a cup of tea with Gordon, and then head back to the Queen to say I was handing over?' I said I am sure he would let you have one last weekend at Chequers. Once we had got all that out of the way, he said my note made perfect sense, and he basically bought into it as the best way to proceed. He said GB is easily the most able person there and we have to try to engage him. I said you understand this means endorsement and he said yes, and provided he worked with him he was happy to do that. I went over it with Alan and Sally and later showed them the note too. Sally was convinced it was the only way to go. Alan didn't like it but agreed. He clearly felt TB should have sacked him ages ago, but that ship had sailed, and though clearly this was not good news for him, or his role in the campaign, I think he understood it had to be.

I talked later to Anji who had been at Sue [Nye]'s who said GB felt the meeting had been good, and got us into a better position. I felt the narrative was clear – TB fronts the campaign, shows he has a lot left to offer, but also that when he goes GB will be there to take over. I sent the note to GB once I knew TB was broadly happy with it. We had an office meeting on the grid and story development. It was easier now that I felt I could slot in GB at various points. Flight was still dominating, and now the Tories had named a blind German student as our mole – wrongly. I said the line should be this is panic leading to paranoia and now farce.

Wednesday 30 March

I hated being in the house on my own and was missing Fiona and the kids, who were on their way back from Scotland. School dinners was running big and though on one level it was fine it felt a bit weak, a celeb chef [Jamie Oliver] driving the policy debate. TB was out doing another masochism TV job on Sky which went off OK, but I could tell he was getting a bit fed up with being abused by the public. The morning just disappeared in a round of meetings, first the normal meeting, then a grid meeting and then I met the public service SPADS to talk them through where we were. Flight was dying down though John Woodcock got a call from the *Mail* about how we got the tape and we had to sit him down and advise him through that. He was worried about being monstered and also whether it would affect his future. I told him not to worry.

I was finding it hard to work in the office because of noise and distraction. Sue Nye and Spencer came over for a meeting on the TB–GB PEB and in trying to explain we needed candour they seemed to think I was saying they should have big rows in public. The point I was making, and made later to GB, was that if they were just two politicians in suits, they would not convince. It had to be real and rooted in how they are, but also try to break through the one dimension people now know of the relationship, namely it is not good.

TB was seeing GB and was therefore late for the big meeting he wanted. Peter M and AH were there so it was very much old team and felt it. PM gave a pretty good overview, but like all of us he was a bit low on ideas to make it interesting. TB was looking to be New Labour but without provoking the left/right internal splits we had before. He had suggested a series of speeches which were pretty bog standard. DM at least came up with a decent set of talking points to shape the approach on policy. But we were torn – to interest the media we had to be providing new ideas and stories. The public were likely to be just as interested in solidity and stability. Anji's view was that they had basically made up their minds and just wanted it all over quickly. TB felt we were making progress but at the end what had we concluded? – keep doing a bit more interactive, crank up the internet (though Matt said the numbers currently being reached were minimal), better ways of doing speeches, more with the team etc. It was, as DM told me later, a low energy meeting. Had we not had Flight the last few days would have been a lot worse.

During the meeting Sue Nye was texting me asking me to go to see GB as soon as I could. I said we were going over the grid. She said GB was up for speeches on Sunday, Tuesday and Thursday. At the end of TB's meeting I went over to see him. He was by then on the phone to TB trying to rewrite the *Times* article TB had done. He was barking changes at Sue who was dictating to DH who somehow got *The Times* to hold on till after 7. He had all his people in there, an expanding EB, EM wearing a Doncaster badge, Jo Dipple [special advisor] and a couple of HMT people I didn't know. GB had the usual mass of papers in front of him. He had been wound up about what I said about maybe going over the tuition fees argument with TB for the broadcast and he said I thought you didn't want an argument on policy. The point I was making was that they would only get candid moments if they were candid throughout. He felt they should maybe get to a position where 'he' accepts my judgement on the economy and I accept his leadership statesman role e.g. re Africa.

I said we had to get over the formulaic responses e.g. we work together well, friend as well as colleague. They had to take it to a new place. He said the danger was it became an extension of the soap opera because they would be asking, 'Would he stay a full term, would GB be Chancellor?' I said did you read my note? He said yes but it doesn't answer fully. I said I can't give the answers, that's for you two to sort, but it takes you a long way down that road. He said I know you're trying hard to bring us together and get us to the same point but it has to be clearer. I said it's bloody obvious what it is saying but you and he have to discuss any steps that flow from it. 'You cannot expect him to fight a campaign and stand there and say, "I will be gone by x date."'

He went over some of the themes of his speeches in the next phase, where he was obviously going to try to dominate the agenda and there would be a contrast with TB doing less substantial stuff. The new structure he had proposed was an overall strategy. He was being very friendly with me, which made TB a bit edgy and CB positively hostile when I saw her later. 'So you're now helping him to move Tony out I hear?' But I felt we now just had to get GB centrally involved and build a sense of teamship. It would be ragged but as TB said the fact he wants to involve you with his stuff suggests he is moving in the right direction. The chat over dinner with TB etc. was fairly low-key and jokey but he did at least feel we were moving in the right direction. 'Cherie doesn't seem terribly happy with this plan?' I said. He said nor was he, but he realised we needed the campaign fought in the way I had suggested.

Thursday 31 March

DWP had put out some stats which were being spun as living standards falling. It was big in some of the papers and the broadcasters were going on it so AM's pre-Cabinet interview was largely about that but he did fine. I called GB and we agreed he would do clips on his visit and also do the post-Cabinet media. Plus we were working towards the Minghella filming tonight. GB was raging about the DWP and condemned Robert Chote of the Institute of Fiscal Studies as a 'bloody activist' but he did at least agree to do stuff. He also talked me through his economic speech plan. It sounded fine and even if we had 'GB to the rescue' as the media take on it, so what if we signalled we were back motoring on the economy? The morning meeting was fairly indecisive and meandering then another grid meeting then I went to see the *Mirror* – Kevin Maguire and Conor Hanna [deputy editor] – to go over a few ideas for the campaign.

GB had proposed a new structure – TB, JP, AM, Ian McC, AC, PG, MC, SM main team then AM chair organisation team and when on economic plan EB, DA and EM around. AM not happy re DA but otherwise fine. We had the first meeting as a warm-up to the Cabinet. TB was asking GB to go over the economic plan and as ever he took us to a different place re NHS and schools but it was fine and would take us to the economy centre stage. JP looked tired and fell asleep at one point. 'Can you stay awake?' asked TB. 'You leave the old fellers alone!' – JP. It was fairly good humoured though, much more so than in recent weeks, and more importantly, productive. At least we had an economic pitch for the next phase. We debated whether to take on immigration pre-emptively. TB and I were strongly of the view we had to, because it was going to come up big at some point anyway, GB strongly of the view it was a bad idea, that we should stick to our own issues. We also went over what message was needed re health and education. I was saying investment and values, a fairly traditional approach. DH had cameras in for Cabinet, just getting general shots around the table, then after the cameras left and all the apparatchiks trooped in, the Cabinet fell about.

PG did his presentation, but I think the more positive mood had made him too upbeat and TB slipped me a note saying he was always too up or too down and this lacked balance. 'I'm worried about complacency.' TB went through where we were – said anything could happen but we should be confident in the arguments. People didn't want the Tories and didn't take the Lib Dems seriously but they wanted to send us a message. The important point was to get over that we got the message, we heard them. He talked through the idea of continuity with change in the context of doing more better and faster but you could sense people were thinking TB–GB. We have to delegitimise the Tories as a vehicle for protest – they don't deserve support. They haven't changed.

I noticed people nodding a lot less than they used to. They looked worried. GB set out his economic plan, rooted in polling showing a third of our voters potentially drifting away – to Libs or 'will not vote' mainly with a few Tories. He said all our messages had to have forward message, achievement and Tory threat. We had to establish economy then go to NHS and schools campaign. The Tories have abandoned the economy and are instead going on cultural issues. Populism. He said every day not on our issues is a lost day prompting CC to enter the argument we had earlier about immigration. That was the one big negative area for us that I felt we had no choice but to go for it on our terms.

GB set out the key economic facts and the forward policy stuff starting tomorrow with home ownership. He said the economy had to become the aircraft carrier for all other areas. And we had to be confident in making our charge of £35 billion cuts. It was a good presentation, not at odds with what we had been doing. Then AM went through organisation, which was getting there, and a bit of message. CC raised Libs and the extent of their lunacy on crime. PH: 'Can we get direct mail from Mandela?' Otherwise quiet, we managed to avoid the round table of people just chipping in with anecdotes. I liaised with GB re his interviews and his speech tomorrow then saw TB to try to get him in the right frame of mind for the filming.

I liked Minghella. He wanted to have a chat before he started filming so I went over to the Commons where he was setting up with an army of people and was clearly quite nervous about it. We went over how to get stuff out of them. He said having met them he felt TB more instinctively understood what we were trying to do, GB would have to be cajoled. TB arrived first and we left them to chat. GB was late but apologetic. They were both taken aback by the scale of it, the huge silver boxes of gear, the tons of cameras and supporting equipment, and the numbers of people in the crew, all packed into the little room outside. It was certainly not low production.

But TB and GB settled down quickly enough. They sat at the big table and Anthony asked them to write down their assessment of what the other would see as achievements first for the government and later for each other. Both went to the area of the economy, but also winning, and some of the specifics like NMW, Africa. Then he asked them to talk about what they had written. It was stilted at times but much less than it might have been. GB gave the richer values-laden clips and TB was a bit managerial, perhaps because he was the one playing up GB rather than himself, but the words and body language between them were pretty good. Minghella had a nice manner with them, and he was a grown up, so both of them felt they had to go along with it on his terms. And as Mark Lucas said, for political obsessives it was fascinating. We agreed we could use an expanded version for the website.

I watched it on the monitors with Sue, Spencer, Jo etc. and they seemed more relaxed about it by the end. They had been worried that the 'candour' idea would just kick off bad stuff, but once you took the anger out of the discussions, and they could just say what they had thought at different points, and then point to the changes that had been made, it worked. There was less faffing around than might have been expected with so much gear and so many people, and they got through a lot. We stopped after 90 minutes or so when they were beginning to flag, but Anthony seemed happy enough with it. There were even one or two moments, especially when talking about the old days, when the warmth between them seemed real.

Friday 1 April

I went into Vic St where Minghella was setting up for another session. He felt yesterday had gone better than he expected. He felt they had both embraced the idea pretty well, and it had only felt odd on a couple of occasions. He said they already had a lot of strong material and he felt people would have a sense of their stature and strength, and the ability of each to bring something out of the other. He felt TB had done the better job in terms of bringing out GB which meant GB probably delivered the better material. TB arrived early and then GB, angry at the way his *Today* programme interview had gone. I hadn't heard it, but he felt they had their own agenda and that at some point we had to do something about it.

I left them to get on with it then went for the AM morning meeting, still going on half an hour after it had started, and my arrival with Sally gave him the chance to go over it all again. Then to a TB meeting where Penn went through the latest polling which was OK, though we were still not really budging sufficiently and there was still a big grunge factor, a reluctance to give us much credit for anything. The Tories were definitely getting noticed more and PG was worried they were doing well with the 'on your side' issues they were raising. TB again came back to Iraq and got really passionate and worked up when arguing why we could not just leave it lying there, that we had to take it on and make the case, even if it meant reliving all the arguments of the time. I said he was showing the problem people felt – that when it came to Iraq he had a real passion and a real drive, but they did not feel that in the same way when it came to issues of more direct relevance to their lives, like public services or what was happening in their local communities.

Then came what he called 'le cauchemar du jour' [nightmare of the day], Little Ant and Dec, an interview with a couple of kids. We had an hour to prepare and I said the FoI nuts would have a field day when they saw how much time went in the diary to prepare for it. We were also joking about getting the spooks in to find out the questions, and getting regular updates about where the kids were. We had fixed it up at a time we were looking for new forms of engagement, but as we went into it, it did have the feel of something with the capacity to go badly wrong. It would just take one clever quip from one of the kids to take the news on it, and if the producers were worth the salt, they would be lining it up. It was definitely high risk, and TB was ridiculously nervous about it, but in the end it went fine, especially a bit he did with CB at the end, so no problems, we hope. And as I said to him, this would be the only time some of our target audience connected with him at all in the next few weeks.

Then back to Victoria St for the blur that life in there was becoming. I did have a decent session with the press office though re systems and roles. I was dreading the noise levels that would hit us when it kicked off. It was already pretty crowded and loud and I found it quite hard to write in there. Later F and I had a bit of an up and downer over her doing a regular slot with [former editor of the *Daily Telegraph*] Bill Deedes on the campaign for the *Today* programme. I pointed out that I despised the *Today* programme and also that I would be livid if she said anything that caused us aggro during the campaign. I reminded her of what she once said to Helena Kennedy – how we worked all hours God sent to deliver a Labour majority and people like her had a responsibility not to disrupt that, particularly at election times.

Saturday 2 April

The Pope [John Paul II] was clearly on the way out and the coverage was literally wall to wall on TV as people waited for the inevitable and we began to assess how it would affect the start of the campaign. I was getting more and more irritated with the long circular meetings and told Alan he had to chair them more sharply. We drew up a stack of things that needed to be covered in a short space of time once the campaign was underway and they were currently far too discursive. The morning meeting should never be longer than half an hour, if possible a lot shorter. Matt Carter wanted me to do a morning call with regional anchors after the meeting every day and I resisted as that was often the busiest and trickiest part of the day. I said I would do some but not all. I was still worried re systems. E.g. Peter Hain was in the *FT* on pensions yesterday, it had been followed up by several of the papers today, and we had not picked up that the Tories were punting it round.

Even though the Pope was wall to wall, the Tories had a fair few stories up and were doing not bad. We worked out a better system for the dissemination of decisions post-meetings, and also on briefing through the day, then I started to draft TB words for Monday and later AM, MC, Huw Evans and I met to go over the first few days. It was beginning to get there but was still not as strong as I would like it.

JR came in for an OK meeting on health message, where I felt we could be strong if we found ways of linking record to future policy, then he popped up a few minutes later on TV giving interviews outside Westminster Cathedral where he said he was making a 'private visit' to pray for the Pope! Alan was working away on the manifesto and still confident there were new stories in there that would help populate the grid for the campaign proper. He was worried about the electoral fraud case* and an Islam headgear case coming to a head on Monday, and felt they could really hit us at the start. I was getting tired and left late p.m., ran home and then had a kip.

F and I went out with Rory and Calum to La Casalinga. I noticed the other people in the restaurant talking about me, and looking over, and not as friendly as normally happens. I had noticed the same thing running in when one of the guys who goes to the lido shouted out something at me that was not too friendly. Maybe GB's view that the tide was going in the wrong direction was right. Who knows? I just wished the bloody thing was over. As we were at the restaurant word came through the Pope had died so once home, I was in a round of calls with TB, GB and AM, separately, and then a No. 10 conference call. GB felt he should cancel his speech tomorrow. TB, who would have to do words as well as go to the Pope's funeral, agreed and we put out a line about public campaigning being off. MB was due to do *Frost* with Michael Ancram [shadow Foreign Secretary] and Ming Campbell so we went round in circles for a while before eventually pulling that too, though the Tories and LDs decided to carry on. MB said she felt it would not be appropriate and that she would not be able to carry much of a political message, which was probably right.

Sunday 3 April

The general feeling on the conference call, as from GB when he and I spoke last night, was that there had to be some kind of gesture in terms of the campaign re the Pope so we agreed that subject to the Queen still being available on Tuesday we should put things back by one day. TB had felt last night we could probably go ahead as planned

---

* Election Commissioner Richard Mawrey QC upheld allegations of postal fraud relating to six seats won by Labour in Birmingham local elections in 2004. Judge Mawrey said the system was 'wide open to fraud'.

but it would be very messy, especially as we had the vespers service at 4.30 and the Jim Callaghan tributes at 3.30. So after a flurry of calls and then JoP talking to the Palace we put out a line that TB would not be going to the Palace tomorrow. TB was working on the manifesto and had also done some work on words for when he went out to kick things off in the street, based on the draft I did on Friday. But we were all a bit tired in our language. I was feeling really tired and a bit lethargic. I think the building was partly to blame. It was incredibly energy zapping, stuffy and noisy, and as AM said you could do a whole day and not feel you had achieved anything.

I couldn't work out whether these lost days – like the Pope's death or the royal wedding to come [Prince Charles and Camilla were due to marry during the campaign] – were really to our benefit or disadvantage. Part of me felt they prevented us getting our message through to the public in a sustained way. Another part of me felt that the same went for the Tories and they had more to gain from sustained messages 1, because they were less familiar to the public and 2, because the media were still trying to lift them. So on balance a few news sponges in the campaign were probably no bad thing.

What was clear from the polling was that if we could keep on the economy we were fine but the so-called economic plan had been a bit short lived with GB's speech off today and now likely to be overshadowed by Tuesday's announcement when he did the next one. We all went for lunch at the Goulds with the Kinnocks and the Hudsons [Hugh and Marianne]. I couldn't really be arsed with the political discussion. PG had a bit of a pop at one point, when Fiona was talking about us being no different to the Tories on some of the public service areas – echoed by Glenys – and Neil came in on PG's side. Hugh seemed a little taken aback that there was so much angst and argument so close to an election. I went for a run.

Monday 4 April
Mood not great generally. In for a TB 8 a.m. meeting. GB fairly up for things, TB weak. He was going over the next few days in a very desultory fashion, almost like he was talking about someone else. GB full of 'the problem is'. JP livid because he was not consulted about the postponement and had heard it on the media. We were still in a state of flux because of lack of clarity about the Pope's funeral and also that had possible knock-on effects for the royal wedding. Finally later it

emerged the funeral would be on Thursday, the wedding on Friday. Then there was a long meandering discussion about how and when to do Faber defection and Gerald Howarth [Tory MP], who had made a joke about Derek Laud [black Tory speechwriter and lobbyist] that some of his enemies were trying to say was racist. GH was definitely a risk but the general feeling was that we had to do it.

Later I had another long session with TB who felt we had to get up the idea of a battle of two very different agendas. Through the day we had a succession of bad polls, showing the lead shrinking, and the private stuff from the marginals was still giving a lot of worry. It was a weird day though, endless circular discussions about what to do when, most of it beneath the pay grades of all of us, let alone TB, but he was the one dragging us into the weeds again. GB asked PG and me to go over to see him in the Treasury. He said we must get a sharper focus on economic plan/two futures. Agreed.

Ed Balls had the idea of posters setting TB against Howard, and GB against Letwin? The TB–MH ones would say, 'Who do you want to run the country?' and the GB–Letwin posters would say, 'Who do you want to run the economy?' It was a nice simple idea, even if it did mean – and this will have been part of their thinking – that it was TB confirming GB as Chancellor, which he had not done publicly. Later when I put it to TB he thought it was a good idea. Only a few minutes later did the penny drop that it meant confirming GB as Chancellor. I thought it was obvious. He didn't seem to mind. With GB we agreed plans for the next few days, lots of black humour about what we would all do when we lost. I couldn't tell if he was really engaging or still watching to make a move. He was maybe getting worried.

PG felt TB was currently something of a problem with the public. The warmth wasn't there, and there was less 'benefit of the doubt'. I told him later maybe the tide was turning. TB was really keen not to lose *The Sun*. I spoke to Rebekah Wade later to get a feel for where they were, but my sense was they were going to diddle. We saw the *FT* who are also reconsidering. Back for a meeting on manifesto news management, future ads with Trevor B, then a meeting re the grid. Also met Faber to go over what we might do. Long session with TB, AM and the No. 10 team on Howarth, whether and when to exploit the media hoo-ha that had arisen over Derek Laud. The mood around the place was not great. It was a very tight lead for the start of a campaign, way smaller than we had on the eve of the '97 and '01 campaigns. I had a couple of chats with TB towards the end of the day and he seemed OK but we were all feeling a bit worried that the momentum was going in the opposite direction.

Tuesday 5 April

The papers were full of the election and the balance was favourable to the Tories though the narrowing polls did not go as big as they might have done them. I got in to No. 10, and up to see TB. He was in T-shirt and shorts covered with stars and stripes. 'Very on message.' We went over whether he should use a script and lectern or speak with nothing between him and media/public. He was scribbling away when the others came up including the full GB crew. We went over the stuff of today and then back to Howarth. Ian M felt it would be a huge own goal to use it at all, a gift to Howard. Race was such a difficult issue on which to judge the politics. The Tories would make it all about us being PC. TB was also more worried than yesterday and was feeling now it was best to get out through a third party. He was really worried that it would backfire.

The morning meeting was focused, as were others, on the next big events. Howard did his campaign launch at a posh hotel. TB went off to Buck House and then came back to do his words. He was nervous going out and it showed a little when he got going, but it was OK. Then to a GB meeting to fix economic messaging for the next few days. He was working much better. Good background briefing notes. Headache inducing round of meetings. TB called from the car, said he was glad it was up and running finally. He was worried about the marginals operation but felt MH nastiness was not good for the Tories. We were pretty clear about the stages now – establish the economy as the base, manifesto, then focus on health then education, back to the economy. I gave *The Sun* the story about plans for 'trials without defendant' which ended in a big row with RW because they threw it away and stupidly I cc'd my complaint to Les [Hinton], which looked like I was getting too heavy.

PG called after doing some groups. They had shown them the TB and Howard launch events and he said MH won them all. They felt he looked fresh, up for it, offering something distinct. TB had a second term message for third term election. The Tories' tails were up re the polls and any test of vox pop opinion on TV was pretty dire for TB. He was clearly an issue and maybe things were worse than we thought. Alan M was looking a bit hurt re the GBs taking over press conferences. But it was inevitable we were heading to GB confirmation as Chancellor.

I had slept badly – probably because of PG's late call, just before I went to bed, about the groups saying basically MH had cut through in a way TB did not. I said at the 7 a.m. meeting we just weren't sharp enough on message – that we had to get more edge and clarity. There was a general agreement TB did OK yesterday but the statement was too diffuse. He looked a bit alarmed at us all saying he wasn't really cutting through but it was best to face up to it. Yesterday had been OK, not terrible, but not great. We could not win by being average. Howard was starting from a lower base of expectation and he surpassed it. There had to be more to it than more of the same. GB had the line on 'four million new opportunities' which was OK though a lot of the media interest was going to be in TB–GB, as was the case when he did *GMTV* and virtually confirmed GB as staying in the job. We were clearly heading that way.

I wrote a hard line for PMQs and for the press conference and he got the message. His argument was that it would take time to open up an argument about the Tories, which of course it would, and GB was talking about four stages but we had to start hurting them soon. The polling was not good at the moment but we were going to start piling on the pressure now. An economy at risk, translated into various other living standards issues, was where we needed to be. JP had a good line given to us by someone he met on the trail – 'Are you remembering what we're remembering?', in response to their 'Are you thinking what we're thinking?' posters. I wasn't sure about their line. On the one hand, it did get up our negatives, like MRSA or anti-social behaviour, but it didn't give any sense of their alternative. It was also a bit creepy which was a feeling with Howard as leader they should be trying to repel not play to. JP's line worked well in terms of getting stuck into their record. It was a bit alarming how short people's memories were about the last government, and again in one of the groups last night, only one person knew Howard had been a minister.

Balls, Douglas and co. were now pretty much always there with GB but they were being pretty friendly and co-operative. After TB went to *GMTV*, GB called me through and we went over message for the press conference. He was also still worrying re immigration, saying was it in fact an out of touch/trust issue or was it the issue for real?

I felt the latter and we had to deal with it. He said CC didn't really have a plan for it. He also warned me Rover [consortium-owned car manufacturer] would go belly-up as early as today (financial crisis due to falling sales). He was doing the usual scribbling and scrawling but didn't seem on top of things as usual. I was called out to speak to TB re PMQs which was clearly going to be a big one. He was lacking a bit of confidence at the moment which we had to watch, especially as MH so clearly had his tail up.

PMQs was a clear win for MH in the House but OK for TB on TV. Howard looked OTT, TB kept his cool fine, and the clips on the news came over well. You would have to see the whole of the exchanges to see Howard had him a bit worried and defensive. I finished his words for the press conference then he came down and before GB arrived I said he was going to get more 'Will GB be Chancellor after the election?' He said we may as well go a bit further, as the poster launch tomorrow would be another step. PH and a very loquacious Yvette [Cooper, MP wife of Ed Balls] joined us and then we went through the tricky questions. GB was looking unshaven so I suggested he shave and get TV make-up. He was also prowling a bit as we waited to go down.

Packed house, the opening words were too long and first few Q&As too much on the TB–GB soap but then gradually they got into the spending arguments and the media had to take notice. They were both going at it hard. The problem with the media was they thought the election was about them. And they were dim. But it went well, went on for over an hour and once they came back I could tell both thought it had been good. They were pretty hyper and firing on all cylinders. GB was a bit worried that TB went too far in saying we could afford all our plans with the tax revenues already predicted to come in kind of thing. GB felt that though the press had not really wanted to bite on it they were having to get into our basic message. He was consulting me the whole time, which was so different to before, and giving a lot more muscle to the campaign. Also, sorting out the choreography of tomorrow's poster launch was not as painful as usual. TB looked and sounded a bit tetchy at the press conference but I couldn't blame him. They were such total wankers in the main, particularly the main broadcasters who just used these press conferences for grandstanding.

I was working on the briefing about the Minghella election broadcast and later saw an early cut with Mark Lucas etc. He was very emotional about it. Mark was such a team player, had wanted to get a big hitter like Minghella involved to do something different and special and impactful, and this would be. I didn't feel we had the right clips yet but then again there had been so much material. The overall effect was excellent. They had done a terrific job. We would get a lot out of it and today's near confirmation that GB was safe would help now move on to the substance rather than the soap opera. I did an email for TB for the party website contrasting the media soap with the real substance issues.

I nipped down to LA Fitness. I was going to need to keep up on the exercise front. I did a bit on the treadmill and in the changing rooms afterwards a guy came over and said he thought we were strengthening. He said, 'I am a party supporter and I'm glad you're back. They were getting very ragged and I can tell you have sorted them out a bit.' It was certainly the case that the near warfare of a few months ago had abated. The atmosphere in the office was better today but it was going to be tough. Bumped into [Lord] Bernard Donoughue [former Harold Wilson advisor] who said he was glad it was me not him that was back in there. He felt immigration was a real problem. The Tories in Arundel [Howard Flight-vacated seat] selected Nick Herbert [first openly gay Conservative candidate], which was good news for us. Today had been an OK day but watching the news later it was so much filtered through a prism of cynicism and with so much focus on the reporters and what they thought, rather than the politicians and what they said.

Thursday 7 April

We were still trying to get focused on the economy but what was interesting was though we were getting message and image OK, we were not cutting through to the public, whereas the Tories were, and the polls were still narrowing. They had edge, we didn't. MH was hitting a message, TB wasn't. But TB was still sure we had the time to get a proper message up and start to tear them apart. The Tories' selecting Herbert was running fine but I was worried it would again just stop us getting up a message. GB left the morning meeting early to go off to do *Today* but needless to say they didn't let him do Herbert much and instead it was all us and tax. TB had a pretty dire cold but was lasering his mind on the whole economic stuff. We had the Balls posters to launch and could get going on the economy again. It turned into a bit of a mess at the launch because the press office got a bit heavy with the media without need. But it was definitely growing as a problem that the media thought it was all about them not us or the people. The mediation stuff was beginning to annoy. I saw the latest cut of the PEB and it had gone back, a fair bit. Too many cooks maybe. I told Anthony to get it back to the original vision.

I was briefing the film overnight and with a picture for the *Mirror* to placate them in advance as we had decided to give the Tony–Gordon joint interview to the *News of the World*. But never mind the *Mirror*, it sparked another almighty row with RW. She went totally berserk, shouting and ranting, threatening all manner of retribution, saying we treated her like the *Mail*, and we had played into Kavanagh's hands etc., that he was pushing them to back the Tories and if we helped the other papers like this, it would help him. It was partly about the *Mirror* but the real problem was helping the *NotW*. I spoke to Les, who was aware of [*News of the World* editor] Andy Coulson's bid for the two of them together, and who felt she was overreacting. GB felt sure Trevor K was stirring it, and had been calling me about other things, and been reasonably friendly, to avoid me thinking it was him stirring.

I went into a seemingly never-ending round of calls – RW, TK, Les, Pascoe-Watson, Coulson – and RW and I really had a major set-to. I ended up losing it a bit, said if she had a problem with papers in the same group, it was up to her to sort it out. But we had a campaign to run and we could not keep everyone happy all of the time. She said, 'You will pay for this. You use me when it suits you but then think nothing of doing something like this.' I said take it up with Les and Andy, as it was Andy's idea not mine, and I told her to be in touch when she had calmed down. I was working up scripts re the PEB and trying to work towards the weekend. I read the manifesto later and felt it was a lot stronger than the earlier drafts, and would work well.

Friday 8 April

TB was in Rome for the Pope's funeral but GB came in for the morning meeting, said he thought he and TB should go to Longbridge [Rover plant], and we had to show we were doing all we could for Rover.* The fact he was suggesting doing it with TB showed the progress we'd made. I spoke to TB in Rome after we heard Howard was doing

---

* The Phoenix Consortium had taken over ailing MG Rover in 2000 but had never succeeded in making the business profitable. It now reported debts of more than £1.4 billion. Despite the government initially offering to support an alliance between MG Rover and the Shanghai Automotive Industry Corporation, the company placed itself in administration.

immigration in Telford on Sunday. He was fretting about the seating at the funeral, because he was going to be very close to Robert Mugabe [corrupt President of Zimbabwe]. 'Just nut him,' I suggested. 'Let's liven things up like JP did in '01.' 'I think ignoring him might be easier, but I wouldn't put it past him coming over for a rant.' It was a massive event obviously and taking a lot of the media attention for the day. TB looked fine on all the live coverage but somehow the Beeb managed to edit the bulletins to make him look like a total twat, just a couple of cutaways where he was looking a bit isolated and snooty.

Rebekah called up for a friendly chat, as if nothing had happened yesterday, total sweetness and light. She wanted a piece with GB today as offered by GB yesterday, but she also wanted something with CB and was clearly stressed out. She later emailed an apology for losing it with me yesterday, and said she was taking a few days off but I could call if urgent. GB had seen Les earlier and told me he had done his best to assure him we were going to be New Labour if he took over some time in the future. He sent Les the education mini-manifesto. He had called me earlier to say that he thought I should brief out he had largely done the economic and education chapters of the manifesto. AM later called and said it was not true, he had not really been involved. AM was a bit down about stuff generally and he knew there was going to be lots of talk in the media of GB taking over at his expense, but he was still just chugging on. I worked on the overnight briefing then went for a long manifesto meeting to go over all the stories and events we could mine from it. AM and I had a call with CC who wanted to do immigration soon. We agreed to get out manifesto plans, do a website piece from CC and maybe do a story we had lined up re Gerald Howarth. GB and CC were up for it, TB was not.

Working on the scripts for weekend. GB calling every half-hour on the way to Longbridge. TK and GPW there to see GB for the interview we had fixed with Rebekah and Les but they complained he didn't really open up. GB called me and said it was the most aggressive interview he had ever endured, and TK was really going mainly on Europe and trying to go for a TB–GB row, hardly anything else. They just weren't interested in the things their readers might be. He was sure Trevor was still trying to push for a change of endorsement. My sense from Rebekah was different, but the interview certainly sounded like a non-meeting of minds, like they had got his back up and he just closed down. It was still a bloody nightmare dealing with these people. Lots of traffic re *Sun*, *Mirror* and it was all reminding me why I was right to leave.

The Rover visit went OK and was certainly the right thing to do. As to why GB was so on board, TB said he had worked out if he was not New Labour he would not get support. The noise in the office was at times unbearable. I ended up borrowing Jo Gibbons's iPod, and listening to music as I wrote, which was better, and when I needed to write stuff like speeches or briefing notes, going to one of the offices with Parna and dictating. TB called after he got back from Birmingham and was still confident the argument had not begun. He said he would not rest until he had got this attack argument sorted. The briefing systems were going OK. The staff team was really beginning to gel. We did a website piece to raise funds and start to present ourselves as financial underdogs. An Aussie woman came in and said Lynton Crosby was a nasty piece of work and we should go for him. The *Mirror* were on the case anyway. GB called after I got home and was worried TB was hemming him in on spending. We were still going round in circles re the Gerald Howarth situation especially after we heard that Howard was doing immigration at a big rally in Telford.

I was about to go to bed when Clive called to tell me he had sorted his forty-four names for the squad and it did not include Jonny Wilkinson. He had talked it over with him and agreed they would keep it under review and if he got fully fit, and some matches under belt and was up for it he would take him. He wouldn't be isolated though so Phil Vickery and Mike Tindall (both injured) would be notable absentees too. He said this is one intense guy. He doesn't know if he's coming or going, he's not getting great advice and he keeps going on about being unworthy of all the attention when he's barely played – when most people think he is one of, if not the, best player alive. At first I thought it was odd but then the logic of not selecting him straight up became clearer. We discussed the idea of letting it out there in advance to stop it being the story when the squad was announced but then we agreed there was no point. The other shock – to me – was that he was taking twenty players from England. Yet he said that if he picked a Test team today it would probably only have two maybe three English players. I rewrote the speech on economy and education for Monday and got to bed at 1.

Saturday 9 April

Considering how bad it might have been the Rover coverage was not a total disaster. The news was now moving on to the royal wedding but

April '05: Howard moves onto immigration

we were still working away on the Sundays with a stack of different briefings for different papers. We were getting CC words onto the website re immigration then after SM spoke to Charles Wardle [former Tory minister], he was up for doing something to have a go at Howard's policies on immigration. I called him and we put together a plan, including to come in and do a briefing tomorrow. He was pretty gung ho even though they would go for him and resurrect any bad stories they could find about him. The attack unit had got hold of a UNHCR [United Nations High Commissioner for Refugees] press release attacking the Tory claims that there were five processing centres in North Africa. I briefed *The Independent*, who were keen. I called Roger Alton to push education and then the polls came in. OK. But there was still too much immigration out there. The morning conference call went through plans for the next couple of days but then came back to immigration and whether to do Howarth. TB said he was really nervous about doing it, felt there would come a point when the Tories would over-reach on this and then we could deploy it. I was worried it was an excuse never to do it but then we agreed if MH went really OTT we would do Howarth.

Meanwhile TB was asking AA to draft an education speech for tomorrow so I realised I would have to go up to make it more connecting and prosaic. I drafted a Sedgefield speech, did a fundraiser email for Matt Carter and delayed departure in case we were going to detonate Howarth. TB was now sure we should wait. He and I talked it over four or five times at one point with Peter M who agreed with me the best reason was to make them feel a bit disabled about going nasty on immigration again. We were now also thinking up ways of getting Crosby in lights. Parna and I got the 5.40 train to Durham, working on the speech on the way up, chatting to Balls re Tory demolition day. I then had what I thought had the potential to be a great idea to make the manifesto launch more interesting – launch it with loads of ministers, even the whole Cabinet, all making short statements that were values, policy, dividing line and something that said, 'We will in the future…'. I had a bit of a manic flow for half an hour or so, and just banged out a big note on it. Loved it. I spoke to TB and JP who liked it too. It would be big, bold, ballsy and show we had a big team with strength in depth and everyone had things to say, past, present, future.

Sunday 10 April
I worked on a new briefing at Myrobella. It was odd to be juggling

TB and Clive Woodward big speeches on such different things. Clive called before seven. The Wilkinson plan was definitely on. It was a bit of a nightmare trying to make sure I could be at all the main events for him while also doing for TB what he needed. It might be a struggle to do the manifesto and the Lions launch on the same day. TB had redrafted the speech again, taking in a mix of my and Andrew's stuff. It was now very crunchy re education though MH was likely to take the day. He had nothing new to say but the language on immigration was really strong and would carry. GWB and TB had discussed the Tory strategy in the margins of the Pope's funeral and Bush had said as far as he could see they were going always for the lowest common denominator. TB was in OK form but CB was cool and distant, with both of us I thought. When Hilary C asked her if she was going to go up with TB at the end of the speech she just said, 'No.' The typist was getting stressed out and at one point I was sure we were not going to get it done in time, but we just about got there. We had three clear sections – ten facts of change since '97, ten things done, ten education plans for the future. It was actually a good speech but I was pretty sure the broadcasters would lead with MH and immigration. Wardle was a big help for us and I did a conference call before his presser, which he seemingly did well. We could not get the broadcasters to pick up on the UNHCR story which had it been us being criticised would have led the news all day. I had a chat with Alex F – pissed off about losing at Norwich yesterday – who was doing the rally tomorrow, and just talked him through what it would entail.

The speech finally done after a fair bit of last-minute-itis, we set off for Trimdon. He was doing it in the Labour Club main room, and got a nice reception but I noticed that when I watched in the bar (TB having said I shouldn't go in the room because they would film me) most of the guys in there weren't watching. TB did OK though there was bizarre Ozzy Osborne lookalike in the shot. TB was sweating a lot but it was all right. He was worrying re *The Sun* and must have asked me half a dozen times whether to call RW. Bruce [Grocott] was up there and on great form and everyone seemed to think we were OK but there was a lot of stuff out there and it was all immigration led. I don't think any of us felt really confident that we really knew what was going on at the moment.

We were still ahead in the polls and yet most people you saw said they never met anyone with a kind word to say about TB. On the plane down we chatted over what to do in the next stages of the campaign.

He was working on the Tuesday document attacking the Tories on tax and spend. The question was whether we could get the argument heard. GB was still too much focused on booming out facts and figures, TB was too up in the air, other ministers were not involved that much and so were probably thinking the centre wasn't hacking it. Ian McC said tuition fees was a much bigger problem than Iraq.

I got back to work on TB words for tomorrow. He was confident we could turn immigration our way but PG and I were not so confident. PG did groups in Edgware which were dire, totally dire. A group of women ranting re immigration and all said they would vote Tory. This could be grim. He said he actually felt a bit sick by the end of it. They just came up with wave after wave of negativity. Yet the state of the parties polls were still OK-ish. I wondered if we were missing something. Out for dinner at Tessa's but the boys and David and I mainly watched the golf while Fiona went off on one about TB and education. Louisa called to go over final details for the Lions launch tomorrow and then I had a nice chat with Brian O'Driscoll at his hotel. He was pretty made up about being made captain and also said he was sure we could win, even if he knew it was going to be tough.

Monday 11 April
I had been kind of dreading these three days because of juggling the election and the Lions launch but in fact we were about to hit the two days that could really turn things I think. We had finally decided to go ahead with the education–economy launch as a positive event this morning and agreed to 7.20 a.m. so people could get to the Tory launch as well. We were starting to pound them fairly heavily and we sensed things moving our way even if the press were still not keen to give us anything. But we had to keep pushing in the face of their desire to do us over. They were saying, 'How can you say the Tories are both doing cuts and also doing spending increases?' The point was this was their contradiction.

We did an OK pre-meeting and really felt better about things. TB said later he and GB were working better than at any time since before John Smith's death and it was because GB realised he needed something of what TB gave. He was even maybe thinking that he would have been the big target by now had TB gone. I then set off with Parna for the Heathrow hotel where Clive was announcing the squad for NZ, on the way dictating a planning note on the election launch. TB had signed up to the idea on Sunday and today I squared JP and GB. It could be parodied as some kind of weird Beam Me Up Scotty quiz show, but equally it could be absolutely brilliant. Policy rich. Values rich. Programme for third-term government. Delivery. Team. I dictated to Parna in the car then got to the hotel and worked with Clive on his speech, which he wanted to rehearse a couple of times.

All the coaches were gathering and enjoying it I think, though one or two were a bit peed off CW had not really consulted too widely on selection. We went over all the possible difficult questions, watched the brilliant video to announce the team, and then got going. It was nice being out of the election bubble for a while. AM called after the Tory manifesto launch and said the problem was that TB was all argument and MH was all message. Wrong call. I got Howard's speech through and it was absolutely pathetic. Just the messages strung together. They had gone for message alone, but without the policy back up. I thought it was pathetic, useless. We can kill these fucking people. I dictated a few lines and agreed we needed a presser p.m. with Ruth Kelly and one or two others to hit back on the public service agenda.

The Lions' launch at the Heathrow Hilton went fine. The video was great but sadly we couldn't show it on the broadcasts. At the Q&A the media were fairly cowed, very different to the politicos. We were in good shape. CW did fine, said later he enjoyed it. Brian O'Driscoll did fine in his Q&A and then pictures. There were mild gasps when they realised Wilkinson was not announced, but CW dealt with it fine and they got out the point that he might make it yet. I did the rounds with CW's interviews while doing more notes re our launch and also responding to the Tories. I got back to the office and sorted Alex for his words at the rally in Manchester.

TB did not call as much today which probably meant he was working OK with GB. The rally speeches were terrific. The other thing I was getting up was a Dorset South situation, the Tory candidate doctoring a picture of an asylum seeker to make the leaflet say something different.* We went for it with Baldwin who was really up for it and we ended up on page one again. Got Beth Breeze our candidate in Maidstone involved too because it had Ann Widdecombe in the picture.

---

* Michael Howard had to issue a public condemnation of candidate Ed Matts after it was revealed that he had altered a photograph to reflect the Tories' hardline stance on immigration. The original showed Matt supporting a local failed asylum seeker and her family; the doctored version had the family's picture replaced by a 'controlled immigration' slogan.

Good day on that front and the Tories' manifesto didn't do well. TB said he felt settled by it. Clive sent a message as I was getting into bed saying thanks, and he was really looking forward to it now.

Tuesday 12 April

The Lions press came out OK. Only the *Mail* bothered much with me having been there. CW did fine and generally all was OK. We were now on to the Tory attack and the Treasury team had done a good document on Tory claims on commitments on spending, and promises on tax, which was going to start the demolition. AD was doing a lot of the detail. It was a heavy and substantial piece of work and the Tory stuff was starting to unravel even before we went in for the press conference e.g. suddenly Letwin unpicking one or two of the commitments in there. All our guys were on form, and I could sense the press beginning to turn. Afterwards people were on a bit of a high, because it had definitely landed a blow, then we worked out plans for tomorrow before they set off for Scotland. TB was calling the whole time to ask about tomorrow. I could tell he also felt things had turned our way a bit. So much of this was about confidence, his in particular. He had been dipping a bit of late, focusing on small stuff not big stuff, but had got his mojo back a bit in the last couple of days.

We were also managing to get up the idea of us having greater strength in depth, which was another reason for the team launch of the manifesto. I loved the idea. It had first come to me on the train to Durham and then when I was on the treadmill in the gym later that evening, and the news was on, I had a really strong sense of how it could look, and had started to draw it up in detail, and designed the set. It would definitely work, I was sure of it now.

George Osborne [shadow Chief Secretary to the Treasury] went on Sky and said tax cuts would not happen until the second year of a Tory government and we pounced. Ed Miliband and Spencer Livermore both said it would have more effect if I called the broadcasters and pushed them on to it, so I did. Then the Tories started saying different things on police numbers and council tax so we were really pushing the line that they were unravelling under the slightest of pressure. Meanwhile we had JR down in Dorset South chasing the Tory candidate. So we had two stories of the Tories unravelling and Howard was a bit on the run. I was sure we could get Crosby's horrible gypsy-baiting, anti-foreigner, dog-whistle shit to backfire all over them. The mood in the office had really picked up a couple of gears, and we could be sure it had dropped at Tory HQ. I felt the campaign picking up and really motoring.

I was down to do a paid speech at the Dorchester to the construction industry. It went fine, and even though I reckoned a lot were natural Tories, I didn't sense any real feeling for Howard, and actually the mood about TB was OK. Q&A good including a question from [Lord] Norman Fowler [former Tory minister], who I had a bit of banter with. He was actually very sound on the media, and we had a chat about that afterwards. There was a Tory candidate there, whose name I didn't get, but he did say 'I found your presentation rather alarming.' Why? 'Because you seemed to set out some very good reasons why you might possibly win big again.' Good response all round. I am sure the general mood was pro-Tory, in so far as how they would vote themselves, but most of them seemed to think we would win again. I didn't sense from Fowler any notion at all that he thought they would win.

I got back for a stack of meetings on the launch, including with TB and GB on the overall pitch of it. TB was wanting a phrase to push on the progressive stuff. He also felt GB should do something very New Labour. I felt we could afford to be reasonably prosaic. The Tories had stumbled and that allowed us to go for serious and substance and we needed more of that, less the new lines here and there. Alan M was worried the pitch was not New Labour enough. The good news was TB and GB were working pretty well together, or at least they had today. GB was definitely operating in a totally different way. JP was the one who was a bit offside, not in a difficult way, but I got the feeling he was feeling a bit unloved, no doubt because of all the focus on TB–GB. I didn't think he was in the right frame of mind for the *Today* programme tomorrow and he agreed to come off provided he did it later in the campaign. He was worried people would say he had been pulled. I said I would make sure they didn't, and we got MB on instead and I briefed her.

Then another hour-long meeting with TB–GB to go over the manifesto. They were both worried my manifesto launch idea, with the whole of the Cabinet standing there at lecterns, would look a bit too much like a weird kind of prayer meeting. But they were up for it. We settled on the idea of Forward not Back as the backdrop, seven lecterns with TB in the middle, GB, JP plus the main public service people up front, the rest of the Cabinet seated in an arc behind them. It was not quite the original look I had but it would work well.

All the hacks were saying tax was the story, and they were going to press hard on National Insurance. We had to have a line leaning against NI rises, but GB was not keen. The BBC coverage was dire, all playing into the Tory narrative, but we had nobody with the balls to attack them. I nipped out for a meeting with some of the Lions journos and go over the NZ issues, and it was fine. They were a lot calmer than the political hacks, and although I knew they might make me a story, I didn't sense deep hostility. I was trying to persuade them that I could help them get more access and better coverage. Back for more TB–GB, just pinning down last details on manifesto planning, then home, late.

Wednesday 13 April

We had set up the manifesto OK. TB was redoing his words at No. 10, GB was doing his in his little office at Victoria St, banging away on the keyboard with the usual force and making loads of typos. I had to watch his bit didn't become longer than TB's but we just about got it sorted in time to leave. The TB words were good, the other ministers were up for it, though I had a spat with CC claiming he never saw the note I did setting out how it was all going to go. I got all our changes put in, then slotted in a shortened version of GB. GB's big worry 'was how do we get up a bigger story than tax?' Balls came round and said, 'Look, Gordon doesn't think he can raise this himself but what about TB makes clear there will be a smooth transition some time during the Parliament?' I laughed. He said it is the logical conclusion of your note, the one on how they are going to be campaigning together. I said maybe, but is it sensible to say so on the day of your manifesto launch?

GB clearly had said something similar to TB because when I joined him, he asked me what I thought about mentioning transition. I said it was too weakening to do it today. It would become the only thing out of the whole event, which had the potential to work on so many levels and be so much richer than yet another personality story. He agreed but said maybe he should say New Labour is now entrenched and when the time comes or some such phrase, make it clear GB would be the right guy. GB had joined us. He wanted him to say 'seamless transition' but that made it sound like he was already set upon it. I said we cannot have as the story from the manifesto launch the idea that he is on his way to the exit door. Maybe, said GB, but your note does lead you logically to this position. Maybe, I said, but not today. I laughed again. To be fair, he smiled back, and TB did too.

We all knew that the strategy we had stitched together in Fife was that they came together for the campaign and at some time in the future TB helped GB take over. But the idea of doing it today was a non-starter. GB must know that. Maybe he was just pinning us down a bit more, I don't know. They never give up, I'll give them that. The posters had taken us a notch closer to stating the obvious and now they wanted to ratchet up a few more notches. It wasn't going to happen, not publicly, but in our minds it was. Perhaps that was their game today, I don't know. I couldn't decide if he was pressing this now for that, the obvious reason, or because he wanted something other than tax to be the main focus. Maybe a bit of both.

Once we had finished the script we headed for the Mermaid Theatre. Quite a buzz around the place. The set was great and despite the obvious 'You are the weakest link' jokes once people saw all the lecterns standing there, it looked terrific. TB didn't want to rehearse but we said he had to as this was more complicated than most launch-type events, and we did and it was the better for it. After TB did his first spiel Matt Carter played TB as the other ministers stayed where they were, and I was pretty clear it was going to go well. GB was so onside at the moment it was ludicrous. He was up for doing it again 'just to make sure we all know what we are doing'. Then he, TB and I met in the River Room and we returned to the theme of succession, TB saying he was worried re lame duckery if he went too far in indicating he would be going. GB was still pushing for 'seamless transition'. I said the furthest he should go is say that 'when the time comes' he would support GB, but not be clear about when that time might be. In the end he did neither but the language between them was clear enough. At one point GB went out to get something and TB and I were left in there, just the two of us. He said 'I think I'm doing the right thing. He is streets ahead of the rest and so long as the direction is set as New Labour then I have to let go once I'm out of here.'

The two of them were getting on better than for ages and even the hacks were sensing something real, that it wasn't just sprayed on and spun for the campaign. I was getting on really well with GB who was asking me for my opinion on pretty much everything he did, and giving me his on pretty much everything else. How much better would we have been these last few years if it could have been like this the whole time though? I think what had happened was TB genuinely came to see he had to get him in harness and GB genuinely came to see if he was to be successful he had to be New Labour. The atmosphere had really improved and we were definitely making inroads. TB was fulsome. He said I should take the credit because I had broken through the mist and the mistrust and got them working together again. He said I was the only one of his people GB really respected and that was out of a certain fear. GB only really respected strength and ability.

We went down to go over things with the Cabinet and though the second-rank people who were not going to speak directly were probably pissed off, it really worked. Jo Gibbons, Parna, Catherine Rimmer and I were watching it at the back and it looked terrific. Both Catherine and Parna whispered 'fantastic' as it came to an end. PG was watching on TV, texted me half a dozen times to say how good it was. The contrasts with the Tories were glaring. It showed we had a team. Strength in depth. Detail. Substance. A record. Plans. Also Letwin had done a presser beforehand making clear they couldn't rule out NI rises too which took a lot of heat off us on tax. TB was on better form than for ages, really confident and strong. GB was fulsome. Afterwards we went into a little huddle and agreed don't put GB on for the after-match interviews because they would take us to tax. We went for AD instead. I watched Howard's press conference. He looked a bit desperate thrashing around and again unable to say anything on tax. GB was very chatty again asking if FM was going for a seat, saying it would be good if she did. The mood backstage afterwards was excellent, and even the sceptics and the cynics about the mass lectern plan felt it had really looked like a proper big, strong, substantial launch.

I went back to Vic St and started to work on the economy speech for tomorrow. I was going slightly bonkers with the constant post-mortem and analysis of media that went on and the fact people kept complaining about the BBC but did nothing about it. But everyone seemed to think today went pretty well and there was a little group that applauded me back in. It had been one of those ideas that would have led to a lot of blame-gaming had it gone wrong. The GB lot even were pretty warm. There was a good buzz around the place now. Howard looked dire. We went round the next few days, agreed to do a new pledge card with tax and trail TB's economy speech tomorrow. Plus we were doing a pretty devastating film on Howard tomorrow too.

I left early to meet Clive and Jayne Woodward and head for William Ellis [AC's sons' school] where Clive was opening the new gym and doing sports prizes. Derek John [chair of governors] was getting stuff signed for his family, Richard Tanton [head teacher] went on too long and also forgot Rory when he was handing out the trophies.

I was speaking next and so did it myself but R was really pissed off with Tanton. Clive was good at the Q&A and the kids clearly warmed to him and admired him. I could sense that from the way they listened, really intently.

CW and Jayne came back for dinner, really nice evening and F seemed happy enough. They were a really close couple, and he obviously relied on her hugely. I think Fiona got a sense for the first time really just how big a deal a Lions tour of NZ was, and she liked his analysis of how to deal with different characters. He had been terrific at the school, though he was still much more shy in public than his persona would suggest. He was saying he thought I would make an actual difference, beyond the comms, because I would develop real relationships with the players and they would want advice on all sorts of things that affected performance. He reckoned once the election was over, if I wasn't going back I should knock politics on the head and set up a sports consultancy, that he could see all sorts of teams, organisations, events and individuals wanting the kind of support I had been giving to him.

Thursday 14 April

As often after a big day, I woke up feeling flat and depressed. The Tories seized on the Kamel Bourgass case ending yesterday [Algerian illegal immigrant who had murdered a policeman] to go on the attack on asylum and we didn't get our defences up properly until JR did the rounds and attacked them over identity cards and terror vote.* We got AM to do a clip in Croydon that we would have an ID card bill in the next Queen's Speech. But he also got verballed into saying we apologised for PC Oake's death. CC went even further later. As I said to AM at least your fuck-up will be covered up by a bigger one. TB spoke to the widow. He had spoken to her a few times since his death, as well as going to his funeral.

We finished his economy speech which was OK without having real cut-through, then he went back to the school in Enfield that he opened in '97. It was amazing to think the kids who started aged eleven then were now past school age. We had the usual round of meetings but

---

* Michael Howard said Tony Blair's failure over asylum had led to Bourgass being able to murder PC Stephen Oake and plot to spread poisions in Manchester in 2003. Howard said 'chaos in our asylum system' enabled Bourgass to stay in the UK.

April '05: TB at 'New Labour' school opened in 1997

people were a bit tired and flagging. The best points of the day were the election broadcast screening, which went down well, and the Lib Dem manifesto launch which was a total shambles. Charlie [Kennedy] looked shattered but worse, he appeared not to know what his own tax plans were. I went to the gym, then to Pret to get a salad, where the guy on the counter said, loudly, that it was 'on the house because you're helping keep a Labour government'. That was nice of him, but I was feeling down all day.

TB got back for a strategy meeting to get the next few days focused. GB was doing a schoolgate campaign tomorrow with HH [Harriet Harman], trying to translate the economy to language that connected better with women. Then into the NHS over the weekend and cut-through on that. Penn was in for the next meeting. He felt we needed an immigration day soon, that it was still the issue with the greatest potential to harm us. Also he felt that TB had to watch he didn't weaken himself with the GB situation. I had a long chat with GB about the future of the party. He said we needed better women. He felt Fiona should be an MP. He felt I should go for a seat or if not go in the Lords, but whatever I did I ought to be a minister. I was wasted doing what I did. He said you have shown what you can do in the last few weeks, things nobody else can do, and that includes Tony and me, and you would be a terrific minister. I said I would think about it, but please don't underestimate how much I am doing all this under duress. I know, he said, I understand. But he said that I was one of the few people around really able to spot talent and inspire other people and that was a talent that should be put to the broadest possible use.

He said he was always struck by how the people who worked direct to me seemed to take real inspiration, and were dedicated. 'That is leadership,' he said. He was really pushing DA and EM and said, 'You may hate him and think he's terrible but Ed B is the best there is at economics.' I said I really don't hate him but I wish he would give up some of the dark arts, and be straight with us. We were closeted away for half an hour or so, and he was very warm and friendly. He was incredibly impressive when he was firing on all cylinders as now, and it was just so sad, and annoying, that he couldn't be like this all the time. He still felt TB should have gone a bit further yesterday. He also said that if he did take over at any point, he would want to involve me as much as possible, preferably as a minister.

TB was more relaxed about the asylum situation than I thought he would be. We were still struggling to move opinion in certain parts of the electorate. But equally things felt like we were on a roll and going for it, and they certainly didn't feel like that a few weeks ago. A few days ago even.

Friday 15 April

In fairly early and TB GB in for a strategy meeting. We agreed that if as expected Rover finally went under TB and GB should go up there. We were doing fine on families though MH was going for asylum again and going to a Sikh temple as cover. We had a TB visit then he did Jeremy Vine, badly, with a sense he was pinned down on Iraq and he didn't really get himself out of it. He was nothing like as good as he used to be at framing interviews on his own terms, and we were far too accepting of the media's agenda and questioning. Rover going under was the big story of the day. Howard was also going for us on postal votes. Matt C gave me stuff on postal voting to give to Tom Baldwin re how the Tories were the ones who pushed for the current system. Did another MB speech re Howard and got her on to Sky. What was annoying was how ministers didn't come up with their own ideas and their own content for this kind of thing though at least MB did it when we produced the material. JP called in for a chat before doing a C4 interview on postal votes and said the mood out there was fine. He had been in half a dozen marginals and the mood had definitely shifted our way a bit. TB was also reporting a good reception pretty much everywhere he went. I was doing a TB piece for the *Mirror* with an NHS petition, then got Tessa doing the media rounds.

I had a meeting with Mark Lucas on the next broadcasts. The one on Howard was going down really well in the office. We need big time to get up his record in government. AM left early so I chaired most of the meetings and we got through them a lot quicker. TB told me Peter M was furious at the way I had worked up GB into such a dominant position. He felt we had ceded far too much. I was still of the view that we could only win well if we all worked together and if he had driven a hard bargain, so be it. The campaign was going a lot better. He said Peter felt GB would have come round eventually, because he would have done anything to avoid being blamed for a poor result. I disagreed, said as it seemed TB was never going to sack or move him, they had to work together.

At a meeting with the agency they said as the Tories had faded again the voters were getting angry with us again and they were rejecting lots of the pledges as just more of the same that wouldn't be delivered. TB felt Alan M should be focusing on marginals activity, which he was really worried about. I did MB's speech and then when we heard the Tories were doing 'Tax Sunday' I chatted with TB and GB and did an overnight briefing on how we could further undermine their economic credibility when they did tax cuts. I enjoyed telling George Jones [*Telegraph*] that our recent cranking of the gears was in part born of their leader on how the Tories' dog-whistle tactics had gone far enough.

Sally M and PG were both trying to persuade me to go for a seat. It didn't appeal. I spent too many days at the moment willing this to be all over, just as I had spent too many of the latter days in No. 10 wishing I was somewhere else. I knew the game, and I knew myself, well enough to know that if my heart was not 100 per cent in it, there was no way it would work. I think I could not have got through recent weeks at all if I thought I was straight back into it after the election. Sally said she was worried about the calibre of candidates, and of the lack of talent coming through. GB called from Birmingham to go over a tax briefing. He was with TB on the train and it was interesting how TB would come on with questions for me to answer about where we go next, GB would have his own ideas and push forcefully. In addition to Peter M bending his ear about Gordon, TB had seen JR for a drink last night who was really pissed off at the GB love-in. Tessa told me TB was throwing away his authority, and would make himself a lame duck.

I was getting a fair bit of flak for GB being so strong in the campaign now, but I was still convinced we had the balance right. TB had not thrown in the towel, far from it. But we had always known the economy was the key to this campaign, and we now had that up in lights. The way Tessa talked, it was as though if we won TB would be strong and secure and there for ever after, and the GB thing would just go away. It wouldn't. I understood the angst as well as anyone, but once it was clear the nuclear option was not a runner, then I really did believe we had no option but to do this the way we were. How TB handled it after the election would depend partly on the result of course, but also on the dynamics of the campaign and of what followed. I think Peter felt GB had outflanked me, but so far as I was concerned my main mission in recent weeks had been to build the campaign, to get TB and GB in sync, without undermining TB's authority fatally. I think I had done that. They didn't. Fine. I was still feeling low though, and tired, and am writing this at 1.30 a.m. with the rest of the house fast asleep, but somehow knowing even though I am knackered I don't think I will sleep well.

Saturday 16 April

Rover went as well as it could have done considering how grim it was. The aim today was to move to health with a TB–JR press conference plus petition, JR speech and TB visit with CB. Howard helped with a leaflet up north totally misrepresenting the MRSA figures, another mistake, another piece of OTT opportunism which was leading the news by the end of the day. TB came in for 8 and was in real pain because of a twisted disc. He had mentioned it earlier in the week but said it was getting worse, and felt like toothache in the middle of his back. He was very unconfident and a bit panicky today. We also agreed it was time to start saying things about the nature of Howard's nasty campaign. We had loads of stuff to pour into the Sundays. Andy McSmith [*Independent on Sunday*] did me over, taking my briefing on TB–GB working together as me being authorised to organise a handover. Ludicrous, but I suspect he may have been pushed in that direction by the GB lot. Perhaps he was put up to it, I don't know.

We were waiting for Tory tax cuts, which they had been trailing for a while, which in the end came as help for pensioners' savings. TB lacked oomph and passion at the presser and we had a post-mortem afterwards. I felt he went into the media agenda the whole time and communicated a sense they were his equal. He needed more authority and passion and needed to start answering their small questions with big answers. Also JR spoke too often and too long and had to be spoken to about that. It was OK but not great. I said we had lost the art of ensuring our message got heard. We gave then too much choice about what to take. JR got a bit sniffy about it when I said so, but TB got the point and was fine about it. It was always difficult getting the balance between motivating and improving on the one hand, and knocking his confidence on the other. But I really felt we had to up our game.

I briefed several of the Sundays. The *Sunday Telegraph* and the *News of the World* had very good polls for us, too good in a way. I felt we had to keep a sense of this being close, and a real choice, otherwise we would not keep the idea of the choice of two futures in people's minds, and it would become a referendum on us. PG had said the groups were beginning to reflect the point Penn made, that people were moving away from us again as the Tories' threat receded. I also

April '05: Post-mortem after 'low oomph' press conference

felt no sense of a campaign locally, close to home. Alan said the same about his patch in Darlington. News wise we had an OK day. TB now wanted us to build the sense that the Tories' campaign deserved to be punished, which it did.

MH had another little stump speech which had a go at me and Peter M. Pathetic, and so divorced from where he needed to be. It was quieter in the office but TB was calling regularly, trying to make sure we were getting the ducks in a row for their tax cuts. I think we were. The plan was an AD–EB–DM briefing tomorrow, then TB GB with a new document Monday. The GB lot were now being unbelievably co-operative, bringing over drafts the whole time for me to OK them etc. We were going for NHS names to back us. Also trying to take forward the conditional voting idea for Muslims; the notion that we should generate a sense of people saying 'I disagree with them on this (e.g. Iraq) but I still prefer Labour to Tory and I'm voting Labour.'

Sunday 17 April

Marathon day, absolutely beautiful and I was really wishing I was doing it. The polls were good – too good – and the papers were by and large OK. After the morning call, mainly focused on plans to pre-empt the Tory tax plans which they had briefed overnight, I left the office and had a little wander on the marathon route. Lovely atmosphere. I bumped into Roger Bannister and had a nice chat with him. Haile Gebrselassie's team invited me to the Millennium Marathon in Addis. Cherie was there and was friendly enough. Rory came sixth in his junior race, and seemed pleased. TB called and we agreed we must get the focus back on health. GB was back and we met up at Victoria St to go over the Howard presser on the pensions rebate plan. GB was tired, and not really up for doing a press conference himself. In the end MH didn't really fly and we had AD/AM/Balls to rebut. I had a good meeting with Penn who had done a note on mid-campaign assessment. He felt we had done the economy part of the campaign so far pretty well, and also successfully managed the idea of TB GB working together well. But we needed to do immigration, work out where we were likely to win back Lib Dems, and have a deeper sense of values.

I took the meeting and then on the drive to Wales, where I was meeting up with the Lions, I dictated to Parna a long note on what we did well so far (six or seven things) and what we did less well (maybe ten). I was in full flow and put together a detailed note for the next few days, health leading to economy / education with TB GB again and then immigration, maybe with Howarth. Then I did a draft speech for tomorrow's rally on health.

TB was having a day off, and watched Man U thrash Newcastle (4–1) in the FA Cup semi-final. I had a big argument with JR on NHS charges because I felt he was confusing the argument. The media were resisting our pitch on this because it sounded like we were saying the Tories would charge for all ops. In fact the actual policy was bad, and wide open to attack, so we didn't need to overdo it. The Tories got a bit of a hit out of pensions but I felt it did not cause as much excitement as they would have been expecting with a £1.7 billion ticket attached.* I said to GB he seemed tired after the US trip. He said he was, it had been hard pounding and he hadn't slept much on the way back, but he would get back in gear. He wanted us to get moving on the public services agenda now. TB at one point said he found it scary the extent to which the whole campaign had to rely on me, him, GB and Alan in particular. I said I didn't mind so long as he understood I was off on 6 May. But SM, PG, Pat McF were pushing me to get a seat and GB was clearly signalling a position with him if I wanted it.

I arrived at the Vale of Glamorgan hotel where the Lions squad had gathered. Dinner with Ben [Wilson, former No. 10 press officer who was joining AC's Lions media team], Bill Beaumont and John Feehan. The players seemed in good form. Several of them wore glasses – Brian O'Driscoll, Martin Corry, Denis Hickie – and it was extraordinary how different they looked. I chatted to a few of them but still had loads more election work to do and went to my room. Jack Straw called. He said there had been a definite dip in his canvas returns in the last few days. He felt Iraq was damaging us more than we thought and he was picking up more negativity about TB than was coming through in the polls.

Monday 18 April

I was up before 6, out for an OK run, then dialled in for the TB, GB etc. meeting. TB was as wet as yesterday when he was in a bit of a flap about the charges issue. Today it was how to get up health. I was arguing we had to do it by doing it. 'What do you mean?' he said. I said we say we are doing it and then we do it. We start laying the

---

* The Tories announced plans for a tax cut to reward people who saved towards pensions. The tax breaks for savers would cost £1.7 billion.

ground and then we make sure the speech is strong and the substance is real. It is not rocket science. It was going to help us that the Tories were doing health today so we could start to trail our stuff as a counter to that. The call went on for 40 minutes, complete with all the irritating background noise coming from the meeting, and I'm not sure we achieved that much. Later we agreed we would do a press conference in Birmingham tomorrow on public health with women ministers. GB was wanting DA to do an education presser with RK on Wednesday. I'd wanted to do progress in regional cities but they were keen to push for another day re women's vote etc. OK by me.

The rest of the day I was largely taken up with Lions business. The video guy had done some terrific films on Lions history, and the intro music was terrific. Then Humphrey Walters, who had done some motivational coaching for Clive with England, did a couple of sessions, some drawing on his sailing exploits, then culminating in a big exercise where we all put on white overalls and did a kind of mix of quiz and painting. I was teamed up with Steve Thompson and Danny Grewcock [players]. We had to get lots of right answers to qualify for paints and brushes, then had to work out who had the canvas that was next to ours, and link up. There was a fair amount of grumbling but when the whole thing was done, we had painted a giant mural with the logo and a sense of what we wanted the tour to be. It was actually pretty breathtaking.

They were generally an OK crowd. The Irish players seemed the most interested in politics, especially Shane Horgan and Denis Hickie. Martin Corry probably the most interested of the English. All the gear for the trip was in a big room, and I was kitted out, including for the suit, with Lewis Moody, who had some pretty impressive scars. Will Greenwood [player] very friendly. Ditto Andy Robinson. I think they thought it was quite interesting to have me around, particularly with the election on. At lunch I sat and chatted with Neil Back [player], Corry, and a very quiet Gavin Henson. Matt Dawson [player] was pretty noisy. Clive came in, said he had just been listening to a phone-in, someone called me despicable and another woman defended me. Most of the players seemed fine but Ben [Wilson] said later after I left that he had to defend me with some of them, that the Welsh and the Irish were all fine but he reckoned one or two of the English boys totally bought the *Mail* agenda on me.

In general the set-up seemed pretty professional. Players very focused, not universally responsive to the speeches they were getting from the coaches though I think they did pretty well and CW was good. Ian McGeechan made the best speech re the game generally. I got driven to Birmingham to meet TB. He was a bit frazzled but we got the speech done OK before heading for the rally. Beverley Knight [singer] provided a bit of glamour and entertainment. JR was a bit windy again. It was an OK event but not that great. PG's polls were not so good, especially women. The Libs were doing too well. Iraq and tuition fees were driving a lot of support for them.

Tuesday 19 April

I was on the conference call first thing and TB was a bit wet again, saying how we had to get the focus on health. The polls were bad for the Tories and talk was starting to bubble up about their strategy. The worry for us was that we got too soon to a sense of meltdown for them. But there was no point us pretending; Howard was coming under fire on immigration too. The sense was that they had become obsessed and were feeding off fear rather than dealing with a genuine problem. I did TB's words and then had a long meandering call with AM and JR who was still wanting us to focus on charges in a way that I felt was too all-embracing and would damage the overall case. I had a session with Matthew Taylor to rewrite the argument and make the policy section much more 'many not the few' in tone and detail, and leading to an attack on them based on the idea of a two-tier health service.

TB was out doing local radio when Howard did a press conference attacking us for lying in leaflets and petitions on health and calling for the withdrawal of all posters/leaflets etc. I wrote a tough line in response. TB was doing a press conference with Tessa, Margaret Hodge and Melanie Johnson [MPs]. We had to cut their words down a bit. TB was on form and most of the questions were on our agenda. It was a little worrying that some of them were starting to talk about the idea of a third landslide. I was watching from the side with Bruce and Parna. Bruce was smiling in that way he has when he thinks everything is going OK.

Another *Sun–Mirror* problem. We had agreed to a TB–CB joint talk for *The Sun* but it would send the *Mirror* off the radar again so we needed to think of something for them too. Off to the train, and I did a note on the theme of the Tories deserving to lose, which I turned into a speech for Jack Straw to do in Blackburn. TB was worried about the shape of the campaign. I bumped into George Osborne in the cafe next to the office and he looked petrified. Their campaign was faltering and people felt it. Did a meeting to agree the next press ads, then to a Penn meeting with TB – the poll lead was OK and the vote was coming back but we needed a big operation on the Lib Dems. I wanted to do a big Saturday postal vote pitch with TB, GB and MB but GB was due to be in Scotland. We needed to do the choice big time on Saturday. The new Pope [Benedict XVI] was unveiled as we were in the middle of another planning meeting. The atmosphere in the office was better than for a while.

Wednesday 20 April

TB wanted me to go up to Leeds to help prepare him for *Newsnight* later on, so after the morning call, I set off by train. The Tories had come up with a shift of policy on revaluation which totally dominated the call. JP was on stressing the need to emphasise fairness more than we had been doing. I wrote up a line on the Tory shift – opportunism because a week ago MH said the opposite, remember the poll tax, plus they're cutting grant. I got the line to TB prior to his *GMTV* joint interview with GB which went OK. I was also working on AM's script for the presser, saying go up front on council tax and go really hard. But he lacked a bit of confidence and oomph at the moment. These situations required total confidence and we didn't show that. We lacked trust for these things – wrongly in my view – in JP. GB was OK in theory about doing a clip in his speech but not up for doing a round at Millbank, though I did manage to persuade him to be beamed in from Scotland for an event on Saturday on postal vote turnout. I also had to persuade TB who had been fancying a day off.

Ruth Kelly was in for the press conference this morning. I told her she may get asked re the new Pope. She smiled. I suggested saying her faith was not an election issue but we will have good relations with the Vatican. On the train I worked on TB's asylum and immigration speech. PG was calling me endlessly through the day as was Alan. PG felt Alan had not really punched through on the council tax message, said we were not hitting hard enough and that whenever I was out of Victoria St the place slightly fell apart. AM was constantly moaning about the BBC but failing to do anything about it. I worked on the speech on the way up. The attack team had got hold of a Lynton Crosby memo which showed a bit of panic and also exposed their strategy. I was pressing DH to go for the broadcasters after the news at lunchtime which everyone said was dire for us, total hit for them. I texted Marr and Nick Robinson to say it was not their job to try to keep the Tories afloat when they were sinking. Marr was a real problem. He had a particularly silly column today in the *Telegraph* saying journalists were keeping the campaign alive. TB did a kind of open air surgery and it went OK though needless to say the only one the BBC covered was an anti-war protestor.

We were doing the interview with Jeremy Paxman in the offices of a Leeds law firm. The interview was OK, TB strong on Iraq and pretty good all round. He was often better when the questioning was tougher. Clive texted me, said he had watched it and thought we had nothing to worry about. It still felt a bit grungy though and as we drove around the place, there was not much sense of their being a big campaign on. Hardly any posters out there. Worrying. On the flight back, TB and I chatted re GB. He felt it had been the right thing to get him back in. He felt he and GB were something special and Peter M and I the only two who got near in terms of having a special political talent. He said it was actually a shame I had never gone for a seat. I said if I had I would not have done the job I did, and I doubt another elected politician could have got them working together. He liked the asylum draft and wanted to build it up. There was even an opportunity now, so badly had the Tories handled it, to make asylum a net plus for us.

Rebekah Wade called and said *The Sun* was 'coming out tonight with red smoke over Wapping'. I had a long chat with her and she was clearly still smarting re me going to Les. Trevor K looked pretty sick doing his interviews on why *The Sun* was still backing us. The news was bad on council tax and PG said if GB and I were not there, things just fall apart.* The clips the Beeb used from TB on Iraq on *Newsnight* were strong. He has to show that kind of passion for the domestic agenda. *The Guardian* were splashing on the Crosby letter we had given them. [He had written to party candidates warning that they were entering 'a difficult period' and urging them to remain focused.]

* Following a Tory claim that the government's revaluation of property was a 'stealth tax' that would cost 7 million homeowners an average of £270 a year, Local Government Minister Nick Raynsford said that Labour's plans no longer included creating higher council tax bands in high-priced housing areas.

Thursday 21 April

Crime figures day, and though they were not as bad as feared, we knew there would be the usual row about what they meant. Then a toddler's mum was stabbed, which became the backdrop. *The Guardian* splashed on the Crosby memo but they kind of missed the point, going on the fear of losing rather than the strategy being exposed. At the morning meeting we agreed GB should join the press conference to do a pre-emptive response to the move to cut stamp duty briefed by the Tories overnight, last piece in the jigsaw. We also went over the weekend and got their agreement to do a big number on Saturday, with TB on the choice and GB on Libs and apathy. JP called in and he and I had long chat afterwards. He seemed OK, and felt the mood out there was all right. He said, 'You must keep at him to go for the Liberals. He doesn't like doing it but it's important. They are doing well under the radar. We are all guns blazing at the Tories, which is right, but the Libs are taking support away right now.'

GB was firing, had some great stuff from Tory candidate leaflet promises. TB's *Newsnight* had gone down well, and he seemed a lot more confident, did a terrific Radio 5 phone-in. He called me after and said 'I don't want to play to your prejudices but those BBC people positively hate us.' Then he was off to Rochdale, and he said the mood there was OK. He was on much better form but we still needed to lift it.

I had a morning of back-to-back meetings, day-to-day grid, last ten days, broadcasts. I lost it with them all at one point when they said both Tony and Gordon were against the idea of a video beamed into one of our events from Africa. I spoke to GB and in fact all he had said was he was worried about the cost of sending Hilary Benn [International Development Secretary] and would it not be better to get a celeb to do it? I asked June Sarpong and she suggested Lisa I'Anson [DJ and broadcaster]. I spoke to her and it was sorted. She was thrilled to be asked. Also Penn's polling had not been that hot on the idea of Clinton campaigning so we decided that it was better BC was beamed into the Africa event rather than came for the last few days. I was writing some decent stuff at the moment. I couldn't work in the open plan office but used TB's office and dictated to Parna and managed to get some really strong lines going. I was slightly starting to feel the pressure though. I said to Jo Gibbons it was driving me crazy the pressures they all put me under. She said I was the only one who could go to both TB and GB, and JP, and so it was inevitable. Nobody else could make anything happen because they were either

TB or GB people, Alan felt squeezed and it was inevitable the pressure came on me.

Fourteen days to go. Jo was a great help. So were Parna, Darren Murphy, Huw Evans and Matthew Doyle. In fact the team in the office more generally was coming together well. Matthew Taylor was on form. DH was handling the lobby much better. A problem emerged about the idea of a visit to Calais for a speech on asylum and immigration, because the election rules agreed by TB meant he could not go near a government establishment. Howard had already been refused a visit to asylum venues for the same reason. I was now doing wall to wall meetings but felt at least we were moving forward. I was really pleased with 'the choice' script for Saturday. We were getting a lot of reports of low Tory morale. And a hilarious moment when I got a cab home and the driver said he had been thinking of voting Tory but he was appalled at their hypocrisy on waste. Why so? Because he took someone from Buckingham Gate to their HQ in Victoria St – 'Crosby his name was – on account.' The weather had been nice today as well which helped the mood and cheered up TB a bit. He was still coughing though and the back pain was still there. I noticed in a walking shot on TV that he had looked really stiff and I could tell he was hiding a grimace. I felt we needed more TB–GB, more team and more of a message re education. We had won the first stages on the economy, we had just about done what we needed to on health, and Howard and co. were just bouncing around, not really landing blows, or sticking to one issue long enough to hurt us. Two weeks out from polling day, we were certainly not in landslide territory but I think we should be OK.

Friday 22 April

We were on to, finally, addressing the final piece of the jigsaw, asylum and immigration. We ought to get to the top of the news all day. I got in for conference call, then TB called and sounded a bit unsure about it all. JoP and I went over to No. 10. Jonathan walked so fast and my calf was playing up. TB was up in the flat scribbling away and had done a very good balanced intro. It got the argument right and would both make TV and hit the serious commentators. It was interesting, a proper argument, and a political risk which the media would like. But hopefully it meant the public would see we got it, we understood the issue from every angle, including their concerns and in some cases their anger, while the Tories just wanted to exploit the issue and tap into the anger. TV had been a real problem in this campaign. In most elections it was the press that trivialised and the telly that held the debate up a little, made it a bit more elevated. This time if anything the situation was reversed. A great example today of how much they felt the election was about them not the issues, the politicians or the public.

I spent half an hour or so briefing Marr and Robinson about what TB was saying. Marr's worry was how could he make it about the Lib Dems because he was out on the road with Charlie Kennedy today? Robinson doorstepped TB aggressively at the end of his speech asking why there were no non-white faces at the event – in fact there were. TB was absolutely livid, because Robinson's undertone was an accusation of racism. He kept calm on camera but later had a real go. I sent Robinson a text saying when will they realise elections are not about them but about people. 'Serious speech deserves serious coverage.' All they seemed to think of was how could they get their own mugs on the box, and how could they make the viewer and listener feel even more cynical? But today went fine taken as a whole. It was unbelievably hot in the office and really hard to concentrate but I did an OK note on the next few days. And overall I was glad we had done immigration and asylum on our terms, even if the coverage was all through the prism of campaign tactics.

Saturday 23 April

Lower-key coverage for the speech than I expected. This was the problem at the moment. The debate never stayed in the same place for more than half a day. Today we were doing the first of the 'Vote for what you value' posters, and a big presser including GB whacking the Lib Dems and MB making an appeal to rural voters. GB didn't quite hit the Libs as hard as I had hoped but it was OK. I had been in No. 10 yesterday and some of the people there were saying they were worried the TB–GB thing would fall apart again the minute I left, the day after the election. I mentioned it to Parna who said, 'Why don't you go back full time?' I said I really didn't want to do that. What about as a part-time consultant? I said I kind of did that anyway. Yes, but formally, taking meetings, holding things together? The problem was you couldn't do that part time. And how long before it got as bad as it had got before I left in '03? I could only really tolerate recent weeks because I felt there was an endpoint.

I did a memo on strategy which Darren [Murphy] accidentally put into a package of material being put together for David Cracknell on the *Sunday Times*. The content was fine but they spun it against us with a headline 'Campbell – we're home and dry.' Wrong message. It was total dishonesty as a piece of reporting, but it would give the right-wing papers an excuse for a go at us. I decided we should put the whole thing on the website and make the point that the whole game for them now was how to depress turnout – the Queensland strategy (when one side essentially threw in the towel, said they couldn't win and for people to vote for them on that basis). It would also show to those who could be bothered to read it how my old line about the real spin doctors being the hacks was so true. Other Sundays were going on Tory problems and divisions on strategy. TB was OK at the press conference if lacking in oomph then he set off to Chequers to work on his Africa speech. I had noted a definite shift back to us among taxi drivers. A bit of a flurry later with the *Mail* splashing on a claim to have seen the legal advice re the Iraq war.

Sunday 24 April

The Libs were moving to Iraq while Howard, for the second day running, was calling TB a liar. The more unpleasant he became, the more he was damaging himself. I don't think he could do any other way. TB felt confident we could do to Kennedy on Iraq what we had done to MH on immigration, expose it as a tactic to avoid the issues most people were most concerned about, and show them as politicians only interested in exploiting problems and never in solving them. I don't think the public see Charles in anything like the same way as Howard, but we could definitely win the argument we were the only party with an agenda for the future across the board, on all the domestic issues. The Sundays were fairly quiet, my memo had gone in the wrong direction, but TB was still very keen to get up the nature of the Tory campaign. He was also keen to get some politics into the event at the Old Vic tonight. I did a note on clips for TB then watched Howard's speech. He looked very old and weak and out of place. David Davies called after reviewing the papers on *Frost* and said morale around the MH team did not seem high.

AM was in chirpier mood. GB was working on his speech for today and also for tomorrow re economy, worrying as ever how we make the economy an issue. I said we just had to, by saying that is what we were doing. Bit of a faux pas when I said something re how ghastly the BBC campaign coverage was in front of Sue Nye [wife of Gavyn Davies, former chairman of the BBC]. Off to the Old Vic, TB had the [Sir John] Gielgud [eminent late actor] dressing room, GB Lilian Baylis [theatrical producer]. Weirdly, as we arrived I was on the phone to Gary Philips [headteacher] at Lilian Baylis School, fixing a visit on Tuesday. I had a good chat with GB before TB arrived and he was on OK form and feeling more confident. He always seemed a bit nervous before a speech but not today. He said Howard was definitely fading at the right time for us. We had lined up for Bill Clinton to be beamed in and I sent through a note via Sara Latham that he should say, 'If you value it, vote for it.'

TB was a bit late and because of technology problems the event was delayed a little but in the end we got both links to work. Bill C was awesome as ever. Lisa I'Anson, who was doing the Africa leg, was brilliant – lively and bubbly and said straight out 'Vote Labour.' John O'Farrell, Arabella Weir [comedian, actress and writer], June Sarpong and Dermot O'Leary [broadcaster] all good in their own way. BC top as ever, bang on message, and he could still wow an audience just by being part of the event. It was a good event, full of values and strong messages about what we believed in, and why those things were very different to the Tories.

Back to Vic St for a meeting with the Big Guns plus their teams re next few days. We agreed we had to go on offensive against the Libs the more they came at us on Iraq. Also that we had to make more of the nature of Tory campaign, partly for the public and also to keep eroding their morale. We were getting feedback that things were not great in there. Plus we had to really sharpen the focus on marginals. TB was really exercised by this last point, partly spooked by some of the stuff PG was reporting back from groups, though reading between the lines I sensed some potential Labour–Tory switchers were coming back to us because they didn't rate Howard and co., but they were not exactly going to be running to the polling station in a state of joy.

GB's thinking was that we had to have a bigger picture message to root the focus on the marginals. Also how do we keep going on the economy when the media just see it as a given than we are strong there? It was definitely a bit of a problem. *The Times* would not take a letter from businessmen supporting us but we got it into the *FT* and the Tory business manifesto was making no impact. I had another chat with GB who was planning in his speech to the British Chambers of

Commerce tomorrow to throw up a new flank on the euro. Later we got more decent polling in. Howard was definitely bringing people to us. But we really had to watch turnout and expose their plan of deliberately depressing turnout by making people feel we had won already.

Monday 25 April

OK coverage for all of yesterday's events but Iraq was going big because of the Libs going on it and because of the attack on TB as a liar. Good coverage in the broadsheets re the business scene, the *FT* splashing on the letter *The Times* wouldn't take and the British Chambers of Commerce boss backing GB. But it was clear Iraq was going to be the main thing. All three big guns were at the morning meeting, and we agreed TB had to be confident and really defend the policy. We had to get up the line that the others went on it because they had nothing to say about other stuff. He was getting quite steely re the Libs and saying he will go for them after the election. GB was pushing hard against the euro again. TB was keen for us to get up the Tories' 'backdoor strategy' – they know they cannot be elected on what they stand for so they will try to stop people voting and hope enough of their own supporters turn out anyway. I sensed the media growing more bored, which was another potential problem for us.

We launched a 'Vulcan hunt' squad for sightings of John Redwood tomorrow [referring to Redwood's similarity to *Star Trek*'s Vulcan Mr Spock]. Also at the ad meeting we agreed to new press ads using red–blue arrows to carry key messages about them and us. Alex had helped me get David Moyes [Everton manager] for tomorrow's Liverpool rally and Bobby Robson [former England manager] for a grassroots football event. I called them both to talk through what was needed. I wrote words for TB, RK and Gary Philips for tomorrow's Lilian Baylis School visit which I felt was really going to be good, having been there myself a while back. I asked Gary if he was able to be political – he said, 'What's the worst that can happen – they say I'm speaking out of turn?'

We finally decided it was time to complain about the Beeb and did it via a JP letter, though I took out a line saying they were biased because they were so sore about Hutton. It was interesting though that even though they had decided Iraq was the main story of the election today, they would not take Iraqis who wanted to say Iraq was a better place as a result of Saddam falling, even though we had lots of them willing to be interviewed. I went for a swim at LA Fitness and a woman stopped me while I was swimming to say she had wobbled a bit on Iraq but she was voting for us for the third time. She had been a Tory till '97. That cheered me up.

Tuesday 26 April

Another concerted effort to get up education with the Lilian Baylis School visit but the Tories were doing well with personal attacks and there was a big story running with the Brian Sedgemore [Labour MP] defection from us to the Libs. We agreed not to go for him, point out that he was not even a candidate [Sedgemore was standing down at the election]. JP called in a rage because he had Greenpeace protestors on his roof at home in Hull which we had to deal with – tough line, lean on broadcasters not to send sat vans. As ever he was worried about Pauline having to deal with stuff like this on her own. He was off on one of his spectacular rants about how a combination of media and protest groups was making politics all but impossible. I said as long as the police were on top of it, Pauline would be fine, and the danger was us overreacting and giving them even more coverage and eating into what we were trying to get up. I think he was particularly sore because to be fair to JP he had banged the green drum pretty loud in government.

The school visit was actually the kind of event that would have got good coverage a few years ago but the nature of debate was now so different. Even this close to an election, the idea of them just covering what the leaders did and said, and then having the analysis, had all but gone. They were constantly on the lookout for the stuff that went wrong, or which fitted the pre-set agenda, and pretty much nothing else. So the line was today was 'overshadowed' by Iraq because that is what they had decided to go on, and TB was 'seeking to avoid questions', blah. It was a fantastic school and by and large everything went really well, though there were one or two boos from a couple of kids. Then there was a buzz that a kid had been glassed and for a while everyone thought it was in the school. It turned out not to be so and Kate [Garvey] was livid when TB was so obviously relieved that it had not happened while he was on the premises.

David Moyes called, said he had to go to a match in Italy tonight and so couldn't do the rally. I called Gordon Taylor [Professional Footballers' Association chief executive] who got me Phil Thompson [former

Liverpool player]. I didn't know he was Labour but was sound as a bell when we spoke. It turned out his son was a friend of Euan [Blair]'s. He also reminded me Howard had called for Gerard Houllier [former Liverpool manager] to be sacked. I had forgotten about that. Another piece of Howard nastiness coming back to harm him. Howard was a Liverpool fan but not well liked, he said.

The Tories were now launching a 'TB liar' poster. They had pretty much given up on a positive message about themselves and were just going to go at us, and TB in particular, on trust. They were also developing the idea of the election as the opportunity to 'send a message' to the government – in other words all part of the Queensland strategy; give the sense of having given up on winning, and hope they depress our vote and pick up a few of their own. When TB arrived we had a long discussion on how to deal with it. It was unusual to be faced with the line that the race was over so far from the end. We agreed our response should be rooted in policy and we worked up a couple of good clips on it.

Then to the helicopter, then the car and TB constantly asking, 'How're we doing, what's really going on out there?' We were running a dull but worthy campaign, it was solid and the line was getting through that the Tories were not fit for government, and that for all the anger over some issues, and all the divisions over the Parliament, we deserved another term. All the speakers were good at the rally, and TB was on excellent form. Phil Thompson top bloke. I wish we had known earlier he was so Labour. Back to the hotel to work on the next speech with TB and AA, another go at getting up on education. It was strong enough but it was a struggle to get up these policy based speeches in the way we used to. Writing this in the early hours, having tried and failed to get to sleep.

Wednesday 27 April

We finished the speech, which was fine, but the Tory attacks were running as the top news stories again. I did a note to GB to say that a big defence of TB by him would fly. To Bolton in the convoy, working on clips of the Tories going negative, negative, negative while we were still focused on education, education, education. TB did it well. To Manchester in the car with TB, and he was a bit fretful again. He had a chat with Paul Keating [former Australian PM]. I spoke to him too and he was on his usual splendidly irreverent form... 'They're fuckers and you've got to fucking beat them.' I reminded him of the time I asked him to try and teach Tony to hate Tories as much as he did. 'Ah, he maybe has a point,' he said, 'but you and I know it's good to go over the top at them every now and then.' Then he repeated, 'You've got to fucking beat them, and keep them fucking beat!' We agreed to draft up an article for him not least re the Queensland strategy.

I had a chat with Seb Coe who wanted me to check out rumours that the French were giving out Legion d'Honneur medals to lots of IOC people. Seb was doing really well but there was a problem if the IOC were going to fall for a bit of underhand stuff. I got back to London, into a few meetings to sort out the next few days, then *Channel 4 News* came on with what they clearly hoped and believed was a bombshell. They had the Attorney General's advice on Iraq.* They had probably had it for a while. Certainly whoever leaked it had had it for a while and was doing this at a time of maximum impact. You could sense people in party HQ getting nervy the moment the headlines came on. The whole place fell really quiet so both DH and I started making a bit of a noise to make sure nobody briefed out that the place had fallen silent when the bombshell dropped. It had, though. Bad moment. Really bad, and clearly part of a strategy from somewhere and all the harder to deal with because we couldn't be sure who was pushing this stuff out.

It played into where the Tories were, though, and what they were trying to do in terms of painting TB as a liar, and further eroding trust. We had to go into damage limitation mode, not helped by TB going straight into his 'It's ridiculous' routine. I drafted a line for [Lord Peter] Goldsmith [Attorney General] to put out. We had to get him in though, as this was going to be really tricky. Phil Bassett said the AG was keen to put out a longer statement. We needed to fight back and make clear the advice was proof of our case not the opposite. We had to be clear and push back hard. Adam Boulton was fine, said it does not establish we lied at all, and Marr was not as bad as he might have been.

Goldsmith came in and after we had a long call with TB and JS we agreed that we should put out an AG statement but that Jack should do the clips and interviews. Goldsmith was looking a bit agonised and was fussing over every word. Phil said he was really worried how all

* A summary of Lord Goldsmith's advice to the Prime Minister included his view that 'we would need to demonstrate hard evidence of non-compliance and non-cooperation. Given the structure of the resolution [1441] as a whole, the views of UNMOVIC and IAFA [weapons inspection authorities] will be highly significant in this respect.'

this affected his reputation in the legal world. I said bugger that – we are in middle of an election, this stuff is being drip-dripped against us and we have to show some fight. Bottom line – he concluded there was a legal base for action. It took a while to agree the statement. It was OK in the end though the papers would be a zoo. TB was strong and robust and getting angry about the nature of the debate. Part of the day had been fine but this brought back a lot of memories of all the late nights and the difficult moments re Iraq. GB was also calling the whole time trying to unpick plans we had made for tomorrow. I could see Goldsmith found this difficult, being dragged right into the campaign in this way, but I guess it was inevitable it was going to happen at some point. We had a chat about who might have pushed it out, but you can go mad worrying about that stuff. It had happened, it was not what we wanted, but we had got through worse and had to get through this.

Thursday 28 April

In early for a chat with TB. Media as expected. BBC wanking on endlessly. *Mail* vile. Etc. But as Tim said when he came in it had the feel of a mini-frenzy which could blow over fairly easily. It had definitely been a big bad moment but the issues having been gone over ad nauseam, via all the media coverage and the inquiries, there was nothing really new of substance other than the fact of them having the piece of paper. PG said there had been some groups done last night and the general feeling was of C4 overcooking it. I agreed with TB that he must stick to what we had planned for the day and also do some business launch words. He was fine, said he rather relished the argument. I chaired a conference call and agreed we should do TB hitting back followed by the Iraqi deputy PM standing up for what we did, then JP to go for Howard in a big way. I worked on JP's speech and a line for ministers before we set off.

Catherine was with us and en route down the Strand we were reminiscing about the journey to the Hutton Inquiry when she broke down in tears after we walked through the demo. We arrived at Bloomberg [in Finsbury Square], which was an odd but rather interesting building with an odd and interesting atmosphere. My campaign rule about 'If you see fruit, eat it' was tested because there was fruit everywhere you looked. We were taken to a room downstairs and spent half an hour going over tough questions. TB was pretty fired up. He was slightly

April '05: Goldsmith unhappy being dragged into campaign

in his boxer mode, pacing up and down, occasionally shrugging, occasionally smiling. Both GB and Patricia Hewitt were excellent. When GB was asked at the press conference if he would have done exactly same re Iraq had he been PM, he just said, 'Yes,' straight out no messing. He was strong on detail too and TB's tone and manner with the hacks was good.

As they came off stage I was pretending to sing an Elvis song – 'The Wonder of You' – into a mic and someone photographed me, and later the *Standard* ran as a story about me whispering to them via invisible earpieces when they were on the platform. Tossers. The Iraqis were obviously a little worried about the electoral scene and not wanting to get overly involved though the DPM was helpful enough. The problem was that the media really felt they had a bone and would keep this going on their terms if they could. TB said later he could not recall a campaign in which so much was thrown at one leader personally. There had to be more of a sense of the Cabinet fighting back for him. I felt GB, JP, Pat all did well today, and JR and MB had been doing loads as well. After the presser we had half an hour to work out where we were on things before heading back. We had to get the debate back to the economic choice. We agreed after tortuous discussion, with TB, GB and me at one end of the room, and some of the others coming in and out chipping in views, that we would get TB and GB out together in a couple of visits, one to demolish the Tories, the other the Libs. We had to fight all the way now.

GB was a bit down about the prospects of getting up the economy in the closing stages but we just had to do it. We had to be really strong and focused now. He felt there were a lot of seats around the place we had lost. By now there were almost a dozen people in the room, and he asked me out on to the main floor at Bloomberg, to get away from all the chatter, and said he really wanted to get things back to stability v risk up in lights, but he didn't quite know how. I said we just had to set our minds to do it, and then do it, and not let anyone stop us. As the thing got towards the end, the more distilled our message, the more they would take it, even if reluctantly. We were still conflicted about how to deal with Libs but there was no doubt the LDs were on the up, with the Tories stuck but their Queensland strategy beginning to work. I said to TB my hatred of media stemmed from fact they had helped reduce any sense that politics really mattered. We agreed the plans for the next 24 hours – more joint campaigning, get up the choice. TB was starting to get angry re the nature of the debate, particularly the way the BBC was framing it. I sent a message to Tessa saying it was ridiculous to renew their Charter just before an election. They pocketed that then went right back to pushing the cynical agenda. TB said he had never known such a poor level of coverage of a debate. Silly superficial people. That being said, he and GB had been on good form today and that permeated through the coverage.

We got Paul Keating's piece back which was great. Also a good piece from Joe Haines [Harold Wilson's press secretary] on 1970. I got a cab back to Vic Street, and another good driver. He said TB was 'good for the image of the country'. There was a phone-in going on in the background on Iraq, and most of the calls were negative, but he said, 'People have made up their minds on that one. If you were losing this 'cos of Iraq, you'd have lost it already.' I did a round of meetings to keep the show on the road, did a rallying pep talk for staff and spads etc. I said it was closer than people thought, the Tories were deliberately trying to depress the vote, we had to tell ourselves every morning that was left that we could still lose, and do every single thing we could to stop that happening, get stuck in, not stand on ceremony, totally go for it and no messing, every single one of you could have the ideas that made the difference, so have them, and make them happen by letting us know what they are.

Carol Linforth [party official] had asked me to do it because she said yesterday they had really taken a hit over the AG advice story and they needed to be bolstered again. I told them every campaign had big bad moments, we had had ours and now we were heading into the final run. If the Tories had anything better to throw at us, they would have done it by now. Over to No. 10 to brief TB for *Question Time*. He was looking tired despite having had a nap and despite, he said, having had a good visit with GB. Mark Penn was there and he took him through his note and recommendations. A lot of this was about undecided women. We went through some of the tough questions likely to come up tonight and he seemed OK. He got irritated when we said it was all about performance. But it was. So much was about him, and he had to embrace that to get up to his top level.

PH came over with speeches etc. then I set off home to watch. Kennedy was up first, was fine if a bit superficial but he was clearly becoming a bit more popular the more people saw of him. He had stumbled at the start of the campaign but had grown into it. Howard was poor and looked old and nasty. Ann Widdecombe had so done him with her 'something of the night' comment because it came through the more people saw of him trying to be nice or reasonable, and then he slipped so easily into being nasty. TB was OK but he was sweating a lot. He was good on substance and tone, didn't get rattled on the difficult stuff, defended himself well and got really passionate on education especially, but it was definitely not a clear hit. We had to keep going now, sharpen message, up the game and just go for it. We had to watch that the worries re turnout didn't depress morale. Alan Milburn's head had dropped a bit in the last few days. John Reid was losing a bit of strength too. I was worried about doing Saturday without TB GB overly involved.

Friday 29 April

The plan was to do a poster launch highlighting the economic choice as being TB–GB v Howard and Letwin, then to Wales to whack the Tories, then meet up with JP in Shipley to do likewise with the Libs. It was interesting that the Tories were moving off Iraq, so they must be getting feedback from groups and from candidates that the TB–liar attack was not going through, and quite possibly backfiring. Very mixed views on TB's *Question Time* performance. He hated it, felt he had not been on form. David M thought it was terrific. Brendan Foster called me and said he thought it was the best he had seen him in ages, and that he would really have connected. I was somewhere between the two, though through the day I picked up a lot of good vibes about it. The thing that always seemed to work was the comparison with Howard. The only story running out of it was people saying TB had not known what he was talking about on the problem of getting a GP appointment within 48 hours. I cheered him up a bit by reminding him that the story that ran after *Question Time* in 2001 was JP thumping the guy with the mullet in Wales.

My first meeting once I got in was with him and GB, trying to decide how better to get up the choice. They were both a bit down about our inability to get up a clear message, but equally they were letting it affect their own performance. Partly to make TB realise we had not been getting at him personally yesterday, I said these last few days were about energy and performance, and a lot of that fell on them. It is only a few days. We have to keep going, and the answer to the question 'How do we keep getting up the choice?' is 'We keep getting up the choice.' GB's people had done a very good report on the progress in every seat but GB kept saying the battle was being fought in headlines. That was only true up to a point. The media were finding the campaign quite dull because they felt we were winning, but we had to keep focused on the public not the press. 'But what do we do if the press don't carry the message?' They both asked it in different ways. Answer: we just keep going.

We were all getting a bit tired now, but we had to find the energy from somewhere. I said the Sundays would no doubt have more stuff to get them down, so it is important they don't let it. They set off, with TB a bit subdued, not helped by a bad cough, which hurt his back every time he coughed, and also a lack of clarity or confidence of message again. Their events went fine but there was definitely a thing creeping into the background mood music that GB was growing in stature while TB was shrinking a bit. We had to keep an eye on that. I know that Peter M was winding up TB on the rare occasions they spoke to say we had made a mistake in letting GB take so much of the stage of the campaign. I think TB still felt we had done the right thing, or perhaps that we had had no choice if we were going to get GB engaged, but it was not good if GB was being built not on his own account but at TB's expense. I am sure there was a bit of that going on, and that some of his supporters would be briefing it, but when TB had been under pressure in the last few days, GB had helped not hindered.

I locked myself away in TB's office at Vic St for a while and worked on JP's words on the Libs, and then a few extracts for the various rallies on Sunday. GB was calling me as often as TB these days, later because he was worried about an interview he had done with the *Telegraph* which they were spinning as him saying he wanted to change the rules re how Parliament voted for war. When he called he always made the main point and then made it repeatedly, in this case that nobody should react and we should say he and 'Blair' had said the same thing. I said 'I thought he was Tony again these days,' and he laughed. 'Come on, I have been doing everything you asked.' I could tell he was a little worried though.

Alan was up north and felt the Libs were a real danger but he said people did start to come back on the 'one in ten' point – if we reminded them that it took just one in ten not to vote and the Tories were in. We had to drive the Tory backdoor strategy hard now and I decided to do a Sunday briefing. I gave out stacks of stuff on it, not least from the Australian experience, helped by Keating's analysis, but also some of our friends in the ALP [Australian Labor Party] had sent through some interesting background. The Sundays were interested in it but to be honest they were not really buying any message of us suggesting we thought the Tories could win.

I chaired a conference call with the regional press officers who felt they were not getting enough time for the local press on visits. I said we would try to rectify that. I then ran through the last few days with them and as I did so I felt the plans were not strong enough, so I called another meeting with the team here to try to harden things up. I was worried that the Tories' last 72-hour plans would be better than ours. The Sunday briefing went fine but we had to set out the message more clearly that if people voted anything but Labour they got a Tory government. TB's evening rally went OK but when he called me afterwards he admitted he was not firing properly yet. I said it would come, we had always had this little wobble before the last few days, but he was not so sure. He said he felt a bit tired and discombobulated again. The media had clearly not picked up on the lack of confidence. Someone had said to Nick Robinson that we were on for another three-figure majority so I called him to give him a flavour of the Sunday briefing. I wondered if it was the Tories talking up the scale of defeat now.

I was getting a bit worried about the team in Vic St. Alan had dipped a bit, probably in the main because of the GB situation. Matt Carter was being very cautious, and worrying a lot about finances, which was fair enough but the mood music was not helpful. The agency was not firing as it normally did, and nor was TB. It was really odd to hear everyone outside the campaign talking about the size of the majority and yet inside it did not have a winning feel.

Saturday 30 April

TB did OK out of last night's rally. I had felt exhausted last night, but slept through to seven, which was exceptional, when GB called. He was still fretting about the *Telegraph*, which was leading the BBC radio news. He said we had to go into action on it, and say it echoed what TB had said many times, namely Parliament would get a vote on war except in exceptional circumstances. I think he knew he had fucked up, and had probably been verballed into giving them a headline they wanted, to keep the whole Iraq thing going. It certainly meant it was going to be harder to get up health which is what we had been planning for. The Sunday briefing had gone fine and it was at least out there now, the idea that the Tories were the ones talking down their own chances as a way of getting people to stay at home, or vote against us without fearing it would mean a Tory government. By the end of the day we managed to get health running OK on the bulletins. There was not much sense of the Tories on policy today, and they were playing into the media agenda of talking tactics the whole time.

I waited at home till Grace was up so we could give her her birthday presents then headed in. I was conscious that I had barely been there in recent weeks, and also that I would be heading to the other side of the world quite soon. Grace said later the best present would be that I didn't go to New Zealand, which tugged away at me all day. JR was doing the health stuff and did fine. When he was good, he was terrific. TB had *Frost* tomorrow and I was working on that. I felt we had to use it to get up leadership, and rather than try to shirk away from Iraq, take it on as an issue of leadership. I called around some of the others, who were instinctively nervous about it. GB and I spoke several times and at least he had seen how if we kept banging on about something – e.g. health today – eventually the broadcasters would feel they had to cover it. He was sounding a bit nervous though, which was not the right mindset before the health rally later. I said he needed to get the Iraq vote thing out of his head, it was done, it was not nearly as bad as the AG moment the other night, and it would blow over. The public were more interested in the economy and health, and he had a big role to play in getting them up today.

I did a note to TB re *Frost*, took a meeting to finalise plans for the week ahead then left early for Grace's party. TB called a couple of times, and signed up to the note re *Frost*, which I started to brief out on the notion that even where we had unpopular positions, TB beat Howard hands down on leadership. I spoke to David [Frost] to tell him what we were saying and where we were strategically going into the last phase. He said he felt we had had a better campaign than we realised, and that the Tory stuff had all been a bit piddling by comparison. Most of the Sunday heavies had varying difficult stories re Iraq. It was interesting though that the Tories were not really piling in. TB felt they were all handlable individually.

Another leaked document in the *Sunday Times*, [Lord] Mike Boyce [former Chief of Defence Staff] in *The Observer* seemingly saying he had never seen the full legal advice, another legal opinion story in the IoS – but the combined effect would not be great. Added to which if David F felt he had to raise them all tomorrow, it was easy for TB to take them where we wanted to be, on people needing to make a judgement about what leadership meant in the modern age. TB v Howard,

April '05: More Iraq pressure in Sunday press

even for all the wobbles and the problems we had, was a no brainer. Otherwise the papers, like the campaign, were a bit dull.

Sunday 1 May

I was in fairly early and set up a conference call pre-*Frost*. TB's cough was grim, every few seconds, and he was still struggling to get exactly where he needed to be re message. We knew Iraq would run again but he wanted to take it to leadership by the end of the day. We worked up a line to take re the various Iraq stories in the Sundays. Boyce had denied the story in *The Observer* to the Beeb but it was odd that it had popped up like that. TB and I agreed we should say the Tories were continuing to push on what happened in the past in Iraq – a policy they supported at the time – because they had nothing to say about the future of Britain. His interview was OK but no more than that. No big bollocks dropped, a few decent clips, but lacking in real oomph and energy. The back and the cough were really becoming problems. I could tell that he was holding back on the voice because he was worried about setting off the cough, and he seemed a bit drained of energy. It was not the best shape to be in at this stage. I was also a bit worried in that he seemed to think he did really well. I didn't say what I really thought because I was a bit worried about undermining his confidence when he wasn't exactly on top form, but I did say we lacked sharpness of message and performance at the moment.

I did a briefing for all the political editors building out from the stuff in the Sundays on the Tory backdoor strategy. The attack unit had produced a good pack of documents and Marr and Robinson both seemed to get the point. Off to Hove by train, working on TB's words. Blunkett was there when we arrived. He was worrying about what job he would get if (I think he said when) we got back. I said we really had to hammer the no complacency buttons but he said, 'There is nobody alive who thinks we won't win. They have thrown everything they have and they are still not making inroads.' He started to bend my ear re GB, and I said I was unlobbyable because as of 6 May, I was off again. He said that was when he hoped to arrive. I got the feeling he thought he might be in the running for GB's job which, given the nature of the campaign, was unlikely bordering on impossible. He seemed pretty down about things. I think he finds the whole grind of campaigning a lot harder because of the blindness and the extra pressure seems to bring out the insecurities too.

The event was OK but TB really had to work hard to lift the crowd. He had done a couple of other rallies earlier and was looking and sounding a bit shagged out. Energy feeding from speaker to crowd and back again was so important at this stage, but it wasn't really happening just now. He hadn't wanted to use a text which was fine, but it was hard work driving these events to the top of the agenda. We came back by helicopter, on the flight trying to work out which bids to do in the last few days. TB and CB had done their interview with *The Sun* and alarmingly Rebekah seemed very excited about something Cherie had said about their sex life, and doing it five times a night.

Monday 2 May

The day started with TB late, his cough still bad, and with GB not wanting to come in until we had TB there. So we sat chatting with JP but not getting very far. JP and I were on the same page on the Liberals, namely that they were taking votes from us which was helping the Tories, but shipping votes to the Tories in Tory–Lib marginals. TB grew more and more angry through the day as it became clearer and clearer what was going on. He developed the line that a disastrous Tory campaign was in danger of being rescued by a disastrous Lib Dem campaign. We finally agreed we had to get on to the economy all day if possible but as GB said the whole thing was now totally dogged by Iraq. I think he was overstating a bit because of his little mis-step with the *Telegraph*. We set off for a school in Wimbledon, having organised today's press conference there to show we were totally focused on marginals and the economy. They didn't really buy the one in ten line on our poster and I spent a lot of the day explaining it to the hacks. I thought we had done enough groundwork on the Queensland strategy stuff but they felt it was too big a leap to make. The argument was getting through though that a Lib Dem vote could help in the Tories by the back door.

Then news came through that a British soldier had been killed in Iraq. The sinking feeling I always got when I heard of these deaths, especially in Iraq, felt even heavier; having just about got through the weekend and all the AG leaks and other stuff, now the media had a perfectly legitimate reason to keep going on Iraq. TB was feeling very down and didn't look fired up at the presser. The news of the death had got to him a bit and it took a while to recover. We were hitting SE marginals so we headed on the bus to Ikea in Croydon where he and GB did a visit while I started to plan for Wednesday. Then via train to Gillingham. I did a briefing on the one in ten on the train while Oonagh Blackman interviewed TB and GB together for the *Mirror*. The problem with the press was that they just couldn't see the Tories winning, and so they felt this was all a bit tactical. But when we got them on to strategy and big message, they resisted that too. Oonagh seemed happy enough, the visit went fine, then TB, GB and I had a meeting on plans for the last 48 hours.

We agreed we had to do one more press conference so we settled on Wednesday with the whole Cabinet, to provide an echo of the team messages from the manifesto launch. We decided to keep going tomorrow with blitzes of marginal, focusing on the threat to mortgages from the Tories and hitting the Libs on drugs. Even though the last few days had been ragged, the basic messages were getting through, though GB was getting down at our inability to get above Iraq in headline terms. There was worse to come later when the soldier's widow – though later it turned out they were separated – attacked TB personally for his death. That really got him down again and of course some of the tough leadership clips from earlier could seem a little heartless used in the context of a soldier's death.

The bulletins were fine apart from Iraq, but he still felt we had to be making the case for the policy in the context of the leadership required in the world. Amid the grim context, the press did for some reason suddenly start to go with the 'one in ten' line after the briefing on the train, and pretty much on our terms. The *Mirror* was going a bit downscale but still being helpful. I was dreading when *The Sun* interview came out, as Rebekah kept dropping hints about the interview on their sex life. We took a helicopter to St Albans but I stayed in the car to do some work while TB went out and about. I had rather forgotten that feeling of losing sense of time and place when out campaigning. I was knackered by the time we got back but they were waiting for me to take a meeting on the last election broadcast, which was pretty good, and I also had to start working on the script for Wednesday and the last press conference.

I was really into the campaign treadmill now. I did another little pep talk for staff and said these last days would be over in no time so we had to milk every single minute and make sure we got something out of every single thing we did. Never mind people saying we had it in the bag; we had to think and act as though we were fighting for our lives. I went back to No. 10 and talked over the reshuffle with TB. He asked me if I had enjoyed coming back and I said up to a point, but I would be glad to be getting away again. He said he couldn't thank me enough for the difference I had made and if ever I wanted to come back, in whatever way I wanted, I could. He was definitely going to give David M a decent job, maybe health. Maybe education for Alan M. He was not sure what to do with JR – one of FCO, Defence or Home. I said he also had to watch not giving too many of the top jobs to GB people. I could defend the strategy we had deployed re GB for the campaign but there is no doubt it weakened TB a little and enough was enough on that.

We went out to the garden, where it was way too hot for me, and he had another go asking if I didn't fancy coming back. He said the thing he really missed when I wasn't around was my strategic mind and my toughness. I said he had never really lost the mind bit. Yes, but it is different when you are here, physically here, and that has been what has helped in recent weeks. People respect you, from JP and GB down, and that makes a big difference to me. There is always a little bit of fear you generate and I am going to need that, he said. I said the last few months had basically had me back in situ as before. I am not saying I haven't enjoyed it in some ways but part of the reason has been having the feeling that I have a get-out clause, and I have had the Lions to think about as a distraction.

He asked if I could imagine working for GB. Not full time I said. It may be at some point I need to come back either to help him see him off, if things go bad, or if things go better to help make the transition. I told him GB had asked if I wanted to be a minister, but I said I just didn't have the hunger right now. He said you on half hunger is as good as most on full, so don't rule it out. I got home to Grace going on about her latest obsession – getting a bloody horse. It did remind me though that I had been seeing a lot less of them again.

Tuesday 3 May

Unsurprisingly most of the papers were going pretty big on the widow of the solider killed in Iraq, so there was every chance Iraq would dominate the agenda right through to Thursday. PG sent a note through saying there had been a fair bit of slippage to the Lib Dems and he was not sure we could win it back. We needed GB to do a big 'Come home to Labour' message to people we had lost through Iraq or tuition fees or whatever. I was worried we lacked the time now to get over all the messages we needed to. GB and I had a chat in his office before he set off to do his interviews. He said the truth is we had had a lot of bad luck through the campaign. He was a lot less hostile when talking about TB, and he said he was grateful I had helped get them working together. His people had also been a lot more co-operative in the last few days. I said it would do them no harm, and everyone a lot of good, if they could carry on in that vein. He said it would not be easy if I wasn't around. People had been saying that we had done what it took to get power. Catherine MacLeod [political editor, *The Herald*] said later that was what she liked about us. We were driven by beliefs to do it and so we did what it took.

TB came in later and looked very down. He felt there was nothing we could say about the widow. If he tried to reach out to her, people would misinterpret it in the current atmosphere, and if he did it privately there was a danger of the same outcome. Though they were separated, the reality is she carried a lot of power in what she said, and the sight of the children suddenly without a dad was heartbreaking. I said all we could do in these circumstances was keep going with basic messages particularly on the economy. When GB came back from his round of interviews he said it was basically pretty much all about Iraq, and very difficult.

We set off together by helicopter – TB, GB, Sue Nye, me and the detectives. We worked on message all the way, landing in Gloucester. We agreed that after the mortgages speech [illustrating how mortgage rates had almost halved since Labour came to power] TB should do a brief dignified clip about the dead soldier but he was then harangued by someone claiming to be an ex-Labour voter and so Iraq was up again. What we couldn't work out was whether there was a real appetite for changing votes on this. We had to keep going with the basic message but in truth it was hard to read. We sensed the Tories were flatlining and we were shipping votes to the Libs but it was hard to be totally sure exactly what was going on. TB and GB were getting on well, and GB genuinely supportive over the fact that TB was being hit so hard.

Next stop the Wrekin, where all the candidates who had come in from around the area seemed pretty happy with the way things were going. Otis Ferry [son of musician Bryan] was out with some anti-war people, including one yelling I had blood on my hands. TB did a good stump speech and GB was fine on values but it wasn't really razor sharp, certainly not what we needed right now. There was such a reluctance to cover the economy. TB said there had been something of a media conspiracy to make Iraq the issue to hurt us. He was nonetheless OK mood wise and through the day we had a few laughs particularly at him being *Heat* magazine torso of the week, which he said I was suppressing. He was really focused now on the Libs. But our main challenge had to be to get the Labour/Tory choice back up in lights. I did some more work on a script for tomorrow then back to the chopper again and off to Ribble Valley, a mums' event not really made for a full-frontal attack on the Libs, so he pulled back a bit.

Off to the Lowry hotel in Manchester to prepare for TB's Channel 4 interview. He did OK. The story seemed to be him ruling out a rise in NICs [National Insurance contributions]. We had an hour or so drive to the evening rally, during which I was trying to get Rebekah to take out or tone down the 'five times a night' line from the *Sun* interview. TB was horrified at the thought of them leading on it. I persuaded them to take it out of the standfirst but not the copy, which is about the best I could have done. TB's clips from the rally were spot on, mix of economy and the Tory strategy to depress the vote. Back to the chopper for a long flight home, starting to think about the *Today* programme interview which was bound to be Iraq-dominated. At one point we were both staring out of the window, down at all the lights in the towns and villages we were passing, and I knew we were thinking the same thing. 'Have they decided, and have they decided the right way?' I fell asleep eventually and woke as we flew in over London, which looked stunning. 'Right then Ali,' TB said in his mock Burnley accent, 'another couple of days and I'll be joining you down t'job centre.' I got home, wrote a note on last day message, sent it round, did diary, now in bed.

Wednesday 4 May

Up really early and off to Vic St to dump bags, finalise words for the day and head off to No. 10. TB was in the usual T-shirt and underpants look and we were going over Iraq pre-*Today*, which everyone was dreading a bit. Also the overnight polls showed the Libs still coming up so it was all a bit tough with a day to go. What was clear was there was no sign people wanted the Tories back and so we had to just keep going with the same basic messages and try to get the Libs fixed. TB genuinely thought they had fought a useless campaign and were helping the Tories rather than themselves. The papers were not as bad as they might have been but we still didn't feel totally confident about where we were. We set off for *GMTV*, where Fiona Phillips

May '05: TB horror at Sun lead on Cherie 'five times a night'

and Lorraine Kelly were really friendly and warm. The interview was fine and he did some good message re the economy and he was fine tone wise. Then to Millbank, where Humphrys was not as bad as he might have been, let TB deliver economic message without too much interruption, zoned in on trust and Iraq but TB just kept a good tone and it was fine. 0–0 draw. The usual tensions between me and the *Today* people.

Lots of ribbing around the place re the TB–CB sex interview but it was OK. The *Mirror* people were not as pissed off as I expected them to be. I was dealing with Conor Hanna [*Mirror*] re front pages and getting TB GB handwritten letters. I was starting to feel really tired. After *Today* I got into the car with TB and though we had a police bikes escort we took ages to get to Finchley. We all felt surely we were going to win OK, with the polls fairly stable and lots of signs of the Tories fading. The news last night was dire for them. They were in real trouble but we could still not be sure exactly what was happening with the Libs – they could take enough off us to do a lot of damage. It was nice just chewing the fat and I said to him what Parna had said, and GB had intimated too – that people were worried I would go and they would be back to infighting. He shrugged, said it was entirely possible. 'GB had been good for the campaign but he has the capacity to turn bad if he feels it suits him. And he would see a shrunken majority as a sign my days are numbered.'

The press conference was fine though because we were late ministers were a bit pissed off and as it was outside central London there was a smaller media turnout too. There was no question he could not answer and the event looked good. The ministers seemed in OK mood, though some probably felt it was a lot of hours to give up on eve of poll without a role other than being an extra. But once it all got underway, I think they could feel it would have the right impact.

We set off for the Elstree helipad with AD and PH. The choppers were late but eventually we took off and headed for Rossendale, where he was speaking at the same venue I had done a while back. I got him to do the handwritten note the *Mirror* wanted on the way. Once we got into a car, he was into his staring out of the window, asking me what was going on out there, did they want us back, were they crazy enough to want the Tories, were we underestimating the damage those wretched Libs had done? We invented a new concept – helicopter focus groups – people who were attracted enough by the noise to come over and talk to us when we landed. Most were friendly. We also had a chat about the reshuffle. He made the point that the one everyone referred to as 'botched' had in fact been successful – Charlie Falconer and John Reid in particular – whereas the unbotched one was not. Kay Burley [Sky News] was on to me close to tears, begging for an interview with him, which eventually I agreed to. Off with AD to Dumfries, as in '97, got message pretty clear now and it was going fine media wise. *Sun* and *Mirror* both coming good as we neared the end.

Russell Brown [Dumfries MP] was looking a bit nervous. We visited exactly the same places as last time. OK mood. Off to Scarborough. Honing message all the time and by the rally he was strong, though he went on too long and had a big problem landing – he had about half a dozen different endings to the speech. He did a very good three minutes live on the BBC Six O'clock. JP joined us and was fussing a bit. Both of them spoke for too long, but the clips were good. The polls had us with leads between three and six, but the Libs were still picking up. We didn't really go for them in time. Alex called, said he had seen the news and felt we were looking like we were peaking at the right time. He felt Howard had disappeared and wasn't sure people took Charlie seriously. I put him on for a little chat with TB. I won the bet with TB about which clips would make the news. I was feeling pretty shagged by the time we made the last leg of the trip, to Sedgefield. Kate Garvey had a do for the whole on the road team, who had been brilliant, especially on these running around all over the place days, and I went to that for a bit. But I was desperate for some rest, even if tomorrow was going to be a quieter day.

Thursday 5 May

Out for a run, fairly windy in parts but I was moving well. I was still worried about the Lib Dems and we were getting a lot of anecdotal feedback to that effect. Meeting with TB, Jonathan, Sally and Bruce on the reshuffle. There was an amazing note from Charles Clarke in which he was talking about himself in the third person... 'Charles Clarke should stay as Home Secretary.' TB wanted to go over possible changes to the machinery of government. The main proposal was a new finance and strategy committee made up of TB, GB, JP and the chief secretary. TB said the only question was whether GB was going to co-operate fully. The aim was to bind him in more closely but it was not clear whether this would work. TB said he was worried with me gone again we would lose the main conduit we had had politically to GB. Sally said he was impossible and would go back to being so the moment the election was over. The money was going to be even tighter this time and that meant more fights over the policy agenda. We are not on the same priority paths, he said. In the end it was all down to TB and GB and could they work together in government again as they had kind of done in the last few weeks? TB did not look overly hopeful.

Bruce and Sally kept reporting every little piece of anecdotage and the picture was very mixed. I said I had woken up feeling we were nearer 70 than 90. Based on what, TB said? Based on nothing. But I did feel we had not gone for Lib Dems in the way we should have done and also that we should have done a better job exposing the Tory marginals strategy. Also Iraq was really hitting us and the Tories were getting their vote out. I felt waves of sadness through the day, not really knowing why, and beginning to feel pissed off that for the third time in a row, it looked like I would not be enjoying a winning election night. TB kept twittering on about what the result might be and we kept saying there was nothing to do so could we get on with something else, like the reshuffle? He said the problem was the major-ity would dictate how much authority he had and whether he could do all the things he wanted to. We went through the reshuffle – fairly modest but it wouldn't be easy. JP came over to talk through his role, TB convinced he was better off without a department to run. A lot of black humour re the GB lot. The civil service view of both Douglas and Yvette [Cooper] was that they were not good at making decisions, but I was always a bit wary of these Whitehall notes on ministers. TB said GB was pushing for Harriet [Harman] as deputy leader.

GB called and was very warm and friendly again. He said it was really important that my role was properly reflected in all the briefings. I said I really didn't mind. I had been glad to come back and help and I was glad I was leaving again. He laughed, said well thanks anyway. He said the campaign had been a joke until I came back and rescued it but 'I can't believe you're buggering off on a fucking rugby tour'. He chatted over the Scottish scene and also the seats he had visited that we were going to lose. I said it was important the team thing kept going. He said the next stages were a bit out of his hands. He didn't sound too sure of the future. As with TB he talked round in circles and repeated himself the whole time when he was articulating a new argument. I said he really must try to build on the way he and TB and the teams had worked together. The best path to him taking over was co-operation not confrontation. He said he might need to call on me when it came to transition. I said all I cared about was Labour winning and Labour governments doing good things. He said I know, and I suspect you are as disappointed as I am that we have not done more.

I went off for a kip, but loads of people were just calling and either passing on a bit of anecdotage or assuming I would know what was happening. Dinner at Myrobella. Sally had the exit polls – 37–32–22. PG was saying we might get a majority of 80 but the BBC and others were agreeing around the 66 mark. TB looked very down, sitting in the corner, for some reason wearing a donkey jacket. Euan was really nice to him, 'Hey Dad it's another win, how many leaders have won three elections? And if you had won this [majority] in 1997, we'd have been pretty chuffed.' There was definitely something in that, that '97 and '01 had been so big, anything that cut big time into it was a problem.

After it became clear we were talking nearer 50 than 90, TB asked me, SM, Jonathan and Bruce to go through to his little office. He said if it was fifty or less he thought it was difficult to stay on. It was such a big hit on his authority and he wouldn't be able to maintain real command and control. I said it was still a working majority and he should not get so down about it. He seemed very down though as we went over the line to use at the count. I felt it was best to say that this was a historic third term etc. but the country clearly wanted Labour back with a reduced majority and that is what the country had delivered. It was now time to focus on the priorities of the people. Iraq had been divisive but it was now time to unite and move on.

He went upstairs as more results came in and SM was getting bad news from various places. She was really down at one point, said, 'It could be meltdown.' I went upstairs to the bedroom and he was sitting in a chair looking grey and tired. 'I think if it's fifty it is very difficult,' he said. It will be more than that, I said, but a majority is a majority. A few better results came through. There seemed to be a bit of a north/south thing going on but then we heard we were losing Manchester Wythenshawe to the Libs. But we held Hove and Dumfries. Lots of anti-war seats were being lost and Tories doing better in some places than others but basically flatlining. TB was really quite down at one point, almost quitting down. I said, 'For God's sake Tony, till New Labour we had not won two full terms and here we are on the brink of getting a majority big enough to do three full terms. Do not get down about this.' I did a conference call and we agreed we had to say historic third term etc. as per my briefing note of earlier. I sent it through to GB who didn't respond.

I was doing notes and calls and trying to keep spirits up. Kate said she was really worried about how grim he seemed to feel. Sally, Jonathan and I were trying to get him in the right place for the speech he would have to make at the count. We left at around one. I had a little session with him to try to lift him a bit and go over the words. I then did a BBC interview and I sensed they felt things were not as bad as we did. The main picture was clear – TB back but with a reduced majority. It was not great but nor was it a disaster. A win is a win and though the majority is well down that is not something we should overlook, or let anyone else overlook. I said if we had been told this was what was on offer in '97 we would have taken it.

At the count Reg Keys [independent candidate whose son had been killed in Iraq] had a real go at TB and he had to stand there and take it. His own speech was very subdued. I got a few texts from people at HQ to the effect that he needed to lift his mood a bit. People down there were actually feeling OK. TB was emanating a lack of confidence. He was way too downbeat. So we raised the mood a bit when we got to Trimdon. There was a good atmosphere and he was clearly feeling a bit better. It was an amazing thing we had done yet there were too many people who would present victory as defeat.

Clive W texted to say had voted Labour purely for TB and me. I got a lovely message from Catherine McLeod who said the interview I did with her for the BBC from the Sedgefield count had reminded her more than anything why she is Labour and how much they owed me. Jonathan Pearse [special advisor] said there had been a spontaneous round of applause at the club when I came on. TB was very up and down about things. So much of it was about Iraq, and he knew that and so probably felt it more than most. The death of the soldier and the attack by the widow, and then the speech by Reg Keys at the count, it had hit him hard, even if he felt totally solid on the policy then and now. It was possible to look at the result and say given how unpopular the Iraq policy was it was all the more amazing we won at all. The Libs had definitely swept up a lot of votes on the back of it. I felt a lot of the lost support could be won back, but his mindset was all wrong at the moment. I said 'you're not going to do something daft are you? You do realise you've won again and it is a perfectly serviceable majority.' He said 'I just feel we could and should have done better.' 'We won,' I said. 'Now lift the mood for fuck's sake.'

We headed for the airport and on the plane down Alan Milburn said he felt there was a bad message for TB in there. A lot of the people who had only voted for us because of TB/New Labour had gone, and it was not certain they would come back. Also GB had been supportive because it suited him, but he was bound to feel TB was weakened by this, he would go straight back to his old ways and TB would not have me there to help keep him in check. Alan seemed a bit down. The results were coming thick and fast. Lost Barbara Roche [Hornsey and Wood Green]. Peter Bradley [The Wrekin]. A few surprises. Held Dorset South. We landed and then got a fast car convoy to the National Portrait Gallery. We all got a fantastic reception as we filed in. GB was there with Sarah but we didn't speak much. He called me later, left a message on the phone saying I had transformed things, and he hoped TB appreciated that but if he and I had been brought in properly a bit earlier it could all have been very different. He felt I had done all I could but it wasn't enough. We didn't deal with Iraq and trust properly 'and that issue is still there'. That part of the message sounded a bit menacing, the rest was very warm.

JP came over, shook hands and just said thanks. PG gave me a big hug, and said if I had not been there they could have gone into meltdown. Matt Carter said much the same. I'm not sure that was right but I know I had made a difference. I also knew I wanted out again. TB's speech went fine. Though he was genuinely disappointed, he managed to hide it, thanked the campaign team, set out the message for the coming term. By now though I was keen to get away. There was a lot of drink flowing, a fair bit of ligging. I was now beginning to share TB's sense of disappointment at the result. It was light by the time I left and I got a really nice reception from people as I was walking to Victoria Street. A few people were shouting out congratulations from cars, quite a lot of thumbs up from people on buses and passers by, and some nice comments and conversations, but I felt a bit low about it all. Ed Stourton [BBC] did an interview with me on the move as I headed to the office to clear my desk, just shovelled everything into my bag.

I went round and said goodbye to a few people and then as I made it for the door, there was a spontaneous round of applause. I stopped and looked back and there was a standing ovation going on, which I found really moving. I felt like these were the people I really loved working with, yet I was still sure I was right not to be going back. Hilary Coffman shouted out, 'You'll be back.' I shook my head, waved at her and walked out. I felt my eyes filling with tears, and was glad to be on my own in the lift. I went to the toilet, locked myself in a cubicle, put my head against the door and just let it all out. I had been really touched by such a reaction from the party staff, but I was also relieved, and above all absolutely exhausted. I must have looked like I was crying when I got into the cab home. 'You should be happy,' the driver said. 'Three in a row.'

Index

Bolland, Mark 61
Bono 313, 316, 325, 331–2
Boorman, Charley 326
Booth, Lauren 127
Boothroyd, Betty 92
Bosch, Olivia 16
Bostock, Tom 9–10, 50, 89–90, 114,
    207–8, 342
Botham, Ian 255, 260
Boulton, Adam 356, 364, 375, 476–7
Bourgass, Kamel 538
Bower, Tom 52
Bowman, John 239
Boyce, Mike, Lord 564, 565
Boycott, Geoff 260
BP (British Petroleum) 119
Bradshaw, David 30, 59, 121
Bragg, Melvyn 314, 315
Braithwaites, Rodric 29
Breakfast with Frost (TV show) 78–9, 123,
    257–8, 272, 326
    and campaign 564, 565
Breeze, Beth 532
Bremer, Paul 130
Bremner, Rory 360
Brighouse, Tim 53
British and Irish Lions 322–3, 332–3,
    362, 363, 544, 545–6
    and launch 532, 533
    and management 381–3, 385–6
    and tour 399–400
British National Party (BNP) 212, 247
Brown, Gordon 10, 28, 88, 476, 576
    and 2005 election 204, 205, 206, 209,
        367–8
    and Africa 389–90, 392, 405, 406
    and Bank of England 196
    and Blair 49–50, 75–8, 134–5, 235–6,
        289, 324
    and campaign 383–4, 417–18, 449–51,
        461–2, 467–8, 502–7
    and Campbell 4–5, 20–21, 212–14,
        216, 539, 573–4
    and China 448–9, 452
    and conference 43, 44–5, 46, 48
    and Dacre 277, 279, 355–6
    and Europe 63, 64, 72
    and joint campaigning 507–12,
        513–14, 516–17, 535–7, 541–2
    and the media 373, 379

and Milburn 108–9
and Murdoch 193
and Peston 396–7, 401, 404, 410
and Prescott 13, 17, 247–8, 288
and unpopularity 58, 73–4, 237–8
Brown, Nick 137, 140
Brown, Sarah 213
Brown, Terry 60
Brown, Tina 9, 31
Browne, John 119, 125
Browne, Sir Nicholas 166
Brown's Britain (Peston) 396, 398, 401,
    404, 406, 410
Bruce, Fiona 364, 365
Brunson, Mike 144
Burnley FC 18–19, 59–60, 108, 121,
    182–4, 227
    and fundraising 126, 129, 130, 153,
        313, 433
Burrell, Paul 61
Bush, George W. 23, 48, 72, 100, 530
    and Brown 505
    and election 342, 343–4, 345, 347
    and Iraq 147, 321
    and Middle East 216
    and Murdoch 193
    and UK visit 83, 84–5, 86, 87, 88–9
Business Appointments Commission 91
Butler Inquiry 154, 156, 251–2, 266,
    269–70, 279
    and Campbell 285
    and publication 286, 287
Byers, Steve 69, 108–9, 111, 118, 179
    and resignation 378

Caborn, Dick 34, 77, 165–6, 247
Cahill, Kevin 363
Calais 550
Caldecott, Andrew 37, 38, 39, 40, 41
Calendar Girls (film) 12–13
Callaghan, James 499–500
Camara, Mo 175–6
Cameron, David 147
Campbell, Donald (father) 7, 19, 77, 133,
    134, 137–9, 150–51, 157
    and death 290–96, 297–9
Campbell, Menzies 326
Cancun News Corp trip 104–5, 190–94
Caplin, Carole 17, 30
Carr, Jimmy 198

O'Leary, Dermot 553
Oliver, Jamie 488, 512
Oliver, Ted 241
Olympic Games 67, 127, 128, 301–4
    and Coe 218, 231, 256
    see also International Olympic
        Committee (IOC)
Omand, David 16, 142
Order in Council 9, 14
Osborne, George 533, 547
Osborne, Ian 112, 119, 126–7
O'Sullivan, Eddie 371
Ovett, Steve 230, 231

Palestine 385
Panorama (TV show) 134, 135
Paphitis, Theo 176, 178–9
Pardew, Alan 60
Park, Richard 259
Parkinson, Michael 198, 287, 300–301
Pascoe-Watson, George 455, 457
Paxman, Jeremy 99, 147, 548
Payne, Michael 302–3
Peacock, Matt 91
Pearse, Jonathan 575
Penn, Mark 402–3, 408, 424–5, 459, 477,
    543
pensions 5, 7, 445, 518, 543, 544
Peston, Robert 103, 396, 398, 401, 404,
    406, 410
Phelps, Michael 302
Phillips, Fiona 251, 570
Phillips, Gary 228–9, 554
Phillips, Melanie 53
Phillis, Bob 9, 101, 112–13, 246
Pickup, Cathy 4
Pienaar, John 113
Pollard, Eve 61
Pollard, Nick 375, 387
Pollard, Stephen 374, 377
Portillo, Michael 178, 345
postal voting 540, 547
Powell, Jonathan 15, 49, 102, 139–40,
    238–9
    and Butler Inquiry 286, 287
    and Hutton publication 142, 143
    and Mandelson 280, 281
Prebble, Stuart 155, 162, 249, 284
    and Armstrong 267, 268
    and Ferguson 232, 239

Prescott, John 13, 17, 179, 251, 555
    and 2005 election 206, 209, 549, 576
    and Brown 76, 77–8, 134–5, 247–8,
        315, 397–8
    and campaign planning 427–9, 430,
        431–2, 445–6, 488–9
    and housing 412–13
    and punch 177, 229
Preston, Roz 89
Prime Minister's Questions (PMQs) 524
Private Eye (magazine) 15, 165
Prodi, Romano 17
Promise 401, 415
Public Administration Committee 43,
    245–6
Purnell, James 311

Al Qaeda 262, 277
Qatar 259–60, 261–3
Queen's Speech 357
Queensland strategy 552, 556, 557, 559,
    566
Question Time (TV programme) 560–61

Ramsay, Gordon 318–19
Ramsey, Louise 372
Randall, Jeff 65–6
Reagan, Ronald 265–6
Rebuck, Gail 7, 17–18, 32, 42, 58–9, 274
    and Harper Collins 125, 160–61
Redmond, Phil 186
Redwood, John 497, 554
Reid, John 27, 69, 147, 148, 251
religion 492–3
Rice, Condoleeza 441
Richards, Dave 86
Richards, Keith 200
Riley, Ian 197
Rimmer, Catherine 21, 35
Roberts, Ivor 66
Robinson, Andy 371, 466, 545
Robinson, Nick 149, 356, 477, 548, 551,
    563
Robinson, Tony 276
Robson, Bobby 554
Rogers, Heather 41
Ronson, Gail 69
Ross, Jonathan 309
Rover 524, 526, 528, 540, 543
Rowson, Martin 285